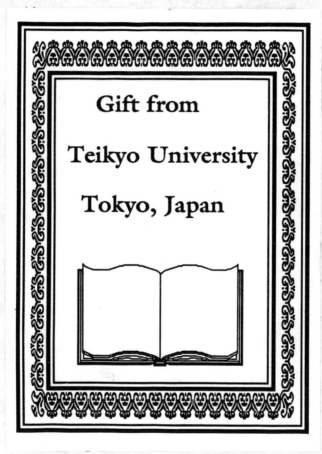

Gift from

Teikyo University

Tokyo, Japan

BEGINNING JAPANESE

PART II

by *Eleanor Harz Jorden*
with the assistance of Hamako Ito Chaplin

90-356

CHARLES E. TUTTLE COMPANY
Suido 1-chome, 2-6, Bunkyo-ku, Tokyo

Published by the Charles E. Tuttle Company, Inc.
of Rutland, Vermont and Tokyo, Japan
with editorial offices at
Suido 1-chome, 2-6, Bunkyo-ku, Tokyo, Japan
by special arrangement with
Yale University Press, New Haven, Connecticut

First Tuttle edition, 1974
Fourteenth printing, 1990

ISBN 0-8048-1575-5
PRINTED IN JAPAN

For

Temmy
Tabby
Telly

NOTE

This volume is a continuation of BEGINNING JAPANESE, Part I.
A description of romanization, special symbols, procedures, etc.
appears in the Introduction to that volume.

Contents

Contents   xiii

Lesson 21. Inns and Hotels

BASIC DIALOGUES: FOR MEMORIZATION

(a)

Clerk

1. Welcome.   I⌐rassyaima⌐se.

Smith

2. Do you have a room [for] tonight?   Ko⌐ñbañ he⌐ya⌐ (g̃a) a⌐rima⌐su ka⌐

Clerk

    promise <u>or</u> appointment
       <u>or</u> engagement   yakusoku <u>or</u> oyakusoku †

3. Are you expected?   O⌐yakusoku de gozaima⌐su ka⌐

Smith

4. No, I don't have a reservation
(but) . . .   Iie, ya⌐kusoku wa arimase⌐ñ g̃a_

Clerk

    Japanese-style room   nihoñma
    nothing but Japanese-style
      rooms   nihoñma sika /+ negative/

5. We have nothing but Japanese-
style rooms. How about [one of
them]?   Ni⌐hoñma sika gozaimase⌐ñ g̃a, i⌐ka⌐g̃a de gozaimasu ka⌐

      being new   a⌐tara⌐sikute
      is broad <u>or</u> wide <u>or</u> spacious
         <u>or</u> big in area   hi⌐ro⌐i /-ku/
      is new and large   a⌐tara⌐sikute hi⌐ro⌐i
      Japanese-style room <u>or</u>
         parlor   za⌐siki⌐ <u>or</u> ozasiki +
      a Japanese-style room which
         is new and large   a⌐tara⌐sikute hi⌐ro⌐i zasiki

6. We have a new (and) large Japa-
nese-style room (but) . . .   A⌐tara⌐sikute hi⌐ro⌐i o⌐zasiki g̃a gozaima⌐su g̃a_

Smith

      being a Japanese-style room   nihoñma de
7. A Japanese-style room will be
fine.   Ni⌐hoñma de ke⌐kkoo desu.

(b)

Smith

with bath	huroba-tuki
room with bath	hu⌐roba-tuki no heya⌐
8. Do you have a room with bath?	Hu⌐roba-tuki no heya⌐ (g̈a) a⌐rima⌐su ka⌐

Clerk

Western-style room	yooma
be free for use or unoccupied	aite (i)ru
9. We have Western-style rooms with bath, but tonight they're taken (lit. aren't free) (but)...	Huroba-tuki no yo⌐oma wa gozaima⌐su g̈a, ko⌐ñbañ wa äite o⌐rimase⌐ñ g̈a_
quiet	si⌐zuka /na/
being quiet	si⌐zuka de
is quiet and large	si⌐zuka de hi⌐ro⌐i
a Japanese-style room that is quiet and large	si⌐zuka de hi⌐ro⌐i zasiki
one room	hi⌐to⌐-ma
10. There's one large, quiet Japanese-style room free (but)...	Si⌐zuka de hi⌐ro⌐i o⌐zasiki g̈a hito⌐-ma a⌐ite orima⌐su g̈a_

Smith

being that	sore de
11. That will be fine.	So⌐re de ke⌐kkoo desu.

(c)

(Smith and Tanaka are stopping at a Japanese inn.)

Room-girl

bath	o⌐hu⌐ro+
go into the bath or take a bath	o⌐hu⌐ro ni ⌐ha⌐iru
12. Wouldn't you like to take a bath?	O⌐hu⌐ro ni o⌐hairi ni narimase⌐ñ ka⌐

Smith

be too hot	a⌐tusug̈i⌐ru /-ru/
13. I'd like to (go in) but it's too hot.	Ha⌐irita⌐i ñ desu g̈a, a⌐tusug̈ima⌐su yo.

Room-girl

usual or regular or ordinary	hutuu
14. It's [the] usual [temperature], isn't it?	Hutuu de gozaimasyoo?

Tanaka

is lukewarm	nu⌐ru⌐i /-ku/
15. Americans prefer a lukewarm bath (lit. alternative) (so...)	A⌐merika⌐ziñ wa nu⌐ru⌐i hoo g̈a o⌐suki da⌐ kara_

Room-girl

16. Well then, I'll make it lukewarm   Zya˺a, nu˺ruku i˥tasima˩su kara—
    (so. . .)

. . .

Room-girl

17. Shall I serve dinner?[1] (Lit.   O˻syokuzi ni itasimasyo˺o ka.
    Shall I make it dining?)

Tanaka

    Japanese eating tray   ozeñ⁺
18. Yes. Bring out the trays.   E˺e. O˻zeñ (o) da˺site.

Room-girl

    Japanese-style food   wasyoku
    nothing but Japanese-style   wasyoku sika /+ negative/
    food
19. We have nothing but Japanese-   Wa˻syoku sika gozaimase˺ñ ḡa—
    style food (but). . .

Smith

    being Japanese-style food   wasyoku de
20. Japanese-style food will be fine. Wa˻syoku de ke˺kkoo desu.

    drinking water   no˻mi˺mizu
21. Please bring some drinking   No˻mi˺mizu mo mo˥tte˩ kite kudasai.
    water, too.

. . .

Tanaka

    is severe   hi˻do˺i /-ku/
    wind   kaze
22. What an awful wind!   *Hi˻do˺i ka˻ze de˺su ˻ne˺e.

(to the room-girl)

    brazier   hi˺bati
23. Say, it's grown cold so bring a   Tyo˺tto; sa˺muku ˥na˩tta kara,
    hibati, will you?   hi˺bati (o) mo˥tte˩ kite ne?

(d)

Mr. Tanaka

    is sleepy   nemui /-ku/
24. Oh, I'm sleepy!   A˺a nemui.

Mr. Yamamoto

25. Me too.   Boku mo.

---

[1] Or breakfast or lunch, depending on the time of day.

(to room-girl)

go to bed <u>or</u> go to sleep	neru /-ru/
Japanese quilt	hutoñ
spread out (on the floor, ground, table, etc.)	siku /-u/

26. We're going to go to bed soon now (already) so spread out the quilts.

Mo⌐o ne⌐ru⌐ kara, hutoñ (o) siite.

bug <u>or</u> insect	musi
is frequent <u>or</u> is much <u>or</u> are many	o⌐o⌐i /-ku/
mosquito net	kaya

27. And we want a mosquito net too, because there are a lot of bugs.

Sore kara; mu⌐si (ḡa) oo⌐i kara, ka⌐ya mo tano⌐mu yo.

Room-girl

get up <u>or</u> wake up	o⌐ki⌐ru /-ru/

28. Certainly. What time will you get up?

Ha⌐i. Nañ-zi ni o⌐oki ni narima⌐su ka↲

Mr. Yamamoto (to room-girl)

wake [someone] up	o⌐ko⌐su /-u/

29. Would you wake us at 7 o'clock? [That's] because we're taking an 8:30 train.

Si⌐ti⌐-zi ni o⌐ko⌐site ku⌐rena⌐i ka↲ Ha⌐ti-zi-ha⌐ñ no ki⌐sya⌐ ni no⌐ru⌐ kara.

Mr. Tanaka (to room-girl)

shoes	ku⌐tu⌐
shine <u>or</u> polish	miḡaku /-u/
man's suit	sebiro
pressing iron <u>or</u> pressing	airoñ
apply <u>or</u> suspend <u>or</u> hang	ka⌐ke⌐ru /-ru/
press with an iron	a⌐iroñ o kake⌐ru
press a suit (lit. apply an iron to a suit)	sebiro ni a⌐iroñ o kake⌐ru

30. Say! I'd like to have these shoes shined and this suit pressed (but)...

Ano ne! Ko⌐no kutu⌐ (o) mi⌐ḡaite, kono sebiro ni a⌐iroñ (o) ka⌐kete mo⌐raita⌐i ñ da kedo↲

Room-girl

consent to <u>or</u> agree to	syooti-suru

31. Certainly.

Syo⌐oti-itasima⌐sita.

. . .

Mr. Tanaka

is noisy	ya⌐kamasi⌐i /-ku/

32. What a racket in the next room! (Lit. The next room is noisy, isn't it!)

To⌐nari no heya⌐ (wa) ya⌐kamasi⌐i ⌐ne⌐e.

Mr. Yamamoto

33. Yeah. They said this (place)   N̄. Koko (wa) ⌈si⌉zuka na he⌐ya⌐
    was a quiet room (but). . .   da tte (i)⌐tta⌐ kedo⌣

(e)

Smith

    rather good inn or inn on   i⌐i hoo no ryŏkañ
      the good side
    one night   hi⌐to⌐-bañ
34. How much is the usual rather   Hutuu no ⌈i⌉i hoo no ryokañ (wa)
    good inn, for one night?   hi⌐to⌐-bañ i⌐kura-ḡu⌐rai desyoo ka.

Tanaka

35. Hmm. I wonder if it wouldn't   Sa⌐a. Ni⌐señ-eñ-ḡu⌐rai kara zya
    be from about ¥2000 [up].   ⌐na⌐i desyoo ka ⌐ne⌐e.

Smith

    with meals   syokuzi-tuki
36. Is that with meals?   Sore (wa) syo⌐kuzi-tuki de⌐su ka⌣

Tanaka

    with two meals   nisyoku-tuki
37. It's with two meals.   Ni⌐syoku-tuki de⌐su yo⌣

Smith

    meaning   i⌐mi
    the expression (lit. one)   ni⌐syoku-tuki⌐ tte i⌐u⌐ no
      said quote with two meals
    what meaning? (lit. mean-   do⌐o iu ⌐i⌐mi
      ing said how?)
38. With two meals? What does   Nisyokutuki? Ni⌐syoku-tuki⌐ tte i⌐u⌐
    'with two meals' mean?   no (wa) ⌐do⌐o iu ⌐i⌐mi desu ka⌣

Tanaka

    be included   ha⌐itte (i)ru
    noon or daytime   hi⌐ru⌐
    separate   betu /na or no/
39. It means that (lit. it is the mean- A⌐sa to ba⌐ñ no syokuzi (ḡa) ha⌐itte
    ing said quote) the morning and   (i)te, hiru no syokuzi wa be⌐tu da⌐
    evening meals are included and   tte iu ⌐i⌐mi desu yo. .
    the noon meal is separate.

NOTES ON THE BASIC DIALOGUES

1. Remember that -ma⌐se imperatives are used primarily by women and by
   service personnel.

3. Note also yakusoku-suru 'make a promise or appointment or engagement.'

4. 'but—is it possible to get a room anyway?'

6. 'but—would that be all right?'
   The opposite of hiˉroˉi is seˉmaˉi /-ku/ 'is narrow or cramped or small in area.'
   Zaˉsikiˉ refers to a Japanese-style room in an inn, and a Japanese-style parlor in a private home.

8. The -tuki of huroba-tuki is derived from tuˉku 'become attached.' Compare also syokuzi-tuki (Sentence 36) and nisyoku-tuki (Sentence 37).

9. 'but—would another kind of room be all right?'

10. 'but—would that be all right?'

12. The hot Japanese bath is an attraction of Japanese-style inns. A bath which the average American considers hot, a Japanese usually considers to be lukewarm (nuˉruˉi).
    Oˉhuˉro is used commonly by both men and women. The less polite equivalent is huˉroˉ.

15. 'so—the bath here seems too hot for him.'
    With the polite osuki ⵏ alternant, this sentence would not be said by an American.

16. 'so—it will be all right then.'

18. The less polite zeñ is rarely used in conversation.

19. 'but—is that all right?'
    With wasyoku compare yoosyoku 'Western-style food.'

21. When there is any doubt about sanitary conditions and the purity of the noˉmiˉmizu, ask for yuˉzaˉmasi 'water which has been boiled.'

26. Hutoñ refers to the large Japanese sleeping quilts which are spread out on the tatami each night and taken up each morning.

27. The opposite of oˉoˉi is suˉkunaˉi /-ku/ 'is rare or is scarce or are few.'
    Oˉoˉi and suˉkunaˉi do NOT precede the word they describe: thus, yaˉmaˉ ḡa oˉoˉi 'there are many mountains' (i.e. 'the mountains are many'), which is similar in meaning, though not in pattern, to yaˉmaˉ ḡa taˉkusañ aˉru. Note the following common patterns: X ḡa [or no] oˉoˉi Y 'a Y with lots of X' (example: yaˉmaˉ ḡa [or no] oˉoˉi tokoro 'a place with lots of mountains' [lit. 'a mountains-are-many place']) and X ḡa [or no] suˉkunaˉi Y 'a Y with few or little X' (example: yaˉmaˉ ḡa [or no] suˉkunaˉi tokoro 'a place with few mountains' [lit. 'a mountains-are-few place']).

29. Oˉkoˉsu is the transitive partner of intransitive oˉkiˉru (Sentence 28).

30. 'but—can it be done?'
    Kaˉkete moˉraitaˈi ñ da kedo is the informal equivalent of kaˉkete moˉraitaˈi ñ desu keredo.

31. Syoˉoti-(ita)simaˉsita is similar in meaning and usage to kaˉsikomarimaˉsita.

33. 'but—it isn't, is it!'

39. Hi⌐ru˥ has two meanings: it means 'daytime,' the opposite of yo˥ru 'night-time'; it also means 'twelve o'clock noon.' With the latter meaning, it has a commonly occurring polite alternant o⌐hi˥ru +.

Betu is one of a limited group of nominals which may be followed by na or no when describing a following nominal.

GRAMMATICAL NOTES

1. Adjectivals: Gerund

The adverbial of adjectivals is made by dropping the -i of the citation form and adding -ku (cf. Lesson 2, Grammatical Note 1). If the citation form is unaccented, the adverbial is also unaccented. If the citation form is accented, the adverbial is accented. (With -nai negatives and -tai 'want to' words, the accent remains on the same syllable; with most other adjectivals, the accent usually moves one syllable closer to the beginning of the word—for example, wa⌐kara˥nai > wa⌐kara˥naku; no⌐mita˥i > no⌐mita˥ku; si⌐ro˥i > si⌐ro-ku. [1])

The gerund of adjectivals is made by adding -te to the adverbial. It is always accented: if the adverbial is accented, the derived gerund is accented on the same syllable; if the adverbial is unaccented, the derived gerund is regularly accented on the syllable immediately preceding the -kute ending.

Examples:

Citation Form (Informal Non-past)	Adverbial	Gerund
abunai 'is dangerous'	abunaku	a⌐buna˥kute
ti⌐isa˥i 'is small'	ti˥isaku	ti˥isakute
na˥i 'isn't in a place,' 'haven't'	na˥ku	na˥kute
ta⌐be˥nai 'doesn't eat'	ta⌐be˥naku	ta⌐be˥nakute
ta⌐beta˥i 'want to eat'	ta⌐beta˥ku	ta⌐beta˥kute
oisii 'is delicious'	oisiku	o⌐isi˥kute
i˥i or yo˥i 'is good'	yo˥ku	yo˥kute
nemui 'is sleepy'	nemuku	ne⌐mu˥kute
sa⌐mu˥i 'is cold'	sa˥muku	sa˥mukute
omoi 'is heavy'	omoku	o⌐mo˥kute
si⌐ro˥i 'is white'	si˥roku	si˥rokute

Like verbal and copula gerunds, an adjectival gerund occurs within a sentence, ending a sequence which is coordinate with what follows (cf. Lesson 7, Grammatical Note 5, and Lesson 10, Grammatical Note 3).

Examples:

Two sentences (informal style): Hi⌐ro˥i. 'It's large.'
                                 Su⌐zusi˥i. 'It's cool.'
One sentence (informal style): Hi⌐rokute su⌐zusi˥i. 'It's large and it's cool.'

---

[1] Many adjectivals in this last group now occur with an alternate accent which follows the pattern of the first two groups. Thus: si˥roku ~ si⌐ro˥ku.

Two sentences (formal style): Hiˌroˈi desu. 'It's large.'
Suˌzusiˈi desu. 'It's cool.'
One sentence (formal style): Hiˈrokute suˌzusiˈi desu. 'It's large and it's cool.'

Remember that words like siˈzuka 'quiet,' kiˈree 'pretty,' geˈñki 'healthy,' byooki 'sick,' etc., are nominals, and the -kute ending occurs only at the end of adjectivals. When the first of a pair of sentences ends in a nominal + √da, the first sequence of the corresponding compound sentence ends in nominal + de (the copula gerund) as described in Lesson 10, Grammatical Note 3.

Compare: Two sentences: Siˈzuka desu. 'It's quiet.' (nominal + desu)
Suˌzusiˈi desu. 'It's cool.'
One sentence: Siˈzuka de suˌzusiˈi desu. 'It's quiet and it's cool.'
and: Two sentences: Yaˈkamasiˈi desu. 'It's noisy.' (adjectival + desu)
Aˈtuˈi desu. 'It's hot.'
One sentence: Yaˈkamaˈsikute aˈtuˈi desu. 'It's noisy and it's hot.'

A sentence modifier may include an adjectival gerund. In Basic Sentence 6 of this lesson, the nominal ozasiki 'room' is described by the single compound sentence aˈtaraˈsikute hiˈroˈi 'it is new and it is large,' i.e. 'a room that is new and large,' 'a new and large room.' With this, compare the sequence aˈtarasiˈi hiˈroˈi ozasiki 'a new, large room,' in which ozasiki is described by two sentences—aˈtarasiˈi 'it is new' and hiˈroˈi 'it is large.' Both kinds of sequence occur commonly.

Additional examples:

Koˈno koohiˈi wa oˈisiˈkute yaˈsuˈi desu. 'This coffee is good and it's cheap.'

Otaku no oniwa wa ˈhiˈrokute ˈkiˈree desu ˈneˈe. 'Your garden is large and beautiful, isn't it.'

Uti ḡa ˈseˈmakute, niwa ḡa hiˈroˈi. 'The house is small and the garden is big.'

Iˈti-ḡatuˈ ḡa aˈttakaˈkute, ni-ˈḡatuˈ ḡa ˈsaˈmukatta. 'January was warm and February was cold.'

Aˈtukute ˈkoˈi otya ḡa suˈkiˈ desu. 'I like tea that's hot and strong.'

Oˈokikute oˈmoi niˈmotu ḡa arimasu. 'I have some luggage that is big and heavy.'

2. Compound Verbals

A COMPOUND VERBAL consists of a verbal stem (the -maˈsu form minus -maˈsu) or adjectival stem (the citation form minus final -i) or a nominal, compounded with a following verbal. Compounds ending in suˈḡiˈru 'exceed' (like aˈtusuḡiˈru 'be too hot') indicate excessive degree. For example:

taˈbe (stem of taˈbeˈru 'eat') + suˈḡiˈru = taˈbesuḡiˈru 'overeat'
noˈmi (stem of noˈmuˈ 'drink') + suˈḡiˈru = noˈmisuḡiˈru 'drink too much'
tukai (stem of tukau 'use') + suˈḡiˈru = tuˈkaisuḡiˈru 'overuse'
taˈka (stem of taˈkaˈi 'is expensive') + suˈḡiˈru = taˈkasuḡiˈru 'be too expensive'

o͞oki (stem of o͞oki⌐i 'is big') + su⌐g̃i⌐ru = o͞okisug̃i⌐ru 'be too big'
o͞o (stem of o͞o⌐i 'is much' or 'are many') + su⌐g̃i⌐ru = o͞osug̃i⌐ru 'be too much' or 'be too many'
ge⌐ñki 'peppy' + su⌐g̃i⌐ru = ge⌐ñkisug̃i⌐ru 'be too peppy'

Note also:

nori (stem of noru 'ride') + kaeru[1] 'change [something]' = no⌐rikae⌐ru 'change vehicles'
to⌐ri (stem of to⌐ru 'take') + kaeru[1] 'change [something]' = torikaeru 'exchange'

Included among compound verbals is the large group of words consisting of a nominal + suru 'make' or 'do': for example, kekkoñ 'marriage' + suru = kekkoñ-suru[2] 'marry'; beñkyoo 'study' [noun] + suru = beñkyoo-suru 'study' [verb].

Actually, formal verbals are compounds, consisting of a verbal stem + the verbal -ma⌐su (which differs from other verbals in that it never occurs independently, and has no meaning other than formality). Thus:

ta⌐be (stem of ta⌐be⌐ru 'eat') + -ma⌐su (formality) = ta⌐bema⌐su 'eat (formal word)'

3. Particle sika 'only,' 'nothing but'

Particle sika following a nominal or a nominal + particle[3] occurs with negative (never affirmative) inflected expressions and is equivalent to English 'only + an affirmative,' 'nothing but + an affirmative,' or 'except + a negative.'

Examples:

   a. (1) Su⌐ko⌐si arimasu. 'There's a little.'
      (2) Su⌐ko⌐si sika a⌐rimase⌐ñ. 'There's only a little.'

   b. (1) Ta⌐naka-sañ g̃a kima⌐sita. 'Mr. Tanaka came.'
      (2) Ta⌐naka-sañ sika kimase⌐ñ desita. 'No one came but Mr. Tanaka.'

   c. (1) Te⌐ñpura o tabema⌐sita. 'I ate tempura.'
      (2) Te⌐ñpura sika tabemase⌐ñ desita. 'I didn't eat anything but tempura.'

   d. (1) Ni⌐ho⌐ñ ni arimasu. 'It's in Japan.'
      (2) Ni⌐ho⌐ñ ni sika a⌐rimase⌐ñ. 'It's only in Japan.'

---

[1] Kaeru /-ru/ 'change [something],' not to be confused with ka⌐eru /-u/ 'return.'

[2] The hyphen in -suru compounds is an arbitrary convention which has no phonetic value.

[3] The particle is not wa, g̃a, or o.

4. Ni⌐hoñma de ke⌐kkoo desu

A nominal (by itself or with following particles) + de (the gerund of da) +
√i⌐i or √yorosii or ke⌐kkoo or √ka⌐mawa⌐nai means 'being [the nominal],
it's all right,' 'it will be fine if it's [the nominal],' '[the nominal] is agreeable (on this occasion) to me.' So⌐no mama⌐ de ⌐i⌐i (Lesson 16) is another
example of this pattern.
   Do not confuse X de ⌐i⌐i and X wa (or g̱a) ⌐i⌐i. Compare:

   Te⌐ekoku-ho⌐teru wa ⌐i⌐i desu. 'The Imperial Hotel is good or nice or
      pleasant.'
   Te⌐ekoku-ho⌐teru de ⌐i⌐i desu. 'The Imperial Hotel will be fine.' (used,
      for example, when deciding on a place to stay, or meet, or eat, etc.)

   Ko⌐re wa i⌐i desu. 'This is good or nice or fine.'
   Ko⌐re de i⌐i desu. 'If it's this, it will be agreeable.' or 'With this, I've
      had enough.' or 'This will be all right (on this occasion or in these cir-
      cumstances).'

5. Informal Requests Ending in ku⌐rena⌐i ka

Requests ending in ku⌐dasaimase⌐ñ ka (Lesson 7, Grammatical Note 4) are
polite and formal. An informal equivalent, ending in ku⌐dasara⌐nai?, occurs
predominantly in women's speech. The plain equivalent of ku⌐dasaimase⌐ñ ka
is ku⌐remase⌐ñ ka (Lesson 17, Grammatical Note 1), and two of its informal
equivalents are ku⌐rena⌐i ka, which occurs in men's speech, and kurenai?,
which occurs in both men's and women's speech. For example, all the following mean 'would you do it for me?' (lit.'won't you give me doing?'):

	Formal	Informal
Polite	Si⌐te kudasaimase⌐ñ ka⌣ (MW)	Si⌐te kudasara⌐nai? (W) [1]
Plain	Si⌐te kuremase⌐ñ ka⌣ (MW)	Si⌐te kurena⌐i ka⌣ (M)
		Site kurenai? (MW)

   Ku⌐rena⌐i ka is the first example of question particle ka ending an informal sentence. All informal questions introduced previously have ended in
question intonation without ka: for example, Iku? 'Are you going?' I⌐i? 'Is
it all right?' Kore? 'This?'
   Informal questions ending with ka occur predominantly in men's speech,
and except for a few combinations (ku⌐rena⌐i ka is one of them) are typical of
abrupt speech.
   Before ka, da is regularly lost. One informal equivalent of So⌐o desu ka
is So⌐o ka.

---

[1] Predominantly.

6. C o u n t e r s :   -<u>ma</u> 'room,' -<u>bañ</u> 'night'

-<u>Ma</u> combines with numerals of Series II—but only rarely with numerals higher than seven—to count the number of room units. The numbers from one to seven are:

hi˹to˺-ma	'1 room'
hu˹ta-ma˺	'2 rooms'
mi˹-ma	'3 rooms'
yo˺-ma	'4 rooms'
i˹tu˺-ma	'5 rooms'
mu˺-ma	'6 rooms'
na˹na˺-ma	'7 rooms'
i˹ku-ma [1]	'how many rooms?'

The counter -<u>bañ</u> combines with numerals of Series II to count nights. Hi˹to˺-bañ '1 night' and <u>huta-bañ</u> '2 nights' occur commonly, and <u>mi˺-bañ</u> '3 nights,' <u>yo˺-bañ</u> '4 nights,' and <u>i˹tu˺-bañ</u> '5 nights' are heard occasionally, but the occurrence of this counter with higher numbers is rare. The corresponding question word is i˹ku-bañ 'how many nights?'

DRILLS

A. Substitution Drill

1.	A Japanese-style room will be fine.	Ni˹hoñma de ke˹kkoo desu. [2]
2.	A Western-style room will be fine.	Yo˹oma de ke˹kkoo desu.
3.	Chopsticks will be fine.	Ha˹si de ˥ke˦kkoo desu.
4.	The same will be fine.	O˹nazi de ke˹kkoo desu.
5.	One-way will be fine.	Ka˹tamiti de ke˹kkoo desu.
6.	An ordinary inn will be fine.	Hu˹tuu no ryokañ de ke˹kkoo desu.
7.	A small television will be fine.	Ti˹isa˺i ˥te˦rebi de ˥ke˦kkoo desu.
8.	Lukewarm, as it is, will be fine.	Nu˹ru˺i ma˥ma˦ de ˥ke˦kkoo desu.
9.	A Japanese one will be fine.	Ni˹hoñ no˺ de ˥ke˦kkoo desu.
10.	As far as the station will be fine.	E˹ki made de ˥ke˦kkoo desu.

---

[1] <u>Iku-</u> regularly compounds with counters which combine with Series II numerals, to form the corresponding question word. (Compare i˹ku-tu 'how many units?') Some Japanese also use <u>iku-</u> with other counters: for example, i˹ku-niñ 'how many people?'

[2] Practice this drill with i˹i desu and yo˹rosi˺i desu as well as ke˹kkoo desu.

B. Substitution Drill

1. Are your children going to go to bed already?

Okosañ (wa) ⌐mo⌐o ne⌐ma⌐su ka⌐

2. Are your children in bed (or asleep) already?

Okosañ (wa) ⌐mo⌐o ne⌐te (i)ma⌐su ka⌐

3. Are your children up (or awake) already?

Okosañ (wa) ⌐mo⌐o ⌐o⌐kite (i)masu ka⌐

4. Are your children going to get up already?

Okosañ (wa) ⌐mo⌐o o⌐kima⌐su ka⌐

5. Are your children going to take a bath already?

Okosañ (wa) ⌐mo⌐o o⌐hu⌐ro ni ha⌐irima⌐su ka⌐

6. Are your children taking a bath already?

Okosañ (wa) ⌐mo⌐o o⌐hu⌐ro ni ⌐ha⌐itte (i)masu ka⌐

7. Are your children going to eat already?

Okosañ (wa) ⌐mo⌐o ta⌐bema⌐su ka⌐

8. Are your children eating already?

Okosañ (wa) ⌐mo⌐o ⌐ta⌐bete (i)masu ka⌐

C. Substitution Drill

1. It was a place with lots of bugs.

Musi no[1] o⌐o⌐i to⌐koro⌐ desita yo⌐

2. It was a house with lots of windows.

Ma⌐do no o⌐o⌐i u⌐ti de⌐sita yo⌐

3. It was a street with lots of shops.

Mise no o⌐o⌐i mi⌐ti de⌐sita yo⌐

4. It was a school with lots of teachers.

Se⌐ñse⌐e no o⌐o⌐i ga⌐kkoo de⌐sita yo⌐

5. It was an inn with lots of guests.

Kyaku no o⌐o⌐i ryo⌐kañ de⌐sita yo⌐

6. It was an inn with few guests.

Kyaku no su⌐kuna⌐i ryo⌐kañ de⌐sita yo⌐

7. It was a station with few porters.

Akaboo no su⌐kuna⌐i ⌐e⌐ki desita yo⌐

8. It was a room with few lights.

De⌐ñki no su⌐kuna⌐i he⌐ya⌐ desita yo⌐

9. It was a spring with little rain.

A⌐me no su⌐kuna⌐i ⌐ha⌐ru desita yo⌐

10. It was a hotel with few Japanese rooms.

Zasiki no su⌐kuna⌐i ⌐ho⌐teru de⌐sita yo⌐

D. Substitution Drill

1. There's nothing but a Western-style room. Is that all right?

Yo⌐oma sika arimase⌐ñ ḡa, ka⌐maimase⌐ñ ka⌐

---

[1] Particle no in all the sentences of this exercise may be replaced by ḡa. Practice both alternants.

2. There's nothing but a Japanese-style room. Is that
all right?

Ni⌐hoῆma sika arimase⌐n ̄ga, ka-
⌐maimase⌐n ka⌐

3. There's nothing but Western-
style food. Is that all right?

Yo⌐osyoku sika arimase⌐n ̄ga, ka-
⌐maimase⌐n ka⌐

4. There's nothing but cold water. Is that all right?

Mi⌐zu sika arimase⌐n ̄ga, ka⌐mai-
mase⌐n ka⌐

5. There's nothing but a small
room. Is that all right?

Se⌐ma⌐i he⌐ya⌐ sika a⌐rimase⌐n ̄ga,
ka⌐maimase⌐n ka⌐

6. There's nothing but an old
magazine. Is that all right?

Hu⌐ru⌐i za⌐ssi sika arimase⌐n ̄ga,
ka⌐maimase⌐n ka⌐

7. There's nothing but a small
hibachi. Is that all right?

Ti⌐isa⌐i ⌐hi⌐bati sika a⌐rimase⌐n
̄ga, ka⌐maimase⌐n ka⌐

8. There's nothing but a morning train. Is that all right?

A⌐sa no ki⌐sya⌐ sika a⌐rimase⌐n
̄ga, ka⌐maimase⌐n ka⌐

9. There's nothing but a ticket
for next week. Is that all
right?

Ra⌐isyuu no kippu sika arimase⌐n
̄ga, ka⌐maimase⌐n ka⌐

10. There's nothing but one
from yesterday. Is that all
right?

Ki⌐noo no⌐ sika a⌐rimase⌐n ̄ga,
ka⌐maimase⌐n ka⌐

E. Substitution Drill

1. [He] said that this was a
quiet room but . . . [1]

Koko (wa) ⌐si⌐zuka na he⌐ya⌐ da
tte (i)⌐tta⌐ kedo⌐

2. [He] said that the bath was
lukewarm but . . .

O⌐hu⌐ro ̄ga nu⌐ru⌐i tte (i)⌐tta⌐ ke-
do⌐

3. [He] said that he would get
up early this norning but . . .

Ke⌐sa ⌐ha⌐yaku o⌐ki⌐ru tte (i)⌐tta⌐
kedo⌐

4. [He] said that there was
plenty of gasoline left
but . . .

Gasoriῆ ̄ga zyu⌐ubu⌐n no⌐ko⌐tte
(i)ru tte (i)⌐tta⌐ kedo⌐

5. [He] said there were few
bugs but . . .

Mu⌐si ̄ga sukuna⌐i tte (i)⌐tta⌐ ke-
do⌐

6. [He] said that he wouldn't
go through Osaka but . . .

O⌐osaka (o) toora⌐nai tte (i)⌐tta⌐
kedo⌐

7. [He] said that the winters
here were severely cold
but . . .

Ko⌐ko no huyu⌐ (wa) ⌐hi⌐doku sa-
⌐mu⌐i tte (i)⌐tta⌐ kedo⌐

8. [He] said that this was most
important but . . .

Ko⌐re ̄ga itibaῆ taisetu da⌐ tte
(i)⌐tta⌐ kedo⌐

9. [He] said that this room was
large and cool but . . .

Ko⌐no heya⌐ (wa) ⌐hi⌐rokute su-
⌐zusi⌐i tte (i)⌐tta⌐ kedo⌐

10. [He] said that he would shine
these shoes for me but . . .

Ko⌐no kutu⌐ (o) mīgaite kureru⌐
tte (i)⌐tta⌐ kedo⌐

---

[1] 'but—it isn't true, is it,' 'but—I'm not sure,' etc.

F. Substitution Drill

(Insert the substitution item in the model sentence as a modifier of
he⌐ya¬, with or without <u>no</u> or <u>na</u> as required.)

1. It's a large room.   Hi⌐ro¬i he⌐ya¬ desu yo⌐
2. It's a quiet room.   Si⌐zuka na he⌐ya¬ desu yo⌐
3. It's the next room.   To⌐nari no heya¬ desu yo⌐
4. It's a ¥2000 room.   Ni⌐señ-eñ no heya¬ desu yo⌐
5. It's a room with bath.   Hu⌐roba-tuki no heya¬ desu yo⌐
6. It's a small room.   Se⌐ma¬i he⌐ya¬ desu yo⌐
7. It's a strange room.   He⌐ñ na he⌐ya¬ desu yo⌐
8. It's a fine room.   Ri⌐ppa na heya¬ desu yo⌐
9. It's a noisy room.   Ya⌐kamasi¬i he⌐ya¬ desu yo⌐
10. It's my room.   Wa⌐takusi no heya¬ desu yo⌐

G. Substitution Drill

(Insert the substitution item in the model sentence in whatever form
or with whatever particle required.)

1. Shall I serve (lit. make [it])   Syo⌐kuzi ni simasyo¬o ka.
    dinner?
2. Shall I make [it] lukewarm?   Nu⌐ruku si⌐masyo¬o ka.
    /nu⌐ru¬i/
3. Shall I make [it] the oppo-   Ha⌐ñtai ni simasyo¬o ka.
    site? /hañtai/
4. Shall I separate [them]?   Be⌐tu ni simasyo¬o ka.
    /betu/
5. Shall I put [them] together?   I⌐ssyo ni simasyo¬o ka.
    /issyo/
6. Shall I make [it] hot?   A⌐tuku si⌐masyo¬o ka.
    /a⌐tu¬i/
7. Shall I fill [it]? /ippai/   I⌐ppai ni simasyo¬o ka.
8. Shall I make [it] wide?   Hi⌐roku si⌐masyo¬o ka.
    /hi⌐ro¬i/
9. Shall I chill [it]? /tumetai/   Tu⌐metaku simasyo¬o ka.
10. Shall I empty [it]? /ka⌐ra¬/   Ka⌐ra¬ ni si⌐masyo¬o ka.

H. Substitution Drill (based on Grammatical Note 2)

1. I'd like to take a bath but   O⌐hu¬ro ni ha⌐rita¬i ñ desu ḡa,
    it's too hot.   a⌐tusugima¬su yo.
2. I'd like to buy [it] but it's Ka⌐ita¬i ñ desu ḡa, ta⌐kasugima¬su
    too expensive. /kau, ta-   yo.
    ⌐ka¬i/
3. I'd like to go but it's too   I⌐kita¬i ñ desu ḡa, to⌐osugima¬su
    far. /iku, tooi/   yo.
4. I'd like to take [it] but it's Mo⌐tte ikita¬i ñ desu ḡa, o⌐mosu-
    too heavy. /motte iku,   ḡima¬su yo.
    omoi/

5. I'd like to put [it] in but it's
    too big. /ireru, oꜛokiꜜi/

6. I'd like to read [it] but it's
    too difficult. /yoꜜmu, mu-
    zukasii/

7. I'd like to eat [it] but it's too
    spicy. /taꜛbeꜜru, kaꜛraꜜi/

8. I'd like to drink [it] but it's
    too strong. /noꜜmu, koꜜi/

Iꜛretaꜜi ñ desu ḡa, oꜛokisuḡimaꜜsu
yo.

Yoꜛmitaꜜi ñ desu ḡa, muꜛzukasisu-
ḡimaꜜsu yo.

Taꜛbetaꜜi ñ desu ḡa, kaꜛrasuḡimaꜜsu
yo.

Noꜛmitaꜜi ñ desu ḡa, koꜛsuḡimaꜜsu
yo.

I. Grammar Drill (based on Grammatical Note 3)

> Tutor: Niꜛhoñma ḡa arimaꜜsu. 'There are Japanese-style rooms.'
> Student: Niꜛhoñma sika arimaseꜜñ. 'There are only Japanese-style
>   rooms.'

1. Aꜛmerikaꜜziñ no toꜛmodati
    (ḡa) miemaꜜsita.

2. Aꜛno hasiꜜ (o) waꜛtarimaꜜ-
    sita.

3. Hoꜜñya e iꜛkimaꜜsita.

4. Hiꜛtoꜜ-ma aꜛite (i)maꜜsu
    yo⌐

5. Watakusi no kuꜛroꜜi kuꜛtuꜜ
    (o) miꜛḡakimaꜜsita.

6. Haꜜha ni iꜛimaꜜsita ḡa⌐

7. Aꜛno siḡoto (o) nokosimaꜜ-
    sita.

8. Hiꜛtoꜜ-bañ toꜛmarimaꜜsita.

Aꜛmerikaꜜziñ no toꜛmodati sika
miemaseꜜñ desita.

Aꜛno hasiꜜ sika waꜛtarimaseꜜñ desita.

Hoꜜñya e sika iꜛkimaseꜜñ desita.

Hiꜛtoꜜ-ma sika aꜛite (i)maseꜜñ
yo⌐

Watakusi no kuꜛroꜜi kuꜛtuꜜ sika
miꜛḡakimaseꜜñ desita.

Haꜜha ni sika iꜛimaseꜜñ desita ḡa⌐

Aꜛno siḡoto sika nokosimaseꜜñ desita.

Hiꜛtoꜜ-bañ sika toꜛmarimaseꜜñ desita.

J. Grammar Drill (based on Grammatical Note 1)

> Tutor: Aꜛtarasiꜜi desu. Hiꜛroꜜi desu. 'It's new. It's large.'
>   (two sentences)
> Student: Aꜛtaraꜜsikute hiꜛroꜜi desu. 'It's new and large.' (one sen-
>   tence)

1. Seꜛmaꜜi desyoo? Aꜛtuꜜi de-
    syoo?

2. Miꜛti ḡa semaꜜi. Ziꜛdoosya
    ḡa ooꜜi.

3. Huꜛyuꜜ ḡa saꜛmuꜜi desu.
    Naꜛtuꜜ ḡa aꜛtuꜜi desu.

4. Aꜛno ryokañ no heyaꜜ wa
    siꜜzuka desu. Geꜜñkañ wa
    yaꜛkamasiꜜi desu.

5. Kono mizu wa tuꜛmetaꜜi.
    Oꜛisiꜜi.

Seꜛmakute aꜛtuꜜi desyoo?

Miꜛti ḡa seꜛmakute, zidoosya ḡa
oꜛoꜜi.

Huꜛyuꜜ ḡa ꜛsaꜜmukute, naꜛtuꜜ ḡa
aꜛtuꜜi desu.

Aꜛno ryokañ no heyaꜜ wa ꜛsiꜜzuka
de, geꜜñkañ wa yaꜛkamasiꜜi desu.

Kono mizu wa tuꜛmetaꜜkute oꜛisiꜜi.

6. Haʳyaʼi aʳtarasiʼi ʰdeˑñsya   Haʼyakute aʳtarasiʼi ʰdeˑñsya ni
   ni noʳrimaˑsita.   noʳrimaˑsita.
7. Siʼzuka na ʳkiʼree na ryo-   Siʼzuka de ʳkiʼree na ryoʰkañ ni
   ʰkañ ni tomarimaˑsita.   tomarimaˑsita.
8. Noʳtta kisyaʼ wa oʼsoʼkatta.   Noʳtta kisyaʼ wa oʼsoʼkute kiʼtana-
   Kiʳtanaʼkatta.   katta.

K. Level Drill[1] (based on Grammatical Note 5)

       Tutor: Kaʼite kuʰdasaimaseʼñ ka⌐
                                 Oʳkaki ni naʼtte kuʰdasaimaseˑñ ka⌐
       Male student: Kaʼite kuʰrenaˑi ka⌐
       Male or female student: Kaʼite kurenai?

1. Huʳtoñ (o) siite kudasaima-   Huʳtoñ (o) siite kurenaˑi ka⌐
   seˑñ ka⌐
   Huʳtoñ (o) osiki ni naʼtte   Hutoñ (o) siite kurenai?
   kuʰdasaimaseˑñ ka⌐
2. Aʳsita no aʼsa ʳhaʼyaku   Aʳsita no aʼsa ʳhaʼyaku oʳkoʼsite
   oʳkoʼsite kuʰdasaimaseˑñ   kuʰrenaˑi ka⌐
   ka⌐
   Aʳsita no aʼsa ʳhaʼyaku oʼo-   Aʳsita no aʼsa ʳhaʼyaku oʳkoʼsite
   kosi ni naʼtte kuʰdasaima-   kurenai?
   seˑñ ka⌐
3. Moʳo sukoʼsi ʳmaʼtte kuʰda-   Moʳo sukoʼsi ʳmaʼtte kuʰrenaˑi ka⌐
   saimaseˑñ ka⌐
   Moʳo sukoʼsi oʼmati ni naʼ-   Moʳo sukoʼsi ʳmaʼtte kurenai?
   tte kuʰdasaimaseˑñ ka⌐
4. Giʳñza maʼde noʳsete kuda-   Giʳñza maʼde noʳsete kurenaˑi ka⌐
   saimaseˑñ ka⌐
   Giʳñza maʼde oʼnose ni naʼ-   Giʳñza maʼde nōsete kurenai?
   tte kuʰdasaimaseˑñ ka⌐
5. Gaʳkkoo no maʼe de oʳroʼ-   Gaʳkkoo no maʼe de oʳroʼsite ku-
   site kuʰdasaimaseˑñ ka⌐   ʰrenaˑi ka⌐
   Gaʳkkoo no maʼe de oʼoro-   Gaʳkkoo no maʼe de oʳroʼsite ku-
   si ni naʼtte kuʰdasaimaseˑñ   renai?
   ka⌐
6. Oʳtonari no Itoo-sañ (o)   Oʳtonari no Itoo-sañ (o) yoñde
   yoñde kudasaimaseʼñ ka⌐   kurenaˑi ka⌐
   Oʳtonari no Itoo-sañ (o)   Otonari no Itoo-sañ (o) yoñde
   oyobi ni naʼtte kuʰdasaima-   kurenai?
   seˑñ ka⌐
7. Moʳo sukoʼsi ʳoʼoki na ʰkoˑe   Moʳo sukoʼsi ʳoʼoki na ʰkoˑe de
   de iʰtte kudasaimaseˑñ ka⌐   iʰtte kurenaˑi ka⌐
   Moʳo sukoʼsi ʳoʼoki na ʰkoˑe   Moʳo sukoʼsi ʳoʼoki na ʰkoˑe de
   de oʰssyaˑtte kuʰdasaima-   itte kurenai?
   seˑñ ka⌐

---

[1] In each case the sentences on the right are the plain informal equivalents
of the sentences on the left.

8. Si⌐o⌐ to ko⌐syo⌐o (o) ⌐to⌐-
   tte ku⌐dasaimase⌐ñ ka⌐
   Si⌐o⌐ to ko⌐syo⌐o (o) o⌐tori
   ni na⌐tte ku⌐dasaimase⌐ñ
   ka⌐

Si⌐o⌐ to ko⌐syo⌐o (o) ⌐to⌐tte ku⌐re-
na⌐i ka⌐
Si⌐o⌐ to ko⌐syo⌐o (o) ⌐to⌐tte kurenai?

L. Expansion Drill

1. I don't need [it].
   I don't need a mosquito net.
   There aren't many (lit.
      they are few) so I don't
      need a mosquito net.
   There aren't many bugs so
      I don't need a mosquito
      net.

I⌐rimase⌐ñ yo⌐
Ka⌐ya wa irimase⌐ñ yo⌐
Su⌐kuna⌐i kara, ka⌐ya wa irima-
se⌐ñ yo⌐
Mu⌐si ḡa sukuna⌐i kara, ka⌐ya wa
irimase⌐n yo⌐

2. I didn't go in.
   It was dirty so I didn't go
      in.
   It was lukewarm and dirty
      so I didn't go in.
   The bath was lukewarm
      and dirty so I didn't go in.
   The bath at that inn was
      lukewarm and dirty so I
      didn't go in.

Ha⌐irimase⌐ñ desita.
Ki⌐tana⌐katta kara, ha⌐irimase⌐ñ
desita.
Nu⌐rukute ki⌐tana⌐katta kara, ha⌐i-
rimase⌐ñ desita.
O⌐hu⌐ro wa ⌐nu⌐rukute ki⌐tana⌐katta
kara, ha⌐irimase⌐ñ desita.
A⌐no ryokañ no ohu⌐ro (wa) ⌐nu⌐ru-
kute ki⌐tana⌐katta kara, ha⌐irima-
se⌐ñ desita.

3. He says there isn't.
   He says there's only one
      room.
   I don't know but he says
      there's only one room.
   I don't know what kind of
      room it is but he says
      there's only one (room).
   I don't know what kind of
      room the room that's
      available is, but he says
      there's only one (room).
   I don't know what kind of
      room the room that's
      available tonight is, but
      he says there's only one
      (room).

A⌐rimase⌐ñ te.
Hi⌐to⌐-ma sika a⌐rimase⌐ñ te.
Si⌐rana⌐i kedo, hi⌐to⌐-ma sika a⌐ri-
mase⌐ñ te.
Do⌐ñna he⌐ya⌐ ka si⌐rana⌐i kedo,
hi⌐to⌐-ma sika a⌐rimase⌐ñ te.
A⌐ite (i)ru heya⌐ (wa) ⌐do⌐ñna he-
⌐ya⌐ ka si⌐rana⌐i kedo, hi⌐to⌐-ma
sika a⌐rimase⌐ñ te.
Ko⌐ñbañ a⌐ite (i)ru heya⌐ (wa) ⌐do⌐-
ñna he⌐ya⌐ ka si⌐rana⌐i kedo, hi-
⌐to⌐-ma sika a⌐rimase⌐ñ te.

4. It's bad.
   I don't feel well.
   I don't feel at all well.
   This morning I don't feel
      at all well.
   I drank too much so this
      morning I don't feel at
      all well.

Wa⌐ru⌐i desu yo⌐
Gu⌐ai ḡa waru⌐i desu yo⌐
To⌐ttemo guai ḡa waru⌐i desu yo⌐
Ke⌐sa wa to⌐ttemo guai ḡa waru⌐i
desu yo⌐
No⌐misuḡita⌐[1] kara, ke⌐sa wa to-
⌐ttemo guai ḡa waru⌐i desu yo⌐

---

[1] Alternate accent: no⌐misu⌐ḡita.

I drank too much sake so this morning I don't feel at all well.	Sa⌐ke (o) nomisuḡita⌐ kara, ke⌐- sa wa to⌐ttemo guai ḡa waru⌐i desu yo⌐
I drank too much sake last night so this morning I don't feel at all well.	Yuube sa⌐ke (o) nomisuḡita⌐ kara, ke⌐sa wa to⌐ttemo guai ḡa wa- ru⌐i desu yo⌐

5. It's all right.   I⌐i desu.

That one will be all right.   So⌐re de i⌐i desu.

There isn't [one] so that   Na⌐i kara, so⌐re de i⌐i desu.
one will be all right.

There's nothing but that   So⌐no hi⌐bati sika ⌐na⁴i kara,
hibachi so that will be   so⌐re de i⌐i desu.
all right.

Tonight there's nothing but   Ko⌐ñbañ wa so⌐no hi⌐bati sika
that hibachi so that will be   ⌐na⁴i kara, so⌐re de i⌐i desu.
all right.

I'd like to buy [one] but to-   Ka⌐ita⁴i ñ desu ḡa; ko⌐ñbañ wa
night there's nothing but   so⌐no hi⌐bati sika ⌐na⁴i kara,
that hibachi so that will   so⌐re de i⌐i desu.
be all right.

I'd like to buy a big heater   O⌐oki⌐i su⌐to⁴obu (ḡa) ka⌐ita⁴i ñ
but tonight there's noth-   desu ḡa; ko⌐ñbañ wa so⌐no ⌐hi⌐-
ing but that hibachi so   bati sika ⌐na⁴i kara, so⌐re de
that will be all right.   i⌐i desu.

I'd like to buy a big heater   Asita o⌐oki⌐i su⌐to⁴obu (ḡa) ka-
tomorrow, but tonight   ⌐ita⁴i ñ desu ḡa; ko⌐ñbañ wa
there's nothing but that   so⌐no ⌐hi⌐bati sika ⌐na⁴i kara,
hibachi so that will be   so⌐re de i⌐i desu.
all right.

It's grown cold so I'd like   Sa⌐muku ⌐na⁴tta kara, asita
to buy a big heater to-   o⌐oki⌐i su⌐to⁴obu (ḡa) ka⌐ita⁴i
morrow, but tonight   ñ desu ḡa; ko⌐ñbañ wa so⌐no
there's nothing but that   ⌐hi⌐bati sika ⌐na⁴i kara, so⌐re
hibachi so that will be   de i⌐i desu.
all right.

It's grown awfully cold so   Hi⌐doku ⌐sa⁴muku ⌐na⁴tta kara,
I'd like to buy a big   asita o⌐oki⌐i su⌐to⁴obu (ḡa)
heater tomorrow, but   ka⌐ita⁴i ñ desu ḡa; ko⌐ñbañ wa
tonight there's nothing   so⌐no ⌐hi⌐bati sika ⌐na⁴i kara,
but that hibachi so that   so⌐re de i⌐i desu.
will be all right.

SUPPLEMENTARY CONVERSATION

Smith: Go⌐meñ-kudasa⌐i. Ko⌐obe no ⌐Su⌐misu desu ḡa, ko⌐ñbañ o⌐negai-sima⁴su.
Clerk: I⌐rassyaima⌐se. Su⌐misu-sama de irassyaimasu ne? O⌐mati-site ori-
  ma⌐sita. Do⌐ozo o⌐aḡari-kudasaima⁴se. Yooma wa ti⌐isa⌐i no sika go⌐zai-
  mase⁴ñ ḡa, hurobatuki no ⌐i⌐i za⌐siki⌐ ḡa go⌐zaima⁴su ḡa_
Smith: Za⌐siki no ho⌐o ḡa ⌐i⁴i desu yo.
Room-girl: Do⌐ozo kotira e. O⌐ni⌐motu wa?
Smith: So⌐re dake⌐ desu.
Room-girl: Wa⌐takusi ḡa motte mairima⌐su. O⌐ni⌐kai de gozaimasu.

Room-girl: Ko⌐tira de gozaima⌐su. Do⌐ozo.
Smith: *Hi⌐rokute ⌐ki⌐ree na za⌐siki⌐ desu ⌐ne⌐e. A⌐a, u⌐mi ḡa mi⌐ema⌐su ⌐ne⌐e.
Room-girl: O⌐ni⌐motu wa ko⌐tira ni ooki-itasima⌐su.
Smith: A⌐a, do⌐o mo.
Room-girl: Su⌐ḡu ⌐hi⌐bati o mo⌐tte mairima⌐su. Su⌐to⌐obu o o⌐tuke-itasi-masyo⌐o ka.
Smith: Hi⌐bati de ⌐ke⌐kkoo desu.
Room-girl: O⌐so⌐reirimasu ḡa, kore ni o⌐namae o oneḡai-itasima⌐su.
Smith: Nihoñḡo de?
Room-girl: Ha⌐a, o⌐neḡai-itasima⌐su.
Smith: *A⌐ñmari zyoozu⌐ zya a⌐rimase⌐ñ ḡa—

                              . . .

Room-girl: A⌐ri⌐ḡatoo gozaimasita. *Zu⌐ibuñ o⌐zyoozu de irassyaima⌐su ⌐ne⌐e. A⌐sita⌐ wa na⌐ñ-zi-ḡo⌐ro o⌐tati ni narima⌐su ka—
Smith: Ha⌐to ni no⌐rima⌐su kara, ha⌐ti-zi-ha⌐ñ ni ko⌐ko o tatita⌐i ñ desu.
Room-girl: Sa⌐yoo de gozaima⌐su ka. Wa⌐karima⌐sita. Su⌐ḡu o⌐hu⌐ro ni o⌐hairi ni narima⌐su ka—
Smith: Iie, a⌐to de hairimasu. Su⌐ḡu o⌐zeñ o da⌐site kudasai.
Room-girl: Osyokuzi wa yōosyoku to wasyoku to ⌐do⌐tira ḡa yo⌐rosi⌐i de-syoo ka.
Smith: Wa⌐syoku o oneḡai-sima⌐su.
Room-girl: Ha⌐a. Syo⌐oti-itasima⌐sita. O⌐nomi⌐mono wa?
Smith: Bi⌐iru o. Sore kara, yu⌐za⌐masi o mo⌐tte⌐ kite kudasai.
Room-girl: Syo⌐oti-itasima⌐sita. Su⌐ḡu o⌐zeñ o motte mairima⌐su. Go⌐meñ-kudasaima⌐se.
Smith: O⌐neḡai-sima⌐su.

                    English Equivalent

Smith: Excuse me. I'm [Mr.] Smith from Kobe. I'd like [a room for] to-night.
Clerk: (Welcome.) You're Mr. Smith, is that right? We were expecting you. Please come in. We have only a small Western-style room (lit. as for Western-style rooms, we have only a small one) but we have a nice Jap-anese-style room with bath . . .
Smith: I prefer the Japanese-style room.
Room-girl: This way please. Your luggage?
Smith: That is all I have.
Room-girl: I'll take it. [The room] is upstairs.

                              . . .

Room-girl: Here it is. Please [go in].
Smith: What a beautiful big (lit. large and beautiful) room. Oh, you can see the ocean, can't you.
Room-girl: I'll put your bag here.
Smith: Oh, thanks.
Room-girl: I'll bring a hibachi right away. Shall I turn on the heater?
Smith: A hibachi will be fine.

Room-girl: Excuse me but may I have your name on this [piece of paper]?
Smith: In Japanese?
Room-girl: Yes, please.
Smith: I'm not very good . . .

. . .

Room-girl: Thank you. [Looking at writing] You're very good [at writing]!
   About what time are you leaving tomorrow?
Smith: I'm taking the Hato so I'd like to leave here at 8:30.
Room-girl: Oh, I see. Are you going to take a bath right away?
Smith: No, I'll take it later. Please bring dinner right away.
Room-girl: For dinner which would you prefer—Western-style food or Jap-
   anese-style food?
Smith: I'd like Japanese food.
Room-girl: All right. What would you like to drink?
Smith: [I'd like] some beer. And would you bring some drinking water that
   has been boiled?
Room-girl: Certainly. I'll serve your dinner right away. Excuse me.
Smith: (Please do as I requested.)

EXERCISES

1. Practice asking and answering questions about meaning, using the patterns of Basic Sentences 38 and 39. (Warning: Don't attempt to say anything you aren't sure of!)

   Examples: Na⌐o˥su to i┝u┤ no wa ⌐do˥o iu ┝i┤mi desu ka⌐
             Na⌐o˥su to i┝u┤ no wa ⌐yo˥ku suru to iu ┝i┤mi desu.
             Hu⌐robatuki to iu˥ no wa ⌐do˥o iu ┝i┤mi desu ka⌐
             Hu⌐robatuki to iu˥ no wa hu⌐roba˥ ḡa ⌐tu˥ite (i)ru to iu
             ┝i┤mi desu.

2. At an inn

   a. Ask the clerk:

       (1) if he has a room with a bath.
       (2) if he has a quiet room.
       (3) if he has a large and cool room.
       (4) if he has a Western-style room.
       (5) how much it will be for one night.
       (6) if that includes meals.

   b. Tell the room-girl:

       (1) to shine your shoes.
       (2) to press this suit.
       (3) that you want to take a bath but you don't know where it is.
       (4) that the bath is too hot.
       (5) that you want some drinking water.
       (6) to bring dinner.

    (7) that Japanese food will be fine.

    (8) that you'd like sukiyaki.

    (9) to spread the futon.

(10) that you'd like a mosquito net because there are a lot of bugs.

(11) that you don't need a mosquito net because there aren't many bugs.

(12) to wake you at 7:30 because you are going to take a 9 o'clock train.

Lesson 22. Services

BASIC DIALOGUES: FOR MEMORIZATION

(a)

Mr. Tanaka

hair (on the head)	ka⌐mi⌐
is long	na⌐ḡa⌐i /-ku/
barber or barbershop	tokoya
even going	i⌐tte⌐ mo
it's all right even if [some- one] goes or may go	i⌐tte⌐ mo ⌐i⌐i

1. My hair has grown long so I'd (just) like to go to the barber- shop. May I go now?

Ka⌐mi⌐ ḡa ⌐ha⌐ḡaku ⌐na⌐tta kara, tyo⌐tto to⌐koya e ikita⌐i ñ desu ḡa; i⌐ma i⌐tte⌐ mo ⌐i⌐i desu ka⌐

Mr. Smith

2. Yes, that will be all right.

E⌐e, i⌐i desu yo⌐

however or but	ke⌐redo
come back	ka⌐ette kuru

3. But I'd like you to come back by 3 o'clock.

Ke⌐redo, sa⌐ñ-zi made ni ⌐ka⌐ette kite mo⌐raita⌐i ñ desu yo.

business affairs or matter to attend to	yo⌐o or yoozi

4. [That's] because I have some- thing I must attend to, too, and I'm going out.

Bo⌐ku mo yoozi ḡa a⌐tte, de⌐ka- keru⌐ kara.

(at the barbershop)

Barber

what kind of style?	do⌐ñna huu /na/
into what kind of style?	do⌐ñna huu ni

5. How shall I cut (lit. do) it?

Do⌐ñna huu ni i⌐tasimasyo⌐o ka.

Mr. Tanaka

is short	mi⌐zika⌐i /-ku/
clip or mow	karu /-u/

6. The front is fine as it is so clip [just] the sides and back short.

Ma⌐e wa ko⌐no mama⌐ de ⌐i⌐i kara, yoko to usiro (o) mi⌐zika⌐ku ka⌐tte kudasa⌐i.

Barber

7. Shall I wash your hair (lit. head) too?

A⌐tama⌐ mo a⌐raimasyo⌐o ka.

23

Mr. Tanaka

beard	hig̃e
shave	so¹ru /-u/

8. Yes, wash my hair and give me   E¹e, a¹tama¹ mo aratte, hi⌐ge mo
   a good shave, too.   yo¹ku ⌐so⁴tte.

(b)

Smith

bicycle	ziteñsya [1]
lend or rent (to someone)	kasu /-u/
look for	saḡasu /-u/

9. I'm looking for a place that   Zi⌐teñsya (o) kasu tokoro¹ (o)
   rents bicycles . . .   sa⌐ḡasite (i)ma⁴su ḡa—

Tanaka

bicycle shop or dealer	ziteñsyaya
it is the expectation that [someone] rents	kasu hazu da

10. They're supposed to rent [them]   A⌐no ziteñsyaya de kasu hazu
    at that bicycle shop.   de¹su yo—

(at the bicycle shop)

Smith

11. Is anyone here? (Lit. Excuse   Go⌐meñ-kudasa¹i.
    me.)

Shopkeeper (coming from back of shop)

12. (Welcome.)   Irassyai—

Smith

the report is that [someone] rents	ka⌐su so¹o da

13. They say that you rent bicycles   Otaku de zi⌐teñsya (o) kasu so¹o
    at your place . . .   desu ḡa—

Shopkeeper

14. Yes, indeed. This way, please.   Ha¹i ⌐ha⁴i. Do¹ozo kotira e.

(c)

Customer (holding a ¥1000 bill)

15. Can you change this?   Ko⌐maka¹ku de⌐kima⁴su ka—

Cab-driver (checking his money)

money	kane or okane +
it is the expectation that there was	a¹tta hazu da
not at all	zeñzeñ /+ negative/

---

[1]
Has accented alternant: zi⌐te¹ñsya.

16. I thought I had (lit. there ought
    to have been) some small
    change . . . I'm sorry but I
    don't have any at all.

Ko⌐maka⌐i okane (ḡa) ⌐a⌐tta ha⌐zu
de⌐su ḡa— Su⌐mimase⌐ñ ḡa, zeñzeñ arimase⌐ñ.

(d)

Customer (Man)

use   tukau /-u/
deliver   to⌐doke⌐ru /-ru/

17. I want to use this on Tuesday
    morning so I'd like to have it
    delivered to my home by
    then . . .

Kore (wa) ka⌐yoo no a⌐sa tu⌐kaita⌐i
kara, so⌐re ma⌐de ni ūti e to⌐do-
kete mo⌐raita⌐i ñ da ḡa ⌐ne⌐e.

Salesgirl

place where one lives   to⌐koro⌐ or otokoro ⌐
onto this place   koko ni

18. Certainly. Would you please
    write your name and address
    here?

Syo⌐oti-itasima⌐sita. Onamae to otokoro (o) kōko ni o⌐kaki ni na⌐tte
ku⌐dasaimase⌐ñ ka—

Customer

even borrowing   ka⌐rite⌐ mo
it's all right even if [some-   ka⌐rite⌐ mo ⌐i⌐i
    one] borrows or may bor-
    row

19. May I borrow this pencil?

Ko⌐no eñpitu (o) karite⌐ mo ⌐i⌐i?

Salesgirl

charge or cost   dai or odai +
even receiving   i⌐tadaite⌐ mo
whether receiving now or   i⌐ma i⌐tadaite⌐ mo o⌐todoke-
    receiving at the time   sita to⌐ki ni i⌐tadaite⌐ mo
    [someone] has delivered
    [it]

20. Certainly. . . . You can pay
    now or when it's delivered
    (but). . . . (Lit. As for the charge,
    whether I receive it now or re-
    ceive it at the time I have de-
    livered, it's all right but . . .)

Do⌐ozo. . . . Odai wa ⌐i⌐ma i⌐ta-
daite⌐ mo o⌐todoke-sita to⌐ki ni
i⌐tadaite⌐ mo ⌐ke⌐kkoo de gozaimasu ḡa—

Customer

pay   ha⌐ra⌐u /-u/
receipt   uketori

21. I'll pay now so would you write
    a receipt?

I⌐ma ha⌐ra⌐u kara, uketori (o)
⌐ka⌐ite ku⌐rena⌐i ka—

(after receiving receipt)

don't forget   wa⌐surena⌐i de (kudasai)

22. Well then, by Tuesday morning   Zya⌐a, ka⌐yoo no a⌐sa made ni ne?
     —all right? Don't forget, will   Wa⌐surena⌐i de (kudasai) ne?
     you?

(e)

Mrs. Tanaka

     maid   zyotyuu
     according to the talk of a   zyo⌐tyuu no hanasi⌐ de wa
        maid
     the report is that it's de-   o⌐isii so⌐o da
        licious
23. According to (the talk of) our   U⌐ti no zyotyuu no hanasi⌐ de wa
     maid, (the report is that) the   a⌐no mise no oni⌐ku (wa) ⌐ya⌐sukute
     meat at that store is cheap and   o⌐isii so⌐o desu yo⌐
     good.

Mrs. Yamamoto

24. That's what they say!   So⌐o desu tte ⌐ne⌐e.

     stop in   yoru /-u/
25. I haven't gone [there] yet but   Ma⌐da i⌐kimaseñ kedo, yo⌐tte mi-
     shall we stop in and see?   masyo⌐o ka.

     sell   uru /-u/
     the report is that [some-   u⌐tte (i)ru so⌐o da
        one] is selling
26. (Because) I hear they are al-   I⌐tu mo ⌐i⌐i o⌐ni⌐ku (o) u⌐tte (i)ru
     ways selling good meat.   so⌐o desu kara.

(at the butcher's)
Mrs. Tanaka (pointing)

     beef   gyuuniku
     is soft <u>or</u> tender <u>or</u>   ya⌐waraka⌐i /-ku/
        pliable
27. Is that beef tender?   Sono gyuuniku (wa) ya⌐waraka⌐i
                                            desu ka⌐

Butcher

     is delicious <u>or</u> is skillful   u⌐ma⌐i <u>or</u> ñ⌐ma⌐i /-ku/
28. Yes, indeed. It's very good.   Ha⌐i ⌐ha⌐i. *N̄⌐ma⌐i desu yo⌐

Mrs. Tanaka

     one gram   i⌐ti-gu⌐ramu
29. Well then, I'd like 500 grams.   Zya⌐a, go⌐hyaku-gu⌐ramu oneḡai-
                                            simasu.

     use for sukiyaki   sukiyaki ni tukau
     as much as possible   narubeku
     is thin (of flat objects)   usui /-ku/
     cut as thin as possible   na⌐rubeku usuku ki⌐ru
30. I'm going to use [it] for sukiya-   Su⌐kiyaki ni tukaima⌐su kara, na-
     ki so please cut [it] as thin as   ⌐rubeku usuku ki⌐tte kudasai.
     possible.

NOTES ON THE BASIC DIALOGUES

3. Like particle keredo, this ke˥redo, which occurs at the beginning of sentences, also has alternants ke˥redomo and ke˥do.

6. Ka˥mi˥ o kǎru is ordinarily used in reference to clipping hair, and ka˥mi˥ o ˥ki˥ru in reference to cutting hair. Karu is used more commonly by men, and ki˥ru by women.

9. 'but—do you know of one?'
   Compare: So˥re o kasite ima˥su. 'I'm lending or renting that (to someone)'; So˥re o karite ima˥su. 'I'm borrowing or renting that (from someone).'

11. See Lesson 12, Notes on the Basic Dialogues, 26.

13. 'but—is it true?'
    Note the use of otaku in reference to a shop.

15. Ko˥maka˥ku de˥ki˥ru means literally 'can make to occur in small units.'

16. 'but—I can't seem to find it.'
    The polite okane is the more common alternant in conversation. There are a few examples of zeñzeñ + an affirmative: for example, ze˥ñzeñ tiǧa˥u 'be completely different'; ze˥ñzeñ dame˥ da 'be no good at all,' 'be completely broken.'

17. 'but—you understand, don't you.'
    To˥doke˥ru is the transitive partner of intransitive to˥do˥ku /-u/ 'reach' or 'be delivered.'

20. 'but—which do you prefer?'
    Otodoke-sita is the humble equivalent of to˥do˥keta (cf. Lesson 13, Grammatical Note 4).

27. Note also butaniku 'pork.'
    The opposite of ya˥waraka˥i is katai /-ku/ 'is hard or tough or stiff or firm.'

28. U˥ma˥i in some of its occurrences is equivalent to zyo˥ozu˥ da and in others to oisii, but it is a less formal word.

30. The opposite of usui is atui 'is thick (of flat objects).' Note the difference in accent between this atui and a˥tu˥i 'is hot'; but in some positions —for example, before √de˥su ˙and kara, where non-past adjectivals are regularly accented on the next-to-last syllable—this distinction disappears: a˥tu˥i desu 'it is thick' or 'it is hot,' a˥tu˥i kara 'because it is thick' or 'because it is hot.'

GRAMMATICAL NOTES

1. hazu

   Hazu 'expectation' is a nominal which is always preceded by a modifier

—usually a sentence modifier (cf. Lesson 19, Grammatical Note 1). It is regularly followed by √da (no before another nominal), or by particle wa or ḡa + √na'i. Hazu implies expectation imposed by circumstances: the most common English equivalents in the affirmative are 'is expected to,' 'is supposed to,' 'ought to,' 'should,' [1] etc.; for the negative hazu wa (or ḡa) ⌐na'i, the most common equivalents are 'there's no expectation,' 'there's no reason to expect,' etc. The subject of a hazu modifier is rarely the speaker.

Examples:

A⌐sa'tte made ni ko⌐re o yo'mu hazu desu. 'He's expected to read this by tonight.'

Wa⌐ka'tta ha⌐zu de'su ḡa— 'He ought to have understood but . . .'

Kore yori so⌐re no ho'o ḡa ta⌐ka'i hazu desu. 'That one should be more expensive than this one.'

Tanaka-sañ wa o'naka no guai ḡa he'ñ da kara, kyo'o wa na'ni mo ta-be'nai hazu desu. 'There's something wrong with Mr. Tanaka's stomach so he isn't expected to (lit. he is expected not to) eat anything today.'

A⌐ratta' kara, ki⌐ree na hazu desu. 'I washed [it] so it should be clean.'

Ku⌐ru hazu no hito ḡa ⌐ma'da ki⌐mase'ñ kara, tyo'tto ⌐ma'tte kudasai. 'The man who is supposed to come hasn't come yet so just a minute.'

Byo'oki da' kara, ku⌐ru hazu wa ⌐na'i yo. 'He's sick so there's no reason to expect that he will come.' (Man talking)

Ya⌐kusoku da' kara, i⌐kanai hazu wa arimase'ñ. 'He has (lit. it is) an appointment, so there's no reason to expect he won't go.'

So⌐ñna hazu wa arimase'ñ yo⌣ 'There's no reason to expect anything like that.'

2. ── so'o √da

So'o √da following a sentence ending in the informal style means that the information contained in the sentence is being reported at second hand: 'it is said that ──,' 'I hear that ──,' 'the report is that ──,' etc. Following an accented word or phrase, so'o regularly loses its accent.

Examples:

Tanaka-sañ wa a̅sita Yo⌐kohama e tu'ku soo desu. 'I hear that Mr. Tanaka is arriving in Yokohama tomorrow.'

A⌐tarasi'i zi⌐do'osya o ka⌐tta so'o desu. 'I hear you bought a new car.'

Ho⌐kka'idoo wa to'temo samu'i soo desu. 'They say that Hokkaido is very cold.'

Yo⌐katta soo da kara, mi⌐ta'i ñ desu yo⌣ 'I hear it was good so I want to see it.'

So⌐no kata' wa ⌐mo'o i⌐rassyara'nai soo desu. 'The report is that he isn't coming any more.'

----

[1] I. e. 'ought to,' or 'should' because it is natural and a matter of course, not because it is a moral obligation.

Soꜟo da soo desu ꜠neꜟe. 'That's what they say!'
A꜠no zibikiꜟ wa niꜟseñ-eñ daꜟtta soo desu. 'They say that dictionary
was ¥ 2000.'

When the information is attributed to a specific source, there is an introductory sequence like — no haꜟnasiꜟ de wa 'according to the talk of —.'
The soꜟo √da following is further indication that information is being reported at second hand.

3. Negative Requests

An informal non-past negative (i. e. a -nai adjectival) + copula gerund de
+ kudasai is a negative imperative meaning 'please don't —.'

Examples:

Iꜟsoḡaꜟnai de kudasai. 'Please don't hurry.'
Waꜟsurenaꜟi de kudasai. 'Please don't forget.'
Soꜟo ossyaraꜟnai de kudasai. 'Please don't say that.'

Kudasai may be replaced by kuꜟrenaꜟi ka, kuꜟdasaimaseꜟñ ka, etc., with
the same differences of politeness and formality that apply in affirmative requests.
A -nai adjectival + de (i. e. the pattern described above without kudasai)
in sentence-final position, or pre-final before a sentence particle, is an informal negative request.

Examples:

Aꜟkenaꜟi de. 'Don't open [it].'
Tuꜟkawanaꜟi de yo. 'Don't use [it]!'
Moꜟo siꜟnaꜟi de ne? 'Don't do it any more—will you?'

4. Gerund + mo; Permission

A gerund—verbal, adjectival, or copula— + mo means 'even being or doing so-and-so,' 'even if it is so-and-so,' 'even if [someone] does so-and-
so.' Before mo, a normally unaccented gerund acquires an accent on the
final syllable.

Examples:

Kiꜟiteꜟ mo waꜟkaraꜟnai. 'Even if I listen, I don't understand.'
Aꜟnaꜟta ḡa iꜟtteꜟ mo waꜟtakusi wa ikimaseꜟñ. 'Even if you go, I'm not
going.'
Toꜟoꜟkute mo iꜟkitaꜟi ñ desu. 'Even if it's far, I want to go.'
Aꜟnaꜟta ḡa iꜟkanaꜟkute mo waꜟtakusi wa ikimaꜟsu. 'Even if you don't
go, I'm going.'
Yoꜟmitaꜟkute mo muꜟzukasisuḡimaꜟsu kara— 'Even if I want to read it,
it's too difficult so . . .'

Ni-⌐too de⌐ mo ta⌐ka⁴i desu yo⌣ 'Even if it's second class it's expensive.'

O⌐mosi⌐roku ⁺na⁴kute mo ⌐yo⌐nde kudasai. 'Even if it's not interesting,
please read it.'

Su⌐ki⌐ zya ⁺na⁴kute mo ⌐ta⌐bete yo. 'Even if you don't like it, eat it!'

A pair of such gerund + _mo_ phrases is equivalent to English 'whether it's
— or — ,' 'whether [someone] does — or — .'

Examples:

Ki⌐ite⌐ mo ki⌐kana⌐kute mo wa⌐kara⌐nai. 'Whether I listen or don't listen, I don't understand.'

Ko⌐ohi⌐i wa ⌐a⌐tukute mo tu⌐meta⌐kute mo su⌐ki⌐ desu. 'Whether coffee is hot or cold, I like it.'

Go⌐zibun de site⌐ mo si⌐te moratte⌐ mo ka⌐maimase⌐n. 'It doesn't matter whether you do it yourself or have it done.'

Ka⌐ita⌐kute mo ka⌐itaku na⌐kute mo o⌐kane ḡa na⌐i kara⌐ 'Whether I
want to buy it or don't want to buy it, I have no money so . . . '

I⌐t-too de⌐ mo ni-⌐too de⌐ mo ta⌐ka⌐i desu yo⌣ 'Whether it's first class
or second class, it's expensive.'

Gerund + _mo_ + $\left\{ \begin{array}{l} \sqrt{i}i \\ \sqrt{yorosii} \\ \sqrt{ka⌐mawa⌐nai} \end{array} \right\}$ means 'even being _or_ doing so-and-so,

it's all right _or_ it doesn't matter.' This pattern is used in requesting and
granting permission: when the gerund is affirmative, permission to do or be
so-and-so is requested (in questions) or granted (in statements); when the
gerund is negative, permission not to do or be so-and-so is requested (in
questions) or granted (in statements).

Examples:

Tu⌐katte⌐ mo ⌐i⌐i desu ka⌣ 'May I use it?' (Lit. 'Even using, is it all
right?')

Ka⌐ette mo yo⌐rosi⌐i desu ka⌣ 'May I go home?'

So⌐re o ta⌐bete mo ⌐i⌐i desu. 'You may eat that.'

Sa⌐mukute mo ka⌐maimase⌐n. 'Even if it's cold, it doesn't matter.'

Ni-⌐too de⌐ mo ⌐i⌐i desu ka⌣ 'Will it be all right even if it's second
class?'

I⌐ma si⁺na⁴kute mo ⁺i⁴i desu ka⌣ 'Is it all right (even) if I don't do it
now?'

I⌐soḡa⌐nakute mo ⌐i⌐i desu. 'You don't have to hurry.' (Lit. 'Even if
you don't hurry it's all right.')

A⌐sita ko⌐nakute mo ka⌐maimase⌐n ka⌣ 'Do you mind (even) if I don't
come tomorrow?'

An affirmative answer to a request for permission may be do⌐ozo or ha⁴i
or √i⌐i or a repetition of all or part of the request without ka, etc.

The negative answer to a request for permission depends on whether the
request is affirmative or negative. In denying permission for someone to do
something, tyo⌐tto⌐ or a negative imperative may be used:

Si⌐te⌐ mo ⌐i⌐i desu ka⌣ 'May I do [it]?'

Tyо̀tto‿ 'I'm afraid not.'   or   Si̋naꞈi de kudasai.   'Please don't do [it].'

In denying permission NOT to do something, tyо̀tto‿ or an affirmative imperative or an appropriate affirmative gerund + moraitai may be used:

Si̋naꞈkute mo ꞈi̋ꞈi desu ka‿ 'Is it all right if I don't do [it]?'
Tyо̀tto‿ 'I'm afraid not.'   or   Si̋ꞈte kudasai.   'Please do [it].'
or   Si̋ꞈte moraita̋ꞈi ñ desu ḡa‿ 'I'd like to have you do [it] . . . '

Other kinds of negative replies will be introduced later.

5. Counter -guramu

The counter -guramu combines with numerals of Series I to count grams.[1]
The numbers from one to ten are:

i̋ꞈti-gűꞈramu	'1 gram'	roꞈku-gűramu	'6 grams'
ni-ꞈgűꞈramu	'2 grams'	naꞈna-gűramu	'7 grams'
saꞈñ-gűꞈramu	'3 grams'	haꞈti-gűramu	'8 grams'
yoꞈñ-gűꞈramu	'4 grams'	kyűꞈu-gűramu	'9 grams'
go-ꞈgűꞈramu	'5 grams'	zyűꞈu-gűramu	'10 grams'
	naꞈñ-gűramu	'how many grams?'	

DRILLS

A. Substitution Drill

1. There isn't any of that at all.   Sore wa zeꞈñzeñ arimaseꞈñ.

2. I don't understand that at all.   Sore wa zeꞈñzeñ wakarimaseꞈñ.

3. There isn't enough of that at all.   Sore wa zeꞈñzeñ tarimaseꞈñ.

4. That doesn't matter at all.   Sore wa zeꞈñzeñ kamaimaseꞈñ.

5. That I don't use at all.   Sore wa zeꞈñzeñ tukaimaseꞈñ.

6. That doesn't hurt at all.   Sore wa zeꞈñzeñ itaꞈku aꞈrima-seꞈñ.

7. That isn't heavy at all.   Sore wa zeꞈñzeñ omoku arima-seꞈñ.

8. That isn't tasty at all.   Sore wa zeꞈñzeñ uꞈmaku aꞈri-maseꞈñ.

9. That isn't pretty at all.   Sore wa zeꞈñzeñ kiꞈree zya aꞈrimaseꞈñ.

10. That isn't the same at all.   Sore wa zeꞈñzeñ onazi zya ari-maseꞈñ.

---

[1] 500 grams = approximately 1.1 lbs.

B. Substitution Drill

1. Can you change [it] (i. e. break it up into small pieces?	Ko⌐maka⌐ku de⌐kima⌐su ka⌐
2. I changed [it].	Ko⌐maka⌐ku si⌐ma⌐sita.
3. I made [it] long.	Na⌐gaku si⌐ma⌐sita.
4. Can you make [it] long?	Na⌐gaku de⌐kima⌐su ka⌐
5. Can you make [it] short?	Mi⌐zika⌐ku de⌐kima⌐su ka⌐
6. I made [it] short.	Mi⌐zika⌐ku si⌐ma⌐sita.
7. I made [it] thin.	U⌐suku sima⌐sita.
8. Can you make [it] thin?	U⌐suku dekima⌐su ka⌐
9. Can you make [it] thick?	A⌐tuku dekima⌐su ka⌐
10. I made [it] thick.	A⌐tuku sima⌐sita.

C. Substitution Drill

1. May I ask?	Ki⌐ite⌐ mo ⌐i⌐i desu ka⌐
2. May I come?	Ki⌐te⌐ mo ⌐i⌐i desu ka⌐
3. May I cut [it]?	Ki⌐tte⌐ mo ⌐i⌐i desu ka⌐
4. May I go up?	A⌐gatte⌐ mo ⌐i⌐i desu ka⌐
5. May I give [it to him]?	A⌐gete⌐ mo ⌐i⌐i desu ka⌐
6. May I get up?	O⌐kite mo ⌐i⌐i desu ka⌐
7. May I get off?	O⌐rite mo ⌐i⌐i desu ka⌐
8. May I put [it down]?	O⌐ite⌐ mo ⌐i⌐i desu ka⌐
9. May I go home?	Ka⌐ette mo ⌐i⌐i desu ka⌐
10. May I apply [it]?[1]	Ka⌐kete mo ⌐i⌐i desu ka⌐
11. May I write [it]?	Ka⌐ite mo ⌐i⌐i desu ka⌐
12. May I do [it]?	Si⌐te⌐ mo ⌐i⌐i desu ka⌐
13. May I spread [it] out?	Si⌐ite⌐ mo ⌐i⌐i desu ka⌐
14. May I read [it]?	Yo⌐nde mo ⌐i⌐i desu ka⌐
15. May I call [him]?	Yo⌐nde⌐ mo ⌐i⌐i desu ka⌐

D. Substitution Drill

(Insert the substitution item in its appropriate form.)

1. May I go now?	I⌐ma i⌐tte⌐ mo ⌐i⌐i desu ka⌐
2. May I use this telephone? /kono deñwa (o) tukau/	Ko⌐no deñwa (o) tukatte⌐ mo ⌐i⌐i desu ka⌐
3. May I just stop in at that store? /tyo⌐tto a⌐no mise⌐ ni yŏru/	Tyo⌐tto a⌐no mise⌐ ni yo⌐tte⌐ mo ⌐i⌐i desu ka⌐
4. May I spread the quilts now? /i⌐ma hŭtoñ (o) siku/	I⌐ma hu⌐toñ (o) siite⌐ mo ⌐i⌐i desu ka⌐
5. May I get off at the next corner? /tu⌐gi⌐ no ⌐ka⌐do de o⌐ri⌐ru/	Tu⌐gi⌐ no ⌐ka⌐do de ⌐o⌐rite mo ⌐i⌐i desu ka⌐

---

[1] Or, depending on context, 'May I telephone?' 'May I press it?' etc.

6. May I smoke? /ta⌐bako (o)
   no⌐mu/

   Ta⌐bako (o) no⌐ñde mo ⌐i⌐i desu
   ka⌐

7. May I throw away these little things? /kono ko⌐maka⌐i
   mo⌐no⌐ (o) sūteru/

   Kono ko⌐maka⌐i mo⌐no⌐ (o) su⌐tete⌐
   mo ⌐i⌐i desu ka⌐

8. May I have a friend write
   it? /to⌐modati ni ka⌐ite
   morau/

   To⌐modati ni ka⌐ite mo⌐ratte⌐ mo
   ⌐i⌐i desu ka⌐

9. May I go home early?
   /ha⌐yaku ⌐ka⌐eru/

   Ha⌐yaku ⌐ka⌐ette mo ⌐i⌐i desu ka⌐

10. May I open the window?
    /ma⌐do (o) ākeru/

    Ma⌐do (o) a⌐kete⌐ mo ⌐i⌐i desu ka⌐

E. Substitution Drill

(Insert the substitution item in its appropriate form.)

1. It doesn't matter whether
   you go or not.

   I⌐tte⌐ mo i⌐kana⌐kute mo ka⌐mai-
   mase⌐ñ yo⌐

2. It doesn't matter whether
   you want to go or not.
   /ikitai/

   I⌐kita⌐kute mo i⌐kitaku na⌐kute mo
   ka⌐maimase⌐ñ yo⌐

3. It doesn't matter whether
   you use [it] or not. /tukau/

   Tu⌐katte⌐ mo tu⌐kawana⌐kute mo
   ka⌐maimase⌐ñ yo⌐

4. It doesn't matter whether
   you're good [at it] or not.
   /zyo⌐ozu da/

   Zyo⌐ozu⌐ de mo zyo⌐ozu⌐ zya ⌐na⌐-
   kute mo ka⌐maimase⌐ñ yo⌐

5. It doesn't matter whether
   you write [it] or not.
   /ka⌐ku/

   Ka⌐ite mo ka⌐ka⌐nakute mo ka⌐mai-
   mase⌐ñ yo⌐

6. It doesn't matter whether
   you do [it] or not. /suru/

   Si⌐te⌐ mo si⌐na⌐kute mo ka⌐maima-
   se⌐ñ yo⌐

7. It doesn't matter whether
   you want to do [it] or not.
   /sitai/

   Si⌐ta⌐kute mo si⌐taku na⌐kute mo
   ka⌐maimase⌐ñ yo⌐

8. It doesn't matter whether
   it's interesting or not.
   /o⌐mosiro⌐i/

   O⌐mosi⌐rokute mo o⌐mosi⌐roku
   ⌐na⌐kute mo ka⌐maimase⌐ñ yo⌐

9. It doesn't matter whether
   it's an express or not.
   /kyuukoo da/

   Kyu⌐ukoo de⌐ mo kyu⌐ukoo zya na⌐-
   kute mo ka⌐maimase⌐ñ yo⌐

10. It doesn't matter whether
    it's heavy or not. /omoi/

    O⌐mo⌐kute mo o⌐moku na⌐kute mo
    ka⌐maimase⌐ñ yo⌐

F. Substitution Drill

1. I'm looking for a place
   where they rent bicycles.

   Zi⌐te⌐ñsya (o) ka⌐su tokoro⌐ (o)
   sa⌐gasite (i)ma⌐su ga⌐

2. I'm looking for a place
    where they're selling bra-
    ziers.

Hi˥bati (o) u˥tte (i)ru tokoro˥ (o)
sa˥ḡasite (i)ma˥su ḡa_

3. I'm looking for a place
    where they check baggage.

Ni˥motu (o) a˥zuka˥ru to˥koro˥ (o)
sa˥ḡasite (i)ma˥su ḡa_

4. I'm looking for a place
    where there aren't many
    bugs.

Mu˥si ḡa¹ sukuna˥i to˥koro˥ (o) sa-
˥ḡasite (i)ma˥su ḡa_

5. I'm looking for a place
    where the tempura is good.

Te˥ñpura ḡa¹ uma˥i to˥koro˥ (o) sa-
˥ḡasite (i)ma˥su ḡa_

6. I'm looking for a place
    where the summers are
    cool.

Na˥tu˥ ḡa¹ su˥zusi˥i to˥koro˥ (o) sa-
˥ḡasite (i)ma˥su ḡa_

7. I'm looking for a place
    where the winters are
    warm.

Hu˥yu˥ ḡa¹ a˥ttaka˥i to˥koro˥ (o) sa-
˥ḡasite (i)ma˥su ḡa_

8. I'm looking for a place
    where it's all right to
    smoke.

Ta˥bako (o) no˥ñde mo ˥i˥i to˥koro˥
(o) sa˥ḡasite (i)ma˥su ḡa_

9. I'm looking for a place
    where it's all right to talk
    in a loud voice.

O˥oki na ˥ko˥e de ha˥na˥site mo
˥i˥i to˥koro˥ (o) sa˥ḡasite (i)ma˥su
ḡa_

10. I'm looking for a place
    where I don't have to wait.

Ma˥ta˥nakute mo ˥i˥i to˥koro˥ (o)
sa˥ḡasite (i)ma˥su ḡa_

G. Substitution Drill

(Insert the substitution items in their appropriate forms.)

1. Please cut the meat as thin
    as possible.

Ni˥ku˥ (o) na˥rubeku usuku ki˥tte
kudasai.

2. Please clip the back as
    short as possible. /usiro,
    mi˥zika˥i, karu/

Usiro (o) na˥rubeku mizika˥ku ka-
˥tte kudasa˥i.

3. Please deliver the paper as
    early as possible. /siñbuñ,
    ha˥ya˥i, to˥doke˥ru/

Siñbuñ (o) na˥rubeku ha˥yaku to-
˥do˥kete kudasai.

4. Please stop the car as near
    as possible. /kuruma, ti-
    ˥ka˥i, tomeru/

Kuruma (o) na˥rubeku tika˥ku to-
˥mete kudasa˥i.

5. Please draw the map as big
    as possible. /ti˥zu, o˥oki˥i,
    ka˥ku/

Ti˥zu (o) na˥rubeku o˥okiku ˥ka˥-
ite kudasai.

6. Please define this (lit. say
    the meaning of this) as
    simply as possible. /ko˥no
    i˥mi, yasasii, iu/

Ko˥no i˥mi (o) na˥rubeku yasasiku
itte kudasa˥i.

---

¹ Or no.

7. Please make the bath as hot
   as possible. /oᴖhuᴖro,
   aᴦtuᴗi, suru/

8. Please make the coffee as
   strong as possible. /ko-
   ᴖohiᴗi, koᴗi, suru/

9. Please cut the vegetables
   as fine as possible. /ya-
   sai, koᴖmakaᴗi, kiᴖru/

Oᴖhuᴖro (o) naᴖrubeku aᴗtuku siᴗ̄te
kudasaᴗi.

Koᴖohiᴗi (o) naᴖrubeku koᴗku siᴗ̄te
kudasaᴗi.

Yasai (o) naᴖrubeku komakaᴗku
ᴖkiᴗtte kudasai.

H. Grammar Drill (based on Grammatical Note 1)

Tutor: Kyoᴗoto e ikimasu.   'He's going to go to Kyoto.'
Student: Kyoᴗoto e iᴗ̄ku hazu deᴗsu. 'He's expected to go to Kyoto.'

1. Raineñ Toᴖodai ni hairimaᴗ-
   su.
2. Moᴗo Yoᴖkohama ni tukimaᴗ-
   sita.
3. Koᴖko deᴗ wa niᴖhoñḡo (o)
   hanasimaᴗsu.
4. Toᴖdoᴗketa toki ni haᴖraimaᴗ-
   sita.
5. Osake to tabako (o) ya-
   ᴖmemaᴗsita.
6. Moᴖratteᴗ kara ᴖsuᴗḡu wa-
   ᴖtasimaᴗsu.
7. Moᴗo ᴖkuᴗ-zi da kara,
   oᴗkite (i)masu.
8. Oᴖnazi gakkoo deᴗsu kara,
   moᴗo Taᴖnaka-sañ ni aimaᴗ-
   sita.

Raineñ Toᴖodai ni haᴗiru hazu
desu.
Moᴗo Yoᴖkohama ni tuᴗita hazu
desu.
Koᴖko deᴗ wa niᴖhoñḡo (o) hanaᴗ-
su hazu desu.
Toᴖdoᴗketa toki ni haᴖraᴗtta hazu
desu.
Osake to tabako (o) yaᴖmeta
hazu deᴗsu.
Moᴖratteᴗ kara ᴖsuᴗḡu waᴖtasu
hazu deᴗsu.
Moᴗo ᴖkuᴗ-zi da kara, ᴖoᴗkite
(i)ru hazu desu.
Oᴖnazi gakkoo deᴗsu kara, moᴗo
Taᴖnaka-sañ ni aᴗtta hazu desu.

I. Grammar Drill (based on Grammatical Note 2)

Tutor: Niᴖhoñḡo ḡa yoᴗku dekimasu. 'He can speak Japanese
         well.'
Student: Niᴖhoñḡo ḡa yoᴗku deᴗ̄kiᴗ̄ru soo desu. 'They say he can
         speak Japanese well.'

1. Suᴖkoᴗsi sika noᴗ̄koᴗ̄tte
   (i)ᴗnaᴗ̄i keredo, zyuᴖubuᴗñ
   desu.
2. Huᴗyuᴗ ḡa ᴗnaᴗ̄ḡakute, naᴖtuᴗ
   ḡa miᴖzikaᴗi desu.
3. Roᴖku-ḡatuᴗ ni wa ᴖaᴗme
   ḡa ᴖyoᴗku hurimasu.
4. Yuube gaᴖiziñ sika miemaᴗ-
   seᴗñ desita.
5. Okane ḡa taᴖrinaᴗkatta kara,
   tomodati kara suᴖkoᴗsi
   kaᴖrimaᴗsita.

Suᴖkoᴗsi sika noᴗ̄koᴗ̄tte (i)ᴗnaᴗ̄i
keredo, zyuᴖubuᴗñ da soo desu.
Huᴗyuᴗ ḡa ᴗnaᴗ̄ḡakute, naᴖtuᴗ ḡa
miᴖzikaᴗi soo desu.
Roᴖku-ḡatuᴗ ni wa ᴖaᴗme ḡa ᴖyo-
ku ᴗ̄huᴗ̄ru soo desu.
Yuube gaᴖiziñ sika mieᴖnakatta
soo desu.
Okane ḡa taᴖrinaᴗkatta kara, tomodati kara suᴖkoᴗsi kaᴖrita
soᴗo desu.

6. Teⁿki no ⌐iᴬi hi ni wa ⌐u⌐mi ḡa miemasu.

     Teⁿki no ⌐iᴬi hi ni wa ⌐u⌐mi ḡa miᵗe⌐ru soo desu.

7. Koko no osasimi (wa) a⌐tara⌐sikute o⌐isi⌐i desu.

     Koko no osasimi (wa) a⌐tara⌐sikute o⌐isii so⌐o desu.

8. Ta⌐isi⌐kañ no siḡoto (o) ya⌐meta⌐i desu.

     Ta⌐isi⌐kañ no siḡoto (o) ya⌐metai so⌐o desu.

9. Zya⌐ma ni na⌐ru kara, mo⌐tte ikimaseñ.

     Zya⌐ma ni na⌐ru kara, mo⌐tte ikanai so⌐o desu.

10. Kyo⌐o wa ⌐geᴬñki da keredo, ki⌐no⌐o wa byo⌐oki de⌐sita.

     Kyo⌐o wa ⌐geᴬñki da keredo, ki⌐no⌐o wa byo⌐oki da⌐tta soo desu.

11. Hutuu wa ⌐sa⌐ñ-zi made da keredo, kyo⌐o wa ⌐yo⌐-zi made desu.

     Hutuu wa ⌐sa⌐ñ-zi made da keredo, kyo⌐o wa ⌐yo⌐-zi made da soo desu.

12. Okosañ (wa) mi⌐ñna ozyo⌐-osañ de, miñna ke⌐kkoñ-site (i)ma⌐su.

     Okosañ (wa) mi⌐ñna ozyo⌐osañ de, miñna ke⌐kkoñ-site (i)ru so⌐o desu.

J. Grammar Drill (based on Grammatical Note 3)

     Tutor: I⌐tte kudasa⌐i. 'Please go.'
     Student: I⌐kana⌐i de kudasai. 'Please don't go.'

1. Mi⌐zika⌐ku ka⌐tte kudasaᴬi.

     Mi⌐zika⌐ku ka⌐ranaᴬi de kudasai.

2. So⌐o itte kudasa⌐i.

     So⌐o iwana⌐i de kudasai.

3. A⌐merika no okane de ha-ra⌐tte kudasai.

     A⌐merika no okane de harawa⌐nai de kudasai.

4. E⌐eḡo (o) hana⌐site kudasai.

     E⌐eḡo (o) hanasa⌐nai de kudasai.

5. Ku⌐ruma no kaḡi⌐ (o) ⌐ka⌐-kete kudasai.

     Ku⌐ruma no kaḡi⌐ (o) ka⌐ke⌐nai de kudasai.

6. Su⌐to⌐obu (o) ke⌐site kuda-sa⌐i.

     Su⌐to⌐obu (o) ke⌐sana⌐i de kudasai.

7. Hu⌐ru⌐i sⁱⁱñbuñ ya zassi (o) su⌐tete kudasa⌐i.

     Hu⌐ru⌐i sⁱⁱñbuñ ya zassi (o) su⌐te-na⌐i de kudasai.

8. Ko⌐maka⌐i mo⌐no⌐ᴬ (o) si-⌐matte kudasa⌐i.

     Ko⌐maka⌐i mo⌐no⌐ᴬ (o) si⌐mawana⌐i de kudasai.

K. Response Drill

     Tutor: Kyo⌐oto e i⌐ku⌐ desyoo ka. 'Do you suppose he is going to go to Kyoto?'
     Student: Ikanai hazu wa a⌐rimaseñ yo⌐ 'There's no reason to ex-pect he won't go.'

1. Kyo⌐o ha⌐ra⌐u desyoo ka.

     Ha⌐rawa⌐nai hazu wa a⌐rimase⌐ñ yo⌐

2. Okane (o) ka⌐site kureru⌐ desyoo ka.

     Kasite kurenai hazu wa a⌐rima-se⌐ñ yo⌐

3. E⌐ki de ⌐ni⌐motu (o) a⌐zu⌐-keta desyoo ka.

     A⌐zuke⌐nakatta hazu wa a⌐rimase⌐ñ yo⌐

4. Kotosi dāiḡaku ni ⌐ha⌐iru desyoo ka.

     Ha⌐ira⌐nai hazu wa a⌐rimase⌐ñ yo⌐

Drills   37

5. Koñna siḡoto (wa) de⌐ki˺ru   De⌐ki˺nai hazu wa a⌐rimaseñ˺ yo⏝
   desyoo ka.
6. Asuko kara ki⌐koeru˺ de-   Kikoenai hazu wa a⌐rimaseñ˺ yo⏝
   syoo ka.
7. Uketori (o) ta⌐no˺ñda de-   Ta⌐noma˺nakatta hazu wa a⌐rima-
   syoo ka.   se˺ñ yo⏝
8. Zyotyuu ni tu⌐taeta˺ desyoo   Tu⌐taena˺katta hazu wa a⌐rima-
   ka.   se˺ñ yo⏝

L. Response Drill

       Tutor: Si⌐te˺ mo ⌐i˺i desu ka⏝ 'May I do [it]?'
       Student: E˺e, si⌐te˺ mo ⌐i˺i desu yo⏝ 'Yes, you may do [it].' or
                Iie, si⌐na˺i de kudasai. 'No, please don't do [it].'

    1. Tomodati ni ⌐mi˺sete mo   E˺e, mi⌐sete mo ⌐i˺i desu yo⏝
       ⌐i˺i desu ka⏝ /e˺e/
    2. Ma˺do (o) ⌐si˺mete mo ⌐i˺i   Iie, si⌐me˺nai de kudasai.
       desu ka⏝ /iie/
    3. Koko de ⌐ma˺tte mo ⌐i˺i   E˺e, ma⌐tte mo ⌐i˺i desu yo⏝
       desu ka⏝ /e˺e/
    4. Ha⌐itte mo ⌐i˺i desu ka⏝   Iie, ha⌐ira˺nai de kudasai.
       /iie/
    5. Tukue no ue no zassi (o)   E˺e, yo⌐ñde mo ⌐i˺i desu yo⏝
       ⌐yo˺ñde mo ⌐i˺i desu ka⏝
       /e˺e/
    6. Ne⌐ko (o) ⌐da˺site mo ⌐i˺i   Iie, da⌐sa˺nai de kudasai.
       desu ka⏝ /iie/
    7. Kore (o) ko⌐no hako ni   E˺e, i⌐rete˺ mo ⌐i˺i desu yo⏝
       irete˺ mo ⌐i˺i desu ka⏝
       /e˺e/
    8. Osara (o) ko⌐no todana ni   Iie, si⌐mawana˺i de kudasai.
       simatte˺ mo ⌐i˺i desu ka⏝
       /iie/
    9. Tyo˺tto sa⌐ñpo-site˺ mo   E˺e, sa⌐ñpo-site˺ mo ⌐i˺i desu
       ⌐i˺i desu ka⏝ /e˺e/   yo⏝
   10. A⌐ratte˺ mo ⌐i˺i desu ka⏝   Iie, a⌐rawana˺i de kudasai.
       /iie/

M. Response Drill

       Tutor: Si⌐na˺kute mo ⌐i˺i desu ka⏝ 'Is it all right if I don't do
                [it]?'
       Student: E˺e, si⌐na˺kute mo ⌐i˺i desu yo⏝ 'Yes, you don't have
                to do [it].' or Iie, si⌐te kudasa˺i. 'No, please do [it].'

    1. Kyo˺o gi⌐ñkoo e ikana˺kute   E˺e, i⌐kana˺kute mo ⌐i˺i desu
       mo ⌐i˺i desu ka⏝ /e˺e/   yo⏝
    2. A⌐iroñ (o) kake˺nakute mo   Iie, ka⌐kete kudasai.
       ⌐i˺i desu ka⏝ /iie/
    3. Tu⌐kue no ue˺ (o) ka⌐tazuke-   E˺e, ka⌐tazuke˺nakute mo ⌐i˺i
       ke˺nakute mo ⌐i˺i desu ka⏝   desu yo⏝
       /e˺e/

4. Ni⌐hoñɡo (o) hanasa⌐nakute
   mo ⌐i⌐i desu ka◡ /iie/   Iie, ha⌐na⌐site kudasai.

5. Asita i⌐na⌐kute mo ⌐i⌐i
   desu ka◡ /e⌐e/   E⌐e, i⌐na⌐kute mo ⌐i⌐i desu yo◡

6. Ko⌐ñbañ be⌐ñkyoo-sina⌐kute
   mo ⌐i⌐i desu ka◡ /iie/   Iie, be⌐ñkyoo-site kudasa⌐i.

7. Si⌐buya de norikae⌐nakute
   mo ⌐i⌐i desu ka◡ /e⌐e/   E⌐e, no⌐rikae⌐nakute mo ⌐i⌐i desu
                                   yo◡

8. Si⌐ñbuñ (o) sikana⌐kute mo
   ⌐i⌐i desu ka◡ /iie/   Iie, si⌐ite kudasa⌐i.

9. Asita ⌐ko⌐nakute mo ⌐i⌐i
   desu ka◡ /e⌐e/   E⌐e, ko⌐nakute mo ⌐i⌐i desu yo◡

10. U⌐siro no ta⌐iya o to⌐rikae-
    na⌐kute mo ⌐i⌐i desu ka◡   Iie, to⌐rikaete kudasa⌐i.
    /iie/

N. Expansion Drill

1. Which shall we make it?   Do⌐tira ni si⌐masyo⌐o ka.
   It doesn't matter but which   Ka⌐maimase⌐ñ ɡa, do⌐tira ni si-
   shall we make it?   ⌐masyo⌐o ka.
   Even if it's Thursday it   Mo⌐kuyo⌐o de mo ka⌐maimase⌐ñ
   doesn't matter but which   ɡa, do⌐tira ni si⌐masyo⌐o ka.
   shall we make it?
   Whether it's Wednesday or   Su⌐iyo⌐o de mo mo⌐kuyo⌐o de mo
   Thursday it doesn't mat-   ka⌐maimase⌐ñ ɡa, do⌐tira ni si-
   ter, but which shall we   ⌐masyo⌐o ka.
   make it?

2. I hear it's a day off.   Ya⌐sumi⌐ da soo desu.
   I hear that Friday is a day   Ki⌐ñyo⌐o wa ya⌐sumi⌐ da soo desu.
   off.
   I hear that next Friday is   Ra⌐isyuu no kiñyo⌐o wa ya⌐sumi⌐
   a day off.   da soo desu.
   According to what the   Se⌐ñse⌐e no ha⌐nasi⌐ de wa ra⌐i-
   teacher says, next Friday   syuu no kiñyo⌐o wa ya⌐sumi⌐ da
   is a day off.   soo desu.

3. He is expected to go . . .   I⌐ku hazu de⌐su ɡa◡
   It's his job so he is ex-   Si⌐ɡoto da⌐ kara, i⌐ku hazu de⌐su
   pected to go . . .   ɡa◡
   Even if he doesn't want to   I⌐kitaku na⌐kute mo; si⌐ɡoto da⌐
   go, it's his job so he is   kara, i⌐ku hazu de⌐su ɡa◡
   expected to go . . .
   Whether he wants to go or   I⌐kita⌐kute mo i⌐kitaku na⌐kute mo;
   not, it's his job so he is   si⌐ɡoto da⌐ kara, i⌐ku hazu de⌐su
   expected to go . . .   ɡa◡

4. There's no reason to ex-   Na⌐i hazu wa a⌐rimase⌐ñ yo◡
   pect that there isn't any.

There's no reason to expect that there isn't any at all.	Ze⌐ñzeñ na⌐i hazu wa a⌐rimase⌐ñ yo⌣
I can't tell for sure but there's no reason to expect that there isn't any at all.	Ha⌐kki⌐ri wa⌐karimase⌐ñ ḡa, ze⌐ñ-zeñ na⌐i hazu wa a⌐rimase⌐ñ yo⌣
I can't tell for sure how much is left but there's no reason to expect that there isn't any at all.	I⌐kura no⌐ko⌐tte (i)ru ka ha⌐kki⌐ri wa⌐karimase⌐ñ ḡa, ze⌐ñzeñ na⌐i hazu wa a⌐rimase⌐ñ yo⌣

5.
You'd better drink [it].	No⌐nda hoo ḡa ⌐i⌐i desu yo⌣
You'd better drink [it] quickly.	Ha⌐yaku ⌐no⌐nda hoo ḡa ⌐i⌐i desu yo⌣
It's medicine so you'd better take it quickly.	Ku⌐suri da⌐ kara, ha⌐yaku ⌐no⌐nda hoo ḡa ⌐i⌐i desu yo⌣
Even if it's bitter, it's medicine, so you'd better take it quickly.	Ni⌐ḡakute mo; ku⌐suri da⌐ kara, ha⌐yaku ⌐no⌐nda hoo ḡa ⌐i⌐i desu yo⌣
Whether it's sweet or bitter, it's medicine, so you'd better take it quickly.	A⌐ma⌐kute mo ⌐ni⌐ḡakute mo; ku⌐suri da⌐ kara, ha⌐yaku ⌐no⌐nda hoo ḡa ⌐i⌐i desu yo⌣

6.
He is expected to come . . .	Ku⌐ru ha⌐zu de⌐su ḡa—
He is expected to come on time . . .	Zi⌐kañ-do⌐ori [ni] ⌐ku⌐ru ha⌐zu de⌐su ḡa—
Even if it doesn't rain (lit. fall) he is expected to come on time . . .	Hu⌐ra⌐nakute mo, zi⌐kañ-do⌐ori [ni] ⌐ku⌐ru ha⌐zu de⌐su ḡa—
Whether it rains (lit. falls) or not he is expected to come on time . . .	Hu⌐tte⌐ mo hu⌐ra⌐nakute mo, zi-⌐kañ-do⌐ori [ni] ⌐ku⌐ru ha⌐zu de⌐su ḡa—
Whether it rains or not he is expected to come on time . . .	A⌐me ḡa hu⌐tte⌐ mo hu⌐ra⌐nakute mo, zi⌐kañ-do⌐ori [ni] ⌐ku⌐ru ha⌐zu de⌐su ḡa—
He has an appointment so whether it rains or not he is expected to come on time . . .	Ya⌐kusoku ḡa a⌐ru kara; a⌐me ḡa hu⌐tte⌐ mo hu⌐ra⌐nakute mo, zi-⌐kañ-do⌐ori [ni] ⌐ku⌐ru ha⌐zu de⌐su ḡa—
He has a firm appointment so whether it rains or not he is expected to come on time . . .	Ka⌐tai yakusoku ḡa a⌐ru kara; a⌐me ḡa hu⌐tte⌐ mo hu⌐ra⌐nakute mo, zi⌐kañ-do⌐ori [ni] ⌐ku⌐ru ha⌐zu de⌐su ḡa—

QUESTION SUPPLEMENT

(based on the Basic Dialogues)

(a) 1. Tanaka-sañ wa ⌐do⌐ko e i⌐kima⌐sita ka⌐ Do⌐o site?
     2. Su⌐misu-sañ wa ⌐do⌐o site Tanaka-sañ ni ⌐sañ-zi made ni ⌐ka⌐ette
         mo⌐raita⌐i ñ desu ka⌐
     3. Tanaka-sañ wa ⌐do⌐ñna huu ni to⌐koya ni site moraima⌐sita ka⌐

(b) 4. Su⌐misu-sañ wa ⌐na⌐ni o sa⌐ḡasite ima⌐sita ka⌐
     5. Ano ziteñsyaya de zi⌐teñsya o kasu so⌐o desu ḡa, ho⌐ñtoo de⌐su ka⌐

(d) 6. Okyakusañ wa ⌐do⌐o site ka⌐tta mono⌐ o ka⌐yo⌐o made ni to⌐do⌐kete
         mo⌐raita⌐i ñ desu ka⌐
     7. Okyakusañ wa ka⌐rita eñpitu de ⌐na⌐ni o ka⌐kima⌐sita ka⌐
     8. Okyakusañ wa ⌐i⌐tu ha⌐raima⌐sita ka⌐
     9. Okyakusañ wa ⌐na⌐ni o ⌐ka⌐ite mo⌐raima⌐sita ka⌐

(e) 10. A⌐no mise⌐ wa ⌐do⌐ñna ni⌐ku⌐ o u⌐tte ima⌐su ka⌐
     11. Ta⌐naka-sañ no o⌐kusañ wa ⌐da⌐re kara so⌐o kikima⌐sita ka⌐
     12. Ta⌐naka-sañ no o⌐kusañ wa ⌐na⌐ni o ka⌐ima⌐sita ka⌐
     13. Ta⌐naka-sañ no o⌐kusan wa ⌐do⌐o site so⌐no niku⌐ o u⌐suku ki⌐tte
          mo⌐raima⌐sita ka⌐
     14. Da⌐re ḡa Ta⌐naka-sañ no o⌐kusañ to issyo ni ni⌐ku⌐ya ni yo⌐tte
          mima⌐sita ka⌐

SHORT SUPPLEMENTARY DIALOGUES

1. Secretary: Ko⌐ñna hu⌐u ni si⌐ma⌐sita ḡa, i⌐ka⌐ḡa desyoo ka.
    Smith: A⌐a, to⌐temo ki⌐ree desu ⌐ne⌐e. Do⌐o mo go⌐ku⌐roosama⌐

2. Smith: Ni⌐hoñzi⌐ñ wa ko⌐ñna hu⌐u na ⌐go⌐hañ ḡa o⌐suki da so⌐o desu
           ⌐ne⌐e.
    Tanaka: E⌐e. Da⌐isuki desu yo⌐

3. A: Ka⌐sima⌐su ka⌐
    B: E⌐e. I⌐ti⌐-neñ dake ka⌐sita⌐i ñ desu ḡa⌐

4. A: Ka⌐rima⌐su ka⌐
    B: E⌐e. I⌐ti⌐-neñ dake ka⌐rita⌐i ñ desu ḡa⌐

5. A: Kinoo ⌐Sa⌐too-sañ kara de⌐ñwa ḡa arima⌐sita ḡa, o⌐ka⌐asañ ḡa byo-
         ⌐oiñ ni ha⌐itta soo desu.
    B: So⌐o desu ka. So⌐re wa ikemase⌐ñ ⌐ne⌐e.

6. A: Yosida-sañ ⌐kyo⌐o ⌐ku⌐ru?
    Mr. B: Ko⌐nai soo da yo⌐
    A: So⌐o?
    Mr. B: Byo⌐oki da so⌐o da yo.

7. A: Kyo⌐o Ta⌐naka-señse¬e ḡa mi⌐e¬ru desyoo?
   B: Mo⌐o su⌐ḡu mi⌐e¬ru ha⌐zu de¬su ḡa_ Ni¬-zi no ya⌐kusoku de¬su ka-
   ra.
   A: Ta⌐naka-señse¬e no hoka ni ⌐do¬nata ḡa ⌐ku¬ru ha⌐zu de¬sita ka_
   B: Yo⌐sida-sañ mo ku⌐ru hazu desyoo?

8. A: O⌐tya a¬ru?
   Mr. B: Na¬i hazu wa ⌐na¬i yo_ — i¬tu mo ⌐a¬ru kara.

9. Maid (coming from telephone): O⌐kusama_ Da⌐ñnasa¬ma wa ⌐ma⌐da ka-
   ⌐isya e otuki ni nara¬nai soo desu.
   Mistress: Tu⌐ka¬nai hazu wa a⌐rimase¬ñ — ha¬yaku u⌐ti o de¬ta kara.
   He¬ñ desu ⌐ne¬e.

10. Teacher A: A⌐no ku⌐rasu[1] ko⌐marima¬su ⌐ne¬e. Ko⌐no ho¬ñ o ⌐mo⌐o be⌐ñ-
    kyoo-sita hazu de⌐su ḡa, na⌐ni mo wakarimase¬ñ ⌐ne¬e.
    Teacher B: A⌐no ku⌐rasu no hi⌐to¬ wa ūti de ze⌐ñzeñ beñkyoo-sina¬i ka-
    ra, wa⌐ka¬ru hazu wa a⌐rimase¬ñ yo.

11. Student: O⌐zyama-site¬ mo yo⌐rosi¬i desyoo ka.
    Teacher: Do⌐ozo ⌐do¬ozo. Betu ni i⌐soḡa¬siku ⌐na¬i kara go⌐eñryo na⌐ku.

12. Smith: Ke⌐sa sī̄ḡoto ḡa ta⌐kusañ a¬ru kara, o⌐kyakusa¬ñ ḡa ki⌐te¬ mo
    a⌐rimase¬ñ yo_
    Secretary: U⌐eda-sañ no oyakusoku wa do⌐o nasaimasu ka_
    Smith: U⌐eda-sañ ni¬ wa a⌐ima¬su ḡa, ho⌐ka no hito¬ wa da⌐me¬ desu.

13. Maid: I¬ma ⌐pa¬ñ o ka⌐tte mairima¬su ḡa, mi¬ruku wa ka⌐wana¬kute mo
    yo⌐rosi¬i desyoo ka.
    Mistress: A¬a, mi¬ruku mo ka⌐tte¬ kite kudasai.

14. A: Mo⌐o ta⌐no¬ñda ⌐ho¬ñ ḡa ⌐ki¬ta ha⌐zu da¬ kara, ho⌐ñya e itte to⌐tte¬
    kima⌐su. I¬ma ha⌐rawa¬nakute mo ⌐i¬i desyoo?
    Mr. B: E¬e. A¬to de ⌐bo¬ku ḡa ha⌐ra¬u kara, ⌐i¬i desu yo_

15. A: A⌐tu¬i desu ⌐ne¬e. Ma⌐do o mi⌐ñna akete¬ mo su⌐zu¬siku na⌐rimase¬ñ
    ⌐ne¬e.
    B: Tu⌐metai mono¬ o ⌐no¬ñde, su⌐ko¬si ya⌐sumimasyo¬o ka.
    A: So⌐o simasyo¬o.

16. A: A¬me ḡa hu⌐tte¬ iru kara, Tanaka-sañ ⌐ko¬nai desyoo ⌐ne¬e.
    B: Iie. Ku⌐ru hazu desu yo_ Hu⌐tte¬ mo hu⌐ra¬nakute mo ⌐ku¬ru tte
    i⌐tta¬ kara.

17. Employee: Asita yo⌐ozi¬ ḡa gozaima⌐su kara, o⌐soku kite¬ mo yo⌐rosi¬i
    desyoo ka.
    Employer: Tyo⌐tto_ A⌐sita¬ wa tōtemo i⌐soḡasi¬i kara. Hoka no hi wa?

---

[1] 'Class.'

Employee: Zya⌐a, ki⌐ñyo⌐o de mo yo⌐rosi⌐i desu g̱a‿
Employer: So⌐o site kudasa⌐i.

18. A: Mu⌐zukasi⌐i desyoo?
     B: Zeñzeñ. Kore wa ko⌐domo de⌐ mo de⌐ki⌐ru ñ desu yo‿

English Equivalents

1. Secretary: I did it like this. How do you like it? (Lit. How is it?)
    Smith: Oh, that's very pretty! Thanks for your trouble.

2. Smith: They say that Japanese like this kind of (or style of) rice, don't
    they.
    Tanaka: Yes, we like it very much.

3. A: Are you going to rent it (i.e. to someone)?
    B: Yes, I'd like to rent it for just one year . . .

4. A: Are you going to rent it (i.e. from someone)?
    B: Yes, I'd like to rent it for just one year . . .

5. A: There was a telephone call from Mr. Sato yesterday. The report is
    that his mother has entered the hospital.
    B: Oh? That's too bad.

6. A: Is Mr. Yoshida coming today?
    Mr. B: They say he isn't coming.
    A: Oh?
    Mr. B: They say he's sick.

7. A: Dr. Tanaka is going to come today, isn't he?
    B: He should come any minute now . . . (Because) he has (lit. it is) a
    2 o'clock appointment.
    A: Who was supposed to come besides Dr. Tanaka?
    B: Mr. Yoshida is supposed to come too, isn't he?

8. A: Is there any tea?
    Mr. B: There should be (lit. there's no reason to expect that there isn't
    any) — since there always is some.

9. Maid: Madam. They say that Mr. —— (lit. the master) hasn't arrived
    at the office yet.
    Mistress: He should have arrived (lit. there's no reason to expect that
    he hasn't arrived) — since he left the house early. Isn't that strange!

10. Teacher A: That class is troublesome, isn't it. They're supposed to
     have studied this book already but they don't understand anything, do
     they.
     Teacher B: The people in that class don't study at home at all, so there's
     no reason to expect them to understand.

11. Student: May I interrupt you?
    Teacher: Certainly. I'm not especially busy so come right ahead.

12. Smith: I have a lot of work this morning so even if any visitors come, I
    won't see them.
    Secretary: What will you do about Mr. Ueda's appointment?
    Smith: Mr. Ueda I'll see, but not any other people.

13. Maid: I'm going to go and buy some bread now. I don't have to buy any
    milk, do I?
    Mistress: Oh, (go and) buy some milk too.

14. A: The books that were ordered should have come by now so I'll go to
    the bookstore and get them (lit. come having taken [them]). I don't
    have to pay now, do I?
    Mr. B: No (i.e. that's right). I'll pay later so don't bother.

15. A: Isn't it hot! Even if you open all the windows it doesn't get cool, does
    it.
    B: Shall we have something cold to drink and rest for a little while?
    A: Let's do that.

16. A: It's raining so Mr. Tanaka probably won't come, will he.
    B: Yes (i.e. that's not right), he should come. (Because) he said that
    he'd come whether it rained or not.

17. Employee: I have some business to attend to tomorrow so would it be
    all right if I came late?
    Employer: That's a bit inconvenient. (Because) tomorrow we're going
    to be very busy. How about another day?
    Employee: Well then, (even being) Friday will be all right . . .
    Employer: Please make it then (lit. that way).

18. A: It's difficult, isn't it?
    B: Not at all. This, even (being) a child can do.

EXERCISES

1. Tell the barber:

    a. to give you a shave.
    b. to cut your hair short.
    c. to wash your hair.

2. Tell the butcher:

    a. you want 500 grams of beef.
    b. to cut it as thin as possible.
    c. to deliver it as quickly as possible.

3. Ask the clerk in the store:

       a. if you may borrow his pencil.
       b. to write a receipt for you.
       c. to deliver these things to your home by 3 tomorrow.
       d. if he can change this (i. e. money).

4. Tell a friend that you have heard that:

       a. the barber next to the station is very good.
       b. the fish at that fish market is usually not fresh.
       c. they sell American newspapers and magazines at that bookstore.
       d. he is looking for a new house.

5. Ask permission to:

       a. come in.
       b. look at that.
       c. read that.
       d. smoke.
       e. use the telephone.
       f. come late tomorrow.
       g. go home early today.
       h. wait here.
       i. open the window.
       j. eat this.
       k. drink this.
       l. give this to the children.
      m. give this to the teacher.
       n. rest a little.
       o. pay now.

6. Practice the Basic Dialogues with appropriate variations, including variations in politeness and formality levels.

Lesson 23. Clothing

BASIC DIALOGUES: FOR MEMORIZATION

(a)

Maid

1. Are you going out tonight? Koˉnbañ oˉdekake deˉsu ka↲

Mr. Tanaka

    early evening   yuūgata
    it is a matter of going out   deˈkakeruˉ ñ da

2. Yes, I am going out toward evening (lit. from early evening on). Aˈa, yuˈuˉgata kara dekakeruˉ ñ da yo↲

    change clothes   kiˈkaˉeru /-ru/ [1]
    go having changed clothes   kiˈkaˈete (i)ku
    shirt   waisyatu
    navy blue   koˈñ

3. I'm going to change clothes before I go so get out a clean white shirt and my navy blue suit. Kiˈkaˈete (i)ˈkuˈ kara, siˈroˈi ˈkiˈree na waisyatu to ˈkoˈñ no seˈbiro (o) daˈsite.

    shoes on the new side **or** the newer shoes   aˈtarasiˈi hoo no kutu
    put on **or** wear (on the feet or legs)   haku /-u/
    go [somewhere] wearing (on the feet or legs)   haite (i)ku

4. And I'm going to wear my new(er) black shoes so shine them. Sore kara; aˈtarasiˈi hoo no kuˈroˈi kuˈtuˈ (o) haˈite (i)kuˈ kara, miḡaite.

Maid

    coat (full-length)   oˈobaa
    put on **or** wear (on the body)   kiru /-ru/
    go [somewhere] wearing (on the body)   kite (i)ku

5. Are you going to wear an overcoat? Oˈobaa (o) kiˈte (i)rassyaimaˈsu ka↲

---

[1] Alternate accent: kiˈkaeˈru.

Mr. Tanaka

snow	yu⌐ki⌐
6. Yes, of course I am (going to wear one). (Because) they say that tonight it's going to snow.	A⌐a, mo⌐ti⌐roñ kite (i)ku yo⌟ Koñ-bañ wa yu⌐ki⌐ ḡa ⌐hu⌐ru soo da kara.

Maid

hat	boosi or o⌐bo⌐osi⁺
put on or wear (on the head)	ka⌐bu⌐ru /-u/
go [somewhere] wearing (on the head)	ka⌐bu⌐tte (i)ku
7. Then you are going to wear a hat too, aren't you?	Zya⌐a, o⌐bo⌐osi mo ka⌐bu⌐tte (i)ra-ssyaimasu ka⌟

Mr. Tanaka

8. Yes, I am (going to wear one).	A⌐a, ka⌐bu⌐tte (i)ku yo⌟

. . .

umbrella	ka⌐sa
it is a matter of looking for	sa⌐ḡasite (i)ru⌐ ñ da
9. I'm looking for my umbrella. . . Oh! [This is where] it was.	Ka⌐sa (o) sa⌐ḡasite ru⌐ ñ da ḡa⌟ A. A⌐tta.

(b)

Mrs. Tanaka

Western-style clothing	yoohuku or o⌐yo⌐ohuku⁺
dry [something] out or air [something]	ho⌐su /-u/
a matter of having [something] aired	ho⌐site mo⌐raita⌐i no
10. I want to have all the clothes that are over there aired to-day.	Kyo⌐o sŏko no yoohuku (o) miñna ⌐ho⌐site mo⌐raita⌐i no.

Maid

trousers	zu⌐boñ
11. Do you mean these trousers too?	Ko⌐no zuboñ mo desu ka⌟

Mrs. Tanaka

dry cleaning	do⌐raikuri⌐iniñḡu
a matter of sending out for dry cleaning	do⌐raikuri⌐iniñḡu ni ⌐da⌐su no
12. No, the things that are on top of that chair are to be sent out for dry cleaning.	Iie, a⌐no isu no ue⌐ ni ⌐a⌐ru mo⌐no⌐ wa do⌐raikuri⌐iniñḡu ni ⌐da⌐su no yo⌟

Maid

sweater	se⌐e⌐taa⌐

13. What are you going to do with this sweater?

Ko⌐no se⌐etaa (wa) ⌐do⌐o nasaimasu ka↲

Mrs. Tanaka

launder	señtaku-suru⌐
a matter of laundering	se⌐ñtaku-suru⌐ no

14. That's to be laundered at home.

So⌐re wa uti de señtaku-suru⌐ no.

Maid

socks or stockings	ku⌐tu⌐sita
gloves	te⌐bu⌐kuro

15. Shall I put away these socks and gloves and things?

Kono ku⌐tu⌐sita ya te⌐bu⌐kuro (wa) si⌐maimasyo⌐o ka↲

Mrs. Tanaka

16. Yes, in the top drawer.

E⌐e, ue no hikidasi ni.

. . .

a matter of not going in	ha⌐ira⌐nai no

17. Won't they go in?

Ha⌐ira⌐nai no?

method or way of doing	sikata
it can't be helped or nothing can be done	si⌐kata ḡa na⌐i or syo⌐o ḡa na⌐i
middle	mañnaka

18. If it's full it's full so put them in the middle drawer or the bottom one. (Lit. It can't be helped so it will be all right whether it's the middle drawer or the bottom one.)

Si⌐kata ḡa na⌐i kara, ma⌐ñnaka no hikidasi de⌐ mo si⌐ta no⌐ de mo ka⌐mawa⌐nai wa↲

(c)

Tanaka

it is a matter of having bought	ka⌐tta⌐ ñ da

19. Excuse me but where did you buy that suit?

Si⌐tu⌐ree desu ḡa, sono sebiro (wa) ⌐do⌐ko de ka⌐tta⌐ ñ desu ka↲

Smith

send (of things)	okuru /-u/
it is a matter of having had [something] sent	o⌐kutte moratta⌐ ñ da

20. I had my mother in the States send it [to me].

A⌐merika no ha⌐ha ni o⌐kutte moratta⌐ ñ desu yo.

Tanaka

	American-made	Amerika-see
	it is a matter of being American-made	A⌐merika-see na⌐ ñ da
21.	Oh, do you mean it's American-made?	A⌐a, A⌐merika-see na⌐ ñ desu ka.

	material or cloth	ki⌐zi
22.	What is this material?	Ko⌐no ki⌐zi (wa) ⌐na⌐ñ desyoo ka.

Smith

	cotton	momeñ
	dacron	da⌐kuroñ
23.	It's cotton and dacron.	Momeñ to ⌐da⌐kuroñ desu yo.

Tanaka

	synthetic fibers	kaseñ
	strong or firm or durable or healthy	zyoobu /na/
	it is strong and what is more—	zyo⌐obu da⌐ si
24.	The synthetics nowadays are good because they are rugged and what is more they are cheap (isn't that true).	Kono-ḡoro no kaseñ wa zyo⌐obu da⌐ si, sono ue ya⌐su⌐i kara; i⌐i desu ⌐ne⌐e.

(d)

Smith

	pattern	gara
	gaudy or bright or loud[1]	ha⌐de⌐ /na/
	plain or subdued or quiet[1]	zi⌐mi⌐ /na/
25.	This pattern is a little loud (so) please show me one that's plainer.	Kono gara (wa) su⌐ko⌐si ha⌐de⌐ da kara, mo⌐tto zi⌐mi⌐ na no (o) ⌐mi⌐sete kudasai.

(looking at others brought by the clerk)

26.	I wonder which one would be best.	Do⌐re ḡa i⌐tibañ i⌐i desyoo ka ⌐ne⌐e.

Clerk

	solid color	mu⌐zi
	suit or be becoming	ni⌐a⌐u /-u/
	it is a matter of being becoming	ni⌐a⌐u ñ da
	isn't it a matter of being becoming?	ni⌐a⌐u ñ zya nai? or o⌐niai ni na⌐ru ↑ ñ zya nai?
27.	Among these three, wouldn't the gray solid-color one be most becoming?	Ko⌐no mi-ttu⌐ no u⌐ti de⌐ wa, haii-ro no ⌐mu⌐zi no ḡa i⌐tibañ oniai ni na⌐ru ñ zya ⌐na⌐i desyoo ka.

---

[1] Of color, style, taste, etc.

Smith

| decide or settle | kimeru /-ru/ |
| decide on this one | kore ni kimeru |

28. Well then, I'll take (lit. decide on) this one.   Zya⌐a, ko⌐re ni kimemasyo⌐o.

(e)

Smith

| shape or style | katati or ka⌐ta⌐ |
| make | tu⌐ku⌐ru /-u/ |

29. I'd like to have a suit of this (kind of) style made. Can you do it right away?   Koñna kata(ti)[1] no sebiro (o) tu-⌐ku⌐tte mo⌐raita⁴i ñ desu ḡa, su⌐ḡu de⌐kima⌐su ka⌐

Tailor

30. Yes, I'll do it right away . . .   Ha⌐a, su⌐ḡu i⌐tasima⁴su ḡa⌐

Smith

[I] have decided and what is more—	ki⌐meta⌐ si
make the same as this	kore to onazi ni suru
it is a matter of making	su⌐ru⌐ ñ da
measurements	suñpoo
measure	ha⌐ka⌐ru /-u/
take measurements	su⌐ñpoo o haka⌐ru

31. The material I've decided on, and the style is to be (made) the same as this, so shall I have the measurements taken now?   Ki⌐zi wa ki⌐meta⁴ si, kata(ti)[1] wa ko⌐re to onazi ni suru⌐ ñ da kara; i⌐ma su⌐ñpoo (o) haka⌐tte mo⌐raimasyo⁴o ka.

Tailor

32. Certainly.   Syo⌐oti-itasima⌐sita.

. . .

Smith (trying on the finished suit)

jacket	uwaḡi
length	na⌐ḡasa
is tight	kitui /-ku/

33. The length of the jacket is just right but it's a little tight.   Uwaḡi no ⌐na⌐ḡasa wa tyo⌐odo i⁴i ñ desu ḡa, tyo⌐tto ki⌐tu⌐i ñ desu yo.

---

[1] Accent of contracted alternant: ka⌐ta⌐ wa.

Tailor

worry	siñpai or gosiñpai ↑
34. I can make it bigger (lit. wide) so don't worry.	Hi˥roku de˥kima˥su kara, go˥siñpai na˥ku.

ADDITIONAL VOCABULARY

1. I'd like to buy a <u>man's suit</u>. What place would be good? — Se˥biro ḡa kaita˥i ñ desu ḡa, do˥ko ḡa ˥i˥i desyoo ka.

woman's suit	su˥utu
skirt	su˥ka˥ato
blouse	bu˥ra˥usu
dress (one-piece)	wa˥ñpi˥isu
handkerchief	hañkati
comb	ku˥si˥
eyeglasses	me˥ḡane
handbag	ha˥ñdoba˥kku
necktie	ne˥kutai
belt (man's)	bañdo
belt (woman's)	beruto
Japanese-style clothing	wahuku
underwear	sitaḡi
kimono	kimono
coat	haori
sash	o˥bi
wooden clogs	geta
sandals	zoori
socks	ta˥bi
summer kimono	yukata
quilted kimono	ta˥ñze˥ñ

(coat through quilted kimono bracketed as: Japanese-style clothing)

2. Is that suit [made of] <u>synthetic fabric</u>? — Ano sebiro wa <u>ka˥señ</u> de˥su ka⌣

silk	ki˥nu
wool	ke or u˥uru
flax or linen	a˥sa˥

3. Which <u>necktie</u> are you going to <u>wear</u>? — Do˥no <u>nekutai</u> o <u>si˥te</u> ikima˥su ka⌣

wear a sash	o˥bi o si˥me˥ru /-ru/
wear a belt	bañdo /or beruto/ o suru
wear eyeglasses	me˥ḡane o ka˥ke˥ru /-ru/
wear gloves	te˥bu˥kuro o hameru /-ru/

NOTES ON THE BASIC DIALOGUES

3. Ki⌐ka⌐eru: compare no⌐rika⌐eru 'change vehicles' and <u>torikaeru</u> 'ex-
    change.' Ki⌐ka⌐eru is a compound of <u>kiru</u> 'wear' (sentence 5 below) and
    <u>kaeru</u> 'change.'
    <u>Waisyatu</u> usually refers to the kind of man's shirt worn with a necktie.

4. Compare a⌐tarasi⌐i kutu 'new shoes' and a⌐tarasi⌐i hoo no kutu 'shoes
    which are new compared with others.'
    In the combinations <u>haite iku</u>, <u>kite iku</u> (sentence 5), and ka⌐bu⌐tte iku
    (sentence 7), <u>iku</u> can of course be replaced by its polite equivalents ma⌐-
    iru⌐ and i⌐rassya⌐ru⌐.

9. Note the use of the past tense a⌐tta 'it was [here].'

12. Do⌐raikuri⌐iñg̃u is often shortened to <u>dorai</u>.

14. <u>Señtaku</u> is a nominal meaning 'laundering.' Note also <u>señtakuya</u> 'laun-
    dry (i.e. a store)' or 'laundryman' and <u>señtakumono</u> 'laundry (i.e. things
    to be washed).'

18. <u>Syoo</u>, a contraction of <u>siyoo</u> which is equivalent in meaning to <u>sikata</u>, is
    an informal word.

28. <u>Kimeru</u> is the transitive partner of intransitive <u>kimaru</u> /-u/ 'be decided.'
    Particle <u>ni</u> is the <u>ni</u> of goal. Compare: <u>hi o kimeru</u> 'decide the day'
    and <u>sono hi ni kimeru</u> 'decide on that day.'

31. Particle <u>ni</u> is the <u>ni</u> of goal: 'make into the same as this.'

34. Go⌐siñpai na⌐ku 'let there be no worry': compare go⌐enryo na⌐ku and
    o⌐kamai na⌐ku (Lesson 18, Grammatical Note 5). <u>Siñpai</u> also occurs in
    the compound verbal <u>siñpai-suru</u> 'worry.'

GRAMMATICAL NOTES

1. Extended Predicates

    A major sentence (cf. Lesson 4, Grammatical Note 5) in Japanese is one
which ends with, or consists of, an inflected word (non-past or past or tentative or imperative) with or without following sentence particles. The shortest
possible major sentences belong to one of the following types:

    (1) A verbal or adjectival alone.

        Examples: Wa⌐ka⌐ru. 'It's clear.' (Informal)
                   Wa⌐karima⌐sita. 'It was clear.' (Formal)
                   I⌐kimasyo⌐o. 'Let's go.' (Formal)
                   I⌐rassyaima⌐se. 'Go!' or 'Come!' or 'Stay!' (Formal)
                   Sa⌐mu⌐i. 'It's cold.' (Informal)
                   A⌐tukatta. 'It was hot.' (Informal)

    (2) The copula √da and what immediately precedes it, including one ver-
        bal, adjectival, or nominal (i.e. the sequence begins with a verbal, ad-
        jectival, or nominal, and ends with √da).

Examples: Wa⌐karimase⌐ñ desita. 'It wasn't clear.' (Formal)
Sa⌐mu⌐i desu. 'It's cold.' (Formal)
A⌐tukatta desyoo. 'It was probably hot.' (Formal)
So⌐o da. 'That's right.' (Informal)
Ho⌐ñ desu. 'It's a book.' (Formal)
Ko⌐re de⌐sita. 'It was this.' (Formal)
O⌐nazi desyo⌐o. 'It's probably the same.' (Formal)
Sa⌐ñ-zi made desu. 'It's until 3 o'clock.' (Formal)
So⌐re da⌐tta desyoo. 'It was probably that.' (Formal)

Such sequences will hereafter be referred to as PREDICATES. Longer major sentences end with—rather than consist of—a predicate, with or without following sentence particles.

For every non-past and past predicate, there is a corresponding form which will hereafter be called an EXTENDED PREDICATE. An extended predicate, meaning literally 'it is a matter of ——,' is a sequence consisting of two predicates: (1) a non-past or past predicate (usually informal) plus (2) an immediately following second predicate consisting of the nominal ñ (the contracted form of no[1]) 'matter,' 'case' + da (or a more formal/polite equivalent). Before this ñ/no, as before no meaning 'one(s),' the na alternant of da occurs. Accentuation before the two no's is also the same.

Thus, a formal predicate, non-past or past, has as its extended equivalent its informal equivalent (with da becoming na) + ñ desu.

Examples:

Formal Predicate	Formal Extended Predicate
wa⌐karima⌐su 'it's clear'	wa⌐ka⌐ru ñ desu 'it's a matter of being clear'[2]
wa⌐karima⌐sita 'it was clear'	wa⌐ka⌐tta ñ desu 'it's a matter of having been clear'
wa⌐karimase⌐ñ 'it isn't clear'	wa⌐kara⌐nai ñ desu 'it's a matter of not being clear'
wa⌐karimase⌐ñ desita 'it wasn't clear'	wa⌐kara⌐nakatta ñ desu 'it's a matter of not having been clear'
i⌐kita⌐i desu 'I want to go'	i⌐kita⌐i ñ desu 'it's a matter of wanting to go'
ta⌐ka⌐i desu 'it's expensive'	ta⌐ka⌐i ñ desu 'it's a matter of being expensive'
ta⌐kakatta desu ⎫ 'it was expensive' ta⌐ka⌐i desita ⎭	ta⌐kakatta ñ desu 'it's a matter of having been expensive'

---

[1] The uncontracted form often occurs in polite or precise speech, and also in some specific constructions—for example, in women's informal speech, as noted below.

[2] These are literal equivalents.

Formal Predicate	Formal Extended Predicate
to⌐modati de⌐su 'it's a friend'	to⌐modati na⌐ ñ desu 'it's a matter of being a friend'
to⌐modati de⌐sita 'it was a friend'	to⌐modati da⌐tta ñ desu 'it's a matter of having been a friend'
sa⌐ñ-zi made desu 'it's until 3 o'clock'	sa⌐ñ-zi made na ñ desu 'it's a matter of being until 3 o'clock'

The formal extended predicate can be made polite by replacing final desu with de gozaimasu.

The extended equivalent of an informal predicate, non-past or past, is formed by adding ñ da (but before ñ, da becomes na). Thus:

Informal Predicate [1]	Informal Extended Predicate [1]
wa⌐ka⌐ru	wa⌐ka⌐ru ñ da
wa⌐ka⌐tta	wa⌐ka⌐tta ñ da
wa⌐kara⌐nai	wa⌐kara⌐nai ñ da
wa⌐kara⌐nakatta	wa⌐kara⌐nakatta ñ da
ikitai	i⌐kita⌐i ñ da
ta⌐ka⌐i	ta⌐ka⌐i ñ da
ta⌐kakatta	ta⌐kakatta ñ da
tomodati da	to⌐modati na⌐ ñ da
to⌐modati da⌐tta	to⌐modati da⌐tta ñ da
sa⌐ñ-zi made da	sa⌐ñ-zi made na ñ da

Informal extended predicates ending in da are typical of men's speech. As equivalents in sentence-final position and before yo, ne⌐e, and ne, women [2] use extended predicates ending in uncontracted no without following da. Thus:

Informal Predicate [1]	Informal Extended Predicate [1] (alternate form)
wa⌐ka⌐ru	wa⌐ka⌐ru no
wa⌐ka⌐tta	wa⌐ka⌐tta no
wa⌐kara⌐nai	wa⌐kara⌐nai no
wa⌐kara⌐nakatta	wa⌐kara⌐nakatta no
ikitai	i⌐kita⌐i no
ta⌐ka⌐i	ta⌐ka⌐i no
ta⌐kakatta	ta⌐kakatta no

---

[1] The English equivalents are the same as for the formal predicates above.

[2] While the occurrence of any nominal + yo, ne⌐e, or ne is typical of women's speech, ordinarily nominals in sentence-final position occur in the speech of both men and women. However, the occurrence of this no in sentence-final position — particularly in statements — is more typical of women's speech.

Informal Predicate [1]	Informal Extended Predicate [1] (alternate form)
tomodati da	to⌐modati na⌐ no
to⌐modati da⌐tta	to⌐modati da⌐tta no
sa⌐ñ-zi made da	sa⌐ñ-zi made na no

Women also use formal inflected forms in the first part of this kind of extended predicate. Wa⌐karima⌐su no is more formal than wa⌐ka⌐ru no, but less formal than wa⌐ka⌐ru ñ desu.

Predicates ending with a tentative form of da (for example, de⌐syo⌐o) also have extended equivalents. A formal predicate ending with de⌐syo⌐o has as its extended equivalent the corresponding non-past or past informal predicate + ñ desyoo. Thus:

Formal Predicate	Formal Extended Predicate
wa⌐ka⌐ru desyoo 'it's probably clear'	wa⌐ka⌐ru ñ desyoo 'it's probably a matter of being clear' [2]
wa⌐ka⌐tta desyoo 'it probably was clear'	wa⌐ka⌐tta ñ desyoo 'it's probably a matter of having been clear'
wa⌐kara⌐nai desyoo 'it probably isn't clear'	wa⌐kara⌐nai ñ desyoo 'it's probably a matter of not being clear'
wa⌐kara⌐nakatta desyoo 'it probably wasn't clear'	wa⌐kara⌐nakatta ñ desyoo 'it's probably a matter of not having been clear'
i⌐kita⌐i desyoo 'he probably wants to go'	i⌐kita⌐i ñ desyoo 'it's probably a matter of wanting to go'
ta⌐ka⌐i desyoo 'it's probably expensive'	ta⌐ka⌐i ñ desyoo 'it's probably a matter of being expensive'
ta⌐kakatta desyoo 'it probably was expensive'	ta⌐kakatta ñ desyoo 'it's probably a matter of having been expensive'
to⌐modati desyo⌐o 'it's probably a friend'	to⌐modati na⌐ ñ desyoo 'it's probably a matter of being a friend'
to⌐modati da⌐tta desyoo 'it probably was a friend'	to⌐modati da⌐tta ñ desyoo 'it's probably a matter of having been a friend'
sa⌐ñ-zi made desyoo 'it's probably until 3 o'clock'	sa⌐ñ-zi made na ñ desyoo 'it's probably a matter of being until 3 o'clock'

---

[1] The English equivalents are the same as for the formal predicates above.

[2] These are literal equivalents.

An extended predicate ending in desyoo can be made polite by replacing desyoo with de gozaimasyoo.

Grammatically speaking, an extended predicate consists of a nominal ñ/no + √da predicate, with the nominal preceded by a sentence modifier.

Extended predicates occur both in sentence-final position and within a sentence. A predicate and its corresponding extended predicate are almost equivalent in meaning. However, the extended predicate is a more indirect form, and hence is often described as softer and less abrupt. Often, the extended predicate with ñ is a pattern of familiarity (note that in the Basic Sentences of this lesson, the employer uses the extended-predicate pattern in addressing the maid, but not vice versa). Thus, the most significant difference between i⌐kima⌐su and i⌐ku⌐ ñ desu, apart from a structural difference, is stylistic. It might be compared to the kind of difference that exists between English pairs like 'Why are you going?' and 'Why is it you're going?'; 'Who doesn't understand?' and 'Who is it that doesn't understand?'; etc.

Additional examples:

Do⌐ko e i⌐ku⁴ ñ desu ka⌐ 'Where are you going?'
Do⌐tira mo onazi na⌐ ñ desu yo. 'They are both the same!'
Zu⌐ibuñ ta⌐ka⌐i ñ da yo. 'It is awfully expensive!' (man speaking)
So⌐o na no yo. 'That's the way it is!' (woman speaking)
O⌐mosiro⌐i ñ desyoo? 'It is interesting, isn't it?'
Kyo⌐oto e i⌐rassya⁴ru ñ de gozaimasu ka⌐ 'Do you mean you're going to Kyoto?'
I⌐ku⌐ ñ da ḡa, i⌐kitaku na⌐i yo. 'I am going but I don't want to go!' (man speaking)
Te⌐ñpura wa tabe⌐ru ñ desu ḡa, sa⌐simi⌐ wa ta⌐be⌐nai ñ desu yo. 'I do eat tempura but I don't eat sashimi.'
U⌐ti da⌐tta ñ desu ḡa, i⌐ma wa ryo⌐ori⌐ya ni ⌐na⁴tte iru ñ desu yo⌐ 'It was a house but now it's become a restaurant.'

The negative of an extended predicate, with √da following ñ/no replaced by its negative equivalent, occurs in questions which expect agreement on the part of the person addressed. Thus: ni⌐a⌐u ñ zya a⌐rimase⁴ñ ka 'isn't it (a matter of being) becoming?' 'don't you agree that it's becoming?' and ni⌐a⌐u ñ zya ⌐na⁴i desyoo ka 'wouldn't it be (a matter of being) becoming?' 'wouldn't you agree that it is becoming?'

2. Verbals: Honorific Equivalents Ending in √da

A nominal consisting of the polite prefix o- + a verbal stem (i.e. the -ma⌐su form minus -ma⌐su) [1] followed by √da, is an honorific replacement for the corresponding verbal. Like o-stem + ni √na⌐ru, it is not used in reference to the speaker; however, the o-stem + ni √na⌐ru construction is slightly more polite.

In its non-past form, the o-stem + √da pattern refers to present, future, or repeated action. Thus, O⌐hanasi de⌐su ka⌐ means, depending on context, 'Are you talking?' or 'Are you going to talk?' or 'Do you talk?'; it is an honorific equivalent of both Ha⌐na⌐site imasu ka⌐ and Ha⌐nasima⌐su ka⌐ .

---

[1] The resulting nominal is unaccented.

Examples:

Oᒐyobi deˀsu kaˌ 'Are you calling me?'
Oˀwakari deˀsita kaˌ 'Did you understand?'
Oᒐtanomi de gozaimaˀsita kaˌ 'Did you order?'
Oᒐtutome zya arimaseˀn̄ kaˌ 'Aren't you working?'
Oisoḡi desyoo? 'You're in a hurry, aren't you?'
Oᒐdekake daˀ karaˍ 'Since you're going out . . .

WARNING: Not every verbal has this kind of polite equivalent. Use only those you have heard or checked with a native speaker.

3. Particle <u>si</u> 'and'

The particle <u>si</u> 'and,' 'and what is more' follows inflected words (verbals, adjectivals, and √<u>da</u>), non-past or past or tentative, informal or formal. It usually ends with comma intonation.

Compare the following three types of examples, all containing 'and' in their English equivalents:

(1) hoᒐn̄ to zǎssi 'books and magazines'
   Tookyoo ya Ōosaka 'Tokyo and Osaka and such places'

(2) Uᒐti e kaˀette, neᒐmaˀsita. 'I returned home and went to bed.'
   Seˀmakute aᒐtuˀi. 'It is small and it is hot.'
   Koᒐre wa Taˀroo de, soᒐre wa Ziˀroo desu. 'This is Taro and that is Jiro.'

(3) Haˀnasimaˀsu si, kaᒐkimaˀsu. 'He speaks and what is more, he writes.'
   Seˀmaˀi si, aᒐtuˀi. 'It's small and what is more, it's hot.'
   Byoᒐoki daˀ si, iᒐkitaku naˀi. 'I'm sick and what is more, I don't want to go.'

In examples of the first kind, <u>to</u> and <u>ya</u> 'and' connect nominals.

In examples of the second kind, the gerund indicates an action or state coordinate with what follows: 'A is true AND B is true'; if, as in the first example under (2), the action of the gerund is not simultaneous with that of what follows, the order of inflected forms is chronological: 'A happens AND THEN B happens.' If a connective follows the gerund, it is often <u>sore kara</u> 'and then,' 'after that.'

In examples of the third kind, an inflected word followed by particle <u>si</u> furnishes one bit of evidence in a series, all of which are contributing to a single result: thus, in the examples above, 'he speaks and what is more, he writes—therefore he is proficient'; 'it's small and what is more, it's hot—therefore it's not a desirable room'; 'I'm sick and what is more, I don't want to go—therefore I'm not going.' There is not a chronological significance in the order of inflected words connected by <u>si</u>. If a connective occurs at the beginning of the second (or later) clause, it is often <u>sono ue</u> 'on top of that,' 'what is more.'

Accentuation before <u>si</u> is the same as accentuation before <u>kara</u> 'so' and <u>desyoo</u>: in general, a normally unaccented verbal acquires an accent on its

final syllable; a normally unaccented adjectival acquires an accent on its pre-
final syllable; and √da following an unaccented word or phrase is accented.

Examples:

> Yo⌐ku ta┌bema⌐su si, yo⌐ku ne┌ma⌐su kara; mo┌o su⌐g̃u ┌ge⌐n̄ki ni ┌na⌐ru
> desyoo. 'He eats well and he sleeps well so he'll probably get strong
> very soon now.'
> A┌no⌐ hito wa ni┌hon̄go mo de⌐kita si, e┌ego mo dekima⌐sita yo⌣ 'He
> could speak Japanese and could speak English too.'
> Ko┌no apa⌐ato wa sa┌mu⌐i si, ti┌isa⌐i desu. 'This apartment is cold, and
> what's more, it's small.'
> Ni┌ku⌐ mo ┌na⌐i si, sa┌kana mo arimase⌐n̄. 'There's no meat and there's
> no fish either.'
> A┌no zi⌐syo wa ┌o⌐okikatta si, ta⌐kakatta kara; ka┌imase⌐n̄ desita. 'That
> dictionary was big and it was expensive so I didn't buy it.'
> Koko wa ┌ki⌐ree da si, su⌐zusi┌i si, si⌐zuka da kara; su┌ki⌐ desu. 'I
> like this place because it's pretty and it's cool and it's quiet.'
> I⌐i ┌ki⌐zi datta si, ya⌐sukatta kara; ta┌kusan̄ kaima⌐sita. 'It was nice
> material and what's more it was cheap so I bought a lot.'

In all the above sentences, sono ue may be inserted following si.

4. Nominals Ending in -sa

An adjectival stem (i.e. the citation form minus its final -i) + -sa is a
nominal indicating the extent of the adjectival quality. The accent of the -sa
word is, with few exceptions, the same as the accent of the adverbial (-ku form)
of the corresponding adjectival.

Examples:

na┌ga⌐i 'is long'	na⌐gasa 'length'
o┌oki⌐i 'is big'	ookisa 'size'
a┌tu⌐i 'is hot'	a⌐tusa 'heat'
atui 'is thick'	atusa 'thickness'
hi⌐ro┌i 'is big (in area)' or 'is wide'	hi⌐rosa 'area' or 'width'
ko⌐i 'is strong or thick (of liquids); is dark (of colors)'	ko⌐sa 'strength or thickness (of liquids); darkness (of colors)'

5. Multiple Modifiers

A nominal may be described by more than one modifier, each of which retains its original form:

> ta┌ka⌐i bu┌ra⌐usu 'an expensive blouse'; ko⌐n̄ no bu┌ra⌐usu 'a navy blue
> blouse'; ta┌ka⌐i ┌ko⌐n̄ no bu┌ra⌐usu 'an expensive, navy blue blouse'
> a┌tarasi⌐i boosi 'a new hat'; ku┌ro⌐i boosi 'a black hat'; a┌tarasi⌐i ku┌ro⌐i
> boosi 'a new, black hat'
> wa┌takusi no se⌐etaa 'my sweater'; mi⌐dori no ┌se⌐etaa 'a green sweater';
> watakusi no ┌mi⌐dori no ┌se⌐etaa 'my green sweater'

kiˈree na ˋoˈobaa 'a pretty coat'; haˈiiro no ōobaa 'a gray coat'; kiˈree na haˈiiro no ōobaa 'a pretty, gray coat'

In some cases, the modifier itself is modified. Thus:

uˈsui haiiro no zidōosya 'a light gray car'
waˈtakusi no tomodati no zidōosya 'my friend's car'

Compare the intonation patterns of the two preceding groups of examples. Given Modifier A + Modifier B + Nominal[1]: if Modifier A describes the nominal, then Modifier B is pronounced as if it were at the beginning of a new sentence; if Modifier A describes Modifier B, then both regularly belong to the same accent phrase. Thus:

usui hāiiro no waisyatu 'a thin, gray shirt' (i.e. a gray shirt that's thin; Modifier A [usui] modifies waisyatu and Modifier B [haiiro] is pronounced as if at the beginning of a new sentence)

usui haiiro no waisyatu 'a light gray shirt' (i.e. a shirt that's light gray; Modifier A [usui] modifies Modifier B [haiiro] and both belong to the same accent phrase)

oˈokiˈi tañsu no hikidasi 'a big, bureau drawer' (i.e. a bureau drawer that's big; Modifier A [oˈokiˈi] modifies hikidasi and Modifier B [tañsu] is pronounced as if at the beginning of a new sentence)

oˈokiˈi tañsu no hikidasi 'a drawer of the big bureau' (Modifier A [oˈokiˈi] modifies Modifier B [tañsu] and both belong to the same accent phrase)

The same distinction applies when Modifier A is a demonstrative (kono, sono, etc.) and Modifier B contains a nominal. Thus:

kono ziˈdoˈosya no ˋeˈñziñ 'this car-engine' (i.e. this engine that belongs to a car; Modifier A [kono] modifies eñziñ and Modifier B [ziˈdoˈosya] is pronounced as if at the beginning of a new sentence)

koˈno zidōosya no ˋeˈñziñ 'the engine of this car' (Modifier A [kono] modifies Modifier B [ziˈdoˈosya] and both belong to the same accent phrase)

DRILLS

A. Substitution Drill

(Use whatever gerund is appropriate with the given substitution item.)

1. He's wearing a navy blue suit.
   Koˈñ no seˈbiro (o) kite (i)maˈsu yo⌣

2. He's wearing black shoes.
   Kuˈroˈi kuˈtuˈ (o) haˈite (i)maˈsu yo⌣

3. He's wearing a funny hat.
   Oˈkasiˈi boˈosi (o) kabuˈtte (i)masu yo⌣

4. He's wearing a loud necktie.
   Haˈdeˈ na ˈneˈkutai (o) siˈte (i)maˈsu yo⌣

---

[1] With normal, non-contrastive intonation. Not included here are special cases comparable to English 'a BLUE car, not a GREEN car.'

5. He's wearing new gloves.
A⌐tarasi⌐i te⌐bu⌐kuro (o) ha⌐mete (i)ma⌐su yo⌐

6. She's wearing a pretty obi.
Ki⌐ree na ⌐o⌐bi (o) ⌐si⌐mete (i)ma-su yo⌐

7. He's wearing big glasses.
O⌐oki⌐i ⌐me⌐ḡane (o) ⌐ka⌐kete (i)masu yo⌐

8. She's wearing a wide skirt.
Hi⌐ro⌐i su⌐ka⌐ato (o) ha⌐ite (i)ma⌐su yo⌐

9. He's wearing a stunning kimono.
Ri⌐ppa na kimono (o) kite (i)ma⌐su yo⌐

10. He's wearing woolen trousers.
U⌐uru no zu⌐bo⌐ñ (o) ha⌐ite (i)ma⌐su yo⌐

B. Substitution Drill

(Use whatever gerund is appropriate with the given substitution item.)

1. Are you going to wear a (man's) suit to the theater?
Gekizyoo e se⌐biro (o) kite iku⌐ ñ desu ka⌐

2. Are you going to wear a (woman's) suit to the theater?
Gekizyoo e ⌐su⌐utu (o) ki⌐te iku⌐ ñ desu ka⌐

3. Are you going to wear Western-style clothing to the theater?
Gekizyoo e yo⌐ohuku (o) kite iku⌐ ñ desu ka⌐

4. Are you going to wear Japanese-style clothing to the theater?
Gekizyoo e wa⌐huku (o) kite iku⌐ ñ desu ka⌐

5. Are you going to wear a kimono to the theater?
Gekizyoo e ki⌐mono (o) kite iku⌐ ñ desu ka⌐

6. Are you going to wear zori to the theater?
Gekizyoo e zo⌐ori (o) haite iku⌐ ñ desu ka⌐

7. Are you going to wear a hat to the theater?
Gekizyoo e bo⌐osi (o) kabu⌐tte i⌐ku⌐ ñ desu ka⌐

8. Are you going to wear a yukata to the theater?
Gekizyoo e yu⌐kata (o) kite iku⌐ ñ desu ka⌐

9. Are you going to wear a haori to the theater?
Gekizyoo e ha⌐ori (o) kite iku⌐ ñ desu ka⌐

10. Are you going to wear a dress to the theater?
Gekizyoo e wa⌐ñpi⌐isu (o) ki⌐te iku⌐ ñ desu ka⌐

C. Substitution Drill

1. We decided on that teacher.
A⌐no señse⌐e ni ki⌐mema⌐sita.

2. We decided on the teacher (i.e. who the teacher is to be).
Se⌐ñse⌐e o ki⌐mema⌐sita.

3. The teacher decided [it].
Se⌐ñse⌐e ḡa ki⌐mema⌐sita.

4. The teacher has been decided on.
Se⌐ñse⌐e ḡa ki⌐marima⌐sita.

5. It was decided on Friday.[1]   Ki⌐ñyo˥o ni ki⌐marima˥sita.
6. We decided on Friday.[1]   Ki⌐ñyo˥o ni ki⌐mema˥sita.
7. We decided on the day   Hi ⌐o˥ kimema˥sita.
   (i.e. what day it is to be).

D. Substitution Drill

1. Is this to be put away?   Kore (wa) si⌐mau˥ ñ desu ka⌐
   (Lit. As for this, is it a
   matter of putting it away?)
2. Is this to be put in?   Kore (wa) i⌐reru˥ ñ desu ka⌐
3. Is this to be taken out?   Kore (wa) ⌐da˥su ñ desu ka⌐
4. Is this to be aired?   Kore (wa) ⌐ho˥su ñ desu ka⌐
5. Is this to be measured?   Kore (wa) ha⌐ka˥ru ñ desu ka⌐
6. Is this to be sent?   Kore (wa) o⌐kuru˥ ñ desu ka⌐
7. Is this to be laundered?   Kore (wa) se⌐ñtaku-suru˥ ñ desu
                                         ka⌐
8. Is this to be thrown away?   Kore (wa) su⌐teru˥ ñ desu ka⌐
9. Is this to be wiped off?   Kore (wa) hu⌐ku˥ ñ desu ka⌐
10. Is this to be fixed?   Kore (wa) na⌐o˥su ñ desu ka⌐

E. Substitution Drill

(Insert the substitution item in its appropriate form.)

1. I want to have a (man's)   Sebiro (o) tu⌐ku˥tte mo⌐raita˥i
   suit made. Can you do it   ñ desu ḡa, su⌐ḡu de⌐kima˥su ka⌐
   right away?
2. I want to have this watch   Kono tokee (o) na⌐o˥site mo⌐rai-
   fixed. Can you do it right   ta˥i ñ desu ḡa, su⌐ḡu de⌐kima˥su
   away? /kono tokee (o)   ka⌐
   na⌐o˥su/
3. I want to have this chair   Kono isu (o) to⌐do˥kete mo⌐raita˥i
   delivered. Can you do it   ñ desu ḡa, su⌐ḡu de⌐kima˥su ka⌐
   right away? /kono isu (o)
   to⌐doke˥ru/
4. I want to have this dress   Ko⌐no wañpi˥isu (o) se⌐ñtaku-site
   laundered. Can you do it   moraita˥i ñ desu ḡa, su⌐ḡu de-
   right away? /ko⌐no wañ-   ⌐kima˥su ka⌐
   pi˥isu (o) se⌐ñtaku-suru/
5. I want to have this car   Kono kuruma (o) mi⌐ḡaite morai-
   polished. Can you do it   ta˥i ñ desu ḡa, su⌐ḡu de⌐kima˥su
   right away? /kono kuruma   ka⌐
   (o) mi⌐ḡaku/

---

[1] Two possible meanings, depending on context: (1) 'the day decided on was
Friday' (ni = particle of goal); (2) 'the day the decision was made was Friday' (ni = particle of time).

6. I want to have my hair cut (i.e. clipped). Can you do it right away? /ka⌐mi⌐ (o) ka̅ru/

Ka⌐mi⌐ (o) ka⌐tte moraita¹i ñ desu ḡa, su̅gu de⌐kima⌐su ka⌐

7. I want to have my hair cut. Can you do it right away? /ka⌐mi⌐ (o) ⌐ki¹ru/

Ka⌐mi⌐ (o) ⌐ki⌐tte mo⌐raita¹i ñ desu ḡa, su̅gu de⌐kima⌐su ka⌐

8. I want to have these dishes washed. Can you do it right away? /kono osara (o) a̅rau/

Kono osara (o) a⌐ratte moraita¹i ñ desu ḡa, su̅gu de⌐kima⌐su ka⌐

9. I want to have this (man's) suit pressed. Can you do it right away? /kono se-biro ni a⌐iroñ (o) kake¹ru/

Kono sebiro ni a⌐iroñ (o) ka¹kete mo⌐raita¹i ñ desu ḡa, su̅gu de-⌐kima⌐su ka⌐

10. I want to have a new cup-board made. Can you do it right away? /a⌐tarasi¹i todana (o) tu⌐ku¹ru/

A⌐tarasi¹i todana (o) tu⌐ku⌐tte mo-⌐raita¹i ñ desu ḡa, su̅gu de⌐ki-ma¹su ka⌐

F. Substitution Drill

1. The length is just right but it's a little tight.

Na¹ḡasa wa tyo⌐odo i¹i ñ desu ḡa, tyo¹tto ki⌐tu¹i ñ desu yo.

2. The size is just right but it's a little short.

O⌐okisa wa tyoodo i¹i ñ desu ḡa, tyo¹tto mi⌐zika¹i ñ desu yo.

3. The thickness is just right but it's a little tough.

A⌐tusa wa tyoodo i¹i ñ desu ḡa, tyo¹tto ka⌐ta¹i ñ desu yo.

4. It's just strong enough but it's a little cold.

Ko¹sa wa tyo⌐odo i¹i ñ desu ḡa, tyo¹tto tu⌐meta¹i ñ desu yo.

5. The speed is just right but it's a little expensive.

Ha¹yasa wa tyo⌐odo i¹i ñ desu ḡa, tyo¹tto ta⌐ka¹i ñ desu yo.

6. The color is just right but it's a little long.

I¹ro⌐ wa tyo⌐odo i¹i ñ desu ḡa, tyo¹tto na⌐ḡa¹i ñ desu yo.

7. The style is just right but it's a little big.

Ka⌐tati wa tyoodo i¹i ñ desu ḡa, tyo¹tto o⌐oki¹i ñ desu yo.

8. The pattern is just right but it's a little small.

Ga⌐ra wa tyoodo i¹i ñ desu ḡa, tyo¹tto ti⌐isa¹i ñ desu yo.

G. Grammar Drill (based on Grammatical Note 1)

Tutor: I⌐kima¹su. (regular predicate)   ⎫
Student: I⌐ku¹ ñ desu. (extended predicate) ⎬ 'I[¹ll] go.'
                                              ⎭

1. A⌐merika e okurima¹su ka⌐

A⌐merika e okuru¹ ñ desu ka⌐

2. Ma¹da to⌐dokimase¹ñ ka⌐

Ma¹da to⌐doka¹nai ñ desu ka⌐

3. Mo¹o su⌐ñpoo (o) hakarima¹-sita yo⌐

Mo¹o su⌐ñpoo (o) haka⌐tta ñ desu yo⌐

4. A⌐tarasi¹i siḡoto (wa) a⌐si-ta¹ kara desu ka⌐

A⌐tarasi¹i siḡoto (wa) a⌐sita¹ kara na ñ desu ka⌐

5. So⌐no niku⌐ (wa) ka⌐ta⌐i   So⌐no niku⌐ (wa) ka⌐ta⌐i ñ desu ka⌐
   desu ka⌐
6. So⌐no wañpi⌐isu (wa) Hu-   So⌐no wañpi⌐isu (wa) Hu⌐rañsu-see
   ⌐rañsu-see de⌐su ka⌐   na⌐ ñ desu ka⌐
7. O⌐ka⌐sikatta desu yo⌐   O⌐ka⌐sikatta ñ desu yo⌐
8. Ka⌐maimase⌐ñ desita yo⌐   Ka⌐mawa⌐nakatta ñ desu yo⌐
9. Ki⌐no⌐o made byo⌐oki de⌐-   Ki⌐no⌐o made byo⌐oki da⌐tta ñ desu.
   sita.
10. Zyo⌐obu zya arimase⌐ñ ka⌐   Zyo⌐obu zya na⌐i ñ desu ka⌐

H. Grammar Drill [1] (based on Grammatical Note 1)

> Man: I⌐ku⌐ ñ da yo⌐ (extended predicate,   ⎫
>   informal men's speech)   ⎪
>   ⎬ 'I['ll] go.'
> Woman: I⌐ku⌐ no yo⌐ (extended predicate,   ⎪
>   informal women's speech)   ⎭

1. A⌐merika e okuru⌐ ñ da yo⌐   A⌐merika e okuru⌐ no yo⌐
2. Ma⌐da to⌐doka⌐nai ñ da yo⌐   Ma⌐da to⌐doka⌐nai no yo⌐
3. Mo⌐o su⌐ñpoo (o) haka⌐tta   Mo⌐o su⌐ñpoo (o) haka⌐tta no yo⌐
   ñ da yo⌐
4. A⌐tarasi⌐i siḡoto (wa) a⌐si-   A⌐tarasi⌐i siḡoto (wa) a⌐sita⌐ kara
   ta⌐ kara na ñ da yo⌐   na no yo⌐
5. So⌐no niku⌐ (wa) ka⌐ta⌐i ñ   So⌐no niku⌐ (wa) ka⌐ta⌐i no yo⌐
   da yo⌐
6. So⌐no wañpi⌐isu (wa) Hu-   So⌐no wañpi⌐isu (wa) Hu⌐rañsu-see
   ⌐rañsu-see na⌐ ñ da yo⌐   na⌐ no yo⌐
7. O⌐ka⌐sikatta ñ da yo⌐   O⌐ka⌐sikatta no yo⌐
8. Ka⌐mawa⌐nakatta ñ da yo⌐   Ka⌐mawa⌐nakatta no yo⌐
9. Ki⌐no⌐o made byo⌐oki da⌐-   Ki⌐no⌐o made byo⌐oki da⌐tta no yo⌐
   tta ñ da yo⌐
10. Zyo⌐obu zya na⌐i ñ da yo⌐   Zyo⌐obu zya na⌐i no yo⌐

I. Level Drill (based on Grammatical Note 2)

> Tutor: De⌐kakema⌐su ka⌐ (formal plain)   ⎫
>   ⎬ 'Are you going out?'
> Student: O⌐dekake de⌐su ka⌐ (formal honorific) ⎭

1. I⌐soḡima⌐su ka⌐   O⌐isoḡi de⌐su ka⌐
2. Su⌐ḡu wa⌐karima⌐sita ka⌐   Su⌐ḡu o⌐wakari de⌐sita ka⌐
3. Ta⌐naka-señse⌐e (ḡa) yo⌐ñde   Ta⌐naka-señse⌐e (ḡa) o⌐yobi de⌐su
   (i)ma⌐su yo⌐   yo⌐
4. Do⌐nata (o) ⌐ma⌐tte (i)masu   Do⌐nata (o) o⌐mati de⌐su ka⌐
   ka⌐
5. Ra⌐zio (o) ki⌐ite (i)ma⌐su   Ra⌐zio (o) o⌐kiki de⌐su ka⌐
   ka⌐
6. Mo⌐o ka⌐erima⌐su ka⌐   Mo⌐o o⌐kaeri de⌐su ka⌐

---

[1] For a man student, the tutor gives the form on the right and the student gives
the form on the left. For a woman student, the opposite procedure is used.

J.　Expansion Drill

1. Do you have any material?
   Do you have any solid-color material?
   Do you have any white solid-color material?
   Do you have any white solid-color material that's linen?

   Ki⌐zi ḡa a⌐rima⌐su ka⌐

   Mu⌐zi no ⌐ki⌐zi ḡa a⌐rima⌐su ka⌐

   Si⌐ro⌐i ⌐mu⌐zi no ⌐ki⌐zi ḡa a⌐rima⌐su ka⌐

   Asa no si⌐ro⌐i ⌐mu⌐zi no ⌐ki⌐zi ḡa a⌐rima⌐su ka⌐

2. How much is one meter?
   How much is the material by the meter?
   How much is the woolen material by the meter?
   How much is the black woolen material by the meter?
   How much is that black woolen material by the meter?

   I⌐ti-me⌐etoru ⌐i⌐kura?

   Ki⌐zi i⌐ti-me⌐etoru ⌐i⌐kura?

   U⌐uru no ⌐ki⌐zi i⌐ti-me⌐etoru ⌐i⌐kura?

   Ku⌐ro⌐i ⌐u⌐uru no ⌐ki⌐zi i⌐ti-me⌐etoru ⌐i⌐kura?

   Sono ku⌐ro⌐i ⌐u⌐uru no ⌐ki⌐zi i⌐ti-me⌐etoru ⌐i⌐kura?

3. I'm looking for [it] (but). . .
   I'm looking for material (but) . . .
   I'm looking for solid-color material (but). . .
   I'm looking for solid-color material of a conservative color (but). . .
   I'm looking for solid-color material of a more conservative color (but). . .

   Sa⌐ḡasite (i)ru⌐ ñ desu ḡa_

   Ki⌐zi (o) sa⌐ḡasite (i)ru⌐ ñ desu ḡa_

   Mu⌐zi no ⌐ki⌐zi (o) sa⌐ḡasite (i)ru⌐ ñ desu ḡa_

   Zi⌐mi⌐ na i⌐ro⌐ no ⌐mu⌐zi no ⌐ki⌐zi (o) sa⌐ḡasite (i)ru⌐ ñ desu ḡa_

   Mo⌐tto zi⌐mi⌐ na i⌐ro⌐ no ⌐mu⌐zi no ⌐ki⌐zi (o) sa⌐ḡasite (i)ru⌐ ñ desu ḡa_

4. Let's go to the sea[shore].
   It's hot so let's go to the sea[shore].
   It's a holiday and what's more it's hot so let's go to the sea[shore].
   Today it's a holiday and what's more it's hot so let's go to the sea[shore].

   ⌐U⌐mi e i⌐kimasyo⌐o.

   A⌐tu⌐i kara, u⌐mi e i⌐kimasyo⌐o.

   O⌐yasumi da⌐ si, a⌐tu⌐i kara; u⌐mi e i⌐kimasyo⌐o.

   Kyo⌐o wa o⌐yasumi da⌐ si, a⌐tu⌐i kara; u⌐mi e i⌐kimasyo⌐o.

5. It wore out. (Lit. It became no good.)
   It wore out right away.
   It's supposed to be durable but it wore out right away.

   Da⌐me⌐ ni na⌐rima⌐sita yo⌐

   Su⌐ḡu da⌐me⌐ ni na⌐rima⌐sita yo⌐

   Zyo⌐obu na hazu de⌐su ḡa, su⌐ḡu da⌐me⌐ ni na⌐rima⌐sita yo⌐

It's made of synthetic fibers so it's supposed to be durable but it wore out right away.	Ka⌐se̅n de tuku⌉tte ⌐a˩ru kara, zyo-⌐obu na hazu de˥su ḡa; su⌐ḡu da-⌐me˩ ni na⌐rima˩sita yo⌟
This sweater is made of synthetic fibers so it's supposed to be durable but it wore out right away.	Ko⌐no se̅e̅taa wa ka⌐se̅n de tuku⌉tte ⌐a˩ru kara, zyo⌐obu na hazu de˥su ḡa; su⌐ḡu da⌐me˩ ni na⌐rima˩sita yo⌟

6. I don't feel very well.

Tyo⌉tto ki⌐moti ḡa waru⌉i n̄ desu yo.

Today I don't feel very well.

Kyo⌉o wa ⌐tyo⌉tto ki⌐moti ḡa waru⌉i n̄ desu yo.

I ate a lot so today I don't feel very well.

Ta⌐kusan̄ ta⌐beta kara, kyo⌉o wa ⌐tyo⌉tto ki moti ḡa waru⌉i n̄ desu yo.

On top of that I ate a lot so today I don't feel very well.

Sono ue ta⌐kusan̄ ta⌐beta kara, kyo⌉o wa ⌐tyo⌉tto ki⌐moti ḡa waru⌉i n̄ desu yo.

I drank a lot and on top of that I ate a lot so today I don't feel very well.

Ta⌐kusan̄ no⌉n̄da si, sono ue ta-⌐kusan̄ ta⌐beta kara; kyo⌉o wa ⌐tyo⌉tto ki⌐moti ḡa waru⌉i n̄ desu yo.

I drank a lot and on top of that I ate a lot, with a friend, so today I don't feel very well.

Tomodati to issyo ni ta⌐kusan̄ no⌉n̄da si, sono ue ta⌐kusan̄ ta⌐beta kara; kyo⌉o wa ⌐tyo⌉tto ki⌐moti ḡa waru⌉i n̄ desu yo.

Yesterday I drank a lot and on top of that I ate a lot, with a friend, so today I don't feel very well.

Ki⌐no⌉o wa to̅modati to issyo ni ta⌐kusan̄ no⌉n̄da si, sono ue ta-⌐kusan̄ ta⌐beta kara; kyo⌉o wa ⌐tyo⌉tto ki⌐moti ḡa waru⌉i n̄ desu yo.

SHORT SUPPLEMENTARY DIALOGUES

1. Guest: Sayoonara.
   Hostess: Mo⌉o o⌐kaeri de gozaima˩su ka⌟
   Guest: E⌉e. Kyo⌉o wa ⌐tyo⌉tto i⌐soḡima˩su kara_

2. Smith: Kinoo ha⌐zi⌉mete Ta⌐naka-san̄ no otaku e ikima˩sita ḡa, ano
   hen̄ wa *mi⌐ti ḡa yo⌉ku a⌐rimase⌉n̄ n̄e⌉e.
   Yamamoto: Su⌐ḡu o⌐wakari de˥sita ka⌟
   Smith: Iie. Zu⌐ibun̄ sa⌐ḡasima˩sita yo.

3. Maid: Na⌉ni o ki⌐te irassyaima˩su ka⌟
   Mr. Tanaka: Ko⌉n̄ no sebiro kite, ku⌐ro⌉i kutu haite iku yo.
   Maid: Waisyatu wa si⌐ro⌉i no de gozaimasu ka⌟
   Mr. Tanaka: E⌉e, so⌉o.

4. Tanaka: Hi⌐do⌐i yu⌐ki¬ desu yo⌐
 Smith: Zya⌐a, a⌐tui o⌐obaa o ki⌐te ikimasyo¬o.

5. Host: Yo⌐ku i⌐rassyaima¬sita. Do⌐ozo o⌐hairi-kudasa¬i.
 Smith (entering and removing overcoat): Si⌐tu⌐ree-simasu.
 Host: A⌐a, bo⌐ku no uti wa sa⌐mu⌐i desu kara, do⌐ozo ⌐o⌐obaa o ki⌐ta
  mama¬ de⌐
 Smith: Sita ni ta⌐kusañ kite orima⌐su kara, do⌐ozo go⌐siñpai na⌐ku.

6. Smith: Kyo⌐o wa ūti kara ⌐ta⌐kusii de ki⌐ta¬ ñ desu yo⌐
 Tanaka: Kuruma wa?
 Smith: E⌐ñziñ no guai ḡa ⌐he⌐ñ ni ⌐na¬ttyatta kara, si⌐kata ḡa na⌐katta
  ñ desu.

7. Smith: Sore Mãtumoto-sañ no otaku desyoo?
 Tanaka: O⌐taku da⌐tta ñ desu ḡa, i⌐ma wa ryo⌐kañ ni na⌐tta ñ desu yo⌐
  Matumoto-sañ wa ko̊ko o kasite a⌐tarasi⌐i u⌐ti ni ha¬itta soo desu.
 Smith: So⌐o na ñ desu ka.

8. Mrs. Tanaka: Ano si⌐ro⌐i ⌐ki⌐ree na ⌐se¬etaa ta⌐ka⌐i no?
 Mrs. Yamamoto: Zu⌐ibuñ ta⌐ka¬i no yo⌐ Na⌐na-señ-eñ na⌐ no yo⌐

9. Tanaka: Ano ⌐si⌐ro to ⌐ku¬ro no ⌐se¬etaa ta⌐ka⌐i?
 Mr. Yamamoto: Zu⌐ibuñ ta⌐ka¬i ñ da yo⌐ Na⌐naseñ-eñ na⌐ ñ da yo.

10. Tanaka: Wa⌐ka⌐ru?
 Mr. Yamamoto: Bo⌐ku wa wa⌐kara¬nai ñ da yo.
 Miss Itoo: Wa⌐takusi mo wakara⌐nai no yo.

11. Customer: A⌐o⌐i ⌐ki⌐nu no ⌐ne¬kutai ⌐mi¬sete⌐
 Salesgirl: Kore wa i⌐ka⌐ḡa de gozaimasu ka.
 Customer: Tyo⌐tto ha⌐de⌐ zya ⌐na¬i desyoo ka.
 Salesgirl: Zya⌐a, mu⌐zi no wa i⌐ka⌐ḡa de gozaimasu ka⌐
 Customer: A⌐a, so⌐no ho⌐o ḡa ni⌐aima¬su yo.

12. Tanaka: Kyo⌐o ohima?
 Yamamoto: Kyo⌐o wa ⌐go⌐ḡo de⌐kakeru¬ si, yuuḡata to⌐modati ḡa ku⌐ru
  kara⌐
 Tanaka: Zya⌐a mata.

13. Mr. Smith: Bo⌐ku no ⌐ho¬ñ si⌐rimase⌐ñ ka⌐
 Tanaka: So⌐ko ni arimase⌐ñ ka⌐
 Mr. Smith: Ko⌐re wa Tanaka-sañ no⌐ da si, so⌐re wa Yosida-sañ no⌐ da
  si⌐
 Tanaka: Zya⌐a, to⌐nari no heya⌐ zya ⌐na¬i desyoo ka.

14. Mrs. Tanaka: Kinoo ko⌐no ne⌐kutai o ka⌐ima¬sita ḡa; syu⌐ziñ ḡa ha⌐de-
  suḡi⌐ru tte i⌐ima¬sita kara, to⌐rikaete moraita⌐i ñ desu ḡa⌐
 Salesgirl: Do⌐ozo. Kotira ni ⌐mo⌐tto zi⌐mi⌐ na no ḡa ta⌐kusañ gozai-
  ma⌐su kara, o⌐suki na⌐ no o⌐

15. Smith: A⌐kai wañpi⌐isu o kite ru a⌐no⌐ hito ⌐To⌐siko-sañ?
    Yamamoto: E⌐e. Ha⌐de⌐ na hito desyoo?
    Smith: Zu⌐ibuñ.

16. Young Man A: Ku⌐ruma ḡa kaita⌐i ñ da kedo; ti⌐ti⌐ mo syo⌐oti-sina⌐i si,
    o⌐kane mo na⌐i si— Syo⌐o ḡa na⌐i ⌐ne⌐e.
    Young Man B: Bo⌐ku mo so⌐o datta kara, zi⌐teñsya o kattyatta⌐ yo.

English Equivalents

1. Guest: Good-bye.
   Hostess: Are you going home already?
   Guest: Yes. (Because) today I'm in a bit of a hurry . . .

2. Smith: Yesterday I went to Mr. Tanaka's for the first time. The roads
   aren't good around there, are they.
   Yamamoto: Were you able to find it right away?
   Smith: No. I searched an awful lot.

3. Maid: What are you going to wear (lit. go wearing)?
   Mr. Tanaka: I'm going to wear my navy blue suit and (I'm going to wear)
   black shoes.
   Maid: And your shirt—will it be a white one?
   Mr. Tanaka: Yes, that's right.

4. Tanaka: It's snowing hard, you know. (Lit. It's severe snow, you know.)
   Smith: Then I guess I'll wear (lit. go wearing) a heavy (lit. thick) overcoat.

5. Host: I'm so glad you've come. Please come in.
   Smith: (Excuse me—i.e. for entering your home).
   Host: My house is cold so please leave your coat on (lit. please, being
   the condition of having put on a coat).[1]
   Smith: I'm wearing a lot underneath so please don't worry.

6. Smith: You know, I came from home by taxi today.
   Tanaka: What happened to your car?
   Smith: The engine went bad (lit. the condition of the engine became strange)
   so there was nothing I could do.

7. Smith: That's Mr. Matsumoto's house, isn't it?
   Tanaka: That was his house but now it's become an inn. They say that
   Mr. Matsumoto is renting this place (i.e. to someone) and he has gone
   into a new house.
   Smith: Is that the way it is.

---

[1] Japanese homes are usually much colder than American homes in winter.
When Americans visit Japanese homes, their hosts are often concerned about
the difference in temperature.

8. Mrs. Tanaka: Is that pretty, white sweater expensive?
    Mrs. Yamamoto: It's very expensive. Why, it's ¥7000.

9. Tanaka: Is that black and white sweater expensive?
    Mr. Yamamoto: It's very expensive. Why, it's ¥7000.

10. Tanaka: Do you understand?
    Mr. Yamamoto: I don't understand.
    Miss Ito: I don't understand either.

11. Customer: Let me see a blue silk necktie.
    Salesgirl: How about this one?
    Customer: Don't you think that's a little loud?
    Salesgirl: Then how about a solid-color one?
    Customer: Oh, that suits me better.

12. Tanaka: [Are you] free today?
    Yamamoto: Today I'm going out in the afternoon, and a friend is coming
      in the early evening, so. . .
    Tanaka: Then [I'll ask you] again [sometime].

13. Mr. Smith: Don't you know [where] my book [is]?
    Tanaka: Isn't it there?
    Mr. Smith: This is Mr. Tanaka's (one) and that is Mr. Yoshida's (one)
      and. . .
    Tanaka: Then wouldn't it be in the next room?

14. Mrs. Tanaka: I bought this necktie yesterday but my husband said that
      it's too loud so I'd like to have it exchanged. . .
    Salesgirl: Certainly. There are lots of more conservative ones [over]
      here so [please choose] one that you'd like.

15. Smith: [Is] that person wearing the red dress Toshiko?
    Yamamoto: Yes. She's quite a number, isn't she?
    Smith: Very much so!

16. Young Man A: I want to buy a car but my father won't say yes and I don't
      have the money and. . . There's nothing I can do!
    Young Man B: I was in the same boat so I ended up buying a bicycle.

EXERCISES

1. Ask the salesgirl to show you:

        a.   that blue linen material.
        b.   that black cotton skirt.
        c.   that brown belt (man's).
        d.   that red silk necktie.
        e.   the gray umbrella in the middle.
        f.   that obi on the bottom.

      g. that white wool sweater.
      h. some gray woolen trousers.
      i. that dark green furoshiki.
      j. some blue solid-color silk material.

2. Tell the tailor:

      a. that your jacket is too tight.
      b. that your trousers are too long.
      c. to make your coat smaller.
      d. to shorten your dress.
      e. that you want to have a suit made.
      f. that you want to have a black silk dress made.

3. Practice conversations between a customer and a clerk. Make your conversations as natural-sounding and as lively as possible. The customer is looking for the following:

      a. 3 1/2 meters of black woolen material, solid color, not more than ¥ 2500 a meter. [1]
      b. 5 meters of navy blue silk material, not more than ¥ 800 a meter. [1]
      c. a white cotton shirt for a six-year-old boy, for about ¥ 700.
      d. a silk necktie, conservative pattern, about ¥ 800.
      e. a large white sweater for a man, about ¥ 4000.

4. Ask someone (informally):

      a. to have your white suit dry-cleaned.
      b. to look for your old black umbrella.
      c. to air your brown overcoat.
      d. to iron your navy blue trousers as quickly as possible.
      e. to launder this sweater and these gloves.
      f. to shine all the shoes that are dirty.
      g. to get out your new gray sweater.
      h. to put your handkerchiefs in the top drawer.
      i. to put your socks in the middle drawer.
      j. to put your shirts in the bottom drawer.

5. Using colored pictures of people, practice describing in Japanese what they are wearing, within the limits of the vocabulary and constructions you have learned.

6. Practice the Basic Dialogues with appropriate variations, including variations in level.

---

[1] I˺ti-me˹etoru 'one meter.'

Lesson 24. Professions and Occupations

BASIC DIALOGUES: FOR MEMORIZATION

(a)

Smith

1. What kind of work are you doing?

   Doⁿna si˥ḡoto (o) site (i)ma˩su
   ka⌐

Tanaka

factory	ko⌐oba⌐ or ko⌐ozyo⌐o
work (verb)	hataraku /-u/

2. I'm working in a factory.

   Ko⌐oba⌐ de ha˥taraite (i)ma˩su.

   lens — reⁿzu

3. I'm employed (lit. it is a matter
   of) making lenses.

   Reⁿzu (o) tu⌐ku˥tte (i)ru ñ desu.

Smith

4. About how long have you been
   doing [this]?

   Doⁿno-ḡurai site (i)ma⌐su ka⌐

Tanaka

since a long time ago or since way in the past	zu˥tto ma⌐e kara
how many years it comes to	naⁿñ-neñ ni ˥na˩ru ka
commit to memory	o⌐boe⌐ru /-ru/
remember clearly or remember exactly	ha⌐kki⌐ri o⌐bo⌐ete (i)ru

5. (It's) since a long time ago, but
   I don't remember exactly how
   many years it comes to.

   Zu˥tto ma⌐e kara desu ḡa,
   naⁿñ-neñ ni ˥na˩ru ka ha⌐kki⌐ri
   o⌐bo⌐ete (i)⌐na⌐i ñ desu.

(b)

Smith

government employee	ko⌐omu⌐iñ
practice a profession	suru
work as a government employee	ko⌐omu⌐iñ o suru

6. You are working as a government employee, aren't you?

   A⌐na⌐ta (wa) ko⌐omu⌐iñ (o) si˥te
   (i)ru˧ ñ desyoo?

Tanaka

former time	mo⌐to
year before last	o⌐to⌐tosi
company employee	ka⌐isya⌐iñ

70

7. No. I used to (lit. as for for-   Iie. Mo⌐to⌐ wa ᴸso⌐o desita ḡa;
   mer time it was that way), but   o⌐to⌐tosi yamete, ka⌐isya⌐iñ ni
   I quit the year before last and   na⌐rima⌐sita.
   became a company employee.

                              Smith

   without interruption   zutto
8. Have you been in the same   Zu⌐tto onazi kaisya ni iru⌐ ñ
   company the whole time?   desu ka⌐

                              Tanaka

   beginning   hazime
   electric company   de⌐ñkiḡa⌐isya
   employ   ya⌐to⌐u /-u/
   receive employment or   ya⌐to⌐tte morau
     be employed
   not even one year   i⌐ti⌐-neñ mo / + negative/
   without doing or instead   si⌐na⌐i de or se⌐zu¹ ni
     of doing
   insurance company   ho⌐keñḡa⌐isya
   undergo change   kawaru /-u/
   change to an insurance   ho⌐keñḡa⌐isya ni kawaru
     company
9. No. At the beginning I was em-   Iie. Hazime wa de⌐ñkiḡa⌐isya ni
   ployed by the electric company,   ya⌐to⌐tte mo⌐raima⌐sita ḡa; i⌐ti⌐-
   but without working there (lit.   neñ mo so⌐ko no siḡoto (o) si-
   without doing the work of that   na⌐i de, ho⌐keñḡa⌐isya ni ka⌐wa-
   place) even a year, I changed   tta⌐ ñ desu yo.
   to an insurance company.

                              Smith

   previous company   ma⌐e no kaisya
10. Excuse me [for asking] but why   Si⌐tu⌐ree desu ḡa, do⌐o site ᴸma⌐e
    is it you quit the previous com-   no kaisya (o) ya⌐meta⌐ ñ desu ka⌐
    pany?

                              Tanaka

   salary   kyu⌐uryoo
11. The salary was—you know!   Kyu⌐uryoo ḡa ⌐ne⌐e.

                              (c)

                         Mr. Tanaka

12. Are you going to go to work at   Asoko ni ⌐ha⌐iru ñ desu ka⌐
    (lit. enter) that place?

                            Yamamoto

   seem to be difficult or   mu⌐zukasii yo⌐o da
     appear difficult

----
¹ Has unaccented alternant.

13. I want to (enter) but it seems to be difficult.

Ha⌐irita⌐i ñ desu ḡa, mu⌐zukasii yo⌐o desu.

as many as ten days or all of ten days

too-ka mo / + affirmative/

a reply or answer

he⌐ñzi⌐

14. I've been waiting for all of ten days now but an answer hasn't come yet.

Mo⌐o to⌐o-ka mo ma⌐tte (i)ru ñ desu ḡa, ma⌐da he⌐ñzi⌐ ḡa ⌐ko⌐- nai ñ desu yo⌐

mail
get in touch or contact
story (or talk) that they'd get in touch with me

yuubiñ
reñraku-suru
re⌐ñraku-site kureru tte iu hanasi⌐

15. The story was that they'd get in touch with me by mail but . . .

Yu⌐ubiñ de reñraku-site kureru tte iu hanasi⌐ datta ñ desu ḡa—

Mr. Tanaka

can do [it] like you
a person who can do work
a person who is able to do the work like you
surely or positively or certainly

a⌐na⌐ta no yoo ni de⌐ki⌐ru
si⌐ḡoto no deki⌐ru hito
a⌐na⌐ta no yoo ni si⌐ḡoto no deki⌐ru hito
kitto

16. People who are able to do the work like you are few [and far between] so certainly a favorable answer will come soon now.

A⌐na⌐ta no yoo ni si⌐ḡoto no de- ki⌐ru hito (wa) su⌐kuna⌐i kara, kitto mo⌐o su⌐ḡu ⌐i⌐i he⌐ñzi⌐ ḡa ki⌐ma⌐su yo.

call to mind or recall

o⌐moida⌐su /-u/

17. Oh, yes! Say! I just remembered—you know?

A⌐a, so⌐o da. Ano ⌐ne⌐e. I⌐ma o⌐moida⌐sita ñ desu ḡa ne?

secretary

hi⌐syo⌐

18. A friend of mine is a secretary at that place.

Boku no tomodati ḡa a⌐suko no hisyo⌐ desu yo.

in [such] a way that [some-one] tries asking
tell [someone] to try asking

ki⌐ite mi⌐ru yoo ni

ki⌐ite mi⌐ru yoo ni ïu

19. Shall I (just) tell her to try asking?

Tyo⌐tto, a⌐no⌐ hito ni ki⌐ite mi⌐ru yoo ni i⌐imasyo⌐o ka.

Yamamoto

thing (intangible) or act or fact

ko⌐to⌐

20. Would that (lit. that kind of thing) be possible?

So⌐ñna koto⌐ (ḡa) de⌐ki⌐ru desyoo ka.

Mr. Tanaka

21. Yes, of course.

E⌐e, mo⌐ti⌐roñ.

      without worrying <u>or</u>   si⌐ṅpai-sina¬i de <u>or</u> si⌐ṅpai-
        instead of worrying   se¬zu[1] ni
22. Wait (lit. be waiting) a minute   Si⌐ṅpai-sina¬i de, tyo⌐tto ⌐ma¬tte
    and don't worry.   (i)te kudasai.

      ask [someone] to try asking   ki⌐ite mi¬ru yoo ni ta⌐no¬mu
23. (Because) I'll telephone right   I¬ma deṅwa-site, ki⌐ite mi¬ru yoo
    now and ask her to try inquiring.   ni ta⌐nomima¬su kara.

                    Yamamoto

24. Well, I'll leave it up to you   Zya¬a, yo⌐rosiku oneḡai-sima¬su.
    (lit. I ask you [to treat me]
    favorably).

                       (d)

               (At a soba shop)

               Mr. Yamamoto

      lunch   hirumesi[2]
      not come any more (lit.   mo¬o ⌐ko¬naku ⌐na⁺ru
        become non-coming any
        more)
25. Tanaka doesn't come for lunch   Tanaka-kuṅ ⌐mo¬o hi⌐rumesi ni
    any more, does he.   ko¬naku ⁺na⁺tta ⌐ne¬e.

                      Mr. Ito

      not a bit   ti⌐tto¬ mo /+ negative/
26. We don't see him a bit these   Kono-ḡoro ti⌐tto¬ mo a⁺wa⁺nai
    days, do we.   ⌐ne¬e.

        finally <u>or</u> in the end   to¬otoo
        seem to have ended up quit-   ya⌐metyatta yo¬o da
          ting
27. He kept saying that he'd quit   Asuko (o) yǎmeru yǎmeru tte
    that place. It looks as if he   i⌐tte (i)ta¬ kedo, to¬otoo ya⁺me-
    finally did (quit)!   tyatta yo¬o da ⌐ne¬e.

               Mr. Yamamoto

      is boring   tu⌐ma¬ṅnai /-ku/
      continue [something]   tuzukeru /-ru/
      without continuing <u>or</u>   tu⌐zukena¬i de <u>or</u> tuzu-
        instead of continuing   kezu ni[3]
      work that is more interest-   mo⌐tto o⌐mosi¬rokute ⌐kyu¬-
        ing and pays a good sal-   uryoo no ⌐i¬i siḡoto
        ary
      almost (lit. as if) every day   ma⌐initi no yo¬o ni

---

[1] Has unaccented alternant.

[2] Man's word.

[3] Has accented alternant: tu⌐zuke¬zu.

28. You know, he used to say al-   Añna tu⌐ma⌐ñnai siḡoto (o) tuzu-
    most every day that instead of   kezu ni, mo⌐tto o⌐mosi⌐rokute ⌐kyu⌐-
    continuing boring work like   uryoo no ⌐i⌐i si⌐ḡoto ḡa sita⌐i tte;
    that, he wanted to do work that   ma⌐initi no yo⌐o ni i⌐tte (i)ta⌐ ñ
    was more interesting and paid   da yo⌐
    a good salary.

                                  Mr. Ito

    be(come) found   mitukaru /-u/
    it is probably a case of   mi⌐tukatta⌐ ñ daroo
      having been found (in-
      formal)
29. He must surely have found a   Kitto ⌐i⌐i siḡoto ḡa mi⌐tukatta⌐ ñ
    good job. (Lit. It must surely   daroo.
    be the case that good work has
    been found.)

                                    (e)

                                  Tanaka

30. You are doing difficult work,   Mu⌐zukasii osi⌐ḡoto (o) si⌐te
    aren't you! Isn't is a strain?   (i)rassya⌐ru ñ desu ⌐ne⌐e. Tai-
                                           heñ desyoo?

                                  Smith

    finally or barely or   yatto
      with difficulty
    make a mistake   ma⌐tiḡae⌐ru /-ru/
    without making a mistake   ma⌐tiḡae⌐nai de or
      or instead of making a   ma⌐tiḡae⌐zu ni
      mistake
    in [such] a way that it is   de⌐ki⌐ru yoo ni
      possible
    reach the point where it   de⌐ki⌐ru yoo ni ⌐na⌐ru
      is possible
31. Yes. I have finally reached the   E⌐e. Kono-ḡoro ya̋tto ma⌐ti-
    point nowadays where I can do   ḡae⌐zu ni de⌐ki⌐ru yoo ni na-
    it without making mistakes   ⌐rima⌐sita keredo—
    but . . .

                       ADDITIONAL VOCABULARY

I don't remember for sure but isn't   Ha⌐kki⌐ri o⌐bo⌐ete (i)⌐mase⌐ñ
he a bank employee?   ḡa, gi⌐ñko⌐oiñ zya a⌐rimase⌐ñ
                                           ka⌐

              carpenter   da⌐iku
              company president   syatyoo
              dentist   ha⌐isya
              diplomat   ga⌐iko⌐okañ

doctor (medical)	isya or oisyasañ [†]
driver or chauffeur	uˈñteˈñsyu
eye doctor or oculist	meˈisya
factory worker	kooiñ
farmer	hyaˈkusyoˈo
fisherman	ryoˈosi
foreign trader	boˈoekiˈsyoo
gardener	uekiya
laborer	roˈodoˈosya
lawyer	beˈñḡoˈsi
manager	siˈhaˈiniñ
missionary	seˈñkyoˈosi
newspaperman	kiˈsya or siˈñbuñkiˈsya
nurse	kaˈñḡoˈhu
office worker	ziˈmuˈiñ
professor	kyoozyu
pupil	seˈeto
salaried man or white-collar worker	saˈrariˈimañ
salesgirl	uriko
serviceman (i.e. member of the armed forces)	guñziñ
shop employee	miˈse no hitoˈ or teñiñ
student	gakusee
waiter/waitress or steward/stewardess or bar-boy or office boy	kyuˈuzi [1] or booi [2]

NOTES ON THE BASIC DIALOGUES

2. Koozyoo usually refers to a large factory, whereas koˈobaˈ often refers to a small factory or workshop.

Compare: hataraku 'work'
          siḡoto o suru 'do work'
          tuˈtomeˈru 'become employed'

A place word + particle de occurs with the first two expressions, indicating the place where work is performed; an organizational word + particle ni with tuˈtomeˈru indicates the organization for which one works:

          giñkoo de hataraite iru 'be working at a bank'
          giñkoo de siḡoto o site iru 'be doing work at a bank'
          giˈñkoo ni tutoˈmete iru 'be working for a bank'

4. Note the use of the non-past, indicating that an action or state is still continuing.

5. Zuˈtto maˈe means literally 'before by far,' i.e. 'way before.'

8. See 4 above.

---

[1] Male or female.

[2] Male.

Zutto 'by far' and zutto 'without interruption,' 'continuous' are distinguished only by context.

9. Particle wa following hazime is the wa of comparison.
Hazime also occurs followed by particle ni, indicating the time when something happens.
Kaisya ~ de⌐ŋkiḡa⌐isya, ho⌐keŋḡa⌐isya: There are many Japanese words beginning with k-, s-, t-, or h- whose initial sound changes when the word becomes the second part of a compound. The change, IF IT OCCURS (it is impossible to predict), is as follows:

   k > ḡ
      Example: Ku⌐tu⌐ 'shoes'
                naḡaḠutu 'boots'

   s > z
      Example: Su⌐ki⌐ 'pleasing'
                sakeZuki 'sake lover,' 'drinker'

   t before a, e, o > d; elsewhere, t > z
      Examples: Tana 'shelf'
                 hoñDana 'bookshelf'

                 Tyawañ '(tea)cup'
                 ko⌐ohiiZya⌐wañ 'coffee cup'

                 Ti 'blood'
                 hanaZi 'nosebleed'

   h > b (or, sometimes, p)
      Examples: Hako 'box'
                 hoñBako 'bookcase'

                 Hya⌐ku⌐ '100'
                 sa⌐ñByaku '300'
                 ro⌐pPyaku⌐ '600'

Kawaru is the intransitive partner of transitive kaeru 'change [something]' which has occurred in compounds no⌐rikae⌐ru 'change vehicles,' torikaeru 'exchange,' and ki⌐kae⌐ru 'change clothes.'

11. Ga here is the emphatic subject particle: 'It was the salary [that was the cause of my leaving].'

14. See 4 above.
He⌐ñzi⌐: note also he⌐ñzi⌐ (o) suru 'make an answer,' 'answer (verb).'

15. 'but—I haven't heard anything yet.'

17. O⌐bo⌐ete iru (sentence 5) means 'remember' in the sense of 'be in a state of having committed to memory,' whereas o⌐moida⌐su means 'remember' in the sense of 'call back to mind.'
Ga here indicates that the speaker is about to go on to explain what it is he just recalled.

25. Me⌐si⌐ is a less formal equivalent of go⌐han. Note also: asamesi 'break-fast' and bañmesi 'dinner' (i. e. 'evening meal').
The use of na⌐ru indicates that a change has taken place: '[He used to come here for lunch but] he doesn't come any more.' See Lesson 10, Grammatical Note 4.

26. Titto is an alternant of tyo⌐tto which occurs before mo.

28. Tu⌐ma⌐ññai is the contracted alternant of tu⌐mara⌐nai.
Tuzukeru is the transitive partner of intransitive tuzuku /-u/ '[some-thing] continues.'

29. Mitukaru is the intransitive partner of transitive mitukeru /-ru/ 'find [something].'

31. 'but — it is still difficult.'
Ma⌐tiḡae⌐ru is the transitive partner of intransitive ma⌐tiḡa⌐tu /-u/ 'be wrong.'

GRAMMATICAL NOTES

1. yo⌐o

Yo⌐o is a nominal meaning 'manner' or 'likeness' or 'resemblance'; it is a na word, and it is always preceded by a modifier. It regularly loses its accent following an accented word or phrase.

Like other na words, yo⌐o occurs followed by √da or by the particle ni of manner (cf. Lesson 15, Grammatical Note 5).

A modifier preceding yo⌐o may be a sentence modifier, a nominal + par-ticle no, or a demonstrative (kono, sono, etc.).

Yo⌐o regularly indicates resemblance or approximation or what seems or appears to be; it has many different English equivalents depending upon the words that surround it. Study the following combinations carefully:

(1) —— yo⌐o √da 'it seems —— ,' 'it appears —— ,' 'it is like —— '

Examples:

Wa⌐ka⌐ru yoo da. 'He seems to understand.'
Ki⌐eta yo⌐o desu. 'It seems to have gone out.'
Ta⌐ka⌐i yoo desita. 'It seemed expensive.'
O⌐bo⌐ete i⌐nai yo⌐o desu. 'It appears that he doesn't remember.'
O⌐suki na yo⌐o de gozaimasu. 'It seems as if he likes it.'
Ki⌐nu no yoo desyoo? 'It's like silk, isn't it?'
So⌐no yo⌐o desita. 'It was like that.'

(2) —— yo⌐o na X[1] 'an X that seems —— ,' 'an X of the kind that —— ,' 'an X that is like —— '

---

[1] X, here, stands for any nominal.

Examples:

Ze⌐nzeñ beñkyoo-sinai yo⌐o na gakusee desu. 'He's a student of
the kind that never studies.'

Ta⌐naka-sañ no yo⌐o na tomodati wa su⌐kuna⌐i desu. 'Friends like
Mr. Tanaka are rare.'

(3) ―― yo⌐o ni 'in the manner of ――,' 'like ――,' 'as ――,' 'in
such a way that ――,' 'so that ―― '

Examples:

Ma⌐e ni i⌐tta yo⌐o ni, sore wa da⌐me⌐ desu. 'As I said before,
that's no good.'

Wa⌐surenai yo⌐o ni i⌐tte kudasa⌐i. 'Don't forget to go.' (Lit.
'Please go, in a manner of not forgetting.')

Ho⌐kka⌐idoo no yoo ni sa⌐mu⌐i desu. 'It's cold, like Hokkaido.'

A⌐na⌐ta no yoo ni wa de⌐kimase⌐ñ. 'I can't do it the way you can.'

Ko⌐ko kara mie⌐ru yoo ni ⌐o⌐okiku ⌐ka⌐ite kudasai. 'Please write
large, in such a way that I can see it from here.'

Da⌐re mo oki⌐nai yoo ni ⌐ti⌐isa na ⌐ko⌐e de ha⌐na⌐site kudasai.
'Please talk in a low voice so that no one wakes up.'

Note the following special combinations containing ―― yo⌐o ni:

(a) ―― yo⌐o ni iu 'tell [someone] to ―― '

Examples:

De⌐ñwa-suru yo⌐o ni i⌐tte kudasa⌐i. 'Please tell him to telephone.'

A⌐no⌐ hito ni ⌐ma⌐do o a⌐keru yo⌐o ni i⌐ima⌐sita. 'I told him to
open the window.'

Na⌐ni mo iwanai yo⌐o ni i⌐tte kudasa⌐i. 'Tell him not to say
anything.'

(b) ―― yo⌐o ni ⌐na⌐ru 'reach the point where ―― '

Examples:

Su⌐ko⌐si wa⌐ka⌐ru yoo ni na⌐rima⌐sita. 'I've reached the point
where I understand a little.'

Mo⌐o hatarakanai yo⌐o ni na⌐rima⌐sita. 'He's reached the point
where he doesn't work any more.'

(c) ―― yo⌐o ni suru 'act in such a way that ――.'

Example:

Ha⌐yaku zyo⌐ozu⌐ ni ⌐na⌐ru yoo ni si⌐te ima⌐su ⌐ga_ 'I'm trying
to become proficient quickly but . . . ' (Lit. 'I'm acting in
such a way that I become proficient quickly but . . . ')

When yo⌐o is preceded by a negative, and suru occurs in an imperative
or request form, the combination is a polite negative request, less direct
than the [a]nai de kudasai pattern.

Example: Tu⌐kawanai yo⌐o ni site kudasai. 'Please don't use it.'
(Lit. 'Please act in a not-using way.')

2. Alternate Negative Adverbial; -_zu ni_ and -_nai de_

All adjectivals have an adverbial form ending in -ku, derived from the informal non-past (for example, o⌐okiku from o⌐oki˺i, ta⌐beta˺ku from ta⌐beta˺i, ta⌐be˺naku from ta⌐be˺nai, etc.). In addition, negative adjectivals (those ending in negative -_nai_) have a second adverbial form which will hereafter be referred to as the ALTERNATE NEGATIVE ADVERBIAL or, more simply, the -ZU FORM. It is made from a -_nai_ form by replacing the final -_nai_ with -_zu_ (except for the irregular _sezu_ from _sinai_).

Examples: [1]

VERBAL	NEGATIVE ADJECTIVAL		
Informal Non-past (= Citation form)	Informal Non-past	Adverbial	Alternate Adverbial [2]
ta⌐be˺ru 'eat'	ta⌐be˺nai	ta⌐be˺naku	ta⌐be˺zu
mi˺ru 'see'	mi˺nai	mi˺naku	mi˺zu
ma˺tu 'wait'	ma⌐ta˺nai	ma⌐ta˺naku	ma˺tazu
ka⌐eru 'return'	ka⌐era˺nai	ka⌐era˺naku	ka⌐erazu
kau 'buy'	kawanai	kawanaku	kawazu
ha⌐na˺su 'talk'	ha⌐nasa˺nai	ha⌐nasa˺naku	ha⌐na˺sazu
ka˺ku 'write'	ka⌐ka˺nai	ka⌐ka˺naku	ka˺kazu
i⌐so�{g}u 'be in a hurry'	i⌐so̱ga˺nai	i⌐so̱ga˺naku	i⌐so̱gazu
yobu 'call'	yobanai	yobanaku	yobazu
yo˺mu 'read'	yo⌐ma˺nai	yo⌐ma˺naku	yo˺mazu
o⌐ssya˺ru 'say'	o⌐ssyara˺nai	o⌐ssyara˺naku	o⌐ssya˺razu
iku 'go'	ikanai	ikanaku	ikazu
ku˺ru 'come'	ko˺nai	ko˺naku	ko˺zu
suru 'do'	sinai	sinaku	sezu

The -_zu_ form + particle _ni_ of manner occurs within sentences meaning 'without doing so-and-so' or 'instead of doing so-and-so.'

Examples:
Be⌐nkyoo-sezu ni Gi⌐nza e ikima˺sita. 'Instead of studying, he went to the Ginza.'
Nani mo iwazu ni de⌐ma˺sita. 'He left, without saying anything.'
Su⌐npoo o hakara˺zu ni tu⌐ku˺tte simatta. 'He finished making it without taking the measurements.'

---

[1] There is no -_zu_ form corresponding to the verbal a˺ru, in spoken Japanese.

[2] It is impossible to make any simple, meaningful statement about the accent of -_zu_ forms. For some speakers, their accent coincides with that of the corresponding citation form, but many have alternate accents.

In the above examples, the -zu negative + ni may be replaced by the corresponding -nai form + de (gerund of da), without any significant change in
meaning. Thus:

> Beⁿkyoo-sinai de Giⁿza e ikimasita.
> Naⁿni mo iwanai de demasita.
> Suⁿpoo o hakaranai de tukutte simatta.

In this use, the two patterns are interchangeable except that -zu ni is less
common in the spoken language, particularly in women's speech.

WARNING: -Nai de patterns — but NOT -zu ni patterns — also occur in negative requests. (Example: Tukawanai de (kudasai). 'Don't use it.' Cf. Lesson 22, Grammatical Note 3.)

3. daroo

The informal equivalent of formal tentative desyoo is daroo. Like desyoo, daroo loses its accent following an accented word or phrase, and the
accent of words and phrases before daroo is the same as before desyoo.
Daroo, like desyoo, may be preceded by informal verbals, non-past and
past; adjectivals, non-past and past; informal datta; nominals; and particles.[1]

> Kuru daroo. 'He probably comes.' or 'He'll probably come.'
> Wakatta daroo. 'He probably understood.'
> Takai daroo.[2] 'It's probably expensive.'
> Yokatta daroo.[3] 'It probably was all right.'
> Amerikaziñ datta daroo.[3] 'It probably was an American.'
> Kore daroo. 'It's probably this one.'
> Kyooto kara daroo. 'It's probably from Kyoto.'

Daroo occurs at the end of informal sentences, before sentence particles
(including ka), and before ga 'but,' predominantly in men's speech. In
formal and informal sentences, in the speech of men and women, it occurs
in quotations and before certain particles, such as kara 'so.' Thus:

> Dekiru daroo? (M) 'You can do it, can't you?'
> Boku daroo ka. (M) 'Do you think it's me?'
> Samui daroo ga, oobaa wa iranai. (M) 'It's probably cold, but I don't
>   need a coat.'
> Muzukasii daroo to iimasita. 'He said it would probably be diffi-
>   cult.'
> Yoru daroo tte. 'He says he'll probably stop in.'

---

[1] But unlike desyoo, daroo does not also follow formal inflected forms.

[2] An alternate form of informal non-past adjectival tentative consists of an
adjectival stem + -karoo. Thus: takakaroo.

[3] The contracted equivalent of -katta daroo is -kattaroo and of datta daroo
is dattaroo. Thus: yokattaroo, Amerikaziñ dattaroo.

Sa⌐mu⌐i daroo kara, o⌐obaa o ki⊦masyo⌐o. 'It will probably be cold so I guess I'll wear a coat.'

Other uses of da⌐ro⌐o will be introduced later.

4. Particle mo Following a Number

An extent expression consisting of a number or quantity word + particle mo, followed by an affirmative, means 'as much as ——,' 'as many as ——,' 'all of ——,' indicating that in the given context, the amount is large.

Examples:

I⌐ti-zi⌐kañ mo ma⊦tima⌐sita. 'I waited all of an hour.'
Si⌐ti⌐-neñ mo i⊦ma⌐sita. 'I was there as long as seven years.'
Ni-⌐señ-eñ mo kakarima⌐su yo⌐. 'It will take as much as ¥2000.'
Sore o ha⌐ñbu⌐ñ mo tu⊦kaima⌐sita. 'I used as much as a half of that.'

An extent expression consisting of a number or quantity word + particle mo, followed by a negative, means 'not even ——,' indicating that in the given context, the amount is small.

Examples:

I⌐p-puñ mo ma⊦timase⌐ñ desita. 'I didn't wait even one minute.'
Su⌐kosi mo wakarimase⌐ñ. 'I don't understand at all (lit. even a little).'
Hi⌐to-ri mo kimase⌐ñ desita. 'Not a single person came.'
Isu wa hi⌐to-tu mo na⌐i. 'There isn't even one chair.'

5. ko⌐to⌐

Ko⌐to⌐, a nominal which is always preceded by a modifier, refers to 'things' in an intangible sense, whereas mo⌐no⌐ is a concrete 'thing.' Compare:

So⌐ñna koto⌐ wa o⌐mosiro⌐i. 'Things (i. e. facts or acts) like that are interesting.'

and:

So⌐ñna mono⌐ wa o⌐mosiro⌐i. 'Things (i. e. objects) like that are interesting.'

—— to (or [t] te) iu koto (lit. 'the thing said quote —— ') occurs as an equivalent of English 'the fact that ——.' Thus:

de⌐ki⌐ru to[1] iu koto 'the fact that it's possible'
a⌐tarasi⌐i to[1] iu koto 'the fact that it's new'
ko⌐nakatta to[1] iu koto 'the fact that [someone] didn't come'
to⌐modati da⌐ to[1] iu koto 'the fact that [someone] is a friend'

A nominal X + no + ko⌐to⌐ is an equivalent of English 'things pertaining to X,' '[things] about X.' Thus: u⌐ti no koto⌐ 'things pertaining to the house'; A⌐merika no koto⌐ '[things] about America.'

---

[1] Or tte.

Additional examples:

Ni⌐hoñ no koto⌐ wa ⌐yo⌐ku wa⌐karima⌐su ⌐ne⌐e. 'You understand a great
deal about Japan, don't you!'
Ni⌐hoñgo o beñkyoo-site iru tte iu koto⌐ wa si⌐rimase⌐ñ desita.'I didn't
know (the fact) that you were studying Japanese.'
Ko⌐syoo da to iu koto⌐ o wa⌐surema⌐sita. 'I forgot (the fact) that it was
(lit. is) broken.'

Ko⌐to⌐ directly preceded by an informal non-past verbal (meaning literally
'the act of —— ') occurs as an equivalent of English 'to do so-and-so' or
'doing so-and-so' in expressions like:

Sa⌐ñpo-suru koto⌐ ḡa su⌐ki⌐ desu. 'I like to take walks.'
Zi⌐teñsya ni no⌐ru koto⌐ ḡa ki⌐rai de⌐su. 'I hate to ride on bicycles.'
Ya⌐su⌐mu koto ḡa ta⌐isetu de⌐su. 'It is important to rest.'

DRILLS

A. Substitution Drill

1. He is (i.e. is working as) a government employee, isn't he?	A⌐no⌐ hito (wa) ko⌐omu⌐iñ (o) si⌐te (i)ru⌐ ñ desyoo?
2. He is (i.e. is working as) a teacher (or doctor), isn't he?	A⌐no⌐ hito (wa) <u>se⌐ñse⌐e</u> (o) si⌐te (i)ru⌐ ñ desyoo?
3. She is (i.e. is working as) a nurse, isn't she?	A⌐no⌐ hito (wa) <u>ka⌐ñḡo⌐hu</u> (o) si⌐te (i)ru⌐ ñ desyoo?
4. He is (i.e. is working as) a doctor, isn't he?	A⌐no⌐ hito (wa) <u>i⌐sya⌐</u> (o) site (i)ru⌐ ñ desyoo?
5. He is (i.e. is working as) a dentist, isn't he?	A⌐no⌐ hito (wa) <u>⌐ha⌐isya</u> (o) si⌐te (i)ru⌐ ñ desyoo?
6. He is (i.e. is working as) an oculist, isn't he?	A⌐no⌐ hito (wa) <u>⌐me⌐isya</u> (o) si⌐te (i)ru⌐ ñ desyoo?
7. He is (i.e. is working as) a missionary, isn't he?	A⌐no⌐ hito (wa) <u>se⌐ñkyo⌐osi</u> (o) si⌐te (i)ru⌐ ñ desyoo?
8. He is (i.e. is working as) a carpenter, isn't he?	A⌐no⌐ hito (wa) <u>⌐da⌐iku</u> (o) si⌐te (i)ru⌐ ñ desyoo?
9. He is (i.e. is working as) a lawyer, isn't he?	A⌐no⌐ hito (wa) <u>be⌐ñḡo⌐si</u> (o) si⌐te (i)ru⌐ ñ desyoo?
10. He is (i.e. is working as) a newspaperman, isn't he?	A⌐no⌐ hito (wa) <u>ki⌐sya⌐</u> (o) si⌐te (i)ru⌐ ñ desyoo?

B. Substitution Drill

1. The work is fine but it's the salary [that's the problem].	Si⌐goto wa i⌐i kedo, kyu⌐uryoo ḡa ⌐ne⌐e.
2. The teacher is fine but it's the pupils [that are the problem].	<u>Se⌐ñse⌐e</u> wa ⌐i⌐i kedo, <u>se⌐eto</u> ḡa ⌐ne⌐e.

3. The husband is fine but it's the wife [that's the problem]. — Go⌐syu¬ziñ wa ⌐i⁴i kedo, o⌐kusañ ḡa ⌐ne¬e.

4. The room is fine but it's the meals [that are the problem]. — He⌐ya¬ wa ⌐i⁴i kedo, syokuzi ḡa ⌐ne¬e.

5. The style is fine but it's the pattern [that's the problem]. — Ka⌐tati wa i⌐i kedo, gara ḡa ⌐ne¬e.

6. The material is fine but it's the color [that's the problem]. — Ki¬zi wa ⌐i⁴i kedo, i⌐ro¬ ḡa ⌐ne¬e.

7. The inside is fine but it's the outside [that's the problem]. — Na⌐ka wa ⌐i⁴i kedo, so⌐to ḡa ⌐ne¬e.

8. The house is fine but it's the furniture [that's the problem]. — U⌐ti wa i⌐i kedo, ka⌐ḡu ḡa ⌐ne¬e.

C. Substitution Drill

1. I worked for two years. — Ni¬-neñ ha⌐tarakima⁴sita.
2. I worked for as long as two years. — Ni¬-neñ mo ha⌐tarakima⁴sita.
3. I didn't work for even two years. — Ni¬-neñ mo ha⌐tarakimase¬ñ de-sita.
4. I worked for only two years. — Ni¬-neñ sika ha⌐tarakimase¬ñ de-sita.
5. I didn't work for two years (—but I did work). — Ni¬-neñ wa ha⌐tarakimase¬ñ de-sita.
6. I did work for two years. — Ni¬-neñ wa ha⌐tarakima⁴sita.
7. I worked for just two years. — Ni¬-neñ dake ha⌐tarakima⁴sita.

D. Substitution Drill

1. It appears that he's going to quit. — Ya⌐meru yo¬o desu.
2. They say that he's going to quit. — Ya⌐meru so¬o desu.
3. He's expected to quit. — Ya⌐meru hazu de¬su.
4. I plan to quit. — Ya⌐meru tumori de¬su.
5. He'll probably quit. — Ya⌐meru desyo¬o.
6. He said that he would quit. — Ya⌐meru to iima¬sita.
7. He said that he had quit. — Ya⌐meta to iima¬sita.
8. He probably quit. — Ya⌐meta desyo¬o.
9. He's supposed to have quit. — Ya⌐meta hazu de¬su.
10. They say he quit. — Ya⌐meta so¬o desu.
11. It appears that he quit. — Ya⌐meta yo¬o desu.

E. Substitution Drill

1. He's like you.
2. It seems difficult.
3. It appears that he isn't
    coming any more.
4. It's like this.
5. He seems to have made a
    mistake.
6. It appears that he doesn't
    remember.
7. It seems to be strong.
8. He doesn't seem to be
    busy.
9. It doesn't seem to be full.
10. He seems to have changed
    to an American company.

A⌐na⌐ta no yoo desu.
Mu⌐zukasii yo⌐o desu.
Mo⌐o ⌐ko⌐nai yoo desu.

Ko⌐no yo⌐o desu.
Ma⌐tiḡa⌐eta yoo desu.

O⌐bo⌐ete (i)⌐nai yo⌐o desu.

Zyo⌐obu na yo⌐o desu.
I⌐soḡa⌐siku ⌐na⌐i yoo desu.

I⌐ppai zya na⌐i yoo desu.
A⌐merika no kaisya ni kawatta
    yo⌐o desu.

F. Substitution Drill

1. Tell [him] to try asking.

2. Tell [him] to continue
    yesterday's work.
3. Tell [him] to send it as
    soon as possible.
4. Tell [him] to polish the
    car.
5. Tell [him] to check the
    luggage.
6. Tell [him] to (go) walk(ing).

7. Tell [him] to transfer to
    the bus.
8. Tell [him] not to overwork.

9. Tell [him] not to smoke
    here.
10. Tell [him] not to lock it.

Ki⌐ite mi⌐ru yoo ni i⌐tte kuda-
    sa⌐i.
Kinoo no siḡoto (o) tu⌐zukeru
    yo⌐o ni i⌐tte kudasa⌐i.
Na⌐rubeku ha⌐yaku o⌐kuru yo⌐o
    ni i⌐tte kudasa⌐i.
Zidoosya (o) mi⌐ḡaku yo⌐o ni
    i⌐tte kudasa⌐i.
Ni⌐motu (o) a⌐zuke⌐ru yoo ni
    i⌐tte kudasa⌐i.
A⌐ru⌐ite i⌐ku yo⌐o ni i⌐tte kuda-
    sa⌐i.
Ba⌐su ni no⌐rikae⌐ru yoo ni i⌐tte
    kudasa⌐i.
Ha⌐tarakisuḡi⌐nai yoo ni i⌐tte
    kudasa⌐i.
Koko de ta⌐bako (o) noma⌐nai
    yoo ni i⌐tte kudasa⌐i.
Ka⌐ḡi⌐ (o) ka⌐ke⌐nai yoo ni i⌐tte
    kudasa⌐i.

G. Substitution Drill

1. Nowadays it's reached the
    point where he can do it.
2. Nowadays it's reached the
    point where he understands
    well.
3. Nowadays it's reached the
    point where it's upsetting.

Kono-ḡoro de⌐ki⌐ru yoo ni na-
    ⌐rima⌐sita.
Kono-ḡoro ⌐yo⌐ku wa⌐ka⌐ru yoo
    ni na⌐rima⌐sita.
Kono-ḡoro ko⌐ma⌐ru yoo ni na-
    ⌐rima⌐sita.

4. Nowadays it's reached the point where he studies hard.

Kono-ḡoro ⌈yo⌉ku be⌐ŋkyoo-suru yo⌐o ni na⌐rima⌐sita.

5. Nowadays it's reached the point where he drinks too much.

Kono-ḡoro no⌈misuḡi⌉ru yoo ni na⌐rima⌐sita.

6. Nowadays it's reached the point where he often makes mistakes.

Kono-ḡoro ⌈yo⌉ku ma⌐tiḡae⌐ru yoo ni na⌐rima⌐sita.

7. Nowadays it's reached the point where he uses Japanese a good deal.

Kono-ḡoro ni⌈hoñḡo (o) yo⌉ku tu-⌐kau yo⌐o ni na⌐rima⌐sita.

8. Nowadays it's reached the point where it rains every day.

Kono-ḡoro ⌈a⌉me ḡa ⌈ma⌉initi ⌐hu⌐-ru yoo ni na⌐rima⌐sita.

H. Substitution Drill

1. Don't forget to write big.

Wa⌈surenai yo⌉o ni ⌈o⌉okiku ⌐ka⌐ite kudasai.

2. Write big, as I told you before.

Ma⌉e ni i⌐tta yo⌐o ni ⌈o⌉okiku ⌐ka⌐ite kudasai.

3. Write big, the same as this.

Ko⌈re to onazi yo⌉o ni ⌈o⌉okiku ⌐ka⌐ite kudasai.

4. Write big, the way Mr. Tanaka [does].

Ta⌉naka-sañ no yo⌉o ni ⌈o⌉okiku ⌐ka⌐ite kudasai.

5. Write big, like this.

Ko⌈no yo⌉o ni ⌈o⌉okiku ⌐ka⌐ite ku-dasai.

6. Write big, so that I can see it from here.

Ko⌈ko kara mie⌉ru yoo ni ⌈o⌉okiku ⌐ka⌐ite kudasai.

I. Substitution Drill

1. I'd like to join [it] but it seems to be difficult.

Ha⌈irita⌉i ñ desu ḡa, mu⌈zukasii yo⌉o desu.

2. I'd like to buy [it] but it seems to be expensive. /kau, ta⌈ka⌉i/

Ka⌈ita⌉i ñ desu ḡa, ta⌈ka⌉i yoo desu.

3. I'd like to take [it] but it seems to be heavy. /mo-tte iku, omoi/

Mo⌈tte ikita⌉i ñ desu ḡa, o⌈moi yo⌉o desu.

4. I'd like to wear [it] but it seems to be small. /kiru, ti⌈isa⌉i/

Ki⌈ta⌉i ñ desu ḡa, ti⌈isa⌉i yoo desu.

5. I'd like to try riding [in it] but it seems to be dangerous. /no⌈tte mi⌉ru, abunai/

No⌈tte mita⌉i ñ desu ḡa, a⌈bunai yo⌉o desu.

6. I'd like to use [it] but it seems to be dirty. /tukau, ki⌈tana⌉i/

Tu⌈kaita⌉i ñ desu ḡa, ki⌈tana⌉i yoo desu.

J. Substitution Drill

1. I don't remember for sure how many years it comes to.
    Naⁿ-nen ni ʰnaᵗru ka haʳkkiˀri oʳboˀete (i)ʰnaˀi ñ desu.

2. I've already forgotten how many years it comes to.
    Naⁿ-nen ni ʰnaᵗru ka moˀo wa-surete simaimaˀsita.

3. I don't know how many years it comes to.
    Naⁿ-nen ni ʰnaᵗru ka siʳrimaseⁿ.

4. I can't tell how many years it comes to.
    Naⁿ-nen ni ʰnaᵗru ka waʳkari-maseˀñ.

5. Shall I ask and see how many years it comes to?
    Naⁿ-nen ni ʰnaᵗru ka kiʳite mi-masyoˀo ka.

6. Please say how many years it comes to.
    Naⁿ-nen ni ʰnaᵗru ka iʳtte kuda-saˀi.

7. Would you find out how many years it comes to?
    Naⁿ-nen ni ʰnaᵗru ka siʳraˀbete kuʰremaseᵗñ ka⌐

8. He told me how many years it comes to.
    Naⁿ-nen ni ʰnaᵗru ka oˀsiete ku-remaˀsita.

K. Substitution Drill

1. He kept saying that he would quit. It looks as if he finally did (quit)!
    Yameru yāmeru tte iʳtte (i)taˀ kedo, toˀotoo yaʰmetyatta yoᵗo desu ʰneˀe.

2. He kept saying that he would go. It looks as if he finally did (go)! /iku/
    Iku īku tte iʳtte (i)taˀ kedo, toˀotoo iʰttyatta yoᵗo desu ʰneˀe.

3. He kept saying that he would sell [it]. It looks as if he finally did (sell)! /uru/
    Uru ūru tte iʳtte (i)taˀ kedo, toˀotoo uʰttyatta yoᵗo desu ʰneˀe.

4. He kept saying that he would do [it]. It looks as if he finally did (do)! /suru/
    Suru sūru tte iʳtte (i)taˀ kedo, toˀotoo siʰtyatta yoᵗo desu ʰneˀe.

5. He kept saying that he would give [it to him]. It looks as if he finally did (give)! /aḡeru/
    Aḡeru āḡeru tte iʳtte (i)taˀ kedo, toˀotoo aʰḡetyatta yoᵗo desu ʰneˀe.

6. He kept saying that he would go home. It looks as if he finally did (go home)! /kaˀeru/
    Kaˀeru ʳkaˀeru tte iʳtte (i)taˀ kedo, toˀotoo ʰkaᵗettyatta yoo desu ʰneˀe.

7. He kept saying that he would decide. It looks as if he finally did (decide)! /kimeru/
    Kimeru kīmeru tte iʳtte (i)taˀ kedo, toˀotoo kiʰmetyatta yoᵗo desu ʰneˀe.

8. He kept saying that he would take [it]. It looks as if he finally did (take)! /toˀru/
    Toˀru ʳtoˀru tte iʳtte (i)taˀ kedo, toˀotoo ʰtoᵗttyatta yoo desu ʰneˀe.

L. Grammar Drill (based on Grammatical Note 1)

> Tutor: I⌐kana¬i de kudasai.   ⎫
> Student: I⌐kanai yo¬o ni site kudasai. ⎬ 'Please don't go.'
>   ⎭

1. Eeḡo (o) tu⌐kawana¬i de   Eeḡo (o) tu⌐kawanai yo¬o ni site
   kudasai.   kudasai.
2. Ma⌐tiḡae¬nai de kudasai.   Ma⌐tiḡae¬nai yoo ni site kudasai.
3. Wa⌐surena¬i de kudasai.   Wa⌐surenai yo¬o ni site kudasai.
4. I⌐soḡa¬nai de kudasai.   I⌐soḡa¬nai yoo ni site kudasai.
5. Ko⌐ko de¬ wa tâbako   Ko⌐ko de¬ wa tâbako (o) no⌐ma¬-
   (o) no⌐ma¬nai de kudasai.   nai yoo ni site kudasai.
6. Okane (o) ka⌐rina¬i de ku-   Okane (o) ka⌐rinai yo¬o ni site
   dasai.   kudasai.

M. Grammar Drill (based on Grammatical Note 2)

> Tutor: Ma⌐tiḡae¬nai de si┗ma┛sita.   ⎫ 'He did it without making
> Student: Ma⌐tiḡae¬zu ni si┗ma┛sita.   ⎬   a mistake.'
>   ⎭

1. Ha⌐tarakana¬i de zu⌐tto   Hatarakazu ni zu⌐tto nete (i)ma¬-
   nete (i)ma¬sita.   sita.
2. Ya⌐suma¬nai de zu⌐tto ha-   Ya⌐suma¬zu ni zu⌐tto hataraite
   taraite (i)ma¬sita.   (i)ma¬sita.
3. Ha⌐rawa¬nai de ⌐de¬te si┗-   Ha⌐rawa¬zu ni ⌐de¬te si┗maima┛-
   ┗maima┛sita.   sita.
4. Wa⌐surena¬i de âsita ⌐ha¬-   Wasurezu ni âsita ⌐ha¬yaku ki┗te┛
   yaku ki┗te┛ kudasai.   kudasai.
5. Ho⌐n̄¬ (o) ┗mi┛nai de mo⌐o   Ho⌐n̄¬ (o) ┗mi┛zu ni mo⌐o iti-do
   iti-do itte kudasa¬i.   itte kudasa¬i.
6. O⌐yu (o) tukawana¬i de   Oyu (o) tukawazu ni a⌐ratte ku-
   a⌐ratte kudasa¬i.   dasa¬i.
7. Su⌐n̄poo (o) hakara¬nai de   Su⌐n̄poo (o) hakara¬zu ni tu⌐ku¬-
   tu⌐ku¬tte si┗maima┛sita.   tte si┗maima┛sita.
8. Na⌐ni mo iwana¬i de de-   Nani mo iwazu ni de⌐ma¬sita.
   ⌐ma¬sita.

N. Level Drill [1]

1. Zutto onazi kaisya ni iru?   Zu⌐tto onazi kaisya ni ima¬su
                                  ka⌐
2. Ma⌐tiḡa¬eta daroo? (M)   Ma⌐tiḡa¬eta desyoo?
3. Mo⌐o ⌐ko¬naku ┗na┛tta ⌐ne¬e.   Mo⌐o ⌐ko¬naku na┗rima┛sita ⌐ne¬e.
   (M)
4. Do⌐o site yameta no? (W)   Do⌐o site ya┗meta┛ n̄ desu ka⌐
5. Ki⌐tto so⌐o daroo ┗ne┛e. (M)   Ki⌐tto so⌐o desyoo ┗ne┛e.

---

[1] In each case the sentence on the right is the formal equivalent of the sentence on the left.

6. A⌐sita⌐ made ni re⌐ñraku-
   site kurena⌐i ka⌐ (M)

   A⌐sita⌐ made ni re⌐ñraku-site ku-
   remaseñ ka⌐

7. Tu⌐ma⌐ñnakatta daroo?
   (M)

   Tu⌐mara⌐nakatta desyoo?

8. O⌐kime ni na⌐tta? (W)

   O⌐kime ni narima⌐sita ka⌐

O. Expansion Drill

1. Please write.

   Ka⌐ite kudasai.

   Please write your address.

   O⌐tokoro (o) ka⌐ite kudasai.

   I'll get in touch with you
   so please write your
   address.

   Re⌐ñraku-sima⌐su kara, o⌐tokoro
   (o) ka⌐ite kudasai.

   I ll get in touch with you
   by mail so please write
   your address.

   Yu⌐ubiñ de reñraku-sima⌐su kara,
   o⌐tokoro (o) ka⌐ite kudasai.

2. [They]'re few [and far be-
   tween], aren't they?

   Su⌐kuna⌐i daroo?

   Americans are few [and
   far between], aren't
   they?

   A⌐merika⌐ziñ wa su⌐kuna⌐i daroo?

   Americans who can do [it]
   are few [and far between],
   aren't they?

   De⌐ki⌐ru A⌐merika⌐ziñ wa su⌐ku-
   na⌐i daroo?

   Americans who can [speak]
   Japanese are few [and
   far between], aren't
   they?

   Ni⌐hoñgo no deki⌐ru A⌐merika⌐-
   ziñ wa su⌐kuna⌐i daroo?

   Americans who can [speak]
   Japanese like that doctor
   are few [and far between],
   aren't they?

   A⌐no oisyasañ no yo⌐o ni Ni⌐hoñ-
   go no deki⌐ru A⌐merika⌐ziñ wa
   su⌐kuna⌐i daroo?

3. It was the answer.

   He⌐ñzi⌐ datta ñ desu yo.

   The answer was (lit. it
   was an answer which
   said) that they had decided.

   Ki⌐meta⌐ tte iu he⌐ñzi⌐ datta ñ
   desu yo.

   The answer was that they
   had decided on another
   person.

   Ho⌐ka no hito⌐ ni ki⌐meta⌐ tte iu
   he⌐ñzi⌐ datta ñ desu yo.

   I waited but the answer
   was that they had de-
   cided on another person.

   Ma⌐tima⌐sita ğa, ho⌐ka no hito⌐
   ni ki⌐meta⌐ tte iu he⌐ñzi⌐ datta ñ desu yo.

   I waited all of three weeks
   but the answer was that
   they had decided on
   another person.

   Sa⌐ñ-syu⌐ukañ mo ma⌐tima⌐sita
   ğa, ho⌐ka no hito⌐ ni ki⌐meta⌐
   tte iu he⌐ñzi⌐ datta ñ desu yo.

4. I've reached the point
   where I understand.

   I've reached the point
   where I understand a
   little.

   I've reached the point
   where I understand a
   little these days.

   It used to be difficult, but
   I've reached the point
   where I understand a
   little these days.

   At the beginning it was
   difficult, but I've
   reached the point where
   I understand a little
   these days.

Wa⌐ka⌐ru yoo ni na⌐rima⌐sita.

Su⌐ko⌐si wa⌐ka⌐ru yoo ni na⌐ri-
ma⌐sita.

Kono-ḡoro su⌐ko⌐si wa⌐ka⌐ru yoo
ni na⌐rima⌐sita.

Mu⌐zukasi⌐katta ñ desu ḡa, kono-
ḡoro su⌐ko⌐si wa⌐ka⌐ru yoo ni
na⌐rima⌐sita.

Ha⌐zime wa muzukasi⌐katta ñ
desu ḡa, kono-ḡoro su⌐ko⌐si wa-
⌐ka⌐ru yoo ni na⌐rima⌐sita.

5. I don't remember.
   I don't remember any more.
   I don't remember any
   more what year it was.
   I hired [her] but I don't
   remember any more
   what year it was.
   I hired [her] a long time
   ago but I don't remember
   any more what year it
   was.
   I hired that secretary a
   long time ago but I don't
   remember any more
   what year it was.

O⌐bo⌐ete (i)⌐na⌐i ñ desu.
Mo⌐o o⌐bo⌐ete (i)⌐na⌐i ñ desu.
Na⌐ñ-neñ datta ka ⌐mo⌐o o⌐bo⌐ete
(i)⌐na⌐i ñ desu.
Ya⌐toima⌐sita ḡa, na⌐ñ-neñ datta
ka ⌐mo⌐o o⌐bo⌐ete (i)⌐na⌐i ñ desu.

Zu⌐tto ma⌐e ni ya⌐toima⌐sita ḡa,
na⌐ñ-neñ datta ka ⌐mo⌐o o⌐bo⌐ete
(i)⌐na⌐i ñ desu.

So⌐no hisyo⌐ (o) zu⌐tto ma⌐e ni
ya⌐toima⌐sita ḡa, na⌐ñ-neñ datta ka ⌐mo⌐o o⌐bo⌐ete (i)⌐na⌐i ñ
desu.

6. I went to bed.
   I went to bed early.
   I went to bed early without
   studying.
   I had a headache so I went
   to bed early without
   studying.
   Last night I had a headache
   so I went to bed early
   without studying.

Ne⌐te simaima⌐sita.
Ha⌐yaku ne⌐te simaima⌐sita.
Beñkyoo-sezu ni ⌐ha⌐yaku ne⌐te
simaima⌐sita.
A⌐tama⌐ ḡa ⌐i⌐takatta kara, beñkyoo-sezu ni ⌐ha⌐yaku ne⌐te
simaima⌐sita.
Yuube a⌐tama⌐ ḡa ⌐i⌐takatta kara,
beñkyoo-sezu ni ⌐ha⌐yaku ne⌐te
simaima⌐sita.

SUPPLEMENTARY CONVERSATIONS

(with questions)

1. Smith: Hi⌐do┐i ┌a┙me desu ⌐ne┐e. Ki⌐no┐o wa ┌do┙o desita ka⌐
   Tanaka: Ki⌐no┐o mo ┌kyo┙o no yoo desita yo⌐ O⌐osaka wa do┐o desita ka⌐
   Smith: Oosaka wa ki⌐no┐o wa ┌i┐i ┌te┙ñki datta ñ desu ga ⌐ne┐e.

   a. Kinoo ⌐Su┐misu-sañ mo Tanaka-sañ mo ko⌐ko ni ima┐sita ka⌐
   b. Kinoo koko wa ⌐do┐ñna ┌te┙ñki desita ka⌐

2. Secretary: Otaku kara o⌐de┐ñwa desu ga⌐
   Smith: I⌐ma i┐so̅gasi┐i kara, sa⌐ñ-zi su̅gi┐ ni ma⌐ta kake┐ru yoo ni i┌tte kudasa┙i.

   a. Da┐re ga sa┌ñ-zi su̅gi┙ ni ma┌ta deñwa o kake┙ru desyoo ka.

3. Smith: A⌐tarasi┐i hi⌐syo┙ wa ⌐ma┐da?
   Tanaka: E┐e. Ke┐sa hi⌐syo┐ ni na⌐rita┙i tte iu hito ga go-⌐ni┐ñ mo ki┌ta┙ ñ desu ga, i┐i hito wa da⌐re mo ina┐katta ñ desu.

   a. Tanaka-sañ wa ⌐mo┐o a⌐tarasi┐i hi⌐syo┙ o ya⌐toima┐sita ka⌐
   b. Ke┐sa ┌ki┙ta hito wa ⌐do┐ñna hi┌to de┙sita ka⌐

4. Tanaka: Hi⌐do┐i yu⌐ki┙ desita ⌐ne┐e. Zi⌐mu┐syo e i⌐kima┐sita ka⌐
   Smith: Iie. Zi⌐mu┐syo e ikazu ni u⌐ti de si̅goto o sima┐sita yo⌐

   a. Su┐misu-sañ wa ⌐do┐o site u┌ti de si̅goto o sita┙ ñ desyoo ka.

5. A: Na⌐rubeku nihoñ̅go o tukau yo┐o ni si┌te iru┙ ñ desu ga, *mu⌐zukasi┐i desu ⌐ne┐e—nihoñ̅go wa.
   B: Su┐gu de⌐ki┙ru yoo ni ┌na┙ru kara, da⌐izyo┐obu desu yo.

   a. A┐-sañ wa ni⌐hoñzi┐ñ desyoo ka. Do┐o site wa┌karima┙su ka⌐

6. Tanaka: Ko⌐no deñwa wa kosyoo da┐ kara, tu⌐kawanai yo┐o ni site kuda- sai.
   Smith: Ko⌐ma┐ru kara, ha┐yaku na⌐o┐site mo┌raimasyo┙o.
   Tanaka: Mo┐o ta⌐no̅nda ñ desu ga; kyo┐o wa i⌐so̅gasi┐i kara, a⌐sita ku┐ru soo desu.

   a. Da┐re ga a┌sita ku┙ru hazu desu ka⌐

7. Tanaka: Zyo⌐oñzu-sañ wa⌐ka┐tta desyoo ka.
   Smith: Wa⌐kara┐nakatta yoo desu ⌐ne┐e.
   Tanaka: Zya┐a, mo┐o iti-do iimasyo┐o ka.
   Smith: E┐e, so┐o site kudasa┐i.

   a. Tanaka-sañ wa ⌐do┐o site mo┐o iti-do iima┙su ka⌐

8. Smith: Zyo꜒oñzu-sañ wa nꜞhoñḡo ḡa niꜛhoñziꜞñ no yoo ni deꜛkimaꜜsu
ꜛneꜞe. Doꜜko de beꜛñkyoo sitaꜜ ñ desyoo ka⌐

Tanaka: Zyo꜒oñzu-sañ desu ka⌐ Oꜛkaꜜasañ ḡa niꜛhoñziꜞñ de, zuꜛtto kodomo no tokiꜞ kara Niꜛhoꜞñ ni iꜛmaꜜsu kara; eꜛeḡo yoꜞri ni-
ꜛhoñḡo no hoꜜo ḡa zyoꜛozuꜞ na ñ desu yo⌐

Smith: So꜒o desu ka. Zyaꜜa, hoñtoo ni niꜛhoñziꜞñ to oꜞnazi yoꜜo ni
deꜛkiꜞru haꜛzu deꜜsu ꜛneꜞe.

a. Zyo꜒oñzu-sañ no nihoñḡo wa ꜜdoꜜo desu ka⌐
b. Zyo꜒oñzu-sañ wa éeḡo to nihoñḡo to ꜜdoꜛtira ḡa zyoꜛozuꜞ
desu ka⌐
c. Zyo꜒oñzu-sañ wa ꜛdoꜜko de niꜛhoñḡo o naraꜜtta ñ desu ka⌐

9. Smith (conducting interview): Aꜞnaꜜta ꜛꜞꜞmaꜜ zyoꜛtyuu site ruꜞ ñ desu ka⌐
Miss Yamamoto: Haꜜa. Oꜛtoꜞtosi made koꜛoiñ o site ori-
maꜜsita ḡa; yamete, sore kara zyoꜛtyuu
o site orimaꜜsu.

Smith: Iꜞma haꜛtaraite imaꜜsu ka⌐
Miss Yamamoto: Haꜜa. Sibuya [1] no giꜛñkoꜞoiñ no uti de hataraite orimasu.

Smith: Do꜒o site ꜛiꜜma no uti yaꜛmetaꜜi ñ desu
ka⌐
Miss Yamamoto: Daꜛñnasaꜞma ḡa Oꜛosaka no giñkoo ni oka-
wari ni narimaꜜsu kara.

Smith: Aꜜa, waꜛkarimaꜜsita. Koko ni nămae to
deꜛñwabaꜞñḡoo ꜛkaꜜite kudasai. Do꜒yoo
maꜜde ni deꜛñwa de reñraku-simaꜜsu
kara.

Miss Yamamoto: Oꜛneḡai-itasimaꜜsu.

a. Yamamoto-sañ wa ꜛꜞꜞtu kara zyoꜛtyuu
o site imaꜜsu ka⌐
b. Iꜞma ꜜdoꜜko de haꜛtaraite imaꜜsu ka⌐
c. Do꜒o site yaꜛmetaꜜi ñ desu ka⌐
d. Suꜞmisu-sañ wa ꜛꜞꜞtu made ni ꜛnaꜞñ de
reꜛñraku-simaꜜsu ka⌐

EXERCISES

1. Complete each of the following sentences with an appropriate ending:

a. Mo꜒to wa Aꜛmerika de hataraite imaꜜsita ḡa, iꜞma wa ——— .
b. Mo꜒to wa niꜛhoñḡo o beñkyoo-site imaꜜsita ḡa, iꜞma wa ——— .
c. Mo꜒to wa keꜛkkoñ-site imaꜜsita ḡa, iꜞma wa ——— .
d. Mo꜒to wa tuꜛtoꜞmete iꜛmaꜜsita ḡa, iꜞma wa ——— .
e. Mo꜒to wa koꜛomuꜞiñ o siꜛte imaꜜsita ḡa, iꜞma wa ——— .
f. Mo꜒to wa guꜛñziñ deꜜsita ḡa, iꜞma wa ——— .
g. Mo꜒to wa suꜛkiꜞ desita ḡa, iꜞma wa ——— .
h. Mo꜒to wa oꜛmosiꜞrokatta ñ desu ḡa, iꜞma wa ——— .
i. Mo꜒to wa ꜛyaꜜsukatta ñ desu ḡa, iꜞma wa ——— .

---

[1] Section of Tokyo.

    j. Mo⌐to wa a⌐buna⌐katta ñ desu ḡa, i⌐ma wa ——— .
    k. Mo⌐to wa o⌐so⌐katta ñ desu ḡa, i⌐ma wa ——— .
    l. Mo⌐to wa ya⌐sasi⌐katta ñ desu ḡa, i⌐ma wa ——— .

2. Ask Mr. Tanaka what kind of work he does.
    Mr. Tanaka answers that:

    a. he is a bank employee.
    b. he is a newspaperman.
    c. he practices law in Yokohama.
    d. he is a company employee but he wants to become a school
        teacher.
    e. he used to work in a factory but now he is an embassy driver.
    f. he works for the American Consulate in Kobe.
    g. he isn't employed.
    h. he is still a student, but in April, he will join the Bank of Japan.

3. Interview a prospective employee. Find out his name, address, telephone
    number, age, present place and kind of employment, reasons for wanting
    to leave, salary, English ability. At the end of the interview, tell him you
    will get in touch with him tomorrow morning.

4. Give the substance of each of the Basic Dialogues in narrative, non-dia-
    logue form, including as many details as possible. For example (Dia-
    logue a):

        Tanaka-sañ wa ⌐reñzu o tu⌐ku⌐ru ko⌐oba⌐ de hataraite imasu.
    Zu⌐tto ma⌐e kara so⌐ñna siḡoto o site ima⌐su ḡa, na⌐ñ-neñ ni ⌐na⌐-
    ru ka Tãnaka-sañ wa ha⌐kki⌐ri o⌐bo⌐ete i⌐mase⌐ñ.

Lesson 25. At the Office

BASIC DIALOGUES: FOR MEMORIZATION

(a)

Tanaka (to friend)

reception desk
1. I wonder where the reception desk is.

2. Oh, I see.

uketuke
Uketuke (wa) ⌈do⌉tira desyoo ˥ne˥e.

A, wa⌈karima⌉sita.

Receptionist

some business or some matter to be attended to

3. Can I help you? (Lit. Is it some matter you wish to attend to?)

na⌉ni ka ⌈yo⌉o or na⌉ni ka go⌈yo⌉o ˥

Na⌉ni ka go⌈yo⌉o desyoo ka.

Tanaka

4. We'd like to see Mr. Ueda . . .

Ministry of Education
introduction
5. We've come through the introduction of Mr. Yamamoto at the Ministry of Education.

U⌈eda-sañ ni ome ni kakarita⌉i ñ desu ḡa—

mo⌈ñbu⌉syoo
syookai or gosyookai ˥
Mo⌈ñbu⌉syoo no Ya⌈mamoto-sañ no gosyookai de mairima⌉sita.

Receptionist

conference
in the middle of a conference
can receive or can be received
can't I have you come?

6. He's in conference now so—I'm sorry but—would you come again [some other time]?

ka⌉iḡi
kaiḡi-tyuu

moraeru /-ru/ or itadakeru ˥ /-ru/
ki⌈te⌉ moraenai? or i⌈ra-ssya⌉tte ˥ itadakenai ˥? or i⌈ra⌉site ˥ itadakenai ˥?

I⌉ma ka⌈iḡi-tyuu de gozaima⌉su kara; su⌈mimase⌉ñ ḡa, ma⌈ta ira⌉-site i˥tadakemase˥ñ ka—

circumstances or conditions

7. Is that convenient for you? (Lit. How are the conditions for you?)

tuḡoo or gotuḡoo ˥

Gotuḡoo (wa) i⌈ka⌉ḡa de gozaiması ka.

Tanaka

can come   ko⌐rare⌐ru /-ru/
8. We can't come any more today   Kyo⌐o wa ⌐mo⌐o ko⌐raremase⌐ñ
     so I guess we'll come tomor-   kara, a⌐sita mairimasyo⌐o.
     row.

(b)

Tanaka

come to see [someone]   a⌐i ni ⌐ku⌐ru or o⌐me ni
                              kaka⌐ri ni ⌐ma⌐iru ‖
9. I've come to see Mr. Yama-   Ya⌐mamoto-sañ ni ome ni kaka⌐ri
     moto...   ni ma⌐irima⌐sita ḡa—

Secretary

can't I have you wait?   ma⌐tte moraenai? or o⌐mati
                             ni na⌐tte ‖ itadakenai ‖?
10. Mr. Yamamoto stepped out   Yamamoto-sañ (wa) ⌐tyo⌐tto o⌐de-
     for a moment but he'll be   kake ni narima⌐sita ḡa; su⌐ḡu o⌐ka-
     back soon so would you wait?   eri ni narima⌐su kara, o⌐mati ni
                             na⌐tte i⌐tadakemase⌐ñ ka—

Tanaka

11. Yes, that will be all right.   E⌐e, ke⌐kkoo desu.

Secretary

sit down (on a chair)   ka⌐ke⌐ru /-ru/
12. Please have a seat.   Do⌐ozo, o⌐kake-kudasa⌐i.

· · ·

Tanaka (to Yamamoto, after talking with him)

various(ly)   iroiro
helpful service   se⌐wa⌐ or o⌐se⌐wa ‖
13. I'm much obliged to you.   Iroiro o⌐se⌐wa ni na⌐rima⌐sita.

a time when you are busy   o⌐isoḡasi⌐i ‖ tokoro
14. Thank you very much for your   O⌐isoḡasi⌐i to⌐koro⌐ (o) ⌐do⌐o mo
     time when you are [so] busy.   a⌐ri⌐ḡatoo gozaimasita.

(c)

Tanaka

can read or can be   yo⌐me⌐ru /-ru/
     read
15. Can you read this?   Yo⌐mema⌐su ka—

Yamamoto

letter   teḡami
16. It's a letter [written] in Eng-   Eeḡo no teḡami desyo⌐o? Ze⌐ñ-
     lish, isn't it? I can't read   zeñ yome⌐nai ñ desu yo—
     it at all.

Tanaka

can read English · · · · · · · · · · · · · e⌐ego ḡa yome⌐ru
somebody who can read · · · · · da⌐re ka e⌐ego ḡa yome⌐ru
English · hito <u>or</u> da⌐re ka e⌐ego
                                                                    no yome⌐ru hito

17. Well then, isn't there some-   Zya⌐a, koko ni ⌐da⌐re ka e⌐ego
    body here who can read   (no) yome⌐ru hito (wa) i⌐mase⌐ñ
    English?   ka⌐

Yamamoto

can speak <u>or</u> can be · · · · · · · · · ha⌐nase⌐ru /-ru/
    spoken

18. Hmmm. Mr. Matsuda can   Sa⌐a. Ma⌐tuda-sañ wa suko⌐si
    speak a little but I wonder   ha⌐nase⌐ru ñ desu ḡa, so⌐no te-
    who would be (the one) able   ḡami (ḡa) yome⌐ru no wa ⌐da⌐re
    to read that letter.   desyoo ⌐ne⌐e.

(d)

Tanaka

all day long · · · · · · · · · · · · · · · iti-niti-zyuu
19. Are you going to work all   Kyo⌐o mo i⌐ti-niti-zyuu ha⌐taraki-
    day today too?   ma⌐su ka⌐

Smith

half-day · · · · · · · · · · · · · · · · · · ha⌐ñniti⌐
20. No, today is just half-day . . .   Iie, kyo⌐o wa ha⌐ñniti dake⌐ desu
                                         ḡa—

Tanaka

movie · e⌐eḡa [1]
go to see · · · · · · · · · · · · · · · · · mi⌐ ni iku
21. Then wouldn't you [like to] go   Zya⌐a, go⌐ḡo i⌐ssyo ni ⌐e⌐eḡa (o)
    to see a movie with me in the   ⌐mi⌐ ni i⌐kimase⌐ñ ka⌐
    afternoon?

Smith

somewhere <u>or</u> some · · · · · · · · do⌐ko ka
    place
go somewhere · · · · · · · · · · · · · do⌐ko ka e iku
go to eat · · · · · · · · · · · · · · · · · ta⌐be ni iku
22. Yes, I'd like to. After we see   E⌐e, yo⌐roko⌐ñde. Mi⌐te kara,
    it, let's go somewhere to eat.   do⌐ko ka e ⌐ta⌐be ni i⌐kimasyo⌐o.

Tanaka

23. Yes, let's do that.   E⌐e, so⌐o simasyo⌐o.

(e)

Smith

overwork · · · · · · · · · · · · · · · · · ha⌐tarakisuḡi⌐ru /-ru/

---

[1] Has unaccented alternant.

must not overwork	ha⌐tarakisu⌐gite wa ı̈kenai or ha⌐tarakisu⌐gitya ı̈kenai
24. Mr. Yoshida. You know you mustn't overwork, don't you?	Yosida-sañ. Ha⌐tarakisu⌐gitya i⌐kena⌐i ñ desyoo?
can rest	ya⌐sume⌐ru /-ru/
25. Can't you rest for a little while?	Su⌐ko⌐si ya⌐sume⌐nai ñ desu ka⌐

Mr. Yoshida

within today or before today is over	kyoo-zyuu ni
26. I want to finish doing all of this work today so [I'll have to do] a little more.	Kyoo-zyuu ni ko̐no sig̊oto (o) ⌐ze⌐ñbu si⌐te simaita⌐i kara, mo⌐o suko⌐si—
summer vacation take a summer vacation	na⌐tuya⌐sumi na⌐tuya⌐sumi o ⌐to⌐ru
27. I'm going to take my summer vacation starting (lit. from) tomorrow, you know.	A⌐sita⌐ kara ⌐bo⌐ku (wa) na⌐tuya⌐sumi (o) ⌐to⌐ru ñ desu yo.

(f)
Mr. Tanaka

must not drink or smoke	no⌐ñde wa ı̈kenai or no⌐ñzya ı̈kenai
28. You mustn't smoke here.	Koko de ta⌐bako (o) no⌐ñzya ı̈kenai yo⌐

Mr. Yamamoto

29. Why?	Na⌐ze?

Mr. Tanaka

30. You say "Why?". . . It says so—over there!	Na⌐ze tte⌐ Soo ⌐ka⌐ite ⌐a⌐ru yo—asuko ni⌐

Mr. Yamamoto

notice	ki ⌐ga tu⌐ku
31. Oh! I didn't notice.	A, ki ⌐ga tuka⌐nakatta.

NOTES ON THE BASIC DIALOGUES

5. De here is the particle of means: 'we have come by means of the introduction——.'
   Note also the verbal syookai-suru 'introduce': A o B ni syookai-suru
   'introduce A to B.'

6. With kaigi-tyuu compare hanasi-tyuu 'in the middle of talking' and si-
   goto-tyuu 'in the middle of work.'

7. Note the common combinations tu⌜ḡoo ḡa i⌝i 'is convenient for someone' (lit. 'circumstances are good') and tu⌜ḡoo ga waru⌝i 'is inconvenient for someone' (lit. 'circumstances are bad').

8. Wa here is the particle of comparison: 'Today (in contrast with other days) we can't come any more so we'll come tomorrow.'

9. 'but—will it be possible for me to see him?'

12. Ka⌜ke⌝ru refers to sitting on a chair or other raised object, in contrast with the verbal suwaru /-u/, which refers to sitting Japanese-style on the floor or ground.

13. Iroiro, meaning 'in many ways,' 'variously,' can occur without a following particle as an expression of manner, modifying an inflected word or phrase. When it describes a following nominal, iroiro occurs with no or na and means 'various,' 'many kinds of.'

14. Note: X (o) a⌜ri⌝ḡatoo 'thank you for X.' The o is frequently omitted. To⌜koro⌝ is a nominal which sometimes refers to time and sometimes to place. Compare ma⌝e 'time before' or 'place in front.'

20. 'but—why do you ask?'

22. Particle e may be replaced by ni.

27. Na⌜tuya⌝sumi: note also a⌜kiya⌝sumi 'autumn vacation,' hu⌜yuya⌝sumi 'winter vacation,' ha⌜ruya⌝sumi 'spring vacation.'

30. Tte is the quotative. See the latter part of Grammatical Note 1 in Lesson 18.

31. Note: X ni ki ⌜ḡa tu⌝ku 'notice X.'

GRAMMATICAL NOTES

1. The Potential

Yo⌜me⌝ru 'can read' or 'can be read'	is the POTENTIAL equivalent of	yo⌝mu 'read'
Ko⌜rare⌝ru 'can come'		ku⌝ru 'come'
Moraeru 'can receive' or 'can be received'		morau 'receive'
Itadakeru↓ 'can receive' or 'can be received'		itadaku↓ 'receive'

Most verbals have corresponding potential verbals meaning 'can do so-and-so' or 'so-and-so can be done.' To make the citation form of the potential of:

-ru verbals: Substitute -rare-ru for final -ru
Example: akeru 'open' ~ akerareru 'can open' or 'can be opened'

-u verbals: Substitute -e-ru for final -u[1]
Example: ka⌝ku 'write' ~ ka⌜ke⌝ru 'can write' or 'can be written'

---

[1] But for iku 'go' there are alternate potential forms: ikareru and ikeru.

-aru verbals: [1] Substitute -ar-e-ru for final -aru
      Example: oˢsyaˈru 'say' ~ oˢsyareˈru 'can say' or 'can be said'
Irregular verbals: kuˈru 'come' ~ koˈrareˈru or koˈreˈru 'can come'
                 suru 'do' ~ deˈkiˈru 'is possible' or 'can do'
                 (Deˈkiˈru is regularly used as the potential equivalent
                 not only of independent suru but also of suru at the
                 end of compounds.)

A potential is accented if the verbal from which it is derived is accented. The accent of the citation form is on the next-to-last syllable.

All potentials are themselves verbals of the -ru group. Thus, the potential of akeru has such forms as:

Informal non-past (= citation form): akerareru
Stem: akerare
Informal past: akerareta
Gerund: akerarete
Formal non-past: akeraremasu

Although there is some variation, in the speech of most Japanese, potentials are intransitive—that is, their usage parallels that of waˈkaˈru 'be clear,' iru 'be necessary,' zyoˈozuˈ da 'be proficient,' suˈkiˈ da 'be pleasing,' etc., in occurring with particles wa and ḡa but not o (direct object particle). Study the following pairs of examples:

Taˈnaka-sañ ḡa yomimaˈsita. 'Mr. Tanaka read [it].'
Taˈnaka-sañ ḡa yomemaˈsita. 'Mr. Tanaka was able to read [it].'

Siˈñbuñ o yomimaˈsita. 'I read the newspaper.'
Siˈñbuñ ḡa yomemaˈsita. 'I was able to read the newspaper.' (Lit.'The newspaper could be read.'

Tanaka-sañ wa siˈñbuñ o yomimaˈsita. 'Mr. Tanaka read the newspaper.'
Tanaka-sañ wa siˈñbuñ ḡa yomemaˈsita. 'Mr. Tanaka was able to read the newspaper.' (Lit. 'As for Mr. Tanaka, the newspaper was able to be read.')

Siñbuñ wa Taˈnaka-sañ ḡa yomimaˈsita. 'Mr. Tanaka read the newspaper (in contrast with other things).'
Siñbuñ wa Taˈnaka-sañ ḡa yomemaˈsita. 'Mr. Tanaka was able to read the newspaper (in contrast with other things)'

Additional examples:

Kyoˈo wa iˈkaremaˈsu ḡa, aˈsitaˈ wa iˈkaremaseˈñ. 'Today I can go but tomorrow I can't (go).'
Niˈhoñḡo ḡa kakemaˈsu ka⌡ 'Can you write Japanese?'
Iˈsoḡasiˈi soo desu kara, aˈeˈnai desyoo. 'They say he's busy so you probably won't be able to see him.'
Aˈsita korareˈnai hito ˈdaˈre? 'Who [is] the person who can't come tomorrow?'
Kiˈppu ḡa kaenaˈkatta kara, koˈñbañ uˈti ni iru tumori deˈsu. 'I couldn't buy a ticket so I plan to stay at home tonight.'

---

[1] Potentials of -aru verbals are comparatively rare.

A verbal gerund + √moraenai or √itadakenai [†] 'cannot receive' occurs in questions as a request, meaning literally 'can't I receive the doing of something (by someone)?' In many—but not all—contexts, the 'someone' is 'you,' i.e. the person addressed.

Thus:

	Informal	Formal
Plain	Katte moraenai?	Ka⌐tte moraemase⌐n̄ ka⌣
Polite	Katte itadakenai?	Ka⌐tte itadakemase⌐n̄ ka⌣
	(Women's speech)	
or (more polite)	O⌐kai ni na⌐tte itadakenai? (Women's speech)	O⌐kai ni na⌐tte i⌐tadakemase⌐n̄ ka⌣

All the above examples mean 'Could I have [you] [1] buy it for me?' 'Would [you] [1] buy it for me?' (Lit. 'Can't I receive buying?').

Compare:

	Informal	Formal
Plain	Katte kurenai?	Ka⌐tte kuremase⌐n̄ ka⌣
Polite	Ka⌐tte kudasara⌐nai?	Ka⌐tte kudasaimase⌐n̄ ka⌣
	(Women's speech)	
or (more polite)	O⌐kai ni na⌐tte ku⌐dasara⌐nai? (Women's speech)	O⌐kai ni na⌐tte ku⌐dasaimase⌐n̄ ka⌣

All of these examples mean 'Would you buy it for me?' (Lit. 'Won't you give me buying?')

These patterns closely resemble each other and are often interchangeable, but those using √moraenai and √itadakenai are less direct and more impersonal. Compare tu⌐ku⌐tte moraitai 'I want to have it made (i.e. by someone)' (lit. 'I want to receive making') and tu⌐ku⌐tte kudasai 'please make it (i.e. YOU make it)' (lit. 'give me making').

NOTE: There is an alternant for the potential, consisting of a non-past informal verbal[2] (citation form) + ko⌐to⌐ ḡa/wa √de⌐ki⌐ru (lit. 'the act of doing so-and-so is possible'). Compare:

Su⌐misu-sañ wa ni⌐hoñḡo ḡa yomema⌐su ka⌣ 'Can Mr. Smith read Japanese?' (Lit. 'As for Mr. Smith, can Japanese be read?')

Su⌐misu-sañ wa ni⌐hoñḡo o yo⌐mu koto ḡa de⌐kima⌐su ka⌣ 'Can Mr. Smith read Japanese?' (Lit. 'As for Mr. Smith, is the act of reading Japanese possible?')

Ha⌐nasema⌐su ḡa, ze⌐ñzeñ kakemase⌐n̄ ⌐ne⌐e. 'He can talk but he can't write at all, can he.'

Ha⌐na⌐su koto wa de⌐kima⌐su ḡa, ze⌐ñzeñ ka⌐ku koto wa de⌐kimase⌐n̄ ⌐ne⌐e. 'He can talk but he can't write at all, can he.'

In conversation, the potential forms discussed at the beginning of this note are more common than the corresponding expressions ending in —— ko⌐to⌐ ḡa/wa √de⌐ki⌐ru.

---

[1] Or someone else, depending on context.

[2] I.e. a verbal which is not a potential.

2. Prohibition: Gerund + wa + √ikenai

A gerund (verbal, adjectival or copula) + particle wa + √ikenai 'it won't do' is an expression of prohibition: '[you] must not do so-and-so' or 'it must not be so-and-so' (lit. 'as for doing or being so-and-so, it won't do'). In normal rapid speech, a -te + wa sequence is usually contracted to -tya or -tyaa, and a -de + wa sequence to -zya or -zyaa.

Examples:

Si⌐te⌐[1] wa ikenai. or (more commonly) Si⌐tya⌐a ikenai. 'You must not do it.'

So⌐re o ta⌐betya ikenai. 'You must not eat that.'

Ko⌐tira ni ha⌐ittya i⌐kemase⌐n. 'You must not come in here.'

Si⌐rokutya i⌐kemase⌐n. 'It must not be white.'

Sa⌐n-too zya⌐a[2] i⌐kemase⌐n. 'It must not be third class.'

This pattern occurs in strong negative replies to affirmative requests for permission. Thus:

Tu⌐katte⌐ mo ⌐i⌐i desu ka↲ 'May I use it?'

Tu⌐kattya⌐a i⌐kemase⌐n. 'You must not (use).'

The pattern also occurs in questions. The most common English conversational equivalent is 'can't I do so-and-so?' or 'can't it be so-and-so?' (lit. as for doing or being so-and-so, won't it do?'). Note the affirmative and negative replies:

Tu⌐kattya⌐a i⌐kemase⌐n ka↲ 'Can't I use it?'

(a) E⌐e. Tu⌐kattya⌐a i⌐kemase⌐n. 'No (i.e. that's right). You can't (or must not) use it.'

(b) Iie. Tu⌐katte⌐ mo ⌐i⌐i desu. 'Yes (i.e. that's wrong). You may (or can) use it.'

3. Indefinites: Interrogatives + ka

The indefinite particle ka following an interrogative makes the interrogative into its corresponding indefinite. Thus:

na⌐ni 'what?' and na⌐ni ka 'something,' 'anything'

da⌐re 'who?' and da⌐re ka 'someone,' 'somebody,' 'anyone,' 'anybody'

do⌐ko 'where?' and do⌐ko ka 'somewhere,' 'anywhere,' 'some place'

i⌐tu 'when?' and i⌐tu ka 'some time'

do⌐tira 'which (of two)?' and do⌐tira ka 'either one'

do⌐re 'which (of three or more things)?' and do⌐re ka 'some one or any one (of three or more things)'

---

[1] Before wa, a normally unaccented gerund acquires a final-syllable accent. The contraction of -te⌐ wa is usually tya⌐a.

[2] Here zya⌐a is a contraction of gerund de⌐ (from da) + wa. Elsewhere in this pattern, it is a contraction of the -de⌐ ending of a verbal gerund + wa.

These indefinites usually occur without a following particle as subjects and objects, but they are regularly followed by particles other than <u>wa</u>, <u>g̃a</u>, and <u>o</u>. Thus:

> Da� re ka ki⌐ma⌐sita. 'Someone has come.'
> Na⌐ni ka ta⌐bemasyo⌐o. 'Let's eat something.'
> Do⌐tira ka ku⌐dasa⌐i. 'Please give me either one.'

but:

> Da⌐re ka kara ki⌐kima⌐sita. 'I heard it from someone.'
> Do⌐ko ka e i⌐kima⌐sita. 'He went somewhere.'
> Da⌐re ka ni tu⌐ku⌐tte mo⌐raima⌐sita. 'He had it made by someone.'

When an appropriate indefinite describes a nominal—or, more commonly, a phrase ending with a nominal—it makes the nominal indefinite. Thus:

> na⌐ni ka o⌐mosiro⌐i ⌐ho⌐n̄ 'some interesting book'
> da⌐re ka ⌐yo⌐ku hataraku hito 'some person who works hard'
> do⌐ko ka ⌐si⌐zuka na ryokan̄ 'some quiet inn'
> i⌐tu ka i⌐soḡa⌐siku ⌐na⌐i toki 'some time when you're not busy'

4. Questions without <u>ka</u>

It was mentioned in Lesson 1, Grammatical Note 2, that while all sentences ending with question particle <u>ka</u> are questions, not all questions end with <u>ka</u>.

Questions without <u>ka</u> are of two basic kinds. In the first type—which has occurred frequently in previous lessons—the sign of the question is final question-mark intonation.

> Compare: Wa⌐ka⌐ru. 'It's clear.'
>   Wa⌐ka⌐ru? 'Is it clear?'

Examples of this kind also occur in formal style, particularly in the speech of women:

> Wa⌐karima⌐su. 'It's clear.'
> Wa⌐karima⌐su?[1] 'Is it clear?'

In the second kind of question without <u>ka</u>—occurring in this lesson for the first time—the sign of the question is an interrogative word (for example, na⌐n̄, do⌐ko, do⌐tira, do⌐re, etc.). Such questions usually end with a tentative form and period intonation.

Examples:

> Da⌐re desyoo. 'Who would that be?' 'Who is it?'
> Sore ⌐na⌐n̄ daroo. 'What would that be?' 'What is that?'
> Do⌐o simasyoo. 'What'll we do?'

5. Verbal Stems in Purpose Expressions

A verbal stem (the -<u>ma⌐su</u> form minus -<u>ma⌐su</u>) occurs as an independent

---

[1] In such cases, final syllable -<u>su</u> regularly has its voiced alternant instead of -<u>sɥ</u>.

word preceding the particle ni of purpose. A word of motion—√iku, √ku⅂ru, etc.—always follows. The combination is a purpose expression: 'go, come, etc. in order to do so-and-so.' Thus:

mi⅂ ni iku 'go to see'
ka⌈i ni ku⅂ru 'come to buy'
ku⌈ruma o nao⅂si ni iku 'go to fix the car'
be⌈n̄kyoo-si ni ku⅂ru 'come to study'
to⅂ri ni i⌈rassya⅂ru 'go or come to pick up'
i⌈tadaki ni ma⅂iru 'go or come to get'
ta⅂be ni ⌈ka⅂eru 'return home to eat'

6. -zyuu 'throughout'

A time or place nominal X compounded with -zyuu (or -tyuu) means 'throughout X' or 'all through X.' A -zyuu compound is unaccented. Thus:

kotosi-zyuu 'throughout this year'
iti-ḡatu-zyuu 'all through January'
ik-kaḡetu-zyuu 'all month long' (lit. 'throughout one month')
hito-ban̄-zyuu 'all night long' (lit. 'throughout one night')
Nihon̄-zyuu 'throughout Japan'

When the particle ni of time follows a -zyuu compound of time,[1] the combination means 'within such-and-such a period of time,' i.e. before the stated time is over. Thus:

kotosi-zyuu ni 'within this year'
kon̄syuu-zyuu ni 'within this week'

Additional examples:

Gu⌈ai ḡa wa⅂rukatta kara, iti-niti-zyuu ya⌈su⅂n̄de imasita.
'I didn't feel well so I took it easy all day long.'
Kyonen̄-zyuu O⌈osaka de hataraite ima⅂sita.
'I was working in Osaka all last year.'
Kon̄na ⌈ti⅂isa na mi⌈se⅂ wa Ni⌈hon̄-zyuu ni arima⅂su.
'Small shops like these are all over Japan.'
Kotosi-zyuu ni a⌈tarasi⅂i uti o tu⌈ku⅂tte mo⌈raita⅂i n̄ desu ḡa_
'I want to have a new house built within this year . . .'
Ko⅂no ho⌈n̄ wa kyo⌈o-zyuu ni yomita⅂i n̄ desu ḡa_
'I'd like to read this book before the day is over . . .'

DRILLS

A. Substitution Drill

1. Thank you very much for your time when you are [so] busy.	O⌈isoḡasi⅂i tokoro ⌈do⅂o mo a⌈ri⅂ḡatoo gozaimasita.

[1] Usually NOT a number compound.

2. Thank you very much for the letter.

Teḡami ˹doˀo mo a˹riˀḡatoo gozaimasita.

3. Thank you very much for the interesting book.

Oˈmosiroˀi ˥hoˀñ ˹doˀo mo a˹riˀḡatoo gozaimasita.

4. Thank you very much for the new magazine.

A˹tarasiˀi zassi ˹doˀo mo a˹riˀḡatoo gozaimasita.

5. Thank you very much for the pretty furoshiki.

Kiˀree na hurosiki ˹doˀo mo a˹riˀḡatoo gozaimasita.

6. Thank you very much for the telephone call.

Oˈdeˀñwa ˹doˀo mo a˹riˀḡatoo gozaimasita.

7. Thank you very much for the English newspaper.

Eeḡo no siñbuñ ˹doˀo mo a˹riˀḡatoo gozaimasita.

8. Thank you very much for the delicious candy.

Oˈisii okaˀsi ˹doˀo mo a˹riˀḡatoo gozaimasita.

B. Substitution Drill

1. I'd like to do this work (within) today . . .

Kyoˈo-zyuu ni kono siḡoto (o) sitaˀi ñ desu ḡa—

2. I'd like to do this work (within) this week . . .

Koˈñsyuu-zyuu ni kono siḡoto (o) sitaˀi ñ desu ḡa—

3. I'd like to do this work (within) this month . . .

Koˈñḡetu-zyuu ni kono siḡoto (o) sitaˀi ñ desu ḡa—

4. I'd like to do this work (within) this year . . .

Koˈtosi-zyuu ni kono siḡoto (o) sitaˀi ñ desu ḡa—

5. I'd like to do this work all day long . . .

Iˈti-niti-zyuu kono siḡoto (o) sitaˀi ñ desu ḡa—

6. I'd like to do this work all week long . . .

Iˈs-syuukañ-zyuu kono siḡoto (o) sitaˀi ñ desu ḡa—

7. I'd like to do this work all month long . . .

Iˈk-kaḡetu-zyuu kono siḡoto (o) sitaˀi ñ desu ḡa—

8. I'd like to do this work all year long . . .

Iˈti-neñ-zyuu kono siḡoto (o) sitaˀi ñ desu ḡa—

C. Substitution Drill

1. Could(n't) I have you read the letter from Mr. Tanaka?

Tanaka-sañ kara no teḡami (o) ˹yoˀñde iˈtadakemaseˀñ ka— [1]

2. Could(n't) I have you read the letter from Mr. Tanaka?

Tanaka-sañ kara no teḡami (o) ˹yoˀñde moˈraemaseˀñ ka— [2]

3. I had [him] read the letter from Mr. Tanaka.

Tanaka-sañ kara no teḡami (o) ˹yoˀñde moˈraimaˀsita. [2]

4. [He] read the letter from Mr. Tanaka for me.

Tanaka-sañ kara no teḡami (o) ˹yoˀñde kuˈremaˀsita. [2]

5. Would(n't) you read the letter from Mr. Tanaka for me?

Tanaka-sañ kara no teḡami (o) ˹yoˀñde kuˈremaseˀñ ka— [2]

---

[1] Polite.

[2] Plain.

6. Would(n't) you read the letter from Mr. Tanaka for me?

Tanaka-sañ kara no teḡami (o) ⌐yoˉñde kuᴿdasaimaseˉñ ka⌐ [1]

7. Please read the letter from Mr. Tanaka.

Tanaka-sañ kara no teḡami (o) ⌐yoˉñde kudasai.

8. I had [him] read the letter from Mr. Tanaka.

Tanaka-sañ kara no teḡami (o) ⌐yoˉñde iᴿtadakimaˉsita. [1]

D. Substitution Drill

1. Would you come again tomorrow?

Maᴿtaˉ asita irassyaˉtte iᴿtadakemaseˉñ ka⌐

2. Would you wait a moment?

Syoˉosyoo oᴿmati ni naˉtte iᴿtadakemaseˉñ ka⌐

3. Would you sit here?

Koᴿtira ni kaˉkete iᴿtadakemaseˉñ ka⌐

4. Would you get in touch [with me] today?

Kyoˉo-zyuu ni reñraku-site itadakemaseˉñ ka⌐

5. Would you lend me a little money?

Okane (o) suᴿkoˉsi kaᴿsite itadakemaseˉñ ka⌐

6. Would you wake me early tomorrow morning?

Aˉsita no aˉsa ⌐haˉyaku oᴿkoˉsite iᴿtadakemaseˉñ ka⌐

7. Would you show me the letter from the teacher?

Seᴿñseˉe kara no teḡami (o) ⌐miˉsete iᴿtadakemaseˉñ ka⌐

8. Would you say it once more?

Moˉo iti-do itte itadakemaseˉñ ka⌐

9. Would you speak in Japanese?

Niᴿhoñḡo de hanaˉsite iᴿtadakemaseˉñ ka⌐

10. Would you call Mr. Ueda who is next door?

Oᴿtonari no Ueda-sañ (o) yoñde itadakemaseˉñ ka⌐

a. Repeat the above drill, substituting moᴿraemaseˉñ for iᴿtadakemaseˉñ.

b. Repeat the above drill, substituting an honorific gerund for each of the plain gerunds. For example, in the third sentence kaᴿkete will be replaced by oᴿkake ni naˉtte.

E. Substitution Drill (based on Grammatical Note 2)

1. You mustn't overwork.

Haᴿtarakisuˉḡityaa iᴿkemaseˉñ yo⌐

2. You mustn't use [it].
/tukau/

Tuᴿkattyaˉa iᴿkemaseˉñ yo⌐

3. You mustn't open [it].
/akeru/

Aᴿketyaˉa iᴿkemaseˉñ yo⌐

4. You mustn't close [it].
/simeru/

Siˉmetyaa iᴿkemaseˉñ yo⌐

5. You mustn't go in.
/haˉiru/

Haˉittyaa iᴿkemaseˉñ yo⌐

---

[1] Polite.

6. You mustn't wash [it].   Aʳrattyaʾa iʳkemaseʾñ yo⌐
   /arau/
7. You mustn't drink [it].   Noʾñzyaa iʳkemaseʾñ yo⌐
   /noʾmu/
8. You mustn't quit.   Yaʳmetyaʾa iʳkemaseʾñ yo⌐
   /yameru/

a. Repeat the above drill using the uncontracted gerund + <u>wa</u> sequences
   (for example, haʳtarakisuꜝgite wa).

F. Response Drill (based on Grammatical Note 2)

     Tutor: Siʳteʾ mo ʳiʾi desu ka⌐   'May I do it?'
     Student: Iie. Siʳtyaʾa iʳkemaseʾñ yo⌐   'No. You must not do it.'

1. Kodomo (o) oʳkoʾsite mo   Iie. Oʳkoʾsityaa iʳkemaseʾñ yo⌐
   ʳiʾi desu ka⌐
2. Asita ʳoʾkite mo ʳiʾi desu   Iie. Oʳkityaa iʳkemaseʾñ yo⌐
   ka⌐
3. Aʳmerika no okane de   Iie. Haʳraʾttyaa iʳkemaseʾñ
   haraʾtte mo ʳiʾi desu ka⌐   yo⌐
4. Iʳma no siḡoto (o) tu-   Iie. Tuʳzuketyaʾa iʳkemaseʾñ
   ʳzuketeʾ mo ʳiʾi desu ka⌐   yo⌐
5. Kyoʾo ʳhaʾyaku ʳkaʾette   Iie. Kaʾettyaa iʳkemaseʾñ yo⌐
   mo ʳiʾi desu ka⌐
6. Aʾnoʾ hito ni kiʳiteʾ mo   Iie. Kiʳityaʾa iʳkemaseʾñ yo⌐
   ʳiʾi desu ka⌐
7. Peʾñ de ⌐kaꜝite mo ʳiʾi   Iie. Kaʾityaa iʳkemaseʾñ yo⌐
   desu ka⌐
8. Kiʳmono (o) kiteʾ mo ʳiʾi   Iie. Kiʳtyaʾa iʳkemaseʾñ yo⌐
   desu ka⌐
9. Taʳkusañ katteʾ mo ʳiʾi   Iie. Kaʳttyaʾa iʳkemaseʾñ yo⌐
   desu ka⌐
10. Kaʳḡiʾ (o) ⌐kaꜝkete mo   Iie. Kaʾketyaa iʳkemaseʾñ yo⌐
    ʳiʾi desu ka⌐

G. Response Drill (based on Grammatical Note 2)

     What does the <u>Haʾi.</u> or <u>Iie.</u> answer (as indicated by the tutor) mean,
     in response to the following questions? Use the -te mo ʳiʾi desu
     or -tyaa iʳkemaseʾñ pattern.

1. Koʳno sakana (o) taʾbetyaa   Taʾbete mo ʳiʾi desu.
   iʳkemaseʾñ ka⌐ . . . Iie.
2. Oʳhuʾro ni ʳhaʾitte mo ʳiʾi   Haʾittyaa iʳkemaseʾñ.
   desu ka⌐ . . . Iie.
3. Uʳe no hikidasi ni iretyaʾa   Iʳretyaʾa iʳkemaseʾñ.
   iʳkemaseʾñ ka⌐ . . . Haʾi.
4. Taʳbako (o) noʾñde mo ʳiʾi   Noʾñde mo ʳiʾi desu.
   desu ka⌐ . . . Haʾi.

5. Asita ya⌐su⌐nzyaa i⌐kema-   Ya⌐su⌐nde mo ⌐i⌐i desu.
   se⌐n ka◡. . . . Iie.

6. Tu⌐gi⌐ no ⌐ka⌐do (o) ma-   Ma⌐gattya⌐a i⌐kemase⌐n.
   ⌐gatte⌐ mo ⌐i⌐i desu
   ka◡. . . . Iie.

7. Ko⌐ko no mizu (o) no⌐n-   No⌐nzyaa i⌐kemase⌐n.
   zyaa i⌐kemase⌐n ka◡. . . .
   Ha⌐i.

8. Ko⌐no te⌐gami (o) sutete⌐   Su⌐tete⌐ mo ⌐i⌐i desu.
   mo ⌐i⌐i desu ka◡. . . . Ha⌐i.

H. Grammar Drill (based on Grammatical Note 3)

Tutor: Da⌐re ga si⌐ma⌐sita ka◡   'Who did it?'
Student: Da⌐re ka si⌐ma⌐sita ka◡   'Did somebody do it?'

1. Do⌐ko de ha⌐taraite (i)ru⌐   Do⌐ko ka de ha⌐taraite (i)ru⌐ n
   n desu ka◡   desu ka◡

2. Do⌐nata ga so⌐o ossyaima⌐-   Do⌐nata ka so⌐o ossyaima⌐sita
   sita ka◡   ka◡

3. Do⌐re (o) tu⌐kaimasyo⌐o   Do⌐re ka tu⌐kaimasyo⌐o ka.
   ka.

4. I⌐tu o⌐me ni kakarimasyo⌐o   I⌐tu ka o⌐me ni kakarimasyo⌐o
   ka.   ka.

5. Na⌐ni (o) sa⌐gasite (i)ru⌐   Na⌐ni ka sa⌐gasite (i)ru⌐ n desu
   n desu ka◡   ka◡

6. Do⌐ko e i⌐kimasyo⌐o ka.   Do⌐ko ka e i⌐kimasyo⌐o ka.

I. Grammar Drill (based on Grammatical Note 5)

Tutor: A⌐soko de sima⌐sita. 'He did it'
Student: Asoko e si ⌐ni ikima⌐sita. 'He went there to do it.'

1. A⌐tarasi⌐i ⌐re⌐sutoran de   A⌐tarasi⌐i ⌐re⌐sutoran e ⌐go⌐han
   ⌐go⌐han (o) ta⌐bema⌐sita.   (o) ⌐ta⌐be ni i⌐kima⌐sita.

2. Se⌐nse⌐e no otaku de o⌐tya   Se⌐nse⌐e no otaku e o⌐tya (o)
   (o) nomima⌐sita.   no⌐mi ni i⌐kima⌐sita.

3. Kyo⌐oto de ha⌐tarakima⌐-   Kyo⌐oto e ha⌐taraki ni ikima⌐-
   sita.   sita.

4. A⌐no ee⌐ga⌐kan de Hu⌐ransu   A⌐no ee⌐ga⌐kan e Hu⌐ransu no ee⌐ga
   no ee⌐ga (o) mima⌐sita.   (o) mi⌐ ni i⌐kima⌐sita.

5. Ho⌐ken⌐ga⌐isya de to⌐modati   Ho⌐ken⌐ga⌐isya e to⌐modati ni a⌐i
   ni aima⌐sita.   ni i⌐kima⌐sita.

6. De⌐pa⌐ato de a⌐tarasi⌐i bo-   De⌐pa⌐ato e a⌐tarasi⌐i bo⌐osi (o)
   ⌐osi (o) kaima⌐sita.   kai ni ikima⌐sita.

7. Gin⌐koo de o⌐kane (o) ka-   Gin⌐koo e o⌐kane (o) kari ni iki-
   rima⌐sita.   ma⌐sita.

8. Yu⌐ubi⌐nkyoku de te⌐gami   Yu⌐ubi⌐nkyoku e te⌐gami (o) da⌐si
   (o) dasima⌐sita. [1]   ni i⌐kima⌐sita.

_____
[1] Te⌐gami o da⌐su 'mail a letter.'

J. Grammar Drill (based on Grammatical Note 1)

> Tutor: To (o) si⌐mema⌐sita ka⌐ 'Did you shut the door?'
> Student: To (ḡa) si⌐merarema⌐sita ka⌐ 'Were you able to shut the door?'

1. Asita mata ki⌐ma⌐su ka⌐   Asita mata ko⌐rarema⌐su ka⌐
2. Nihoñḡo (o) yo⌐mima⌐su ka⌐   Nihoñḡo (ḡa) yo⌐mema⌐su ka⌐
3. So⌐ñna mono⌐ (wa) ⌐do⌐ko   So⌐ñna mono⌐ (wa) ⌐do⌐ko de ka-
   de ka┌ima┐su ka⌐   ┌ema┐su ka⌐
4. Syo⌐kudoo no ma⌐do (o)   Syo⌐kudoo no ma⌐do (ḡa) a⌐kera-
   a⌐kema⌐sita ka⌐   rema⌐sita ka⌐
5. A⌐sita⌐ made ni re⌐ñraku-   A⌐sita⌐ made ni re⌐ñraku-dekima⌐-
   sima⌐su ka⌐   su ka⌐
6. A⌐na⌐ta (wa) byo⌐oki de⌐   A⌐na⌐ta (wa) byo⌐oki de⌐ mo ko⌐no
   mo ko⌐no siḡoto (o) tu-   siḡoto (ḡa) tuzukerarema⌐su ka⌐
   zukema⌐su ka⌐
7. Ni⌐hoñ no okane de ha-   Ni⌐hoñ no okane de haraema⌐-
   raima⌐sita ka⌐   sita ka⌐
8. Sono siḡoto (wa) o⌐taku   Sono siḡoto (wa) o⌐taku de deki-
   de sima⌐sita ka⌐   ma⌐sita ka⌐
9. Ko⌐ñsyuu mo raisyuu mo   Ko⌐ñsyuu mo raisyuu mo ikare-
   ikima⌐su ka⌐   ma⌐su ka⌐
10. Ka⌐ḡi⌐ (ḡa) ka⌐ka⌐tte (i)ta   Ka⌐ḡi⌐ (ḡa) ka⌐ka⌐tte (i)ta kara,
    kara, ha⌐ira⌐nakatta.   ha⌐ire⌐nakatta.

K. Substitution Drill

1. Isn't there someone here   Koko ni ⌐da⌐re ka e⌐eḡo ḡa[1] yo-
   who can read English?   me⌐ru hito (wa) i⌐mase⌐ñ ka⌐
2. Isn't there someone here   Koko ni ⌐da⌐re ka hu⌐rañsuḡo ḡa
   who knows (lit. can do)   deki⌐ru hito (wa) i⌐mase⌐ñ ka⌐
   French?
3. Isn't there someone here   Koko ni ⌐da⌐re ka tyu⌐uḡokuḡo ḡa[1]
   who can write Chinese?   kake⌐ru hito (wa) i⌐mase⌐ñ ka⌐
4. Isn't there someone here   Koko ni ⌐da⌐re ka do⌐ituḡo ḡa[1]
   who understands German?   waka⌐ru hito (wa) i⌐mase⌐ñ ka⌐
5. Isn't there someone here   Koko ni ⌐da⌐re ka su⌐peiñḡo (o)
   who is studying Spanish?   beñkyoo-site (i)ru hito⌐ (wa)
                                                 i⌐mase⌐ñ ka⌐
6. Isn't there someone here   Koko ni ⌐da⌐re ka e⌐eḡo ḡa[1] beñ-
   who wants to study Eng-   kyoo-sitai hito⌐ (wa) i⌐mase⌐ñ
   lish?   ka⌐
7. Isn't there someone here   Koko ni ⌐da⌐re ka ni⌐hoñḡo ḡa
   who can teach Japanese?   osierareru hito⌐ (wa) i⌐mase⌐ñ
                                                 ka⌐
8. Isn't there someone here   Koko ni ⌐da⌐re ka ro⌐siaḡo ḡa ha-
   who can speak Russian?   nase⌐ru hito (wa) i⌐mase⌐ñ ka⌐

---
[1] Or no.

L. Expansion Drill

1. [He] can't speak, can he.

[He] can't speak very
well, can he.

[He] can read but he
can't speak very well,
can he.

[He] can read English
but he can't speak very
well, can he.

That student can read
English but he can't
speak very well, can
he.

Haˡnasemaseˡn̄ ˡneˡe.

Aˡn̄mari hanasemaseˡn̄ ˡneˡe.

Yoˡmemaˡsu ḡa, aˡn̄mari hanase-
maseˡn̄ ˡneˡe.

Eˡeḡo wa yomemaˡsu ḡa, aˡn̄mari
hanasemaseˡn̄ ˡneˡe.

Ano gakusee (wa) eˡeḡo wa yomemaˡsu ḡa, aˡn̄mari hanasemaseˡn̄
ˡneˡe.

2. I probably can't do it.

I probably can't do it all.

I probably can't do it all
within this week.

I am doing [it] but I probably can't do it all
within this week.

I am doing [it] all day long,
but I probably can't do
it all within this week.

I am doing [it] every day
all day long, but I
probably can't do it all
within this week.

That work I am doing
every day all day long,
but I probably can't do
it all within this week.

Deˡkiˡnai desyoo.

Zeˡn̄bu wa deˡkiˡnai desyoo.

Koˡn̄syuu-zyuu niˡ wa ˡzeˡn̄bu wa
deˡkiˡnai desyoo.

Siˡte (i)ruˡ n̄ desu ḡa, koˡn̄syuu-
zyuu niˡ wa ˡzeˡn̄bu wa deˡkiˡnai desyoo.

Iˡti-niti-zyuu site (i)ruˡ n̄ desu
ḡa, koˡn̄syuu-zyuu niˡ wa ˡzeˡn̄-
bu wa deˡkiˡnai desyoo.

Maˡiniti iˡti-niti-zyuu site (i)ruˡ
n̄ desu ḡa, koˡn̄syuu-zyuu niˡ
wa ˡzeˡn̄bu wa deˡkiˡnai desyoo.

Sono siḡoto (wa) ˡmaˡiniti iˡti-
niti-zyuu site (i)ruˡ n̄ desu ḡa,
koˡn̄syuu-zyuu niˡ wa ˡzeˡn̄bu
wa deˡkiˡnai desyoo.

3. I wasn't able to borrow
[it].

He was out so I wasn't
able to borrow [it].

I went but he was out so
I wasn't able to borrow
[it].

I went to borrow [it] but
he was out so I couldn't
(borrow).

I went to borrow a book
but he was out so I
couldn't (borrow).

I went to a friend's house
to borrow a book but he
was out so I couldn't
(borrow).

Kaˡriraremaseˡn̄ desita.

Ruˡsu datta kara, kaˡriraremaseˡn̄
desita.

Iˡkimaˡsita ḡa; ruˡsu datta kara,
kaˡriraremaseˡn̄ desita.

Kaˡri ni ikimaˡsita ḡa; ruˡsu datta
kara, kaˡriraremaseˡn̄ desita.

Hoˡn̄ (o) kaˡri ni ikimaˡsita ḡa;
ruˡsu datta kara, kaˡriraremaseˡn̄
desita.

Tomodati no uti e ˡhoˡn̄ (o) kaˡri
ni ikimaˡsita ḡa; ruˡsu datta kara,
kaˡriraremaseˡn̄ desita.

4. It would be good,
   wouldn't it.

   It would be best,
   wouldn't it.

   I wonder who would be
   best.

   I'd like to be taught (but)
   I wonder who would be
   best.

   I'd like to be taught
   French (but) I wonder
   who would be best.

   I'd like to be taught
   French by a person
   who's good at it (but)
   I wonder who would
   be best.

   I'd like to be taught
   French by some person
   who's good at it (but) I
   wonder who would be
   best.

I⌐i desyoo ⌐ne⌐e.

I⌐tibañ i⌐i desyoo ⌐ne⌐e.

Da⌐re ḡa i⌐tibañ i⌐i desyoo ⌐ne⌐e.

O⌐siete moraita⌐i ñ desu ḡa,
da⌐re ḡa i⌐tibañ i⌐i desyoo
⌐ne⌐e.

Hu⌐rañsuḡo (o) osiete moraita⌐i
ñ desu ḡa, da⌐re ḡa i⌐tibañ
i⌐i desyoo ⌐ne⌐e.

Zyo⌐ozu⌐ na hito ni hu⌐rañsuḡo
(o) osiete moraita⌐i ñ desu ḡa,
da⌐re ḡa i⌐tibañ i⌐i desyoo
⌐ne⌐e.

Da⌐re ka zyo⌐ozu⌐ na hito ni
hu⌐rañsuḡo (o) osiete moraita⌐i
ñ desu ḡa, da⌐re ḡa i⌐tibañ
i⌐i desyoo ⌐ne⌐e.

5. I've become upset.

   I've become upset be-
   cause [he] doesn't
   listen.

   I've become upset be-
   cause [he] doesn't
   listen at all.

   I've become upset be-
   cause that child doesn't
   listen at all.

   [I] said it but I've become
   upset because that child
   doesn't listen at all.

   [I] said that he mustn't,
   but I've become upset
   because that child
   doesn't listen at all.

   [I] told him that he
   mustn't forget, but I've
   become upset because
   that child doesn't listen at all.

   [I] told him that he
   mustn't forget because
   it is important, but
   I've become upset be-
   cause that child doesn't
   listen at all.

Ko⌐ma⌐ttyatta.

Ki⌐kana⌐i kara, ko⌐ma⌐ttyatta.

Ze⌐ñzeñ kikana⌐i kara, ko⌐ma⌐-
ttyatta.

A⌐no⌐ ko (wa) ze⌐ñzeñ kikana⌐i
kara, ko⌐ma⌐ttyatta.

I⌐tta⌐ kedo; a⌐no⌐ ko (wa) ze⌐ñzeñ
kikana⌐i kara, ko⌐ma⌐ttyatta.

I⌐kena⌐i tte i⌐tta⌐ kedo; a⌐no⌐ ko
(wa) ze⌐ñzeñ kikana⌐i kara,
ko⌐ma⌐ttyatta.

Wa⌐suretya⌐a i⌐kena⌐i tte i⌐tta⌐
kedo; a⌐no⌐ ko (wa) ze⌐ñzeñ
kikana⌐i kara, ko⌐ma⌐ttyatta.

Ta⌐isetu da⌐ kara, wa⌐suretya⌐a
i⌐kena⌐i tte i⌐tta⌐ kedo; a⌐no⌐
ko (wa) ze⌐ñzeñ kikana⌐i kara,
ko⌐ma⌐ttyatta.

I told him that he mustn't forget because it is important, but I've become upset because that child doesn't listen at all.	Bo⌐ku (wa); ta⌐isetu da⌐ kara, wa-⌐suretya⌐a i⌐kena⌐i tte i⌐tta⌐ kedo; a⌐no⌐ ko (wa) ze⌐ñzeñ kikana⌐i kara, ko⌐ma⌐ttyatta.

6. Would you come?

Ki⌐te⌐ i⌐tadakemase⌐ñ ka⌐

Would you come again?

Ma⌐ta kite⌐ i⌐tadakemase⌐ñ ka⌐

Would you come again after three?

Sa⌐ñ-zi suḡi⌐ ni ma⌐ta kite⌐ i⌐tadakemase⌐ñ ka⌐

He's supposed to come back about three so would you come again after three?

Sa⌐ñ-zi-ḡo⌐ro ⌐ka⌐eru ha⌐zu de⌐su kara, sa⌐ñ-zi suḡi⌐ ni ma⌐ta kite⌐ i⌐tadakemase⌐ñ ka⌐

He isn't in but he's supposed to come back about three so would you come again after three?

I⌐mase⌐ñ ḡa; sa⌐ñ-zi-ḡo⌐ro ⌐ka⌐eru ha⌐zu de⌐su kara, sa⌐ñ-zi suḡi⌐ ni ma⌐ta kite⌐ i⌐tadakemase⌐ñ ka⌐

He isn't at his desk (lit. seat) but he's supposed to come back about three so would you come again after three?

O⌐se⌐ki ni i⌐mase⌐ñ ḡa, sa⌐ñ-zi-ḡo⌐ro ⌐ka⌐eru ha⌐zu de⌐su kara, sa⌐ñ-zi suḡi⌐ ni ma⌐ta kite⌐ i⌐ta-dakemase⌐ñ ka⌐

He isn't at his desk [just] now but he's supposed to come back about three so would you come again after three?

I⌐ma o⌐se⌐ki ni i⌐mase⌐ñ ḡa; sa⌐ñ-zi-ḡo⌐ro ⌐ka⌐eru ha⌐zu de⌐su kara, sa⌐ñ-zi suḡi⌐ ni ma⌐ta kite⌐ i⌐tadakemase⌐ñ ka⌐

QUESTION SUPPLEMENT

(based on the Basic Dialogues)

(a) 1. Tanaka-sañ wa ⌐da⌐re ni a⌐ita⌐i ñ desu ka⌐
     2. Da⌐re no syookai de ki⌐ma⌐sita ka⌐
     3. Yamamoto-sañ wa ⌐do⌐ko ni tu⌐to⌐mete imasu ka⌐
     4. Ueda-sañ wa ⌐i⌐ma hi⌐ma de⌐su ka⌐
     5. Tanaka-sañ wa ⌐kyo⌐o ma⌐ta korarema⌐su ka⌐ I⌐tu ma⌐ta ku⌐ru desyoo ka.

(b) 6. Yamamoto-sañ wa zi⌐mu⌐syo ni i⌐ma⌐sita ka⌐
     7. Yamamoto-sañ wa ⌐kyo⌐o zi⌐mu⌐syo e ⌐ka⌐eru ha⌐zu de⌐sita ka⌐
     8. Tanaka-sañ wa Ya⌐mamoto-sañ ni awa⌐nai de so⌐no⌐ hito no zi-⌐mu⌐syo o de⌐ma⌐sita ka⌐
     9. Tanaka-sañ wa Ya⌐mamoto-sañ to hana⌐site kara ⌐na⌐ñ te i⌐ima⌐-sita ka⌐

(c) 10. Yamamoto-sañ wa ⌐ee⌐ḡo ḡa yo⌐mema⌐su ka⌐
    11. Ma⌐tuda-sañ wa do⌐o desu ka⌐
    12. Tanaka-sañ wa ⌐na⌐ni o ⌐yo⌐nde mo⌐raita⌐i ñ desu ka⌐

(d) 13. Su⌉misu-sañ wa ⌈kyo⌉o na⌈ñ-zi-ḡo⌉ro made ha⊦taraku⊣ desyoo ka.
14. Tanaka-sañ wa ⌈go⌉ḡo ⌈do⌉ko e i⊦ku tumori de⊣su ka⌣
15. Su⌉misu-sañ mo i⌈kima⌉su ka⌣
16. E⌈ḡa o mi⌉te kara ⌈na⌉ni o su⊦ru tumori de⊣su ka⌣

(e) 17. Yosida-sañ wa ⌈do⌉o site ya⊦sumemase⊣ñ ka⌣
18. Yosida-sañ wa a⌈sita⌉ mo ha⊦taraku⊣ desyoo ka.
19. I⌉ma hu⌈yu⌉ desyoo ka. Do⌉o site wa⊦karima⊣su ka⌣

(f) 20. Koko de ⌈na⌉ni o si⊦te⊣ wa i⊦kemase⊣ñ ka⌣
21. Tanaka-sañ wa ⌈do⌉o site wa⊦karima⊣sita ka⌣
22. Ya⌈mamoto-sañ mo sono koto⌉ o si⊦tte ima⊣sita ka⌣
23. Tanaka-sañ to Yamamoto-sañ wa o⌈toko⌉ desyoo ka, o⌈ñna⌉ desyoo ka. Do⌉o site wa⊦karima⊣su ka⌣

SHORT SUPPLEMENTARY DIALOGUES

1. Hotel guest: Ma⌉da o⊦hu⌉ro ni ⊦ha⊣ittya i⌈kenai?
Room-girl: A⌉tuku ⊦na⊣tta yoo de go⊦zaima⊣su kara, mo⌉o o⌈hairi ni na⌉tte mo yo⌈rosi⌉i desyoo.

2. Mr. Tanaka: Tadaima.
Maid: O⌈kaeri-nasaima⌉se. Ni-⌈zi-ḡo⌉ro ⌈do⌉nata ka i⌈rassyaima⌉sita yo⌣
Mr. Tanaka: Da⌉re daroo.
Maid: O⌈namae wa ukaḡaimase⌉ñ desita ḡa, ha⌈tati-ḡu⌉rai no o⌈ñna no kata⌉ desita.
Mr. Tanaka: A⌉a ⌈so⌉o. Zya⌉a, Yo⌈sida-sañ daro⌉o.

3. Smith: Ti⌈isa⌉i ha⊦iza⊣ra mo⌈o hito⌉-tu ⌈do⌉ko ka ni ⌈a⌉ru ha⊦zu de⊣su ḡa— Aa— A⌈rima⌉sita.
Tanaka: A⌉a, so⌈re o saḡasite⌉ ta ñ desu ka.

4. Smith: Asita ⌈bo⌉ku no zi⊦mu⊣syo e ki⌈mase⌉ñ ka⌣
Tanaka: A⌈sita⌉ desu ka⌣ A⌈sita⌉ yori ki⌈ñyo⌉o no hoo ḡa tu⌈ḡoo ḡa i⌉i ñ desu ḡa—
Smith: Zya⌉a ki⌈ñyo⌉o ni ⊦do⊣ozo.

5. Smith: Do⌉ko ka ⌈si⌉zuka na ki⊦ssa⊣teñ de o⌈tya o nomimase⌉n ka⌣
Tanaka: E⌉e, so⌈o simasyo⌉o. A⌈no yotukado ni a⌉ru no ḡa ⊦i⊣i desyoo?

6. Smith: Kono mizu no⌈mema⌉su ka⌣
Tanaka: Iie, da⌈me⌉ desu yo. Zyotyuusañ o yoñde, no⌈mi⌉mizu o mo⊦raimasyo⊣o.

7. Smith: So⌈no hako no na⌉ka ni ⌈mo⌉tto i⊦rerareru⊣ desyoo?
Tanaka: Iie. Mo⌉o i⌈ppai de⌉su kara.

8. Customer: Uketori ⌈ka⌉ite mo⊦raemase⊣ñ ka⌣
Salesgirl: Su⌉ḡu o⊦kaki-sima⊣su kara, syo⌉osyoo o⊦mati-kudasa⊣i.

9. Smith: Ki⌐koemase⌐ñ desita kara; su⌐mimase⌐ñ ḡa, mo⌐o iti-do ossya⌐tte
i⌐tadakemase⌐ñ ka⌐
Tanaka: To⌐nari no heya⌐ ḡa ya⌐kamasi⌐i desu ⌐ne⌐e. Si⌐zuka ni su⌐ru
yo⌐o ni i⌐imasyo⌐o.

10. Smith: Sa⌐too-sañ wa?
Tanaka: Tyo⌐tto ta⌐bako o kai ni ikima⌐sita. Su⌐ḡu ka⌐erima⌐su yo⌐

English Equivalents

1. Hotel guest: Can't I take a bath yet?
Room-girl: It seems to be (lit. have become) hot so you may go in now.

2. Mr. Tanaka: I'm back.
Maid: (Welcome back.) Someone came here at about two o'clock.
Mr. Tanaka: Who would that be?
Maid: I didn't ask her name . . . It was a woman about twenty years old.
Mr. Tanaka: Oh. In that case, it must be Miss Yoshida.

3. Smith: There should be one more small ashtray somewhere . . . Uh . . .
Here it is.
Tanaka: Oh, is that what you were looking for?

4. Smith: Will (lit. won't) you come to my office tomorrow?
Tanaka: Tomorrow? Friday is more convenient than tomorrow but . . .
Smith: Then [come] on Friday, by all means.

5. Smith: Wouldn't you [like to] have tea at some quiet tearoom?
Tanaka: Yes, let's do that. The one at that intersection would be nice,
wouldn't it?

6. Smith: Can you drink this water?
Tanaka: No, that's no good. Let's call the maid and get some drinking
water.

7. Smith: You can put more into that box, can't you?
Tanaka: No. (Because) it's full already.

8. Customer: Would you write a receipt for me?
Salesgirl: I'll write it right away (so) just a moment please.

9. Smith: I couldn't hear so—I'm sorry but—could I have you say it once
more?
Tanaka: Isn't the next room noisy! Let's tell them to be quiet.

10. Smith: [Where is] Mr. Sato?
Tanaka: He just went to buy some cigarettes. He'll be back in a minute.

EXERCISES

1. Make up conversations appropriate to the following situations. Keep your conversations lively — within the limits of the Japanese you have drilled on. Be careful to use appropriate politeness and formality levels.

    a. Mr. Smith from the American Embassy arrives at Mr. Tanaka's office to find that Mr. Tanaka has gone to the Embassy to see him.

    b. A lone American who speaks Japanese, but obviously cannot read it, is smoking in an area where several signs are posted which read "Danger! No Smoking!"

    c. A Russian who speaks only Russian arrives in Mr. Tanaka's office and is greeted by a Japanese-speaking receptionist and other office workers who discuss what is best to do.

2. (a) Ask if it is forbidden to:

a.	come in.	n.	stay here.
b.	smoke.	o.	listen.
c.	look at that.	p.	wait here.
d.	eat this.	q.	rest for a while.
e.	drink this.	r.	put these things away.
f.	go home early.	s.	write on this paper.
g.	come again tomorrow.	t.	have (lit. receive) this.
h.	open the window.	u.	exchange this.
i.	turn on the radio.	v.	deliver the desk tonight.
j.	throw away these let-ters.	w.	park (lit. stop) the car here.
k.	use the telephone.	x.	remove the ashtrays.
l.	show this to a friend.	y.	board the train now.
m.	borrow this pencil.		

   (b) Give the <u>iie</u> answer for each of the questions in the preceding exercise.

Lesson 26. Weather

BASIC DIALOGUES: FOR MEMORIZATION

(a)

Tanaka

climate   kikoo
think   o⌐mo⌐u /-u/
what do you think?   do⌐o o⌐mo⌐u

1. What do you think of the climate here?   Koko no kikoo (wa) ⌐do⌐o omoimasu ka⌐

Smith

think that it's good   i⌐i to o⌐mo⌐u

2. I don't think it's very pleasant (but). . .   A⌐ñmari i⌐i to wa o⌐moimase⌐ñ ḡa—

Tanaka

is muggy <u>or</u> sultry   mu⌐siatu⌐i /-ku/

3. The summers are awfully muggy, aren't they?   Na⌐tu⌐ (wa) ⌐zu⌐ibuñ mu⌐siatu⌐i ñ desyoo?

Smith

mildew   kabi
come out <u>or</u> spring up
    <u>or</u> grow   ha⌐e⌐ru /-ru/

4. Yes. [Things] get moldy (and). . .   E⌐e. Ka⌐bi ḡa hae⌐ru si—

(b)

Smith

rainy season   tuyu

5. It will be the rainy season soon now, won't it?   Mo⌐o su⌐ḡu tu⌐yu ni narima⌐su ne?

Tanaka

middle   na⌐kaba⌐
begin [something]   hazimeru /-ru/
begin falling   hu⌐rihazime⌐ru /-ru/
think that it probably
  begins (<u>or</u> will begin)
  falling   hu⌐rihazime⌐ru daroo to
                    o⌐mo⌐u

6. Yes. I think that it will probably begin raining (lit. falling) (from) about the middle of this month.   E⌐e. Koñḡetu no na⌐kaba-ḡo⌐ro kara hu⌐rihazime⌐ru daroo to omoimasu.

Smith

[something] continues	tuzuku /-u/
7. About how long does it last?	Do⌐no-g̃urai tuzukima⌐su ka↵

Tanaka

year	to⌐si⌐
depend <u>or</u> rely	yoru /-u/
depending on the year <u>or</u> according to the year	to⌐si⌐ ni yotte
think that it was about 20 days	ha⌐tu-ka-g̃u⌐rai datta to o⌐mo↑u
8. It's different depending on the year, but I think that it was about 20 days last year.	To⌐si⌐ ni yotte ti⌐g̃aima⌐su g̃a, kyo⌐neñ wa ha⌐tu-ka-g̃u⌐rai datta to omoimasu.

Smith

unpleasant	i⌐ya⌐ /na/
9. Isn't it awful—the rainy season.	I⌐ya⌐ desu ⌐ne⌐e—tuyu wa.

(c)

Tanaka

begin to fall	hu⌐tte⌐ kuru
10. It's begun to rain.	A⌐me g̃a hu⌐tte⌐ kimasita yo↵

. . .

cease	yamu /-u/
11. It has stopped already.	Mo⌐o ya⌐mima⌐sita.
clear up	ha⌐re⌐ru /-ru/
looking as if it is about to clear up	ha⌐reso⌐o /na/
appear <u>or</u> seem <u>or</u> look	mi⌐e⌐ru /-ru/
sun	hi
emerge	de⌐te kuru
12. It looks as if it's going to clear—since the sun has come out.	Ha⌐reso⌐o ni mi⌐ema⌐su yo↵—hi ⌐g̃a de⌐te ki⌐ma⌐sita kara.

Smith

think that it doesn't (<u>or</u> will not) fall	hu⌐ra⌐nai to o⌐mo↑u
13. I don't think that it's going to rain any more so let's go out.	Mo⌐o hu⌐ra⌐nai to o⌐moima⌐su kara, de⌐kakemasyo⌐o.
14. Won't you stop in at my house for a minute?	Tyo⌐tto u⌐ti ni yorimase⌐ñ ka↵

Tanaka

let's go or I guess I'll go (informal)	ikoo
think I'll go	i⌐koo⌐ to omo⌐u⌐
with much trouble or on purpose or with special kindness	se⌐kkaku⌐
it's kind of you to ask me but	se⌐kkaku⌐ desu ḡa

15. I'm thinking of going to the bank now (lit. from this point) so—it's kind of you to ask me but—I'm afraid not, today.

Kore kara gi⌐ṅkoo e ikoo to omo⌐tte (i)masu kara; se⌐kkaku⌐ desu ḡa, kyo⌐o wa ⌐tyo⌐tto_

last week	seṅsyuu
be about to go or try to go	ikoo to suru
when I was about to go or when I tried to go	i⌐koo to sita to⌐ki [ni]
whatever happens or by all means	do⌐o site⌐ mo

16. Last week when I was about to go to the bank a friend came and I couldn't go, so today no matter what happens [I must go].

Seṅsyuu gi⌐ṅkoo e ikoo to sita to⌐ki [ni] tomodati ḡa kite, i⌐ka-rena⌐katta kara; kyo⌐o wa do⌐o site⌐ mo_

(d)

Mrs. Tanaka

blow	⌐hu⌐ku /-u/
cold-looking	sa⌐muso⌐o /na/

17. An awful wind is blowing and it looks cold, doesn't it.

Hi⌐do⌐i ka⌐ze ḡa hu⌐ite (i)te, sa-⌐muso⌐o ⌐ne⌐e.

Mr. Tanaka

cloud up	ku⌐mo⌐ru /-u/
begin to cloud up	ku⌐mo⌐tte kuru

18. It's begun to cloud up, hasn't it.

Ku⌐mo⌐tte kita ⌐ne⌐e.

looking as if it is about to fall	hu⌐riso⌐o /na/

19. It looks as if it's going to snow.

Yu⌐ki⌐ ḡa hu⌐riso⌐o da yo_

Mrs. Tanaka

freeze	kooru /-u/
be frozen	kootte (i)ru
think that it probably is (or will be) dangerous	a⌐buna⌐i to o⌐mo⌐u

20. The roads are frozen so I
    think it will probably be
    dangerous . . .

Mi⌐ti ḡa kootte (i)ru⌐ kara, a⌐bu-
na⌐i to o⌐mo⌐u ñ da kedo—

Mr. Tanaka

21. Don't worry. I'll be careful
    (lit. because I'll go care-
    fully).

Da⌐izyo⌐obu da⌐izyo⌐obu. Ki⌐otu-
ke⌐te (i)⌐ku⌐ kara.

22. Well, goodbye.

Zya⌐a, i⌐tte kima⌐su.

Mrs. Tanaka

23. Goodbye.

I⌐tte (i)rassya⌐i.

(e)

Mrs. Tanaka

24. Good morning.

O⌐hayoo gozaima⌐su.

Mrs. Yamamoto

25. Good morning.

O⌐hayoo gozaima⌐su.

    is cold

o⌐samuu gozaima⌐su +

26. It's awfully cold. Is every-
    one [in your family] well?

Zu⌐ibuñ o⌐samuu gozaima⌐su ḡa,
mi⌐na⌐sama o⌐ge⌐ñki de (i)rassyai-
masu ka—

Mrs. Tanaka

27. Yes, thank you.

A⌐ri⌐ḡatoo gozaimasu. Okaḡesa-
ma de.

    a cold
    become fashionable or
      popular or prevalent
    be fashionable or
      popular or prevalent
    baby

kaze
ha⌐ya⌐ru /-u/

ha⌐ya⌐tte (i)ru

a⌐katyañ

28. There are a lot of colds going
    around this year. [Is] your
    baby [all right]?

Kotosi wa ka⌐ze ḡa haya⌐tte orimasu ḡa, o⌐taku no a⌐katyañ wa?

Mrs. Yamamoto

    is big
    is weak or frail or
      delicate or poor in
      health
    worry

o⌐okyuu gozaimasu +
yo⌐wa⌐i /-ku/

siñpai-suru

29. He (lit. our child) is big,
    but he's delicate so I am
    always worrying . . .

Uti no ko wa ⌐o⌐okyuu gozaimasu
ḡa; yo⌐wa⌐i kara, i⌐tu mo siñpai-
site—

Mrs. Tanaka

    sturdy-looking or
    healthy-looking

zyoobusoo /na/ or
ozyoobusoo ⁺ /na/

30. He looks sturdy but. . .   Oˈzyoobusoo de (i)rassyaimaˈsu
                                                 keredo‿

Mrs. Yamamoto

    shopping   kaimono or okaimono +
31. Are you going shopping now?   Kore kara oˈkaimono ni irassyai-
                                                 maˈsu ka‿

Mrs. Tanaka

    take the trouble to come   seˈkkaku kuˈru
    finish [something]   suˈmaseˈru /-ru/
    want to finish   suˈmasetoˈo gozaimasu +
32. Yes. Since I took the trouble   Haˈa. Sekkaku Giˈñza maˈde ma-
    to come all the way to the   ˈirimaˈsita kara, kaˈimono (o)
    Ginza, I'd like to finish my   sumasetoˈo gozaimasu.
    shopping.

ADDITIONAL VOCABULARY

1. Wasn't the heavy rain yes-   Kiˈnoo no ooaˈme (wa) taˈiheñ
    terday terrible!   deˈsita ˈneˈe.

        sudden shower   niˈwakaaˈme
        sudden (evening) shower   yuudati
        strong wind   oˈokaˈze [1]
        storm   aˈrasi
        gale   boˈohuˈu
        typhoon   taˈihuˈu
        heavy snow   ooyuki
        snow storm   huˈbuki
        hail   arare or hyoˈo
        thunder   kaˈminariˈ
        lightning   iˈnabiˈkari

2. Look at the sky.   Soˈra o ˈmiˈte kudasai.

        cloud   kuˈmo
        moon (or month)   tuˈkiˈ
        star   hosi
        rainbow   niˈziˈ

3. It's thundering, isn't it.   Kaˈminariˈ ḡa naˈtte [2] (i)maˈsu
                                                 ˈneˈe.

4. There's lightning, isn't there.   Iˈnabiˈkari ḡa siˈte (i)maˈsu
                                                 ˈneˈe.

---

[1] Alternate accents: oˈokazeˈ, ookaze.

[2] Naru /-u/ 'sound,' 'ring,' 'roar,' 'rumble.'

NOTES ON THE BASIC DIALOGUES

2. 'but—that is just my opinion.'

4. 'and—various other things happen that prove it's muggy.'
    Note also: ha⌐ ḡa ha⌐e⌐ru 'cut a tooth.'

5. The rainy season in Japan begins about the middle of June and usually
    lasts for three or four weeks.

6. Na⌐kaba⌐ is regularly used in reference to the middle of a period of time.
    The intransitive partner of transitive hazimeru is hazimaru /-u/
    '[something] begins.' Both these verbals may be preceded by a time ex-
    pression + kara ('begin at [lit. from] a given time') or, less commonly,
    a time expression + ni ('begin at a given time').

7. The transitive partner of intransitive tuzuku is tuzukeru /-ru/ 'con-
    tinue [something]' (Lesson 24).

11. Yamu '[it] ceases' is the intransitive partner of transitive yameru /-ru/
    'stop doing [something]' (Lesson 14).

15. With kore kara 'from this point,' 'after this,' compare sore kara
    'from that point,' 'after that.'
    Se⌐kkaku⌐ desu ḡa_ occurs as an apologetic refusal of an invitation or
    offer: 'you took the trouble to ask me but . . .' or 'you showed special
    kindness in asking me but . . .'
    Se⌐kkaku⌐ also occurs (cf. Sentence 32, following) as an expression of
    manner, without following particle: se⌐kkaku ku⌐ru 'come on purpose,'
    'take the trouble to come,' 'come specially.' In such occurrences, it
    regularly loses its accent.

28. The more formal alternant of a⌐katyañ is akañboo.
    Note also kaze o hiku /-u/ 'catch a cold.'

31. Ni here is the ni of purpose: 'go for shopping.'

32. Su⌐mase⌐ru is a transitive verbal derived from the intransitive verbal
    su⌐mu /-u/ 'come to an end.'

GRAMMATICAL NOTES

1. Verbals: Informal Tentative

The formal tentative of verbals ends in -masyo⌐o and means 'let's do so-
and-so' or 'I guess I'll do so-and-so.' To make the informal equivalent:

-ru Verbals: Drop final -ru of the citation form and add -yoo.
-u Verbals: Drop final -u of the citation form and add -oo.
Irregular Verbals: ku⌐ru — ko⌐yo⌐o
                   suru — siyoo

If the citation form of a verbal is accented, the informal tentative is accented,
on the next-to-last syllable. The informal tentative of an unaccented verbal
occurs with unaccented and accented alternants.

Examples:

INFORMAL NON-PAST	TENTATIVE	
(= Citation form)	Informal	Formal
akeru ‘open’	akeyoo [1]	a⌐kemasyo¬o
ta⌐be¬ru ‘eat’	ta⌐beyo¬o	ta⌐bemasyo¬o
iru ‘be in a place’	iyoo [1]	i⌐masyo¬o
mi¬ru ‘see’	mi⌐yo¬o	mi⌐masyo¬o
ma¬tu ‘wait’	ma⌐to¬o	ma⌐timasyo¬o
ka⌐e¬ru ‘return’	ka⌐ero¬o	ka⌐erimasyo¬o
kau ‘buy’	kaoo [1]	ka⌐imasyo¬o
ha⌐na¬su ‘talk’	ha⌐naso¬o	ha⌐nasimasyo¬o
kiku ‘ask,’ ‘listen’	kikoo [1]	ki⌐kimasyo¬o
i⌐so¬ḡu ‘be in a	i⌐soḡo¬o	i⌐soḡimasyo¬o
hurry’		
yobu ‘call’	yoboo [1]	yo⌐bimasyo¬o
yo¬mu ‘read’	yo⌐mo¬o	yo⌐mimasyo¬o

In informal sentences, the informal tentative occurs in sentence-final position and pre-final before particles. In these positions, it occurs more commonly in the speech of men than of women. In formal and informal sentences, in the speech of men and women, it occurs in quotations. Thus:

Ikoo. ‘Let’s go.’ or ‘I guess I’ll go.’
Do¬o siyoo. ‘What’ll we do?’ or ‘What’ll I do?’
Mo¬o suko¬si no⌐mo¬o yo. ‘Let’s drink a little more!’
Ta⌐beyo¬o ne? ‘Let’s eat, shall we?’
I¬ma dekakeyoo to i⌐ima⌐sita. ‘He suggested we leave now.’ (Lit.‘He
    said quote let’s leave now.’)
I⌐soḡo¬o tte. ‘He suggested we hurry.’ (Lit. ‘Quote let’s hurry.’)

For additional uses, see Notes 2 and 3 following.

2. ——— to √o⌐mo¬u

A sentence ending with an informal non-past or past or tentative followed by the quotative to[2] + √o⌐mo¬u means ‘think /that/ ——— .’

Examples:

I⌐ku to omoima⌐su. ‘I think I (or someone) will go.’
Wa⌐ka¬tta to omoimasu. ‘I think I (or someone) understood.’
To⌐ttemo i¬i to o⌐moima⌐sita. ‘I thought it was very good.’
Mu⌐zukasi¬katta to omoimasu. ‘I think it was difficult.’
Ta¬naka-sañ wa byooki da to omoima¬su. ‘I think Mr. Tanaka is sick.’

---

[1] Has accented alternant, with accent on the next-to-last syllable.

[2] Before √o⌐mo¬u, the quotative to is not interchangeable with /t/ te.
For some speakers, accentuation before to is the same as before kara, no,
etc., with all verbal tentative forms accented on the next-to-last syllable.

Bo⌐ku no datta to omoimasu. 'I think it was mine.'
Ko⌐nai daroo to o⌐moima⌐sita. 'I thought he probably wouldn't come.'
Ni⌐hoñzi⌐ñ daroo to omoimasu. 'I think he's probably a Japanese.'

In examples like the first two above, context usually determines whether the subject of the quotation and the subject of √o⌐mo⌐u are the same or different; but there is often a contrast in meaning between (a) verbal non-past or past + daroo to √o⌐mo⌐u 'think that someone (else) probably does or will do or did so-and-so' (subject of the first inflected expression different from the subject of √o⌐mo⌐u), and (b) verbal tentative + to √o⌐mo⌐u 'think of doing so-and-so,' 'plan to do so-and-so' (subject of tentative and o⌐mo⌐u the same):

(a) Ka⌐u daro⌐o to omoimasu. 'I think he'll probably buy [it].'
(b) Ka⌐oo to omoima⌐su. 'I think I'll probably buy [it].' or 'I plan to buy [it].'
     Ka⌐oo to omo⌐tte imasu. 'I'm thinking of buying [it].'

The examples under (b) are similar to, but less definite than, Ka⌐u tumori de⌐su. 'I intend to buy [it].'

When a tentative question precedes to √o⌐mo⌐u, the most common English equivalent is 'I wonder if —— .' Thus:

Ta⌐bako o yameyo⌐o [1] ka to o⌐mo⌐tte imasu. 'I'm wondering if I should give up smoking.' (Lit. 'I'm thinking, "Shall I give up tobacco?"')
Mo⌐o ka⌐ero⌐o ka to o⌐mo⌐tte imasu. 'I'm wondering if I should go home (already) now.'

Note the following two types of negatives:

Byo⌐oki ni nara⌐nai to omoimasu. 'I don't think he'll get sick'—i.e. my thought is that he will not get sick.
Byo⌐oki ni na⌐ru to wa o⌐moimase⌐ñ. 'I don't think he'll get sick'— i.e. that he will get sick is not what I think.

3. Verbal Tentative + to + √suru

An informal tentative verbal + to + √suru means 'be about to —— ,' 'make as if to —— ,' 'try (unsuccessfully) to —— .' It often occurs in the middle of a sentence, followed by a statement of what prevented the completion of the action.

Examples:

De⌐yo⌐o to si⌐ta to⌐ki [ni], a⌐me ga hu⌐rihazimema⌐sita.
'Just as I was about to go out, it began to rain.'
Si⌐ñbuñ o kaoo to sita to⌐ki [ni], to⌐modati ni a⌐tte ka⌐imase⌐ñ desita.
'Just as I was about to buy a paper, I met a friend and I didn't buy it.'

---

[1]
Before some particles—for example, ka—a normally unaccented informal tentative regularly acquires an accent on its pre-final syllable.

Aꜛmaꜜdo o aꜛkeyoo to simaꜜsita ḡa, zeꜛñzeñ akeraremaseꜜñ desita.
   'I tried to open the shutters but I couldn't open them at all.'
Haꜛiroꜜo to siꜜmaꜜsita ḡa, kaꜛḡiꜜ ḡa kaꜛkaꜜtte ita kara—
   'I tried to go in but it was locked so . . . '
Waꜜtakusi ḡa kaoo to sita zidoꜜosya wa, goꜛzyuu hatiꜜ-neñ no ꜛSiꜜbo-
   ree desu.
   'The car I tried to buy is a '58 Chevrolet.'

With this pattern, compare gerund + √miꜛru (Lesson 19, Grammatical Note 3):

Haꜜitte miꜜmaꜜsita.
   'I tried going in'—i.e. I did actually go in.
Haꜛiroꜜo to siꜜmaꜜsita ḡa—
   'I tried to go in but [I couldn't].'

4. Polite Adjectivals

To make a formal polite adjectival:

change final $\left\{ \begin{array}{c} \underline{-ai} \\ \underline{-oi} \\ \underline{-ui} \\ \underline{-ii} \end{array} \right\}$ of the plain informal (= citation form) to $\left\{ \begin{array}{c} \underline{-oo} \\ \underline{-oo} \\ \underline{-uu} \\ \underline{-yuu} \end{array} \right\}$ and

add <u>gozaimasu</u> (or <u>gozaimasita</u> or <u>gozaimasyoo</u>). Some adjectivals also add
the polite prefix <u>o-</u> in the polite form. In most cases, an adjectival which
has an accent in the plain informal is also accented in the polite, one syllable
nearer the beginning of the word.

Examples:

Informal Plain	Formal Plain	Formal Polite
itadakitai	iꜛtadakitaꜜi desu	iꜛtadakitoo gozaimaꜜsu
		'I'd like to receive'
hiꜛroꜜi	hiꜛroꜜi desu	hiꜜroo gozaimasu
		'it's wide'
yaꜛsuꜜi	yaꜛsuꜜi desu	yaꜜsuu gozaimasu
		'it's cheap'
yorosii	yoꜛrosiꜜi desu	yoꜛrosyuu gozaimaꜜsu
		'it's all right'

Some polite adjectivals occur very commonly: oꜛhayoo gozaimaꜜsu (from
haꜛyaꜜi 'is early'), oꜛmedetoo gozaimaꜜsu (from meꜛdetaꜜi 'is auspicious'),
aꜛriꜛḡatoo gozaimasu (from aꜛriḡataꜜi 'is grateful'), oꜛatuu gozaimaꜜsu (from
aꜛtuꜜi 'is hot'), oꜛsamuu gozaimaꜜsu (from saꜛmuꜜi 'is cold'). Many adjectivals have a polite equivalent which occurs only rarely in actual conversation.

The formal polite negative of adjectivals is the formal plain negative,
with aꜛrimaseꜜñ replaced by goꜛzaimaseꜜñ. Thus:

Informal Plain	Formal Plain	Formal Polite
aꜜtuku ꜜnaꜜi	ꜛaꜜtuku aꜛrimaseꜜñ	aꜜtuku goꜛzaimaseꜜñ
		'it isn't hot'

Except for those which are used as special greetings, polite adjectivals are used much more commonly by women than by men.

5. Nominals Ending in -soo

A nominal consisting of a verbal stem (the -ma⌐su form minus -ma⌐su) or an adjectival stem (the non-past minus -i) or a nominal (usually a na word) + -soo means '—— looking,' 'looking as if [it] would or will be ——.' The compound is accented on its pre-final syllable.[1] Thus:

> de⌐kiso⌐o 'looking [as if it would be] possible'
>   (from de⌐ki⌐ru 'be possible')
> a⌐tuso⌐o 'hot-looking,' 'looking as if it would be hot'
>   (from a⌐tu⌐i 'is hot')
> i⌐kitaso⌐o 'looking as if he would want to go'
>   (from ikitai 'want to go')
> zyoobusoo 'strong-looking,' 'looking as if it would be strong'
>   (from zyoobu 'strong')

Two irregular formations must be noted: (1) the -soo word derived from i⌐i/yo⌐i 'is good' is yo⌐saso⌐o 'looking [as if it would be] good'; (2) -soo words derived from informal negatives ending in -nai end in -nasasoo (and the -soo word derived from na⌐i 'there isn't any' is na⌐saso⌐o 'looking as if there wouldn't be any').

-Soo words are na words: they occur followed by √da (including na before a following nominal) or the particle ni of manner. Thus:

> O⌐isiso⌐o desu. 'It's delicious-looking.' 'It looks [as if it would be]
>   delicious.'
> O⌐isiso⌐o na o⌐ka⌐si desu. 'It's delicious-looking cake.'
> O⌐isiso⌐o ni miemasu. 'It looks as if it would be delicious.' (Lit. 'It
>   appears in a delicious-looking manner.')

Note the following negative constructions, which differ grammatically but can be used almost interchangeably:

> De⌐kinasaso⌐o desu. 'It looks [as if it will be] impossible.'
> De⌐kiso⌐o zya a⌐rimase⌐n. 'It doesn't look [as if it will be] possible.'
> De⌐kiso⌐o ni wa mi⌐emase⌐n. 'It doesn't look as if it will be possible.'
>   (Lit. 'It doesn't appear in a possible-looking manner.')

-Soo words imply evidence based on the senses—particularly sight—and usually indicate an action or state that has not yet occurred or been realized, in reference to the given context. Patterns with yo⌐o 'manner,' on the other hand, include various kinds of evidence (including sight) and usually refer to an already occurring action or already existing state. Compare:

> De⌐kiso⌐o desu ne⌐e. 'He looks as if he will be able to do it, doesn't
>   he!' (said, perhaps, because he looks bright, capable, strong, etc.)

---

[1] However, the -soo derivative of an unaccented verbal or adjectival or nominal sometimes occurs without an accent.

De⌐ki⌐ru yoo desu ⌐ne⌐e. 'He seems to be able to do it, doesn't he!'
(based on some kind of evidence I have—perhaps the results of his
first attempt)

A⌐tuso⌐o desu ⌐ne⌐e. It looks /as if it would be/ hot!' (for example,
said of a winter coat on a hot summer's day)

A⌐tu⌐i yoo desu ⌐ne⌐e. 'It seems to be hot, doesn't it.' (for example,
said of something that is steaming)

Ya⌐metaso⌐o desu ⌐ne⌐e. 'He looks as if he is going to want to quit,
doesn't he!' (said, perhaps, on the basis of the expression of his
face)

Ya⌐metai yo⌐o desu ⌐ne⌐e. 'He seems to want to quit, doesn't he!'
(said, perhaps, because of rumors I have heard)

WARNING: Do not confuse compounds in -soo with informal sentences
followed by so⌐o da (Lesson 22, Grammatical Note 2). Thus:

Sa⌐muso⌐o desu. 'It looks /as if it would be/ cold.'
but:
Sa⌐mu⌐i soo desu. 'They say it's cold.'

Ge⌐ñkiso⌐o desu. 'He's healthy-looking.'
but:
Ge⌐ñki da soo desu. 'They say he's well.'

6. Intransitive Verbals + √ku⌐ru

The gerund of an intransitive verbal (i.e. one that never takes a direct
object) + √ku⌐ru 'come' indicates the gradual coming into being of an action
or state. (Compare English 'I've come to like it here'; 'You'll come to re-
gret it'; etc.)

Examples:

tu⌐ka⌐rete kuru 'grow tired,' 'begin to tire'
wa⌐ka⌐tte kuru 'come to understand,' 'reach understanding'
ko⌐otte ku⌐ru 'begin to freeze'

In this pattern, √ku⌐ru must follow the gerund immediately. Compare:

Koko e i⌐so⌐ide ki⌐ma⌐sita. 'I came here in a hurry,' which has an al-
ternant (differing only in emphasis):
I⌐so⌐ide ko⌐ko e kima⌐sita. Here the gerund is the gerund of manner
(Lesson 20, Grammatical Note 1).

7. Compound Verbals Ending in √-hazimeru

A compound verbal consisting of a transitive or intransitive verbal stem
(the -ma⌐su form minus -ma⌐su) + √-hazimeru 'begin' means 'begin doing
so-and-so.' The compound is accented on the next-to-last syllable, (or [al-
ternate accent] is unaccented). Examples:

ta⌐be⌐ru 'eat'	ta⌐behazime⌐ru 'begin eating'
a⌐ru⌐ku 'walk'	a⌐rukihazime⌐ru 'begin walking'
yo⌐mu 'read'	yo⌐mihazime⌐ru 'begin reading'
suru 'do'	si⌐hazime⌐ru 'begin doing'

The combination of a verbal gerund + √ku⌐ru, described in the previous note, indicates a more gradual beginning than a √-hazimeru compound.

DRILLS

A. Substitution Drill

1. It's different depending on the year.	To⌐si⌐ ni yotte tiḡaimasu.
2. It's different depending on the month.	Tu⌐ki⌐ ni yotte tiḡaimasu.
3. It's different depending on the day.	Hi ⌐ni yotte tiḡaima⌐su.
4. It's different depending on the time.	Zi⌐kañ ni yotte tiḡaima⌐su.
5. It's different depending on the place.	To⌐koro ni yotte tiḡaima⌐su.
6. It's different depending on the person.	Hi⌐to ni yotte tiḡaima⌐su.
7. It's different depending on the thing.	Mo⌐no⌐ ni yotte tiḡaimasu.
8. It's different depending on the store.	Mi⌐se⌐ ni yotte tiḡaimasu.
9. It's different depending on the weather.	Te⌐ñki ni yotte tiḡaimasu.

B. Grammar Drill (based on Grammatical Note 7)

Tutor: Mo⌐o si⌐ḡoto o sima⌐sita. 'I've done the work already.'
Student: Mo⌐o si⌐ḡoto o sihazimema⌐sita. 'I've begun to do the work already.'

1. A⌐me ḡa hu⌐rima⌐sita.	A⌐me ḡa hu⌐rihazimema⌐sita.
2. A⌐katyañ (wa) ⌐mo⌐o ⌐go⌐-hañ o ta⌐bema⌐sita.	A⌐katyañ (wa) ⌐mo⌐o ⌐go⌐hañ o ta-⌐behazimema⌐sita.
3. Ho⌐ñ (o) ⌐ka⌐ita desyoo ka.	Ho⌐ñ (o) ka⌐kihazimeta⌐ desyoo ka.
4. A⌐tarasi⌐i ka⌐mi⌐ (o) tu⌐kaimasyo⌐o ka.	A⌐tarasi⌐i ka⌐mi⌐ o tu⌐kaihazi-memasyo⌐o ka.
5. Mo⌐o Ta⌐naka-sañ ḡa ka⌐-ita ⌐ho⌐ñ (o) yo⌐mima⌐-sita.	Mo⌐o Ta⌐naka-sañ ḡa ka⌐ita ⌐ho⌐ñ (o) yo⌐mihazimema⌐sita.
6. Mo⌐o si⌐taku (o) sima⌐-sita.	Mo⌐o si⌐taku (o) sihazimema⌐sita.

C. Grammar Drill (based on Grammatical Note 5)

Tutor: Sa⌐mu⌐i desu ⌐ne⌐e. 'Isn't it cold!'
Student: Sa⌐muso⌐o desu ⌐ne⌐e. 'Doesn't it look cold!'

1. Wa⌐karimaꞌsu ⌐neꞌe—ano   Wa⌐karisoꞌo desu ⌐neꞌe—ano kodo-
   kodomo wa.   mo wa.
2. So⌐re wa dekimaꞌsu ḡa—   So⌐re wa dekisoꞌo desu ḡa—
3. So⌐re wa dekimaseꞌñ ḡa—   So⌐re wa dekinasasoꞌo desu ḡa—
4. A⌐no mise no okaꞌsi (wa)   A⌐no mise no okaꞌsi (wa) oꞌisisoꞌo
   oꞌisiꞌi desu ⌐neꞌe.   desu ⌐neꞌe.
5. Oꞌtaku no boꞌttyañ (wa)   Oꞌtaku no boꞌttyañ (wa) geꞌñkisoꞌo
   ⌐geꞌñki desu ⌐neꞌe.   desu ⌐neꞌe.
6. Keꞌsa kaⸯtta hoꞌñ (wa)   Keꞌsa kaⸯtta hoꞌñ (wa) oꞌmosiro-
   oꞌmosiroꞌi desu ⌐neꞌe.   soꞌo desu ⌐neꞌe.
7. Te⌐ḡami (wa) arimaseꞌñ   Te⌐ḡami (wa) nasasoꞌo desu ḡa—
   ḡa—
8. Ko⌐ñna kiꞌzi (wa) zyo-   Ko⌐ñna kiꞌzi wa zyo⌐obusoo deꞌsu
   ꞌobu deꞌsu ⸯneⸯe.   ⸯneⸯe.

D. Level Drill [1] (based on Grammatical Note 4)

1. Uti no ko (wa) oꞌokiꞌi   Uti no ko (wa) ⌐oꞌokyuu gozai-
   desu ḡa—   masu ḡa—
2. Kyoꞌo wa ⌐aꞌtuku aꞌrima-   Kyoꞌo wa ⌐aꞌtuku goꞌzaimaseñ
   señ ⌐neꞌe.   ⌐neꞌe.
3. Kono sakana (wa) oꞌisiꞌi   Kono osakana (wa) ⌐oisyuu gozai-
   desyoo?   masyoo?
4. Otaku no niwa (wa) hiꞌroꞌi   Otaku no oniwa (wa) ⌐hiꞌroo go-
   desu ⌐neꞌe.   zaimasu ⌐neꞌe.
5. A⌐ñna monoꞌ (wa) taꞌkaꞌi   A⌐ñna monoꞌ (wa) ⌐taꞌkoo gozai-
   desu ⌐neꞌe.   masu ⌐neꞌe.
6. Yo⌐rosiꞌi desyoo?   Yorosyuu gozaimasyoo?
7. Tu⌐kaꞌrete (i)masu kara,   Tu⌐kaꞌrete orimasu kara, su⌐koꞌsi
   su⌐koꞌsi ya⌐sumitaꞌi desu.   ya⌐sumitoꞌo gozaimasu.
8. So⌐no hoꞌñ (wa) a⌐ñmari   So⌐no hoꞌñ (wa) a⌐ñmari omosiꞌ-
   omosiⸯroku aⸯrimaseⸯñ.   roku goꞌzaimaseⸯñ.

E. Substitution Drill

1. Since I took the trouble   Se⌐kkaku kitaꞌ kara, su⌐masetaꞌi
   to come, I'd like to   ñ desu ḡa—
   finish [it].
2. Since I took the trouble   Se⌐kkaku tukuꞌtta kara, tu⌐kaitaꞌi
   to make [it], I'd like to   ñ desu ḡa—
   use [it]. /tu⌐kuꞌru,
   tukau/
3. Since I took the trouble   Se⌐kkaku kattaꞌ kara, yo⌐mitaꞌi
   to buy [it], I'd like to   ñ desu ḡa—
   read [it]. /kau, yoꞌmu/

---

[1] Each sentence on the right is the polite equivalent of the corresponding
sentence on the left.

4. Since I took the trouble
   to write [it], I'd like to
   show [it to him]. /ka⌐ku,
   mi⌐se⌐ru/

   Se⌐kkaku ka⌐ita kara, mi⌐seta⌐i ñ
   desu ḡa—

5. Since I took the trouble
   to fix [it], I'd like to sell
   [it]. /na⌐o⌐su, uru/

   Se⌐kkaku nao⌐sita kara, u⌐rita⌐i ñ
   desu ḡa—

6. Since I took the trouble
   to get [it] out, I'd like
   to take [it]. /da⌐su,
   motte iku/

   Se⌐kkaku da⌐sita kara, mo⌐tte iki-
   ta⌐i ñ desu ḡa—

7. Since I took the trouble
   to come, I'd like to see
   [it]. /ku⌐ru, mi⌐ru/

   Se⌐kkaku kita⌐ kara, mi⌐ta⌐i ñ
   desu ḡa—

F. Level Drill [1] (based on Grammatical Note 1)

1. Zya⌐a, i⌐kimasyo⌐o.
   Zya⌐a, i⌐ko⌐o.

2. To⌐nari no heya⌐ de sa-
   ⌐ḡasite mimasyo⌐o.
   To⌐nari no heya⌐ de sa⌐ḡasite
   miyo⌐o.

3. Asita ⌐ha⌐yaku o⌐kima-
   syo⌐o.
   Asita ⌐ha⌐yaku o⌐kiyo⌐o.

4. Mu⌐koo no seki⌐ ni ka-
   ⌐kemasyo⌐o.
   Mu⌐koo no seki⌐ ni ka⌐keyo⌐o.

5. O⌐soku na⌐tta kara, ka-
   ⌐erimasyo⌐o.
   O⌐soku na⌐tta kara, ka⌐ero⌐o.

6. Se⌐ñse⌐e kara mo⌐ratta
   zibiki⌐ (o) tu⌐kaimasyo⌐o.
   Se⌐ñse⌐e kara mo⌐ratta zibiki⌐
   (o) tu⌐kao⌐o.

7. Bi⌐iru (o) ⌐i⌐p-pai no-
   ⌐mimasyo⌐o.
   Bi⌐iru (o) ⌐i⌐p-pai no⌐mo⌐o.

8. I⌐ya⌐ da kara, ya⌐mema-
   syo⌐o.
   I⌐ya⌐ da kara, ya⌐meyo⌐o.

9. Ko⌐ñbañ yo⌐ohuku (o)
   kimasyo⌐o.
   Ko⌐ñbañ yo⌐ohuku (o) kiyo⌐o.

10. A⌐sita no a⌐sa ⌐ta⌐kusii
    de ki⌐masyo⌐o.
    A⌐sita no a⌐sa ⌐ta⌐kusii de ko-
    ⌐yo⌐o.

G. Substitution Drill (based on Grammatical Note 3)

1. I tried to go but I
   couldn't (go).
   I⌐koo to sima⌐sita ḡa, i⌐karema-
   se⌐ñ desita.

2. I tried to open [it] but I
   couldn't (open). /akeru/
   A⌐keyoo to sima⌐sita ḡa, a⌐kera-
   remase⌐ñ desita.

3. I tried to close [it] but I
   couldn't (close).
   /si⌐me⌐ru/
   Si⌐meyo⌐o to si⌐ma⌐sita ḡa, si⌐me-
   raremase⌐ñ desita.

4. I tried to continue [it]
   but I couldn't (continue).
   /tuzukeru/
   Tu⌐zukeyoo to sima⌐sita ḡa, tu⌐zu-
   keraremase⌐ñ desita.

---

[1] Each sentence on the right is the informal equivalent of the corresponding
sentence on the left.

5. I tried to get up but I
   couldn't (get up).
   /o˹ki˺ru/

   O˹kiyo˺o to si⁺ma⁴sita ḡa, o˹kira-
   remase˼ñ desita.

6. I tried to read [it] but
   I couldn't (read).
   /yo˼mu/

   Yo˹mo˼o to si⁺ma⁴sita ḡa, yo˹me-
   mase˼ñ desita.

7. I tried to cut [it] but I
   couldn't (cut). /ki˼ru/

   Ki˹ro˼o to si⁺ma⁴sita ḡa, ki˹rema-
   se˼ñ desita.

8. I tried to put [it] on but
   I couldn't (put on).
   /kiru/

   Ki˹yoo to sima˼sita ḡa, ki˹rarema-
   se˼ñ desita.

9. I tried to come but I
   couldn't (come). /ku˼ru/

   Ko˹yo˼o to si⁺ma⁴sita ḡa, ko˹rare-
   mase˼ñ desita.

10. I tried to fix [it] but
    I couldn't (fix).
    /na˹o˼su/

    Na˹oso˼o to si⁺ma⁴sita ḡa, na˹ose-
    mase˼ñ desita.

H. Substitution Drill (based on Grammatical Note 3)

1. Just as I was about to
   go, a friend came and
   I couldn't (go).

   I˹koo to sita to˼ki /ni/ tõmodati
   ḡa kite, i˹karena˼katta ñ desu
   yo.

2. Just as I was about to
   go out, a friend came
   and I couldn't (go out).
   /de˼ru/

   De˹yo˼o to si⁺ta to⁴ki /ni/ tõmodati ḡa kite, de˹rare˼nakatta ñ
   desu yo.

3. Just as I was about to
   go in, a friend came and
   I couldn't (go in).
   /ha˼iru/

   Ha˹iro˼o to si⁺ta to⁴ki /ni/ tõmodati ḡa kite, ha˹ire˼nakatta
   ñ desu yo.

4. Just as I was about to
   begin [it], a friend came
   and I couldn't (begin).
   /hazimeru/

   Ha˹zimeyoo to sita to˼ki /ni/ tõmodati ḡa kite, ha˹zimerarena˼-
   katta ñ desu yo.

5. Just as I was about to
   telephone, a friend
   came and I couldn't
   (telephone). /de˹ñwa
   (o) kake˼ru/

   De˹ñwa (o) kakeyo˼o to si⁺ta to⁴-
   ki /ni/ tõmodati ḡa kite, ka˹ke-
   rare˼nakatta ñ desu yo.

6. Just as I was about to
   write [it], a friend came
   and I couldn't (write).
   /ka˼ku/

   Ka˹ko˼o to si⁺ta to⁴ki /ni/ tõmodati ḡa kite, ka˹ke˼nakatta ñ
   desu yo.

7. Just as I was about to
   look at [it], a friend
   came and I couldn't
   (look). /mi˼ru/

   Mi˹yo˼o to si⁺ta to⁴ki /ni/ tõmodati ḡa kite, mi˹rare˼nakatta ñ
   desu yo.

8. Just as I was about to
   eat [it], a friend came
   and I couldn't (eat).
   /ta˹be˼ru/

   Ta˹beyo˼o to si⁺ta to⁴ki /ni/ tõmodati ḡa kite, ta˹berare˼naka-
   tta ñ desu yo.

9. Just as I was about to
rest, a friend came and
I couldn't (rest).
/ya⌐su⌐mu/

Ya⌐sumo⌐o to si⌐ta to⌐ki /ni/ tōmodati ḡa kite, ya⌐sume⌐nakatta
ñ desu yo.

10. Just as I was about to
make [it], a friend
came and I couldn't
(make). /tu⌐ku⌐ru/

Tu⌐kuro⌐o to si⌐ta to⌐ki /ni/ tōmodati ḡa kite, tu⌐kure⌐nakatta
ñ desu yo.

I. Substitution Drill (based on Grammatical Note 2)

1. I'm thinking of going tonight . . .

Ko⌐ñbañ i⌐koo to omo⌐tte (i)masu
ḡa―

2. I'm thinking of going out
tonight . . . /dekakeru/

Ko⌐ñbañ de⌐kakeyoo to omo⌐tte
(i)masu ḡa―

3. I'm thinking of studying
tonight . . .
/beñkyoo-suru/

Ko⌐ñbañ be⌐ñkyoo-siyoo to omo⌐tte
(i)masu ḡa―

4. I'm thinking of stopping
in tonight . . . /yoru/

Ko⌐ñbañ yo⌐roo to omo⌐tte (i)masu
ḡa―

5. I'm thinking of wearing
Western-style clothing
tonight . . . /yoohuku
(o) kiru/

Ko⌐ñbañ yo⌐ohuku (o) kiyoo to
omo⌐tte (i)masu ḡa―

6. I'm thinking of going to
bed early tonight . . .
/ha⌐yaku neru/

Ko⌐ñbañ ⌐ha⌐yaku ne⌐yoo to omo⌐tte
(i)masu ḡa―

7. I'm thinking of listening
to the radio tonight . . .
/ra⌐zio (o) kiku/

Ko⌐ñbañ ⌐ra⌐zio (o) ki⌐koo to omo⌐-
tte (i)masu ḡa―

8. I'm thinking of watching
television tonight . . .
/te⌐rebi (o) ⌐mi⌐ru/

Ko⌐ñbañ ⌐te⌐rebi (o) mi⌐yo⌐o to
o⌐mo⌐tte (i)masu ḡa―

9. I'm thinking of writing
letters tonight . . .
/te⌐ḡami (o) ka⌐ku/

Ko⌐ñbañ te⌐ḡami (o) kako⌐o to o⌐mo⌐-
tte (i)masu ḡa―

10. I'm thinking of going
home early tonight . . .
/ha⌐yaku ⌐ka⌐eru/

Ko⌐ñbañ ⌐ha⌐yaku ka⌐ero⌐o to o⌐mo⌐-
tte (i)masu ḡa―

J. Grammar Drill (based on Grammatical Note 2)

Tutor: I⌐koo to omoima⌐su. 'I think I'll probably go.'
Student: I⌐ku daro⌐o to omoimasu. 'I think he'll probably go.'

1. I⌐ma no siḡoto (o) ya-
⌐meyoo to omoima⌐su.

I⌐ma no siḡoto (o) ya⌐meru daro⌐o
to omoimasu.

2. Zi⌐mu⌐syo (o) ka⌐tazu-
keyo⌐o to omoimasu.

Zi⌐mu⌐syo (o) ka⌐tazuke⌐ru daroo
to omoimasu.

3. Ko⌐domo ni yaroo to
omoima⌐su.

Ko⌐domo ni yaru daro⌐o to omoimasu.

4. Se⌐ñse⌐e ni a⌐ḡeyoo to   Se⌐ñse⌐e ni a⌐ḡeru daro⌐o to
   omoima⌐su.   omoimasu.
5. O⌐hu⌐ro ni ha⌐iro⌐o to   O⌐hu⌐ro ni ⌐ha⌐iru daroo to omo-
   omoimasu.   imasu.
6. Ge⌐ta (o) hakoo to omo-   Ge⌐ta (o) haku daro⌐o to omoi-
   ima⌐su.   masu.
7. Bo⌐osi (o) kaburo⌐o to   Bo⌐osi (o) kabu⌐ru daroo to omo-
   omoimasu.   imasu.
8. Kodomo (o) o⌐ite ikoo [1] Kodomo (o) o⌐ite iku daro⌐o to
   to omoima⌐su.   omoimasu.

K. Grammar Drill (based on Grammatical Note 2)

           Tutor: Wa⌐karima⌐sita. 'I've understood.'
           Student: Wa⌐ka⌐tta to omoimasu. 'I think I've understood.'

1. A⌐me ḡa ya⌐mima⌐sita.   A⌐me ḡa ya⌐ñda to omoima⌐su.
2. Kotosi ka⌐ze ḡa haya⌐tte   Kotosi ka⌐ze ḡa haya⌐tte (i)ru to
   (i)masu.   omoimasu.
3. Ko⌐ñna ho⌐ñ (wa) tu⌐mara- Ko⌐ñna ho⌐ñ (wa) tu⌐mara⌐nai
   ra⌐nai desu.   to omoimasu.
4. Koñḡetu no na⌐kaba⌐   Koñḡetu no na⌐kaba⌐ kara da
   kara desu.   to omoimasu.
5. Mo⌐o rok-ka⌐ḡetu tuzu-   Mo⌐o rok-ka⌐ḡetu tuzuku to omo-
   kimasu.   imasu.
6. So⌐no ka⌐iḡi (wa) o⌐to⌐-   So⌐no ka⌐iḡi (wa) o⌐to⌐tosi datta
   tosi desita.   to omoimasu.
7. Ta⌐naka-sañ no yo⌐o na   Ta⌐naka-sañ no yo⌐o na se⌐ñse⌐e
   se⌐ñse⌐e wa su⌐kuna⌐i   wa su⌐kuna⌐i to omoimasu.
   desu.
8. Kinoo no siḡoto (wa)   Kinoo no siḡoto (wa) mu⌐zukasi⌐-
   mu⌐zukasi⌐katta desu.   katta to omoimasu.

L. Response Drill (based on Grammatical Note 2)

           Tutor: A⌐tu⌐i desu ka⌐ 'Is it hot?'
           Student: (a) A⌐tu⌐i to wa o⌐moimase⌐ñ ḡa⌐ ⎱
                    (b) A⌐tuku ⌐na⌐i to omoimasu.   ⎰ 'I don't think it's hot.'

1. Asuko no kikoo (wa)   I⌐i to wa o⌐moimase⌐ñ ḡa⌐
   ⌐i⌐i desu ka⌐   Yo⌐ku ⌐na⌐i to omoimasu.

2. Tanaka-sañ no eeḡo   U⌐ma⌐i to wa o⌐moimase⌐ñ ḡa⌐
   (wa) u⌐ma⌐i desu ka⌐   U⌐maku ⌐na⌐i to omoimasu.

3. Are wa ko⌐oba⌐ desu   Ko⌐oba⌐ da to wa o⌐moimase⌐ñ ḡa⌐
   ka⌐   Ko⌐oba⌐ zya ⌐na⌐i to omoimasu.

4. Ko⌐ñna ki⌐zi (wa) yo-   Yo⌐wa⌐i to wa o⌐moimase⌐ñ ḡa⌐
   ⌐wa⌐i desu ka⌐   Yo⌐waku ⌐na⌐i to omoimasu.

---
[1] <u>Oite iku</u> 'leave behind (i. e. go having left [something]).'

5. Ki⌐marima⌐sita ka⌐   Ki⌐matta⌐ to wa o⌐moimase⌐n̄ ḡa—
                                     Ki⌐marana⌐katta to omoimasu.

6. A⌐n̄na mono⌐ (wa) zyo-   Zyo⌐obu da⌐ to wa o⌐moimase⌐n̄ ḡa—
   ⌐obu de⌐su ka⌐   Zyo⌐obu zya na⌐i to omoimasu.

7. A⌐suko no natu⌐ (wa) mu-   Mu⌐siatu⌐i to wa o⌐moimase⌐n̄ ḡa—
   ⌐siatu⌐i desu ka⌐   Mu⌐sia⌐tuku ⌐na⌐i to omoimasu.

8. Ko⌐no wan̄pi⌐isu (wa) ha-   Ha⌐desuḡi⌐ru to wa o⌐moimase⌐n̄
   ⌐desuḡima⌐su ka⌐   ḡa—
                                     Ha⌐desuḡi⌐nai to omoimasu.

M. Expansion Drill

1. [It] continues.   Tu⌐zukima⌐su.
   [It] lasts about 20 days.   Ha⌐tu-ka-ḡu⌐rai tuzukimasu.
   [It] begins about the   Na⌐kaba-ḡo⌐ro kara hazimatte,
   middle and lasts about   ha⌐tu-ka-ḡu⌐rai tuzukimasu.
   20 days.
   [It] begins about the   Roku-ḡatu no na⌐kaba-ḡo⌐ro kara
   middle of June and   hazimatte, ha⌐tu-ka-ḡu⌐rai tuzu-
   lasts about 20 days.   kimasu.
   The rainy season be-   Tuyu wa rŏku-ḡatu no na⌐kaba-
   gins about the middle   ḡo⌐ro kara hazimatte, ha⌐tu-ka-
   of June and lasts   ḡu⌐rai tuzukimasu.
   about 20 days.

2. I go shopping.   Ka⌐imono ni ikima⌐su.
   I go shopping about 9   Ku-⌐zi-ḡo⌐ro kaimono ni ikimasu.
   o'clock.
   I usually go shopping   Taitee ku-⌐zi-ḡo⌐ro kaimono ni
   about 9 o'clock.   ikimasu.
   It's different depending   Hi ⌐ni yotte tiḡaima⌐su ḡa, taitee
   on the day but I usually   ku-⌐zi-ḡo⌐ro kaimono ni ikimasu.
   go shopping about 9
   o'clock.

3. It looks as if there   Na⌐saso⌐o desu ⌐ne⌐e.
   weren't any.
   There's no reason to   Na⌐i hazu wa ⌐na⌐i kedo, na⌐sa-
   expect that there   so⌐o desu ⌐ne⌐e.
   isn't any, but it looks
   as if there weren't
   any.
   Since he said that a lot   Ta⌐kusan̄ noko⌐tte (i)ru tte i⌐tta⌐
   was left there should   kara, na⌐i hazu wa ⌐na⌐i kedo;
   be some, but it looks   na⌐saso⌐o desu ⌐ne⌐e.
   as if there weren't
   any.

4. I think it's good.   I⌐i to omoimasu.
   I think it would be   Si⌐ta ho⌐o ḡa ⌐i⌐i to omoimasu.
   better to do it.

I think it would be better
to make it tomorrow.

A⌐sita⌐ ni si⌐ta ho⌐o ḡa ⌐i⌐i to
omoimasu.

Instead of going today,
I think it would be
better to make it to-
morrow.

Kyo⌐o wa i⌐kana⌐i de, a⌐sita⌐ ni
si⌐ta ho⌐o ḡa ⌐i⌐i to omoimasu.
masu.

Since it's begun to cloud
up, instead of going
today I think it would
be better to make it
tomorrow.

Ku⌐mo⌐tte ⌐ki⌐ta kara; kyo⌐o wa
i⌐kana⌐i de, a⌐sita⌐ ni si⌐ta
ho⌐o ḡa ⌐i⌐i to omoimasu.

5. Is that all right?

Ka⌐maimase⌐ñ ka◡

I'd like to talk. Is that
all right?

Ha⌐nasita⌐i ñ desu ḡa, ka⌐mai-
mase⌐ñ ka◡

I'd like to talk Japanese.
Is that all right?

Ni⌐hoñḡo de hanasita⌐i ñ desu
ḡa, ka⌐maimase⌐ñ ka◡

I'd like to talk Japanese
as much as possible.
Is that all right?

Narubeku ni⌐hoñḡo de hanasita⌐i
ñ desu ḡa, ka⌐maimase⌐ñ ka◡

Since I've studied, I'd
like to talk Japanese
as much as possible.
Is that all right?

Be⌐ñkyoo-sita⌐ kara, narubeku
ni⌐hoñḡo de hanasita⌐i ñ desu
ḡa; ka⌐maimase⌐ñ ka◡

Since I've studied Jap-
anese, I'd like to talk
Japanese as much as
possible. Is that all
right?

Ni⌐hoñḡo (o) beñkyoo-sita⌐ kara,
na⌐rubeku nihoñḡo de hanasita⌐i
ñ desu ḡa; ka⌐maimase⌐ñ ka◡

Since I took the trouble
to study Japanese,
I'd like to talk Japanese
as much as possible.
Is that all right?

Se⌐kkaku nihoñḡo (o) beñkyoo-
sita⌐ kara, na⌐rubeku nihoñḡo
de hanasita⌐i ñ desu ḡa; ka⌐mai-
mase⌐ñ ka◡

6. It's unpleasant, isn't it.

I⌐ya⌐ desu ⌐ne⌐e.

It's unpleasant because
it rains (lit. falls) a
lot.

Yo⌐ku ⌐hu⌐ru kara, i⌐ya⌐ desu
⌐ne⌐e.

It's unpleasant because
it rains a lot.

A⌐me ḡa ⌐yo⌐ku ⌐hu⌐ru kara,
i⌐ya⌐ desu ⌐ne⌐e.

[Things] get moldy and
it rains a lot so it's unpleasant, isn't it.

Ka⌐bi ḡa hae⌐ru si, a⌐me ḡa
⌐yo⌐ku ⌐hu⌐ru kara; i⌐ya⌐ desu
⌐ne⌐e.

It's muggy and [things]
get moldy and it rains
a lot so it's unpleasant,
isn't it.

Mu⌐siatu⌐i si, ka⌐bi ḡa hae⌐ru
si, a⌐me ḡa ⌐yo⌐ku ⌐hu⌐ru
kara; i⌐ya⌐ desu ⌐ne⌐e.

The summer is unpleasant
because it's muggy and
[things] get moldy and
it rains a lot.

Na⌐tu⌐ wa, mu⌐siatu⌐i si, ka⌐bi ḡa
hae⌐ru si, a⌐me ḡa ⌐yo⌐ku ⌐hu⌐ru
kara; i⌐ya⌐ desu ⌐ne⌐e.

The summer here is un-pleasant because it's muggy and [things] get moldy and it rains a lot.	Ko⸢ko no natu⸣ wa, mu⸢siatu⸣i si, ka⸢bi ḡa hae⸣ru si, a⸣me ḡa ⸢yo⸣ku ⸢hu⸣ru kara; i⸢ya⸣ desu ⸢ne⸣e.

SHORT SUPPLEMENTARY DIALOGUES

1. Smith: Ma⸣da yu⸢ki⸣ ḡa hu⸢tte⸣ imasu ka
    Tanaka: Yu⸢ki⸣ wa ya⸢mima⸣sita ḡa, ⸢a⸣me ni na⸢rima⸣sita.
    Smith: I⸢ya⸣ desu ⸢ne⸣e.

2. Mr. Yamamoto: Tanaka-sañ ōsoi ⸢ne⸣e.
    Mr. Okada: Si⸢tu⸣ree-site no⸢mihazimeyo⸣o ka.
    Mr. Yamamoto: So⸢o siyo⸣o.

3. Mrs. Tanaka: So⸢no oka⸣si ōisisoo ⸢ne⸣e.
    Mr. Tanaka: Yo⸢sasoo da ⸢ne⸣e. Ta⸢beyo⸣o ka.
    Mrs. Tanaka: E⸣e, ta⸢bemasyo⸣o.

4. Mr. Tanaka: So⸢to a⸢tusoo da kara, u⸢ti ni iyo⸣o yo.
    Mrs. Tanaka: So⸣o ⸢ne⸣e.

5. Mr. Tanaka: Sa⸣mukatta daroo?
    Mr. Yamamoto: Asi ko⸢orisoo da⸣tta yo.

6. Ueda: Da⸣re ka ⸢ma⸣tte ru ñ desu ka
    Yamamoto: E⸣e. Ta⸢naka-señse⸣e o.
    Ueda: A⸣a, mo⸢o su⸢ḡu ⸢de⸣te kuru to o⸢moima⸣su yo

7. Smith: Mi⸢na⸣sañ o⸢hirugo⸣hañ ⸢do⸣o suru ñ desu ka
    Tanaka: Hi⸢to ni yotte tiḡaima⸣su ḡa, taitee ka⸢isya no so⸣ba ni ⸢a⸣ru
              su⸢si⸣ya ya so⸢ba⸣ya de ta⸢be⸣ru ñ desu yo.

8. Tanaka: Asita se⸢ñse⸣e no otaku e i⸢rassya⸣ru soo desu ḡa; a⸢ru⸣ite
              i⸢rassyaima⸣su ka, ku⸢ruma de irassyaima⸣su ka.
    Smith: Sore wa ⸢te⸣ñki ni yotte ki⸢mema⸣su kara

9. Smith: Sekkaku Ni⸢ho⸣ñ made ki⸢ta⸣ ñ da kara, Kyo⸣oto ya ⸢Na⸣ra e
              i⸢kita⸣i ñ desu yo.
    Tanaka: Do⸣ozo ⸢do⸣ozo. O⸢mosiro⸣i daroo to omoimasu.

10. Tanaka: Asita Ka⸢makura e iko⸣o to o⸢mo⸣tte ru ñ desu ḡa, a⸢na⸣ta mo
              i⸢kimase⸣ñ ka
    Smith: Se⸢kkaku⸣ desu ḡa, a⸢sita⸣ wa ⸢yo⸣o ḡa a⸢rima⸣su kara

11. Tanaka: Hu⸢ru⸣i kuruma ka⸢o⸣o ka to o⸢mo⸣tte ru ñ desu ḡa
    Yamamoto: Ya⸣sukute ⸢i⸣i no ḡa ⸢a⸣ru daroo to o⸢moima⸣su yo

12. Tanaka: O⸢matase-itasima⸣sita. De⸢kakeyo⸣o to sita toki ⸢a⸣me ḡa hu-
              ⸢rihazimema⸣sita kara; ka⸣sa o saḡasite
    Smith: Do⸣o itasimasite. *I⸢ya⸣ na ⸢te⸣ñki desu ⸢ne⸣e.

13. Smith: Ni⸣motu ku⸢ruma no na⸣ka ni i⸢reta⸣ ñ desu ka
    Tanaka: I⸢reyoo to sita⸣ ñ desu ḡa, ka⸢ḡi⸣ ka⸢ka⸣tte ru yoo da kara
    Smith: So⸣o ⸢so⸣o. Ma⸣e ni kā⸢ḡi ⸢ka⸣keta ñ desu ⸢ne⸣e.

14. Tanaka: Koñḡetu kara e┌eḡo o beñkyoo-sihazimeyo┐o to o⊢mo⊣tte ru ñ desu ḡa, da┐re ka zyo┌ozu┐ na se⊢ñse⊣e go┌zo┐ñzi desyoo ka.
    Smith: Sa┐a. Betu ni zyo┌ozu┐ da to wa o⊢moimase⊣ñ ḡa, ka┐nai wa—
    Tanaka: O┐kusama desu ka. O┌siete kudasaima┐su ka‿
    Smith: E┐e, yo┌roko┐ñde. So┌ñna siḡoto ḡa suki┐ desu kara—
    Tanaka: Zya┐a, koñsyuu ōtaku e de┌ñwa o ka┐kete, ki┌mete itadakimasyo┐o.

English Equivalents

1. Smith: Is it still snowing?
   Tanaka: The snow has stopped but it has turned to rain.
   Smith: How awful!

2. Mr. Yamamoto: Isn't Tanaka late!
   Mr. Okada: Shall we go ahead and have a drink? (Lit. Shall we be rude and start drinking?)
   Mr. Yamamoto: Let's do that.

3. Mrs. Tanaka: Doesn't that cake look delicious!
   Mr. Tanaka: It looks good, doesn't it. Shall we have some?
   Mrs. Tanaka: Yes, let's.

4. Mr. Tanaka: It looks hot outside so let's stay home.
   Mrs. Tanaka: That's right.

5. Mr. Tanaka: It was cold, wasn't it?
   Mr. Yamamoto: My feet felt as if they'd freeze!

6. Ueda: Are you waiting for someone?
   Yamamoto: Yes. For Dr. Tanaka.
   Ueda: Oh, I think he'll come out any minute now.

7. Smith: What do all of you do for lunch?
   Tanaka: It depends on the person but we usually eat at places like sushi shops and soba shops that are near the office.

8. Tanaka: I hear that you are going to go to the teacher's house tomorrow. Are you going to walk there or go by car?
   Smith: That I'll decide depending on the weather so [I don't know yet].

9. Smith: Since I've come all the way to Japan, I'd like to go to places like Kyoto and Nara.
   Tanaka: Please do. I think that you'd probably enjoy it.

10. Tanaka: I'm thinking of going to Kamakura tomorrow. Wouldn't you like to go too?
    Smith: It's kind of you to ask me but tomorrow I have some business I must attend to so . . .

11. Tanaka: I'm wondering if I should buy a used (lit. old) car . . .
    Yamamoto: I think there are probably some good cheap ones.

12. Tanaka: I'm sorry to have kept you waiting. Just as I was about to start out, it began to rain, so I looked for an umbrella and . . .
    Smith: Don't mention it. Isn't it awful weather!

13. Smith: Did you put the luggage in the car?
    Tanaka: I tried to put it in, but it seems to be locked so [I couldn't].
    Smith: That's right. I locked it a while ago, didn't I.

14. Tanaka: I've been thinking that I'd start studying English this month.
              Do you know some good teacher?
    Smith: I don't think she's especially good, but my wife . . .
    Tanaka: Your wife? Will she teach me?
    Smith: Yes, she'd be glad to. (Because) she likes that kind of work.
    Tanaka: Well then, I'll telephone your home this week and have it set-
              tled.

EXERCISES

1. Take turns asking and answering questions based on the Basic Dialogues.
   The student who is answering questions should do so without referring to
   the text.

2. Take turns asking and answering questions about the climate of places
   you know. Practice using words from the Additional Vocabulary as well
   as those which occur in the Basic Dialogues.

3. You have just returned from a trip. Give the following replies to Mr. Tanaka's question, 'How was the weather?':

   a. It was very pleasant.
   b. It rained every day.
   c. It was awfully muggy.
   d. It was snowy and cold.
   e. It was hot.

4. Tell Mr. Tanaka that:

   a. it's raining.
   b. it's snowing.
   c. it has started to rain.
   d. it has stopped snowing.
   e. it has begun to cloud up.
   f. it has begun to clear up.
   g. it is very windy.

Lesson 27. Outings

BASIC DIALOGUES: FOR MEMORIZATION

(a)

Tanaka

1. Doesn't it rain (lit. fall) a lot!   *Yo⌐ku hu⌐rima⌐su ⌐ne⌐e.

Smith

2. There really is a great deal of rain this year, isn't there!   *Hoñtoo ni ko̅tosi wa ⌐a⌐me g̅a o⌐o⌐i desu ⌐ne⌐e.

      is amazing or unusual or unexpected   me⌐zurasi⌐i /-ku/

      is unusually good   me⌐zura⌐siku ⌐i⌐i

3. Yesterday was unusually nice (weather) but [we haven't had much weather like that].   Ki⌐no⌐o wa me⌐zura⌐siku ⌐i⌐i ⌐te⌐ñki desita g̅a—

Tanaka

      the country   inaka

      cherry tree or cherry blossom   sakura

4. Yesterday I went to the country to see the cherry blossoms . . .   Kinoo i̅naka e sa⌐kura (o) mi⌐ ni itte ⌐ne⌐e.

Smith

5. Oh.   A⌐a, so⌐o.

Tanaka

      completely   su⌐kka⌐ri

      bloom   saku /-u/

      be in bloom   saite (i)ru

6. They were in full bloom already so they were beautiful.   Mo⌐o su⌐kka⌐ri sa⌐ite (i)ta⌐ kara, ki⌐ree desita yo⌐

Smith

      go out (for a special occasion)   de⌐ru /-ru/

      be out   de⌐te (i)ru

7. A lot of people were out (to see them), weren't they?   Hito (g̅a) ta⌐kusañ de⌐te (i)ta desyoo?

Tanaka

cherry-blossom viewing	ha⌐nami⌐ or ohanami +
people looking at the cherry blossoms	ha⌐nami no hito⌐
filled with people	hi⌐to⌐ de ippai

8. Yes. The park was filled with people looking at the cherry blossoms.

E⌐e. Kooeñ (wa) ha⌐nami no hito⌐ de i⌐ppai de⌐sita yo.

song	u⌐ta⌐
sing	utau /-u/
make noise or be boisterous	sa⌐wa⌐g̃u /-u/
do such things as drinking, singing, and making a racket	no⌐ñdari u⌐tatta⌐ri sa⌐wa⌐i-dari suru

9. They were all drinking sake and singing songs and making a racket...

Miñna o⌐sake (o) no⌐ñdari, u⌐ta⌐ (o) u⌐tatta⌐ri, sa⌐wa⌐idari site—

Smith

10. Oh, my goodness! or You don't say! or Really!

Sore wa sore wa.

Tanaka

box lunch	be⌐ñto⌐o
tree	ki⌐

11. We took our lunch and ate under the trees...

Be⌐ñto⌐o (o) motte (i)tte, ki⌐ no sita de ⌐ta⌐bete—

and or then or and then	sosite
play or amuse oneself	asobu /-u/
come after playing or go and play	a⌐soñde ku⌐ru
return (noun)	ka⌐eri⌐
the return train	ka⌐eri no de⌐ñsya

12. And we amused ourselves (lit. came after amusing ourselves) until evening. The return train was crowded...

Sosite yu⌐ug̃ata ma⌐de a⌐soñde kima⌐sita g̃a, *ka⌐eri no de⌐ñsya (g̃a) ⌐koñde ⌐ne⌐e.

until arriving	tu⌐ku made
stand up	ta⌐tu /-u/
be standing	ta⌐tte (i)ru

13. We were standing all the way until we arrived in Tokyo.

To⌐okyoo e tu⌐ku made, zu⌐tto ta⌐tte (i)masita.

Smith

14. How awful!

So⌐re wa taiheñ de⌐sita ⌐ne⌐e.

Tanaka

therefore <u>or</u> and so <u>or</u> for that reason <u>or</u> that is why	da⌐ kara <u>or</u> de⌐su kara

15. That is why I got completely
 tired out, and today I don't
 have any pep at all.

Da⌐ kara su⌐kka⌐ri tu⌐ka⌐rete simatte, kyo⌐o wa zeñzeñ ⌐geñki
(ḡa) ⌐na⌐i ñ desu.

(b)

(Mr. Tanaka is talking to his good friend, Mr. Yamamoto.)

Mr. Tanaka

wherever [someone]
 goes

do⌐ko e i⌐tte⌐ mo

16. Nowadays wherever you go
 it's crowded; (so) isn't it
 awful!

Kono-ḡoro wa ⌐do⌐ko e i⌐tte⌐ mo
⌐ko⌐mu kara ko⌐ma⌐ru ⌐ne⌐e.

Mr. Yamamoto

on days off

ya⌐sumi no hi⌐ ni wa <u>or</u>
ya⌐sumi no hi⌐ nyaa

not go anywhere
do such things as read
 and see

do⌐ko e mo ikanai
yo⌐ñdari ⌐mi⌐tari suru

17. Uh huh. On days off, instead
 of going anywhere, it's better
 to loaf around at home, reading books and magazines and
 watching television.

N̄. Ya⌐sumi no hi⌐ nyaa; doko e
mo ikazu ni; uti de ⌐ho⌐ñ ya za-
⌐ssi yo⌐ñdari, te⌐rebi ⌐mi⌐tari
site; a⌐sobu ho⌐o ḡa ⌐i⌐i yo.

Mr. Tanaka

not do anything <u>or</u>
 do nothing
nap
take a nap
do something like
 take a nap

nani mo sinai

hirune
hirune (o) suru
hi⌐rune (o) sita⌐ri suru

18. Me—I take a nap or something at home instead of doing anything.

Boku wa na⌐ni mo sina⌐i de, uti
de hi⌐rune sita⌐ri site_

Mr. Yamamoto

whatever [someone] says
the act of resting
resting is best

na⌐ñ te i⌐tte⌐ mo
ya⌐su⌐mu koto
ya⌐su⌐mu koto ḡa i⌐ti⌐bañ
da

19. Whatever you say, on days
 of rest, rest is best.

Na⌐ñ te i⌐tte⌐ mo; ya⌐sumi no
hi⌐ nyaa, ya⌐su⌐mu koto ḡa i⌐ti-
bañ da yo.

Mr. Tanaka

is young	wa⌐ka⌝i /-ku/
the interval during which [someone] is young	wa⌐ka⌝i uti
unconcerned <u>or</u> indifferent <u>or</u> unmoved	heeki /na/

20. Uh huh. While we were young we were a match for everything (but), weren't we.

N̄, wa⌐ka⌝i uti wa, na⌐n̄ de⌝ mo he⌐eki da⌐tta ḡa ⌐he⌝e.

old person	to⌐siyori⌝ [1]
for an old person	to⌐siyori⌝ ni wa <u>or</u> to⌐siyori⌝ nyaa
care-taking	rusubañ
take care of the house during the absence of others	rusubañ (o) suru

21. For old people, it's better to take care of the house while the others are away, than to go out to look at the cherry blossoms.

To⌐siyori⌝ nyaa, ha⌐nami⌝ ni de-⌐kakeru yo⌝ri ru⌐subañ suru ho⌝o ḡa ⌐i⌝i yo.

we <u>or</u> us	bo⌝kutati
gradually	dañdañ
is troublesome <u>or</u> tiresome	me⌐n̄dookusa⌝i /-ku/

22. I suppose we aren't old yet but gradually cherry-blossom viewing has grown to be tiresome, hasn't it.

Bo⌝kutati wa ⌐ma⌝da to⌐siyori⌝ zya ⌐na⌝i daroo kedo, dañdañ ha⌐nami⌝ ḡa me⌐n̄dookusa⌝ku ⌐na⌝tta ⌐he⌝e.

(c)

(A young man is talking to his girl friend.)

Taro

you	kimi
any number of times	na⌝n̄-do mo

23. I telephoned your place any number of times yesterday but no one answered.

Kinoo ki̅mi no toko e ⌐na⌝n̄-do mo de⌐n̄wa-sita⌝ kedo, da⌐re mo de⌝nakatta yo⌐

24. What happened?

Do⌝o sita no? [2]

Haruko

25. Oh, we were (gone) on an excursion to Kamakura.

A⌝a, Ka⌐makura e asobi ni itte⌝ ta no yo⌐

---

[1] Alternate accent: to⌐siyo⌝ri.

[2] Note the use of the ——— no? pattern by a man in talking to his girl friend.

| | is hard of hearing | mi⌐mi⌐ ḡa tŏoi |
| 26. | My grandfather was watching the house but he's hard of hearing so he probably couldn't hear the phone. | O⌐zi⌐isañ ḡa ru⌐subañ site⌐ ta kedo; a⌐no⌐ hito mi⌐mi⌐ ḡa to⌐oi⌐ kara, deñwa ki⌐koena⌐katta ñ desyoo. |

Taro

| 27. | Oh. | So⌐o ka. |
| 28. | How was Kamakura? | Kamakura ⌐do⌐o datta? |

Haruko

29.	It was lots of fun.	To⌐ttemo omosi⌐rokatta wa⌐
	swim	o⌐yo⌐ḡu /-u/
	go sight-seeing	keñbutu-suru
	do such things as swim and go sight-seeing	o⌐yo⌐idari ke⌐ñbutu-sita⌐ri suru
30.	We swam and went sight-seeing . . .	O⌐yo⌐idari ke⌐ñbutu-sita⌐ri site⌐

Taro

| | whenever [someone] goes | i⌐tu i⌐tte⌐ mo |
| 31. | Whenever you go there, that place is always fun, isn't it. | Asuko wa ⌐i⌐tu i⌐tte⌐ mo o⌐mosiro⌐i ⌐ne⌐e. |

NOTES ON THE BASIC DIALOGUES

12. Asobu is the opposite of hataraku. Depending on context, it can mean 'play,' 'be at leisure,' 'have a good time,' 'visit (for pleasure),' 'loaf,' 'be unemployed,' etc.

17. Nya or nyaa is the contracted equivalent of ni wa, used more commonly by men.

20. Uti 'interval' also follows nominals of time + no meaning 'the interval of ——,' 'within ——,' 'during ——.' Examples: i⌐k-ka⌐ḡetu no uti 'within a month'; sono hi no uti 'during that day.' Compare also A to B to C no uti 'among A and B and C' (Lesson 15, Grammatical Note 3).
    Note: heeki de suru 'do [it] with unconcern,' 'make nothing of it'; heeki na kao o suru 'look unconcerned' (lit. 'make an unconcerned face [i. e. expression]').

23. Kimi is the informal equivalent of a⌐na⌐ta, more typical of men's speech. A person addressed as kimi is always a close friend or an inferior of the speaker.

25. Asobi ni iku 'go for fun.' See the note on sentence 12 above.

26. Note the use of the honorific (⌐) o⌐zi⌐isañ in reference to one's own grandfather. This is normal usage among young people, as a sign of respect for age.

GRAMMATICAL NOTES

1. The Representative

Miˈtari		miˈru 'see.'
Yoˈndari		yoˈmu 'read.'
Noˈndari		noˈmu 'drink.'
Saˈwaˈidari	is the REPRESENTATIVE of	saˈwaˈḡu 'make noise.'
Oˈyoˈidari		oˈyoˈḡu 'swim.'
Siˈtaˈri		suru 'do.'

Inflected words (verbals, adjectivals, and copula) have REPRESENTATIVE forms which are made by adding -ri to the corresponding past. If the past is accented, the representative is accented on the same syllable; if the past is unaccented, the representative is accented on the next-to-last syllable (ta). Thus:

	Non-past	Past	Representative
Verbals	taˈberu 'eat'	taˈbeta	taˈbetari
	kau 'buy'	katta	kaˈttaˈri
	oˈssyaˈru 'say'	oˈssyaˈtta	oˈssyaˈttari
	kuˈru 'come'	kiˈtaˈ [1]	kiˈtaˈri
Adjectivals	aˈtuˈi 'is hot'	aˈtukatta	aˈtukattari
	akai 'is red'	aˈkaˈkatta	aˈkaˈkattari
	iˈi/yoˈi 'is good'	yoˈkatta	yoˈkattari
	taˈbeˈnai 'doesn't eat'	taˈbeˈnakatta	taˈbeˈnakattari
	taˈbetaˈi 'want to eat'	taˈbetaˈkatta	taˈbetaˈkattari
Copula	da	daˈtta	daˈttari

A formal verbal ending in -maˈsu has a corresponding representative ending in -maˈsitari.

The representative is a tenseless form. It is used to indicate one action or state among several; [2] these may or may not be specifically mentioned. Most commonly, representatives occur in pairs, A and B, followed by √suru 'do.' A and B may follow each other directly (in which case they are never the same word) or they may be preceded by modifiers (in which case they may be the same or different words).

Such a combination of representatives plus √suru may refer (1) to typical actions or states (that is, those mentioned represent a longer list of similar actions or states): 'do (or be) such things as A and B,' 'do (or be) A and B and so on.'

Examples:

Saˈra o arattaˈri, heˈyaˈ o kaˈtazuˈketari site imasu.
    'She's washing the dishes, straightening up the rooms, and so on.'

---

[1] Alternate accent: kiˈta.

[2] The several actions or states may be different or the same one repeated.

Be⌐ñkyoo-sita⌐ri, te⌐gami o ka⌐itari si⌐ma⌐sita.
  'I did things like studying and writing letters.'
Ho⌐ñ o ⌐yo⌐ñdari, za⌐ssi o yoñdari simasu.
  'I read books and (I read) magazines and so on.'

And/or the combination may refer (2) to repeated or alternating actions or
states: 'keep doing A and B' or 'do A and B, A and B.'

  Examples:

De⌐tari ⌐ha⌐ittari si⌐ma⌐sita.
  'He kept going out and coming in.'
A⌐tukattari ⌐sa⌐mukattari simasu.
  'It's hot and cold, hot and cold.'
A⌐tuku ⌐na⌐ttari, sa⌐muku ⌐na⌐ttari simasu.
  'It gets hot and (gets) cold, hot and cold.'

And/or the combination may refer (3) to differing actions or states of members of a group, occurring at the same time: 'some do A while others do
B.'

  Example:

Tomodati wa; de⌐ñsya ni no⌐tta⌐ri, zi⌐buñ no kuruma ni notta⌐ri site
  i⌐kima⌐sita.
  My friends went, some in the (electric) train and some in their own
    cars.'

Representative forms may also occur singly or in groups of three or more,
with the same kinds of meanings. [1] Thus:

U⌐ti o soozi-sita⌐ri si⌐ma⌐sita.
  'She cleaned the house and so on.'
Ko⌐nakattari si⌐ma⌐su kara, ko⌐ma⌐tte imasu.
  'It's annoying because time and again he doesn't come.'
Be⌐ñkyoo-sita⌐ri, ho⌐ñ o ⌐yo⌐ñdari, te⌐gami o ka⌐itari si⌐ma⌐sita.
  'I did things like studying and reading books and writing letters.'
Sara wa, ka⌐tta⌐ri tu⌐katta⌐ri ko⌐wa⌐sitari site imasu.
  'I keep buying, using, and breaking plates.'
Tomodati wa; de⌐ñsya ni no⌐tta⌐ri, ba⌐su ni no⌐tta⌐ri, zi⌐buñ no ku-
  ruma ni notta⌐ri site i⌐kima⌐sita.
  'My friends went, some in (electric) trains, some in busses, and
    some in their own cars.'

A representative form—or a sequence of such forms—is not always immediately followed by √suru. It sometimes occurs at the end of an accent
phrase without following particle, as a modifier of an inflected word or phrase,
and sometimes it immediately precedes √da. The uses of the representa-
tive(s) in such cases are the same—to indicate typical, repeated, alternating,
and/or distributive actions or states. Thus:

Be⌐ñkyoo-sita⌐ri, te⌐gami o ka⌐itari, to⌐temo isoga⌐sikatta.
  'What with studying and writing letters (and so on), I was very busy.'

---
[1] Obviously there are no examples of a single representative form having
the last-mentioned kind of meaning.

A⌐me dattari, yu⌐ki⌐ dattari desu.
'It's (being) rain and snow, rain and snow.'

Additional examples:

Ni⌐ho⌐n̄ e ki⌐te⌐ kara, ma⌐initi ni⌐hon̄go o hana⌐sitari ⌐yon̄dari si⌐te ima⌐su kara; zu⌐ibun̄ zyo⌐ozu⌐ ni na⌐rima⌐sita.
'Ever since coming to Japan, he's been speaking and reading Japanese every day, so he's grown to be awfully good at it.'
Okaḡesama de ⌐zu⌐ibun̄ ⌐ge⌐n̄ki ni ⌐na⌐tte; ne⌐ta⌐ri ⌐o⌐kitari de⌐ki⌐ru yoo ni na⌐rima⌐sita.
'I'm much better, thank you, and I've reached the point where I can alternate between being in bed and getting up.'
A⌐no mise no mono⌐ wa; to⌐ki⌐ ni yotte, ya⌐sukattari ⌐ta⌐kakattari su⌐ru yo⌐o desu.
'The things in that store seem to be sometimes cheap and sometimes high, depending on the time.'
A⌐no⌐ hito wa; hi ni yotte, yo⌐ku be⌐n̄kyoo-sita⌐ri ze⌐n̄zen̄ sina⌐kattari su⌐ru⌐ n̄ desu.
'He goes back and forth between studying hard and not studying at all, depending on the day.'
Kono-ḡoro wa; a⌐me dattari yu⌐ki⌐ dattari site, i⌐i ⌐te⌐n̄ki no hi wa ze⌐n̄zen̄ na⌐i n̄ desu.
'It keeps raining and snowing these days, and there are no pleasant days at all.'
Ho⌐ka no hito no heya⌐ o, kikazu ni a⌐keta⌐ri si⌐te⌐ wa i⌐kemase⌐n̄.
'You mustn't open [the door of] other people's rooms (or do other such things) without asking.'

2. Interrogative + mo

In previous lessons, there have been a few occurrences of interrogatives (question words like da⌐re 'who?' do⌐ko 'where?' etc.) followed by particle mo:

Da⌐re mo demase⌐n̄. 'Nobody answers.'
I⌐tu mo go-⌐zi-han̄-ḡo⌐ro kaerimasu. 'I always go home at about 5:30.'

In general, it can be said that an interrogative + mo before a negative has an all-exclusive meaning, and before an affirmative an all-inclusive meaning; but occurrences before negatives are more numerous.

The following chart includes the more frequent kinds of occurrence:

Interrogative	+ mo	+ Negative	+ Affirmative
da⌐re 'who?'	da⌐re mo	'nobody,' 'not anybody'	
na⌐ni 'what?'	na⌐ni mo	'nothing,' 'not anything'	
do⌐ko 'what place?'	do⌐ko mo	'no place,' 'not any place'	
i⌐tu 'when?'	i⌐tu mo		'always'
do⌐tira 'which (of 2)?'	do⌐tira mo	'neither one,' 'not either one'	'both'

---

[1] Interrogative + mo often occurs with an unaccented alternant.

Interrogative	+ _mo_	+ Negative	+ Affirmative
do¬re 'which (of 3 or more)?'	do¬re mo	'not one (of 3 or more)'	'every one (of 3 or more)'
i¬kura 'how much?'	i¬kura mo	'no large amount'	
i¬ku-tu 'how many?'	i¬ku-tu mo	'no large number'	'a large number'
do¬no eñpitu[1] 'which pencil?'	do¬no eñpi-tu[1] mo	'no pencil'	'every pencil'
do¬ñna eñpitu[1] 'what kind of pencil?'	do¬ñna eñ-pitu[1] mo	'no kind of pencil'	'every kind of pencil'
na¬ñ-boñ[2] 'how many long cylindrical units?'	na¬ñ-boñ mo	'no large number of long cylindrical units'	'a large number of long cylindrical units'

Remember that _mo_ replaces particles g̱a, wa, and o but follows other particles. Compare:

Da⌐re g̱a ki┌ma┐sita ka⌐   Da⌐re mo kimase┐ñ desita.
  'Who came?'   'Nobody came.'
Na⌐ni o ta┌bema┐sita ka⌐   Na⌐ni mo tabemase┐ñ desita.
  'What did you eat?'   'I didn't eat anything.'
Da⌐re ni ki┌kima┐sita ka⌐   Da⌐re ni mo kikimase┐ñ desita.
  'Whom did you ask?'   'I didn't ask anybody.'
Do⌐ko e i┌kima┐sita ka⌐   Do⌐ko e mo ikimase┐ñ desita.
  'Where did you go?'   'I didn't go anywhere.'

Additional Examples:

Da⌐re mo wakarimase┐ñ. 'Nobody understands.'
Na⌐ni mo wakarimase┐ñ. 'I don't understand anything.'
Do⌐ko de mo hataraite imase┐ñ. 'I'm not working anywhere.'
I┐tu mo de⌐ki┌ru tte i┌ima┐su g̱a, de⌐kimase┐ñ ⌐ne┐e. 'He always says that he can do it, but he can't, can he!'
Hu┌ta-tu kaima┐sita g̱a, do⌐tira mo yo┌ku a┌rimase┐ñ. 'I bought two but neither one is [any] good.'
Uti no ko wa do⌐tira mo oñna┐ desu. 'Our children are both girls.'
Kinoo a⌐tarasi┐i zassi o ta⌐kusañ kaima┐sita g̱a, ma┐da do⌐re mo yomi-mase┐ñ. 'Yesterday I bought lots of new magazines but I haven't read any of them yet.'
Koko ni ni⌐hoñg̱o no ho┐ñ g̱a ta⌐kusañ arima┐su g̱a, dore mo mu⌐zuka-si┐i desu. 'There are lots of Japanese books here but every one of them is difficult.'
Su┌ko┐si wa a⌐rima┐su g̱a, i┌kura mo arimase┐ñ. 'There is a little but there isn't any large amount.'
Mi-┌ttu-g̱u┐rai i┌rima┐su g̱a, i┌ku-tu mo i┌rimase┐ñ. 'I need about three but I don't need a large number.'

---

[1] Eñpitu represents any nominal.

[2] Hoñ /-boñ/ represents any counter.

Hoñ wa iꜜku-tu mo arimaꜜsu ḡa, yoꜜmu zikañ ḡa aꜛrimaseꜜñ kara‿ 'I have any number of books but I have no time to read so. . . '

Koko no ꜛdoꜜno kimono mo ꜛkiꜜree zya aꜛrimaseꜜñ ˥neꜜe. 'Not one of the kimonos here is pretty, is it!'

Koꜛre mo simaitaꜜi ñ desu ḡa, doꜛno hako mo iꜛppai deꜜsu kara‿ 'I'd like to put these away too, but every box is full so. . . '

Kono-ḡoro ꜛdoꜛnna ziꜛdoꜜosya mo ꜛyaꜜsuku aꜛrimaseꜜñ. 'Nowadays no kind of car is cheap.'

Siꜛroꜜi kaꜛmiꜜ wa ꜛmaꜜda aꜛrimaꜜsu ḡa, aꜛoꜜi kaꜛmiꜜ wa ꜛmoꜜo naꜛñ-mai mo arimaseꜜñ. 'There is still some white paper but there aren't many more sheets of blue paper.'

Eꜜñpitu wa naꜛñ-boñ mo aꜛrimaꜜsu ḡa, peꜜñ wa ꜛiꜜp-poñ sika aꜛrimaseꜜñ. 'I have any number of pencils but I have only one pen.'

3. doꜜko e iꜛtteꜜ mo

Reread Lesson 15, Grammatical Note 4.

A verbal or adjectival gerund plus particle <u>mo</u> — as well as the copula gerund <u>de</u> plus <u>mo</u> — may follow an interrogative; the sequence has a generalized rather than an interrogative meaning, and is tenseless.

Compare the following pairs:

Naꜜñ desu ka‿ 'What is it?'   naꜜñ de mo 'whatever it is,' 'no matter what it is'

Naꜜni ḡa aꜛrimaꜜsu ka‿ 'What is there?'   naꜜni ḡa ꜛaꜜtte mo 'whatever there is,' 'no matter what there is'

Naꜜni o taꜛbemaꜜsu ka‿ 'What are you going to eat?'   naꜜni o ꜛtaꜜbete mo 'whatever [someone] eats,' 'no matter what [someone] eats'

Doꜜko e iꜛkimaꜜsu ka‿ 'Where are you going?'   doꜜko e iꜛtteꜜ mo 'wherever [someone] goes,' 'no matter where [someone] goes'

Doꜜko kara kiꜛmaꜜsu ka‿ 'Where do you come from?' [1]   doꜜko kara kiꜛteꜜ mo 'wherever [someone] comes from,' 'no matter where [someone] comes from'

Daꜜre ḡa kiꜛmaꜜsu ka‿ 'Who is coming?'   daꜜre ḡa kiꜛteꜜ mo 'whoever comes,' 'no matter who comes'

Daꜜre ni aꜛitaꜜi ñ desu ka‿ 'Who is it you want to see?'   daꜜre ni aꜛitaꜜkute mo 'whomever [someone] wants to see,' 'no matter whom [someone] wants to see'

Naꜜñ-zi ni iꜛkitaꜜi ñ desu ka‿ 'At what time do you want to go?'   naꜜñ-zi ni iꜛkitaꜜkute mo 'at whatever time [someone] wants to go,' 'no matter what time [someone] wants to go'

---

[1] I. e. in general, whenever you come here.

Examples:

Do⁷ko e i⁺tte⁴ mo To⁽okyoo wa yakamasi⁷i kara, su⌐ki⁷ zya ⌐na⁷i ñ desu.
  'No matter where I go Tokyo is noisy so I don't like it.'
Mo⁷o ⌐yo⁷ku na⌐rima⁴sita kara, na⁷ni o si⁺te⁴ mo ka⌐maimase⁷ñ.
  'I've recovered now so whatever I do it's all right.'
Do⁷no zi⁺biki⁴ o ⌐mi⁴te mo, ko⌐no i⁷mi wa wa⌐karimase⁷ñ desita.
  'No matter what dictionary I looked at, I couldn't tell the meaning of
  this.'
I⁷tu ko⌐no depa⁴ato ni ki⁺te⁴ mo, hi⌐to⁷ de i⌐ppai de⁷su ⌐ne⁴e.
  'No matter when you come to this department store it's filled with
  people, isn't it!'
I⌐kura ⌐ma⁴tte mo, a⌐no⁷ hito wa ki⌐mase⁷ñ desita.
  'No matter how long I waited, he didn't come.'
I⌐kura ⌐ta⁴kakute mo, a⌐re ga kaita⁷i ñ desu.
  'No matter how (much) expensive it is, that's the one I want to buy.'

4. Sentence-final Gerund [+ ne⁷e] in Non-request Sentences

Reread the note on fragments (Lesson 4, Grammatical Note 5).

In conversation, a gerund (verbal, adjectival, or copula) ending in suspensive intonation ( ) or a gerund + ne⁷e often occurs in sentence-final position, when the speaker is about to say more that is coordinate with what has just been said ('X is true and—Y is true'), or when the speaker assumes that the listener understands something coordinate without his continuing ('X is true and—you know the rest').

Usually each such occurrence of ne⁷e following a gerund is acknowledged by the listener either by word or gesture.

For examples, see Basic Sentences 4, 9, 11, 12, 18, and 30 in this lesson.

5. Verbal + made

Made was introduced previously, following a nominal of place meaning 'as far as,' and following a nominal of time meaning 'until,' 'up to and including.'

In this lesson, it follows a verbal in its informal non-past (NEVER past) form, meaning 'until.' The subject of the verbal, if expressed, is usually followed by particle ga. Thus:

  ku⁷ru made 'until [someone] comes or came'
  se⌐ñse⁷e ga ⌐ku⁴ru made 'until the teacher comes or came'

A sequence consisting of a verbal + made is accented on the verbal; the verbal acquires an accent on its final syllable if it is normally unaccented.

Examples:

  Ta⌐naka-sañ ga ku⁷ru made ⌐ma⁴tte kudasai.
    'Please wait until Mr. Tanaka comes.'
  Hu⁷ne ga ⌐de⁴ru made Yo⌐kohama ni ima⁷sita.
    'I stayed in Yokohama until the ship left.'

A⌈tarasi⌉i no o mo⌐rau⌐ made hu⌐ru⌐i no o tukaimasu.
'Until I get a new one I'll use the old one.'

6. Particle <u>ni</u> of Reference

The particle <u>ni</u> follows a nominal indicating the person in reference to whom something is true.

Examples:

A⌈na⌉ta ni ti⌐isasuḡi⌐ru kara_
'Since it's too small for you...'
To⌐siyori⌉ ni wa mu⌐zukasi⌐i desyoo ḡa, wa⌐ka⌉i hito ni wa he⌐eki de⌐su.
'For old people it's probably difficult but for young people it's nothing at all.'

7. Pluralizing Suffixes

Most Japanese nominals do not distinguish between singular and plural; but bo⌉ku 'I,' watukusi 'I,' kimi 'you,' and a⌈na⌉ta 'you,' which are always singular, are exceptions. The plural of these words is made by adding one of a number of pluralizing suffixes, for example -<u>tati</u> or the honorific -ḡata † . [1] Other nominals denoting persons, which in their basic form refer to one or more than one without distinction, may also occur with these suffixes to denote specific plurals. Thus:

hi⌐to⌉ 'person' or 'persons' or 'people'—but hi⌐to⌉tati 'persons' or 'people'
kodomo 'child' or 'children'—but ko⌐domo⌉tati 'children'
hya⌐kusyo⌉o 'farmer' or 'farmers'—but hya⌐kusyo⌉otati 'farmers'
ka⌐ta⌉† 'person' or 'persons' or 'people'—but ka⌐ta⌉ḡata † 'persons' or 'people'

Note also: Tanaka-sañ-tati 'Mr. Tanaka and the others (of a particular group).'

DRILLS

A. Substitution Drill

1. For old people it's in-   To⌐siyori⌉ ni wa o⌐mosiro⌐i de-
    teresting (but)... [2]   su ḡa_
2. For old people it's dif-   To⌐siyori⌉ ni wa <u>mu⌐zukasi⌐i</u>
    ficult (but)...   <u>desu</u> ḡa_
3. For old people it's bor-   To⌐siyori⌉ ni wa <u>tu⌐marana⌐i</u>
    ing (but)...   <u>desu</u> ḡa_

_____

[1] -Ḡata is never added to bo⌉ku, watakusi, or kimi since it is an honorific (†) suffix.

[2] 'but—not for everyone.'

4. For old people it's easy
   (but)...
   To⌐siyori⌐ ni wa ya⌐sasi⌐i desu
   ḡa—

5. For old people it doesn't
   matter (but)...
   To⌐siyori⌐ ni wa ka⌐maimase⌐ñ
   ḡa—

6. For old people it's important (but)...
   To⌐siyori⌐ ni wa ta⌐isetu de⌐su
   ḡa—

7. For old people it's possible (but)...
   To⌐siyori⌐ ni wa de⌐kima⌐su ḡa—

8. For old people it's clear
   (but)...
   To⌐siyori⌐ ni wa wa⌐karima⌐su
   ḡa—

B. Substitution Drill

1. There's really a lot of
   rain, isn't there.
   A⌐me ḡa ho⌐ñtoo ni oo⌐i desu
   ne⌐e.

2. There's really a lot of
   snow, isn't there.
   Yu⌐ki⌐ ḡa ho⌐ñtoo ni oo⌐i desu
   ne⌐e.

3. There's an amazing
   amount of snow, isn't
   there.
   Yu⌐ki⌐ ḡa me⌐zura⌐siku o⌐o⌐i desu
   ne⌐e.

4. There's unusually little
   snow, isn't there.
   Yu⌐ki⌐ ḡa me⌐zura⌐siku su⌐kuna⌐i
   desu ne⌐e.

5. There are unusually few
   cherry trees, aren't
   there.
   Sakura ḡa me⌐zura⌐siku su⌐kuna⌐i
   desu ne⌐e.

6. There are very few
   cherry trees, aren't
   there.
   Sakura ḡa to⌐ttemo sukuna⌐i desu
   ne⌐e.

7. The cherry trees are
   very pretty, aren't they.
   Sakura ḡa to⌐ttemo ki⌐ree desu
   ne⌐e.

8. The trees are very
   pretty, aren't they.
   Ki⌐ ḡa to⌐ttemo ki⌐ree desu ne⌐e.

9. The trees are awfully
   pretty, aren't they.
   Ki⌐ ḡa zu⌐ibuñ ⌐ki⌐ree desu ne⌐e.

10. There are an awful lot
    of trees, aren't there.
    Ki⌐ ḡa zu⌐ibuñ o⌐o⌐i desu ne⌐e.

C. Substitution Drill (based on Grammatical Note 5)

1. I waited until I arrived
   in Tokyo.
   To⌐okyoo e tu⌐ku made ma⌐tima⌐-
   sita.

2. I waited until a friend
   came.
   To⌐modati ḡa ku⌐ru made ma⌐ti-
   ma⌐sita.

3. I waited until the ship
   went out.
   Hu⌐ne ḡa ⌐de⌐ru made ma⌐tima⌐-
   sita.

4. I waited until the movie
   began.
   E⌐eḡa ḡa hazimaru⌐ made ma⌐ti-
   ma⌐sita.

5. I waited until everyone
   stood up.
   Mi⌐ñna⌐ ḡa ⌐ta⌐tu made ma⌐tima⌐-
   sita.

6. I waited until the candy
   got hard.
   O⌐ka⌐si ḡa ka⌐taku na⌐ru made
   ma⌐tima⌐sita.

7. I waited until my car
   got old.

Kuˡruma ḡa huˡruku ᴷnaᴷru made
maˡtimaˡsita.

8. I waited until I recovered.

Geⁿki ni ᴷnaᴷru made maˡtima-
sita.

D. Substitution Drill

1. It's best to rest.

Yaˡsuˡmu koto ḡa iˡtiˡbañ desu.

2. It's important to rest.

Yaˡsuˡmu koto ḡa taˡisetu deˡsu.

3. It's important to go to
   bed early.

Haˡyaku neᴷru kotoˡ ḡa taˡisetu
deˡsu.

4. It's important to study
   at home.

Uˡti de beñkyoo-suru kotoˡ ḡa taˡisetu deˡsu.

5. I like to study at home.

Uˡti de beñkyoo-suru kotoˡ ḡa suˡkiˡ desu.

6. I like to swim.

Oˡyoˡḡu koto ḡa suˡkiˡ desu.

7. I like to sing (songs).

Uˡtaˡ (o) uᴷtau kotoˡ ḡa suˡkiˡ desu.

8. I like to take baths.

Oˡhuˡro ni ᴷhaˡiru koto ḡa suˡkiˡ
desu.

9. I like to eat with chopsticks.

Oˡhaˡsi de taᴷbeˡru koto ḡa suˡkiˡ
desu.

10. Can you eat with chop-
    sticks?

Oˡhaˡsi de taᴷbeˡru koto ḡa deˡkimaˡsu kaˑ

11. Can you read Japanese?

Niˡhoñḡo (o) yoˡmu koto ḡa deˡkimaˡsu kaˑ

12. Can you fix this watch?

Koˡno tokee (o) naoˡsu koto ḡa deˡkimaˡsu kaˑ

13. Can you walk?

Aˡruˡku koto ḡa deˡkimaˡsu kaˑ

E. Substitution Drill (based on Grammatical Note 1)

1. Singing songs and making
   a racket—you know!

Uˡtaˡ (o) uᴷtattaᴷri saˡwaˡidari
site ᴷneᴷe.

2. Eating and drinking—you
   know! /taˡbeˡru, noˡmu/

Taˡbetari ⁿoⁿdari site ᴷneᴷe.

3. Swimming and taking
   walks—you know!
   /oˡyoˡḡu, sañpo-suru/

Oˡyoˡidari saˡñpo-sitaˡri site
ᴷneᴷe.

4. Going on and off—you
   know! /kieru, tuˡku/

Kiˡetaˡri ˡtuˡitari site ᴷneᴷe.

5. Coming and going—you
   know! /iku, kuˡru/

Iˡttaˡri ˡkiˡtari site ᴷneᴷe.

6. Going out and coming in
   —you know! /deˡru,
   haˡiru/

Deˡtari ˡhaˡittari site ᴷneᴷe.

7. Sometimes understand-
   ing and sometimes not
   understanding—you
   know! /waˡkaˡru, waˡka-
   raˡnai/

Waˡkaˡttari waˡkaraˡnakattari
site ᴷneᴷe.

8. Being hot and cold, hot   Aˈtukattari ˈsaˈmukattari site ˈneˈe.
   and cold—you know!
   /aˈtuˈi, saˈmuˈi/

9. Sometimes tasting good   Oˈisiˈkattari ˈmaˈzukattari site
   and sometimes tasting   ˈneˈe.
   awful—you know!
   /oisii, maˈzuˈi/

10. Raining and snowing,   Aˈme dattari yuˈkiˈ dattari site
    raining and snowing—   ˈneˈe.
    you know! /aˈme da,
    yuˈkiˈ da/

F. Grammar Drill (based on Grammatical Note 3)

> Tutor: Toˈokyoo e itteˈ mo kaˈmaimaseˈñ. 'Even if you go to To-
>   kyo, it doesn't matter.'
> Student: Doˈko e iˈtteˈ mo kaˈmaimaseˈñ. 'Wherever you go it
>   doesn't matter.'

1. Soˈko ni oiteˈ mo kaˈmai-   Doˈko ni oˈiteˈ mo kaˈmaimaseˈñ.
   maseˈñ.

2. Toˈmodati ḡa itteˈ mo   Daˈre ḡa iˈtteˈ mo kaˈmaimaseˈñ.
   kaˈmaimaseˈñ.

3. Siˈḡoto (o) siteˈ mo ka-   Naˈni (o) siˈteˈ mo kaˈmaimaseˈñ.
   ˈmaimaseˈñ.

4. Tiˈisaˈi hoo ni siˈteˈ mo   Doˈtira ni siˈteˈ mo kaˈmaima-
   kaˈmaimaseˈñ.   seˈñ.

5. Iˈtibañ tiisaˈi no ni siˈteˈ   Doˈre ni siˈteˈ mo kaˈmaimaseˈñ.
   mo kaˈmaimaseˈñ.

6. Ni-ˈdo miˈte mo kaˈmai-   Naˈñ-do ˈmiˈte mo kaˈmaimaseˈñ.
   maseˈñ.

7. Aˈsita miˈte mo kaˈmai-   Iˈtu ˈmiˈte mo kaˈmaimaseˈñ.
   maseˈñ.

G. Substitution Drill (based on Grammatical Note 3)

1. Wherever I go it's crowded   Doˈko e iˈtteˈ mo ˈkoˈmu kara,
   (so) it's annoying.   koˈmarimaˈsu.

2. No matter what kind of   Doˈñna yoˈohuku (o) kiteˈ mo
   Western-style clothes I   niˈawaˈnai kara, koˈmarimaˈsu.
   wear they aren't becom-
   ing (so) it's annoying.
   /doˈñna yoohuku (o) kiru,
   niˈawaˈnai/

3. Whatever I learn I for-   Naˈni (o) oˈboˈete mo waˈsure-
   get (so) it's annoying.   ruˈ kara, koˈmarimaˈsu.
   /naˈni (o) oˈboeˈru, wa-
   sureru/

4. Whenever I telephone   Iˈtu deˈñwa-siteˈ mo ˈruˈsu da
   he's out (so) it's annoy-   kara, koˈmarimaˈsu.
   ing. /iˈtu deñwa-suru,
   ˈruˈsu da/

5. However he says it I
   don't understand (so)
   it's annoying. /do⌐o
   iu, wa⌐kara⌐nai/

   Do⌐o i┕tte⌐ mo wa⌐kara⌐nai kara,
   ko⌐marima⌐su.

6. Whatever I ask he
   doesn't know (so) it's
   annoying. /na⌐ni (o)
   kiku, siranai/

   Na⌐ni (o) ki┕ite⌐ mo si⌐rana⌐i kara,
   ko⌐marima⌐su.

7. No matter what kind of
   work I do I get tired
   (so) it's annoying.
   /do⌐nna sig̃oto (o) suru,
   tu⌐kare⌐ru/

   Do⌐nna si┕g̃oto (o) site⌐ mo tu⌐ka-
   re⌐ru kara, ko⌐marima⌐su.

8. No matter how many
   hours I study I can't
   remember (so) it's
   annoying. /na⌐ñ-zi⌐-
   kañ beñkyoo-suru, o⌐bo-
   erare⌐nai/

   Na⌐ñ-zi⌐kañ be┕ñkyoo-site⌐ mo
   o⌐boerare⌐nai kara, ko⌐marima⌐su.

H. Response Drill (based on Grammatical Note 2)

> Tutor: Do⌐ko e i┕kima⌐sita ka↲ 'Where did you go?'
> Student: Do⌐ko e mo ikimase⌐ñ desita. 'I didn't go anywhere.'

1. Da⌐re o ya┕toima⌐sita ka↲
2. Da⌐re g̃a ru┕subañ (o)
   sima⌐su ka↲
3. Do⌐re o tu┕kaima⌐sita
   ka↲
4. Do⌐tira g̃a su┕ki⌐ desu
   ka↲
5. Do⌐ko de ha┕taraite
   (i)ma⌐su ka↲
6. Do⌐re ni i┕rema⌐sita ka↲
7. Na⌐ni g̃a i┕rima⌐su ka↲
8. Do⌐nna ha┕na⌐ g̃a sa┕ite
   (i)ma⌐su ka↲

Da⌐re mo yatoimase⌐ñ desita.
Da⌐re mo rusubañ (o) simase⌐ñ.

Do⌐re mo tukaimase⌐ñ desita.

Do⌐tira mo suki⌐ zya a┕rima-
se⌐ñ.
Do⌐ko de mo hataraite (i)mase⌐ñ.

Do⌐re ni mo iremase⌐ñ desita.
Na⌐ni mo irimase⌐ñ.
Do⌐nna ha┕na⌐ mo sa┕ite (i)ma-
se⌐ñ.

I. Response Drill (based on Grammatical Note 2)

> Tutor: Na⌐ñ-do de┕ñwa-sita⌐ desyoo ka↲ 'How many times do
>   you suppose he called?'
> Student: Na⌐ñ-do mo de┕ñwa-sita⌐ to omoimasu. 'I think he called
>   any number of times.'

1. Do⌐tira g̃a o┕isi⌐i desyoo
   ka.
2. I┕ku-tu mo┕ratta⌐ desyoo
   ka.

Do⌐tira mo oisi⌐i to omoimasu.

I┕kutu mo mo┕ratta⌐ to omoimasu.

3. I˥tu a˥ite (i)ru˧ desyoo ka.

I˥tu mo a˥ite (i)ru˧ to omoimasu.

4. Na˥ñ-mai tu˥kau˧ de-syoo ka.

Na˥ñ-mai mo tu˥kau˧ to omoima-su.

5. Mo˥o na˥ñ-neñ i˥ru˧ de-syoo ka.

Mo˥o na˥ñ-neñ mo i˥ru˧ to omoi-masu.

6. Mo˥o nañ-ka˥ḡetu tu˥zu-ku˧ desyoo ka.

Mo˥o nañ-ka˥ḡetu mo tu˥zuku˧ to omoimasu.

7. Na˥ñ-niñ ˥de˧ru desyoo ka.

Na˥ñ-niñ mo ˥de˧ru to omoimasu.

J. Level Drill [1]

1. To˥siyori˥ nyaa o˥mosi-ro˥i daroo kedo⌣

To˥siyori˥ ni wa o˥mosiro˥i da-roo keredo.

2. Zya˥a, tu˥zukemasyo˥o.

De˥ wa, tu˥zukemasyo˥o.

3. Tu˥ma˥ñnai desyoo—ko˥-˥ñna e˥eḡa ḡa.

Tu˥mara˥nai desyoo—ko˥ñna e˥eḡa ḡa.

4. A˥tta˥kaku na˥rima˥sita ˥ne˥e.

A˥tata˥kaku na˥rima˥sita ˥ne˥e.

5. I˥tte rassya˥i.

I˥tte irassya˥i.

6. Sa˥wa˥izyaa i˥kemase˥ñ yo⌣

Sa˥wa˥ide wa i˥kemase˥ñ yo⌣

7. Sakura wa ˥mo˥o sa˥ite ma˥su ka⌣

Sakura wa ˥mo˥o sa˥ite ima˥su ka⌣

8. Ki˥noo tukattyatta˥ kara, mo˥o a˥rimase˥ñ.

Ki˥noo tukatte simatta˥ kara, mo˥o a˥rimase˥ñ.

K. Expansion Drill

1. I don't go out.
   De˥kakemase˥ñ.

   I don't go out very much.
   A˥ñmari dekakemase˥ñ.

   I don't go out very much these days.
   Kono-ḡoro wa a˥ñmari dekake-mase˥ñ.

   I worry so I don't go out very much these days.
   Si˥ñpai-suru˥ kara, kono-ḡoro wa a˥ñmari dekakemase˥ñ.

   Even if I have someone stay at the house for me I worry, so I don't go out very much these days.
   Ru˥subañ (o) site moratte˥ mo, si˥ñpai-suru˥ kara; kono-ḡoro wa a˥ñmari dekake-mase˥ñ.

   No matter who stays at the house for me I worry, so I don't go out very much these days.
   Da˥re ni ru˥subañ (o) site moratte˧ mo, si˥ñpai-suru˥ kara; kono-ḡoro wa a˥ñ-mari dekakemase˥ñ.

2. I plan to do it.
   Su˥ru tumori de˥su.

   I plan to do things like going sight-seeing.
   Ke˥ñbutu-sita˥ri suru tumori desu.

---

[1] In each case the sentence on the right contains the uncontracted equivalent of contractions in the sentence on the left.

I plan to do things like going to the country and go-
sight-seeing.

I⌐naka e itta⌐ri ke⌐ṅbutu-sita⌐ri
suru tumori desu.

When I am free I plan to do
things like going to the
country and going sight-
seeing.

Hi⌐ma na toki⌐ [ni], i⌐naka e itta⌐-
ri ke⌐ṅbutu-sita⌐ri suru tumori
desu.

Since I took the trouble to
come here, when I am free
I plan to do things like going to the country and going sight-seeing.

Se⌐kkaku kima⌐sita kara; hi⌐ma na
toki⌐ [ni], i⌐naka e itta⌐ri ke⌐ṅ-
butu-sita⌐ri suru tumori desu.

Since I came all the way to
Japan, when I am free I
plan to do things like going
to the country and going
sight-seeing.

Sekkaku Ni⌐ho⌐ṅ e ki⌐ma⌐sita kara;
hi⌐ma na toki⌐ [ni], i⌐naka e itta⌐ri
ke⌐ṅbutu-sita⌐ri suru tumori desu.

3. I stay home.

U⌐ti ni ima⌐su.

I stay home, looking
after the children
and so on.

Ko⌐domo (o) mi⌐tari site, u⌐ti ni
ima⌐su.

I stay home, watching
the house, looking
after the children,
and so on.

Ru⌐subaṅ (o) sita⌐ri ko⌐domo (o)
mi⌐tari site, u⌐ti ni ima⌐su.

I stay home, always
watching the house,
looking after the
children, and so on.

I⌐tu mo ru⌐subaṅ (o) sita⌐ri kodomo (o) mi⌐tari site, u⌐ti ni
ima⌐su.

Instead of going any-
where, I stay home,
always watching the
house, looking after
the children, and so
on.

Do⌐ko e mo ikana⌐i de; i⌐tu mo
ru⌐subaṅ (o) sita⌐ri ko⌐domo (o)
mi⌐tari site, u⌐ti ni ima⌐su.

I'm an old man [1] so in-
stead of going any-
where, I stay home,
always watching the
house, looking after
the children, and so
on.

To⌐siyori⌐ da kara, do⌐ko e mo
ikana⌐i de; i⌐tu mo ru⌐subaṅ (o)
sita⌐ri ko⌐domo (o) mi⌐tari site,
u⌐ti ni ima⌐su.

4. I think it's impossible.

De⌐ki⌐nai to omoimasu.

For old people I think
it's impossible.

To⌐siyori⌐ ni wa de⌐ki⌐nai to
omoimasu.

For young people it's
nothing at all, but for
old people I think it's
impossible.

Wa⌐ka⌐i hito ni wa he⌐eki de⌐su
ga, to⌐siyori⌐ ni wa de⌐ki⌐nai
to omoimasu.

----

[1] Or, of course, 'old woman.'

This kind of work is nothing at all for young people, but for old people I think it's impossible.	Koñna siḡoto wa waꞋkaꞋi hito ni wa heᴸeki deᴸsu ḡa, toꞋsiyoriꞋ ni wa deꞋkiꞋnai to omoimasu.
5. I've reached the point where I understand.	WaꞋkaꞋru yoo ni naᴸrimaᴸsita.
I've gradually reached the point where I understand.	Dañdañ waꞋkaꞋru yoo ni naᴸri-maᴸsita.
I'm doing things like listening to the Japanese radio so I've gradually reached the point where I understand.	NiꞋhoñ no raꞋzio (o) kiᴸitaᴸri siᴸte (i)ruᴸ kara, dañdañ wa-ꞋkaꞋru yoo ni naᴸrimaᴸsita.
I'm doing things like talking with Japanese and listening to the Japanese radio so I've gradually reached the point where I understand.	NiꞋhoñziꞋñ to haᴸnaᴸsitari, NiꞋhoñ no raꞋzio (o) kiᴸitaᴸri siᴸte (i)ruᴸ kara; dañdañ waꞋkaꞋru yoo ni naᴸrimaᴸsita.
I'm doing things like studying and talking with Japanese and listening to the Japanese radio so I've gradually reached the point where I understand.	BeꞋñkyoo-sitaꞋri, niꞋhoñziꞋñ to haᴸnaᴸsitari, NiꞋhoñ no raꞋzio (o) kiᴸitaᴸri siᴸte (i)ruᴸ kara; dañdañ waꞋkaꞋru yoo ni naᴸri-maᴸsita.
I didn't understand but I'm doing things like studying and talking with Japanese and listening to the Japanese radio so I've gradually reached the point where I understand.	WaꞋkaraꞋnakatta keredo; beꞋñkyoo-sitaꞋri, niꞋhoñziꞋñ to haᴸnaᴸsitari, NiꞋhoñ no raꞋzio (o) kiᴸitaᴸri siᴸte (i)ruᴸ kara; dañdañ waꞋkaꞋ-ru yoo ni naᴸrimaᴸsita.
I didn't understand at all but I'm doing things like studying and talking with Japanese and listening to the Japanese radio so I've gradually reached the point where I understand.	ZeꞋñzeñ wakaraꞋnakatta keredo; beꞋñkyoo-sitaꞋri, niꞋhoñziꞋñ to haᴸnaᴸsitari, NiꞋhoñ no raꞋzio (o) kiᴸitaᴸri siᴸte (i)ruᴸ kara; dañdañ waꞋkaꞋru yoo ni naᴸri-maᴸsita.
At the beginning I didn't understand at all but	Hazime wa zeꞋñzeñ wakaraꞋna-katta keredo; beꞋñkyoo-sitaꞋri,

I'm doing things like
studying and talking
with Japanese and
listening to the Jap-
anese radio so I've
gradually reached the
point where I under-
stand.

niˈhoñziˈñ to haˈnaᵈsitari, Niˈhoñ
no raˈzio (o) kiˈitaᵈri siˈte
(i)ruᵈ kara, dañdañ waˈkaˈru
yoo ni naˈrimaᵈsita.

BASIC DIALOGUES: RESTATEMENT

(with questions)

Dialogue (a)

Kotosi wa ˈaˈme ḡa oˈoˈi desu ḡa, kiˈnoˈo wa meˈzuraˈsiku ˈiᵈi ˈteᵈñki
desita. Tanaka-sañ wa kĩnoo ĩnaka e saˈkura o miˈ ni iˈkimaᵈsita. Sakura wa ˈmoˈo saˈite itaˈkara, kiˈree desita. Kooeñ wa haˈnami no hitoˈ de
ĩppai de; miñna oˈsake o noˈñdari, uˈtaˈ o uˈtattaᵈri siˈte imaᵈsita. Tanaka-
sañ wa õbeñtoo o motte itte, kiˈ no sita de taˈbemaᵈsita. Yuˈḡata maˈde
asoñde, sore kara kaˈerimaˈsita. Kaˈeri no deñsya ḡa koˈñde, Toˈokyoo e
tuˈku made zuˈtto taˈtte imasita. Daˈ kara; Tanaka-sañ wa suˈkkaˈri tuˈkaᵈ-
rete simatte, kyoˈo wa zeˈñzeñ geˈñki ḡa ˈnaᵈi soo desu.

Questions:

   1. Koˈtosi no teˈñki wa ˈdoˈo desu ka⌐
   2. Kĩnoo no teˈñki wa ˈdoˈo desita ka⌐
   3. Tanaka-sañ wa kĩnoo ˈnaˈni o siˈmaᵈsita ka⌐
   4. Haˈnami no hitoˈ wa ˈnaˈni o siˈte imaᵈsita ka⌐
   5. Tanaka-sañ wa ˈdoˈko de ˈnaˈni o taˈbemaᵈsita ka⌐
   6. Tanaka-sañ wa ˈkyoˈo wa ˈgeˈñki ḡa ˈnaˈi soo desu ḡa, doˈo site
       desu ka⌐

Dialogue (c)

Taˈroo-sañ wa kĩnoo ˈHaˈruko-sañ no uti e ˈnaˈñ-do mo deˈñwa-simaˈsita
ḡa, daˈre mo demaseˈñ desita. Haˈruko-sañ wa Kãmakura e ãsobi ni itte
ite, ruˈsu desita. Haˈruko-sañ no oˈziˈisañ ḡa ruˈsubañ o site imaˈsita keredo; miˈmiˈ ḡa toˈoiˈ kara, deñwa ḡa kiˈkoenaˈkatta ñ desyoo. Haˈruko-
sañ wa Kãmakura de oˈyoˈidari keˈñbutu-sitaˈri site aˈsobimaᵈsita ḡa, to-
ˈtemo omosiˈrokatta soo desu.

Questions:

   1. Taˈroo-sañ wa kĩnoo ˈHaˈruko-sañ to haˈnasimaˈsita ka⌐ Doˈo site
       desu ka⌐
   2. Daˈre ḡa ruˈsubañ o site imaᵈsita ka⌐
   3. Doˈo site soˈnoˈ hito wa deˈñwa ni deᵈnakatta desyoo ka.
   4. Haˈruko-sañ wa Kãmakura de ˈnaˈni o siˈmaᵈsita ka⌐

SHORT SUPPLEMENTARY DIALOGUES

1. Teacher A: Heꜜñ desu ꞈneꜜe. Suꞈmisu-sañ wa, hi ni yotte, yoꜜku waꜛkaˑ-
ttari zeꜛñzeñ wakaraꞈnakattaꜜri suꜛruˑ ñ desu yo⌐ Doꜜo site
desyoo.
   Teacher B: Hi ni yotte ꜛyoꜜku beꜛñkyoo-sitaˑri zeꜛñzeñ sinaꜜkattari su-
ꜛruˑ kara desyoo?
   Teacher A: Soꜜo desyoo ꞈneꜜe.

2. Taro: Nitiyoo ni Uꜛeno-koꜜoeñ e itte ꞈneˑe.
   Yukio: Aꜜa ꜛsoꜜo.
   Taro: *Zuꜜibuñ hiꜛto ḡa deꜜte ta yo⌐
   Yukio: Soꜜo daroo. Haꞈnami no hitoꜜ daroo? Sakura ꜛdoꜜo datta?
   Taro: Maꜜda suꜛkoꜜsi sika saꜛite inaˑkatta ḡa ꞈneꜜe. Kiꜜ no sita de hiꜛto
ḡa taꜛkusañ noꜛñdari saꜛwaꜜidari site ꞈneˑe.
   Yukio: Kimi mo?
   Taro: Boꜛku wa sake wa dameꜜ da kara ꞈneˑe. Beꜛñtoꜜo ꜛtaˑbete kita
yo.

3. Smith: Aꞈnataḡata niꜜ wa koꜛñna zassi ḡa omosiroˑi desyoo ḡa, waꜛta-
kusiꜜtati ni wa muꜛzukasisuḡiꜜru kara, zeꜛñzeñ omosiꜜroku ꞈnaꜜi
ñ desu yo.
   Tanaka: Moꜛtto yaꜛsasii zassi mo aꜜru kara, soꜛññaꜜ no o ꜛyoꜛñda hoo ḡa
ꜛiˑi desyoo ꞈneꜜe.

4. Mr. Tanaka: Koñna siḡoto wa naꜛñ-ziꜜkañ mo kaꜛkaˑru kara, koꜛñbañ ꜛkaꜛ-
eru made hȍka no siḡoto wa deꜛkiꜜnai to oꜛmoˑu yo⌐
   Secretary: Aꜜa, soꜜo desu ka.
   Mr. Tanaka: Daꜜ kara, daꜜre ḡa kiꜛteˑ mo aꜛeꜜnai ñ da yo.
   Secretary: Waꜛkarimaꜜsita.

5. Tanaka: Kono tuḡi naꜛñyoꜜobi ni kiꜛmasyoˑo ka.
   Smith: Naꜛñyoꜜobi ni kiꜛteˑ mo kaꜛmaimaseˑñ ḡa, aꜛsa no uti ni kiteꜜ
kudasai. Goꜜḡo wa daꜛre mo inaꜜi kara.
   Tanaka: Waꜛkarimaꜜsita. Zyaꜜa, aꜜsa ꜛhaˑyaku kimasu.

English Equivalents

1. Teacher A: Isn't it strange! Depending on the day, Mr. Smith either
understands very well or doesn't understand at all. Why
would that be?
   Teacher B: Wouldn't it be because, depending on the day, he either studies hard or doesn't study at all?
   Teacher A: I guess that's it.

2. Taro: I went to Ueno Park on Sunday . . .
   Yukio: Oh.
   Taro: There were an awful lot of people out.
   Yukio: I guess so. You mean people looking at the cherry blossoms, don't
you? How were the cherry blossoms?
   Taro: There were still only a few in bloom but lots of people were drink-
ing and making a racket under the trees and . . .

Yukio: You too?
Taro: I can't drink sake so . . . I went and ate my lunch.

3. Smith: For you this kind of magazine is probably interesting, but for us
              it isn't at all interesting because it's too difficult.
    Tanaka: There are some easier magazines too so it would probably be
              better to read one like that, wouldn't it.

4. Tanaka: Work like this takes any number of hours so I don't think I can
                do any other work [right up] until I go home tonight.
    Secretary: Oh.
    Tanaka: That's why—no matter who comes—I won't be able to see him.
    Secretary: I see.

5. Tanaka: What day shall I come the next time?
    Smith: It doesn't matter what day you come but please come during the
              morning—since no one is here in the afternoon.
    Tanaka: I see.   Then I'll come early in the morning.

                              EXERCISES

1. Describe a weekend trip—where, how, and with whom you went, what you
    did, what you saw, the weather, etc. Include as many details as possible,
    but restrict yourself to those you are sure you can express in natural Jap-
    anese.

2. Suggest to a Japanese friend that you:

        (a) go to see the cherry blossoms on Sunday.
        (b) go swimming on Saturday.
        (c) go sight-seeing tomorrow afternoon.
        (d) take a box lunch.
        (e) sing some Japanese songs.
        (f) wait here until Taro comes.
        (g) stop in at a tearoom on the way home and have something cold
             to drink.
        (h) telephone Mr. Ueda instead of writing a letter, because letters
             are a chore.

3. Make up ten short dialogues, each one of which contains one of the follow-
    ing:

        a. sosite
        b. da⌐kara
        c. ta⌐betari
        d. su⌐kka⌐ri
        e. me⌐zura⌐siku
        f. wa⌐takusi⌐tati
        g. na⌐ni mo
        h. na⌐n̄-zi⌐kañ mo
        i. na⌐ñ te i⌐tte⌐ mo
        j. ku⌐ru made

Lesson 28. Theater

BASIC DIALOGUES: FOR MEMORIZATION

(a)

Smith

a play or a show	sibai
see (a thing) or look at	haikeñ-suru ⌐ or goʳrañ ni naʳru ⌐

1. Is that a theatrical magazine? I'll have a look at it.
Siʳbai no zassi deˀsu ka⌐ Tyoˀ-tto haikeñ-simasu.

Tanaka

(form of traditional Japanese theater)	kabuki

2. Have you seen kabuki?
Kaʳbuki (o) gorañ ni narimaˀ-sita ka⌐

Smith

by all means	zeˀhí
lead	tureru /-ru/
take (people and animals)	turete (i)ku

3. Not yet; (so) do take me some (lit. one) time.
Maˀda desu kara, zeˀhí iʳti-do turete (i)⁴tte kudasai.

Tanaka

4. Yes, any time at all, when it's convenient for you.
Eˀe, iʳtu deˀ mo, goʳtuḡoo no iˀi toki ni.

Smith

readily or easily	suˀḡu

5. Can tickets be bought easily?
Kippu (wa) ʳsuˀḡu kaʳeruˀ ñ desu ka⌐

Tanaka

problem	moñdai

6. The tickets are the problem but—you know how it is.
Kiʳppu ḡa mondai deˀsu ḡa ⌐ne⁴e.

advance sale	maeuri
not easily or not readily	nakanaka /+ negative/

7. It's better to buy [tickets] in advance but you can't buy them easily.
Maʳeuri (o) katt(e) oˀita hoo ḡa ⌐i⁴i ñ desu ḡa, naʳkanaka kaenaˀi ñ desu yo.

Smith

is difficult to buy	kaʳinikuˀi /-ku/

159

8. In America too, tickets for good shows are hard to buy.	A⌉merika de⌉ mo, i⌉i sibai no kippu (wa) ka⌈iniku⌉i ñ desu yo.
the act of buying	ka⌈u⌉ no
in the process of buying or for buying	ka⌈u⌉ no ni
if or when [someone] does	si⌉ta⌉ra
how or what should [someone] do	do⌉o sitara ⊢i⊣i
9. What should you do to buy tickets?	Ki⌈ppu (o) kau⌉ no ni (wa), do⌉o sitara ⊢i⊣i ñ desyoo ka.

Tanaka

if or when [someone] sees	mi⌉tara
if or when [someone] tries telephoning	de⌈ñwa-site mi⌉tara
10. You inquire by telephone. How would it be if I tried telephoning now? or Why don't I try telephoning now?	De⌈ñwa de kiku⌉ ñ desu ḡa, i⌉ma de⊢ñwa-site mi⊣tara ⊢do⊣o desyoo.

Smith

11. Would you?	O⌈neḡai-sima⌉su.

(b)

Ticket-seller (on the telephone)

(kabuki theater in Tokyo)	Kabukiza
12. Hello. (This is the) Kabukiza.	Mo⌉simosi. Ka⌈bukiza de gozaima⌉su.

Tanaka

evening	yo⌉ru
evening performance	yo⌉ru no bu
13. Do you still have two first-class [tickets] for the evening performance on the tenth?	Too-ka no ⌈yo⌉ru no bu, it-too ⌈ni⌉-mai, ma⌉da ⌈a⌉ru desyoo ka.

Ticket-seller

sellout	urikire
14. We're entirely sold out through the twentieth.	Ha⌈tu-ka ma⌉de ⌈ze⌉ñbu u⌈rikire de gozaima⌉su.
after that or later than that	so⌈re-i⌉ḡo
being after that is all right	so⌈re-i⌉ḡo de yorosii
if it's all right	yo⌈rosi⌉kattara
15. If after that is all right, there are still a few left (but) . . .	So⌈re-i⌉ḡo de yo⊢rosi⊣kattara, ma⌉da su⌈ko⌉si no⊢ko⊣tte orimasu ḡa—

Tanaka

    discuss or talk over   soodañ-suru
16. Well, I'll talk it over; (so) just   Zya⌐a, so⌐odañ-suru⌐ kara, tyo⌐-
    a moment please.   tto ⌐ma⁴tte kudasai.

. . .

17. Hello. I'm sorry to have kept   Mo⌐simosi. O⌐matase-sima⌐sita.
    you waiting. It will be all   Ha⌐tu-ka-i⌐ḡo de mo ⌐i⁴i ñ desu
    right even if it's after the   ḡa_
    twentieth (but) . . .

Ticket-seller

    adjoin   tuzuku /-u/
18. We have two first-class [seats]   Ni⌐zyuu yo-kka no ĩt-too ⌐ni⌐-mai
    for the twenty-fourth but the   go⌐zaima⁴su ḡa, o⌐se⌐ki (ḡa) tu⌐zu-
    seats aren't adjoining. Would   ite orimase⌐ñ ḡa; yo⌐rosi⌐i desyoo
    they be all right?   ka.

Tanaka

    supposing   mo⌐si
    adjoining seats   tu⌐zuita se⌐ki
    if or when there are   a⌐ttara
19. If there are adjoining seats,   Mo⌐si tu⌐zuita se⌐ki ḡa ⌐a⁴ttara,
    even second class will be all   ni-⌐too de⌐ mo ⌐i⁴i desu ḡa_
    right (but) . . .

20. I'd like seats as near the   Narubeku ma⌐ññaka no ho⌐o no
    center as possible.   ⌐se⁴ki (o) oneḡai-simasu.

Ticket-seller

21. We have adjoining second-   Ni⌐zyuu ro⌐ku-niti⁴ no nĩ-too no
    class seats for the twenty-   tu⌐zuita ose⌐ki (ḡa) go⌐zaima⁴su
    sixth (but) . . .   ḡa_

Tanaka

    put aside for future use   to⌐tte oku
22. Then would you put them aside   Zya⌐a, so⌐re (o) to⌐tt(e) oite ku-
    for me? (Because) I'll come   ⌐remase⁴ñ ka‿ Su⌐ḡu ⌐to⌐ri ni
    (lit. go) to pick them up right   i⌐ku⁴ kara.
    away.

23. I'm Yukio Tanaka.   Ta⌐naka Yukio de⌐su.

Ticket-seller

24. Certainly. I'll be waiting   Ka⌐sikomarima⌐sita. Zya⌐a,
    (so) . . .   o⌐mati-site orima⌐su kara.

(c)

Smith

    come to an end   owaru /-u/

the time (lit. one) when   o⌐waru⌐ no
it ends
25. About what time does it end?   O⌐waru⌐ no (wa) na⌐n̄-zi-g̃o⌐ro de-
                                          syoo ka.

Tanaka

the end   owari
26. If you see it from beginning   Ha⌐zime kara owari ma⌐de ⌐mi⌐-
to end it takes all of five   tara, go-⌐zi⌐kan̄ mo ka⌐ka⌐ru n̄
hours.   desu yo⌐

27. Therefore it must end about   Da⌐ kara, o⌐waru⌐ no (wa) zyu-
eleven o'clock. (Lit. As for   ⌐uiti-zi-g̃o⌐ro ni ⌐na⌐ru desyoo
the time when it ends, it   ⌐ne⌐e.
must get to be about
11 o'clock.)

Smith

to that extent   son̄na ni
28. Do you mean it takes that long?   So⌐n̄na ni kaka⌐ru n̄ desu ka.

Tanaka

if it isn't interesting   o⌐mosi⌐roku ⌐na⌐kattara
29. If it isn't interesting you   O⌐mosi⌐roku ⌐na⌐kattara, o⌐wari
don't have to see it through   ma⌐de ⌐mi⌐nakute mo ⌐i⌐i n̄ de-
to the end.   su yo⌐

various dining rooms   iroiro na syokudoo or
                                         iron̄ na syokudoo
curtain or act   ma⌐ku⌐
between acts   maku no aida or makuai
30. There are all kinds of dining   Ka⌐bukiza no na⌐ka ni i⌐ron̄ na
rooms inside the Kabukiza   syokudoo g̃a a⌐tte, makuai ni
and you can eat between the   ta⌐berare⌐ru n̄ desu g̃a –
acts (but). . .

Smith

if or when [someone]   i⌐tta⌐ra
goes
as soon as [someone]   i⌐tta⌐ra ⌐su⌐g̃u
goes
reserve   yoyaku-suru
reserve in advance   yoyaku-site oku
if or when [someone]   yo⌐yaku-sit(e) o⌐itara
reserves in advance
31. How would it be if we reserved   I⌐tta⌐ra ⌐su⌐g̃u te⌐eburu (o) yo-
a table as soon as we got   yaku-sit(e) o⌐itara ⌐do⌐o desyoo.
there (lit. went)?

Tanaka

32. Let's do that.   So⌐o simasyo⌐o.

Smith

this time (i.e. this next time or this last time)	ko˥ndo
plot	su˥zi
simple or brief	kañtañ /na/
explain	setumee-suru

33. Some time when you're free, would you explain briefly the plot of the play we're going to see this time?

I˥tu ka o˩hima na to˩ki /ni/, ko˥ndo ˥mi˩ru si˩bai no su˩zi (o) ka˩ñtañ ni setumee-site ita-dakemase˥ñ ka.

Tanaka

complicated	hukuzatu /na/
anyway or at any rate	to˥nikaku

34. It's rather complicated so I can't explain it very briefly but. . . . Anyway I'll try (do-ing).

Na˩kanaka hukuzatu de˥su kara, a˩ñmari kañtañ ni˥ wa se˩tumee-dekimase˩ñ ga ˥ne˩e. To˥nikaku si˩te mimasyo˩o.

ADDITIONAL VOCABULARY

1. Have you seen ballet yet?

Mo˥o ˩ba˩ree (o) go˩rañ ni nari-ma˥sita ka˩

(a form of classical Japanese drama)	no˥o [1]
(traditional Japanese puppet theater)	bu˥ñraku
modern drama	siñgeki
dance or dancing (Japanese style)	odori
dance or dancing (Western style)	da˥ñsu

2. Do you like this kind of music?

Ko˩ñna oñgaku (wa) o˩suki de˥su ka˩

concert	o˩ñgaku˩kai
orchestra	o˩oke˩sutora
opera	ka˥geki or o˩pera

3. Isn't he good—that musician!

U˩ma˩i desu ˩ne˩e — ano oñgakuka wa.

actor or actress	yakusya or haiyuu
actress	zyoyuu
star (i.e. leading player)	su˩ta˩a

---

[1] Women usually use polite onoo⁺.

NOTES ON THE BASIC DIALOGUES

1. Haikeñ-suru᾿ and go⌐rañ ni na᾿ru᾿ are the polite equivalents of mi᾿ru.
Haikeñ-suru is polite in a humbling sense, and is used most commonly
when the thing looked at belongs to the person addressed (i. e. 'I look at
something of yours'). Go⌐rañ ni na᾿ru is polite in an honorific sense.
Haikeñ and gorañ occur alone and at the end of longer sentences as informal polite requests: Haikeñ. 'Let me see!'; Gorañ. 'Look!'

3. Ze᾿hi occurs most frequently in request sentences and with -tai 'want
to —— ' words.
Note also: tu⌐rete ku᾿ru 'bring (people and animals).'

10. Note the use of g̱a connecting a statement and a closely related question.

13. Yo᾿ru occurs both as a slightly more formal equivalent of bañ meaning
'evening' or 'night,' and as the opposite of hi⌐ru᾿ 'daytime' meaning
'night-time.'
Hiru no bu and ma᾿tinee both occur as equivalents of 'daytime performance.'

15. 'but—would that be all right?'
The opposite of -i᾿g̱o is -i᾿zeñ 'before.' Both words occur directly following time expressions (which lose their accents). Thus: sa⌐ñ-zi-i᾿g̱o
'after 3 o'clock'; ge⌐tuyoobi-i᾿g̱o 'after Monday'; go᾿zyuu roku-neñ-i᾿zeñ
'before '56.'

16. Note also the nominal soodañ 'discussion.'

17. 'but—what seats do you have?'

18. See the note on Sentence 10 above.

19. 'but—do you have any of those?'

21. 'but—would they be all right?'

24. 'so—be sure to come.'

26. The nominal owari is derived from the verbal owaru. A nominal derived from a verbal is regularly the verbal stem (the -ma᾿su form minus
-ma᾿su), with one accent difference: normally a nominal derived from
an accented verbal is also accented, but on its final syllable. Thus: ha-
na̱si᾿ 'talk (noun)' or 'speech' from ha᾿na᾿su 'talk (verb),' ya᾿sumi᾿
'rest (noun),' or 'vacation' from ya⌐su᾿mu 'rest (verb),' ka⌐eri᾿ 'return (noun)' from ka᾿eru 'return (verb),' and koori 'ice (noun)' from
kooru 'freeze (verb).'

28. Note also koñna ni 'to this extent,' añna ni 'to that extent,' and do᾿ñna
ni 'to what extent?'

30. 'but—would you like to do that?'
Iroñ na (+ nominal) is the less formal, more conversational equivalent
of iroiro na (+ nominal). Remember that when iroiro modifies an inflected expression, it occurs without a following particle. Thus: I⌐ro-
iro na koto᾿ o i⁺ima᾿sita. 'I said various things.' But: I⌐roiro hanasi-
ma᾿sita. 'I talked about all sorts of things (lit. variously).' The iroñ
alternant occurs only before na.

33. Note also the nominal setumee 'explanation.'

GRAMMATICAL NOTES

1. The Conditional

Mi˥tara		mi˥ru 'see.'
O˥ita˥ra		oku 'place.'
A˥ttara		a˥ru 'be (in a place)'
	is the CONDITIONAL of	or 'have.'
I˥tta˥ra		iku 'go.'
Si˥ta˥ra		suru 'do.'
Yo˥rosi˥kattara		yorosii 'is all right.'
Na˥kattara		na˥i 'there isn't.'

Inflected words (verbals, adjectivals, and copula) have CONDITIONAL forms, meaning 'if or when so-and-so happens or happened or had happened' or 'if it is or was or had been so-and-so.' A conditional form regularly refers to a single instance; it is never equivalent to 'whenever ——— .'

To form the conditional of any inflected word, add -ra to its past. The accent of a past and its corresponding conditional are the same, except that a verbal conditional derived from an unaccented past is accented on its next-to-last syllable (-ta). Thus:

Verbal: tu˥ku 'arrive'; past, tu˥ita; conditional, tu˥itara [1] 'if or when [someone] arrives or arrived or had arrived'
Adjectival: sa˥mu˥i 'is cold'; past, sa˥mukatta; conditional, sa˥mukattara 'if it is or was or had been cold'
Copula: da; past, da˥tta; conditional, da˥ttara [1]
as in: so˥re da˥ttara 'if it is or was or had been that'
         To˥okyoo kara da˥ttara 'if it is or was or had been from To-kyo'
         i˥ku˥ ñ dattara 'if it is or was or had been a matter of going'

Like the gerund, the conditional is tenseless. Study the following examples, noting particularly how the final inflected forms determine the time:

(a) Kyo˥oto e i˥tta˥ra, Ta˥naka-sañ ni aima˥su.
    'If (or when) I go to Kyoto, I'll see Mr. Tanaka.'
(b) Kyo˥oto e i˥tta˥ra, Ta˥naka-sañ ni aima˥sita.
    'When I went to Kyoto, I saw Mr. Tanaka.'
(c) Kyo˥oto e i˥tta˥ra, Ta˥naka-sañ ni a˥tta ñ desu ga—
    'If I had gone to Kyoto, I would have seen Mr. Tanaka (but)...'

Compare example (b) with:

(d) Kyo˥oto e i˥tta toki˥ ni, Ta˥naka-sañ ni aima˥sita.
    'When I went to Kyoto, I saw Mr. Tanaka.'

Sentence (b) states a condition or set of circumstances and the result, whereas sentence (d) tells at what time an action took place. Sentence (b) answers the question 'under what circumstances?' and (d) answers the question 'when?'

Mo˥si 'supposing' may occur at the beginning of a condition. It is an advance signal of the condition, and emphasizes its suppositional character.

---

[1] A more formal conditional is made by adding -ra to the formal past of of verbals and the copula: thus, tu˥kima˥sitara, de˥sitara.

A condition, consisting of or ending with a conditional, plus do⌐o desu ka, do⌐o desyoo ka, etc. is a suggestion: 'how will or would it be if someone does or did so-and-so?' It is the Japanese equivalent of English 'why don't [you] do so-and-so?' used as a suggestion.

Examples:

Te⌐gami o ka⌐itara ⌐do⌐o desu ka.
'Why don't [you] write a letter?' or
'How will it be if [you] write a letter?'
Se⌐nse⌐e ni ki⌐ita⌐ra ⌐do⌐o desyoo ka.
'Why don't [you] ask the teacher?' or
'How would it be if [you] asked the teacher?'

A condition, consisting of or ending with a conditional, plus √i⌐i 'it's good' is equivalent to English '[someone] should do so-and-so,' i.e. 'if [someone] does so-and-so, it will be good.' This construction frequently occurs with a question word in the condition.

Examples:

Kono miti o ma⌐ssu⌐gu i⌐tta⌐ra ⌐i⌐i desyoo.
'[You] should probably go straight along this street.' (Lit. 'It will probably be good if [you] go straight along this street.')
Do⌐o sitara ⌐i⌐i.
'What should [I] do?' (Lit. If [I] do what, will it be good?)
Do⌐ko de ki⌐ita⌐ra ⌐i⌐i desyoo ka.
'Where should [I] ask?' (Lit. 'If [I] asked where, would it be good?')

Do not confuse the following three kinds of patterns, all of which may contain 'should' in their English equivalents:

Do⌐o i⌐tta⌐ra ⌐i⌐i desyoo ka.
'How should I go?' (Lit. 'If I go how would it be good?')
Ha⌐yaku i⌐tta ho⌐o ga ⌐i⌐i desu yo⌐
'You should go early.' (I.e. 'It would be better to go early.')
Mo⌐o i⌐ru hazu de⌐su ga_
'He should be there already but [I don't know whether he is or not].'
(I.e. 'It is expected that he is there already.')

When a conditional is followed by a past form of i⌐i plus ga [⌐ne⌐e] or ke(re)do [⌐ne⌐e], the combination is equivalent to an English past wish: 'I wish so-and-so had happened.' Thus:

Tanaka-sañ ga ⌐ha⌐yaku ⌐ki⌐tara ⌐yo⌐katta ñ desu ga ⌐ne⌐e.
'I wish Mr. Tanaka had come early.' (Lit. 'If Mr. Tanaka had come early it would have been good but [he didn't], isn't that right.')
Mo⌐tto ⌐hu⌐ttara ⌐yo⌐katta keredo⌐
'I wish it had rained more.' (Lit. 'Although it would have been good if it had rained more [it didn't].')

Additional examples:

Ta⌐naka-sañ ga irassya⌐ttara, de⌐ñwa o ka⌐kete kudasai.
'If (or when) Mr. Tanaka comes, please telephone me.'

Aˈmerika e ittaˈra ˈsuˈgu eˈego ga zyoozuˈ ni ˈnaˈru desyoo.
  'As soon as you go to America, you will probably become proficient
  in English.' (Lit. 'When you go to America, immediately your Eng-
  lish will probably become skillful.')
Aˈnmari taˈkakattara, kaˈwanaˈi de ne?
  'If it's too expensive, don't buy it, will you?'
Taˈbetaˈku ˈnaˈkattara, taˈbeˈnakute mo kaˈmaimaseˈn.
  'If you don't want to eat, you don't have to.'
Oˈdekake ni naritaˈkattara, doˈozo goˈenryo naˈku.
  'If you want to go out, please don't hesitate.'
Iˈi ˈteˈnki dattara iˈkimaˈsu ga, aˈme ga ˈhuˈttara yaˈmemaˈsu.
  'If it's nice weather I'll go, but if it rains, I'll give up [the idea].'
Siˈtte itaˈra siˈnaˈkatta to omoimasu.
  'I think that if he had known, he wouldn't have done it.'
Aˈno sakana o tabeˈnakattara, byoˈoki ni naraˈnakatta desyoo.
  'If I hadn't eaten that fish, I probably wouldn't have gotten sick.'
Koˈraˈretara, zeˈhi kiˈteˈ kudasai.
  'If you can come, by all means do (come).'
Ziˈdoˈosya de iˈkuˈ n dattara, boˈku mo iˈkitaˈkatta n desu yo⌣
  'If it had been a case of going by car, I'd have wanted to go too.'

2. More About Nominal no 'one[s]'

The nominal no 'one' or 'ones' may refer to a person, thing, place, time,
or act, depending on context.

Compare the following examples:

(no referring to person)   Oˈsieruˈ no wa ˈdaˈre desu ka⌣
                           'Who is it who teaches?'
(no referring to thing)   Oˈsieruˈ no wa ˈnaˈn desu ka⌣
                           'What is it you teach?'
(no referring to place)   Oˈsieruˈ no wa ˈdoˈko desu ka⌣
                           'Where is it you teach?'
(no referring to time)   Oˈsieruˈ no wa naˈnyoˈo desu ka⌣
                           'What day is it you teach?'
(no referring to act)   Oˈsieruˈ no wa oˈmosiroˈi desyoo?
                           'Teaching (i.e. the act of teaching) is interesting,
                           isn't it?'

The nominal no referring to 'act,' with an appropriate preceding sentence
modifier, may occur as a grammatical subject, object, topic, goal, etc. Note
the last example above and study the following pairs:

  Koˈnna sibai ga omosiroˈi desu. 'This kind of play is interesting.'
  Koˈnna sibai o miˈru no ga oˈmosiroˈi desu. '(The act of) seeing this
    kind of play is interesting.'

  Niˈhongo no benkyoo o yamemaˈsita. 'I've given up the study of Jap-
    anese.'
  Niˈhongo o benkyoo-suruˈ no o yaˈmemaˈsita. 'I've given up (the act
    of) studying Japanese.'

Su⌐zi wa hu⌐kuzatu de⌐su. 'The plot is complicated.'
Su⌐zi o se⌐tumee-suru⌐ no wa hu⌐kuzatu de⌐su. '(The act of) explain-
    ing the plot is complicated.'

The nominal <u>no</u> referring to an act closely resembles <u>ko⌐to⌐</u> in meaning
and general usage, but depending upon the particular pattern, <u>no</u> may be preferred, or <u>ko⌐to⌐</u> may be preferred, or either one may be used (with the <u>ko-</u>
<u>⌐to⌐</u> alternative slightly more formal). In general, <u>no</u> is more common in
conversation except in a few fixed expressions: for example, —— ko⌐to⌐ g̃a
de⌐ki⌐ru (Lesson 25, Grammatical Note 1, end).

Examples:

A⌐ru⌐ku no wa i⌐ya⌐ desu.
    'I dislike walking.' (Lit. 'The act of walking is displeasing.')
Ni⌐hoñg̃o o beñkyoo-suru⌐ no wa mu⌐zukasi⌐i desu ⌐ne⌐e.
    '(The act of) studying Japanese is difficult, isn't it.'
Ha⌐yaku ne⌐ru⌐ no g̃a su⌐ki⌐ desu.
    'I like going to bed early.' (Lit. 'The act of going to bed early is
    pleasing.')
Ha⌐ya⌐i no wa ⌐ke⌐kkoo desu g̃a, o⌐so⌐i no wa ko⌐marima⌐su.
    '(The act of) being early is fine but (the act of) being late causes
    problems.'

3. —— no ni (wa)

The nominal <u>no</u> occurs preceded by an informal non-past verbal and followed by particles <u>ni (wa)</u>, meaning 'in the process of doing so-and-so.' This
pattern is especially common in general statements.

Examples:

O⌐taku e iku⌐ no ni (wa) Si⌐ñbasi⌐-eki no ⌐so⌐ba o to⌐orima⌐su ka⌐
    'In going to your house, do you pass near Shimbashi Station?'
Kore wa ⌐zu⌐ibuñ a⌐tu⌐i kara, tu⌐metaku suru⌐ no ni (wa) k̃oori g̃a ta-
    ⌐kusañ irima⌐su.
    'This is very hot so in making it cold you need lots of ice.'
Ni⌐hoñg̃o o oboe⌐ru no ni (wa) zi⌐kañ g̃a kaka⌐ru desyoo?
    'It takes time—doesn't it—to learn Japanese?'

4. tu⌐zuita se⌐ki

Intransitive verbals, particularly those meaning 'become so-and-so,' often
occur in the informal past as sentence modifiers of nominals. Thus:

<u>tuzuku</u> 'adjoin'; <u>tu⌐zuita se⌐ki</u> 'adjoining seats' (lit. 'seats that have ad-
    joined')
<u>tu⌐kare⌐ru</u> 'become tired'; <u>tu⌐ka⌐reta hito</u> 'tired person' (lit. 'person
    who has become tired')
<u>ko⌐ware⌐ru</u> 'become broken'; <u>ko⌐wa⌐reta sara</u> 'broken dish'
<u>aku</u> '[something] opens'; <u>a⌐ita ma⌐do</u> 'open window'
<u>no⌐ko⌐ru</u> 'become left behind'; <u>no⌐ko⌐tta mono</u> 'left-over things'
<u>ti⌐g̃a⌐u</u> 'be different' or 'be wrong'; <u>ti⌐g̃a⌐tta hito</u> 'different person' or
    'wrong person'

Less frequently, the corresponding gerund + (i)ru occurs, with about the same meaning (for example, tu⌐ka⌐rete (i)ru hito 'tired person'—lit. 'person who is tired'; ko⌐wa⌐rete (i)ru sara 'broken dish'; etc.).

5. Compound Adjectivals Ending in √-niku⌐i and √-yasu⌐i/ -i⌐i

The stem of a verbal (the -ma⌐su form minus -ma⌐su) compounded with -niku⌐i is an adjectival meaning 'cause difficulty in doing so-and-so.' The stem of a verbal + -yasu⌐i or -i⌐i [1] has the exact opposite meaning. Thus:

ka⌐kiniku⌐i 'cause difficulty in writing'

yo⌐miniku⌐i 'cause difficulty in reading'

wa⌐kariniku⌐i 'cause difficulty in understanding'

o⌐boeniku⌐i 'cause difficulty in remembering'

ka⌐kiyasu⌐i or ka⌐kii⌐i 'make writing easy'

yo⌐miyasu⌐i or yo⌐mii⌐i 'make reading easy'

wa⌐kariyasu⌐i or wa⌐karii⌐i 'make understanding easy'

o⌐boeyasu⌐i or o⌐boei⌐i 'make remembering easy'

Examples:

Ko⌐no kami⌐ wa ka⌐kiyasu⌐i desu. 'This paper is easy to write on.'
Ko⌐no pe⌐ñ wa ka⌐kiyasu⌐i desu. 'This pen is easy to write with.'
Koñna tori wa ta⌐beniku⌐i desu ⌐ne⌐e. 'This kind of chicken is hard to eat, isn't it!'
Ko⌐ñna ha⌐si wa ta⌐beniku⌐i desu ⌐ne⌐e. 'Chopsticks like these are hard to eat with, aren't they!'
Ne⌐niku⌐i ⌐be⌐tto desu ⌐ne⌐e. 'It's a bed that's hard to sleep in, isn't it!'
Tu⌐kaii⌐i zi⌐biki⌐ o ka⌐ima⌐sita yo˿ 'Say, I bought a dictionary that's easy to use.'

DRILLS

A. Substitution Drill

1. I want to go and see, by all means.

Ze⌐hi i⌐tte mita⌐i ñ desu.

2. At any rate, I want to go and see.

To⌐nikaku i⌐tte mita⌐i ñ desu.

3. That is why I want to go and see.

Da⌐ kara i⌐tte mita⌐i ñ desu.

4. After this, I want to go and see.

Kore kara i⌐tte mita⌐i ñ desu.

5. However, I want to go and see.

Ke⌐redo i⌐tte mita⌐i ñ desu.

6. I want to go and see (already) now.

Mo⌐o i⌐tte mita⌐i ñ desu.

---

[1]
The inflection of -i⌐i is the same as that of i⌐i 'is good': -yo⌐ku, -yo⌐kute, etc.

B. Substitution Drill

1. He doesn't readily under-   Na⌐kanaka wakarimase⌐ñ ⌐ne⌐e.
    stand, does he.

2. He doesn't understand at   Ze⌐ñzeñ wakarimase⌐ñ ⌐ne⌐e.
    all, does he.

3. He doesn't understand   A⌐ñmari wakarimase⌐ñ ⌐ne⌐e.
    very well, does he.

4. He doesn't understand   Ma⌐da wa⌐karimase⌐ñ ⌐ne⌐e.
    yet, does he.

5. He doesn't understand   Mo⌐o wa⌐karimase⌐ñ ⌐ne⌐e.
    any more, does he.

6. He doesn't understand   Ti⌐tto⌐ mo wa⌐karimase⌐ñ ⌐ne⌐e.
    a bit, does he.

C. Substitution Drill

1. It would be better to buy   Ma⌐euri (o) katt(e) o⌐ita hoo ḡa
    tickets in advance but I   ⌐i⌐i ñ desu ḡa, na⌐kanaka kae-
    can't buy them easily.   na⌐i ñ desu yo.

2. It would be better to for-   Wa⌐sureta ho⌐o ḡa ⌐i⌐i ñ desu
    get but I can't forget   ḡa, na⌐kanaka wasurerarena⌐i
    easily. /wasureru/   ñ desu yo.

3. It would be better to   O⌐bo⌐eta hoo ḡa ⌐i⌐i ñ desu ḡa,
    learn it but I can't learn   na⌐kanaka oboerare⌐nai ñ desu
    it easily. /o⌐boe⌐ru/   yo.

4. It would be better to fix   Ha⌐yaku na⌐o⌐sita hoo ḡa ⌐i⌐i ñ
    it quickly but I can't fix   desu ḡa, na⌐kanaka naose⌐nai
    it easily. /ha⌐yaku   ñ desu yo.
    na⌐o⌐su/

5. It would be better to quit   Tabako (o) ya⌐meta ho⌐o ḡa ⌐i⌐i
    smoking but I can't quit   ñ desu ḡa, na⌐kanaka yamera-
    easily. /tabako (o)   rena⌐i ñ desu yo.
    ya̅meru/

6. It would be better to turn   A⌐no suto⌐obu (o) ke⌐sita ho⌐o ḡa
    off that heater but I can't   ⌐i⌐i ñ desu ḡa, na⌐kanaka ke-
    turn it off easily. /a⌐no   sena⌐i ñ desu yo.
    suto⌐obu (o) ke̅su/

D. Substitution Drill (based on Grammatical Note 1)

1. If (or when) my friend   To⌐modati ḡa ki⌐tara, so⌐odañ-
    comes, we'll talk it over.   sima⌐su.

2. If my friend had come,   To⌐modati ḡa ki⌐tara, <u>so⌐odañ-
    we would have talked it   sita⌐ ñ desu ḡa</u>_
    over . . .

3. If (or when) my friend   To⌐modati ḡa ki⌐tara, <u>so⌐odañ-
    comes, let's talk it   sima⌐syo⌐o.</u>
    over.

4. If (or when) my friend   To⌐modati ḡa ki⌐tara, <u>so⌐odañ-
    comes, I'd like to talk   sita⌐i ñ desu ḡa</u>_
    it over . . .

5. If (or when) my friend
   comes, I think I'll talk
   it over.

   To⌐modati g̃a ki⌐tara, so⌐odañ-
   <u>siyoo to omoima⌐su</u>.

E. Substitution Drill (based on Grammatical Note 1)

1. If you study, you'll
   probably understand
   very well.

   Be⌐ñkyoo-sita⌐ra, yo⌐ku wa⌐ka⌐ru
   desyoo.

2. If you ask the teacher,
   you'll probably under-
   stand very well.
   /se⌐ñse⌐e ni kiku/

   Se⌐ñse⌐e ni ki⌐ita⌐ra, yo⌐ku wa-
   ⌐ka⌐ru desyoo.

3. If you have the plot explained, you'll probably
   understand very well.
   /su⌐zi (o) setumee-site
   morau/

   Su⌐zi (o) se⌐tumee-site moratta⌐ra,
   yo⌐ku wa⌐ka⌐ru desyoo.

4. If you read this, you'll
   probably understand
   very well. /ko⌐re (o)
   yo⌐mu/

   Ko⌐re (o) yo⌐ñdara, yo⌐ku wa⌐ka⌐-
   ru desyoo.

5. If you continue until the
   end, you'll probably
   understand very well.
   /o⌐wari ma⌐de tuzukeru/

   O⌐wari ma⌐de tu⌐zuketa⌐ra, yo⌐ku
   wa⌐ka⌐ru desyoo.

6. If you see it again, you'll
   probably understand very
   well. /ma⌐ta mi⌐ru/

   Ma⌐ta mi⌐tara, yo⌐ku wa⌐ka⌐ru
   desyoo.

F. Substitution Drill (based on Grammatical Note 1)

1. How would it be if [you]
   tried telephoning now?

   I⌐ma de⌐ñwa-site mi⌐tara ⌐do⌐o
   desyoo.

2. How would it be if YOU
   looked at it? /a⌐na⌐ta
   g̃a go⌐rañ ni na⌐ru/

   A⌐na⌐ta g̃a go⌐rañ ni na⌐ttara
   ⌐do⌐o desyoo.

3. How would it be if I
   looked at it? /watakusi
   g̃a haikeñ-suru/

   Wa⌐takusi g̃a haikeñ-sita⌐ra ⌐do⌐o
   desyoo.

4. How would it be if [you]
   took a friend? /tomodati
   (o) turete (i)ku/

   To⌐modati (o) turete (i)⌐ttara
   ⌐do⌐o desyoo.

5. How would it be if [you]
   went swimming? /o⌐yo⌐g̃i
   ni iku/

   O⌐yo⌐g̃i ni i⌐tta⌐ra ⌐do⌐o desyoo.

6. How would it be if [you]
   stopped in at my house?
   /uti ni yoru/

   U⌐ti ni yotta⌐ra ⌐do⌐o desyoo.

7. How would it be if [you]
   asked someone? /da⌐re
   ka ni ki⌐ku/

   Da⌐re ka ni ki⌐ita⌐ra ⌐do⌐o desyoo.

8. How would it be if [you]   Aˈkaboo (o) tanoˈndara ˈdoˈo de-
   hired a porter? /aˈkaboo   syoo.
   (o) tanoˈmu/

G. Substitution Drill (based on Grammatical Note 1)

1. What should I do?   Doˈo sitara ˈiˈi ñ desyoo ka.
2. When should I take him?   Iˈtu tuˈrete (i)ˈttara ˈiˈi ñ de-
   /iˈtu turete (i)ku/   syoo ka.
3. Where should we discuss   Doˈko de soˈodañ-sitaˈra ˈiˈi ñ
   it? /doˈko de soodañ-   desyoo ka.
   suru/
4. Which song should I sing?   Doˈno uˈtaˈ (o) uˈtattaˈra ˈiˈi ñ
   /doˈno uˈtaˈ (o) utau/   desyoo ka.
5. What should I make?   Naˈni (o) tuˈkuˈttara ˈiˈi ñ de-
   /naˈni (o) tuˈkuˈru/   syoo ka.
6. Whom should I ask?   Daˈre ni kiˈitaˈra ˈiˈi ñ desyoo
   /daˈre ni kiku/   ka.
7. What kind of things   Doˈñna moˈnoˈ (o) taˈbeˈtara ˈiˈi
   should I eat? /doˈñna   ñ desyoo ka.
   moˈnoˈ (o) taˈbeˈru/
8. How many should I buy?   Iˈku-tu kaˈttaˈra ˈiˈi ñ desyoo
   /iˈku-tu kau/   ka.

H. Substitution Drill (based on Grammatical Note 3)

1. What should I do to buy   Kiˈppu (o) kauˈ no ni (wa), doˈo
   tickets?   sitara ˈiˈi ñ desyoo ka.
2. What should I do to re-   Teˈeburu (o) yoyaku-suruˈ no ni
   serve a table?   (wa), doˈo sitara ˈiˈi ñ desyoo
                                ka.
3. What should I do to put   Koˈñna obiˈ (o) siˈmeˈru no ni
   on this kind of obi?   (wa), doˈo sitara ˈiˈi ñ desyoo
                                ka.
4. What should I do to re-   Niˈhoñgo (o) oboeˈru no ni (wa),
   member Japanese?   doˈo sitara ˈiˈi ñ desyoo ka.
5. What should I do to join   Soˈñna kaisya ni haˈiru no ni (wa),
   that kind of company?   doˈo sitara ˈiˈi ñ desyoo ka.
6. What should I do to   Taˈiya (o) toˈrikaeruˈ no ni (wa),
   change a tire?   doˈo sitara ˈiˈi ñ desyoo ka.
7. What should I do to open   Koˈno hikidasi (o) akeruˈ no ni
   this drawer?   (wa), doˈo sitara ˈiˈi ñ desyoo
                                ka.
8. What should I do to check   Niˈmotu (o) aˈzukeˈru no ni (wa),
   baggage?   doˈo sitara ˈiˈi ñ desyoo ka.

I. Substitution Drill (based on Grammatical Note 1)

1. I wish it had rained.   Aˈme ḡa ˈhuˈttara ˈyoˈkatta ke-
                                redo_
2. I wish it hadn't rained.   Aˈme ḡa huˈraˈnakattara ˈyoˈkatta
   /aˈme ḡa huˈraˈnai/   keredo_

3. I wish he had come early. Ha⌐yaku ˥ki˧tara ˥yo˧katta keredo—
   /ha⌐yaku ˥ku˧ru/

4. I wish he hadn't come   O⌐soku ko⌐nakattara ˥yo˧katta
   late. /o⌐soku ko⌐nai/   keredo—

5. I wish it had been in-   O⌐mosi⌐rokattara ˥yo˧katta keredo—
   teresting. /o⌐mosiro⌐i/

6. I wish it hadn't been   Tu⌐mara⌐naku ˥na˧kattara ˥yo˧katta
   dull. /tu⌐mara⌐naku   keredo—
   ˥na˧i/

7. I wish it had been near.   Ti⌐ka⌐kattara ˥yo˧katta keredo—
   /ti⌐ka⌐i/

8. I wish it hadn't been far. To⌐oku na⌐kattara ˥yo˧katta ke-
   /to⌐oku na⌐i/   redo—

9. I wish it had been simple. Ka⌐ñtañ da⌐ttara ˥yo˧katta keredo—
   /kañtañ da/

10. I wish it hadn't been   Hu⌐kuzatu zya na⌐kattara ˥yo˧-
    complicated. /hu⌐ku-   katta keredo—
    zatu zya na⌐i/

J. Substitution Drill (based on Grammatical Note 2)

1. About when is it you're   Ka⌐u⌐ no wa i⌐tu-ḡoro de⌐su ka⌐
   going to buy it?

2. Who is it who's going to   Ka⌐u⌐ no wa da⌐re desu ka⌐
   buy it?

3. What is it you're going   Ka⌐u⌐ no wa na⌐ñ desu ka⌐
   to buy?

4. Which (of three or more)   Ka⌐u⌐ no wa do⌐re desu ka⌐
   is it you're going to
   buy?

5. Which (of two) is it you're   Ka⌐u⌐ no wa do⌐tira desu ka⌐
   going to buy?

6. How much is the one   Ka⌐u⌐ no wa i⌐kura desu ka⌐
   you're going to buy?

7. Where is the one you're   Ka⌐u⌐ no wa do⌐ko desu ka⌐
   going to buy? or
   Where is the one who's
   going to buy it? or
   Where is it you're going
   to buy?

K. Substitution Drill (based on Grammatical Note 2)

1. I like to see plays.   Si⌐bai (o) mi⌐ru no wa su⌐ki⌐
                                    desu.

2. I like to go sight-seeing.   Ke⌐ñbutu-suru⌐ no wa su⌐ki⌐
                                    desu.

3. I dislike going sight-   Ke⌐ñbutu-suru⌐ no wa i⌐ya⌐ desu.
   seeing.

4. I dislike cleaning.   So⌐ozi-suru⌐ no wa i⌐ya⌐ desu.

5. Cleaning is a chore.   So⌐ozi-suru⌐ no wa me⌐ñdookusa⌐i
                                   desu.

6. Doing that kind of work is   So˹nna si͞goto (o) suru˺ no wa
    a chore.   me˹ndookusa˺i desu.

7. Doing that kind of work is   So˹nna si͞goto (o) suru˺ no wa
    difficult   mu˹zukasi˺i desu.

8. Studying Japanese is dif-   Ni˹ho͞ngo (o) be͞nkyoo-suru˺ no wa
    ficult.   mu˹zukasi˺i desu.

L. Response Drill (based on Grammatical Note 5)

        Tutor: Ta˹beniku˺i ñ desu ka⌐   'Is it hard to eat?'
        Student: Iie, {ta˹beyasu˺i} ñ desu.   'No, it's easy to eat.'
                       {ta˹bei˺i   }

1. Sibai no kippu (wa) ka-   Iie, {ka˹iyasu˺i} ñ desu.
    ˹iniku˺i ñ desu ka⌐   {ka˹ii˺i   }

2. Are (wa) si˹yasu˺i ñ desu   Iie, si˹niku˺i ñ desu.
    ka⌐

3. So˹nna kutu˺ (wa) ha˹ki-   Iie, {ha˹kiyasu˺i} ñ desu.
    niku˺i ñ desu ka⌐   {ha˹kii˺i   }

4. Ano kusuri (wa) no˹mi-   Iie, no˹miniku˺i ñ desu.
    i˺i ñ desu ka⌐

5. A˹nna ha˺si (wa) tu˹kai-   Iie, {tu˹kaiyasu˺i} ñ desu.
    niku˺i ñ desu ka⌐   {tu˹kaii˺i   }

6. Ano zassi (wa) yo˹miya-   Iie, yo˹miniku˺i ñ desu.
    su˺i ñ desu ka⌐

M. Expansion Drill

1. Would it be good?   I˺i desyoo ka.
    What should I do?   Do˺o sitara ˺i˺i desyoo ka.
    What should I do with the   Ni˹ku˺ wa ˹do˺o sitara ˺i˺i de-
    meat?   syoo ka.
    What should I do with the   No˹ko˺tta ni˺ku˺ wa ˹do˺o sitara
    left-over meat?   ˺i˺i desyoo ka.

2. It's all right.   I˺i ñ desu yo.
    You don't have to read it.   Yo˹ma˺nakute mo ˹i˺i ñ desu yo.
    You don't have to read it   O˹wari ma˺de yo˹ma˺nakute mo
    to the end.   ˹i˺i ñ desu yo.
    If it's difficult you don't   Mu˹zukasi˺kattara, o˹wari ma˺de
    have to read it to the   yo˹ma˺nakute mo ˹i˺i ñ desu
    end.   yo.
    (Supposing) if it's diffi-   Mo˹si mu˹zukasi˺kattara, o˹wari
    cult you don't have to   ma˺de yo˹ma˺nakute mo ˹i˺i ñ
    read it to the end.   desu yo.

3. How would it be?   Do˺o desyoo.
    Why don't you buy [them]   Ka˹tt(e) o˺itara ˺do˺o desyoo.
    in advance?

Why don't you buy the tickets in advance?	Kippu (o) ka￢tt(e) o￢itara ┌do┤o de-syoo.
Why don't you buy the return tickets in advance?	Kaeri no kippu (o) ka￢tt(e) o￢itara ┌do┤o desyoo.
Why don't you buy the return tickets (in advance) right away?	Su￢g̈u k̄aeri no kippu (o) ka￢tt(e) o￢itara ┌do┤o desyoo.
Why don't you buy the return tickets in advance as soon as you arrive?	Tu￢itara ⌐su￢g̈u k̄aeri no kippu (o) ka￢tt(e) o￢itara ┌do┤o desyoo.

4.
It will probably be(come) late, won't it.	O￢soku na￢ru desyoo ⌐ne￢e.
It will probably end late too, won't it.	O￢waru￢ no mo o￢soku na￢ru desyoo ⌐ne￢e.
If it's late, it will probably end late too, won't it.	O￢so￢kattara, o￢waru￢ no mo o￢soku na￢ru desyoo ⌐ne￢e.
If it's that late, it will probably end late too, won't it.	So￢n̄na ni oso￢kattara, o￢waru￢ no mo o￢soku na￢ru desyoo ⌐ne￢e.
If it starts that late, it will probably end late too, won't it.	Ha￢zimaru￢ no g̈a so￢nna ni oso￢-kattara, o￢waru￢ no mo o￢soku na￢ru desyoo ⌐ne￢e.

5.
I can't go.	I￢karemase￢n̄.
I can't go very easily.	Na￢kanaka ikaremase￢n̄.
Before that I can't go very easily.	So￢no ma￢e wa na￢kanaka ikare-mase￢n̄.
It's all right but before that I can't go very easily.	I￢i n̄ desu g̈a, so￢no ma￢e wa na￢kanaka ikaremase￢n̄.
If it's after the tenth it's all right but before that I can't go very easily.	To￢o-ka-i￢g̈o dattara ┌i┤i n̄ desu g̈a, so￢no ma￢e wa na￢kanaka ikaremase￢n̄.

6.
How would it be?	Do┤o desyoo.
Why don't you buy [it]?	Ka￢tta￢ra ┌do┤o desyoo.
Why don't you buy a new one?	A￢tarasi￢i no (o) ka￢tta￢ra ┌do┤o desyoo.
It takes money so why don't you buy a new one?	O￢kane g̈a kaka￢ru kara, a￢tara-si￢i no (o) ka￢tta￢ra ┌do┤o de-syoo.
It takes an awful lot of money so why don't you buy a new one?	Zu￢ibun̄ o￢kane g̈a kaka￢ru kara, a￢tarasi￢i no (o) ka￢tta￢ra ┌do┤o desyoo.
It takes an awful lot of money to fix [it] so why don't you buy a new one?	Na￢o￢su no ni (wa) ⌐zu￢ibun̄ o￢kane g̈a kaka┤ru kara, a￢tarasi￢i no (o) ka￢tta￢ra ┌do┤o desyoo.

It takes an awful lot of money to fix this so why don't you buy a new one?

Ko⌐re (o) nao⌐su no ni (wa) ⌐zu⌐i-buñ o⌐kane ḡa kaka⁴ru kara, a⌐tarasi⌐i no (o) ka⌐tta⁴ra ⌐do⁴o desyoo.

QUESTION SUPPLEMENT

(based on the Basic Dialogues)

(a) 1. Su⌐misu-sañ wa ⌐mo⌐o kābuki o mi⌐ma⌐sita ka↲
     2. Su⌐misu-sañ wa ka⌐buki ḡa mita⌐i ñ desu ka↲ Do⌐o site wa⌐karima⁴su ka↲
     3. Kabuki no kippu wa ⌐su⌐ḡu ka⌐eru⌐ ñ desu ka↲ Amerika no ⌐i⌐i sibai no kippu wa ⌐do⌐o desu ka↲

(b) 4. Nañ-niti made u⌐rikire de⁴su ka↲
     5. Ni⌐zyuu yo-kka no i⌐t-too no kippu wa, do⌐o site i⌐rimase⁴ñ ka↲
     6. Nañ-niti no kippu ni ki⌐mema⁴sita ka↲ I⌐t-too no kippu de⌐su ka, ni-⌐too no kippu de⌐su ka↲
     7. Tanaka-sañ wa kore kara ⌐na⌐ni o si⌐ma⁴su ka↲

(c) 8. Ka⌐buki no owaru⌐ no wa na⌐ñ-zi-ḡo⌐ro desu ka↲
     9. Ha⌐zime kara owari ma⌐de ⌐mi⁴tara, na⌐ñ-zi⌐kañ ka⌐karima⁴su ka↲
    10. Ha⌐zimaru⌐ no wa ⌐na⌐ñ-zi desu ka↲
    11. Tanaka-sañ to ⌐Su⌐misu-sañ wa ⌐do⌐ko de ta⌐be⁴ru tumori desu ka↲
    12. Ge⌐kizyoo e itta⌐ra ⌐su⌐ḡu, na⌐ni o su⌐ru⌐ desyoo ka.
    13. Su⌐misu-sañ wa Tānaka-sañ ni ⌐do⌐ñna koto o ta⌐nomima⁴sita ka↲
    14. Do⌐o site Tanaka-sañ wa a⌐ñmari kañtañ ni⁴ wa se⌐tumee-deki⁴-nai to i⌐ima⁴sita ka↲

SUPPLEMENTARY CONVERSATION

Tanaka: Su⌐misu-sañ. A⌐zuma-o⌐dori[1] o go⌐rañ ni narima⌐sita ka↲

Mr. Smith: Iie. Na⌐ñ desu ka↲—A⌐zuma-o⌐dori tte i⌐u⁴ no wa. Ni⌐hoñ no odori de⌐su ka↲

Tanaka: O⌐dori dake⌐ zya ⌐na⌐i ñ desu yo↲ Ge⌐esya[2] ḡa suru kabuki de⌐su yo.

Mr. Smith: So⌐o desu ka. Zya⌐a, o⌐ñna⌐ ḡa su⌐ru kabuki de⁴su ka↲

Tanaka: E⌐e. Hutuu no kabuki wa o⌐toko⌐ sika si⌐na⁴i ñ desu ḡa, A⌐zuma-o⌐dori wa ⌐Si⌐ñbasi no ge⌐esya ḡa suru⌐ ñ desu. Ki⌐ree de-su yo↲

Mr. Smith: So⌐o desyoo ⌐ne⌐e. Ze⌐hi tu⌐rete i⁴tte kudasai. Ka⌐bukiza de site iru⌐ ñ desu ka↲

Tanaka: Iie. Ka⌐bukiza no so⌐ba desu ḡa, Si⌐ñbasi-eñbuzyoo[3] tte iu gekizyoo de ⌐i⌐ma si⌐te iru⁴ ñ desu yo↲

---

[1] A special spring entertainment performed in Tokyo.

[2] 'Geisha.'

[3] Name of a Tokyo theater.

Mr. Smith: Kippu wa ꞌsuꞌgu kaꞋeruꞌ ñ desu ka⌣
Tanaka: Iie. Hutuu wa naꞋkanaka kaenaꞌi ñ desu yo.
Mr. Smith: SoꞋre wa komarimaꞌsu Ꞌneꞌe. Doꞌo simasyoo ka.
Tanaka: TuꞋgiꞌ no doꞋyoꞌobi, goꞋtugoo ga yoꞌkattara; kippu ga Ꞌniꞌ-mai
           Ꞌaꞌru ñ desu yo⌣ ToꞋmodati kara morattaꞌ ñ desu ga⌐
Mr. Smith: TuꞋgiꞋ no doꞋyoꞌobi desu ne? NaꞋñ-zi kara desyoo ka.
Tanaka: ZyuꞋuitiꞋ-zi kara desu ga⌐
Mr. Smith: Yoꞌru zya Ꞌnaꞌi ñ desu ne? Zyaꞌa, tyoꞌodo iꞌi desu. DoꞋyoꞌobi
           wa siꞋtiꞋ-zi kara yaꞋkusoku ga aꞌru ñ desu ga⌐
Tanaka: Yo-ꞌzi-hañ-goꞌro oꞋwaru to omoimaꞌsu ga, moꞋsi oꞋmosiꞌroku
           Ꞌnaꞌkattara oꞋwari maꞌde ꞌmiꞌnakute mo Ꞌiꞌi desyoo.
Mr. Smith: OꞋmosiroꞌi to oꞋmoimaꞌsu yo⌣ Boꞌku wa kaꞋbuki ga sukiꞌ de,
           yoꞋku Ꞌmiꞌ ni iꞋkuꞌ ñ desu yo⌣
Tanaka: Zyaꞌa⌐ DoꞋyoꞌobi ni Ꞌdoꞌko de aꞋimasyoꞌo ka. Iꞌma soꞋodañ-site
           okimasyoꞌo. GoꞋzoꞌñzI desu ka⌣—SiꞋñbasi-eñbuzyoo o.
Mr. Smith: Iie, siꞋrimaseꞋñ ga⌐
Tanaka: Zyaꞌa, zyuꞋuitiꞋ-zi zyuꞋugo-huꞌñ mae ni SiꞋñbasiꞋ-eki no Ꞌmaꞌe
           de oꞋmati-simasyoꞌo.
Mr. Smith: Zyaꞌa, zyuꞋugo-huꞌñ mae made ni SiꞋñbasiꞋ-eki no Ꞌmaꞌe ni Ꞌaꞌ-
           ru Ꞌtaꞌkusii no noꞋriba no soꞌba ni iꞋkimaꞌsu kara, oꞋnegai-si-
           maꞌsu. . . .
           A, soꞌo Ꞌsoꞌo. OꞋhiꞌru wa geꞋkizyoo de tabemaꞌsu ka⌣
Tanaka: Soꞌo desu Ꞌneꞌe. SaꞋñdoiꞌttiꞋ to koꞋohiꞌi o moꞋtte iꞌtte, maꞋkuai
           ni tabemasyoꞌo ka.
Mr. Smith: Zyaꞌa, boꞌku ga moꞋtte ikimaꞌsu kara⌐
Tanaka: SoꞋre wa doꞌo mo.

           (Gekizyoo de)

Mr. Smith: Hoñtoo ni Ꞌkiꞌree na oꞋdori deꞌsita Ꞌneꞌe.
Tanaka: KiꞋmonoꞋ mo kiꞋree desita Ꞌneꞌe. SuꞋzi oꞋwakari deꞌsita ka⌣
Mr. Smith: Eꞌe. Maꞌe ni miꞋmaꞌsita kara. TuꞋgiꞋ wa siꞋbai deꞌsu ne?
Tanaka: Eꞌe, soꞌo desu. NaꞋgaꞌI sibai no oꞋwari no hoꞌo no haꞋñbuꞌñ o
           suꞋruꞌ ñ desu yo⌣
Mr. Smith: Aꞌa, soꞌo desu ka. Zyaꞌa, suꞋmimaseꞋñ ga, suꞋzi o kaꞋñtañ ni
           setumee-site kuremaseꞋñ ka.
Tanaka: Yoꞌku oꞋboꞌete iꞋmaseꞋñ kara, tyoꞌtto ꞋmaꞋtte kudasai⌣ PuꞋroguꞋ-
           ramu[2] o Ꞌyoꞌñde miꞋmaꞌsu kara⌐

                        English Equivalent

Tanaka: Mr. Smith. Have you seen the Azuma-odori?
Mr. Smith: No. What is it—(the thing called) the Azuma-odori? Is it Jap-
           anese dancing?
Tanaka: It isn't just dancing. It's kabuki that geisha perform.
Mr. Smith: Really? Then do you mean that it's kabuki that women perform?
Tanaka: Yes. Only men do ordinary kabuki but the Shimbashi geisha do
           the Azuma-odori. It's beautiful, you know.

─────────────
[1] 'Sandwich.'

[2] 'Program.'

Mr. Smith: It must be. Do take me. Are they performing it at the Kabukiza?
Tanaka: No. It's near the Kabukiza but they're performing it now at a theater called the Shimbashi-Embujo.
Mr. Smith: Can you buy tickets easily?
Tanaka: No. Usually you can't buy them easily [at all].
Mr. Smith: That's annoying. What shall we do?
Tanaka: If next Saturday is convenient, I have two tickets. I got them from a friend . . .
Mr. Smith: That's next Saturday you say? What time would it start?
Tanaka: It starts at 11:00 . . .
Mr. Smith: That's not the evening, is it? Then it's just fine. On Saturday, I have an appointment from 7 o'clock [on] but . . .
Tanaka: I think it will be over at about 4:30, but if it's not interesting we won't have to watch it until the end.
Mr. Smith: I think it will be interesting. I like kabuki and I often go to see it.
Tanaka: Then [you'll probably like this]. Where shall we meet on Saturday? Let's talk it over now (in advance). Do you know it—the Shimbashi-Embujo?
Mr. Smith: No, I don't (know it) . . .
Tanaka: Well then, I'll wait [for you] in front of Shimbashi Station at a quarter to eleven.
Mr. Smith: Well then, I'll be (lit. go) near the taxi stand that's in front of Shimbashi Station by a quarter of, so please [look for me].
            . . . Oh, yes.—At noontime will we eat in the theater?
Tanaka: Let me see . . . Shall we take sandwiches and coffee and eat between the acts?
Mr. Smith: In that case, I'll bring [the food] so [don't you bother].
Tanaka: That's very [kind of you].

            (At the theater)

Mr. Smith: It was really beautiful dancing, wasn't it.
Tanaka: The kimono were beautiful too, weren't they. Did you understand the plot?
Mr. Smith: Yes, because I've seen it before. [1] The next is a play, isn't it?
Tanaka: Yes, that's right. They're going to do the second (lit. end) half of a long play.
Mr. Smith: Oh really? In that case, I'm sorry [to bother you] but would you explain the plot to me briefly?
Tanaka: I don't remember it very well so just a moment. (Because) I'll read the program and see.

                                EXERCISES

1. Plan a trip to see kabuki with a friend: decide when you will go, who will buy the tickets, what kind of seats you wish, where you will eat, etc.

2. Using the pattern of Basic Sentence 25 of this lesson, ask Mr. Tanaka:

---

[1] I. e. a performance using the same plot, probably in regular kabuki.

a.   what time he begins work.
b.   what time the show starts.
c.   when it gets to be the rainy season.
d.   when this work will end.
e.   when he will return to Japan.

3.   Tell Mr. Tanaka that:

a.   you dislike walking.
b.   you think riding in Tokyo taxis is dangerous.
c.   you think reading Japanese newspapers is difficult.
d.   you like to eat at Japanese restaurants.
e.   you think seeing kabuki is interesting.
f.   going from here to your house is simple.

4.   You ask the theater employee: She replies:

a.   if there are still three   There are but the seats are
     first-class [tickets] for   not together.
     the afternoon perform-
     ance on the 14th.
b.   if the evening perform-   No, there are still a few
     ance on the 20th is sold   second-class seats left.
     out already.
c.   if these seats [i.e. those   Yes, they are.
     for which you have
     tickets] are together.
d.   if these seats are in   No, they're on the side.
     the middle section.
e.   what time the show   At 5 o'clock.
     begins.
f.   if there is an English   They should be selling them
     program (puroguramu).   over there.
g.   how long the intermis-   Twenty minutes.
     sion is.
h.   if it's all right even if   If you want to eat during the
     you don't reserve a   intermission, it's better to
     table in the dining room.   reserve a table now.

Lesson 29. Renting a House

BASIC DIALOGUES: FOR MEMORIZATION

(a)

Smith

being cool or because
it's cool

su⌐zu⌐sikute

is nice and cool

su⌐zu⌐sikute ⌐i⌐i

1. It's nice and cool here, isn't it!

*Koko (wa) su⌐zu⌐sikute ⌐i⌐i desu ⌐ne⌐e.

house for rent

kasiya

2. Aren't there houses for rent around here?

Kono heñ ni ka⌐siya (ḡa) na⌐i de-syoo ka.

thus or this way
a place like this
being a case of wanting
to rent or because
[someone] wants to rent

ko⌐o
ko⌐o iu tokoro⌐
ka⌐rita⌐i no de

3. (Because) I'd like to rent a summer home in a place like this.

Ko⌐o iu tokoro⌐ ni na⌐tu no uti⌐ (o) ka⌐rita⌐i no de—

Tanaka

be pleasing or appeal
isn't clear whether there
are or not
become vacant

ki ni iru /-u/
a⌐ru ka ⌐do⌐o ka wa⌐kara⌐-nai
aku /-u/

4. Let me see. I can't tell whether or not there's a house of the kind that will appeal to you, but there certainly are vacant houses.

So⌐o desu ⌐ne⌐e. Ki ⌐ni iru yo⌐o na uti (ḡa) ⌐a⌐ru ka ⌐do⌐o ka wa⌐karimaseñ ḡa, aite (i)ru uti wa ki⌐tto arima⌐su yo⌐

Smith

being a case of being
far or because it
is far
town
a town like this

to⌐oi⌐ no de

ma⌐ti⌐
ko⌐o iu mati⌐

5. I wanted to go to Karuizawa but it's too far so I've been looking for a closer place. I think that a town like this is just right.

Ka⌐ruizawa e ikita⌐katta keredo; a⌐ñmari tooi⌐ no de, mo⌐tto ti-⌐ka⌐i to⌐koro⌐ (o) sa⌐ḡasite (i)ma⌐-su ḡa; ko⌐o iu mati⌐ ḡa tyo⌐odo i⌐i to omoimasu.

180

Tanaka (pointing to a house)

6. How would that house be?
Would that be a little [too]
small?

Ano uti (wa)|do⌐o desyoo.[1] Tyo⌐-
tto ti⌐isa⌐i desyoo ka.

Smith

even as a house
7. Yes. Even as just a summer
home that's too small so I'm
afraid that wouldn't do.

u⌐ti⌐ to si⌐te⌐ mo
E⌐e. Na⌐tu dake⌐ no u⌐ti⌐ to si⌐te⌐
mo, ti⌐isasuḡima⌐su kara ⌐tyo⌐tto—

Tanaka (pointing to another house)

inconvenient
8. It's a slightly inconvenient
location but how would that
house be?

hu⌐beñ /na/
Tyo⌐tto ⌐hu⌐beñ na to⌐koro⌐ desu
ḡa, a⌐no uti wa do⌐o desyoo.

isn't clear whether it's
a house for rent or not
9. I can't tell whether it's (a
house) for rent or not but I
think it's vacant.

ka⌐siya ka do⌐o ka wa⌐ka-
ra⌐nai
Ka⌐siya ka do⌐o ka wa⌐karimase⌐ñ
ḡa, a⌐ite (i)ru to omoima⌐su.

Smith

scenery
10. [In] back are the mountains
and [in] front is the ocean
so the scenery is lovely,
isn't it.

ke⌐siki
U⌐siro ḡa yama⌐ de, ma⌐e ḡa
⌐u⌐mi da kara; *ke⌐siki wa ⌐i⌐i
desu ⌐ne⌐e.

as a house
11. As a summer house it would
probably be quite nice!

u⌐ti⌐ to site
Na⌐tu no uti⌐ to si⌐te⌐ wa, na-
⌐kanaka i⌐i desyoo ⌐ne⌐e.

Tanaka

home-owner or landlord
acquaintance
introduce

ya⌐nusi[2]
siriai
syookai-suru or gosyookai-
suru+

12. The owner is an acquaintance
of mine. Shall I introduce
you?

Ya⌐nusi (wa) si⌐riai de⌐su ḡa, go-
⌐syookai-simasyo⌐o ka.

Smith

13. Yes, please. (Because) I do
want to see that house (lit.
have that house shown to
me).

E⌐e oneḡai-simasu. Ze⌐hi a⌐no
uti⌐ (o) ⌐mi⌐sete mo⌐raita⌐i kara.

---

[1] For explanation of special symbol |, see Part I, page xxxvii.

[2] Has unaccented alternant.

(b)

Smith

after it gets to be summer vacation	na˥tuya˥sumi ni ˥na˩tte kara
even if it's just two months	ni-˥ka˥ḡetu da˥ke˩ de mo

14. I'd like to come here after my summer vacation starts. Would you rent [the house] (even) for just two months? — Na˥tuya˥sumi ni ˥na˩tte kara ki˥ta˩i ñ desu ḡa, ni-˥ka˥ḡetu da˥ke˩ de mo ka˥site itadakeru˥ desyoo ka.

Landlord

the rent	ya˥tiñ
being July, August, September	siti-ḡatu hǎti-ḡatu ˥ku˥-ḡatu de
it has become <u>or</u> been decided <u>or</u> been set at <u>or</u> been made into	na˥tte (i)ru

15. The rent has been set at ¥70,000 for July, August, and September (but). . . — Ya˥tiñ (wa); siti-ḡatu hǎti-ḡatu ˥ku˥-ḡatu de, na˥namañ-eñ ni na˥tte orimasu ḡa—

Smith

commute	kayou /-u/

16. Would it be possible to commute as far as Tokyo? — To˥kyoo ma˥de ka˥yoeru˥ desyoo ka.

Landlord

17. Yes. It's a little far but there are people who commute. — E˥e. Tyo˥tto to˥oi˩ keredo, ka˥you hito˥ mo i˥ma˩su yo⌋

Smith

the remaining one month	a˥to no i˥k-ka˩ḡetu

18. Well then, I guess it would be all right if I rented it for three months, took my vacation for two months, and commuted during the remaining month. — Zya˥a, sa˥ñ-ka˥ḡetu karite; ni-˥ka˥ḡetu wa ya˥su˩ñde, a˥to no i˥k-ka˥ḡetu wa ka˥yotta˥ra ˥i˩i desyoo ˥ne˥e.

(c)

Smith

being hot <u>or</u> because it's hot	a˥tukute
be annoying because it's hot	a˥tukute ko˥ma˥ru

19. Tokyo summers are bad because of the heat. How is it here? — To˥okyoo no natu˥ wa ˥a˥tukute ko˥marima˥su ḡa, ko˥ko wa do˥o desyoo ka.

Landlord

being a case of having
been special or be-
cause it was special

to⌐kubetu da⌐tta no de

20. Last year was special so it
was hot here too, but usually
it's very cool.

Kyo⌐neñ wa to⌐kubetu da⁴tta no
de, ko⌐ko mo a⌐tukatta ñ⌐ desu ḡa;
hutuu wa to⌐temo suzusi⌐i ñ desu
yo⌐

Smith

vehicle

norimono

21. What about transportation?

Norimono wa?

Landlord

it's nothing

na⌐ñ de mo na⌐i

22. [To go] to the station it
takes about thirty minutes
if you walk, but in the summer there's a bus so it's
nothing at all.

E⌐ki made (wa) a⌐ru⌐ite sa⌐ñzyup-
puñ-ḡu⌐rai ka⌐karima⁴su ḡa; na-
⌐tu⌐ wa ⌐ba⌐su ḡa ⌐a⌐ru kara, na⌐ñ
de mo arimase⌐ñ yo.

Smith

23. How far do you go for shopping?

Kaimono (wa) ⌐do⌐ko made i⌐ki-
ma⁴su ka⌐

Landlord

there's everything
sake shop
fish market, vegetable
store, sake shop

na⌐ñ de mo a⌐ru
sakaya
sakanaya yáoya sákaya

24. Near the station there's
everything, but we have a
fish market, vegetable
store, and sake shop right
there.

E⌐ki no ⌐so⌐ba ni wa na⌐ñ de mo
arima⌐su ḡa, sakanaya yáoya sákaya wa ⌐su⌐ḡu so⌐ko ni arima⁴su
yo⌐

(d)

Smith

commodity prices

bukka

25. What about prices?

Bukka wa | do⌐o desu ka⌐

Landlord

never

kessite / + negative/

26. They're never high.

Ke⌐ssite ta⌐kaku wa a⌐rimase⁴ñ.

in particular
be surprised or amazed
or startled
being cheap or because
it's cheap
be amazed because it's
so cheap

to⌐ku ni
bi⌐kku⌐ri-suru

ya⌐sukute

a⌐ñmari ya⌐sukute bi⌐kku⌐-
ri-suru

27. In particular, the fish is so
cheap that you'll probably
be amazed.

To˺ku ni sa˹kana ḡa añmari ya˺-
sukute bi˹kku˺ri-nasaru desyoo.

Smith

however or but or
even so

de˺ mo

28. But isn't it the case that
prices go up in summer?

De˺ mo, na˹tu˺ wa bŭkka (ḡa)
a˹ḡaru˺ ñ zya ˪na˪i desyoo ka.

Landlord

merchant or shopkeeper
honest
being a case of being
honest or because
[someone] is honest

syo˺oniñ
syo˹oziki˺ /na/
syo˹oziki˺ na no de

29. The shopkeepers around
here are honest so there's
nothing to worry about.

Ko˹no heñ no syo˺oniñ wa syo-
˹oziki˺ na no de, si˹ñpai arima-
se˺ñ.

non-rice field or dry
field
in spite of the fact
that it is scarce

hatake

su˹kuna˪i no ni

30. And in spite of the fact that
there aren't many farms
(lit. fields) the vegetables
are cheap too.

Sosite; ha˹take ḡa sukuna˪i no
ni, ya˹sai mo yasu˪i ñ desu.

Smith

consider or think over
whether I rent it or not

ka˹ñgae˺ru /-ru/
o˹kari-site˺ mo si˹na˺kute
mo

31. In any case, I'll think it
over for a while, and whether
I rent [the house] or not, I'll
get in touch [with you].

To˺nikaku ˹tyo˺tto ka˪ñḡa˪ete,
o˹kari-site˺ mo si˹na˺kute mo
go˹reñraku-sima˺su.

week end

syuumatu

32. This week end I plan to come
here again so [I'll see you]
again then . . .

Ko˹no syuumatu ni˺ (wa) ma˹ta
kotira e ku˹ru tu˪mori da˪ kara,
so˹no to˺ki /ni/ mata—

(e)

Tanaka

in spite of the fact that
[someone] came

ki˹ta˺ no ni

33. We went to the trouble of
coming here but there
wasn't a good house for
rent, was there.

Se˹kkaku kita˺ no ni, i˪i kasiya
(wa) a˹rimase˺ñ desita ˪ne˪e.

Smith

34. It can't be helped so let's   Si⌐kata ḡa na⌐i kara, mata ra-
    look for one again, next   ⌐isyuu saḡasimasyo⌐o.
    week.

NOTES ON THE BASIC DIALOGUES

3. Note: ko⌐o 'this way,' so⌐o and a⌐a 'that way,' do⌐o 'what way?' or
   'how?'

8. The opposite of hu⌐beñ is be⌐ñri /na/
   Do not confuse be⌐ñri 'convenient' in the sense of 'handy, accessible,
   convenient to use' with tu⌐ḡoo ḡa i⌐i 'is convenient' indicating that
   stated conditions are convenient for someone on a particular occasion.
   A refrigerator is be⌐ñri; having the picnic next Saturday, tu⌐ḡoo ḡa i⌐i.

15. 'but—would this be agreeable to you?'
    Note the polite use of o⌐rima⌐su following a gerund, with an inanimate
    subject.

17. Note particle mo: '[Most people don't commute but] there are also
    people who do commute.'

22. Do not confuse na⌐ñ de mo na⌐i 'it is nothing' with na⌐ñi mo na⌐i 'there
    is nothing' and na⌐ñ de mo a⌐ru 'there is everything'

24. Sakaya refers to a shop where sake is sold in bottles to be taken out.
    Sakaba is a place where sake is drunk. The change of final -e to -a,
    when a word occurs as the first part of a compound, is common. Com-
    pare a⌐me with a⌐maḡa⌐sa 'rain umbrella' and a⌐ma⌐do 'storm shutters.'

26. The wa of comparison may occur within a negative adjectival expres-
    sion: ta⌐kaku wa ⌐na⌐i '[whatever else they may be] expensive they're
    not.'

28. Ke⌐redo (or more formal ke⌐redomo or more informal ke⌐do) 'however'
    is more often used when one speaker adds to what he has previously
    said, whereas de⌐ mo (lit. 'even being [so]') often accompanies a shift
    of speaker.
    The opposite of aḡaru is sa⌐ḡa⌐ru 'go down.' Both are intransitive
    verbals. Their transitive equivalents are a⌐ḡeru 'raise [something]' and
    sa⌐ḡe⌐ru 'lower [something].'

30. Hatake contrasts with ta⌐ 'rice field.' Ta⌐ is a paddy field, while ha-
    take is a dry field where things other than rice are grown.

31. O⌐kari-site⌐ mo si⌐na⌐kute mo is the humble equivalent of ka⌐rite⌐ mo
    ka⌐rina⌐kute mo.

GRAMMATICAL NOTES

1. Gerund Meaning 'because'

A gerund (or a phrase ending with a gerund) that is coordinate with what follows may explain the reason for what follows. Thus:

O⌐hu⌐ro ḡa a⌐tusu⌐ḡite ha⌐irimase⌐n̄ desita. 'The bath was too hot and [so] I didn't go in.' (Lit. 'The bath being too hot, I didn't go in.'

Sa⌐mukute i⌐ya⌐ desu. 'It's cold and [so] I don't like it.' (Lit. 'Being cold, I don't like it.')

Byooki de ki⌐mase⌐n̄ desita. 'He was sick and [so] he didn't come.' (Lit. 'Being sick, he didn't come.')

An extended predicate (cf. Lesson 23, Grammatical Note 1) may also occur in its gerund form as a causal expression: a non-past or past verbal, adjectival, or copula[1] is followed by no[2] + gerund de 'being the case that ——,' 'inasmuch as ——,' 'because ——.' Thus:

Ki⌐noo itta⌐ no de, kyo⌐o wa i⌐kimase⌐n̄. 'Inasmuch as I went yesterday, I'm not going today.' (Lit. 'Being the case that I went yesterday, I'm not going today.')

Hu⌐ru⌐i no de, a⌐tarasi⌐i no ḡa ka⌐ita⌐i n̄ desu ḡa_ 'Inasmuch as it's old I'd like to buy a new one . . .' (Lit. 'Being the case that it's old, I'd like to buy a new one . . .')

Byo⌐oki na⌐ no de, kyo⌐o wa ki⌐mase⌐n̄. 'Because he's sick he isn't coming today.' (Lit. 'Being a case of being sick, today he won't come.')

Thus, the following three sentences all contain causal expressions:

Ta⌐kakatta kara, ka⌐imase⌐n̄ desita. 'It was expensive so I didn't buy it.'

Ta⌐kakatta no de, ka⌐imase⌐n̄ desita. 'Inasmuch as it was expensive I didn't buy it.'

Ta⌐kakute ka⌐imase⌐n̄ desita. 'It was expensive and [so] I didn't buy it.'

Of the three alternatives, the one with no de is most formal.

An adjectival gerund of cause plus i⌐i 'being ——, it's nice' or 'it's nice because it's ——' is the closest Japanese equivalent of English 'it's nice and —— ' (i.e. 'it's —— in a pleasant way'). Thus, tu⌐meta⌐kute ⌐i⌐i 'it's nice and cold'; hi⌐rokute ⌐i⌐i 'it's nice and big.'

The gerund of cause may occur in sentence-final position, or pre-final before ne⌐e, in fragments (cf. Lesson 27, Grammatical Note 4). Thus:

A: I⌐kimase⌐n̄ desita ka_ 'Didn't you go?'

B: E⌐e. A⌐me ḡa ⌐hu⌐tte_ 'No. It was raining and [so I didn't].'

2. —— no ni 'in spite of the fact that —— '

A verbal, adjectival or copula (non-past or past) + nominal no + particle ni 'against' or 'in spite of' occurs in expressions of strong contrast: 'in spite of the fact that ——.'[3] Thus:

---

[1] Remember that the non-past copula form occurring before no is na.

[2] No may be contracted to n̄.

[3] A non-past verbal + no ni 'in spite of the fact that —— ' and a non-past verbal + no ni 'in the process of —— ' are distinguished by context.

Yo͡ku ha˥taraita˧ no ni, ze˥ñzeñ tukaremase˥ñ desita.
'In spite of the fact that I worked hard, I didn't get at all tired.'
Ta͡kakatta no ni, su͡ḡu da͡me˧ ni na˥rima˧sita.
'In spite of the fact that it was expensive, it broke right away.'
Byo͡oki na˧ no ni, ha˥taraki ni kima͡sita.
'In spite of the fact that he's sick, he came to work.'

Compare the following sentences, representing weak and strong degrees
of contrast:

Se˥tumee-site moraima͡sita ḡa, ma͡da wa˥karimase˥ñ.
'I had it explained to me but I still don't understand.'
Se˥tumee-site moratta˧ keredo, ma͡da wa˥karimase˥ñ.
'Although I had it explained to me, I still don't understand.'
Se˥tumee-site moratta˧ no ni, ma͡da wa˥karimase˥ñ.
'In spite of the fact that I had it explained to me, I still don't under-
stand.'

The first two sentences are almost interchangeable, but the third sentence
shows much stronger contrast.

Sekkaku frequently occurs within a —— no ni pattern, meaning 'in spite
of the fact that I took the trouble to —— .' Thus:

Se˥kkaku tuku͡tta no ni, da˥re mo tabemase˥ñ desita.
'In spite of the fact that I took the trouble to make it, nobody ate it.'

3. Quoted Alternate Questions

Review alternate questions in Lesson 12, Grammatical Note 3.

Alternate questions A ka and B ka occur in the informal style, preceding
inflected words like √wa˥kara͡nai 'don't understand' or 'isn't clear,' √sira-
nai 'don't know,' √wasureru 'forget,' etc., meaning 'whether A or B'; in
such occurrences they are called QUOTED ALTERNATE QUESTIONS. Before ka, the informal non-past da is regularly lost.

Examples:

I˥ku˧ ka i˥kana͡i ka si˥rimaseñ.
'I don't know whether he will go or won't go.'
Kore wa zi˥buñ de katta˧ ka, da˥re ka kara moratta˧ ka; wa͡surema͡sita.
'I have forgotten whether I bought this myself or got it from some-
one.' (Lit. 'As for this, did I buy it myself, did I receive it from
someone, I have forgotten.')
Sore wa de˥ki˧ru ka de˥ki˧nai ka, he˥ñzi˧ o site kudasai.
'Please give me an answer [as to] whether it's possible or not.'
A˥ma͡i ka su˥ppa͡i ka si˥rimaseñ ḡa, ta͡bete mimasyoo.
'I don't know whether it's sweet or sour but let's eat it and see.'
A˥no˧ hito no kuruma wa ˥Ho͡odo ka Kya˥dera͡kku ka, o˥bo͡ete i˥maseñ.
'I don't remember whether his car is a Ford or a Cadillac.'
A˥me datta ka, yu˥ki˧ datta ka, o˥bo͡ete i˥maseñ ḡa; sono hi ˥te͡ñki ḡa
͡wa͡rukatta koto wa ͡yo͡ku o˥bo͡ete imasu.
'I don't remember whether it was rain or snow, but the fact that the
weather was bad that day I remember well.'

When the second of a pair of quoted alternate questions is do͡o ka (an informal equivalent of do͡o desu ka) 'how is it?,' the combination is equivalent

to 'whether A *[or not]*.'[1] Thus:

o⌐mosiro⌐i ka tu⌐mara⌐nai ka kĩku 'ask whether it is interesting or dull'

but:

o⌐mosiro⌐i ka ⌐do⌐o ka kĩku 'ask whether it is interesting *[or not]*'

Examples:

Ta⌐naka-sañ wa kima⌐su ğa, Sa⌐too-sañ wa ⌐ku⌐ru ka ⌐do⌐o ka si⌐rima-
se⌐ñ.
'Mr. Tanaka is coming but I don't know whether Mr. Sato is coming
or not.'
Sono zassi wa o⌐mosiro⌐i ka ⌐do⌐o ka wa⌐kara⌐nakatta kara, ka⌐imase⌐ñ
desita.
'I couldn't tell whether that magazine was interesting *[or not]*, so I
didn't buy it.'
O⌐suki ka do⌐o ka ki⌐ite kudasa⌐i.
'Ask him whether he likes it *[or not]*.'
Ho⌐ñtoo ka do⌐o ka si⌐raberare⌐ru desyoo ka.
'Could you find out whether it's true *[or not]*?'

WARNING: Do not confuse quoted alternate questions with gerund + mo +
gerund + mo (Lesson 22, Grammatical Note 4); the English equivalents of
of both contain 'whether.' Compare:

Tanaka-san wa i⌐ku⌐ ka i⌐kana⌐i ka .si⌐rimase⌐ñ.
'I don't know [the answer to the question] whether Mr. Tanaka is go-
ing or (is) not (going).' (Lit. 'Is Mr. Tanaka going, is he not going,
I don't know.')

and:

Ta⌐naka-sañ ğa itte⌐ mo i⌐kana⌐kute mo, wa⌐takusi wa ikimase⌐ñ.
'Whether Mr. Tanaka goes or (does) not (go), I'm not going.' (Lit.
'Even if Mr. Tanaka goes, even if he doesn't go, I am not going.')

4. ―― to site

To site following a nominal is the Japanese equivalent of 'in the capacity
of ――,' 'as ――,' 'for ――.' Thus:

Se⌐ñse⌐e to site i⌐kima⌐sita. 'He went as a teacher.'

A ―― to site phrase as an item of comparison is followed by particle
wa. Thus:

Be⌐ñkyoo-suru mono⌐ to si⌐te⌐ wa, o⌐mosiro⌐i desu.
'As something to study, it's interesting.'
A⌐merika⌐ziñ to si⌐te⌐ wa, ni⌐hoñğo ğa zyoozu⌐ desu.
'His Japanese is good for an American.'

A ―― to site phrase may also be followed by particle mo 'even.' Thus:

A⌐merika no hatake to site⌐ mo o⌐oki⌐i desu.
'It's big even for an American farm (lit. field).'

---

[1] Do⌐o ka usually occurs in the Japanese equivalent, whereas 'or not' is op-
tional in English.

5. Enumeration

In enumeration, two or more nominals, with or without preceding modifiers, may follow one another without intervening particles. Each member of the series regularly begins a new accent phrase (i. e. is pronounced as if at the beginning of a sentence).

Examples:

hoꟹ zǎssi siꟹbuꟹ 'books, magazines, newspapers'
Tookyoo Yŏkohama ᒥKyoꟹoto 'Tokyo, Yokohama, Kyoto'
siᒥroꟹi waᒧꟹpiᐟisu, aᒥoꟹi ᒧseᐟetaa, koꟹꟹ no kutu 'white dress, blue sweater, navy blue shoes'

DRILLS

A. Substitution Drill

1.	It's never high.	Keᒥssite taꟹkaku aᒧrimaseᐟꟹ.
2.	It's not very high.	Aᒥꟹmari taꟹkaku aᒧrimaseᐟꟹ.
3.	It's not a bit high.	<u>Tiᒥttoꟹ mo</u> ᒧtaᐟkaku aᒧrimaseᐟꟹ.
4.	It's not at all high.	<u>Zeᒥꟹzeꟹꟹ</u> taꟹkaku aᒧrimaseᐟꟹ.
5.	It's not especially high.	<u>Beᒥtu ni</u> taꟹkaku aᒧrimaseᐟꟹ.
6.	It's really not high.	<u>Hoᒥꟹtoo wa</u> taꟹkaku aᒧrimaseᐟꟹ.
7.	It's ordinarily not high.	<u>Huᒥtuu wa</u> taꟹkaku aᒧrimaseᐟꟹ.

B. Substitution Drill

1.	It's so cheap that you'll probably be amazed.	Aᒥꟹmari yaꟹsukute, biᒥkkuꟹri-suru desyoo.
2.	It's so simple that you'll probably be amazed.	Aꟹmari <u>kañtañ de</u>, biᒥkkuꟹri-suru desyoo.
3.	It's so complicated that you'll probably be amazed.	Aꟹmari <u>hukuzatu de</u>, biᒥkkuꟹri-suru desyoo.
4.	It's so different that you'll probably be amazed.	Aꟹmari <u>tig̱atte (i)te</u>, biᒥkkuꟹri-suru desyoo.
5.	It's so noisy that you'll probably be amazed.	Aᒥꟹmari <u>yakamaꟹsikute</u>, biᒥkkuꟹri-suru desyoo.
6.	It's so quiet that you'll probably be amazed.	Aᒥꟹmari <u>siᒥzuka de</u>, biᒥkkuꟹri-suru desyoo.
7.	It's so strong that you'll probably be amazed.	Aᒥꟹmari <u>tuᒥyokute</u>, biᒥkkuꟹri-suru desyoo.
8.	It takes so much time that you'll probably be amazed.	Aᒥꟹmari <u>zikañ g̱a kakaꟹtte</u>, biᒥkkuꟹ-ri-suru desyoo.
9.	He's so young that you'll probably be amazed.	Aᒥꟹmari <u>waꟹkakute</u>, biᒥkkuꟹri-suru desyoo.

C. Grammar Drill (based on Grammatical Note 1)

> Tutor: A⌐tu⌉i desu yo↵ 'It's hot.'
> Student: A⌉tukute ko⌐marima⌉su yo↵ 'I'm bothered by the heat.'
> (Lit. 'Being hot, I'm bothered.')

1. Ta⌐ka⌉i desu yo↵   Ta⌉kakute ko⌐marima⌉su yo↵
2. Hu⌉beñ desu yo↵   Hu⌉beñ de ko⌐marima⌉su yo↵
3. Ma⌐tiḡaima⌉su yo↵   Ma⌐tiḡa⌉tte ko⌐marima⌉su yo↵
4. To⌐oi⌉ desu yo↵   To⌐o⌉kute ko⌐marima⌉su yo↵
5. Ta⌐rimase⌉ñ yo↵   Ta⌐rina⌉kute ko⌐marima⌉su yo↵
6. Mu⌐siatu⌉i desu yo↵   Mu⌐sia⌉tukute ko⌐marima⌉su yo↵
7. Hu⌐kuzatu de⌉su yo↵   Hukuzatu de ko⌐marima⌉su yo↵
8. Hu⌐ru⌉i desu yo↵   Hu⌉rukute ko⌐marima⌉su yo↵
9. O⌐mo⌉i desu yo↵   O⌐mo⌉kute ko⌐marima⌉su yo↵
10. Ka⌐bi ḡa haema⌉su yo↵   Ka⌐bi ḡa ha⌉ete ko⌐marima⌉su yo↵

D. Grammar Drill (based on Grammatical Note 1)

> Tutor: Su⌐zusi⌉i desu ⌐ne⌉e. 'Isn't it cool!'
> Student: Su⌐zu⌉sikute ⌐i⌉i desu ⌐ne⌉e. 'Isn't it nice and cool!'

1. Tu⌐meta⌉i desu ⌐ne⌉e.   Tu⌐meta⌉kute ⌐i⌉i desu ⌐ne⌉e.
2. Ha⌐rema⌉sita ⌐ne⌉e.   Ha⌉rete ⌐i⌉i desu ⌐ne⌉e.
3. Ka⌉ñtañ de⌉su ⌐ne⌉e.   Kañtañ de ⌐i⌉i desu ⌐ne⌉e.
4. Ti⌐ka⌉i desu ⌐ne⌉e.   Ti⌐ka⌉kute ⌐i⌉i desu ⌐ne⌉e.
5. Ki⌐ree desu ⌐ne⌉e.   Ki⌐ree de ⌐i⌉i desu ⌐ne⌉e.
6. Hi⌐ro⌉i desu ⌐ne⌉e.   Hi⌉rokute ⌐i⌉i desu ⌐ne⌉e.
7. Be⌉ñri desu ⌐ne⌉e.   Be⌉ñri de ⌐i⌉i desu ⌐ne⌉e.
8. Ka⌐ru⌉i desu ⌐ne⌉e.   Ka⌐ru⌉kute ⌐i⌉i desu ⌐ne⌉e.
9. Si⌉zuka desu ⌐ne⌉e.   Si⌉zuka de ⌐i⌉i desu ⌐ne⌉e.
10. Yo⌉ku ni⌐aima⌉su ⌐ne⌉e.   Yo⌉ku ni⌐a⌉tte ⌐i⌉i desu ⌐ne⌉e.

E. Grammar Drill (based on Grammatical Note 1)

> Tutor: Mo⌉o i⌐tta⌉ kara, mo⌉o i⌐kimase⌉ñ. ⎫ 'Because I already
>   ⎬ went, I won't go
> Student: Mo⌉o i⌐tta⌉ no de, mo⌉o i⌐kimase⌉ñ. ⎭ any more.'

1. Ha⌐zi⌉mete so⌐ñna mono⌐   Ha⌐zi⌉mete so⌐ñna mono⌉ (o)
    (o) ⌐mi⌐ta kara, bi⌐kku⌉ri-   ⌐mi⌐ta no de, bi⌐kku⌉ri-sima-
    simasita.   sita.
2. Ki ⌐ni irana⌉i kara, ya⌐me- Ki ⌐ni irana⌉i no de, ya⌐meta⌉i
    ta⌉i ñ desu ḡa↵   ñ desu ḡa↵
3. Syo⌐oziki⌉ da kara, so⌐ñna   Syo⌐oziki⌉ na no de, so⌐ñna
    koto⌉ wa si⌐mase⌉ñ.   koto⌉ wa si⌐mase⌉ñ.
4. Mo⌉o se⌐tumee-site mora-   Mo⌉o se⌐tumee-site moratta⌉
    tta⌉ kara, wa⌐ka⌉ru hazu   no de, wa⌐ka⌉ru hazu desu.
    desu.
5. Ha⌐take ḡa sukuna⌉i kara,   Ha⌐take ḡa sukuna⌉i no de,
    yasai wa ta⌐ka⌉i ñ desu.   yasai wa ta⌐ka⌉i ñ desu.

6. Be⌐ñkyoo-sina⌐katta kara,
   wa⌐karimase⌐ñ desita.

Be⌐ñkyoo-sina⌐katta no de, wa⌐ka-
rimase⌐ñ desita.

7. A⌐ñmari hukuzatu da⌐tta
   kara, ze⌐ñbu ka⌐ema⌐sita.

A⌐ñmari hukuzatu da⌐tta no de,
ze⌐ñbu ka⌐ema⌐sita.

8. Hu⌐ruku ˧na˦tta kara,
   a⌐tarasi⌐i no ga ka⌐ita⌐i
   ñ desu.

Hu⌐ruku ˧na˦tta no de, a⌐tarasi⌐i
no ga ka⌐ita⌐i ñ desu.

F. Grammar Drill (based on Grammatical Note 2)

> Tutor: Ha⌐take ga sukuna⌐i keredo, yasai wa ya⌐su⌐i ñ desu.
> 'Although there aren't many farms (lit. fields), the vegeta-
> bles are cheap.'
> Student: Ha⌐take ga sukuna⌐i no ni, yasai wa ya⌐su⌐i ñ desu.
> 'In spite of the fact that there aren't many farms, the veg-
> etables are cheap.'

1. Tu⌐ka⌐rete (i)˧ta˦ keredo,
   tu⌐zukema⌐sita.

Tu⌐ka⌐rete (i)˧ta˦ no ni, tu⌐zuke-
ma⌐sita.

2. Ta⌐ ya hǎtake ga o⌐o⌐i
   keredo, bukka wa ta⌐ka⌐i
   ñ desu.

Ta⌐ ya hǎtake ga o⌐o⌐i no ni,
bukka wa ta⌐ka⌐i ñ desu.

3. Hu⌐beñ na to˧koro˦ da
   keredo, ya⌐tiñ wa ta⌐ka⌐i
   ñ desu.

Hu⌐beñ na to˧koro˦ na no ni,
ya⌐tiñ wa ta⌐ka⌐i ñ desu.

4. Se⌐tumee-site morawana⌐-
   katta keredo, ze⌐ñbu wa-
   ⌐karima⌐sita.

Se⌐tumee-site morawana⌐katta
no ni, ze⌐ñbu wa⌐karima⌐sita.

5. Si⌐tya⌐a i⌐kena⌐i tte ˧tta˦
   kedo, sityatta.[1]

Si⌐tya⌐a i⌐kena⌐i tte ˧tta˦ no ni,
sityatta.

6. Mu⌐zukasisugi⌐ru keredo,
   ka⌐emase⌐ñ.

Mu⌐zukasisugi⌐ru no ni, ka⌐ema-
se⌐ñ.

7. Mo⌐to wa ka⌐ñtañ da⌐tta
   keredo, i⌐ma wa ⌐zu⌐ibuñ
   hu⌐kuzatu ni na⌐tte (i)ma-
   su.

Mo⌐to wa ka⌐ñtañ da⌐tta no ni,
i⌐ma wa ⌐zu⌐ibuñ hu⌐kuzatu ni
na⌐tte (i)masu.

G. Substitution Drill

1. In spite of the fact that
   I took the trouble to
   come here, there wasn't
   a good house for rent.

Se⌐kkaku ki̧ta⌐ no ni, i⌐i kǎsiya
(wa) a⌐rimase⌐ñ desita.

2. In spite of the fact that
   I took the trouble to make
   it, nobody ate it.
   /tu⌐ku⌐ru, da⌐re mo ta-
   be⌐nai/

Se⌐kkaku tuku⌐tta no ni, da⌐re
mo tabemase⌐ñ desita.

---

[1] Contracted equivalent of <u>Si⌐te⌐ wa i⌐kena⌐i tte i˧tta˦ keredo, site simatta</u>.

3. In spite of the fact that I
took the trouble to borrow
money, I didn't need it.
/okane o kariru, iranai/

Se⌐kkaku okane (o) karita¬ no ni,
i⌐rimase¬n̄ desita.

4. In spite of the fact that I
took the trouble to buy
it, I didn't use it. /kau,
tukawanai/

Se⌐kkaku katta¬ no ni, tu⌐kaimase¬n̄
desita.

5. In spite of the fact that I
took the trouble to bring
it, nobody looked at it.
/mo⌐tte ku¬ru, da⌐re mo
mi¬nai/

Se⌐kkaku motte¬ kita no ni, da⌐re
mo mimase¬n̄ desita.

6. In spite of the fact that I
took the trouble to get up
early, nobody appeared.
/ha¬yaku o┌ki˧ru, da⌐re
mo mie¬nai/

Se⌐kkaku ha¬yaku ┌o˧kita no ni,
da⌐re mo miemase¬n̄ desita.

H. Substitution Drill

1. I can't tell whether he
can do it or not.

So┌no¬ hito (wa) de⌐ki¬ru ka ┌do˧o
ka wa⌐karimase¬n̄.

2. I don't know whether he
can do it or not.

So┌no¬ hito (wa) de⌐ki¬ru ka ┌do˧o
ka si⌐rimase¬n̄.

3. I don't remember whether
he can do it or not.

So┌no¬ hito (wa) de⌐ki¬ru ka ┌do˧o
ka o⌐bo¬ete (i)¬mase¬n̄.

4. I've forgotten whether he
can do it or not.

So┌no¬ hito (wa) de⌐ki¬ru ka ┌do˧o
ka wa⌐surema¬sita.

5. Please tell me whether
he can do it or not.

So┌no¬ hito (wa) de⌐ki¬ru ka ┌do˧o
ka o⌐siete kudasa¬i.

6. Do you know whether he
can do it or not?

So┌no¬ hito (wa) de⌐ki¬ru ka ┌do˧o
ka go⌐zo¬n̄zi desyoo ka.

I. Grammar Drill (based on Grammatical Note 3)

    Tutor: Ta⌐ka¬i desu ka, ya⌐su¬i desu ka‿   'Is it expensive or is it
               cheap?'
    Student: Ta⌐ka¬i ka ya⌐su¬i ka si⌐rimase¬n̄.   'I don't know whether
               it's expensive or cheap.'

1. Hi⌐syo¬ (o) ya⌐toima¬sita
ka, ya⌐toimase¬n̄ desita
ka‿

Hi⌐syo¬ (o) ya⌐to¬tta ka ya⌐towa¬-
nakatta ka si⌐rimase¬n̄.

2. Ka┌n̄tan̄ de¬su ka, hu⌐ku-
zatu de¬su ka‿

Kan̄tan̄ ka hŭkuzatu ka si⌐rima-
se¬n̄.

3. Me⌐ḡane (o) ⌐ka¬kete (i)ma-
sita ka‿

Me⌐ḡane (o) ⌐ka¬kete (i)ta ka ┌do˧o
ka si⌐rimase¬n̄.

4. A┌ita uti¬ (ḡa) a⌐rima¬su
ka‿

A┌ita uti¬ (ḡa) ⌐a¬ru ka ┌do˧o ka
si⌐rimase¬n̄.

5. Tu┌yo¬i desu ka, yo⌐wa¬i
desu ka‿

Tu┌yo¬i ka yo⌐wa¬i ka si⌐rimase¬n̄.

6. Taˈisiˈkañ desita ka,   Taˈisiˈkañ datta ka ryoˈoziˈkañ
   ryoˈoziˈkañ desita ka⌐   datta ka siˈrimaseˈñ.
7. Syoˈokai-site moraimaˈ-   Syoˈokai-site morattaˈ ka ˈdoˈo
   sita ka⌐   ka siˈrimaseˈñ.
8. Oˈisiˈi desu ka⌐   Oˈisiˈi ka ˈdoˈo ka siˈrimaseˈñ.
9. Guˈñziñ deˈsita ka⌐   Guˈñziñ daˈtta ka ˈdoˈo ka siˈrima-
                                       seˈñ.
10. Kaˈsiya deˈsu ka⌐   Kaˈsiya ka doˈo ka siˈrimaseˈñ.

J. Grammar Drill (based on Grammatical Note 3)

> Tutor: Aˈtaraˈsikute mo ˈhuˈrukute mo kaˈmaimaseˈñ. 'It doesn't
>   matter whether it's new or old.'
> Student: Aˈtarasiˈi ka huˈruˈi ka siˈrimaseˈñ. 'I don't know whether
>   it's new or old.'

1. Yoˈyaku-siteˈ mo siˈnaˈ-   Yoˈyaku-suruˈ ka siˈnaˈi ka siˈri-
   kute mo kaˈmaimaseˈñ.   maseˈñ.
2. Hiˈrokute mo ˈseˈmakute   Hiˈroˈi ka seˈmaˈi ka siˈrimaseˈñ.
   mo kaˈmaimaseˈñ.
3. Waˈkakute mo toˈsiyoriˈ   Waˈkaˈi ka toˈsiyoriˈ ka siˈrima-
   de mo kaˈmaimaseˈñ.   seˈñ.
4. Oˈnazi deˈ mo tiˈgatte   Onazi ka tiˈgatte (i)ruˈ ka siˈri-
   (i)teˈ mo kaˈmaimaseˈñ.   maseˈñ.
5. Kaˈtaˈkute mo yaˈwaraˈ-   Kaˈtaˈi ka yaˈwarakaˈi ka siˈrima-
   kakute mo kaˈmaimaseˈñ.   seˈñ.
6. Haˈtaraiteˈ mo aˈsoñdeˈ   Haˈtarakuˈ ka aˈsobuˈ ka siˈrima-
   mo kaˈmaimaseˈñ.   seˈñ.
7. Beˈñri de mo ˈhuˈbeñ de   Beˈñri ka ˈhuˈbeñ ka siˈrimaseˈñ.
   mo kaˈmaimaseˈñ.
8. Keˈñbutu-siteˈ mo oˈyoˈgi   Keˈñbutu-suruˈ ka oˈyoˈgi ni iˈˈkuˈ
   ni iˈtteˈ mo kaˈmaima-   ka siˈrimaseˈñ.
   seˈñ.

K. Substitution Drill

1. I'm using it as a summer   Sore (o) naˈtu no utiˈ to site
   home.   tukatte (i)masu.
2. I'm using it as a cleaning   Sore (o) zoˈokiñ to site tukatte
   rag.   (i)maˈsu.
3. I'm using it as a baby   Sore (o) <u>aˈkatyañ no ˈbeˈtto</u> to
   bed.   site tukatte (i)masu.
4. I'm using it as a furoshiki.   Sore (o) <u>huˈrosiki</u> to site tukatte
                                  (i)maˈsu.
5. I'm using it as a desk.   Sore (o) <u>tuˈkue</u> to site tukatte
                                  (i)maˈsu.
6. I'm using it as a mos-   Sore (o) <u>kaˈya</u> to site tukatte
   quito net.   (i)maˈsu.
7. I'm using it as an ashtray.   Sore (o) <u>haˈizaˈra</u> to site tukatte
                                  (i)masu.
8. I'm using it as a store.   Sore (o) <u>miˈseˈ</u> to site tukatte
                                  (i)masu.

L. Substitution Drill

1. It's nice as a summer home, isn't it. — Na⌐tu no uti⌐ to si⌐te⌐ wa ⌐i⌐i desu ⌐he⌐e.
2. It's big for a farm (lit. field), isn't it. — Ha⌐take to site⌐ wa <u>hi⌐ro⌐i</u> desu ⌐he⌐e.
3. It's cheap for rent, isn't it. — Ya⌐tiñ to si⌐te⌐ wa <u>ya⌐su⌐i</u> desu ⌐he⌐e.
4. It's complicated for a plot, isn't it. — Su⌐zi to si⌐te⌐ wa <u>hu⌐kuzatu</u> de⌐su ⌐he⌐e.
5. It's long for a winter vacation, isn't it. — Hu⌐yuya⌐sumi to si⌐te⌐ wa <u>na⌐ga⌐i</u> desu ⌐he⌐e.
6. It's slow for an express, isn't it. — Kyu⌐ukoo to site⌐ wa <u>o⌐so⌐i</u> desu ⌐he⌐e.
7. He's heavy for a baby, isn't he. — A⌐katyañ to si⌐te⌐ wa <u>o⌐mo⌐i</u> desu ⌐he⌐e.
8. He's young for a teacher, isn't he. — Se⌐ñse⌐e to si⌐te⌐ wa <u>wa⌐ka⌐i</u> desu ⌐he⌐e.
9. He's nice as a person, isn't he. — Hi⌐to to site⌐ wa <u>⌐i⌐i</u> desu ⌐he⌐e.

M. Expansion Drill

1. I couldn't buy any. — Ka⌐emase⌐ñ desita.

   They were sold out already so I couldn't buy any. — Mo⌐o u⌐rikire da⌐tta kara, ka⌐ema se⌐ñ desita.

   In spite of the fact that I went to buy [them] they were sold out already so I couldn't buy any. — Ka⌐i ni itta⌐ no ni; mo⌐o u⌐rikire da⌐tta kara, ka⌐emase⌐ñ desita.

   In spite of the fact that I went to buy tickets, they were sold out already so I couldn't buy any. — Ki⌐ppu (o) kai ni itta⌐ no ni; mo⌐o u⌐rikire da⌐tta kara, ka⌐emase⌐ñ desita.

   In spite of the fact that I went all the way to the Kabukiza to buy tickets, they were sold out already so I couldn't buy any. — Ka⌐bukiza ma⌐de ki⌐ppu (o) kai ni itta⌐ no ni; mo⌐o u⌐rikire da⌐tta kara, ka⌐emase⌐ñ desita.

   In spite of the fact that I took the trouble to go all the way to the Kabukiza to buy tickets, they were sold out already so I couldn't buy any. — Se⌐kkaku Kabukiza ma⌐de ki⌐ppu (o) kai ni itta⌐ no ni; mo⌐o u⌐rikire da⌐tta kara, ka⌐emase⌐ñ de⌐sita.

2. I'd like to go. — I⌐kita⌐i ñ desu.

   I'd like to go after my summer vacation starts. — Na⌐tuya⌐sumi ni ⌐na⌐tte kara i⌐kita⌐i ñ desu.

Because there are lots of houses for rent, I'd like to go there after my summer vacation starts.

Ka⌐siya⌐ ḡa oo⌉i no de, na⌐tuya⌐su-mi ni ⌐na⁺tte kara i⌐kita⌉i ñ de-su.

Because the scenery is nice and there are lots of houses for rent, I'd like to go there after my summer vacation starts.

Ke⌉siki mo ⌐i⁺i si, ka⌐siya⌐ ḡa oo⌉i no de; na⌐tuya⌐sumi ni ⌐na⁺tte kara i⌐kita⌉i ñ desu.

Because [it] is convenient and the scenery is nice and there are lots of houses for rent, I'd like to go there after my summer vacation starts.

Be⌉ñri da si, ke⌉siki mo ⌐i⁺i si, ka⌐siya⌐ ḡa oo⌉i no de; na⌐tuya⌐su-mi ni ⌐na⁺tte kara i⌐kita⌉i ñ desu.

Because that town is con-venient and the scenery is nice and there are lots of houses for rent, I'd like to go there after my summer vacation starts.

A⌐no mati⌉ (wa) ⌐be⌉ñri da si, ke⌉-siki mo ⌐i⁺i si, ka⌐siya⌐ ḡa oo⌉i no de; na⌐tuya⌐sumi ni ⌐na⁺tte kara i⌐kita⌉i ñ desu.

3. I'll get in touch with you.

Go⌐reñraku-sima⌉su.

Even if I'm not going to rent it I'll get in touch with you.

Ka⌐rina⌉kute mo go⌐reñraku-sima⌉-su.

Whether I rent it or not I'll get in touch with you.

Ka⌐rite⌉ mo ka⌐rina⌉kute mo go⌐reñ-raku-sima⌉su.

I'll think it over a little and whether I rent it or not I'll get in touch with you.

Tyo⌉tto ka⌐ñḡa⁺ete, ka⌐rite⌉ mo ka-⌐rina⌉kute mo go⌐reñraku-sima⌉su.

I can't tell yet, but I'll think it over a little and whether I rent it or not I'll get in touch with you.

Ma⌐da wa⌐karimase⌉ñ ḡa; tyo⌉tto ka⌐ñḡa⁺ete, ka⌐rite⌉ mo ka⌐rina⌉-kute mo go⌐reñraku-sima⌉su.

I can't tell yet whether I'm going to rent it or not, but I'll think it over a little and whether I rent it or not I'll get in touch with you.

Ka⌐riru⌉ ka ⌐do⁺o ka ⌐ma⌉da wa⌐ka-rimase⌉ñ ḡa; tyo⌉tto ka⌐ñḡa⁺ete, ka⌐rite⌉ mo ka⌐rina⌉kute mo go-⌐reñraku-sima⌉su.

4. I think [it] is just fine.

Tyo⌐odo i⌉i to omoimasu.

I think an inn like this is just fine.

Koo iu ryokañ ḡa tyo⌐odo i⌉i to omoimasu.

I've been looking for [one]. I think an inn like this is just fine.

Sa⌐ḡasite (i)ru⌉ ñ desu ḡa, koo iu ryokañ ḡa tyo⌐odo i⌉i to omoimasu.

I've been looking for a
cheaper place. I think
an inn like this is just
fine.

Because it's too expen-
sive I've been looking
for a cheaper place. I
think an inn like this is
just fine.

I wanted to stop [there]
but because it's too ex-
pensive I've been look-
ing for a cheaper place.
I think an inn like this
is just fine.

I wanted to stop at a big
hotel but because they're
too expensive I've been
looking for a cheaper
place. I think an inn
like this is just fine.

Mo˥tto ya˦su˩i to˥koro˥ (o) sa˥g̃a-
site (i)ru˥ ñ desu g̃a, koo iu
ryokañ g̃a tyo˦odo i˩i to omoimasu.

A˦ñmari taka˩i no de, mo˥tto ya-
˦su˩i to˥koro˥ (o) sa˥g̃asite (i)ru˥
ñ desu g̃a; koo iu ryokañ g̃a
tyo˦odo i˩i to omoimasu.

To˥marita˩katta keredo; a˦ñmari
taka˩i no de, mo˥tto ya˦su˩i to-
˥koro˥ (o) sa˥g̃asite (i)ru˥ ñ
desu g̃a; koo iu ryokañ g̃a tyo-
˦odo i˩i to omoimasu.

O˦oki˩i ˥ho˥teru ni to˥marita˥ka-
tta keredo; a˦ñmari taka˩i no de,
mo˥tto ya˦su˩i to˥koro˥ (o) sa˥g̃a-
site (i)ru˥ ñ desu g̃a; koo iu ryokañ g̃a tyo˦odo i˩i to omoimasu.

QUESTION SUPPLEMENT

(based on the Basic Dialogues)

(a) 1. Su˦misu-sañ to Ta˦naka-sañ no hana˩site iru to˥koro˥ wa, do˥ñna to-
        ˥koro˥ desu ka↩

     2. Do˦o site ˥Su˥misu-sañ wa ko̊no heñ ni ka˦siya g̃a a˩ru ka ˥do˩o ka
        ki˥kima˥sita ka↩

     3. Ta˦naka-sañ no heñzi˥ wa?

     4. Su˦misu-sañ wa ˦do˥ko e i˥kita˥katta ñ desu ka↩ Do˦o site ya˥me-
        ma˥sita ka↩ I˥ma ˦do˦ñna to˥koro˥ o sa˥g̃asite ima˥su ka↩

     5. Ha˦zime ni mi˥ta uti wa ˦do˩o site ki ˥ni irimase˥ñ desita ka↩

     6. So˦no tug̃i˥ wa ˦do˦ñna u˥ti de˥sita ka↩ Ka˦siya de˥sita ka↩

     7. Ke˥siki wa ˦do˩o desu ka↩

     8. Tanaka-sañ wa ˦ya˦nusi o si˥tte ima˥su ka↩.

     9. Do˦o site ˥Su˥misu-sañ wa syo˥okai-site moraita˥i ñ desu ka↩

(b) 10. Su˦misu-sañ wa ˥i˥tu ki˥ta˥i ñ desu ka↩

     11. Su˦misu-sañ wa do˦no-g̃urai natu no uti o karita˩i ñ desu ka↩

     12. Ko˦no uti no ya˥tiñ wa ˥i˥kura desu ka↩

     13. Koko wa Tōkyoo kara to˦oi˥ desu ka, ti˥ka˩i desu ka↩

     14. To˥kyoo ma˥de ka˦yoema˥su ka↩

(c) 15. To˦okyoo no natu˥ wa ˦do˩o desu ka↩

     16. Ko˦ko no natu˥ wa hŭtuu ˦do˩o desu ka↩ Kyo˦neñ no na˥tu˥ wa ˦do˩o
        desita ka↩

     17. Kono uti kara ˥e˥ki made a˦ru˩ite do˦no-g̃urai kakarima˥su ka↩

     18. I˥tu mo ˥ba˦su g̃a a˦rima˥su ka↩

     19. E˥ki no ˥so˥ba ni ˦do˦ñna mi˥se˥ g̃a a˦rima˥su ka↩

     20. Do˦ñna mi˥se˥ g̃a ˥su˥g̃u ˥so˥ba ni a˦rima˥su ka↩

(d) 21. Koko no bukka wa ˹doˀo desu ka⌟
    22. Naˀni ga to˞kubetu ni yasuˀi n̄ desu ka⌟
    23. Na˞tu no bukka wa doˀo desu ka⌟
    24. Ko˞ko no yasai wa yasuˀi n̄ desu ga, sore wa kōno hen̄ wa ha˞take
        ga ooˀi kara desu ka⌟
    25. Suˀmisu-san̄ wa kōno uti o ka˞riru ka doˀo ka yānusi ni i˞imaˀsita
        ka⌟
    26. Suˀmisu-san̄ wa kōno syuumatu ni ˹doˀko e i˞ku tumori deˀsu ka⌟
    27. Suˀmisu-san̄ wa ˹yaˀnusi ni ˹doˀn̄na ya˞kusoku o simaˀsita ka⌟

(e) 28. Suˀmisu-san̄ wa rāisyuu ˹doˀo su˞ru tumori deˀsu ka⌟

EXERCISES

1. You have just met the owner of a house in Karuizawa which you are in-
   terested in renting for the summer. Using the Basic Sentences of this
   lesson as a point of departure, discuss the house, including as many questions and details as possible.

2. Make up six short dialogues each one of which contains one of the following:
   a. taˀkakatta no ni
   b. aˀme ga hu˞rihazimeˀta no de
   c. hi˞rune o sitaˀ no ni
   d. to˞siyoriˀ na no de
   e. se˞kkaku kitaˀ no ni
   f. ka˞isya ga tikaˀi no de

Lesson 30. Renting a House (cont.)

BASIC DIALOGUES: FOR MEMORIZATION

(a)

Tanaka

according to what Mr. Ueda says	U┌eda-san̄ no hanasi┐ ni yoru to
a house for rent that seems just right for you	a┌na┐ta ni tyo┌odo i┐i yoo na k┌a┐siya
advertisement	kookoku
an advertisement for a house for rent	kasiya no kookoku
1. According to (what) Mr. Ueda (says), in this morning's paper there was an ad for a house for rent that seems just right for you. Did you see it?	U┌eda-san̄ no hanasi┐ ni yoru to, ke┐sa no sin̄bun̄ ni a┌na┐ta ni tyo┌odo i┐i yoo na ka┌siya no kookoku ḡa a┐tta soo desu ḡa; go┌ran̄ ni narima┐sita ka⌣

Smith

2. I just read it.	Yo┐n̄da to⊢koro⊣ desu.

(handing over newspaper)

This is it. Here.	Ko┌re de┐su yo. Do┐ozo.

Tanaka (after reading the advertisement)

maybe it's good	i┐i ka mo sirenai
3. Oh, this may be good!	A┐a, i┐i ka mo siremasen̄ ┌ne┐e.
agent	bu┌ro┐okaa
4. Why don't you ask the agent and see [about it]?	Bu┌ro┐okaa ni ki┌ite mi┐tara ⊢do⊣o desyoo.

(b)

Smith

facts pertaining to a house	u┌ti no koto┐
concerning facts pertaining to a house	u┌ti no koto┐ de
5. I'd like to inquire about a house . . .	U┌ti no koto┐ de ┌tyo┐tto u┌kaḡai-ta┐i n̄ desu ḡa—
(name of a Japanese newspaper)	A┐sahi

6. I read [about it] in Asahi this   Ke⌐sa ⌐A⌐sahi de yo⌐mima⌐sita ḡa,
    morning. What kind of house   aｈo uti⌐ (wa) ⌐doｈna u⌐ti⌐ desu
    is that (house)?   ka⌐

Agent

      building lot   sikiti
      one tsubo (approximately   hi⌐to⌐-tubo
         6' x 6')
      200 tsubo   ni⌐hyaku⌐-tubo
7. Let's see. The lot is (lit.   So⌐o desu ｈe⌐e. Sikiti (wa) ni⌐hya-
    has) 200 tsubo.   ku⌐-tubo a⌐rima⌐su yo⌐

Smith

8. That's big, isn't it—for in   Hi⌐ro⌐i desu ｈe⌐e — ma⌐ti no na⌐ka
    the city . . .   to si⌐te⌐ wa.

Agent

      three-mat area or room   sa⌐ñ-zyo⌐o
      four-and-one-half-mat   yo-⌐zyo⌐o-hañ
        area or room
      six-mat area or room   ro⌐ku-zyo⌐o
      eight-mat area or room   ha⌐ti-zyo⌐o
      ten-mat area or room   zyu⌐u-zyo⌐o
9. Yes. The house consists of   E⌐e. Uti wa ha⌐ti-zyo⌐o; ro⌐ku-
    (lit. is) an eight-mat room,   zyo⌐o hu⌐ta⌐-ma; yo-⌐zyo⌐o-hañ;
    two six-mat rooms, a four-   sa⌐ñ-zyo⌐o; sore kara, zyu⌐u-
    and-one-half-mat room, a   zyo⌐o no yo⌐oma na⌐ ñ desu ḡa—
    three-mat room, and a
    Western-style room with a
    ten-mat area . . .

Smith

10. I see.   A⌐a, so⌐o.

Agent

      south   minami
      facing south   minamimuki
      exposure to the sun   hiatari
      is sunny   hi⌐atari ḡa i⌐i
11. It's not a very big house, but   A⌐ñmari ooki⌐i u⌐ti⌐ zya ｈa⌐i ñ
    it faces south so it's sunny,   desu ḡa; mi⌐namimuki de⌐su
    and it has a large beautiful   kara, hi⌐atari ḡa yo⌐kute; sore
    garden.   kara, hi⌐ro⌐i ⌐ki⌐ree na ni⌐wa
     ḡa arima⌐su yo⌐

Smith

      equipment or facilities   se⌐tubi
       or accommodations
12. Oh. How is the equipment?   So⌐o desu ka. Se⌐tubi (wa) ⌐do⌐o
     desyoo ka.

Agent

13. It's good—very [good].   I⌐¹i desu yo⌐ — tottemo⌐

Smith

    flushing   suiseñ
14. I suppose the toilet is a   Te⌐a⌐rai (wa) su⌐iseñ desyo⌐o ne?
    flush toilet, isn't it?

Agent

15. Yes, that's right.   E⌐e ⌐so⌐o desu yo⌐

Smith

    running water or   suidoo
      water pipes
16. What about gas [and] running   Ga⌐su, suidoo wa?
    water?

Agent

17. Of course it's running water   Mo⌐ti⌐roñ su⌐idoo de⌐su ga, ano
    but that area doesn't have gas   heñ (wa) ⌐ma⌐da ⌐ga⌐su wa ⌐na⌐i ñ
    yet.   desu yo.

Smith

18. What about the bath?   O⌐hu⌐ro wa?

Agent

    coal   se⌐kita⌐ñ
19. It's [heated with] coal.   Se⌐kita⌐ñ desu.

Smith

    heating   dañboo
20. How about the heating?   Dañboo wa?

Agent

    Western-style building   yookañ
    heating equipment or   da⌐ñboose⌐tubi
      central heating
21. It's not a Western-style   Yo⌐okañ zya na⌐i ñ desu kara,
    building so there's no central   da⌐ñboose⌐tubi (wa) a⌐rimase⌐ñ.
    heating.

        I guess or you might   ma⌐a
          say
        electric heater   de⌐ñkisuto⌐obu
        quilt-covered warming   kotatu
          place
        to the approximate extent   ko⌐tatu-gu⌐rai
          of a kotatsu
22. I guess electric heaters, hi-   Ma⌐a; de⌐ñkisuto⌐obu, hi⌐bati,
    bachi, [and] kotatsu are about   ko⌐tatu-gu⌐rai de⌐
    all [that you could use] . . .

Smith

repairs	syuuzeñ
the tenant (lit. the side	ka⌐riru ho⌐o
that borrows or rents)	
do [it] through the tenant	ka⌐riru ho⌐o de suru

23. The repairs wouldn't have to
be made by the tenant, would
they?

Syuuzeñ (wa) ka⌐riru ho⌐o de si-
⌐na⌐kute mo ⌐i⌐i ñ desyoo ne?

Agent

24. No (lit. that's right), (because)
the landlord makes them.

E⌐e, ya⌐nusi ḡa si⌐ma⌐su kara—

(c)

Landlord (showing the house)

roof	ya⌐ne
fence	ka⌐ki⌐ne
wall	hee
become painful or	i⌐ta⌐mu /-u/
damaged or worn out	
be painful or damaged	i⌐ta⌐ñde (i)ru
or worn out	

25. [Right] now I'm repairing the
roof and (ex)changing the
mats. The fence and wall
are also a bit damaged so
I'm thinking of repairing
them too.

I⌐ma ⌐ya⌐ne (o) na⌐o⌐site, ta⌐ta-
mi (o) torikaete (i)ma⌐su ḡa;
ka⌐ki⌐ne to hee mo ⌐tyo⌐tto i⌐ta-
ñde (i)masu kara, so⌐re mo na-
oso⌐o to o⌐mo⌐tte (i)ru ñ desu.

Smith

wall of a room	kabe

26. How about the walls?

Kabe wa?

Landlord

paint	nuru /-u/
repaint	nu⌐rikae⌐ru /-ru/

27. The walls are clean so I don't
think they'll have to be repainted (lit. I think it will be
all right even if I don't repaint them).

Ka⌐be wa ki⌐ree desu kara, nu-
⌐rikae⌐nakute mo ⌐i⌐i to omoimasu.

Smith

screens	a⌐mi⌐do

28. Are there screens?

A⌐mi⌐do (ḡa) a⌐rima⌐su ka—

Landlord

29. There aren't any but I can
put them on right away.

Na⌐i ñ desu ḡa, su⌐ḡu tu⌐kera-
rema⌐su yo.

Smith

trash   go⌐mi⌐
30. What about trash?   Go⌐mi⌐ wa?

Landlord

trash collector   go⌐mi⌐ya
31. The trash collector comes so   Go⌐mi⌐ya (ḡa) ki┌ma┘su kara, go-
    don't worry about that.   ⌐siñpai na┘ku.

Smith

day after tomorrow   a⌐sa⌐tte
32. Well, I'll bring my wife the   Zya⌐a, a⌐sa⌐tte ⌐ka⌐nai (o) tu┌rete
    day after tomorrow; (so)   kima┘su kara, mo⌐o iti-do mi⌐-
    would you let me see [the   sete i┌tadakemase┘ñ ka.
    house] again [then]?

Landlord

maybe [someone] isn't   i⌐na⌐i ka mo sirenai
there
33. I may not be in but my wife   Wa┌takusi wa ina⌐i ka mo si-
    will be here so come right   ┌remase┘ñ ḡa; ka⌐nai wa o⌐ri-
    ahead.   ma┘su kara, do⌐ozo.

ADDITIONAL VOCABULARY

1. The chimney is damaged so I   E┌ñtotu ḡa ita⌐ñde (i)masu kara,
   want to have it fixed . . .   na┌o┘site mo┌raita┘i ñ desu ḡa—

       floor   yuka
       ceiling   teñzyoo
       gate   mo⌐ñ

2. I'd like to see the southern   Nihoñ no minami no ho⌐o ḡa
   part of Japan . . .   mi┌ta⌐i ñ desu ḡa—

       north   ki┌ta⌐
       east   hi┌ḡasi⌐
       west   nisi

NOTES ON THE BASIC DIALOGUES

1. Note again the occurrence of particle ḡa separating a statement from a
   related question.

6. See preceding note.

9. Ro⌐ku-zyo⌐o hu┌ta┘-ma: note the occurrence of a number directly following a member of an enumerated series.

11. Note also: kitamuki 'facing north,' hiḡasimuki 'facing east,' and nisi-
    muki 'facing west.'

23. Note: syuuzeñ-suru 'repair,' 'fix' is used in reference to houses, machines, watches, etc. Na⌐o¬su is a word of more general use.
For a description of the negative permission pattern, see Lesson 22, Grammatical Note 4.

25. Hee is an outdoor wall, for example one surrounding a house; kabe (Basic Sentence 26) refers most frequently to the plaster walls in a Japanese house.

27. Nu⌐rikae¬ru: compare ki⌐kae¬ru 'change clothes'; no⌐rikae¬ru 'change vehicles'; torikaeru 'exchange.'
For a description of the negative permission pattern, see Lesson 22, Grammatical Note 4.

GRAMMATICAL NOTES

1. to⌐koro¬ [1]

In many of its occurrences, the nominal to⌐koro¬ refers only to spatial location and means 'place.' For example:

Ki¬ree na to⌐koro¬ desu. 'It's a pretty place.'
Ka¬gu o u⌐tte iru tokoro¬ wa ⌐do¬ko desu ka⌟ 'Where is the place where they sell furniture?

But in other contexts, to⌐koro¬ refers to location in time and means 'occasion' or 'moment' or 'point in time.' The words occurring with to⌐koro¬ or the over-all context determines which meaning it has in any given occurrence.

The following examples illustrate some of the uses of to⌐koro¬ as a time word. Note that in other contexts many of these same combinations would refer to place.

to⌐koro¬ + √da

Yo¬mu to⌐koro¬ desu. 'I'm just going to read.'
Yo¬ñde iru to⌐koro¬ desu. 'I'm just reading.'
Yo¬ñda to⌐koro¬ desu. 'I've just read.'
Yo¬ñde ita to⌐koro¬ desu. 'I have just been reading.'
Yo¬mo¬o to si⌐te iru tokoro¬ desu. 'I'm just on the point of reading.'
   or 'I'm just about to read.'
Yo¬mu to⌐koro¬ desita. 'I was just going to read.'
Yo¬ñde iru to⌐koro¬ desita. 'I was just reading.'
Yo¬ñda to⌐koro¬ desita. 'I had just read.'
Yo¬ñde ita to⌐koro¬ desita. 'I had just been reading.'
Yo¬mo¬o to si⌐te iru tokoro¬ desita. 'I was just about to read.'

to⌐koro¬ + o

Se⌐ñse¬e ga ⌐yo¬ñde iru to⌐koro¬ o mi⌐ma¬sita. 'I saw the teacher just as he was reading.'
O⌐isoḡasii tokoro¬ o a⌐ri¬ḡatoo gozaimasita. 'Thank you [for your kindness] just at a time when you are busy.'

---

[1] The contracted equivalent is toko.

$$to^\lceil koro^\rceil + \left|\begin{matrix} e \\ \overline{ni} \end{matrix}\right|$$

Se^⌐ñse⌐e ḡa ⌊yo⌐ñde iru to^⌐koro⌐ $\left|\begin{matrix} e \\ ni \end{matrix}\right|$ ki^⌐ma⌐sita. 'I came just as the teacher was reading.'

The gerund of an intransitive verbal of motion + √iru regularly refers to a state rather than an action:

> ka⌐eru 'return' ~ ka⌐ette iru 'be back'
> ku⌐ru 'come' ~ ki^⌐te⌐ iru 'be here' etc.

However, before to^⌐koro⌐, such combinations often refer to the actual occurrence of the action: ka⌐ette iru tokoro 'just the time when [someone] is returning,' ki^⌐te⌐ iru tokoro 'just the time when [someone] is coming.'

2. ――ka mo sirenai

X + ka mo sirenai (formal, si^⌐remase⌐ñ) means 'maybe X,' 'X may be true.' X consists of, or ends with, a verbal (informal non-past or past), an adjectival (informal non-past or past, affirmative or negative), a nominal, da⌐tta, or a particle. In other words, ka mo sirenai is preceded by an informal sentence, non-past or past, but before ka mo sirenai, the informal non-past copula da is lost.

The accent of inflected words before ka is the same as that before kara, no, keredo, etc. Following an unaccented word or phrase, the ka of ka mo sirenai is accented.

Examples:

> Ku⌐ru ka mo siremaseñ. 'Maybe he'll come.'
> Ki⌐ta ka mo siremaseñ. 'Maybe he has come.'
> Mu^⌐zukasi⌐i ka mo siremaseñ. 'It may be difficult.'
> Mu^⌐zukasi⌐katta ka mo siremaseñ. 'It may have been difficult.'
> I^⌐sya ka⌐ mo siremaseñ. 'He may be a doctor.'
>   (Cf. Isya da. 'He is a doctor.')
> Byo^⌐oki da⌐tta ka mo siremaseñ. 'Maybe he was sick.'
> Bo⌐ku no ka mo siremaseñ. 'Maybe it's mine.'
>   (Cf. Bo⌐ku no da. 'It is mine.')
> To^⌐modati kara ka⌐ mo siremaseñ. 'Maybe it's from a friend.'
>   (Cf. Tomadati kara da. 'It's from a friend.')
> To^⌐modati da⌐ kara ka mo siremaseñ. 'Maybe it's because he's a friend.'
>   (Cf. To^⌐modati da⌐ kara da. 'It's because he's a friend.')
> Ko⌐nai ka mo siremaseñ. 'Maybe he won't come.'
> Mu^⌐zukasiku na⌐i ka mo siremaseñ. 'Maybe it isn't difficult.'
> So⌐o zya ⌐na⌐i ka mo siremaseñ. 'Maybe it isn't so.'

3. ――ni yoru to

A nominal followed by ni yoru to indicates the source of the statement that follows. The source may be a person (se^⌐ñse⌐e ni yoru to 'according to the teacher'), but more often it is a thing (ra^⌐zio ni yoru to 'according to the radio'), particularly something said or written (se^⌐ñse⌐e no ha^⌐nasi⌐ ni yoru to 'according to what the teacher says,' a⌐no hoᐟn̄ ni yoru to 'according to that book'). —— ni yoru to is a rather formal expression.

Most sentences containing —— ni yoru to also contain soᐟo √da (Lesson 22, Grammatical Note 2) as a further indication that the information is second-hand. Thus:

> Keᐟsa moratta teḡami ni yoru to, Tookyoo wa koᐟtosi ⌐zuᐟibuñ saᐟmuᐟi soo desu.
> 'According to a letter I received this morning, (the report is that) Tokyo is awfully cold this year.'
> Toᐟmodati no hanasiᐟ ni yoru to, a⌐no buroᐟokaa wa syoᐟozikiᐟ zya ⌐naᐟi soo desu ḡa; ho⌐n̄too deᐟsu ka↲
> 'According to what a friend tells me, (the report is that) that agent isn't honest. Is that true?'

4. Counters: -tubo, -zyoo

-Tubo is the most common counter of Japanese area measurement for building lots, gardens, houses, etc. One tsubo equals the area covered by two tatami, i.e. approximately 36 square feet. For combinations with numerals from 1 to 10, see the list below noting the mixture of numerals from both series; from 11 on, -tubo combines with numerals of Series I: zyu⌐uiᐟt-tubo '11 tsubo,' zyu⌐uniᐟ-tubo '12 tsubo,' etc.).

-Zyoo is another Japanese area counter, used in measuring the size of rooms. One jo equals the area covered by one tatami, i.e. approximately 18 square feet or exactly ¹/₂-tsubo. -Zyoo combines with numerals of Series I, but only certain combinations occur with any frequency (see the list, following). A numeral compounded with -zyoo, besides indicating an area, may also be used as the name for a room having that area.

Study the following lists:

hi⌐toᐟ-tubo	'1 tsubo'	i⌐ti-zyoᐟo	'1-mat area'
hu⌐taᐟ-tubo	'2 tsubo'	ni-⌐zyoᐟo	'2-mat area'
miᐟ-tubo	'3 tsubo'	sa⌐n̄-zyoᐟo	'3-mat area' or '3-mat room'
yoᐟ-tubo	'4 tsubo'	yo-⌐zyoᐟo-hañ	'4 ¹/₂-mat area' or '4 ¹/₂-mat room'
i⌐tuᐟ-tubo or go ᐟ-tubo	'5 tsubo'		
ro⌐kuᐟ-tubo	'6 tsubo'	ro⌐ku-zyoᐟo	'6-mat area' or '6-mat room'
na⌐naᐟ-tubo	'7 tsubo'		
haᐟt-tubo	'8 tsubo'	ha⌐ti-zyoᐟo	'8-mat area' or '8-mat room'
kyu⌐uᐟu-tubo	'9 tsubo'		
toᐟ-tubo	'10 tsubo'	zyu⌐uᐟu-zyoᐟo	'10-mat area' or '10-mat room'
naᐟn̄-tubo	'how many tsubo?'	naᐟn̄-zyoo	'area of how many mats?'

5. More About -g̃u⌐rai

-G̃u⌐rai 'about' has occurred previously following numbers and indefinite
quantity expressions (cf. Lesson 8, Grammatical Note 5). It may also occur
following non-quantity expressions indicating approximate extent: 'to the extent of ——,' 'about as much as ——,' '—— being about all.'

Examples:

   Kyo⌐neñ wa, a⌐no mise no hito⌐ wa, mi⌐ñna eeg̃o g̃a dekima⌐sita g̃a;
      kotosi wa, Tanaka-sañ, Ya⌐mamoto-sañ-g̃u⌐rai de; ho⌐ka no hito⌐
      wa, ze⌐ñzeñ dekimase⌐ñ.
   'Last year the people in that store could all speak English, but this
      year Tanaka and Yamamoto are about the only ones and the other
      people can't speak at all.'
   Hu⌐zisañ-g̃u⌐rai ⌐ki⌐ree na ya⌐ma⌐ wa, do⌐ko ni mo na⌐i to omoimasu.
   'I don't think there is a mountain as pretty as Fuji (lit. pretty about
      as much as Fuji) anywhere.'

X-G̃u⌐rai usually occurs with an affirmative inflected expression. Compare:

   Yu⌐ki-g̃u⌐rai si⌐ro⌐i desu. 'It's as white as snow.'
with:
   Yu⌐ki⌐ hodo ⌐si⌐roku a⌐rimase⌐ñ. 'It isn't as white as snow.'

DRILLS

A. Substitution Drill

1. It's big, isn't it—for in the city.	Hi⌐ro⌐i desu ⌐ne⌐e — ma⌐ti no na⌐ka to si⌐te⌐ wa.
2. It's weak, isn't it—for a wall.	Yo⌐wa⌐i desu ⌐ne⌐e — <u>he⌐e</u> to site⌐ wa.
3. He's young, isn't he—for a parent.	Wa⌐ka⌐i desu ⌐ne⌐e — <u>o⌐ya⌐</u> to si⌐te⌐ wa.
4. It's pretty, isn't it—for an ad.	Ki⌐ree desu ⌐ne⌐e — <u>ko⌐okoku</u> to site⌐ wa.
5. It's big, isn't it—for a kotatsu.	O⌐oki⌐i desu ⌐ne⌐e — <u>ko⌐tatu</u> to site⌐ wa.
6. It's out of the ordinary, isn't it—for a Western building.	To⌐kubetu de⌐su ⌐ne⌐e —<u>yo⌐okañ</u> to site⌐ wa.
7. It's unusual, isn't it—for a gate.	Me⌐zurasi⌐i desu ⌐ne⌐e — <u>⌐mo⌐ñ</u> to si⌐te⌐ wa.
8. It's dark, isn't it—for the color of a wall.	Ko⌐i desu ⌐ne⌐e — <u>ka⌐be no iro⌐</u> to si⌐te⌐ wa.
9. It's elegant, isn't it—for inn equipment.	Ri⌐ppa de⌐su ⌐ne⌐e —<u>ryo⌐kañ no se⌐tubi</u> to si⌐te⌐ wa.

B. Substitution Drill

1. I'd like to ask about a house...	U⌐ti no koto⌐ de ⌐tyo⌐tto u⌐kagai-ta⌐i ñ desu g̃a_

2. I'd like to ask about kabuki . . . — Ka⌐buki no koto⌐ de ⌐tyo⌐tto u⌐ka-
   ḡaita⌐i ñ desu ḡa_

3. I'd like to ask about kimono . . . — Ki⌐mono no koto⌐ de ⌐tyo⌐tto u⌐ka-
   ḡaita⌐i ñ desu ḡa_

4. I'd like to ask about inns . . . — Ryo⌐kañ no koto⌐ de ⌐tyo⌐tto u⌐ka-
   ḡaita⌐i ñ desu ḡa_

5. I'd like to ask about universities . . . — Da⌐iḡaku no koto⌐ de ⌐tyo⌐tto u⌐ka-
   ḡaita⌐i ñ desu ḡa_

6. I'd like to ask about the rainy season . . . — Tu⌐yu no koto⌐ de ⌐tyo⌐tto u⌐kaḡai-
   ta⌐i ñ desu ḡa_

C. Substitution Drill

1. The lot is (lit. has) 200 tsubo. — Sikiti (wa) ni⌐hyaku⌐-tubo a⌐rima⌐-
   su yo_

2. That house has five rooms. — Ano uti (wa) i⌐tu⌐-ma a⌐rima⌐su
   yo_

3. The parlor is ten mats. — Za⌐siki⌐ (wa) zyuu-zyo⌐o a⌐rima⌐su
   yo_

4. The garden is 50 tsubo. — Niwa (wa) go⌐zyu⌐t-tubo a⌐rima⌐su
   yo_

5. That inn has 100 rooms. — Ano ryokañ (wa) hya⌐ku⌐-ma a⌐ri-
   ma⌐su yo_

6. The study is eight mats. — Syosai (wa) ha⌐ti-zyo⌐o a⌐rima⌐su
   yo_

7. That house for rent is 35 tsubo. — Ano kasiya (wa) ⌐sa⌐ñzyuu ⌐go⌐-
   tubo a⌐rima⌐su yo_

8. The bedroom is six mats. — Siñsitu (wa) ro⌐ku-zyo⌐o a⌐rima⌐su
   yo_

D. Substitution Drill (based on Grammatical Note 3)

1. According to what Mr. Ueda says, it's very interesting. — U⌐eda-sañ no hanasi⌐ ni yoru to,
   to⌐ttemo omosiro⌐i soo desu.

2. According to a letter from an acquaintance, it's very interesting. — Siriai kara no teḡami ni yoru to,
   to⌐ttemo omosiro⌐i soo desu.

3. According to this morning's Asahi, it's very interesting. — Ke⌐sa no ⌐A⌐sahi ni yoru to, to-
   ⌐ttemo omosiro⌐i soo desu.

4. According to the magazine I bought last night, it's very interesting. — Yuube katta zassi ni yoru to,
   to⌐ttemo omosiro⌐i soo desu.

5. According to what I heard on the radio tonight, it's very interesting. — Ko⌐ñbañ kiita ⌐ra⌐zio ni yoru to,
   to⌐ttemo omosiro⌐i soo desu.

6. According to the book I read yesterday, it's very interesting. — Ki⌐noo yo⌐ñda ⌐ho⌐ñ ni yoru to,
   to⌐ttemo omosiro⌐i soo desu.

E. Substitution Drill (based on Grammatical Note 1)

1. I just read the ad.   Ko⌐okoku (o) yo⌐ñda to⌐koro⌐ desu.
2. I'm just repainting the   Ka⌐be (o) nurika⌐ete iru to⌐koro⌐
    walls.   desu.
3. I'm just going to take a   O⌐hu⌐ro ni ⌐ha⌐iru to⌐koro⌐ desu.
    bath.
4. I've just been writing   Te⌐ḡami (o) ka⌐ite (i)ta to⌐koro⌐
    letters.   desu.
5. I'm just about to go   U⌐ti e kaero⌐o to si⌐te (i)ru to-
    home.   koro⌐ desu.
6. I was just about to go   U⌐ti e kaero⌐o to si⌐te (i)ru to-
    home.   koro⌐ desita.
7. I had just had it pressed.   A⌐iroñ (o) ka⌐kete mo⌐ratta toko-
                                         ro⌐ desita.
8. I was just looking up the   De⌐ñwaba⌐ñḡoo (o) si⌐ra⌐bete (i)ru
    telephone number.   to⌐koro⌐ desita.
9. I had just been talking on   De⌐ñwa de hana⌐site (i)ta to⌐koro⌐
    the telephone.   desita.

F. Grammar Drill (based on Grammatical Note 1)

        Tutor: Yo⌐mima⌐sita. 'I read [it].'
        Student: Yo⌐nda to⌐koro⌐ desu. 'I just read [it].'

1. Ka⌐be (o) nutte (i)ma⌐su.   Ka⌐be (o) nutte (i)ru tokoro⌐ desu.
2. Ya⌐ne (o) na⌐osima⌐sita.   Ya⌐ne (o) na⌐o⌐sita to⌐koro⌐ desu.
3. Hu⌐toñ (o) siite (i)ma⌐su.   Hu⌐toñ (o) siite (i)ru tokoro⌐ desu.
4. Da⌐iḡaku (o) dema⌐sita.   Da⌐iḡaku (o) de⌐ta to⌐koro⌐ desu.
5. Ku⌐ruma (o) miḡaite   Ku⌐ruma (o) miḡaite (i)ru tokoro⌐
    (i)ma⌐su.   desu.
6. Ta⌐tami (o) torikaema⌐-   Ta⌐tami (o) torikaeta tokoro⌐
    sita.   desu.
7. De⌐ñwatyoo (o) saḡasite   De⌐ñwatyoo (o) saḡasite (i)ru to-
    ima⌐su.   koro⌐ desu.
8. Su⌐ñpoo (o) hakarima⌐-   Su⌐ñpoo (o) haka⌐tta to⌐koro⌐ desu.
    sita.

G. Substitution Drill

1. [He] came just as [I] was   Ko⌐okoku (o) yo⌐nde (i)ru to⌐koro⌐
    reading the ads.   e ki⌐ma⌐sita.
2. [He] came just when [I]   Ne⌐ta tokoro⌐ e ki⌐ma⌐sita.
    had gone to bed.
3. [He] came just as [I] was   O⌐hu⌐ro ni ⌐ha⌐itte (i)ru to⌐koro⌐ e
    taking a bath.   ki⌐ma⌐sita.
4. [He] came just as [I] was   Syo⌐kuzi no sitaku (o) siyoo to
    about to prepare dinner.   site (i)ru tokoro⌐ e ki⌐ma⌐sita.
5. [He] came just as [I] was   Ku⌐ruma (o) miḡaite (i)ru tokoro⌐
    polishing the car.   e ki⌐ma⌐sita.

6. [He] saw me as [I] was   Ku⌐ruma⌐ (o) miḡaite (i)ru <u>tokoro⌐</u>
   polishing the car.   (o) mi⌐ma⌐sita.

7. [He] saw me as [I] was   O⌐sara (o) aratte (i)ru⌐ tokoro⌐ (o)
   washing the dishes.   mi⌐ma⌐sita.

8. [He] saw me as [I] was   Hu⌐de de ka⌐ite (i)ru⌐ to⌐koro⌐ (o)
   writing with a brush.   mi⌐ma⌐sita.

H. Substitution Drill

1. Maybe there's central   Da⌐ñboose⌐tubi (ḡa) ⌐a⌐ru ka mo
   heating.   siremaseñ.

2. There's probably central   Da⌐ñboose⌐tubi (ḡa) <u>⌐a⌐ru desyoo.</u>
   heating.

3. I think there's central   Da⌐ñboose⌐tubi (ḡa) ⌐a⌐ru to omoi-
   heating.   <u>masu.</u>

4. There's supposed to be   Da⌐ñboose⌐tubi (ḡa) ⌐a⌐ru <u>hazu</u>
   central heating.   <u>desu.</u>

5. They say there's central   Da⌐ñboose⌐tubi (ḡa) ⌐a⌐ru <u>soo desu.</u>
   heating.

6. There's central heating,   Da⌐ñboose⌐tubi (ḡa) ⌐a⌐ru <u>desyoo?</u>
   isn't there?

I. Grammar Drill (based on Grammatical Note 2)

Tutor: I⌐kima⌐su. 'He'll go.'
Student: I⌐ku⌐ ka mo siremaseñ. 'Maybe he'll go.'

1. To⌐modati (o) turete ki-   To⌐modati (o) turete ku⌐ru ka mo
   ma⌐su.   siremaseñ.

2. A⌐no tosiyori⌐ (wa) mi-   A⌐no tosiyori⌐ (wa) mi⌐mi⌐ ḡa to-
   ⌐mi⌐ ḡa to⌐oi⌐ desu.   ⌐oi⌐ ka mo siremaseñ.

3. A⌐no se⌐ki (wa) a⌐ite   A⌐no se⌐ki (wa) a⌐ite (i)ru⌐ ka mo
   (i)ma⌐su.   siremaseñ.

4. Si⌐o⌐ (ḡa) ta⌐rimase⌐ñ.   Si⌐o⌐ (ḡa) ta⌐rina⌐i ka mo sirema-
                               señ.

5. Ka⌐rita⌐ no (wa) o⌐to⌐tosi   Ka⌐rita⌐ no (wa) o⌐to⌐tosi datta ka
   desita.   mo siremaseñ.

6. De⌐ñkisuto⌐obu (ḡa) tu⌐ke- De⌐ñkisuto⌐obu (ḡa) tu⌐kerare⌐na-
   raremase⌐ñ desita.   katta ka mo siremaseñ.

7. Sore (wa) o⌐oki⌐i moñdai   Sore (wa) o⌐oki⌐i mo⌐ñdai ka⌐ mo
   desu.   siremaseñ.

8. Sore (wa) ⌐ma⌐da ki⌐me-   Sore (wa) ⌐ma⌐da ki⌐mena⌐i ka mo
   mase⌐ñ.   siremaseñ.

9. A⌐no kami⌐ (wa) u⌐ketori   A⌐no kami⌐ (wa) u⌐ketori ka⌐ mo
   de⌐su.   siremaseñ.

10. Ta⌐iya (ḡa) pañku-sima⌐-   Ta⌐iya (ḡa) pañku-sita⌐ ka mo
    sita.   siremaseñ.

J. Grammar Drill

Tutor: I⌐ku⌐ ka mo siremaseñ. 'Maybe he'll go.'
Student: I⌐kana⌐i ka mo siremaseñ. 'Maybe he won't go.'

1. I⌐i ka mo siremaseñ.   Yo⌐ku ⌐na⌐i ka mo siremaseñ.
2. A⌐ru ka mo siremaseñ.   Na⌐i ka mo siremaseñ.
3. De⌐kita ka mo siremaseñ.   De⌐ki⌐nakatta ka mo siremaseñ.
4. Tu⌐meta⌐katta ka mo si-   Tu⌐metaku na⌐katta ka mo sire-
    remaseñ.   maseñ.
5. Ka⌐ñtañ da⌐tta ka mo si-   Ka⌐ñtañ zya na⌐katta ka mo sire-
    remaseñ.   maseñ.
6. Be⌐ñri ka mo siremaseñ.   Be⌐ñri zya ⌐na⌐i ka mo sirema-
                                         señ.
7. Ni⌐hoñḡo (ḡa) kake⌐ru ka   Nihoñḡo (ḡa) ka⌐ke⌐nai ka mo si-
    mo siremaseñ.   remaseñ.
8. Da⌐ñboose⌐tubi ka mo si-   Da⌐ñboose⌐tubi zya ⌐na⌐i ka mo
    remaseñ.   siremaseñ.
9. Syuuzeñ wa su⌐ru⌐ ka mo   Syuuzeñ wa si⌐na⌐i ka mo sire-
    siremaseñ.   maseñ.

K. Substitution Drill (based on Grammatical Note 5)

1. There's not a place as   Gi⌐ñza-ḡu⌐rai ka⌐imono ni i⌐i to-
    good as the Ginza for   ko wa ⌐na⌐i.
    shopping.
2. There's not a place as   A⌐no heñ-ḡu⌐rai sa⌐ñpo ni i⌐i to-
    good as around there for   ko wa ⌐na⌐i.
    walking.
3. There's not a place as   Ko⌐no syosai-ḡu⌐rai be⌐ñkyoo ni
    good as this library for   i⌐i toko wa ⌐na⌐i.
    studying.
4. There's not a place as   U⌐eno-kooeñ-ḡu⌐rai ha⌐nami⌐ ni
    good as Ueno Park for   ⌐i⌐i toko wa ⌐na⌐i.
    seeing the cherries.
5. There's not a place as   I⌐naka-ḡu⌐rai ya⌐sumi⌐ ni ⌐i⌐i to-
    good as the country for   ko wa ⌐na⌐i.
    rest.
6. There's not a place as   A⌐no mati-ḡu⌐rai ke⌐ñbutu ni i⌐i
    good as that town for   toko wa ⌐na⌐i.
    sightseeing.

L. Expansion Drill

1. He may not be able to   De⌐ki⌐nai ka mo siremaseñ.
    do it.
    It's raining (lit. falling)   Hu⌐tte⌐ (i)ru kara, de⌐ki⌐nai ka
    so he may not be able   mo siremaseñ.
    to do it.
    It's raining so he may not   A⌐me ḡa hu⌐tte⌐ (i)ru kara, de-
    be able to do it.   ⌐ki⌐nai ka mo siremaseñ.
    [He] said [that] but it's   I⌐tta⌐ keredo; a⌐me ḡa hu⌐tte⌐
    raining so he may not   (i)ru kara, de⌐ki⌐nai ka mo
    be able to do it.   siremaseñ.
    [He] said he'd fix [it]   Na⌐o⌐su tte i⌐tta⌐ keredo; a⌐me
    but it's raining so he may   ḡa hu⌐tte⌐ (i)ru kara, de⌐ki⌐-
    not be able to do it.   nai ka mo siremaseñ.

[He] said he'd fix [it] today but it's raining so
he may not be able to
do it.

KyoＤo naＴoｌsu tte iｆtta⌐ keredo;
aＤme ḡa huｆtte⌐ (i)ru kara, deｒkiｈnai ka mo siremaseñ.

[He] said he'd fix the
damaged places today
but it's raining so he
may not be able to do
it.

Iｒtaｈnda toｆkoro⌐ (o) ｒkyoＤo naＴoｌsu
tte iｆtta⌐ keredo; aＤme ḡa huｆtte⌐
(i)ru kara, deｒkiｈnai ka mo siremaseñ.

[He] said he'd fix the
damaged places in the
roof today but it's
raining so he may not
be able to do it.

YaＤne no iｒtaｈnda toｆkoro⌐ (o)
ｒkyoＤo naＴoｌsu tte iｆtta⌐ keredo;
aＤme ḡa huｆtte⌐ (i)ru kara, deｒkiｈnai ka mo siremaseñ.

The carpenter said he'd
fix the damaged places
in the roof today but
it's raining so he may
not be able to do it.

DaＤiku-sañ ḡa ｒyaＤne no iｒtaｈnda
toｆkoro⌐ (o) ｒkyoＤo naＴoｌsu tte
iｆtta⌐ keredo; aＤme ḡa huｆtte⌐
(i)ru kara, deｒkiｈnai ka mo siremaseñ.

2. Have you seen it?

Goｒrañ ni narimaｈsita ka⌐

The report is that they're
doing a play. Have you
seen it?

Siｒbai (o) site (i)ru soＤo desu ḡa,
goｒrañ ni narimaｈsita ka⌐

The report is that they're
doing a very interesting
play. Have you seen it?

Toｒtemo omosiroＤi siｆbai (o) site
(i)ru soＤo desu ḡa, goｒrañ ni narimaｈsita ka⌐

The report is that they're
doing a very interesting
play in Nihombashi. [1]
Have you seen it?

Nihoñbasi [1] de toｒtemo omosiroＤi
siｆbai (o) site (i)ru soＤo desu
ḡa, goｒrañ ni narimaｈsita ka⌐

According to what the
teacher says, they're
doing a very interest-
ing play in Nihombashi.
Have you seen it?

Seｒñseｈe no haｆnasi⌐ ni yoru to,
Nihoñbasi de toｒtemo omosiroＤi siｆbai (o) site (i)ru soＤo
desu ḡa; goｒrañ ni narimaｈsita
ka⌐

3. It will probably be all
right, won't it?

Iｈi desyoo ne?

I probably don't have to
take it, do I?

Moｒtte ikanaｈkute mo ｒiｈi desyoo
ne?

I probably don't have to
take an umbrella do I?

KaＤsa (o) moｆtte ikanaｌkute mo
ｒiｈi desyoo ne?

The report is that it will
clear so I probably
don't have to take an
umbrella, do I?

HaＤreｒru soo da kara, kaＤsa (o)
moｆtte ikanaｌkute mo ｒiｈi desyoo ne?

---

[1] A section of Tokyo.

The report is that it will
clear tonight so I prob-
ably don't have to take
an umbrella, do I?

Koⁿbañ ha⌐re⌐ru soo da kara, ka⌐-
sa (o) moᴸtte ikana⁴kute mo ⌐i⌐i
desyoo ne?

According to the news-
paper it's going to clear
tonight so I probably
don't have to take an
umbrella, do I?

Siñbuñ ni yoru to, koⁿbañ ha⌐re⌐ru
soo da kara; ka⌐sa (o) moᴸtte
ikana⁴kute mo ⌐i⌐i desyoo ne?

4. I'm looking for [it].

Sa⌐ḡasite (i)ru⌐ ñ desu.

I'm looking for a bigger
one.

Mo⌐tto o⌐oki⌐i no (o) saᴸḡasite
(i)ru⁴ ñ desu.

It's small so I'm looking
for a bigger one.

Ti⌐isa⌐i kara, mo⌐tto o⌐oki⌐i no (o)
saᴸḡasite (i)ru⁴ ñ desu.

Even as a home for the
summer it's small so
I'm looking for a big-
ger one.

Na⌐tu no uti⌐ to siᴸte⁴ mo tiᴸisa⁴i
kara, mo⌐tto o⌐oki⌐i no (o) saᴸḡasite (i)ru⁴ ñ desu.

The equipment is good
too, but even as a home
for the summer it's
small so I'm looking
for a bigger one.

Se⌐tubi mo ᴸi⁴i keredo: na⌐tu no
uti⌐ to siᴸte⁴ mo tiᴸisa⁴i kara,
mo⌐tto o⌐oki⌐i no (o) saᴸḡasite
(i)ru⁴ ñ desu.

[It] is sunny and the equipment is good too, but
even as a home for the
summer it's small so
I'm looking for a big-
ger one.

Hi⌐atari ḡa i⌐i si, se⌐tubi mo ᴸi⁴i
keredo; na⌐tu no uti⌐ to siᴸte⁴
mo tiᴸisa⁴i kara, mo⌐tto o⌐oki⌐i
no (o) saᴸḡasite (i)ru⁴ ñ desu.

That house for rent is
sunny and the equip-
ment is good too, but
even as a home for the
summer it's small so
I'm looking for a big-
ger one.

Ano kasiya wa hi⌐atari ḡa i⌐i si,
se⌐tubi mo ᴸi⁴i keredo; na⌐tu no
uti⌐ to siᴸte⁴ mo tiᴸisa⁴i kara,
mo⌐tto o⌐oki⌐i no (o) saᴸḡasite
(i)ru⁴ ñ desu.

5. You'd better call.

Yo⌐ñda ho⌐o ḡa ᴸi⁴i desu yo⌐

You'd better call a taxi.

Ta⌐kusii (o) yoᴸñda ho⁴o ḡa ᴸi⁴i
desu yo⌐

If you want to go you'd
better call a taxi.

I⌐kita⁴kattara, ta⌐kusii (o) yoᴸñda
ho⁴o ḡa ᴸi⁴i desu yo⌐

If you want to go right
away you'd better call
a taxi.

I⌐ma ⌐suᴸgu iᴸkita⁴kattara, ta⌐kusii
(o) yoᴸñda ho⁴o ḡa ᴸi⁴i desu
yo⌐

If you want to go right
away you'd better call
a taxi.

Mo⌐si ⌐i⌐ma ⌐suᴸḡu iᴸkita⁴kattara,
ta⌐kusii (o) yoᴸñda ho⁴o ḡa ᴸi⁴i
desu yo⌐

It will take all of two or
three hours, so if you

Ni-⌐sañ-zi⌐kañ mo kaᴸka⁴ru kara;
mo⌐si ⌐i⌐ma ⌐suᴸḡu iᴸkita⁴kattara,

want to go right away you'd better call a taxi.	taˈkusii (o) yoˈnda hoˈo ga ˈiˈi desu yo⌣
It will take all of two or three hours more, so if you want to go right away you'd better call a taxi.	Moˈo ni-sañ-ziˈkañ mo kaˈkaˈru kara; moˈsi ˈiˈma ˈsuḡu iˈkitaˈ-kattara, taˈkusii (o) yoˈnda hoˈo ga ˈiˈi desu yo⌣
I'm just fixing [it] but it will take all of two or three hours more, so if you want to go right away you'd better call a taxi.	Naˈoˈsite (i)ru toˈkoroˈ desu ga; moˈo ni-sañ-ziˈkañ mo kaˈkaˈru kara; moˈsi ˈiˈma ˈsuḡu iˈkitaˈ-kattara, taˈkusii (o) yoˈnda hoˈo ga ˈiˈi desu yo⌣
I'm just fixing your car but it will take all of two or three hours more, so if you want to go right away you'd better call a taxi.	Aˈnaˈta no kuruma (o) naˈoˈsite (i)ru toˈkoroˈ desu ga; moˈo ni-sañ-ziˈkañ mo kaˈkaˈru kara; moˈsi ˈiˈma ˈsuḡu iˈkitaˈkattara, taˈkusii (o) yoˈnda hoˈo ga ˈiˈi desu yo⌣
I'm just fixing your car now but it will take all of two or three hours more, so if you want to go right away you'd better call a taxi.	Iˈma aˈnaˈta no kuruma (o) naˈoˈ-site (i)ru toˈkoroˈ desu ga; moˈo ni-sañ-ziˈkañ mo kaˈkaˈru kara; moˈsi ˈiˈma ˈsuḡu iˈkitaˈ-kattara, taˈkusii (o) yoˈnda hoˈo ga ˈiˈi desu yo⌣

SUPPLEMENTARY CONVERSATION

(Mr. Smith unexpectedly meets his friend, Mr. Yamada, on the street.)

Smith: Tyoˈtto siˈtuˈree desu ga, Yaˈmada-sañ zya arimaseˈñ ka⌣

Yamada: Aˈa, Suˈmisu-sañ. Siˈbaˈraku desita ˈneˈe.

Smith: Siˈbaˈraku desita ˈneˈe. Iˈma Toˈokyoo de otutome deˈsu ka⌣

Yamada: Eˈe. Niˈhoñbasi [1] no giñkoo deˈsu. Miˈnaˈsañ oˈgeˈñki? Okosañ ˈzuˈ-ibuñ ˈoˈokiku ˈnaˈtta desyoo ne?

Smith: Okaḡesama de. Oˈtaku mo minaˈsañ oˈgeˈñki desyoo?

Yamada: Eˈe. Aˈriˈḡatoo. Toˈokyoo e kiteˈ kara ni-ˈsyuˈukañ ni naˈrimaˈsu ga, maˈda uˈti ga naˈkute koˈmaˈtte imasu yo.

Smith: Iˈma wa ryoˈkañ deˈsu ka⌣

Yamada: Iie. Boˈku dake giñkoo no tomodati no uti ni ite, kaˈnai ya ko-domo wa ˈmaˈda Oˈosaka de maˈtte iru kara; haˈyaku uˈtiˈ o kaˈ-ritaˈi ñ desu ga; *kasiya wa aˈrimaseñ ˈneˈe.

Smith: Hoˈñtoo ni sukunaˈi desu yo — kasiya wa⌣ Kaˈimaseˈñ ka — uˈtiˈ o.

Yamada: Kasiya mo ˈyatiñ ga taˈkaˈi kara, tiˈisaˈi uˈtiˈ o kaˈtteˈ mo ˈiˈi keredo; aˈru desyoo ka.

Smith: Boˈku no kaisya no hitoˈ ga uˈritaˈi ñ desu yo.

Yamada: Soˈre wa keˈkkoo. Doˈñna uˈtiˈ desyoo.

---

[1] A section of Tokyo.

Smith: Boᒣku wa yoᒣku siᒥranaᒤi kara, soᒣno tomodati to soodañ-sitaᒣra
         ᒥdoᒤo desyoo. Aᒣto de aᒣhaᒤta no hoo e oᒣdeᒣñwa-simasu kara—
Yamada: Doᒣo mo aᒥriᒤgatoo. Boᒣku no meesi deᒣsu. Doᒣozo. Goᒣ-zi made
         giᒥñkoo ni orimaᒤsu kara, oᒣnegai-simaᒣsu.
Smith: Zyaᒣa, goᒣ-zi made ni oᒣdeᒣñwa-simasu kara—
Yamada: Oᒣisogasiᒤi toᒥkoroᒤ o suᒣmimaseᒣñ.
Smith: Iie. Naᒣñ de mo arimaseᒣñ yo.

(After Mr. Yamada has received further details on the telephone, he goes
to see the house that is for sale. He talks to Mr. Goto, the owner.)

Yamada: Goᒣmeñ-kudasaᒤi. Suᒣmisu-sañ no goᒥsyookai de mairimaᒤsita. Uᒣti
         no kotoᒤ de uᒥkagaitaᒤi ñ desu gaᒣ—
Goto: Aᒣa, Yaᒣmada-sañ de irassyaimaᒣsu ne? Yoᒣku iᒥrassyaimaᒤsita.
         Doᒣozo oᒥhairi-kudasaᒤi. Suᒣgu oᒥwakari deᒤsita kaᒧ
Yamada: Eᒣe. Eᒣki no ᒥmaᒤe no koobañ de yoᒣku oᒥsiete moraimaᒤsita ka-
         ra— Kono heñ wa ᒣsiᒣzuka de ᒣiᒣi tokoro desu ᒣneᒣe.
Goto: Eᒣki kara ᒣtyoᒣtto tooᒣiᒤ desu ga, uᒣti ga sukunaᒣkute ᒣiᒣi desyoo?
Yamada: Kono otaku wa iᒣtu-goro noᒤ desu kaᒧ
Goto: Go-ᒣneñ maᒣe ni tuᒥkurimaᒤsita.
Yamada: Oniwa mo naᒣkanaka hiroᒣi desu ᒣneᒣe.
Goto: Eᒣe. Sikiti ga niᒣhyakuᒣ-tubo aᒥrimaᒤsu kara—
Yamada: Uti wa naᒣñ-tubo-guᒤrai desyoo ka.
Goto: Tyoodo ᒣniᒣzyuu ᒣhaᒤt-tubo desu.
Yamada: Kono heñ wa ᒣgaᒣsu wa ᒥdoᒤo desu kaᒧ
Goto: Kyoᒣneñ kara kiᒥteᒤ imasu yoᒧ Oᒣhuᒣro mo ᒥgaᒤsu desu.
Yamada: Zyaᒣa, beᒣñri de ᒣiᒣi desu ᒣneᒣe.
Goto: Eᒣe. Gaᒣsu ga kiᒥteᒤ kara zuᒣtto beᒣñri ni naᒥrimaᒤsita yoᒧ
Yamada: Oᒣheya o miᒣsete iᒥtadakitaᒤi ñ desu gaᒣ—
Goto: Doᒣozo ᒥdoᒤozo. . . . Koᒣtira ga zasikiᒣ de, haᒣti-zyoᒣo desu. Tona-
         ri ga tyanoma de, roᒣku-zyoᒣo desu.
Yamada: Kabe mo tāᒣtami mo ᒣkiᒣree desu ᒣneᒣe.
Goto: Eᒣe. Kyoᒣneñ kaᒣbe o nurikaᒣete taᒣtami mo ataraᒣsiku siᒥmaᒤsita
         kara— Koᒣtira ga roku-zyoᒣo de, mukoo ni kōdomo no tiᒣisaᒣi he-
         ᒥyaᒤ ga aᒥrimaᒤsu ga; saᒣñ-zyoo-guᒣrai desu ga, taᒣtami wa ari-
         maseᒣñ.
Yamada: Zyaᒣa, taᒣtami no heyaᒣ wa ᒣmiᒣ-ma desu ne?
Goto: Soᒣo desu. Daᒣidokoro to hurobaᒣ wa ᒣtyoᒣtto seᒥmaᒤi desu gaᒣ—
         Doᒣozo ᒥmiᒤte kudasai.
Yamada: Tyoᒣodo iᒣi desu ᒣneᒣe. Hiᒣatari mo yoᒣkute, niᒣwa mo hiᒣrokute—
         Suᒣmisu-sañ kara no haᒣnasiᒤ ni yoru to, oᒣuri ni naritaᒣi ñ da
         ᒥsoᒤo desu gaᒣ—
Goto: Eᒣe. Moᒣo suᒣgu ᒣKoᒣobe e iᒥkimaᒤsu kara, kono uti wa uᒥritaᒤi ñ
         desu yo.
Yamada: Iᒣkura-guᒣrai de?
Goto: Soᒣo desu ᒣneᒣe. Suᒣmisu-sañ ni mo ᒣtyoᒣtto oᒥhanasi-simaᒤsita
         gaᒣ; hoᒣka no kataᒣ ni wa hyaᒣku nizyuu-mañ-guᒣrai [1] de uᒥritaᒤi
         to oᒥmoᒤtte imasita gaᒣ; Suᒣmisu-sañ no oᒥtomodati deᒤsu kara,
         moᒣo sukoᒣsi ᒣyaᒣsuku iᒥtasimasyoᒤo.

---

[1]   120 ten thousands = 1,200,000. 'Yen' is understood.

Yamada: So⌐re wa do⌐o mo. Zya⌐a, ka⌐nai to denwa de ⌐yo⌐ku soodañ-site,
         ka⌐nai to issyo ni mo⌐o iti-do—
Goto: Do⌐ozo ⌐do⌐ozo. Su⌐mimase⌐n ḡa; ho⌐ka no hito⌐ mo mi⌐ema⌐su ka-
         ra, na⌐rubeku ha⌐yaku o⌐negai-sita⌐i ñ desu ḡa—
Yamada: Mo⌐ti⌐roñ. Ha⌐tu-ka ma⌐de ni go⌐heñzi-sima⌐su kara—
Goto: O⌐negai-itasima⌐su.
Yamada: Do⌐o mo si⌐tu⌐ree-itasimasita. Zya⌐a, ma⌐ta mairima⌐su kara—
Goto: Do⌐ozo otya o. Ka⌐nai ḡa si⌐taku site orima⌐su kara—
Yamada: O⌐so⌐reirimasu. Do⌐ozo o⌐kamai na⌐ku.

English Equivalents

Smith: Say, excuse me but aren't you Mr. Yamada?
Yamada: Oh, Mr. Smith. I haven't seen you for a long time.
Smith: It <u>has</u> been a long time. Are you working in Tokyo now?
Yamada: Yes. I'm in a bank in Nihombashi. [Is] everyone in your family
         well? Your children must have grown a lot (lit. become very big),
         haven't they?
Smith: [They're fine] thank you. Everyone is well in your family too?
Yamada: Yes, thank you. You know, it's almost (lit. it will become) two
         weeks since I came to Tokyo, but I'm having an awful time because
         I don't have a house yet.
Smith: Are you staying at (lit. is it) an inn now?
Yamada: No. I (only) am staying at the home of a friend from the bank and
         my wife and children are still waiting in Osaka so I'd like to rent a
         house quickly, but there aren't any rentals to be had, are there.
Smith: They're really scarce—houses for rent. Aren't you going to buy (a
         house)?
Yamada: Rented houses are expensive too because of the rent (lit. rented
         houses too, the rent is high) so it would be all right if I bought a
         small house, but I wonder if there are any.
Smith: You know, a man in my company wants to sell [a house].
Yamada: That's wonderful. What kind of house is it?
Smith: I don't know too much about it so why don't you talk it over with
         this (lit. that) friend of mine? I'll put in a call to you later so . . .
Yamada: Thanks very much. Here's my card. Please take it. I'll be at the
         bank until five so would you [call me]?
Smith: Then I'll call you by five (so) . . .
Yamada: I'm sorry [to bother you] when you're so busy.
Smith: Not at all. It's nothing.

. . . .

Yamada: Excuse me. Mr. Smith sent me. (Lit. I've come through the intro-
         duction of Mr. Smith.) I'd like to inquire about the house . . .
Goto: Oh, you're Mr. Yamada, aren't you? I'm so glad you've come.
         Please come in. Did you find [the house] right away?
Yamada: Yes. I got good directions at the police box in front of the station
         so . . . This neighborhood is (a) nice and quiet (place), isn't it.
Goto: It's a bit far from the station, but it's pleasant because there aren't
         many houses, don't you think?

Yamada: About how old is this house? (Lit. This house is of about when?)
Goto: I built it five years ago.
Yamada: The garden is quite big too, isn't it.
Goto: Yes. The lot is (lit. has) 200 tsubo so . . .
Yamada: About how many tsubo is the house?
Goto: It's exactly 28 tsubo.
Yamada: How about gas around here?
Goto: It's been (lit. come) here since last year. The bath is gas too.
Yamada: Then it's nice and convenient, isn't it.
Goto: Yes. Since the gas came it's been (lit. become) much more conven-
         ient.
Yamada: I'd like to have you show me the rooms . . .
Goto: Certainly. This is the parlor and it's eight mats. Next (door) is the
         sitting room and it's six mats.
Yamada: The walls and the tatami are in good shape (lit. clean), aren't they.
Goto: Yes. Last year we repainted the walls and renovated the tatami
         (so) . . . This is a six-mat room and beyond there's a small child's
         room. It's about three mats [in size] but it doesn't have tatami.
Yamada: Then there are three tatami rooms—right?
Goto: That's right. The kitchen and bathroom are a bit small . . . Please
         take a look.
Yamada: It's just right. It's (both) sunny and the garden is big too, and . . .
         According to Mr. Smith, you want to sell . . .
Goto: Yes. We're going to Kobe very soon now so we'd like to sell this
         house.
Yamada: For about how much?
Goto: Hmmm . . . I talked a little [about this] to Mr. Smith too. I was
         thinking that I'd like to sell it for about ¥ 1,200,000 to anyone else
         (lit. other people), but since you're a friend of Mr. Smith's, I'll make
         it a little cheaper.
Yamada: That's very [kind of you]. Well, I'll discuss this with my wife by
         telephone and [then I'd like to come here] once more with her . . .
Goto: By all means. I'm sorry [to mention this] but other people will be
         coming too, so I'd like to ask [that you make it] as soon as possible.
Yamada: Of course. I'll give you an answer by the 20th (so) . . .
Goto: If you would.
Yamada (preparing to leave): Please excuse my rudeness [in barging in].
         Then I'll come here again (so) . . .
Goto: Please [have] some tea. My wife is getting it ready (so) . . .
Yamada: Thank you. Please don't go to any trouble.

EXERCISES

1. Answer an ad for a summer house, checking on the following points:

    a. Location of the house
    b. Rent for two months
    c. Furniture
    d. Running water, electricity, gas, flush toilet, screens, trash
        disposal
    e. Transportation

2. You are considering a house Mr. Tanaka wants to rent.

       As Mr. Tanaka: Mr. Tanaka replies:

        a. how large the lot is.   150 tsubo.

        b. what kind of house it is.   A new Western-style house with southern exposure.

        c. how many rooms are in the house.   Seven rooms.

        d. if there are any tatami rooms.   Yes, two.

        e. about the heating facilities.   There is gas in the house so you use gas heaters.

        f. what kind of bath the house has.   The bath is gas.

        g. who takes care of the repairs.   The landlord.

        h. when you may see the house.   How about tomorrow?

Lesson 31. At a Department Store

BASIC DIALOGUES: FOR MEMORIZATION

(a)

(Mr. Smith and Mr. Brown, accompanied by Mr. Tanaka,
are doing some shopping.)

Smith (at the information desk)

toy
oˈmoˈtya

1. Where [is] the place where
they sell toys?

Oˈmoˈtya utte ru toko ˈdoˈko?

Clerk

counter <u>or</u> selling place
toy counter <u>or</u> toy department

uriba
oˈmotyauˈriba

2. The toy department is on the
third floor.

Oˈmotyauˈriba (wa) saˈñ-ḡai de
gozaimaˈsu.

Smith

3. Thanks.

Doˈo mo.

(to Tanaka)

4. (I think) I'd like to send a
Japanese toy to my daughter
who's in America . . .

Aˈmerika ni iru musumeˈ ni
Niˈhoñ no omoˈtya (o) oˈkutte
yaritai to omoˈtte ˈneˈe.

Tanaka

doll
a doll that's wearing
kimono
dolls and so forth <u>or</u> a
doll for example <u>or</u>
something like a <u>doll</u>

niñḡyoo
kimono (o) kite (i)ru
niñḡyoo
niˈñḡyoo naˈdo <u>or</u>
niˈñḡyoo naˈñka

5. How about something like a
doll dressed in kimono?

Kiˈmono (o) kite (i)ru niñḡyoo
naˈñka (wa) ˈdoˈo desyoo.

one time
two or three times
send, for someone
(lit. give sending)
have at some time sent,
for someone
become broken
have never been broken

ik-kai
ni-sañ-kai
okutte aḡeru

oˈkutte aḡeta kotoˈ ḡa ˈaˈru

koˈwareˈru /-ru/
koˈwaˈreta koto wa ˈnaˈi

218

6. I have sent [them] two or three
    times, but there hasn't been a
    single case of breakage so I
    do think it's safe (but) . . .

Boku (wa) ni-ˈsañ-kai okutte aḡeta kotoꜛ ḡa ˈaꜜru ñ desu ḡa; ko-
ˈwaꜛreta koto (wa) iˈk-kai mo naꜜi
kara, daˈizyoꜜobu da to oˈmoꜜu ñ
desu ḡa—

Smith

gift

okurimono

7. It's a girl so a doll would
    probably make (lit. become)
    a good gift, wouldn't it.

Oˈñnaꜜ no ko da kara, niñḡyoo
wa ˈiꜜi oˈkurimono ni naꜜru desyoo ˈneꜜe.

(b)

(At the doll counter)

Tanaka

second in a series
is second from the left

ni-ˈbañ-meꜜ
hiˈdari kara ni-bañ-meꜜ ni
ˈaꜜru

is cute

kaˈwaiꜜi /-ku/

8. The big doll that's second
    from the left is cute, isn't
    it.

Hiˈdari kara ni-bañ-meꜜ ni ˈaꜜru
oˈokiꜜi niñḡyoo (wa) kaˈwaiꜜi desu
ˈneꜜe.

Smith

price

nedañ

9. Yes. The price is attached,
    isn't it?

Eꜜe. Neˈdañ (ḡa) tuˈite (i)ru desyoo?

Brown

10. It's ¥ 1500.

Seꜜñ goˈhyakuꜜ-eñ desu.

Smith

comparatively

wari ni

11. It's comparatively cheap,
     isn't it.

Waˈri ni yasuꜜi ñ desu ˈneꜜe.

12. I'll take it. (Lit. I guess I'll
     make it that one.)

Soˈre ni simasyoꜜo.

Tanaka

wrap
the interval when [some-
    one] is having [some-
    thing] wrapped
(Japanese game)
(Japanese game)
look in at __or__ peek at

tuˈtuꜜmu /-u/
tuˈtuñde moratte (i)ru
aida

goꜜ
syooḡi
nozoku /-u/

13. While you are having the doll
     wrapped, I'll go and take a
     look at the go and shogi
     counter.

Niˈñḡyoo (o) tutuñde moratte
(i)ru aida ni; tyoꜜtto, goꜜ ya
syooḡi no uˈriba (o) nozoite
kimaꜜsu.

Smith

14. Take your time.   Do⌐ozo go⌐yukku⌐ri.

Tanaka

15. I'll be right back.   Su⌐gu ki⌐ma⌐su yo⌐

(c)

Tanaka (to Brown)

16. There's something that you   A⌐na⌐ta mo ⌐na⌐ni ka mi⌐ta⌐i mo-
     want to look at too, isn't   ⌐no⌐ (ga) ⌐a⌐ru ñ desyoo?
     there?

Brown

     want   ho⌐si⌐i /-ku/
     I want   bo⌐ku ga hosi⌐i
     the thing which I want   bo⌐ku ga hosi⌐i no or
                                          bo⌐ku no hosi⌐i no
     is low   hi⌐ku⌐i /-ku/
17. The thing I want is a low   Bo⌐ku no hosi⌐i no (wa) hi⌐ku⌐i
     table.   te⌐eburu na⌐ ñ desu yo.

     the other day or   kono aida or
     recently   konaida
18. I saw [this] recently when   Konaida, to⌐modati no uti e itta
     I went to a friend's house.   to⌐ki /ni/ ⌐mi⌐ta ñ desu ga; za-
     He's using a tatami-room   siki no teeburu (o) yo⌐oma de
     table in a Western-style   tukatte (i)ru⌐ ñ desu yo.
     room.

19. You know, I thought it was   Na⌐kanaka i⌐i to o⌐mo⌐tta ñ
     quite nice.   desu yo.

Tanaka

     is round   marui /-ku/
     is square   si⌐kaku⌐i /-ku/
20. Which do you like better,   Ma⌐ru⌐i no to si⌐kaku⌐i no to,
     round ones or square ones?   do⌐tira ga o⌐suki de⌐su ka⌐

Brown

     couch or sofa   nagaisu
     is long and slender or   ho⌐sonaga⌐i /-ku/
     is long and narrow
21. I'm going to put it in front   Na⌐gaisu no ma⌐e ni o⌐ku⌐ ñ
     of a couch so I'd prefer a   desu kara, ho⌐sonaga⌐i hoo ga
     long narrow one.   ⌐i⌐i ñ desu yo.

Tanaka

     thing that isn't here or   na⌐i mono
       thing [someone] doesn't
       have
     there isn't a thing they   na⌐i mo⌐no⌐ wa ⌐na⌐i
       don't have

22. It's a big department store so
there probably isn't a thing
they don't have.

Oˈokiˈˈi deˈpaˈato desu kara, naˈi
moˈnoˈ wa ˈnaˈi desyoo ˈneˈe.

Brown

past noon _or_ afternoon
time before eating

hiˈru-sugiˈ
taˈbeˈru mae

23. It's past noon already, but is
it all right if we go to look
at [them] for a minute before we eat?

Moˈo hiˈru-sugiˈ desu ˈga, taˈbe-
ru mae ni ˈtyoˈtto ˈmiˈ ni iˈtteˈ
mo ˈiˈi desu kaـ

Smith

24. Certainly.

Doˈozo ˈdoˈozo.

Tanaka

after having finished

suˈmaˈseta ˈaˈto de

25. After we've finished our
shopping, let's take our time
and have something good to
eat.

Kaˈimono (o) sumaˈseta ˈaˈto de,
naˈni ka uˈmaˈi moˈnoˈ (o) yuˈkku-
ri taˈbemasyoˈo.

vicinity
the sushi shop 'Shintomi'
the tempura shop 'Tenkin'
the soba shop 'Yabu'
Yabu and so forth _or_
Yabu for example _or_
a place like Yabu
guide _or_ show the way

tiˈkaˈku
suˈsiˈya no Siñtomi
teñpuraya no Teñkiñ
soˈbaˈya no Yabu
Yaˈbu naˈdo _or_
Yaˈbu naˈñka
aˈñnaˈi-suru _or_
goˈañnaˈi-suru

26. Near here there are places
like the sushi shop 'Shintomi,'
the tempura shop 'Tenkin,'
and the soba shop 'Yabu'; (so)
I'll take you to a place you'll
like.

Koˈno tikaˈku ni wa, suˈsiˈya no
Siñtomi, teñpuraya no Teñkiñ,
soˈbaˈya no Yaˈbu naˈñka (ga)
ˈaˈru kara; oˈsuki na tokoroˈ e
goˈañnai-simaˈsu yoـ

(d)

Smith

writing brush
ink stick
ink stone
ink stone and so forth
_or_ ink stone for ex-
ample _or_ a thing like
an ink stone

hude
suˈmiˈ
suˈzuriˈ
suˈzuriˈ nado _or_
suˈzuriˈ nañka

27. I just remembered. I'd like
to look at things like writing
brushes, ink sticks, and ink
stones, too. Is that all
right?

Iˈma oˈmoidaˈsita ñ desu ˈga; hude,
sumi, suˈzuriˈ nañka mo miˈtaˈi
ñ desu ˈga; kaˈmaimaseˈñ kaـ

	Japanese syllabary	kana
	Chinese character	kañzi
	practice (noun)	reñsyuu
	practice (verb)	reñsyuu o suru <u>or</u> reñsyuu-suru
28.	I want to practice writing kana and kanji with a brush.	Kana ya kañzi (o) hu⌐de de ka⌐ku re⌐ñsyuu (ḡa) sita⌐i ñ desu yo.

Tanaka

	calligraphy	syuuzi
29.	Oh, calligraphy?	A⌐a, syu⌐uzi de⌐su ka.

Brown

	quote—calligraphy	syuuzi tte
30.	What is 'calligraphy'?	Syuuzi tte, ⌐na⌐ñ desyoo ka.

Tanaka

	way <u>or</u> style of writing	ka⌐kika⌐ta
	the meaning 'practice'	re⌐ñsyuu tte iu i⌐mi
31.	It means 'practice in writing style.'	Ka⌐kika⌐ta no re⌐ñsyuu tte iu i⌐mi desu yo.

(e)

Brown

32.	Oh, I'm hungry.	A⌐a onaka (ḡa) suita.

Smith

33.	Me—I'm thirsty.	Boku wa ⌐no⌐do (ḡa) ka⌐wakima⌐- sita yo.

Tanaka

	while drinking	no⌐mina⌐ḡara
34.	Well then, let's have some beer and eat at the same time (lit. while drinking beer let's eat).	Zya⌐a, bi⌐iru (o) no⌐mina⌐ḡara ta⌐bemasyo⌐o.

ADDITIONAL VOCABULARY

1.	Where is the place where they sell <u>souvenirs</u>?	Mi⌐yaḡe (o) utte (i)ru tokoro⌐ (wa) ⌐do⌐ko desu ka⌐
	curios <u>or</u> antiques	kottoohiñ
	china <u>or</u> pottery	setomono
	kitchen utensils	da⌐idokorodo⌐oḡu <u>or</u> ka⌐ttedo⌐oḡu
	foodstuffs <u>or</u> groceries	syokuryoohiñ
	writing materials	bu⌐ñbo⌐oḡu <u>or</u> bu⌐ñpo⌐oḡu
	yard goods <u>or</u> dry goods	gohukumono

2. What I want is a <u>screen</u>.   Wa⌐takusi no hosi⌐i no (wa) byo-
                                                  ⌐obu na⌐ n̄ desu yo.

    hanging scroll   ka⌐ke⌐mono
    fan (folding)   señsu
    fan (non-folding)   u⌐ti⌐wa
    picture   e⌐
    jewel   hooseki
    pearl   siñzyu

3. The average large depart-   Hutuu no o⌐oki⌐i de⌐pa⌐ato ni
    ment store has a <u>basement</u>.   (wa) ti⌐ka⌐situ (ḡa) arimasu.

    roof garden   okuzyoo
    rest room <u>or</u> lounge   kyu⌐uke⌐esitu

NOTES ON THE BASIC DIALOGUES

4. 'and—that is why I am going to the toy department.'

6. 'but—I can't be sure.'
    Ko⌐ware⌐ru is the intransitive partner of transitive ko⌐wa⌐su /-u/ 'break
    [something].'

13. Note: X ni tu⌐tu⌐mu 'wrap in X.'
    Go⌐ is a complicated game played with markers on a board marked with
    squares. It is extremely popular in Japan. Syooḡi is Japanese chess.
    The verbal √suru occurs with the names of games as the equivalent of
    'play': go⌐ (o) suru 'play go'; syooḡi o suru 'play shogi.'

14. Go⌐yukku⌐ri, the honorific equivalent of yu⌐kku⌐ri 'slowly,' is an invita-
    tion to 'take it easy,' 'don't rush,' 'have a pleasant, unhurried time.'

17. Ho⌐si⌐i: Nominals indicating the person who wants and the thing wanted
    are followed by particle <u>wa</u> or <u>ḡa</u>, depending on emphasis.
    Ho⌐si⌐i is regularly used in expressions of wanting but not in polite re-
    quests. Compare:

    Ta⌐bako ḡa hosi⌐i kara, ta⌐bakoya e itte kima⌐su. 'I want some
        cigarettes so I'm going to the cigar store.'
    with:
    Ta⌐bako (o) oneḡai-sima⌐su. 'I'd like <u>or</u> May I have some ciga-
        rettes.'

    Ta⌐ka⌐i 'is high' is used as the opposite of both ya⌐su⌐i 'is low in price'
    and hi⌐ku⌐i 'is low in height.'

18. <u>Konaida</u> is the contracted, less formal equivalent of <u>kono aida</u>.
    Note the use of ḡa here and in Sentence 27 below, separating an intro-
    ductory statement from a related statement which contains information
    being pointed up or emphasized, or from a related question.

20. Note: <u>maru</u> 'circle' and <u>marui</u> 'is round.'
          si⌐kaku⌐ 'square' and si⌐kaku⌐i 'is square.'

21. Ho⌐so̚naḡa̚i is a compound of the adjectivals ho⌐so̚i 'is thin or small in circumference' and na⌐ḡa̚i 'is long.' The opposite of ho⌐so̚i is hu⌐to̚i /-ku/ 'is thick or big in circumference.'

26. Ti⌐ka̚ku 'vicinity' is a nominal derived from an adjectival (ti⌐ka̚i 'is near'). Compare also to⌐oku̚ 'far distance,' 'the far away' (from tooi 'is far'), and o⌐soku̚ 'late' (from osoi 'is late'), as in o⌐soku̚ made 'until late.'
     The no of su⌐si̚ya no Sintomi, teñpuraya no Teñkiñ, and so⌐ba̚ya no Yabu is the special form of da occurring at the end of a sentence modifier (cf. Lesson 19, Grammatical Note 1).

27. The ink for Japanese brush-writing is made by rubbing an ink stick (su⌐mi̚) against an ink stone (su⌐zuri̚) containing a small amount of water.

28. Native Japanese writing is usually a combination of kana (symbols representing syllables without reference to meaning) and Chinese characters (symbols representing words or meaningful parts of words). The writing of Japanese with Roman letters — as the Japanese in this text — is called ro⌐oma̚zi 'romanization.'
     For particle ḡa, see the end of Note 1 in Lesson 7.

32. Note the informal style. Brown's exclamation is addressed to himself as much as to anyone else.

33. Ka⌐wa̚ku 'become dry' is the intransitive partner of transitive ka⌐waka̚su /-u/ 'dry [something].'

Additional Vocabulary:

     Da⌐idokorodo̚o̚ḡu ~ ka⌐ttedo̚o̚ḡu: Katte is an alternate word for 'kitchen.'
     Do⌐o̚ḡu̚ as an independent word means 'implement,' 'tool,' 'utensil.'

GRAMMATICAL NOTES

1. —— ko⌐to̚ ḡa ⌐a̚ru

     The informal past of a verbal + ko⌐to̚ (nominal meaning 'act' or 'fact') + ḡa (or wa) + a̚ru means '[someone] has, at some time up to the present, done so-and-so.' In question form, the Japanese sequence is equivalent to 'have [you] ever done so-and-so?' The negative —— ko⌐to̚ ḡa (or wa) ⌐na̚i means '[someone] has never done so-and-so.' Thus:

     (a) Hi⌐ko̚oki de i⌐tta koto⌐ ḡa arimasu. 'I have (at some time) gone by plane.'
     (b) Hi⌐ko̚oki de i⌐tta koto⌐ ḡa a⌐rima̚su ka⌐ 'Have you ever gone by plane?'
     (c) Hi⌐ko̚oki de i⌐tta koto⌐ wa a⌐rimase̚ñ. 'I have never gone by plane.'

     The simple past of a verbal refers to past occurrence and may be equivalent to either 'did do' or 'has done,' depending on context. The -ta ko⌐to̚ ḡa ⌐a̚ru sequence means only 'has at some time done.' Thus:

Ka⌐buki o mima⌐sita ka⌐ 'Did you see kabuki?' or 'Have you seen kabuki?'

but:

Ka⌐buki o mi⌐ta koto ḡa a⌐rima⌐su ka⌐ 'Have you ever seen kabuki?'

When a⌐ru occurs in one of its past forms in this pattern, the combination means '[someone] had, at some time up to a given point in the past, done so-and-so.' Thus:

Ni⌐hoñ e ⌐ku⌐ru made wa, ni⌐hoñḡo o kiita koto ḡa a⌐rimaseñ desita. 'Until I came to Japan, I had never heard Japanese.'

A past negative may also precede ko⌐to; the combination means '[someone] has, at some time, not done so-and-so.' In question form, the Japanese sequence is equivalent to 'have [you] ever not done so-and-so?' If ko⌐to is preceded AND followed by a negative, the combination means '[someone] has never not done so-and-so,' i.e. 'there has never been a time when [someone] did not do so-and-so' or '[someone] has always done so-and-so.'

(d) Hi⌐ko⌐oki de i⌐kana⌐katta koto ḡa arimasu. 'I have at some time not gone by plane.'
(e) Hi⌐ko⌐oki de i⌐kana⌐katta koto ḡa a⌐rima⌐su ka⌐ 'Have you ever not gone by plane?'
(f) Hi⌐ko⌐oki de i⌐kana⌐katta koto wa a⌐rimaseñ. 'There has never been a time when I didn't go by plane.'

Corresponding —— ko⌐to ḡa ⌐a⌐ru patterns preceded by a non-past verbal or negative adjectival also occur, meaning 'there are times (or there is never a time) when [someone] does (or doesn't do) so-and-so.' Thus:

(a) Hi⌐ko⌐oki de i⌐ku koto ḡa arimasu. 'There are times when I go by plane.'
(b) Hi⌐ko⌐oki de i⌐ku koto ḡa a⌐rima⌐su ka⌐ 'Do you ever go by plane?'
(c) Hi⌐ko⌐oki de i⌐ku koto wa a⌐rimaseñ. 'There is never a time when I go by plane.'
(d) Hi⌐ko⌐oki de i⌐kanai koto mo[1] arimasu. 'There are times when I don't go by plane.'
(e) Hi⌐ko⌐oki de i⌐kanai koto mo a⌐rima⌐su ka⌐ 'Do you ever not go by plane?'
(f) Hi⌐ko⌐oki de i⌐kanai koto wa a⌐rimaseñ. 'There is never a time when I don't go by plane.'

With the preceding, compare the following, which are similar in meaning:[2]

(a) Tokidoki hi⌐ko⌐oki de ikimasu. 'Sometimes I go by plane.'

The —— ko⌐to ḡa ⌐a⌐ru pattern is used whether an action occurs frequently or only rarely; tokidoki implies comparative frequency, whether used alone (as in the immediately preceding example) or together with the —— ko⌐to ḡa ⌐a⌐ru pattern (for

[1] Note the use of mo: '[Usually I do go by plane but] there are also times when I don't go by plane.'

[2] Sentence (a) here is to be compared with (a) in the preceding group, (c) with (c), etc.

example: Tokidoki hi⌐ko⌐oki de i⌐ku koto⌐ ḡa arimasu. 'Sometimes (there are times when) I go by plane.')

(c) Kessite hi⌐ko⌐oki de i⌐kimase⌐ñ. 'I never go by plane.'
(d) Taitee hi⌐ko⌐oki de ikimasu. 'Usually I go by plane.'
(f) I⌐tu mo hi⌐ko⌐oki de ikimasu. 'I always go by plane.'

2. 'Before,' 'While,' and 'After'

a. 'Before': ma⌐e

Ma⌐e, a nominal meaning 'time before' or 'place in front,' has previously occurred in combinations like zi⌐p-puñ ┌ma⌐e 'ten minutes ago' and
e⌐ki no ┌ma⌐e 'front of the station.' Ma⌐e may also be preceded by a sentence
modifier, ending with or consisting of an informal, NON-PAST verbal; the
sequence means 'before doing so-and-so' or 'before so-and-so happens or
happened.' The subject of the sentence modifier, if expressed, is followed by
ḡa or no. Thus: ta⌐be⌐ru mae 'before eating'; i⌐ku ma⌐e 'before going'; su-
┌ru ma⌐e 'before doing'; to⌐modati ḡa (or no) ku⌐ru mae 'before my friend
comes or came.'

What follows ma⌐e depends upon its relation to what follows in the sentence. When the sequence ending in ma⌐e tells WHEN something happened,
it is followed by particle ni; when the ma⌐e sequence modifies a nominal, it
is followed by no; when it is the topic of comparison, it is followed by wa;
etc.

Examples:
De⌐kakeru ma⌐e ni, tyo⌐tto de⌐ñwa-sita⌐i ñ desu ḡa—
'Before I go out, I'd just like to make a phone call . . . '
So⌐no boosi o kau ma⌐e ni, iti-do ka⌐bu⌐tte ┌mi⌐ta hoo ḡa ┌i⌐i desyoo?
'Before you buy that hat, shouldn't you try it on once?' (lit. 'it would
be better to have tried putting it on once, wouldn't it?')
No⌐bori ḡa (or no) tu⌐ku mae ni, ku⌐dari ḡa tatima⌐sita.
'Before the up-train arrived, the down-train left.'
Ko⌐no kaisya ni tutome⌐ru ┌ma⌐e no siḡoto wa, o⌐mosi⌐roku ┌na⌐katta ñ
desu.
'The work[I did] before working for this company wasn't interesting.'
Ni⌐ho⌐ñ e ┌ku⌐ru mae wa ze⌐ñzeñ nihoñḡo o kikimase⌐ñ desita.
'Before I came to Japan (in comparison with after), I didn't hear Jap-
anese at all.'
Sore wa ┌a⌐u ┌ma⌐e desita.
'That was before I met [him].'

b. 'While': aida and -naḡara

Aida, a nominal meaning 'interval of time or space,' has previously
occurred in combinations like A to B no aida 'between A and B.' Aida may
also be preceded by a sentence modifier ending with (or consisting of) an informal verbal or negative adjectival, non-past or past; most commonly this
is iru, ita, inai, or i⌐na⌐katta (or a more polite equivalent) preceded by a
verbal gerund. The sequence is equivalent to 'while so-and-so is or was
occurring.' The subject of the sentence modifier, if expressed, is followed

by ḡa or no. Thus: ta⌐bete iru aida 'while [someone] is eating'; no⌐nde ita
aida 'while [someone] was drinking'; Tanaka-sañ ḡa (or no) iru aida 'while
Mr. Tanaka is here'; tomodati ḡa (or no) inai aida 'while my friend isn't
here.'

Such a sequence is regularly used (a) when two actions or conditions having different subjects occur concurrently — 'while A is doing or being one
thing, B is doing or being another'; and (b) when one action occurs within
the interval during which another action or condition occurs (in which case
the subjects may be the same or different) — 'at some point (or on occasions)
while A is doing or being one thing, A (or B) does another.'

What follows aida depends upon its relation to what follows in the sentence. When an aida phrase occurs as an extent construction (telling HOW
LONG something happens or happened), it occurs without a following particle; an aida phrase followed by particle ni indicates the interval during
part of which something else happens.

Examples:

Dekakete iru aida, da⌐re ḡa ru⌐subañ o sima⌐su ka⌐
  'While we're out, who'll watch the house?'
A⌐na⌐ta ḡa be⌐ñkyoo-site iru aida ni, watakusi wa ka⌐imono ni itte ki-
  ma⌐su.
  'While you are studying, I'll go and do some shopping (lit. I'll come
    having gone for shopping).'
Tanaka-sañ ḡa to⌐modati to hana⌐site ita aida, bo⌐ku wa ku⌐ruma no
  na⌐ka de ⌐ma⌐tte imasita.
  'While Mr. Tanaka was talking with a friend, I was waiting in the
    car.'
A⌐na⌐ta ḡa te⌐ḡami o yo⌐ñde i⌐rassya⌐ru aida ni, watakusi wa to⌐mo-
  dati ni deñwa-sima⌐su.
  'While you're reading the letter, I'll telephone a friend.'
Kyo⌐oto ni ita aida, yo⌐ku sa⌐simi⌐ o ta⌐bema⌐sita.
  'While I was in Kyoto, I ate sashimi a good deal.'
Ha⌐ha ḡa i̅nai aida, bo⌐ku ḡa zi̅buñ de syo⌐kuzi no sitaku o sima⌐sita.
  'Throughout the time my mother hasn't been here, I've prepared
    the meals by myself.'

When two actions are performed concurrently by the same person(s), a
compound consisting of a verbal stem + -naḡara 'while doing so-and-so'
occurs. If the verbal stem is accented, the derived -naḡara compound is
also accented, on syllable na; otherwise, it is regularly unaccented. Thus:

ta⌐be⌐ru	(stem: ta⌐be)	'eat'	ta⌐bena̅ḡara 'while eating'
ha⌐na⌐su	(stem: ha⌐na⌐si)	'talk'	ha⌐nasina̅ḡara 'while talking'
kiku	(stem: kiki)	'listen'	kikinaḡara 'while listening'
suru	(stem: si)	'do'	sinaḡara 'while doing'

Examples:

Ra⌐zio o kikinaḡara be⌐ñkyoo-sima⌐sita.
  'While listening to the radio, I studied.' or 'I listened to the radio
    and studied at the same time.'
A⌐rukina̅ḡara i⌐roiro hanasimasyo⌐o.
  'Let's talk (about various things) as we walk.'

Syu⌐ziñ wa ⌐ma⌐initi si⌐ñbuñ o yomina⌐ḡara ⌐go⌐hañ o tabemasu.
'Every day my husband eats while reading the paper.'
Ta⌐bena⌐ḡara ta⌐bako o nomima⌐sita.
'While I ate I smoked.'

With the last example, compare:

Tomodati ḡa ⌐ta⌐bete ita aida, watakusi wa ta⌐bako o nomima⌐sita.
'While my friend was eating, I smoked.'

Remember: when YOU whistle while YOU work, use -naḡara; when YOU whistle while SOMEONE ELSE works, use aida.

   c. 'After': a⌐to de

       A⌐to de occurred previously meaning 'later on.' A⌐to is a nominal meaning 'later'; de is the gerund of da, meaning 'being.' Preceded by a sentence modifier consisting of or ending with an informal PAST verbal, it means 'after having done so-and-so.' The subject of the sentence modifier, if expressed, is usually followed by particle ḡa, less commonly by particle no. Thus: ta⌐beta ⌐a⌐to de 'after having eaten'; si⌐ta a⌐to de 'after having done'; to⌐modati ḡa (or, less commonly, no) itta a⌐to de 'after my friend went.'

   Examples:

Ki⌐ita a⌐to de, o⌐moidasima⌐sita.
'After I heard it I remembered.'
U⌐tta a⌐to de, ma⌐ta ho⌐siku na⌐rima⌐sita.
'After I sold it, I began to want it (lit. I became wanting) again.'
Tomodati ḡa ta⌐isi⌐kañ o ya⌐meta a⌐to de ha⌐irima⌐sita.
'I joined [the embassy] after my friend quit (the embassy).'

Kara preceded by a verbal gerund, meaning 'after doing so-and-so,' has occurred previously (cf. Lesson 16, Grammatical Note 2). An informal past + a⌐to de and the corresponding gerund + kara are close in meaning; but the pattern with kara usually implies that two actions follow each other directly or immediately, whereas the construction with a⌐to de occurs when one action takes place any time after—that is, not before—another. Thus:

Ga⌐kkoo o de⌐te kara, so⌐no kaisya ni hairima⌐sita.
'After (i.e. directly after) leaving school, I joined that company.'
but:
Ga⌐kkoo o de⌐ta ⌐a⌐to de, so⌐no kaisya ni hairima⌐sita.
'I joined that company after (i.e. not before) I left school.' (Something else may or may not have intervened.)

3. na⌐ñka ~ na⌐do

Na⌐ñka, or its more formal equivalent na⌐do, following one or more nominals, indicates that the preceding are mentioned as examples of a longer possible list. It often follows a series of nominals joined by particle ya, which also indicates that the words listed are examples of a longer series.

If the preceding word is accented, na⌐ñka and na⌐do lose their accents.

Examples:

waˈtakusi naˈñka 'people like me,' 'I, for example'
kyoˈneñ nado 'last year, for example'
hoˈñ, zassi, siˈñbuñ naˈdo 'books, magazines, newspapers, etc.'
peˈñ ya eˈñpitu naˈñka 'pens and pencils and so on'

A sequence + naˈñka (or naˈdo) occurs in the same kinds of constructions
—and followed by the same particles—as the sequence alone.

Examples:

Toˈkidoki arimaˈsu ḡa, kyoˈneñ nado wa zeˈñzeñ arimaseˈñ desita.
    'Sometimes there are some, but last year, for example, there
    weren't any at all.'
Koˈko niˈ wa, hoˈñ, zassi, siˈñbuñ naˈdo o siˈmatte kudasaˈi.
    'In here, put away the books, magazines, newspapers, and so forth.'
Peˈñ ya eˈñpitu naˈñka o kaˈimaˈsita.
    'I bought pens and pencils and things like that.'

4. Compound Nominals Ending in -kata

A verbal stem (the -maˈsu form minus -maˈsu) + -kata is a nominal
meaning 'manner or way or style of doing so-and-so.' If the verbal stem
is accented, the derived -kata compound is accented on syllable ka; if the
verbal stem is unaccented, the -kata compound is also unaccented. Thus:

kaˈku	(stem: kaˈki)	'write'	kaˈkikaˈta 'way of writing'	
yoˈmu	(stem: yoˈmi)	'read'	yoˈmikaˈta 'way of reading'	
aˈruˈku	(stem: aˈruˈki)	'walk'	aˈrukikaˈta 'way of walking'	
haˈnaˈsu	(stem: haˈnaˈsi)	'talk'	haˈnasikaˈta 'way of talking'	
taˈbeˈru	(stem: taˈbe)	'eat'	taˈbekaˈta 'way of eating'	
suru	(stem: si)	'do'	sikata 'way of doing'	

5. Ordinal Numbers

The addition of the suffix -me to a number changes a cardinal number to
its corresponding ordinal (which is accented on its final syllable). Thus:

niˈ-bañ	'number 2'	and:	ni-ˈbañ-meˈ '2d in a series'
mi-ˈttu	'3 things'	and:	mi-ˈttu-meˈ 'the 3d thing'
yo-neñ	'4 years'	and:	yo-ˈneñ-meˈ 'the 4th year'
go-ˈkaḡetu	'5 months'	and:	go-ˈkaḡetu-meˈ 'the 5th month'
roˈkuˈ-mai	'6 thin, flat units'	and:	roˈku-mai-meˈ 'the 6th thin, flat unit'

Ordinarily, -me is suffixed to numbers above number 1 in any series.

DRILLS

A. Substitution Drill

1. Where is the place where   Oˈmoˈtya (o) uˈtte (i)ru tokoroˈ
   they sell toys?   (wa) ˈdoˈko desu ka‿

2. Where is the place where they are having the conference?

Ka⌐iḡi (o) si⌐te (i)ru tokoro⌐ (wa) ⌐do⌐ko desu ka⌐

3. Where is the place where the children are playing?

Ko⌐domo ḡa asoñde (i)ru tokoro⌐ (wa) ⌐do⌐ko desu ka⌐

4. Where is the place where your husband is working?

Go⌐syuziñ ḡa ha⌐taraite (i)ru tokoro⌐ (wa) ⌐do⌐ko desu ka⌐

5. Where is the place where you are buying your groceries?

Syo⌐kuryo⌐ohiñ (o) ka⌐tte (i)ru tokoro⌐ (wa) ⌐do⌐ko desu ka⌐

6. Where is the place where they are making pottery like this?

Ko⌐o iu setomono (o) tuku⌐tte (i)ru to⌐koro⌐ (wa) ⌐do⌐ko desu ka⌐

7. Where is the place where you are studying Japanese?

Ni⌐hoñḡo (o) beñkyoo-site (i)ru tokoro⌐ (wa) ⌐do⌐ko desu ka⌐

8. Where is the place where they are fixing the screen?

Byo⌐obu (o) nao⌐site (i)ru to⌐koro⌐ (wa) ⌐do⌐ko desu ka⌐

B. Substitution Drill

1. It's comparatively cheap, isn't it!

Wa⌐ri ni yasu⌐i ñ desu ⌐ne⌐e.

2. It's really cheap, isn't it!

Ho⌐ñtoo ni yasu⌐i ñ desu ⌐ne⌐e.

3. It's really cute, isn't it!

Ho⌐ñtoo ni kawai⌐i ñ desu ⌐ne⌐e.

4. It's quite cute, isn't it!

Na⌐kanaka kawai⌐i ñ desu ⌐ne⌐e.

5. It's quite high, isn't it!

Na⌐kanaka taka⌐i ñ desu ⌐ne⌐e.

6. It's a little high, isn't it!

Tyo⌐tto ta⌐ka⌐i ñ desu ⌐ne⌐e.

7. It's a little low, isn't it!

Tyo⌐tto hi⌐ku⌐i ñ desu ⌐ne⌐e.

8. It's awfully low, isn't it!

Zu⌐ibuñ hi⌐ku⌐i ñ desu ⌐ne⌐e.

9. It's awfully thick (around), isn't it!

Zu⌐ibuñ hu⌐to⌐i ñ desu ⌐ne⌐e.

10. It's very thick (around), isn't it!

To⌐ttemo huto⌐i ñ desu ⌐ne⌐e.

C. Substitution Drill

1. Which do you prefer — a round one or a square one?

Ma⌐ru⌐i no to si⌐kaku⌐i no to, do⌐tira ḡa o⌐suki de⌐su ka⌐

2. Which do you prefer — a thin (around) one or a thick (around) one?

Ho⌐so⌐i no to hu⌐to⌐i no to, do⌐tira ḡa o⌐suki de⌐su ka⌐

3. Which do you prefer — an expensive one or a cheap one?

Ta⌐ka⌐i no to ya⌐su⌐i no to, do⌐tira ḡa o⌐suki de⌐su ka⌐

4. Which do you prefer — a low one or a high one?

Hi⌐ku⌐i no to ta⌐ka⌐i no to, do⌐tira ḡa o⌐suki de⌐su ka⌐

5. Which do you prefer — a simple one or a complicated one?

Ka⌐ñtañ na⌐ no to hu⌐kuzatu na⌐ no to, do⌐tira ḡa o⌐suki de⌐su ka⌐

6. Which do you prefer — a far one or a near one?

To⌐oi⌐ no to ti⌐ka⌐i no to, do⌐tira ḡa o⌐suki de⌐su ka⌐

7. Which do you prefer — a bright one or a conservative one?

Ha⌈de⌉ na no to zi⌈mi⌉ na no to, do⌉tira ḡa o⌐suki de⌐su ka↵

8. Which do you prefer — a dark (in color) one or a light (in color) one?

Ko⌉i no to u⌈su⌉i no to, do⌉tira ḡa o⌐suki de⌐su ka↵

9. Which do you prefer — a thin (flat) one or a thick (flat) one?

U⌈su⌉i no to a⌈tu⌉i no to, do⌉tira ḡa o⌐suki de⌐su ka↵

10. Which do you prefer — a light one or a heavy one?

Ka⌈ru⌉i no to o⌈mo⌉i no to, do⌉tira ḡa o⌐suki de⌐su ka↵

D. Substitution Drill

1. It's a girl so a doll would probably make a good gift, wouldn't it.

O⌈ñna⌉ no ko da kara, niñḡyoo wa ⌈i⌉i o⌐kurimono ni na⌐ru desyoo ⌈ne⌉e.

2. It's a boy so a knife would probably make a good gift, wouldn't it.

O⌈toko⌉ no ko da kara, na⌉ihu wa ⌈i⌉i o⌐kurimono ni na⌐ru desyoo ⌈ne⌉e.

3. It's a child so a toy would probably make a good gift, wouldn't it.

Ko⌈domo da⌉ kara, o⌈mo⌉tya wa ⌈i⌉i o⌐kurimono ni na⌐ru desyoo ⌈ne⌉e.

4. It's a Japanese so something from America would probably make a good gift, wouldn't it.

Ni⌈hoñzi⌉ñ da kara, A⌈merika no mono⌉ wa ⌈i⌉i o⌐kurimono ni na⌐ru desyoo ⌈ne⌉e.

5. It's an American so something from Japan would probably make a good gift, wouldn't it.

A⌈merika⌉ziñ da kara, Ni⌈hoñ no mono⌉ wa ⌈i⌉i o⌐kurimono ni na⌐ru desyoo ⌈ne⌉e.

6. It's a woman so flowers would probably make a good gift, wouldn't they.

O⌈ñna no hito⌉ da kara, ha⌈na⌉ wa ⌈i⌉i o⌐kurimono ni na⌐ru desyoo ⌈ne⌉e.

7. It's a student so a book would probably make a good gift, wouldn't it.

Ga⌈kusee da⌉ kara, ho⌈ñ wa ⌈i⌉i o⌐kurimono ni na⌐ru desyoo ⌈ne⌉e.

E. Substitution Drill [1]

1. I think I'd like to send a toy to my daughter . . .

Mu⌈sume⌉ ni o⌈mo⌉tya (o) o⌐kutte yaritai to omo⌐tte ⌈ne⌉e.

2. I think I'd like to send some candy to my son . . .

Musuko ni o⌈ka⌉si (o) o⌐kutte yaritai to omo⌐tte ⌈ne⌉e.

3. I think I'd like to send a book to the teacher . . .

Se⌈ñse⌉e ni ⌈ho⌉ñ (o) o⌐kutte aḡetai to omo⌐tte ⌈ne⌉e.

4. I think I'd like to send some pearls to my wife . . .

Ka⌉nai ni si⌈ñzyu (o) okutte yaritai to omo⌐tte ⌈ne⌉e.

---

[1] Be sure to replace _yaritai_ with _aḡetai_ wherever appropriate.

5. I think I'd like to send
   some Japanese pottery
   to my (younger) sister
   in America . . .

A⌐merika no imooto⌐ ni Ni⌐hoñ no
setomono (o) okutte yaritai to
omo⌐tte ⌐ne⌐e.

6. I think I'd like to send a
   fan to a foreign friend of
   mine . . .

Gaiziñ no tomodati ni se⌐ñsu (o)
okutte ag̃etai to omo⌐tte ⌐ne⌐e.

7. I think I'd like to send
   some fruit to our maid
   who is sick . . .

Byooki no zyotyuu ni ku⌐da⌐mono
(o) o⌐kutte yaritai to omo⌐tte
⌐ne⌐e.

F. Substitution Drill (based on Grammatical Note 4)

1. What a strange way of
   writing!

He⌐ñ na ka⌐kika⌐ta desu ⌐ne⌐e.

2. What a strange way of
   talking! /ha⌐na⌐su/

He⌐ñ na ha⌐nasika⌐ta desu ⌐ne⌐e.

3. What a strange way of
   walking! /a⌐ru⌐ku/

He⌐ñ na a⌐rukika⌐ta desu ⌐ne⌐e.

4. What a strange way of
   saying [it]! /iu/

He⌐ñ na i⌐ikata de⌐su ⌐ne⌐e.

5. What a strange way of
   thinking! /ka⌐ñg̃ae⌐ru/

He⌐ñ na ka⌐ñg̃aeka⌐ta desu ⌐ne⌐e.

6. What a strange way of
   reading [it]! /yo⌐mu/

He⌐ñ na yo⌐mika⌐ta desu ⌐ne⌐e.

7. What a strange way of
   calling! /yobu/

He⌐ñ na yo⌐bikata de⌐su ⌐ne⌐e.

8. What a strange way of
   using [it]! /tukau/

He⌐ñ na tu⌐kaikata de⌐su ⌐ne⌐e.

G. Substitution Drill (based on Grammatical Note 5)

1. It's the second from the
   left.

Hidari kara ni-⌐bañ-me⌐ desu.

2. He's the third person
   from the right.

Mig̃i kara sa⌐ñ-niñ-me⌐ desu.

3. It's the fourth thing from
   the bottom.

Sita kara yo⌐ttu-me⌐ desu.

4. It's the fifth (thin, flat)
   thing from the top.

Ue kara go-⌐mai-me⌐ desu.

5. It's the sixth (long,
   cylindrical) thing from
   the front.

Ma⌐e kara ro⌐p-poñ-me⌐ desu.

6. It's the seventh (vehicle)
   from the back.

Usiro kara na⌐na-dai-me⌐ desu.

H. Substitution Drill

1. I want to practice writing
   with a brush.

Hu⌐de de ka⌐ku re⌐ñsyuu (g̃a)
sita⌐i ñ desu yo.

2. I want to practice singing
   this song.

Ko⌐no uta⌐ (o) u⌐tau reñsyuu (g̃a)
sita⌐i ñ desu yo.

3. I want to practice talking in Japanese.

Ni⌐hoñḡo de hana⌐su re⌐ñsyuu (ḡa) sita⌐i ñ desu yo.

4. I want to practice reading French.

Hu⌐rañsuḡo (o) yo⌐mu re⌐ñsyuu (ḡa) sita⌐i ñ desu yo.

5. I want to practice changing a tire.

Ta⌐iya (o) torikaeru reñsyuu (ḡa) sita⌐i ñ desu yo.

6. I want to practice tying an obi.

O⌐bi (o) si⌐me⌐ru re⌐ñsyuu (ḡa) sita⌐i ñ desu yo.

I. Grammar Drill

Tutor: Ka⌐kika⌐ta (o) re⌐ñsyuu-simasyo⌐o. 'Let's practice writing.'

Student: Ka⌐kika⌐ta no re⌐ñsyuu (o) simasyo⌐o. 'Let's practice writing.' (Lit. 'Let's do writing practice.')

1. Ni⌐hoñḡo (o) reñsyuu-simasyo⌐o.

Ni⌐hoñḡo no reñsyuu (o) simasyo⌐o.

2. Ka⌐na to kañzi (o) reñ-syuu-simasyo⌐o.

Ka⌐na to kañzi no reñsyuu (o) si-masyo⌐o.

3. Syo⌐oḡi (o) reñsyuu-simasyo⌐o.

Syo⌐oḡi no reñsyuu (o) simasyo⌐o.

4. Si⌐bai (o) reñsyuu-simasyo⌐o.

Si⌐bai no reñsyuu (o) simasyo⌐o.

5. Go⌐ (o) re⌐ñsyuu-simasyo⌐o.

Go⌐ no re⌐ñsyuu (o) simasyo⌐o.

J. Grammar Drill

Tutor: Ma⌐do (o) a⌐kema⌐sita. '[I] opened the window.'
Student: Ma⌐do (ḡa) a⌐kima⌐sita. 'The window opened.'

1. O⌐sara (o) kowasima⌐sita.

O⌐sara (ḡa) kowarema⌐sita.

2. Se⌐ñtakumono (o) kawa-kasima⌐sita.

Se⌐ñtakumono (ḡa) kawakima⌐sita.

3. A⌐tarasi⌐i siḡoto (o) ha⌐zimema⌐sita.

A⌐tarasi⌐i siḡoto (ḡa) ha⌐zimari-ma⌐sita.

4. Hi ⌐(o) kimema⌐sita.

Hi ⌐(ḡa) kimarima⌐sita.

5. Ko⌐domo (o) okosima⌐sita.

Ko⌐domo (ḡa) okima⌐sita.

6. De⌐ñki (o) ke⌐sima⌐sita.

De⌐ñki (ḡa) ki⌐ema⌐sita.

7. Te⌐ḡami (o) todokema⌐-sita.

Te⌐ḡami (ḡa) todokima⌐sita.

8. Ku⌐suri (o) kobosima⌐-sita.

Ku⌐suri (ḡa) koborema⌐sita.

K. Expansion Drill (based on Grammatical Note 3)

Tutor: Ni⌐ñḡyoo (wa) do⌐o desyoo. 'How about a doll?'
Student: Ni⌐ñḡyoo na⌐ñka (wa) ⌐do⌐o desyoo. 'How about something like a doll?'

1. O⌐mo⌐tya (wa) ⌐do⌐o desyoo.

O⌐mo⌐tya nañka (wa) ⌐do⌐o desyoo.

2. Hi⌐bati (wa) ⌐do⌐o desyoo.

Hi⌐bati nañka (wa) ⌐do⌐o desyoo.

3. Hu⌐rosiki (wa) do⌐o desyoo.   Hu⌐rosiki na⌐ñka (wa) ˥do⌐o desyoo.
4. O⌐sake (wa) do⌐o desyoo.   O⌐sake na⌐ñka (wa) ˥do⌐o desyoo.
5. O⌐ka⌐si (wa) ˥do⌐o desyoo.   O⌐ka⌐si na⌐ñka (wa) ˥do⌐o desyoo.

L. Grammar Drill

Tutor: Syu⌐uzi to iu⌐ no (wa) ⌐na⌐ñ desyoo. 'What is (the thing
          called) calligraphy?'
Student: Syuuzi tte ⌐na⌐ñ desyoo. 'What is "calligraphy"?'

1. Su⌐zuri⌐ to i˥u˥ no (wa)   Su⌐zuri⌐ tte ⌐na⌐ñ desyoo.
   ⌐na⌐ñ desyoo.
2. Ko⌐tatu to iu⌐ no (wa)   Kotatu tte ⌐na⌐ñ desyoo.
   ⌐na⌐ñ desyoo.
3. Ha⌐nami⌐ to i˥u˥ no (wa)   Ha⌐nami⌐ tte ⌐na⌐ñ desyoo.
   ⌐na⌐ñ desyoo.
4. Syo⌐oḡi to iu⌐ no (wa)   Syoo⌐ḡi tte ⌐na⌐ñ desyoo.
   ⌐na⌐ñ desyoo.
5. Ka⌐ke⌐mono to i˥u˥ no   Ka⌐ke⌐mono tte ⌐na⌐ñ desyoo.
   (wa) ⌐na⌐ñ desyoo.
6. Tu⌐yu to iu⌐ no (wa) ⌐na⌐ñ   Tuyu tte ⌐na⌐ñ desyoo.
   desyoo.

M. Grammar Drill

Tutor: Wa⌐takusi no hosi⌐i no (wa) te⌐eburu na⌐ ñ desu. 'What
          I want is a table.'
Student: Te⌐eburu no hosi⌐i no wa wa⌐takusi na⌐ ñ desu. 'I'm
          the one who wants a table.'

1. Mu⌐sume no hosi⌐i no (wa)   Ni⌐ñḡyoo no hosi⌐i no (wa) mu-
   ni⌐ñḡyoo na⌐ ñ desu.   ⌐sume⌐ na ñ desu.
2. A⌐no⌐ hito no de˥ki˥ru no   Ro⌐siaḡo no deki⌐ru no (wa) a⌐no⌐
   (wa) ro⌐siaḡo na⌐ ñ desu.   hito na ñ desu.
3. To⌐modati no zyoozu⌐ na   Syu⌐uzi no zyoozu⌐ na no (wa) to-
   no (wa) o⌐syu⌐uzi 1 na ñ   ⌐modati na⌐ ñ desu.
   desu.
4. Se⌐ñse⌐e no wa˥ka˥ru no   Do⌐ituḡo no waka⌐ru no (wa)
   (wa) do⌐ituḡo na⌐ ñ desu.   se⌐ñse⌐e na ñ desu.
5. Hi⌐syo no iru⌐ no (wa)   Ka⌐mi no iru⌐ no (wa) hi⌐syo⌐ na
   ka⌐mi⌐ na ñ desu.   ñ desu.
6. Wa⌐tasi no suki⌐ na no   Sa⌐simi no suki⌐ na no (wa) wa-
   (wa) sa⌐simi⌐ na ñ desu.   ⌐tasi na⌐ ñ desu.
7. Ga⌐kusee no sita⌐i no (wa)   E⌐eḡo no reñsyuu no sita⌐i no
   e⌐eḡo no reñsyuu na⌐ ñ   (wa) ga⌐kusee na⌐ ñ desu.
   desu.
8. A⌐no gaiziñ no hanase⌐ru   Hu⌐rañsuḡo no hanase⌐ru no (wa)
   no (wa) hu⌐rañsuḡo na⌐ ñ   a⌐no gaiziñ na⌐ ñ desu.
   desu.

1
  Polite (+) form used more commonly by women.

N. Grammar Drill (based on Grammatical Note 2)

> Tutor: De˹kakema˺sita. So˹no ma˺e ni, ta˹bema˺sita. 'I went out.
>   Before that I ate.'
> Student: De˹kakeru ma˺e ni, ta˹bema˺sita. 'Before going out, I ate.'

1. Ka˹erima˺su.
    So˹no ma˺e ni, ka˹ɡuu˺riba
    (o) no˥zoite kima˦su.

    Ka˹eru mae ni, ka˹ɡuu˺riba (o)
    no˥zoite kima˦su.

2. A˹no isu (o) nurikaema˺su.
    So˹no ma˺e ni, a˹raima˺su.

    A˹no isu (o) nurikae˹ru mae ni,
    a˹raima˺su.

3. Ki˹mema˺su.
    So˹no ma˺e ni, mo˹o tyo˺tto
    so˥odañ-simasyo˦o.

    Ki˹meru ma˺e ni, mo˹o tyo˺tto
    so˥odañ-simasyo˦o.

4. To˹modati ni watasima˺-
    sita.
    So˹no ma˺e ni, hu˹rosiki
    ni tutumima˺sita.

    To˹modati ni watasu ma˺e ni,
    hu˹rosiki ni tutumima˺sita.

5. Sa˹ñpo ni ikima˺sita.
    So˹no ma˺e ni, o˹tya (o)
    nomima˺sita.

    Sa˹ñpo ni iku ma˺e ni, o˹tya (o)
    nomima˺sita.

6. Ki˹sya˺ ni norimasu.
    So˹no ma˺e ni, ki˹ppu (o)
    kaima˺su.

    Ki˹sya˺ ni no˥ru ma˦e ni, ki˹ppu
    (o) kaima˺su.

O. Grammar Drill (based on Grammatical Note 2)

> Tutor: A˹na˺ta wa ni˹ñɡyoo (o) tutu˺ñde moraimasu. Watasi wa
>   ˹go˺ ya syooɡi no u˥riba o nozoite kima˦su. 'You will
>   have the doll wrapped. I'll go and take a look at the go
>   and shogi counter.'
> Student: A˹na˺ta ɡa ni˹ñɡyoo (o) tutu˺ñde moratte (i)ru aida ni,
>   watasi wa ˹go˺ ya syooɡi no u˥riba o nozoite kima˦su.
>   'While you have the doll wrapped, I'll go and take a look
>   at the go and shogi counter.'

1. A˹na˺ta wa de˹ñwa (o)
    kakema˺su.
    Watakusi wa si˹ñbuñ (o)
    katte kima˺su.

    A˹na˺ta ɡa de˹ñwa (o) ka˹kete (i)ru
    aida ni, watakusi wa si˹ñbuñ
    (o) katte kima˺su.

2. A˹na˺ta wa se˹ñse˺e to
    hanasimasu.
    Watakusi wa ta˹bako (o)
    nomima˺su.

    A˹na˺ta ɡa se˹ñse˺e to ha˹na˺site
    (i)ru aida ni, watakusi wa ta-
    ˹bako (o) nomima˺su.

3. A˹na˺ta wa o˹sara (o)
    araima˺su.
    Watakusi wa za˹siki˺ (o)
    katazukemasu.

    A˹na˺ta ɡa o˹sara (o) aratte (i)ru
    aida ni, watakusi wa za˹siki˺
    (o) katazukemasu.

4. A˹na˺ta wa ki˹mono (o)
    kikaema˺su.
    Watakusi wa te˹eburu (o)
    yoyaku-site okima˺su.

    A˹na˺ta ɡa ki˹mono (o) kika˹ete
    (i)ru aida ni, watakusi wa te˹e-
    buru (o) yoyaku-site okima˺su.

5. A⌐na⌐ta wa bu⌐ro⌐okaa to   A⌐na⌐ta ḡa bu⌐ro⌐okaa to soodañ-
   soodañ-simasu.   site (i)ru aida ni, watakusi wa
   Watakusi wa ma⌐ta uti   ma⌐ta uti (o) mi⌐sete morai-
   (o) mi⌐sete moraimasu.   masu.
6. A⌐na⌐ta wa ke⌐ñbutu-   A⌐na⌐ta ḡa ke̅ñbutu-site (i)ru aida
   sima⌐su.   ni, watakusi wa hi⌐rune (o)
   Watakusi wa hi⌐rune (o)   sima⌐su.
   sima⌐su.

P. Grammar Drill (based on Grammatical Note 2)

    Tutor: Bi⌐iru (o) nomimasu. Ta⌐bema⌐su. '[We]'ll drink beer.
             [We]'ll eat.'
    Student: Bi⌐iru (o) no⌐mina⌐ḡara, ta⌐bema⌐su. '[We]'ll eat and
             drink beer at the same time.'

    1. A⌐rukimasyo⌐o. Ha⌐nasi-   A⌐rukina⌐ḡara, ha⌐nasimasyo⌐o.
       masyo⌐o.
    2. U⌐ta⌐ (o) u⌐taima⌐sita.   U⌐ta⌐ (o) utaina⌐ḡara, o⌐sake (o)
       O⌐sake (o) nomima⌐sita.   nomima⌐sita.
    3. Ta⌐bema⌐sita. To⌐modati   Ta⌐bena⌐ḡara, to⌐modati kara no
       kara no teḡami (o) yo-   teḡami (o) yomima⌐sita.
       mima⌐sita.
    4. A⌐sobima⌐sita. Si⌐ḡoto   Asobina⌐ḡara, si⌐ḡoto (o) sima⌐-
       (o) sima⌐sita.   sita.
    5. So⌐o iima⌐sita. He⌐ya⌐   Soo iina⌐ḡara, he⌐ya⌐ kara de⌐ma⌐-
       kara de⌐ma⌐sita.   sita.
    6. Ra⌐zio (o) ki⌐kimasyo⌐o.   Ra⌐zio (o) kikina⌐ḡara, syo⌐kuzi
       Syo⌐kuzi (o) simasyo⌐o.   (o) simasyo⌐o.

Q. Grammar Drill (based on Grammatical Note 2)

    Tutor: Ka⌐imono (o) suma⌐sete kara, ta⌐bemasyo⌐o. 'After fin-
             ishing our shopping let's eat.'
    Student: Ka⌐imono (o) suma⌐seta ⌐a⌐to de, ta⌐bemasyo⌐o.' 'Let's
             eat after (not before) we've finished our shopping.'

    1. So⌐odañ-site⌐ kara, ki⌐me-   So⌐odañ-sita a⌐to de, ki⌐mema⌐-
       ma⌐sita.   sita.
    2. Ka⌐be (o) nurika⌐ete kara,   Ka⌐be (o) nurika⌐eta ⌐a⌐to de,
       ta⌐tami (o) torikaema⌐sita.   ta⌐tami (o) torikaema⌐sita.
    3. Sa⌐kura (o) mi⌐te kara,   Sa⌐kura (o) mi⌐ta ⌐a⌐to de, o⌐beñ-
       o⌐beñtoo (o) tabemasyo⌐o.   too (o) tabemasyo⌐o.
    4. Se⌐tumee-site moratte⌐   Se⌐tumee-site moratta a⌐to de,
       kara, yo⌐ñde mimasyoo.   yo⌐ñde mimasyoo.
    5. Ni⌐ho⌐ñ e i⌐tte⌐ kara, ni-   Ni⌐ho⌐ñ e i⌐tta a⌐to de, ni⌐hoñḡo
       ⌐hoñḡo (o) beñkyoo-   (o) beñkyoo-sihazimema⌐sita.
       sihazimema⌐sita.
    6. De⌐ñki (o) ke⌐site⌐ kara,   De⌐ñki (o) ke⌐sita a⌐to de, ma⌐do
       ma⌐do (o) a⌐kema⌐sita.   (o) a⌐kema⌐sita.

7. A⌐merika e ka⌐ette kara,   A⌐merika e ka⌐etta ˨a˥to de, ta⌐ba-
   ta⌐bako (o) yamema˥sita.   ko (o) yamema˥sita.
8. Ne⌐dañ (o) kiite˥ kara,   Ne⌐dañ (o) kiita a˥to de, ki⌐mema˥-
   ki⌐mema˥sita.   sita.

R. Grammar Drill (based on Grammatical Note 1)

   Tutor: I⌐kima˥su ka⌐ 'Do you (or are you going to) go?'
   Student: I⌐tta koto˥ ga a⌐rima˥su ka⌐ 'Have you ever gone?'

1. O⌐sasimi (o) mesiagari-   O⌐sasimi (o) mesiagatta koto˥ ga
   ma˥su ka⌐   a⌐rima˥su ka⌐
2. Hi⌐ko⌐oki ni no⌐rima˥su   Hi⌐ko⌐oki ni no⌐tta koto˥ ga a⌐ri-
   ka⌐   ma˥su ka⌐
3. O˥kusañ (o) tu⌐rete iki-   O˥kusañ (o) tu⌐rete itta koto˥ ga
   ma˥su ka⌐   a⌐rima˥su ka⌐
4. Hu⌐de de kakima˥su ka⌐   Hu⌐de de ka⌐ita koto ga a⌐rima˥su
                                      ka⌐
5. To⌐okyoo ma⌐de ka⌐yoima˥-   To⌐okyoo ma⌐de ka⌐yotta koto˥ ga
   su ka⌐   a⌐rima˥su ka⌐
6. Yoohukuya ni se⌐biro (o)   Yoohukuya ni se⌐biro (o) tuku⌐-
   tuku⌐tte mo⌐raima˥su ka⌐   tte mo⌐ratta koto˨ ga a⌐rima˥su
                                      ka⌐
7. Ko⌐tatu (o) tukaima˥su ka⌐   Ko⌐tatu (o) tukatta koto˥ ga a⌐ri-
                                      ma˥su ka⌐
8. Hu⌐toñ ni nema˥su ka⌐   Hu⌐toñ ni neta koto˥ ga a⌐rima˥su
                                      ka⌐
9. A˥sahi (o) yo⌐mima˥su ka⌐   A˥sahi (o) ⌐yo⌐ñda koto ga a⌐ri-
                                      ma˥su ka⌐
10. Ka⌐buki (o) mima˥su ka⌐   Ka⌐buki (o) mi⌐ta koto ga a⌐ri-
                                      ma˥su ka⌐

   Give the _iie_ answer for each of the questions in the right-hand
   column above.

S. Grammar Drill (based on Grammatical Note 1)

   (For each sentence on the left, give the approximate meaning equivalent containing _tokidoki_, _i⌐tu mo_, _taitee_, or _kessite_.)

1. Ni⌐hoñ no siñbuñ (o) yo⌐-   Kessite Ni⌐hoñ no siñbuñ (o)
   mu koto wa a⌐rimase˥ñ.   yomimase˥ñ.
2. Hu⌐de de ka⌐ku koto ga   Tokidoki hu⌐de de kakima˥su.
   a⌐rimasu.
3. Ku⌐ruma de ikanai koto˥   Taitee ku⌐ruma de ikima˥su.
   mo arimasu.
4. O⌐soku˥ made ha˧taraku   Tokidoki o⌐soku˥ made hatara-
   koto˨ ga arimasu.   kimasu.
5. Koko ni da⌐re mo inai   I⌐tu mo ko˥ko ni ⌐da⌐re ka imasu.
   koto˥ wa a⌐rimase˥ñ.
6. O⌐boerare˥nai koto mo   Ta⌐itee oboerarema˥su.
   arimasu.

7. Osake nañka (o) nomu koto wa arimaseñ. — Kessite osake nañka (o) nomimaseñ.
8. Gaiziñ da keredo, wakaranai koto wa arimaseñ. — Gaiziñ da keredo, itu mo wakarimasu.

QUESTION SUPPLEMENT

(based on the Basic Dialogues)

(a)
1. Depaato no omotya o utte iru tokoro wa nañ to iimasu ka⌟
2. Omotyauriba wa nañ-ḡai desu ka⌟
3. Sumisu-sañ wa nani o dare ni okutte yaritai ñ desu ka⌟
4. Tanaka-sañ no hanasi ni yoru to, nani ḡa ii okurimono ni naru desyoo ka.
5. Tanaka-sañ wa doo site niñḡyoo o gaikoku e okutte mo daizyoobu da to omoimasu ka⌟
6. Sumisu-sañ wa doo site niñḡyoo wa ii okurimono ni naru to omoimasu ka⌟

(b)
7. Dono niñḡyoo ḡa kawaii ñ desu ka⌟
8. Ikura desu ka⌟
9. Takai ñ desu ka, yasui ñ desu ka⌟
10. Sumisu-sañ wa doñna okurimono ni kimemasita ka⌟
11. Sumisu-sañ ḡa niñḡyoo o tutuñde moratte iru aida ni, Tanaka-sañ wa nani o simasu ka⌟

(c)
12. Buraun-sañ no mitai no wa nañ desu ka⌟
13. Buraun-sañ no tomodati wa zāsiki no teeburu o doko de tukatte imasu ka⌟
14. Buraun-sañ wa doo omoimasita ka⌟
15. Buraun-sañ wa doo site hosonaḡai teeburu ḡa kaitai ñ desu ka⌟
16. Tanaka-sañ wa kaimono o sumasete kara nani o sitai ñ desu ka⌟
17. Depaato no tikaku ni wa doñna taberu tokoro ḡa arimasu ka⌟
18. Tanaka-sañ wa doko e Buraun-sañ o annai-simasu ka⌟

(d)
19. Sumisu-sañ wa niñḡyoo no hoka ni nani ḡa mitai ñ desu ka⌟
20. Doo site soñna mono ḡa kaitai ñ desu ka⌟
21. Syuuzi to iu no wa nañ to iu imi desu ka⌟

EXERCISES

1. Ask the following questions and make up an appropriate answer for each:
   a. Ask a Japanese friend if he has ever been (lit. gone) to America.
   b. Ask who the third man from the right is.

   c. Ask where the toys you bought yesterday are.

   d. Ask your house guest if he would like to take a bath before having dinner.

   e. Ask a friend if he has ever eaten at the Tenkin Tempura Shop.

   f. Ask the maid who broke the big square plate.

   g. Ask if you should wrap the books and magazines together.

   h. Ask a Japanese friend if he ever writes with a brush.

   i. Ask the meaning of 'na⌐o⌐su.'

   j. Ask Mr. Tanaka if he is going to have dinner AFTER he has telephoned to America.

   k. Ask Mr. Tanaka if you may read his newspaper while he is telephoning.

   l. Ask Mr. Tanaka if he will write his address and telephone number in romanization for you.

   m. A visitor is looking for Mr. Smith's office. Ask if you should show him the way.

   n. A Japanese friend is trying to read an English text. Ask if he understands the meaning.

   o. You have been asked to write your name and address. Ask if romanization will be all right.

   p. Ask a friend if he ever eats while reading the paper.

   q. Ask Mr. Tanaka if he started studying English AFTER he went to America.

   r. Ask a friend if he is hungry.

2. Practice the drills of this lesson, changing to informal style wherever possible.

Lesson 32. Sightseeing

BASIC DIALOGUES: FOR MEMORIZATION

(a)

Smith

all directions or everywhere	hoʼoboo
travel	ryokoo-suru
return having traveled	ryoᶜkoo-site kaʼeru

1. Since I came all the way to Japan, (I think) I'd like to travel around before I go home (lit. return home having traveled in all directions) . . .

   Sekkaku Niᶜhoñ e kiᵗtaᐧ ñ desu kara, hoʼoboo ryoᶜkoo-site kae-ritaʼi to oᵗmoimaᐧsu ḡa—

that being the case or accordingly	sore de
troublesome or annoying	meʼewaku /na/ or goᶜmeʼewaku ᐧ /na/
provided it isn't a nuisance for you or unless it's a nuisance for you	goᶜmeʼewaku zya ɦaʼkereba

2. That being the case, if it isn't too much trouble, would you tell me what kind of places I should go to?

   Sore de; goᶜmeʼewaku zya ɦaʼ-kereba, doῆna toᵇkoroᐧ e iᵇttaᐧ-ra ᵇiᐧi ka oᶜsiete kudasaimaseᐧῆ ka.

Tanaka

be useful or serve a purpose	yaᶜkuʼ ni ᵇtaᐧtu /-u/ or oᶜyaku ni taʼtu ᐧ

3. Hmm. Depending on the person, the places one wants to see are different, so I don't know whether I'll be of any use or not . . .

   Saʼa. Hito ni yotte miᶜtaʼi toᵇko-roᐧ ḡa tiᵇḡaimaᐧsu kara, oᶜyaku ni taʼtu ka ᵇdoᐧo ka waᶜkarimaseᐧῆ ḡa—

provided it's a nearby place	tiᶜkaʼi toᵇkoroᐧ nara
famous	yuumee /na/

4. If you mean a nearby place, Nikko is famous.

   Tiᶜkaʼi toᵇkoroᐧ nara, Niᶜkkoo ḡa yuᶜumee deʼsu ɦeʼe.

Smith

5. Oh, that's right.

   Aʼa, soᐧo desu ɦeʼe.

<table>
<tr><td>provided [someone] goes</td><td>iˌkeˈba</td></tr>
</table>

6. How is it most convenient to go
   there? (Lit. In going there, it
   is probably most convenient
   provided you go by what?)

   Aˌsoko e ikuˈ no ni wa, naˈn de
   iˈkeˈba iˈtibañ beˈñri desyoo ka.

Tanaka

7. I guess the electric train is
   best — since there's a special
   express.

   Maˈa, deˌñsya g̃a itibañ iˈi desu
   yo⌐ — toˈkkyuu (g̃a) arimaˈsu
   kara.

Smith

decide to go	iˌku kotoˈ ni suru
provided [someone] decides to go	iˌku kotoˈ ni suˈreˈba
unless [someone] buys in advance	kaˌtte okanaˈkereba
it won't do	naˌraˈnai
must buy in advance	kaˌtte okanaˈkereba naˈraˈ-nai

8. But if I decide to go by
   special express, I suppose
   I'll have to buy a special
   express ticket in advance,
   won't I.

   Deˈ mo; toˈkkyuu de iku kotoˈ ni
   suˈreˈba, toˈkkyuˈukeñ (o) kaˈtte
   okanaˈkereba naˈraˈnai desyoo
   ne?

Tanaka

9. Yes. By the day before
   [you go].

   Eˈe. Maˌe no hiˈ made ni.

(b)

Smith

fishing	turi
hot spring or hot spring resort	oñseñ
hot spring resort where fishing is possible	tuˌri no dekiˈru oñseñ

10. I'd like to try going to a
    quiet hot spring resort
    where I can fish . . .

    Tuˌri no dekiˈru ˌsiˈzuka na
    oñseñ e iˈtte mitaˈi ñ desu g̃a⌐

Tanaka

provided it's Izu	Iˌzu naˈra

11. Oh. If it's Izu, there are
    lots of places like that.

    Aˈa ˈsoˈo. Iˌzu naˈra, soˈñna
    tokoroˈ (g̃a) taˈkusañ arimaˈsu
    yo⌐

Smith (thinking)

island	siˈmaˈ

12. Isn't (lit. wasn't) Izu an
    island?

    Izu (wa), siˌmaˈ zya nakatta ñ
    desu ka⌐

Tanaka

    fairly or rather   ka⌐nari
    peninsula   hañtoo
13. No. It's a fairly large   Iie. Ka⌐nari o┌oki⌐i ha┌ñtoo
    peninsula.   de⌐su yo.

Smith

14. Oh, was that it.   A⌐a, so⌐o desita ka.

(c)

Smith

    Buddhist temple   tera or otera +
    Shinto shrine   zi⌐ñzya
15. I hear that in Kyoto there are   Kyo⌐oto ni wa hu┌ru⌐i o┌tera ya
    many old temples and shrines. zi⌐ñzya (ḡa) o┌o⌐i soo desu ┌ne⌐e.

Tanaka

16. That's right.   E⌐e.

Smith

    Christianity   kirisutokyoo
    church   kyookai
17. Aren't there any Christian   Ki┌risutokyoo no kyookai wa
    churches?   arimase⌐ñ ka↲

Tanaka

    do exist or do have   a⌐ru koto wa ┌a⌐ru
    build or erect   ta┌te⌐ru /-ru/
    newly built thing   a┌tara⌐siku ┌ta⌐teta mono
18. Well, they do exist but there   Ma⌐a, ┌a⌐ru koto wa a┌rima⌐su
    are [only a] few and they're   ḡa; su┌kuna⌐i si, taitee a┌tara-
    usually newly built (things).   siku ┌ta⌐teta mo┌no⌐ desu.

Smith

19. Oh? or Really?   Hoo?

Tanaka

    Shintoism   si⌐ñtoo
    Buddhism   bu⌐kkyoo
    flourishing or prosperous   sakañ /na/
     or thriving or popular
    a place where Buddhism   bu⌐kkyoo to ┌si⌐ñtoo no
    and Shintoism flourish   sakañ na tokoro
20. [That's] because Kyoto is a   Kyo⌐oto wa ┌bu⌐kkyoo to ┌si⌐ñ-
    place where Buddhism and   too no sa┝kañ na tokoro⌐ desu
    Shintoism flourish.   kara.

Smith

21. I see! or To be sure! or   Naruhodo.
    Of course!

(d)

Smith

Honshu		Ho⌐ñsyuu
Hokkaido	4 main	Ho⌐kka⌐idoo
Shikoku	islands	Si⌐ko⌐ku
Kyushu	of Japan	Kyu⌐usyuu

some place to go and see do⌐ko ka ke⌐ñbutu-suru
or some place of tokoro⌐
interest

22. Aren't there some places of Kyu⌐usyuu ni wa ⌐do⌐ko ka ke⌐ñ-
interest in Kyushu? butu-suru tokoro⌐ (wa) a⌐rima-
se⌐ñ ka⌐

Tanaka

23. Certainly there are. A⌐rima⌐su to mo.

beginning with Nagasaki Na⌐ga⌐saki o hazime
or from Nagasaki on
down or to say nothing
of Nagasaki
(mountain in Kyushu) A⌐so
(island in Kyushu) Aosima
(city in Kyushu) Ka⌐gosima

24. [There are] Aso, Aoshima, Na⌐ga⌐saki (o) hazime; A⌐so,
Kagoshima, and so on—to Aosima, Ka⌐gosima na⌐do—
say nothing of Nagasaki.

harbor or port minato
one of the harbors mi⌐nato no hito⌐-tu
a day when the weather te⌐ñki no ⌐i⌐i hi
is nice
view na⌐game⌐
is wonderful su⌐barasi⌐i /-ku/

25. Nagasaki is one of the oldest Na⌐ga⌐saki wa i⌐tibañ huru⌐i mi-
harbors, and on days when ⌐nato no hito⌐-tu da si; te⌐ñki no
the weather is nice, the view ⌐i⌐i hi ni wa, A⌐so no na⌐game⌐
of Aso is wonderful. (wa) su⌐barasi⌐i ñ desu yo⌐

(e)

Smith

26. In Japan, wherever you go, Ni⌐hoñ ni wa; do⌐ko e i⌐tte⌐ mo,
there are things that are un- me⌐zura⌐sikute o⌐mosiro⌐i mo⌐no⌐
usual and interesting, aren't ga arimasu ⌐ne⌐e.
there.

Tanaka

27. There are, aren't there. So⌐o desu ⌐ne⌐e.

Smith

souvenir miyage or omiyage +
buy for a souvenir miyage ni kau

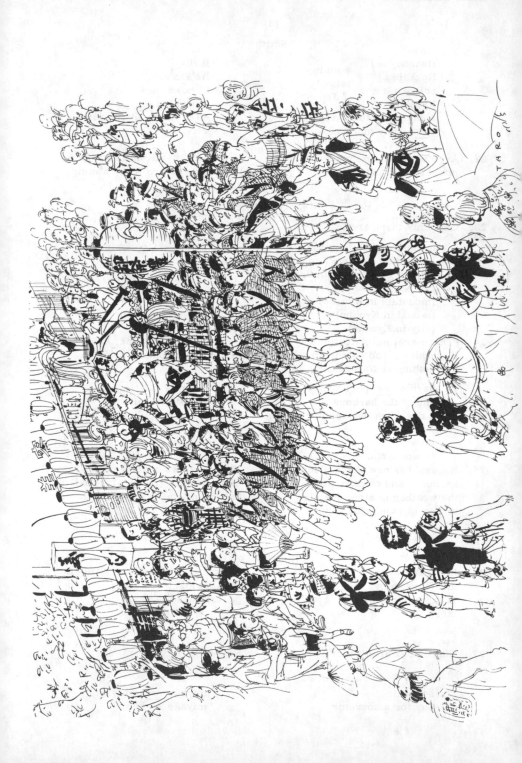

[lit.] become desirous of returning home having bought	ka⌐tte kaerita⌐ku ⌐na⌐ru
28. Whatever I see I want to buy and take home for a souvenir.	Na⌐ni (o) ⌐mi⌐te mo, mi⌐yaḡe ni katte kaerita⌐ku na⌐rima⌐su yo.

Tanaka

29. I guess so.	So⌐o desyoo ⌐ne⌐e.
a country or one's native land or area	kuni or okuni †
of (or from) whatever country things are or things of every country	do⌐no kuni no mo⌐no⌐ de mo
respectively or severally	so⌐re⌐zore
flavor or taste	azi
different flavor	tiḡatta azi
30. [That's] because things of every country have their own different flavor.	Do⌐no kuni no mo⌐no⌐ de mo, so-⌐re⌐zore ti⌐ḡatta azi ḡa arima⌐su kara—
every time [someone] travels	ryo⌐koo-suru tabi⌐ ni
used to buy	ka⌐tta mono⌐ da or ka⌐tta mo⌐n da
31. You know, I too used to buy souvenirs every time I traveled.	Watasi mo ⌐mo⌐to wa ryo⌐koo-suru tabi⌐ ni o⌐miyaḡe (o) katta mon(o)⌐ 1 desu yo.

(f)

Tanaka

geography	ti⌐ri
history	rekisi
provided [someone] knows	si⌐tte (i)re⌐ba
the more [someone] knows	si⌐tte (i)re⌐ba ïru hodo
a trip	ryokoo
32. The more you know Japanese geography and history, the more interesting trips are possible.	Nihon no ⌐ti⌐ri ya rēkisi (o) si⌐tte (i)re⌐ba ïru hodo o⌐mosiro⌐i ryo-⌐koo ḡa deki⌐ru ñ desu ⌐ne⌐e.

Smith

33. That's true, isn't it.	So⌐re wa so⌐o desu ⌐ne⌐e.
concerning history	re⌐kisi ni tu⌐ite
cause or reason or circumstance	wa⌐ke
isn't the case that [someone] doesn't know	si⌐ranai wa⌐ke zya ⌐na⌐i
in a big hurry	o⌐oi⌐soḡi de

---

1 When final o is dropped, mo⌐no⌐ becomes mo⌐ñ.

	one time	ip-peñ
	decide to read	yo⌐mu koto ni suru
34.	It isn't (the case) that I don't know anything at all about geography and history, but I guess I'll (decide to) do some reading again in a big hurry before I start out.	Ti⌐ri ya re⌐kisi ni tu⌐ite, ze⌐ñzeñ siranai wa⌐ke zya ⌐na⌐i ñ desu ḡa; de⌐kakeru ma⌐e ni o⌐oi⌐soḡi de mo⌐o ip-peñ yo⌐mu koto ni si⌐ma-syo⌐o.

Tanaka

35.	Oh?	So⌐o desu ka.
	provided [someone] wants to read	yo⌐mita⌐kereba or o⌐yomi ni narita⌐kereba ⌐
	guidebook	a⌐ññaisyo⌐
36.	If you want to read it, I have a guidebook in English . . .	O⌐yomi ni narita⌐kereba, e⌐eḡo no aññaisyo⌐ (ḡa) a⌐rima⌐su ḡa—

Smith

	borrow	haisyaku-suru ⌐
37.	Oh, then I'd like to borrow it by all means . . .	A. Zya⌐a, ze⌐hi ha⌐isyaku-sita⌐i ñ desu ḡa—

Tanaka

	provided it's all right or agreeable or convenient	yo⌐rosi⌐kereba
	hold or take hold of or have	mo⌐tu /-u/
38.	Certainly. Take it now if you'd like to.	E⌐e, do⌐ozo. Yo⌐rosi⌐kereba, i⌐ma o⌐moti-kudasa⌐i.

ADDITIONAL VOCABULARY

1.	In Japan, wherever you go, there are lanterns.	Ni⌐ho⌐ñ ni wa ⌐do⌐ko e i⌐tte⌐ mo to⌐oroo ḡa arima⌐su ⌐ne⌐e.
	paper lantern	tyo⌐oti⌐ñ
	tower or pagoda	to⌐o
	gateway to Shinto shrine	torii
	festival	maturi or omaturi ⌐
	portable shrine carried about during festivals	mi⌐kosi or o⌐mi⌐kosi ⌐

2.	For sightseers sightseeing busses are best, aren't they?	Ka⌐ñko⌐okyaku ni wa ka⌐ñkooba⌐su ḡa i⌐tibañ i⌐i desyoo?
	sightseeing train	ka⌐ñkoore⌐ssya

3.	Do you like hiking?	Ha⌐ikiñgu ḡa o⌐suki de⌐su ka—

mountain-climbing	ya⌐mano⌐bori
swimming	o⌐yoḡi⌐
golf	go⌐ruhu
tennis	te⌐nisu

4. Isn't (lit. wasn't) that (place)
    a <u>plain</u>?

    Asuko (wa) he⌐eti zya na⌐katta ñ
    desu ka⌐

valley	ta⌐ni⌐
beach	ha⌐ma⌐
cape <u>or</u> promontory	misaki
bay	wa⌐ñ

5. For fishing I usually go to a
    <u>lake</u>.

    Tu⌐ri ni⌐ wa wãtasi (wa) tãitee
    mi⌐zuu⌐mi e ikimasu.

pond	i⌐ke⌐
river	ka⌐wa⌐
canal	u⌐ñḡa

6. Does the continent of Asia
    have many <u>volcanoes</u>?

    A⌐ziya-ta⌐iriku wa ⌐ka⌐zañ ḡa
    o⌐o⌐i ñ desu ka⌐

| forest | hayasi |
| jungle | mituriñ |

7. What (place) is the largest
    <u>country</u> in the world?

    Se⌐ka⌐i de i⌐tibañ hiro⌐i <u>kuni</u>
    (wa) ⌐do⌐ko desyoo ka.

| desert | sabaku |

8. The more you know <u>politics</u>
    the more interesting it gets.

    Se⌐ezi (o) sitte (i)re⌐ba ĩru hodo
    o⌐mosi⌐roku na⌐rima⌐su yo⌐

| economics | ke⌐ezai |
| word <u>or</u> language | ko⌐toba⌐ |

NOTES ON THE BASIC DIALOGUES

10. <u>Turi</u> refers to fishing with a line.

12. Note the use of the past. The speaker is trying to recall something
     from the past: 'Wasn't the information I had the fact that Izu is an is-
     land?'

18. From ta⌐te⌐ru 'build' is derived ta⌐te⌐mono 'building.'

21. <u>Naruhodo</u> means 'of course' following a statement, not in answer to a
     question.

24. <u>X o hazime</u> singles out X as the most important member of a group,
     animate or inanimate.

31. Ta⌐bi⌐ 'time' or 'occurrence' has an alternate form ta⌐ñbi⌐.

34. Wa˥ke: Note also Do˥o iu ˥wa˥ke desu ka. 'What is the reason?'

37. Haisyaku-suru is the humble equivalent of kariru. Haisyaku occurs in
     sentence-final position as an informal polite imperative meaning 'let me
     borrow.'

38. Mo˥tu: compare motte iku 'take' (lit. 'go holding') and mo⌐tte ku˥ru
     'bring' (lit. 'come holding'). Note: X o ⌐mo˥tte imasu '[I] have X' or
     '[I] own X' or '[I] am holding X.'

Additional Vocabulary:

3. Note also ya⌐ma˥ ni noboru 'climb a mountain.'

6. Note riku 'land'; ta˥iriku 'continent.'

                          GRAMMATICAL NOTES

1. The Provisional

I⌐ke˥ba		iku 'go.'
Su⌐re˥ba		suru 'do.'
Yo⌐rosi˥kereba	is the PROVISIONAL of	yorosii 'is good.'
Na˥kereba		na˥i 'isn't.'
Na⌐rita˥kereba		na⌐rita˥i 'want to become.'
Na˥ra		copula da.

Inflected words (verbs, adjectivals, and √da) have PROVISIONAL forms
meaning, in the affirmative, 'provided so-and-so happens or is true,' and
in the negative, 'provided so-and-so doesn't happen or isn't true' or 'unless
so-and-so happens or is true.'

     To form the provisional:

          Verbals, all groups: Drop the final -u of the informal non-past (the
               citation form) and add -eba; if the non-past is accented, the pro-
               visional is accented on the same syllable, and if the non-past is un-
               accented, the provisional is accented on the next-to-last syllable.

          Examples:

               ta⌐be˥ru 'eat': ta⌐be˥reba 'provided [someone] eats'
               kau 'buy': ka⌐e˥ba 'provided [someone] buys'
               i⌐rassya˥ru† 'go,' 'come,' 'be': i⌐rassya˥reba 'provided [some-
                    one] goes or comes or is'
               ku˥ru 'come': ku˥reba 'provided [someone] comes'

          Adjectivals: Drop the final -i of the non-past and add -kereba; the ad-
               jectival provisional is always accented, on the same syllable as the
               corresponding adjectival past and conditional.

          Examples:

               ti⌐isa˥i 'is small': ti⌐isakereba 'provided [something] is small'
               su⌐zusi˥i 'is cool': su⌐zu˥sikereba 'provided it is cool'
               sa⌐mu˥i 'is cold': sa⌐mukereba 'provided it is cold'
               i˥i/yo˥i 'is good': yo˥kereba 'provided [something] is good'

ta⌐be¬nai 'doesn't eat': ta⌐be¬nakereba 'provided [someone] doesn't
eat' or 'unless [someone] eats'
ta⌐beta¬i 'want to eat': ta⌐beta¬kereba 'provided [someone] wants
to eat'

Copula: The provisional of <u>da</u> is na⌐ra¬ or na⌐raba; it loses its accent
following an accented word or phrase.

A sequence consisting of or ending with a provisional states the provision
subject to which something else occurs. The most common English equivalent for both the conditional and the provisional, in the affirmative, is 'if
—— ,' but there is a slight distinction in meaning between the two. Compare:

Ku⌐ruma o utta¬ra, ryo⌐koo-sima¬su. 'If (or when) I sell the car, I'm
going to take a trip.' (This sentence tells what will happen if or
when I sell the car.)

and:

Ku⌐ruma o ure¬ba, ryo⌐koo-sima¬su. 'I'm going to take a trip, if (i.e.
provided) I sell the car.' (This sentence tells under what circumstances I will take a trip.)

In the negative, the conditional corresponds to English 'if not —— ,'
whereas the negative provisional is comparable to English 'unless —— .'
Compare:

Ta⌐naka-sañ ḡa ko¬nakattara, be⌐ñkyoo-sima¬su. 'If Mr. Tanaka doesn't
come, I'll study.' (This sentence tells what will happen if Mr. Tanaka doesn't come.)

and:

Ta⌐naka-sañ ḡa ko¬nakereba, be⌐ñkyoo-sima¬su. 'I'll study unless Mr.
Tanaka comes.' (This sentence indicates an intention to study —
provided Mr. Tanaka doesn't come.)

While the conditional occurs in sentences referring to past, present, or
future time, sentences containing a provisional form usually refer to present
or future time only. However, extended predicates (for example, i⌐ku¬ ñ desu
'it is a matter of going') have provisional equivalents consisting of a non-past
or past + ñ (or <u>no</u>) <u>nara</u>; and when the combination consists of a past + ñ
<u>nara</u>, it refers indirectly to the past (for example, i⌐tta¬ ñ nara 'provided it
is a matter of having gone,' 'provided you DID go'). Thus:

A⌐na¬ta ḡa i˥kuˈ ñ nara, wa⌐takusi mo ikimasyo¬o.
'Provided it involves your going, I'll go too.'
Wa⌐kara¬nakatta ñ nara, do¬o site wa˥karaˈnai tte i˥wanaˈkatta ñ desu
ka↲
'If it's a case of not having understood, why is it you didn't say that
you didn't understand?' (I.e. 'If you didn't understand, why
didn't you say so?')
Ya⌐su¬i ñ nara, ka⌐tte¬ mo ˥iˈi desu.
'Provided it is cheap, you may buy it.'

A provisional followed by i⁷i desu g̱a ¹ —lit. 'provided so-and-so, it is (or will be) fine but' — is a present or future hope or wish, and followed by yo⁷-katta no ni, is a past, contrary-to-fact wish. Thus:

> Ha⁷yaku ʰku⁴reba ʰi⁴i desu g̱a ⌐ne⁷e. 'I hope he comes early, don't you.'
> I⌐re⁷ba ʰi⁴i desu g̱a— 'I hope he's in.'
> Hu⌐ra⁷nakereba ʰi⁴i desu g̱a ⌐ne⁷e. 'I hope it doesn't rain, don't you.'
> Ki⌐ke⁷ba ʰyo⁴katta no ni. 'I wish I had asked.' (Lit. 'In spite of the fact that it was good provided I ask [I didn't].')

Additional examples:

> A⁷sa ⌐ha⌐yaku iʰke⁴ba, a⌐tarasi⁷i saʰkana g̱a kaema⁴su.
> 'You can buy fresh fish, provided you go early in the morning.'
> Te⁷ñki ni ʰna⁴reba, a⌐ru⁷ite ikimasu.
> 'I'll walk there provided it clears (lit. becomes good weather).'
> Sa⁷mukereba, su⌐to⁷obu o tuʰke⁴te kudasai.
> 'Turn on the heater if it's cold.'
> Ni⌐hoñg̱o g̱a wakara⁷nakereba, e⌐eg̱o de itte⁷ mo ka⌐maimase⁷ñ.
> 'You may say it in English, unless you understand Japanese.'
> Ko⌐ohi⁷i g̱a noʰmita⁴kereba; a⌐soko de utte iru⁷ kara, do⁷ozo.
> 'If you want to drink coffee, they're selling it over there so go right ahead.'
> Hu⌐rañsug̱o na⁷ra suʰko⁷si yoʰmema⁴su g̱a, eeg̱o wa ze⌐ñzeñ yomema-se⁷ñ.
> 'Provided it's French I can read it a little, but English I can't read at all.'
> Ba⁷su nara, zyu⌐p-puñ-g̱u⁷rai sika kaʰkarimase⁴ñ.
> 'It takes only about ten minutes, if it's the bus.'

2. 'Must'

A negative provisional ending in -nakereba followed immediately by the negative √na⌐ra⁷nai is an expression of necessity: 'unless [someone] does so-and-so, it won't do (lit. it doesn't become)': that is '[someone] must do so-and-so.' Thus: ta⌐be⁷nakereba naʰra⁴nai '[someone] must eat'; no⌐ma⁷-nakereba naʰra⁴nai '[someone] must drink'; si⌐na⁷kereba naʰra⁴nai '[someone] must do.'

The stronger √ikenai 'it won't do' may be used in place of √na⌐ra⁷nai, particularly when it is the person addressed who is required to do something: 'you must —— .'

Alternating with the negative provisional in this pattern is the negative gerund ending in -nakute + particle wa, usually contracted to nakutya[a] (cf. Lesson 25, Grammatical Note 2). Compare:

> I⌐ttya⁷a ikenai. 'You mustn't go.' (Lit. 'As for going, it won't do.'

and:

> I⌐kana⁷kutyaa ikenai. 'You must go.' (Lit. 'As for not going, it won't do.')

---

¹ Or i⁷i (desu) ke(re)do.

The -nakutyaa alternant is less formal than the -nakereba alternant.

A -nakereba (or -nakutyaa) + naⁿraⁿnai (or ikenai) sequence often occurs in a strong negative reply to a question which asks, 'Is it all right if [I] don't —— ?' (cf. Lesson 22, Grammatical Note 4). Thus:

Iᶠkanaᵓkute mo ᵗiᵗi desu ka⌐ 'Is it all right if I don't go?'
Iie. Iᶠkanaᵓkereba (or iᶠkanaᵓkutyaa) naᵗrimaseᵗñ (or iᵗkemaseᵗñ) yo.
'No. You must go.'

Conversely, in the negative reply to a 'must' question, a negative gerund + mo + iᵓi 'you don't have to ——' occurs. Thus:

Iᶠkanaᵓkereba (or iᶠkanaᵓkutyaa) naᵗrimaseᵗñ ka⌐ 'Must I go?'
Iie. Iᶠkanaᵓkute mo ᶠiᵓi desu yo⌐ 'No. You don't have to go.'

Additional examples:

Koᵗñbañ wa oᶠsokuᵓ made kaᶠisya ni inaᵓkereba naᵗraᵗnai ka mo siᵗrena-ᵗi kara, koᶠrareᵓnai to omoimasu.
'Tonight since I may have to be in the office until late I don't think I can come (lit. I think I can't come).'
Siᶠnaᵓkereba naᵗraᵗnai siᵗḡoto ḡa aᵗru kara, oᶠsaki ni situᵓree-simasu.
'There's work I must do so excuse me for leaving ahead of you.'
Narubeku niᶠhoñḡo o tukau yoᵓo ni siᶠnaᵗkereba naᵗrimaseᵗñ.
'One must try to use Japanese as much as possible.'
Haᵗyaku iᵗkanaᵗkutyaa iᶠkemaseᵓñ yo. 'You must go early!'
Kiᶠnoᵓo wa ᶠnoᵓdo ḡa iᵗtaᵗkute, iti-niti-zyuu neᵗte inaᵓkereba naᵗraᵗ-nakatta ñ desu.
'I had to stay in bed all day yesterday with a sore throat.' (Lit. 'Yesterday my throat being sore, I had to be in bed all day long.')
Aᶠsitaᵓ mo, kyoᵓo no ᵗyoᵗo ni, ᶠhaᵓyaku deᵗkakenaᵗkutyaa naᵗraᵗnai?
'Do you have to go out early tomorrow too, the way [you did] today?'

3. 'The more ——, the more ——'

A sequence containing a provisional + the corresponding citation form + hodo 'extent' occurs in the Japanese equivalent of English sequences having the pattern 'the more X, the more Y' (for example, 'the bigger the better,' 'the higher the fewer,' 'the more I see it the more I want it.'

Examples:

Aᶠtaraᵓsikereba aᶠtarasiᵓi hodo ōisii. 'The fresher the more deli-cious.' (Lit. 'Provided it's fresh, to the extent that it's fresh, it's delicious.')
Oᶠokikereba oᶠokiᵓi hodo ᶠiᵓi desu. 'The bigger the better.' (Lit. 'Provided it's big, to the extent that it's big, it's good.')
Kotira no tuḡoo wa ᶠhaᵓyakereba haᵓyaᵓi hodo ᶠiᵓi ñ desu. 'The ear-lier the better for me.' (Lit. 'As for the circumstances on this [i.e. my] side, provided it's early, to the extent that it's early, it's good.')
Kyoᵓoto no haᵗnasiᵗ o kiᶠkeᵓba kĭku hodo iᶠtte miᵗtaku narimasu.
'The more I hear about Kyoto, the more I want to try and go.' (Lit.

'Provided I hear talk of Kyoto, to the extent that I hear, I become desirous of going and seeing.')

Nihoñgo wa be⌐ñkyoo-sure⌐ba su̅ru hodo mu̅zukasiku na⌐ru yoo desu.
'The more I study Japanese, the more difficult it seems to become.'
(Lit. 'As for Japanese, provided I study, to the extent that I study, it seems to become difficult.')

The corresponding sequence derived from a nominal + √da expression occurs in either of the following forms:

(1) nominal + de ⌐a⌐reba ⌐a⌐ru hodo ——
(2) nominal + <u>nara</u> + nominal + | no / na | hodo ——

Thus: be⌐ñri da 'it's convenient':

Be⌐ñri de ⌐a⌐reba ⌐a⌐ru hodo ta⌐ka⌐i desu.
Be⌐ñri nara ⌐be⌐ñri na hodo ta⌐ka⌐i desu.
'The more convenient it is, the more expensive it is!'

4. —— ko⌐to⌐ ni √suru

A nominal X + particle <u>ni</u> of goal + √<u>suru</u> means 'make [it] to be X,' 'decide on X' (cf. Lesson 14, Grammatical Note 6).

When the nominal is ko⌐to⌐ 'act' preceded by a verbal in its citation form, the combination is equivalent to 'decide to do so-and-so.' Compare:

Ki⌐ñyo⌐obi ni si⌐masyo⌐o. 'Let's decide on Friday'; 'Let's make it Friday.'

and:

I⌐ku koto⌐ ni si⌐masyo⌐o. 'Let's decide to go'; 'Let's plan to go.'

When <u>ko⌐to⌐</u> is preceded by a negative, the combination means 'decide not to do so-and-so.' Thus:

I⌐kanai koto⌐ ni si⌐masyo⌐o. 'Let's decide not to go'; 'Let's plan on not going.'

The use of <u>ko⌐to⌐ ni √suru</u> following a verbal or a negative adjectival implies choosing between two or more alternatives, or deciding on a plan, or changing a plan. Compare:

Ta⌐bemasyo⌐o. 'Let's eat.'

and:

Ta⌐be⌐ru koto ni si⌐masyo⌐o. '[Of the various possible alternatives] let's decide to eat.'

Examples:

A⌐me g̅a hu⌐tta⌐ra, i⌐kanai koto⌐ ni si⌐masyo⌐o.
'Let's decide not to go if it rains.'
A⌐soko de tabe⌐ru koto ni si⌐ta⌐ra ⌐do⌐o desyoo.
'How would it be if we decided to eat over there?'

Kyo⌐o⌐ ⌐ku⌐-zi-hatu Ko⌐obe-iki de ta⌐tu koto ni si˥ma˩sita.
'I have decided to leave today on the 9 o'clock train for Kobe.'
Narubeku e⌐eḡo o tukawanai koto⌐ ni si˥tai to omo˩tte imasu.
'I've been thinking that I'd like to (decide to) avoid using (lit. not to
use) English as much as possible.'

5. a⌐ru koto wa ˥a˩ru

Ko⌐to⌐ wa, preceded by a sentence modifier (consisting of — or ending with
—a non-past or past verbal or adjectival, or a nominal + no or na or datta)
and followed by an independent equivalent of the modifier, is equivalent to 'it
IS so-and-so [but],' 'so-and-so IS true [but],' 'granted so-and-so [but].'
Thus:

ta⌐be⌐ru koto wa ta˥bema˩su ḡa_ '[someone] DOES eat but . . .' (for
   example, as in: 'he DOES eat but he doesn't eat the right things,'
   'he DOES eat but he doesn't eat much,' etc.)
o⌐oki˩i koto wa o˥oki˩i '[it] IS big' (for example, as in: 'it IS big but
   it isn't very good')
byo⌐oki no koto⌐ wa byo˥oki de˩su '[someone] IS sick' (for example,
   as in: 'he IS sick but it isn't serious')
be⌐ñri na ko˥to˩ wa ˥be˩ñri desu 'it IS convenient' (for example, as
   in: 'it IS convenient but it's not a pretty place')

If the inflected word before and after ko⌐to⌐ is a negative, the combination
means 'granted that so-and-so isn't true.' Thus:

A⌐ñmari tabe⌐nai koto wa ta˥be˩nai ñ desu ḡa, si⌐ñpai wa arimase⌐ñ.
'Granted he doesn't eat much, but there's nothing to worry about.'

Additional examples:

Bo⌐ku mo i⌐ku koto⌐ wa i˥kima˩su ḡa, na⌐ñ-zi ni i˥ku˩ ka wa wa⌐kari-
   mase⌐ñ.
'I too AM going, but at what time I'm going I can't tell.'
A⌐no e⌐eḡa wa o⌐mosiro⌐i koto wa o˥mosiro˩i ñ desu ḡa, na⌐ḡasu⌐ḡite_
'That movie IS interesting, but it's too long . . .'
Ano heñ wa ⌐si⌐zuka na ko˥to˩ wa ˥si˩zuka desu ḡa, añmari ⌐be⌐ñri
   zya a˥rimase˩ñ.
'That section IS quiet but it isn't very convenient.'
I⌐ma de mo ⌐ki⌐ree na ko˥to˩ wa ˥ki˩ree desu ḡa; a⌐ki ni ˥na˩ttara,
   mo⌐tto ˥ki˩ree ni na˥rima˩su yo⌐
'Even now it IS pretty, but when autumn comes, it will be(come)
   prettier.'

6. mo⌐no⌐ Referring to Habitual Action

An inflected word in its past-tense form + nominal mo⌐no⌐ (different
from the nominal mo⌐no⌐ 'concrete thing') + √da indicates habitual action:
'used to do or be so-and-so.' The contracted equivalent of mo⌐no⌐ is mo⌐ñ.

Examples:

Ko⌐domo no toki⌐ ni wa, ma⌐ibañ ⌐so⌐hu ni ha⌐nasi⌐ o si˥te moratta
   mono˩ desu.

'When I was a child, I used to have my grandfather tell me a story
   every night.'
Mo⌐to wa ⌐zu⌐ibuñ sa⌐ke o no⌐nda mo⌐no⌐ desu ḡa—
   'I used to drink (sake) a great deal (formerly) but [now I don't].'
A⌐kai mono⌐ wa ko⌐domo sika kina⌐katta mo⌐no⌐ desu ḡa, i⌐ma wa ke-
   ⌐kkoñ-sita hito⌐ de mo ki⌐te ima⌐su ⌐ne⌐e.
'Only children used to wear red (things), but now even married
   people wear it.'
Deñwa wa mi⌐ñna ku⌐rokatta mo⌐no⌐ desu ḡa, kono-ḡoro wa a⌐ka⌐i no
   ya si⌐ro⌐i no mo a⌐rima⌐su ⌐ne⌐e.
'Telephones all used to be black but nowadays there are also red
   ones and white ones (and others), aren't there.'

7. —— ni ⌐tu⌐ite

A nominal X + ni ⌐tu⌐ite means 'about X' or 'concerning X.'

A phrase ending with ni ⌐tu⌐ite occurs (1) without following particle, in
construction with an inflected word or phrase; (2) followed by particle no in
construction with a nominal; (3) followed by particle wa with contrastive
meaning; (4) preceded by an interrogative and followed by particle mo + a
negative, with an all-exclusive meaning.

Examples:

So⌐re ni tu⌐ite se⌐tumee-site kurema⌐sita. 'He explained to me about
   that.'
Ko⌐re ni tu⌐ite ⌐do⌐o omoimasu ka⌐ 'What do you think about this?'
Na⌐ni ni ⌐tu⌐ite ha⌐nasimasyo⌐o ka. 'What shall we talk about?'
Ni⌐ho⌐ñ ni ⌐tu⌐ite desu. 'It's about Japan.'
Ni⌐ho⌐ñ ni ⌐tu⌐ite no ⌐ho⌐ñ o yo⌐mima⌐sita. 'I read a book about Ja-
   pan.'
Ka⌐buki ni tu⌐ite wa na⌐ni mo sirimase⌐ñ. 'About kabuki I know noth-
   ing.'
Na⌐ni ni ⌐tu⌐ite mo ha⌐nasemase⌐ñ. 'I can't talk about anything.'

8. Particles: Sentence-final to mo

The particle sequence to mo occurs following an inflected word—non-
past or past, informal or formal—at the end of a statement which answers a
question. It implies strong emphasis: 'certainly' or 'positively' or 'of
course.'

Examples:

A⌐no⌐ hito ni⌐hoñḡo ḡa deki⌐ru?. . . De⌐ki⌐ru to mo. To⌐ttemo zyoozu⌐
   desu yo⌐
   'Can he speak Japanese?. . . Of course he can. He's very good.'
Ano sakana ta⌐berarema⌐su ka⌐. . . Ta⌐berarema⌐su to mo. O⌐isi⌐i
   desu yo⌐
   'Can you eat that fish?. . . Of course you can eat it. It's delicious.'
A⌐no ho⌐teru ta⌐ka⌐i?. . . Ta⌐ka⌐i to mo.
   'Is that hotel expensive?. . . It certainly is expensive.'

Kono teḡami zi⌐buñ de ka⌉ita?. . . So⌉o da to mo.
   'Did you write this letter by yourself?. . . Certainly (that's right).'
Ma⌉da a⌐rima⌉sita ka⌐. . . A⌐rima⌉sita to mo.
   'Was there still some?. . . Of course there was.'

9. Counter -heñ

The counter -heñ combines with the numerals of Series I to count number
of times or occurrences. It is similar in meaning to counters -do and -kai.

i⌐p-pe⌉ñ 'one time'   ro⌉p-peñ 'six times'
ni-⌐he⌉ñ 'two times'   si⌐ti⌉-heñ or na⌐na⌉-heñ 'seven times'
sa⌉ñ-beñ 'three times'   ha⌉p-peñ or ha⌐ti⌉-heñ 'eight times'
yo⌉ñ-heñ 'four times'   kyu⌉u-heñ 'nine times'
go-⌐he⌉ñ 'five times'   zi⌉p-pe⌉ñ or zyu⌐p-pe⌉ñ 'ten times'

na⌉ñ-beñ 'how many times?'

DRILLS

A. Substitution Drill

(Each cue is given in its independent form. In using it as a sentence
modifier make any changes necessary.)

1. Isn't there some place of   Do⌉ko ka ke⌐ñbutu-suru tokoro⌉
   interest?   (wa) a⌐rimase⌉ñ ka⌐
2. Isn't there some famous   Do⌉ko ka yu⌐umee na tokoro⌉ (wa)
   place? /yuumee da/   a⌐rimase⌉ñ ka⌐
3. Isn't there some pretty   Do⌉ko ka ⌐ki⌉ree na to⌐koro⌉ (wa)
   place? /ki⌉ree da/   a⌐rimase⌉ñ ka⌐
4. Isn't there some place   Do⌉ko ka na⌐ḡame no[1] i⌉i to⌐koro⌉
   with a nice view?   (wa) a⌐rimase⌉ñ ka⌐
   /na⌐ḡame⌉ ḡa ⌐i⌉i/
5. Isn't there some warm   Do⌉ko ka a⌐ttaka⌉i to⌐koro⌉ (wa)
   place? /a⌐ttaka⌉i/   a⌐rimase⌉ñ ka⌐
6. Isn't there some place   Do⌉ko ka ka⌐yoeru tokoro⌉ (wa)
   [I] can commute to?   a⌐rimase⌉ñ ka⌐
   /kayoeru/
7. Isn't there some broken   Do⌉ko ka ko⌐wa⌉reta to⌐koro⌉ (wa)
   place (i. e. part)?   a⌐rimase⌉ñ ka⌐
   /ko⌐wa⌉reta/
8. Isn't there some special   Do⌉ko ka to⌐kubetu na tokoro⌉ (wa)
   place? /tokubetu da/   a⌐rimase⌉ñ ka⌐
9. Isn't there some place   Do⌉ko ka ⌐a⌉tuku ⌐na⌉i to⌐koro⌉
   that isn't hot? /a⌉tuku   (wa) a⌐rimase⌉ñ ka⌐
   ⌐na⌉i/
10. Isn't there some place   Do⌉ko ka su⌐ki⌉i no[1] sa⌐kañ na
    where skiing is popular?   tokoro⌉ (wa) a⌐rimase⌉ñ ka⌐
    /su⌐ki⌉i ḡa sa⌐kañ da/

---

[1] Or ḡa.

B. Substitution Drill

1. Since I came all the way
    to Japan, (I think) I'd
    like to travel around be-
    fore I go home.

    Sekkaku Ni⌐ho꣸n e ki⌐taꔼ ñ desu
    kara, hoꔼoboo ryo⌐koo-site kae-
    ritaꔼi to omoimasu.

2. Since I came all the way
    to Japan, (I think) I'd
    like to see the sights of
    Kyoto before I go home.

    Sekkaku Ni⌐ho꣸n e ki⌐taꔼ ñ desu
    kara, Kyoꔼoto (o) ke⌐ñbutu-site
    kaeritaꔼi to omoimasu.

3. Since I came all the way
    to Japan, (I think) I'd
    like to go to a famous hot
    spring before I go home.

    Sekkaku Ni⌐ho꣸n e ki⌐taꔼ ñ desu
    kara, yuꔼumee na oñseñ e itte
    kaeritaꔼi to omoimasu.

4. Since I came all the way
    to Japan, (I think) I'd
    like to see kabuki before
    I go home.

    Sekkaku Ni⌐ho꣸n e ki⌐taꔼ ñ desu
    kara, ka⌐buki (o) miꔼte ka⌐eri-
    taꔼi to omoimasu.

5. Since I came all the way
    to Japan, (I think) I'd
    like to climb Mt. Fuji
    before I go home.

    Sekkaku Ni⌐ho꣸n e ki⌐taꔼ ñ desu
    kara, Huꔼzisañ ni no⌐botte kae-
    ritaꔼi to omoimasu.

6. Since I came all the way
    to Japan, (I think) I'd
    like to study Japanese
    before I go home.

    Sekkaku Ni⌐ho꣸n e ki⌐taꔼ ñ desu
    kara, ni⌐hoñgo (o) beñkyoo-site
    kaeritaꔼi to omoimasu.

7. Since I came all the way
    to Japan, (I think) I'd
    like to consult with
    Dr. Tanaka before I go
    home.

    Sekkaku Ni⌐ho꣸n e ki⌐taꔼ ñ desu
    kara, Taꔼnaka-señseꔼe to so⌐o-
    dañ-site kaeritaꔼi to omoimasu.

8. Since I came all the way
    to Japan, (I think) I'd
    like to buy some sou-
    venirs before I go home.

    Sekkaku Ni⌐ho꣸n e ki⌐taꔼ ñ desu
    kara, oꔼmiyaḡe (o) katte kaeri-
    taꔼi to omoimasu.

C. Substitution Drill

1. The things of every
    country have their own
    flavor, haven't they.

    Doꔼno kuni no mo⌐noꔼ de mo,
    so⌐reꔼzore ti⌐ḡatta azi ḡa ari-
    maꔼsu ⌐neꔼe.

2. The clothing of every
    country has its own flavor,
    hasn't it.

    Doꔼno kuni no ki⌐mono deꔼ mo,
    so⌐reꔼzore ti⌐ḡatta azi ḡa ari-
    maꔼsu ⌐neꔼe.

3. The drinks of every
    country have their own
    flavor, haven't they.

    Doꔼno kuni no no⌐miꔼmono de
    mo, so⌐reꔼzore ti⌐ḡatta azi ḡa
    arimaꔼsu ⌐neꔼe.

4. The shops of every
    country have their own
    flavor, haven't they.

    Doꔼno kuni no mi⌐seꔼ de mo, so-
    ⌐reꔼzore ti⌐ḡatta azi ḡa arimaꔼsu
    ⌐neꔼe.

5. The furniture of every country has its own flavor, hasn't it.

Do⌐no kuni no ⌐ka⌐ḡu de mo, so-⌐re⌐zore ti⌐ḡatta azi ḡa arima⌐su ⌐ne⌐e.

6. The dolls of every country have their own flavor, haven't they.

Do⌐no kuni no ni⌐ñḡyoo de⌐ mo, so⌐re⌐zore ti⌐ḡatta azi ḡa ari-ma⌐su ⌐ne⌐e.

7. The language of every country has its own flavor, hasn't it.

Do⌐no kuni no ko⌐toba⌐ de mo, so⌐re⌐zore ti⌐ḡatta azi ḡa ari-ma⌐su ⌐ne⌐e.

8. The food of every country has its own flavor, hasn't it.

Do⌐no kuni no ta⌐bemo⌐no de mo, so⌐re⌐zore ti⌐ḡatta azi ḡa ari-ma⌐su ⌐ne⌐e.

D. Substitution Drill

1. If it isn't too much trouble, would you tell me what kind of places I should go to?

Go⌐me⌐ewaku zya ⌐ha⌐kereba, do⌐ñ-na to⌐koro⌐ e i⌐tta⌐ra ⌐i⌐i ka o⌐siete kudasaimase⌐ñ ka.

2. If it isn't too much trouble, would you tell me where I should travel? /Do⌐ko e ryo-⌐koo-sita⌐ra ⌐i⌐i desu ka⌐/

Go⌐me⌐ewaku zya ⌐ha⌐kereba, do⌐ko e ryo⌐koo-sita⌐ra ⌐i⌐i ka o⌐siete kudasaimase⌐ñ ka.

3. If it isn't too much trouble, would you tell me how I should wrap it? /Do⌐o iu ⌐hu⌐u ni tu⌐tu⌐ñ-dara ⌐i⌐i desu ka⌐/

Go⌐me⌐ewaku zya ⌐ha⌐kereba, do⌐o iu ⌐hu⌐u ni tu⌐tu⌐ñdara ⌐i⌐i ka o⌐siete kudasaimase⌐ñ ka.

4. If it isn't too much trouble, would you tell me who should explain it to me (lit. by whom I should have it explained)? /Da⌐re ni se⌐tumee-site moratta⌐ra ⌐i⌐i desu ka⌐/

Go⌐me⌐ewaku zya ⌐ha⌐kereba, da⌐re ni se⌐tumee-site moratta⌐ra ⌐i⌐i ka o⌐siete kudasaimase⌐ñ ka.

5. If it isn't too much trouble, would you tell me how it is most convenient to go? /Na⌐ñ de i⌐ke⌐ba i⌐tibañ be⌐ñri desu ka⌐/

Go⌐me⌐ewaku zya ⌐ha⌐kereba, na⌐ñ de i⌐ke⌐ba i⌐tibañ be⌐ñri ka o⌐siete kudasaimase⌐ñ ka.

6. If it isn't too much trouble, would you tell me what (time) train is fastest to ride on? /Na⌐ñ-zi no ki⌐sya⌐ ni no⌐re⌐ba i⌐tibañ haya⌐i desu ka⌐/

Go⌐me⌐ewaku zya ⌐ha⌐kereba, na⌐ñ-zi no ki⌐sya⌐ ni no⌐re⌐ba i⌐tibañ haya⌐i ka o⌐siete kudasaimase⌐ñ ka.

7. If it isn't too much   Go⌐me¬ewaku zya ⌐ha¬kereba, a⌐ho
   trouble, would you tell   hito¬tati (wa) ⌐da¬re ka o⌐siete
   me who those people   kudasaimase¬ñ ka.
   are? /A⌐ho hito¬tati (wa)
   ⌐da¬re desu ka⌐/
8. If it isn't too much   Go⌐me¬ewaku zya ⌐ha¬kereba, bu¬-
   trouble, would you tell   kkyoo ya ⌐si¬ñtoo (wa) ⌐do¬ñna
   me what kind of things   mo⌐no¬ ka o⌐siete kudasaimase¬ñ
   Buddhism and Shinto are?   ka.
   /Bu¬kkyoo ya ⌐si¬ñtoo (wa)
   ⌐do¬ñna mo⌐no¬ desu ka⌐/

E. Substitution Drill

1. Every time I travel I buy a   Ryo⌐koo-suru tabi¬ ni, o⌐miyaḡe
   souvenir.   (o) kaima¬su.
2. Every time I ride in a   Hi⌐ko¬oki ni no⌐ru tabi¬ ni, byo-
   plane I get sick.   ⌐oki ni narima¬su.
3. Every time I go to Japan,   Ni⌐ho¬ñ e i⌐ku tabi¬ ni, Hu¬zisañ
   I climb Fuji.   ni noborimasu.
4. Every time I rent a house,   Kasiya (o) ka⌐riru tabi¬ ni, ta-
   I change the tatami.   ⌐tami (o) torikaema¬su.
5. Every time I go sightsee-   Keñbutu ni i⌐ku tabi¬ ni, tu⌐ka¬-
   ing, I get tired.   rete simaimasu.
6. Every time I go out, I   De⌐kakeru tabi¬ ni, na¬ni ka wa-
   forget something.   ⌐surete simaima¬su.
7. Every time I repaint [it],   Nu⌐rikae¬ru ta⌐bi¬ ni, ti⌐ḡatta iro¬
   I make [it] a different   ni simasu.
   color.
8. Every time I smoke, my   Tabako (o) ⌐ho¬mu ta⌐bi¬ ni, no¬do
   throat hurts.   ḡa i⌐ta¬ku narimasu.

F. Response Drill (based on Grammatical Note 6)

   Tutor: I⌐tta koto¬ ḡa a⌐rima¬su ka⌐ 'Have you ever gone [there]?'
   Student: E¬e. Mo¬to wa ⌐yo¬ku i⌐tta mono¬ desu. 'Yes. I used to
            go [there] often.'

1. Ryo⌐koo-sita koto¬ ḡa a⌐ri-   E¬e. Mo¬to wa ⌐yo¬ku ryo⌐koo-
   ma¬su ka⌐   sita mono¬ desu.
2. Hu⌐de de ka⌐ita koto ḡa   E¬e. Mo¬to wa ⌐yo¬ku /hu⌐de de/
   a⌐rima¬su ka⌐   ka⌐ita mo⌐no¬ desu.
3. Ryo⌐kañ ni tomatta koto¬   E¬e. Mo¬to wa ⌐yo¬ku /ryo⌐kañ ni/
   ḡa a⌐rima¬su ka⌐   tomatta mono¬ desu.
4. Tu⌐ri ni itta koto¬ ḡa   E¬e. Mo¬to wa ⌐yo¬ku /tu⌐ri ni/
   a⌐rima¬su ka⌐   itta mono¬ desu.
5. Go¬ (o) si⌐tta koto¬ ḡa   E¬e. Mo¬to wa ⌐yo¬ku /⌐go¬ (o)/
   a⌐rima¬su ka⌐   si⌐tta mono¬ desu.
6. Zi⌐teñsya ni notta koto¬   E¬e. Mo¬to wa ⌐yo¬ku /zi⌐teñsya
   ḡa a⌐rima¬su ka⌐   ni/ notta mono¬ desu.

7. Ka⌐buki (o) mi⌉ta koto
   ḡa a⌐rima⌉su ka⌟

8. Ni⌐hoñ no siñbuñ (o)
   yo⌐ñda koto ḡa a⌐rima⌉su
   ka⌟

E⌉e. Mo⌉to wa 「yo⌐ku /ka⌐buki (o)/
mi⌉ta mo⌐no⌉ desu.

E⌉e. Mo⌉to wa 「yo⌐ku /Ni⌐hoñ no
siñbuñ (o)/ yo⌉ñda mo⌐no⌉ desu.

G. Substitution Drill (based on Grammatical Note 7)

1. We talked about history.
   Re⌐kisi ni tu⌉ite ha⌐nasima⌉sita.

2. We talked about geography.
   Ti⌉ri ni tuite ha⌐nasima⌉sita.

3. I'd like to read about geography . . .
   Ti⌉ri ni tuite yo⌐mita⌉i ñ desu ḡa_

4. I'd like to read about Japanese farmers . . .
   Ni⌐hoñ no hyakusyo⌉o ni tuite yo⌐mita⌉i ñ desu ḡa_

5. I'd like to ask about Japanese farmers . . .
   Ni⌐hoñ no hyakusyo⌉o ni tuite ki- 「kita⌉i ñ desu ḡa_

6. I'd like to ask about Buddhism . . .
   Bu⌉kkyoo ni tuite ki⌐kita⌉i ñ desu ḡa_

7. Would you give me some information about Buddhism?
   Bu⌉kkyoo ni tuite o⌐siete kurema- se⌉ñ ka.

8. Would you give me some information about politics and economics?
   Se⌐ezi to ke⌐ezai ni tuite o⌐siete kuremase⌉ñ ka.

9. I'm writing a book about politics and economics.
   Se⌐ezi to ke⌐ezai ni tuite 「ho⌉ñ (o) 「ka⌉ite (i)masu.

10. I'm writing a book about Christianity.
    Ki⌐risutokyoo ni tu⌉ite 「ho⌉ñ (o) 「ka⌉ite (i)masu.

H. Expansion Drill

   Tutor: Tanaka-sañ Ya⌐mamoto-sañ na⌉ñka (ḡa) imasu. /Ikeda- sañ/ 'Mr. Tanaka, Mr. Yamamoto and others are here. /Mr. Ikeda/'
   Student: Ikeda-sañ (o) hazime, Tanaka-sañ Ya⌐mamoto-sañ na⌉ñ- ka (ḡa) imasu. 'Mr. Tanaka, Mr. Yamamoto, and others are here, to say nothing of Mr. Ikeda.'

1. Zassi si⌐ñbuñ na⌉ñka (o) u⌐tte (i)ma⌉su. /ho⌉ñ/
   Ho⌉ñ (o) hazime, zassi si⌐ñbuñ na⌉ñka (o) u⌐tte (i)ma⌉su.

2. Rekisi 「ti⌉ri nañka (o) be⌐ñkyoo-site (i)ma⌉su. /ko⌐toba⌉/
   Ko⌐toba⌉ (o) hazime, rekisi 「ti⌉- ri nañka (o) be⌐ñkyoo-site (i)ma⌉su.

3. Kotatu de⌐ñkisuto⌉obu nañka (o) tu⌐katte ima⌉su. /hi⌉bati/
   Hi⌉bati (o) hazime, kotatu de⌐ñki- suto⌉obu nañka (o) tu⌐katte (i)ma⌉su.

4. O⌐yoḡi⌉ ya 「te⌉nisu mo sa⌐kañ ni narima⌉sita. /go⌉ruhu/
   Go⌉ruhu (o) hazime, o⌐yoḡi⌉ ya 「te⌉nisu mo sa⌐kañ ni narima⌉- sita.

5. Hi⌐syo⌉ mo zyo⌐tyuu mo kima⌉sita. /o⌉kusañ/
   O⌉kusañ (o) hazime, hi⌐syo⌉ mo zyo⌐tyuu mo kima⌉sita.

6. Ta⌐roo-tyañ mo ⌐Zi⌐roo-
   tyañ mo ki⊢ma⊣sita.
   /se⌐ñse⌐e/

Se⌐ñse⌐e (o) hazime, Ta⌐roo-tyañ
mo ⌐Zi⌐roo-tyañ mo ki⊢ma⊣sita.

I. Response Drill (based on Grammatical Note 4)

Tutor: I⌐kimasyo⌐o ka. 'Shall we go?'
Student: E⌐e, i⌐ku koto⌐ ni si⊢masyo⊣o. 'Yes, let's plan to go.'

1. Ya⌐memasyo⌐o ka.

   E⌐e, ya⌐meru koto⌐ ni si⊢masyo⊣o.

2. Ko⌐domo (o) turete ikima-
   syo⌐o ka.

   E⌐e, ko⌐domo (o) turete iku koto⌐
   ni si⊢masyo⊣o.

3. Mo⌐o suko⌐si so⌐odañ-
   simasyo⌐o ka.

   E⌐e, mo⌐o suko⌐si so⌐odañ-suru
   koto⌐ ni si⊢masyo⊣o.

4. Ki⌐mono (o) kimasyo⌐o ka.

   E⌐e, ki⌐mono (o) kiru koto⌐ ni
   si⊢masyo⊣o.

5. Teeburu (o) yo⌐yaku-site
   okimasyo⌐o ka.

   E⌐e, teeburu (o) yo⌐yaku-site oku
   koto⌐ ni si⊢masyo⊣o.

6. Yo⌐osyoku (o) tabemasyo⌐o
   ka.

   E⌐e, yo⌐osyoku (o) tabe⌐ru koto ni
   si⊢masyo⊣o.

7. Hu⌐toñ ni nemasyo⌐o ka.

   E⌐e, hu⌐toñ ni neru koto⌐ ni si-
   ⊢masyo⊣o.

8. Ka⌐ñkooba⌐su ni no⌐rima-
   syo⊣o ka.

   E⌐e, ka⌐ñkooba⌐su ni no⌐ru koto⊣
   ni si⊢masyo⊣o.

J. Response Drill (based on Grammatical Note 5)

Tutor: A⌐rimase⌐ñ ka⌣ 'Aren't there any?'
Student: A⌐ru koto wa a⊢rima⊣su ḡa_ 'There ARE some but. . . .'

1. Wa⌐karimase⌐ñ ka⌣

   Wa⌐karu koto wa wa⊢karima⊣su
   ḡa_

2. Ya⌐ku⌐ ni ta⌐timase⌐ñ ka⌣

   Ya⌐ku⌐ ni ⌐ta⌐tu koto wa ta⊢ti-
   ma⊣su ḡa_

3. Ka⌐wa⌐iku a⌐rimase⌐ñ ka⌣

   Ka⌐wai⌐i koto wa ka⊢wai⊣i desu
   ḡa_

4. Yu⌐umee zya arimase⌐ñ
   ka⌣

   Yu⌐umee na koto⌐ wa yu⊢umee
   de⊣su ḡa_

5. Ni⌐hoñzi⌐ñ zya a⌐rimase⌐ñ
   ka⌣

   Ni⌐hoñzi⌐ñ no koto wa ni⊢hoñzi⊣ñ
   desu ḡa_

6. Tu⌐yoku a⌐rimase⌐ñ ka⌣

   Tu⌐yo⌐i koto wa tu⊢yo⊣i desu ḡa_

7. To⌐kee (o) mo⌐tte (i)⌐ma-
   se⌐ñ ka⌣

   To⌐kee (o) mo⌐tte (i)⊢ru koto⊣ wa
   ⊢mo⊣tte (i)masu ḡa_

8. Re⌐ñsyuu-site (i)mase⌐ñ
   ka⌣

   Re⌐ñsyuu-site (i)ru koto⌐ wa si⊢te
   (i)ma⊣su ḡa_

9. Yo⌐ku a⌐rimase⌐ñ ka⌣

   I⌐i koto wa ⊢i⊣i desu ḡa_

10. Syo⌐oziki⌐ zya a⌐rimase⌐ñ
    ka⌣

   Syo⌐oziki⌐ na koto wa syo⌐⊢oziki⊣
   desu ḡa_

K. Response Drill

Tutor: A⌐rimase⌐ñ ka⌣ 'Aren't there any?'
Student: Na⌐i ⊢wa⊣ke zya a⌐rimase⊣ñ ḡa_ 'It isn't that there aren't
         any but [something else is involved].'

1. De⌐ki¹maseᵓñ ka⌐ De⌐ki¹nai ⌐wa⁴ke zya a⌐rimase⁴ñ g̃a—
2. Hu¹beñ desu ka⌐ Hu¹beñ na ⌐wa⁴ke zya a⌐rimase⁴ñ g̃a—
3. A⌐tta¹kaku a⌐rimase⌐ñ ka⌐ A⌐tta¹kaku ⌐na¹i ⌐wa⁴ke zya a⌐rimase⁴ñ g̃a—
4. Ki⌐koemase⌐ñ ka⌐ Ki⌐koenai wa⁴ke zya a⌐rimase⁴ñ g̃a—
5. Ka⌐maimase⁴ñ ka⌐ Ka⌐mawa¹nai ⌐wa⁴ke zya a⌐rimase⁴ñ g̃a—
6. Ki ⌐ni irimase⁴ñ ka⌐ Ki ⌐ni iranai wa⁴ke zya a⌐rimase⁴ñ g̃a—
7. Ko⌐marima¹su ka⌐ Ko⌐ma¹ru ⌐wa⁴ke zya a⌐rimase⁴ñ g̃a—
8. O⌐yog̃emase⌐ñ ka⌐ O⌐yog̃e¹nai ⌐wa⁴ke zya a⌐rimase⁴ñ g̃a—
9. Hi⌐roku a⌐rimase⌐ñ ka⌐ Hi⌐roku ⌐na¹i ⌐wa⁴ke zya a⌐rimase⁴ñ g̃a—
10. To⌐modati zya arimase⌐ñ ka⌐ To⌐modati zya na¹i ⌐wa⁴ke zya a⌐rimase⁴ñ g̃a—
11. Ti⌐g̃aima¹su ka⌐ Ti⌐g̃au wa⁴ke zya a⌐rimase⁴ñ g̃a—
12. He⌐ta¹ desu ka⌐ He⌐ta¹ na ⌐wa⁴ke zya a⌐rimase⁴ñ g̃a—

L. Substitution Drill (based on Grammatical Note 1)

1. How would it be best to go? (Lit. Provided I go how, would it be best?)

   Na⌐ñ de i⌐ke⁴ba i⌐tibañ i⁴i desyoo ka.

2. What would be best to read? /na⌐ni o ⌐yo⁴mu/

   Na⌐ni (o) ⌐yo⁴meba i⌐tibañ i⁴i desyoo ka.

3. Which would be best to practice? /do⌐re o reñ-syuu-suru/

   Do⌐re (o) re⌐ñsyuu-sure⁴ba i⌐tibañ i⁴i desyoo ka.

4. What time would it be best to come? /na⌐ñ-zi ni ⌐ku⁴ru/

   Na⌐ñ-zi ni ⌐ku⁴reba i⌐tibañ i⁴i desyoo ka.

5. Who would be best to explain it? (Lit. Provided I have it explained by whom, would it be best?) /da⌐re ni setumee-site morau/

   Da⌐re ni se⌐tumee-site mora-e⁴ba i⌐tibañ i⁴i desyoo ka.

6. When would be best to exchange [it]? /i⌐tu tori-kaeru/

   I⌐tu to⌐rikaere⁴ba i⌐tibañ i⁴i desyoo ka.

7. What day would be best to deliver [it]? /na⌐ñyo-obi ni to⌐doke⁴ru/

   Na⌐ñyo⌐obi ni to⌐doke⁴reba i⌐tibañ i⁴i desyoo ka.

8. Where would it be best to put [it] for the time being? /do⌐ko ni oite oku/

   Do⌐ko ni o⌐ite oke⁴ba i⌐tibañ i⁴i desyoo ka.

9. What month would it be   Naᷧñ-ḡatu ni ryoᴦkoo-sureᴵba iᴦti-
   best to travel? /naᷧñ-   bañ iᴵi desyoo ka.
   ḡatu ni ryokoo-suru/
10. How would it be best to   Doᷧo iᴦeᴵba iᴦtibañ iᴵi desyoo ka.
    say it? /doᷧo iu/

M. Grammar Drill (based on Grammatical Note 1)

         Tutor: Aᷧme ḡa hurimasu. 'It rains.'
         Student: Aᷧme ḡa ᴦhuᷧreba ᴦiᴵi desu ḡa ᴦneᷧe. 'I hope it rains . . .'

1. Oᷧkusañ (o) turete kimasu.   Oᷧkusañ (o) tuᴦrete kuᴦreba ᴦiᴵi
                                     desu ḡa ᴦneᷧe.
2. Yuᴦkiᷧ ḡa huᷧrimaseᷧñ.   Yuᴦkiᷧ ḡa huᴦraᷧnakereba ᴦiᴵi de-
                                     su ḡa ᴦneᷧe.
3. Eᷧki de ᴦniᷧmotu (o) azu-   Eᷧki de ᴦniᷧmotu (o) aᴦzukeᴦreba
    kemasu.   ᴦiᴵi desu ḡa ᴦneᷧe.
4. Raᴦisyuu maᷧde tuzuki-   Raᴦisyuu maᷧde tuᴦzukeᴵba ᴦiᴵi
    masu.   desu ḡa ᴦneᷧe.
5. Niᴦhoñḡo ḡa dekimaᷧsu.   Niᴦhoñḡo ḡa dekiᴦreba ᴦiᴵi desu
                                     ḡa ᴦneᷧe.
6. Koᷧñbañ ᴦyoᷧku beñkyoo-   Koᷧñbañ ᴦyoᷧku beᴦñkyoo-sureᴵba
    simasu.   ᴦiᴵi desu ḡa ᴦneᷧe.
7. Kaᴦuᷧ no (o) waᴦsurema-   Kaᴦuᷧ no (o) waᴦsurenaᷧkereba ᴦiᴵi
    seᷧñ.   desu ḡa ᴦneᷧe.
8. Aᷧsa ᴦhaᷧyaku tukimasu.   Aᷧsa ᴦhaᷧyaku ᴦtuᴦkeba ᴦiᴵi desu
                                     ḡa ᴦneᷧe.
9. Bañ osoku deᴦmaseᷧñ.   Bañ osoku ᴦdeᷧnakereba ᴦiᴵi desu
                                     ḡa ᴦneᷧe.
10. Zyuᴦubuᷧñ arimasu.   Zyuᴦubuᷧñ ᴦaᴵreba ᴦiᴵi desu ḡa
                                     ᴦneᷧe.

N. Substitution Drill (based on Grammatical Note 1)

1. If you want to read, I   Yoᷧmitaᷧkereba aᴦñnaisyoᷧ (ḡa)
    have a guidebook . . .   aᴦrimaᴵsu ḡa_
2. If you want to go, there's   Iᴦkitaᷧkereba, kyoᴦokai (ḡa) ari-
    a church . . . /iku, kyoo-   maᷧsu ḡa_
    kai/
3. If you want to visit [them],   Keᴦñbutu-sitaᷧkereba, oᷧtera ya
    there are temples and   ziᴵñzya (ḡa) aᴦrimaᴵsu ḡa_
    shrines . . . /keñbutu-
    suru, oᴦtera ya ziᴵñzya/
4. If you want to rent [it],   Kaᴦritaᷧkereba, iᴵi kaᴦsiya (ḡa)
    there's a nice house for   arimaᷧsu ḡa_
    rent . . . /kariru, iᴵi
    kāsiya/
5. If you want to write [it],   Kaᴦkitaᷧkereba, eᴦñpitu (ḡa) ari-
    I have a pencil . . .   maᷧsu ḡa_
    /kaᴵku, eñpitu/

6. If you want to telephone,   De⌐ñwa (o) kaketa⌐kereba, de⌐ñwa-
   I have a phone book . . .   tyoo (ḡa) arima⌐su ḡa‿
   /de⌐ñwa (o) kake⌐ru,
   deñwatyoo/
7. If you want to buy [any],   Ka⌐ita⌐kereba, i⌐i mi⌐yaḡe (ḡa)
   there are nice souvenirs . . .   arima⌐su ḡa‿
   /kau, i⌐i mi⌐yaḡe/
8. If you want to stop, there's   To⌐marita⌐kereba, i⌐i ryo⌐kañ (ḡa)
   a nice inn . . . /tomaru,   arima⌐su ḡa‿
   i⌐i ryŏkañ/

O. Grammar Drill (based on Grammatical Note 3)

Tutor: Ti⌐ri ya re⌐kisi (o) sitte (i)ma⌐su. '[You] know geography
         and history.'
         O⌐mosiro⌐i ryo⌐koo ḡa dekima⌐su. 'Interesting trips are
         possible.'
Student: Ti⌐ri ya rĕkisi (o) si⌐tte (i)re⌐ba i̅ru hodo o⌐mosiro⌐i ryo-
         ⌐koo ḡa dekima⌐su. 'The more [you] know geography and
         history, the more interesting trips are possible.'

1. Wa⌐ka⌐i desu. Tu⌐yo⌐i desu.   Wa⌐kakereba wa⌐ka⌐i hodo tu⌐yo⌐i
                                    desu.
2. O⌐oki⌐i desu. I⌐i desu.   O⌐okikereba o⌐oki⌐i hodo ⌐i⌐i desu.
3. Añna tokee wa ti⌐isa⌐i   Añna tokee wa ⌐ti⌐isakereba ti-
   desu. Ta⌐ka⌐i desu.   ⌐isa⌐i hodo ta⌐ka⌐i desu.
4. Sikiti wa ma⌐ti⌐ kara   Sikiti wa ma⌐ti⌐ kara to⌐o⌐kereba
   to⌐oi⌐ desu. Ya⌐su⌐i desu.   to⌐oi⌐ hodo ya⌐su⌐i desu.
5. Re⌐ñsyuu-sima⌐su. Zyo-   Re⌐ñsyuu-sure⌐ba su̅ru hodo zyo-
   ⌐ozu⌐ ni na⌐rima⌐su yo‿   ⌐ozu⌐ ni na⌐rima⌐su yo‿
6. Hu⌐kuzatu de⌐su. Mu-   Hu⌐kuzatu de a⌐reba ⌐a⌐ru hodo
   ⌐zukasi⌐i desu.   mu⌐zukasi⌐i desu. [1]
7. Ryo⌐koo-sima⌐su. Ku⌐ni   Ryo⌐koo-sure⌐ba su̅ru hodo ku⌐ni
   e kaerita⌐ku narimasu.   e kaerita⌐ku narimasu.
8. O⌐kane wa arima⌐su.   Okane wa ⌐a⌐reba ⌐a⌐ru hodo
   Ho⌐siku ⌐na⌐ru mo⌐no⌐   ⌐ho⌐siku ⌐na⌐ru mo⌐no⌐ desu.
   desu.

P. Response Drill (based on Grammatical Note 2)

Tutor: Si⌐na⌐kute mo ⌐i⌐i desu ka‿ 'Is it all right if [I] don't do
         it?'
Student: Iie, si⌐na⌐kereba na⌐rimase⌐ñ yo. 'No, [you] must do it.'

1. Tu⌐tuma⌐nakute mo ⌐i⌐i   Iie, tu⌐tuma⌐nakereba na⌐rimase⌐ñ
   desu ka‿   yo.
2. Mi⌐nato ni haira⌐nakute mo   Iie, /mi⌐nato ni/ haira⌐nakereba
   ⌐i⌐i desu ka‿   na⌐rimase⌐ñ yo.

---

[1] Another alternant: Hu⌐kuzatu na⌐ra hŭkuzatu na hodo mu⌐zukasi⌐i desu.

3. Ma⌐initi ka⌐yowana⌐kute   Iie, /ma⌐initi/ ka⌐yowana⌐kereba
   mo ⌐i⌐i desu ka⌐   na⌐rimase⌐ñ yo.

4. A⌐sa⌐tte zya ⌐na⌐kute mo   Iie, a⌐sa⌐tte zya ⌐na⌐kereba na-
   ⌐i⌐i desu ka⌐   ⌐rimase⌐ñ yo.

5. Tu⌐metaku na⌐kute mo ⌐i⌐i   Iie, tu⌐metaku na⌐kereba na⌐ri-
   desu ka⌐   mase⌐ñ yo.

6. Mo⌐o ip-peñ iwana⌐kute mo   Iie, /mo⌐o ip-peñ/ iwana⌐kereba
   ⌐i⌐i desu ka⌐   na⌐rimase⌐ñ yo.

7. Te⌐eburu (o) yoyaku-sina⌐-   Iie, /te⌐eburu (o)/ yoyaku-sina⌐-
   kute mo ⌐i⌐i desu ka⌐   kereba na⌐rimase⌐ñ yo.

8. E⌐ēgo zya na⌐kute mo ⌐i⌐i   Iie, e⌐ēgo zya na⌐kereba na⌐ri-
   desu ka⌐   mase⌐ñ yo.

9. Ma⌐ruku na⌐kute mo ⌐i⌐i   Iie, ma⌐ruku na⌐kereba na⌐rima-
   desu ka⌐   se⌐ñ yo.

10. Ka⌐be (o) nurikae⌐nakute   Iie, /ka⌐be o/ nurikae⌐nakereba
    mo ⌐i⌐i desu ka⌐   na⌐rimase⌐ñ yo.

Repeat the drill above, asking the questions in informal style (i. e.
ending in i⌐i?) and answering informally, using the -nakutyaa na-
⌐ra⌐nai pattern.

Q. Response Drill

   (Give the iie answer for each of the following questions, using a
   'may,' 'must,' 'must not,' or 'don't have to' pattern.)

1. Bu⌐kkyoo to ⌐si⌐ñtoo no   Iie. /Bu⌐kkyoo to ⌐si⌐ñtoo no
   ko⌐to⌐ (o) be⌐ñkyoo-sina⌐-   ko⌐to⌐ wa/ be⌐ñkyoo-sina⌐kute
   kereba na⌐rimase⌐ñ ka⌐   mo ⌐i⌐i desu yo⌐

2. Tu⌐ri ni itte⌐ mo ⌐i⌐i   Iie. /Tu⌐ri ni/ ittya⌐a i⌐kema-
   desu ka⌐   se⌐ñ yo.

3. A⌐ñna⌐i-sinakute mo ⌐i⌐i   Iie. A⌐ñna⌐i-sinakereba na⌐ri-
   desu ka⌐   mase⌐ñ yo.

4. No⌐zoitya⌐a i⌐kemase⌐ñ   Iie. No⌐zoite⌐ mo ⌐i⌐i desu yo⌐
   ka⌐

5. Hu⌐de de ka⌐ite mo ⌐i⌐i   Iie. /Hu⌐de de/ ka⌐ityaa i⌐ke-
   desu ka⌐   mase⌐ñ yo.

6. Ha⌐rawa⌐nakute mo ⌐i⌐i   Iie. Ha⌐rawa⌐nakereba na⌐rima-
   desu ka⌐   se⌐ñ yo.

7. O⌐ñseñ zya na⌐kereba na-   Iie. O⌐ñseñ zya na⌐kute mo ⌐i⌐i
   ⌐rimase⌐ñ ka⌐   desu yo⌐

8. Go⌐mi⌐ (o) i⌐retya⌐a i⌐ke-   Iie. Go⌐mi⌐ (o) i⌐rete⌐ mo ⌐i⌐i
   mase⌐ñ ka⌐   desu yo⌐

SUPPLEMENTARY DIALOGUES

1. Tanaka: I⌐i ⌐te⌐ñki da kara, tu⌐ri ni ikimase⌐ñ ka⌐
   Smith: Se⌐kkaku⌐ da keredo; kyo⌐o wa ba⌐ñ ma⌐de ni si⌐te simawana⌐-
           kereba na⌐ra⌐nai ⌐yo⌐o ḡa ⌐a⌐tte, i⌐karena⌐i ñ desu yo.
   Tanaka: Zya⌐a, hi⌐to⌐ri de i⌐ku koto⌐ ni si⌐ma⌐su yo.
   Smith: Su⌐mimase⌐ñ.

2. Tanaka: Ho⌐oryuuzi [1] tte iu otera go⌐zo⌐ñzi desu ka⌐

     Smith: Iti-do ni⌐hoñzi⌐ñ no tomodati ni tu⌐rete itte moratta koto⌐ ḡa
⌐a⌐ru ñ desu ḡa, zu⌐ibuñ ri⌐ppa na mono⌐ da to o⌐mo⌐tta ñ desu.

   Tanaka: Watasi wa ⌐mo⌐o go-⌐roku-do itta⌐ ñ desu ḡa; mi⌐reba ⌐mi⌐ru
hodo su⌐barasi⌐i to o⌐mo⌐tte, mata ⌐su⌐ḡu i⌐tte mi⌐taku ⌐na⌐ru
ñ desu yo⌐

     Smith: Watasi wa a⌐ñmari yo⌐ku ⌐mi⌐nakatta kara, ze⌐hi ma⌐ta ikita⌐i
ñ desu. I⌐tu ka i⌐ssyo ni tu⌐rete itte kudasaimase⌐ñ ka⌐

   Tanaka: A⌐a, i⌐i desu to mo. I⌐ssyo ni ikimasyo⌐o.

3. Tanaka: Kono heñ ni ka⌐siya ḡa na⌐i desyoo ka ⌐ne⌐e.

    Agent: A⌐rima⌐su ḡa; kono heñ wa ⌐be⌐ñri na to⌐koro⌐ na no de, ya⌐tiñ
ḡa ⌐ka⌐nari ta⌐ka⌐i ñ desu yo⌐

   Tanaka: So⌐o desyoo ⌐ne⌐e. Ya⌐tiñ ḡa a⌐ñmari ta⌐kaku ⌐na⌐kute, be⌐ñri na
to⌐koro⌐ ḡa ⌐a⌐reba ⌐i⌐i ñ desu ḡa⌐

    Agent: Mu⌐zukasi⌐i desu ⌐ne⌐e. Ya⌐tiñ wa ⌐e⌐ki kara to⌐oku na⌐reba ⌐na⌐-
ru hodo ⌐ya⌐suku ⌐na⌐tte imasu ḡa, hu⌐beñ ni mo na⌐rima⌐su
kara ⌐ne⌐e.

4. Tanaka (filling out a form): Su⌐mimase⌐ñ. Tyo⌐tto u⌐kaḡaita⌐i ñ desu
ḡa⌐

    Clerk: Na⌐ñ desyoo ka⌐

   Tanaka: Ko⌐no kami⌐ ni ⌐pe⌐ñ de ka⌐ka⌐nakereba na⌐ra⌐nai ka e⌐ñpitu de
ka⌐ite mo ⌐i⌐i ka u⌐kaḡaita⌐i ñ desu ḡa⌐

    Clerk: Na⌐ñ de ⌐ka⌐ite mo ka⌐maimase⌐ñ ḡa, ha⌐kki⌐ri ⌐ka⌐ite kudasai⌐

5. Tanaka: Ki⌐noo no ka⌐iḡi ni i⌐rassyaima⌐sita ka⌐

     Smith: E⌐e. I⌐tta koto wa i⌐tta⌐ ñ desu ḡa; yo⌐o ḡa ⌐a⌐tte, ha⌐yaku
⌐ka⌐ette si⌐matta⌐ kara, kyo⌐o ⌐da⌐re ka ni ⌐do⌐ñna ko⌐to⌐ o ki⌐-
⌐meta⌐ ka ki⌐kana⌐kereba na⌐ra⌐nai to o⌐mo⌐tte iru ñ desu yo⌐
A⌐na⌐ta wa?

   Tanaka: Watasi wa ⌐ka⌐iḡi no owaru su⌐ko⌐si ⌐ma⌐e ni ka⌐isya e ka⌐ette
ki⌐ta⌐ no de, ka⌐iḡi no ko⌐to⌐ wa na⌐ni mo kikana⌐katta ñ desu
yo⌐

6. Smith: Se⌐tona⌐ikai [2] wa totemo ⌐ke⌐siki ḡa ⌐i⌐i soo desu ḡa, si⌐ma⌐ ḡa
ta⌐kusañ a⌐ru ñ desyoo?

   Tanaka: E⌐e. A⌐wazi [3] o hazime, Syo⌐odo⌐sima [3] nado⌐ Sa⌐ñ-zeñ-ḡu⌐rai
⌐a⌐ru soo desu.

     Smith: Sa⌐ñ-byaku zya ⌐na⌐i ñ desu ka⌐

   Tanaka: Sa⌐ñ-ze⌐ñ desu yo⌐ Miñna ti⌐isa⌐i si⌐ma⌐ desu ḡa⌐

     Smith: I⌐tta koto ḡa ⌐a⌐ru ñ desyoo?

   Tanaka: E⌐e. Mo⌐to wa, ya⌐sumi no toki⌐ ni wa, yo⌐ku i⌐tta mono⌐ desu.

7. Smith: I⌐ma ka⌐erima⌐su ka⌐

   Tanaka: E⌐e, ka⌐ero⌐o to o⌐mo⌐tte imasu ḡa⌐

---

[1] Name of a famous Buddhist temple.

[2] 'Inland Sea.'

[3] Name of island.

Smith: Su⌐gu ⌐ka⌐eru ñ nara, e⌐ki made no⌐tte ikimase⌐ñ ka⌐

Tanaka: A⌐ri⌐ḡatoo. Zya⌐a, e⌐ñryo na⌐ku o⌐negai-sima⌐su.

8. Smith: Ke⌐ñbutu-suru ma⌐e ni ka⌐buki ni tu⌐ite yo⌐mita⌐i ñ desu ḡa, i⌐i ⌐ho⌐ñ ḡa ⌐a⌐ru desyoo ka.

Tanaka: E⌐eḡo no⌐ desu ne?

Smith: Mo⌐ti⌐roñ ⌐so⌐o desu yo.

Tanaka: I⌐roiro arima⌐su ḡa; do⌐no ⌐ho⌐ñ mo so⌐re⌐zore ⌐i⌐i to⌐koro⌐ mo wa⌐ru⌐i to⌐koro⌐ mo ⌐a⌐tte, ko⌐re ḡa itibañ i⌐i to i⌐eru mono⌐ wa ⌐na⌐i ñ desu yo⌐

Smith: Watasi wa si⌐bai ya e⌐eḡa no be⌐ñkyoo o sita koto⌐ wa ⌐na⌐i si; ma⌐a, kañtañ ni ka⌐buki to iu mono⌐ wa ⌐do⌐ñna mo⌐no⌐ ka ⌐yo⌐ñde mi⌐ta⌐i ñ desu ḡa⌐

Tanaka: Zya⌐a, wa⌐tasi ḡa mo⌐tte ru a⌐ñnaisyo⌐ ḡa tyo⌐odo i⌐i ka mo si⌐remase⌐ñ yo⌐ E⌐ mo ⌐ha⌐itte ru si; u⌐sui ho⌐ñ da kara, su⌐gu yo⌐me⌐ru si⌐

Smith: Na⌐ñ te iu ⌐ho⌐ñ desyoo. Hu⌐tuu no ho⌐ñya de ka⌐eru⌐ desyoo ne?

Tanaka: E⌐e, ka⌐eru to omoima⌐su ḡa; wa⌐tasi no⌐ o ⌐yo⌐ñdara ⌐do⌐o desu ka⌐ I⌐ma da⌐re mo yo⌐ñde i⌐mase⌐ñ kara⌐

Smith: Ha⌐isyaku-dekima⌐su ka⌐

Tanaka: Mo⌐ti⌐roñ desu to mo. Tyo⌐tto o⌐mati ni nare⌐reba; o⌐oi⌐soḡi de ŭti e itte, su⌐gu to⌐tte kima⌐su yo⌐

Smith: Do⌐o mo ⌐i⌐tu mo go⌐me⌐ewaku na õneḡai o site, su⌐mimase⌐ñ.

English Equivalents

1. Tanaka: Since it's [such] nice weather, won't you go fishing?

Smith: It's kind of you to ask me but I can't go today because I have some business I must finish up (lit. do completely) by evening.

Tanaka: Then I'll plan to go alone.

Smith: I'm sorry.

2. Tanaka: Do you know the Horyuji Temple?

Smith: I have had a Japanese friend take me once. I thought it was an awfully impressive thing.

Tanaka: I've gone there five or six times already, but the more I see it the more I think that it's wonderful and I (get to) want to try and go again soon.

Smith: Since I didn't see it too well, I want to go again by all means. Won't you take me along some time?

Tanaka: Oh, certainly! Let's go together.

3. Tanaka: I wonder if there aren't any houses for rent around here.

Agent: There are, but since this section is a convenient location the rents are rather high.

Tanaka: I guess that's right. I hope there's a place where the rents aren't too high that's convenient. (Lit. It will be fine if there's a place [described by saying] the rents aren't too high and it's convenient.)

Agent: That's difficult. The farther you get from the station the cheaper the rent gets, but it gets inconvenient too so—you know . . .

4. Tanaka: Excuse me. I'd like to ask you something . . .
   Clerk: What is it?
   Tanaka: I'd like to inquire whether I must write with a pen on this paper,
           or whether I may write with a pencil . . .
   Clerk: It doesn't matter what you write with but please write clearly.

5. Tanaka: Did you go to yesterday's conference?
   Smith: Yes, I did go, but I had some business to attend to and I went
           home early so I've been thinking that I must ask someone today
           what kind of things [they] decided. How about you?
   Tanaka: Since I came back to the office [just] a little before the confer-
           ence ended, I didn't hear anything about the conference.

6. Smith: I hear that the Inland Sea has very beautiful scenery. (Lit. As
           for the Inland Sea, I hear that the scenery is very good.) There
           are lots of islands, aren't there?
   Tanaka: Yes. [There's] Shodoshima, for example, to say nothing of
           Awaji. They say there are about three thousand.
   Smith: Don't you mean three hundred?
   Tanaka: It's three thousand. They're all small islands but [it is three
           thousand].
   Smith: You've gone there, haven't you?
   Tanaka: Yes. I used to go often at vacation time.

7. Smith: Are you going home now?
   Tanaka: Yes, I've been thinking I would . . .
   Smith: If you're going home right away, wouldn't you [like to] ride as
           far as the station?
   Tanaka: Thanks. I'll take you up on that. (Lit. Well, I'll ask you without
           holding back.)

8. Smith: I'd like to read about kabuki before I see it. Is there a good
           book?
   Tanaka: You mean an English one, don't you?
   Smith: Of course (that's right).
   Tanaka: There are all different kinds, but every book has its own good
           points (lit. places) and bad points, and there is no book (lit. thing)
           about which you can say, 'This one is best.'
   Smith: I've never made a study of plays and movies, and I just want to try
           reading briefly what kind of thing (the thing called) 'kabuki' is . . .
   Tanaka: In that case, the guidebook I have may be just right. There are
           pictures in it and it's a thin book so you can read it in no time
           and . . .
   Smith: What's the name of the book? (Lit. It's a book called what?) You
           can probably buy it at a regular bookstore, can't you?
   Tanaka: Yes, I think you can buy it but how about reading mine? No one
           is reading it now so . . .
   Smith: Can I borrow it?
   Tanaka: Of course! If you can wait a minute, I'll rush home (lit. go
           home in a big hurry) and get it (lit. come having picked it up).
   Smith: I hate to bother you all the time. (Lit. I'm very sorry to make
           troublesome requests all the time.)

BASIC DIALOGUES: RESTATEMENT

(as contained in a letter from Tanaka to Smith)

Sekkaku Ni⌐hoñ e o⌐ide ni na⌐tta no de, ho⌐oboo ryo⌐koo-nasa⌐tte o⌐kaeri ni narita⌐i kara, do⌐ñna to⌐koro⌐ e i⌐tta⌐ra ⌐i⌐i ka o⌐siete moraita⌐i to iu o⌐hanasi de⌐su ḡa; hito ni yotte mi⌐ta⌐i to⌐koro⌐ ḡa ti⌐ḡau⌐ no de, o⌐yaku ni ta⌐tu ka ⌐do⌐o ka wa⌐karimase⌐ñ ḡa; mo⌐osiaḡete ¹ mimasyo⌐o.

Ti⌐ka⌐i to⌐koro⌐ nara, Ni⌐kkoo ḡa yu⌐umee de⌐su. Ni⌐kkoo e i⌐ku⌐ no ni wa, to⌐kkyuu ḡa arima⌐su kara, de⌐ñsya de i⌐ku⌐ no ḡa i⌐tibañ be⌐ñri desu. Ke⌐redomo, to⌐kkyuu de iku koto⌐ ni su⌐re⌐ba, ma⌐e no hi⌐ made ni to⌐kkyu⌐-ukeñ o ka⌐tte okana⌐kereba na⌐rimase⌐ñ.

Tu⌐ri no deki⌐ru ⌐si⌐zuka na o⌐ñseñ ni itte mita⌐i to o⌐ssyaima⌐su ḡa, I⌐zu na⌐ra so⌐ñna tokoro⌐ ḡa ta⌐kusañ arima⌐su. Izu wa ⌐ka⌐nari o⌐oki⌐i ha⌐⌐ñtoo de⌐su.

A⌐na⌐ta ḡa o⌐kiki ni na⌐tta yoo ni, Kyo⌐oto wa huru⌐i o⌐tera ya zi⌐ñzya ḡa ta⌐kusañ arima⌐su. Kyo⌐oto wa ⌐bu⌐kkyoo to ⌐si⌐ñtoo no sa⌐kañ na tokoro⌐ desu kara, kirisutokyoo no kyookai mo ⌐a⌐ru ko⌐to⌐ wa a⌐rima⌐su ḡa; su⌐kuna⌐i si, taitee a⌐tara⌐siku ⌐ta⌐teta mo⌐no⌐ desu.

Kyu⌐usyuu ni wa, do⌐ko ka ke⌐ñbutu-suru tokoro⌐ ḡa ⌐a⌐ru ka to iu go⌐situmoñ ² de⌐su ḡa; mo⌐ti⌐roñ arimasu. Na⌐ḡa⌐saki o hazime; A⌐so, Aosima, Ka⌐ḡosima na⌐do desu ḡa; Na⌐ḡa⌐saki wa i⌐tibañ huru⌐i mi⌐nato no hito⌐tu da si, te⌐ñki no ⌐i⌐i hi ni wa, A⌐so no na⌐ḡame⌐ wa su⌐barasi⌐i mo⌐no⌐ desu.

O⌐hanasi no yo⌐o ni, Ni⌐hoñ ni wa ⌐do⌐ko e i⌐tte⌐ mo me⌐zura⌐sikute o⌐mosiro⌐i mo⌐no⌐ ḡa arimasu. Na⌐ni o ⌐mi⌐te mo mi⌐yaḡe ni katte kaerita⌐ku ⌐na⌐ru to o⌐ssya⌐ru keredo; do⌐no kuni no mo⌐no⌐ de mo so⌐re⌐zore ti⌐ḡatta azi ḡa arima⌐su kara, a⌐na⌐ta ḡa so⌐o oomoi ni na⌐ru no wa a⌐tari-mae ³ da to omoima⌐su. Wa⌐takusi mo mo⌐to wa ryo⌐koo-suru tabi⌐ ni mi⌐yaḡe o katta mono⌐ desu.

Ni⌐hoñ no ti⌐ri ya re⌐kisi ni tu⌐ite, mo⌐o go⌐zo⌐ñzi ka mo si⌐remase⌐ñ ḡa; ti⌐ri ya rēkisi wa si⌐tte ireba I⌐ru hodo o⌐mosiro⌐i ryo⌐koo ḡa deki⌐ru kara, o⌐dekake ni na⌐ru ⌐ma⌐e ni, so⌐re ni tu⌐ite ⌐na⌐ni ka I⌐ti-do o⌐yomi ni na⌐ttara i⌐ka⌐ḡa desyoo ka. Yo⌐rosi⌐kattara; wa⌐takusi no tokoro⌐ ni ēego no a⌐ñnaisyo⌐ ḡa a⌐rima⌐su kara, i⌐tu de⌐ mo o⌐moti-kudasa⌐i.

EXERCISES

1. Plan a trip to Kyoto with a friend. Have your conversation cover the fol-
    lowing points:

---

¹ Moosiaḡeṛu ⁺ /-ru/ 'say (to you).'

² Situmoñ (gositumoñ ⁺) 'question.'

³ Atarimae 'natural,' 'proper,' 'reasonable.'

    a. when you will leave
    b. how long you will stay
    c. how you will go
    d. where you will stay (tomaru)
    e. what you want to see
    f. what souvenirs you want to buy

2. Make up 15 short conversations, each one of which contains one of the
    following:

    a. ya⌐ku⌐ ni ⌐ta⌐tu
    b. o⌐oi⌐soḡi de
    c. ta⌐be⌐ru koto wa ta⌐bema⌐su
    d. yo⌐rosi⌐kereba
    e. se⌐ñse⌐e o hazime
    f. go⌐me⌐ewaku zya ⌐na⌐kereba
    g. sekkaku ni⌐hoñḡo o beñkyoo-site iru⌐ ñ desu kara
    h. o⌐okikereba o⌐oki⌐i hodo
    i. sore de
    j. si⌐na⌐kereba na⌐ra⌐nai
    k. ryo⌐koo-suru koto⌐ ni si⌐ma⌐sita
    l. i⌐tta mono⌐ desu
    m. Ni⌐ho⌐ñ ni tuite
    n. de⌐ki⌐nai ⌐wa⌐ke zya ⌐na⌐i
    o. ku⌐ru ta⌐bi⌐ ni

Lesson 33. House Repairs

BASIC DIALOGUES: FOR MEMORIZATION

(a)

Mr. Smith

specialty	señmoñ
specialist <u>or</u> expert	se⌐ñmoñ no hito⌐
isn't so much that [someone] hires (lit. isn't the extent of hiring)	ta⌐no⌐mu hodo zya ⌐na⁺i

1. It's not worth hiring an expert, but I do have all kinds of work that I can't do by myself.

Se⌐ñmoñ no hito⌐ (o) ta⌐no⌐mu hodo zya ⌐na⁺i keredo, zi⌐buñ zya deki⌐nai siḡoto (ḡa) i⌐roiro a⌐ru ñ desu.

for example	ta⌐to⌐eba
shelf	tana
suspend <u>or</u> hang by a string	turu /-u/
move [something]	u⌐ḡoka⌐su /-u/
a grass <u>or</u> weed	ku⌐sa⌐
weed a garden (lit. remove garden weeds)	ni⌐wa no kusa⌐ o ⌐to⌐ru
do such things as suspending, moving, weeding	tu⌐tta⌐ri u⌐ḡoka⌐sitari ⌐to⌐ttari suru

2. For example, they're (lit. being) things like putting up shelves, moving heavy furniture, weeding the garden...

Ta⌐to⌐eba; ta⌐na (o) tutta⌐ri, o⌐moi ka⌐ḡu (o) u⌐ḡoka⁺sitari, ni⌐wa no kusa⌐ (o) ⌐to⌐ttari su⌐ru yo⁺o na ko⌐to⁺ de—

Tanaka

handyman	beñriya

3. Then you should call in a handyman.

Zya⌐a, be⌐ñriya (o) yoñda⌐ra ⌐i⁺i desyoo.

Mr. Smith

what?	e?
business <u>or</u> occupation	syo⌐obai

4. What? Handyman? Is there such a business?

E? Beñriya? So⌐ñna syo⌐obai (ḡa) ⌐a⌐ru ñ desu ka⌐

270

Tanaka

so-and-so	na⌐ninani
service	sa⌐abisu
so-and-so service	na⌐ninani-sa⌐abisu
with the name "So-and-so Service"	na⌐ninani-sa⌐abisu tte iu namae de
do	yaru /-u/
[someone] does for you [1]	yatte kureru

5. Yes. Nowadays there are places of business with the name "So-and-so Service" that do everything for you.

E⌐e. Kono-ḡoro, na⌐ninani-sa⌐a-bisu tte iu namae de, na⌐ñ de⌐ mo ya⌐tte kureru mise⌐ ḡa ⌐a⌐ru ñ desu yo↲

Mr. Smith

6. Really? or You don't say! or No kidding!

Hee?

Tanaka

things that are impossible except for (lit. unless it is) an expert	se⌐ñmoñ no hito⌐ zya ⌐na⌐kereba de⌐ki⌐nai koto
suitable or appropriate	tekitoo /na/
[someone] makes contact for you [1]	reñraku-site kureru
way or manner	to⌐ori
like its name or in accordance with its name	na⌐mae no to⌐ori

7. Of course, [for] things that can't be done except by an expert, they put you in touch with a suitable place in each case, so like their name, they are handy.

Mo⌐ti⌐roñ, se⌐ñmoñ no hito⌐ zya ⌐na⌐kereba de⌐ki⌐nai koto wa, so⌐re⌐zore te⌐kitoo na tokoro⌐ e re⌐ñraku-site kureru⌐ kara; na⌐mae no to⌐ori ⌐be⌐ñri desu yo↲

(b)

(A man from Chiyoda Service comes to see Mr. and Mrs. Smith)

Man

Chiyoda Service person	Ti⌐yoda-sa⌐abisu mo⌐no⌐ ↓

8. I'm (a person) from Chiyoda Service. I've come to inquire about what you want done.

Ti⌐yoda-sa⌐abisu no mo⌐no⌐ de gozaimasu ḡa, go⌐yo⌐o (o) u⌐ka-ḡai ni mairima⌐sita.

Mr. Smith

a good deal or a good many	daibu

---

[1] 'You' here may refer literally to the person addressed, or it may mean 'you' in the indefinite sense of 'one' or 'anyone.'

one thing at a time	hi⌐to-tu-zu⌐tu

9. Oh, there are a good many things that I want to have done so I'll explain them one at a time.

A⌐a, ya⌐tte moraitai koto⌐ (g̃a) da⌐ibu a⌐ru kara, hi⌐to-tu-zu⌐tu se⌐tumee-simasyo⌐o.

Man

10. Certainly.

Ha⌐a ⌐ha⌐a.

Mr. Smith (pointing to fusuma)

tear [something]	ya⌐bu⌐ku /-u/
hole	a⌐na⌐

11. We've torn the fusuma so I'd like to have the holes repaired.

Hu⌐suma (o) yabu⌐ite si⌐matta⌐ kara, tyo⌐tto a⌐na⌐ (o) na⌐o⌐site mo⌐raita⌐i ñ desu.

Man

cause to repair	na⌐osase⌐ru /-ru/
make someone repair	da⌐re ka ni na⌐osase⌐ru

12. Certainly. This I'll have someone repair right away.

Ha⌐a ⌐ha⌐a. Kore wa ⌐su⌐g̃u ⌐da⌐re ka ni na⌐osasema⌐su.

Mr. Smith (pointing to a chair)

screw	ne⌐zi
come off _or_ come out _or_ be taken	to⌐re⌐ru /-ru/

13. Next—the screws of this chair have come out too so. . .

Sore kara ne? Ko⌐no isu no ne⌐zi mo ⌐to⌐rete si⌐matta⌐ kara—

Man

14. Oh, this is simple.

A⌐a, ko⌐re wa kañtañ de gozaima⌐su.

15. I'll bring some new screws.

A⌐tarasi⌐i ⌐ne⌐zi (o) mo⌐tte mairima⌐su.

Mr. Smith

chimney	eñtotu
become blocked _or_ clogged	tu⌐ma⌐ru /-u/
before it gets clogged (lit. in the non-clogged interval)	tu⌐mara⌐nai uti ni
cause to clean	soozi-saseru /-ru/

16. And the chimney—before it gets clogged would you have [someone] clean it (for me)?

Eñtotu mo, tu⌐mara⌐nai uti ni so⌐ozi-sasete kuremase⌐ñ ka—

when it is after clogging	tu⌐ma⌐tte kara da to

17. Because it's awful, (when it is) after it's clogged. . .

Tu⌐ma⌐tte kara da to, ta⌐iheñ de⌐su kara—

Man

18. Yes. Certainly.   Ha⌐a ˥ha˦a. Ka˥sikomarima˥sita.

Mr. Smith

    care or repair (noun)   te˥ire˥
    care for or repair (verb)   te˥ire˥ o suru
19. I guess I'll have the garden   Ni˥wa no teire˥ mo si˥te morai-
    taken care of, too.   masyo˦o.

    lawn   siba
    circumference   mawari
    around the fence   ka˥ki˥ne no mawari ni
    plant (verb)   ueru /-ru/
    [do things like] clipping   ka˥tta˥ri u˥eta˥ri
    and planting
20. Cutting the lawn, planting   Si˥ba (o) katta˥ri, ka˥ki˥ne no
    some trees around the fence. . .   mawari ni ˥ki˥ (o) u˥eta˦ri_

Man

21. Yes, certainly.   Ha⌐a, syo˥oti-itasima˥sita.

    gardener   uekiya
    within the morning   asa no uti /ni/
    cause to visit   ukagawaseru /-ru/
22. There's a good gardener [I   I˥i u˥ekiya (ga) orima˦su kara,
    know] so I'll have him come   asita a˥sa no uti /ni/ ukagawa-
    and see you tomorrow, during   semasyo˥o.
    the morning.

(c)

Mrs. Smith

    curtain   ka˥ateñ
23. Say! I'd like to have this   Ano ne! Ko˥no ki˥zi (o) so˥ko
    material made into curtains   no ka˥ateñ ni si˥te moraita˦i
    for [over] there. Do you   ñ desu kedo, ta˥riru˥ desyoo ka.
    think it's enough?

Man

    isn't any insufficiency   ta˥rinai koto˥ wa ˥na˦i
    back or lining or   u˥ra˥
      wrong side
    when [someone] doesn't   tu˥ke˦nai to
      attach
24. Yes, it's enough all right,   Ha⌐a. Ta˥rinai koto˥ wa go˥zai-
    but I don't think it looks right   mase˦ñ ga; u˥ra˥ (o) tu˥ke˦nai
    without a lining (lit. I think   to, gu˥ai ga waru˥i to omoimasu.
    the condition is bad when you
    don't attach a lining.)

Mrs. Smith

oh!   a꜒ra [1]

25. Oh, really? Well then, make   A꜒ra, so꜒o? Zya꜒a, u꜔ra꜒ (o) tu-
    (lit. attach) a lining, would   ꜔ke꜔te ne?
    you?

> whenever it falls   hu꜒ru to
> leak (verb)   mo꜒ru /-u/
> maid's room   zyotyuubeya

26. Also, I hear that the rain   Sore kara; hi꜒doku ꜔hu꜔ru to,
    leaks in whenever it rains   a꜒me ḡa ꜔mo꜒ru soo desu kara;
    hard, so please look at the   zyo꜔tyuubeya no ya꜒ne mo ꜔mi꜔te
    roof of the maid's room too,   kudasai ne?
    would you?

Mr. Smith (to Mrs. Smith)

27. Oh, there's still [more to be   A. Ma꜒da ꜔a꜔ru ne?
    done], isn't there?

(to man from Chiyoda Service)

> smell or odor   ni꜔o꜒i
> have an odor   ni꜔o꜒i ḡa suru
> box for refuse   gomibako
> lid or cover   huta

28. Let's have the lid of the rub-   He꜒ñ na ni꜔o꜔i ḡa su꜔ru꜔ kara,
    bish box (ex)changed because   go꜔mibako no huta (o) torikaete
    it has a strange smell.   morao꜒o.

Mrs. Smith

29. That's right. We must have   So꜒o desu ꜔ne꜔e. Na꜔rubeku ha꜒-
    that done as quickly as pos-   yaku si꜔te morawana꜔kereba_
    sible.

Mr. Smith

> for the most part or by   daitai
>   and large or generally
> estimate   mitumori
> rough estimate   daitai no mitumori
> cause to know or let   siraseru /-ru/
>   [someone] know

30. Please let me know your rough   A꜔sita no bañ ma꜔de ni da꜔itai
    estimate by tomorrow night.   no mitumori (o) sirasete kudasa꜒i.

> on the basis of that   so꜔no ue꜒ de

31. Let's talk things over again on   So꜔no ue꜒ de ma꜔ta soodañ-sima-
    the basis of that.   syo꜔o.

Man

32. Certainly.   Ha꜒a, syo꜔oti-itasima꜒sita.

---

[1] Woman's exclamation of surprise.

Mrs. Smith

feed <u>or</u> cause to eat   ta⌐besase⌐ru /-ru/
33. At noon I'll feed the gardener   U⌐ekiya no ohi⌐ru wa ko⌐tira de
     so. . . (Lit. As for the gar-   tabesasema⌐su kara—
     dener's noontime, I on my
     part will feed him so. . .)

Man

cause to have   mo⌐tase⌐ru /-ru/
send here <u>or</u> hand over   yo⌐ko⌐su /-u/
  to speaker
send here with a lunch   be⌐ñto⌐o o mo⌐ta⌐sete yo-
                              ⌐ko⌐su
cause to drink <u>or</u> let   no⌐mase⌐ru /-ru/
  [someone] drink
would you make <u>or</u> let   no⌐ma⌐sete i⌐tadakemase⌐ñ
  [someone] drink?   ka
  (lit. can't I receive
  your causing [someone]
  to drink?)
34. No, no! I'll send him here   Iie iie. Be⌐ñto⌐o (o) mo⌐ta⌐sete
     with his lunch so would you   yo⌐kosima⌐su kara, o⌐tya dake
     give him (lit. let him drink)   noma⌐sete i⌐tadakemase⌐ñ ka—
     just tea?

ADDITIONAL VOCABULARY

1. In repairing that you need a   A⌐re o nao⌐su no ni wa, <u>bo⌐o</u>
   <u>stick</u>.   ḡa irima⌐su yo—

      board   i⌐ta
      ladder   hasiḡo
      rope   na⌐wa⌐
      hammer   ka⌐nazu⌐ti
      hatchet <u>or</u> ax   o⌐no
      pliers   pe⌐ñti <u>or</u> yattoko
      saw   no⌐koḡiri⌐
      screwdriver   ne⌐zima⌐wasi
      nail   kuḡi⌐
      tool   do⌐oḡu⌐

2. This kind of thing is made of   Ko⌐o iu mono⌐ wa ⌐ki⌐ de tuku-
   <u>wood</u>.   rimasu.

      brick   re⌐ñḡa
      tile   ta⌐iru
      sand   suna
      dirt   tu⌐ti⌐
      gravel   zyari

3. Please put this in the <u>closet</u>.   Kore (o) o⌐siire⌐ ni irete kudasa⌐i.

     storeroom   mo⌐nooki⌐
     storehouse <u>or</u> godown   ku⌐ra⌐

4. When [you] <u>pull</u> [it] there's   Hi⌐ku⌐ to koma⌐ru kara, ki⌐otuke⌐te.
    trouble so be careful.

[you] push [it]	osu /-u/	T [1]
[you] raise [it]	aḡeru /-ru/	T
[you] lower [it]	sa⌐ḡe⌐ru /-ru/	T
[you] bend [it]	maḡeru /-ru/	T
[you] turn [it] <u>or</u> send [it] around	mawasu /-u/	T
[it] goes around	mawaru /-u/	I [1]
[you] drop [it]	o⌐to⌐su /-u/	T
[it] falls <u>or</u> drops	o⌐ti⌐ru /-ru/	I
[you] throw [it] down <u>or</u> knock [it] down	ta⌐o⌐su /-u/	T
[it] falls over <u>or</u> collapses	ta⌐ore⌐ru /-ru/	I
[you] pick [it] up	hirou /-u/	T
[you] lift [it]	mo⌐tiaḡe⌐ru /-ru/	T
[you] grasp [it]	niḡiru /-u/	T
[you] hit <u>or</u> strike [it]	u⌐tu /-u/	T
[you] mix [it]	ma⌐ze⌐ru /-ru/	T
[it] mixes <u>or</u> mingles	ma⌐zi⌐ru /-u/	I
[you] tie <u>or</u> bind [it]	si⌐ba⌐ru /-u/	T
[you] let [it] go <u>or</u> set [it] free	ha⌐na⌐su /-u/	T
[it] separates <u>or</u> parts (from) <u>or</u> falls apart	ha⌐nare⌐ru /-ru/	I

NOTES ON THE BASIC DIALOGUES

1. <u>Zya</u> is the contracted equivalent of <u>de wa</u>: zi⌐buñ zya deki⌐nai siḡoto
'work which by myself I can't do.'

2. Ta⌐to⌐eba is the provisional of a verbal ta'toe⌐ru /-<u>ru</u>/ 'give an example'
or 'illustrate.'
  U⌐ḡoka⌐su is the transitive partner of intransitive u⌐ḡo⌐ku /-<u>u</u>/ '[some-
thing] moves.'

5. Na⌐ninani: note also da⌐redare 'so-and-so (a person)' and do⌐kodoko
'such-and-such a place.'
  <u>Kureru</u> 'give' occurs with these three meanings: (a) 'someone gives
to me'; (b) 'someone else gives to you'; and (c) 'someone gives to
someone undefined'—cf. Lesson 17, Grammatical Note 1.
  <u>Yaru</u> 'do' is a less formal word than <u>suru</u>. The two verbals are often
interchangeable, but <u>yaru</u> does not occur in compounds like beñkyoo-
<u>suru</u>, <u>kekkoñ-suru</u>, etc.

---

[1] T = transitive; I = intransitive.

7. Yo⌐o means 'way' or 'manner' with emphasis on resemblance, but to⌐-ori means 'way' or 'manner' in the sense of accordance or agreement.

   Compare: Ya⌐kusoku no yo⌐o desu. 'It's like (i.e. resembles) a promise.' and: Ya⌐kusoku no to⌐ori desu. 'It's as [someone] promised,' 'It's in accordance with a promise.' To⌐ori usually occurs without a following particle when it modifies an inflected word or phrase.

8. Note the polite style of speech used by a beñriya in addressing his prospective employer.

11. Ya⌐buku: another transitive verbal meaning 'tear [something]' is ya-⌐buru /-u/. The intransitive partner is ya⌐bureru /-ru/ '[something] tears.'
    Note the combinations a⌐na⌐ o akeru 'make a hole' and a⌐na⌐ ḡa aku 'get a hole [in something].'

12. Kore wa 'this — in comparison with other jobs.'

13. To⌐reru is the intransitive partner of transitive to⌐ru 'take' or 'take away.'

16. The transitive partner of intransitive tu⌐maru is tu⌐meru /-ru/ 'cram' or 'stuff' or 'stop up.'

24. The opposite of u⌐ra⌐ is o⌐mote⌐ 'front surface' or 'outside' or 'right side.'

26. Note: ya⌐ne ḡa ⌐mo⌐ru 'the roof leaks'; ga⌐su ḡa ⌐mo⌐ru 'gas escapes'; ya⌐ne kara ⌐a⌐me ḡa ⌐mo⌐ru 'the roof leaks rain.'

28. With ni⌐o⌐i ḡa suru, compare azi ḡa suru 'have a flavor.' Note the combinations huta o suru 'put a lid on' and X no huta o suru 'put a lid on X.'

29. Lit. 'Unless we have that done as quickly as possible, [it won't do].'

34. Yo⌐ko⌐su refers to the sending of people or things to the place where the speaker now is.

Additional Vocabulary, 4. The intransitive partner of transitive aḡeru is aḡaru /-u/ 'go up' (Lesson 18); of transitive sa⌐ḡeru, sa⌐ḡaru /-u/ 'go down'; and of transitive maḡeru, maḡaru /-u/ 'make a turn' (Lesson 7).

GRAMMATICAL NOTES

1. The Causative

Ta⌐besase⌐ru		ta⌐be⌐ru 'eat.'
Na⌐osase⌐ru		na⌐o⌐su 'repair.'
Ukaḡawaseru	is the CAUSATIVE of	ukaḡau 'visit.'
Siraseru		siru 'come to know.'
Mo⌐tase⌐ru		mo⌐tu 'have.'
No⌐mase⌐ru		no⌐mu 'drink.'
Soozi-saseru		soozi-suru 'clean.'

Most verbals have corresponding CAUSATIVE verbals meaning 'cause [someone] to do so-and-so' or 'make [someone] do so-and-so' or, in some circumstances, 'let [someone] do so-and-so.'

An informal non-past causative is accented if the verbal from which it is derived is accented, and the accent occurs on the next-to-last syllable. To form the causative:

-<u>ru</u> verbals: substitute -<u>sase-ru</u> for the final -<u>ru</u> of the informal non-past (the citation form)

Example: <u>akeru</u> 'open': <u>akesaseru</u> 'make [someone] open'

-<u>u</u> verbals: substitute -<u>ase-ru</u> for the final -<u>u</u> of the informal non-past; when the informal non-past ends in two vowels, substitute -<u>wase-ru</u> for the final -<u>u</u>

Examples: kaꜛku 'write': kaꜛkaseꜛru 'make [someone] write'
tukau 'use': <u>tukawaseru</u> 'make [someone] use'

-<u>aru</u> verbals: causative does not occur

Irregular verbals: kuꜛru 'come': koꜛsaseꜛru 'make [someone] come'
suru 'do': <u>saseru</u> 'make [someone] do'

All causatives are themselves verbals of the -<u>ru</u> group. Thus, the causative of <u>akeru</u> has such forms as:

Informal non-past: akesaseru
Stem: akesase
Informal past: akesaseta
Gerund: akesasete
Conditional: aꜛkesasetaꜛra
Provisional: aꜛkesasereꜛba

The person acted upon (i.e. made to do something) is usually followed by particle <u>ni</u>:

Uꜛnteꜛnsyu ni kuꜛruma o miḡakasemaꜛsita. 'I made the driver polish the car.'

However, with some causatives based on intransitive verbals—namely, those that never occur with direct object particle <u>o</u>—the person made to do something is followed by particle <u>ni</u> or <u>o</u>:

Taꜛroo ni iꜛkasemaꜛsita.
    or   'I made Taro go.'
Taꜛroo (o) iꜛkasemaꜛsita.

But with a few causatives, the person made to do something is followed by <u>o</u> but not <u>ni</u>:

Uꜛti no zyotyuu (o) yamesasemaꜛsita. 'I fired our maid.' (Lit. 'I caused our maid to quit.')

The causative is sometimes equivalent to 'let [someone] do so-and-so,' particularly when a causative gerund is followed by a verbal of giving or receiving. Thus:

Yo⌐ma⌐sete kudasai. 'Please let me read [it].'
Tu⌐kawasete kurema⌐sita. '[He] let me use [it].' (Lit. '[He] gave me
    letting [me] use.')
Ha⌐ikeñ-sasete itadakima⌐su. '(Lit.) I accept your letting me look.'
    (Said by a person about to look at something he has been given per-
    mission to see.)
Ka⌐era⌐sete i⌐tadakemase⌐ñ ka⌐ 'May I go home?' or 'Would you let
    me go home?' (Lit. 'Can't I receive your letting me go home?')

The latter sentence is an extremely polite way of asking permission.

However, depending on context, a causative in combination with a word of
giving or receiving may still mean 'make [someone] do so-and-so.' For example, the first sentence of the preceding group may also mean 'Please
make [someone] read [it].'

In some contexts, a causative which is not followed by a word of giving or
receiving is equivalent to 'let [someone] do so-and-so.' For example:

Kodomo o ni⌐wa de asobasema⌐sita. 'He let the children play in the
    garden.'
Tu⌐kawasete⌐ wa i⌐kemase⌐ñ. 'You mustn't let [them] use [it].'

Be sure to distinguish among the following three kinds of examples:

(a) I⌐kasema⌐sita. 'I had [him] go.'
(b) I⌐tte moraima⌐sita. 'I had [him] go.'
(c) I⌐kasete moraima⌐sita. '[He] let me go.' or 'I had [him] have
    [someone] go.'

Sentence (a) implies that he went because I told him to. Other English equivalents would be 'I made him go' and 'I let him go.' Sentence (b) states that
'I received his going'—that is, 'he went for me.' There is no indication in
the Japanese whether or not he was told to go; the sentence tells only what
was done for me. Sentence (c) also tells what I received: depending on context, either permission to go, or the causing of someone else to go.

The causative and representative may occur together in either one of two
ways:

(a) causative representative verbal(s) + √suru
    or
(b) non-causative representative verbal(s) + √saseru

Example:

ma⌐do o a⌐kesaseta⌐ri si⌐mesa⌐setari suru   'make [someone]
    or   keep opening and
ma⌐do o a⌐keta⌐ri ⌐si⌐metari saseru   shutting the window'

Additional examples:

Zyotyuu ni syo⌐kuzi no sitaku o sasema⌐sita.
    'I had the maid get dinner ready.'
Kodomo ni ⌐go⌐hañ o ta⌐besase⌐nakereba na⌐ra⌐nai kara, si⌐tu⌐ree-
    simasu.
    'I must feed the children so please excuse me.'

Naⁿ-do mo ka⌐ka⌐seta ñ desu ḡa, ma⌐da ⌐yo⌐ku o⌐boe⌐nai yoo desu.
   'I made him write it any number of times, but he doesn't seem to
     have learned it yet.'
Sono a⌐tarasi⌐i zyotyuu wa ze⌐ñzeñ deki⌐nakatta kara, mo⌐o ya⌐mesa-
   sema⌐sita.
   'That new maid couldn't do anything so I've fired her (lit. made her
     quit) already.'
U⌐ñte⌐ñsyu o ⌐ma⌐initi kosasemasu.
   'I have the driver come every day.'
A⌐buna⌐i kara, ti⌐isa⌐i ko ni ⌐ma⌐tti o mo⌐ta⌐sete wa i⌐kemase⌐ñ yo.
   'You mustn't let small children have matches, because it's danger-
     ous.'
I⌐itai koto⌐ ḡa ⌐a⌐ru kara, wa⌐takusi ni⌐ mo i⌐wasete moraita⌐i ñ de-
   su.
   'There are things I'd like to say so I want you to let me speak, too.'
Wa⌐takusi ni⌐ mo ko⌐no deñwa o tukawasete kuremase⌐ñ ka⏌
   'Would you let me use this phone, too?'
O⌐kusama, tyo⌐tto gu⌐ai ḡa wa⌐ruku na⌐rima⌐sita kara, ka⌐era⌐sete i⌐ta-
   dakemase⌐ñ ka⏌
   'Madam, I don't feel well, so may I go home?'
A⌐buna⌐i kara, i⌐so⌐ide na⌐osa⌐sete kudasai.
   'It's dangerous so please have [someone] fix it in a hurry.'

2. Particle <u>to</u> 'with' Following Inflected Words

Particle <u>to</u> 'with' has previously occurred following nominals: for example, to⌐modati to hana⌐sita 'I talked with a friend.'

Particle <u>to</u> may also follow a NON-PAST inflected form—formal or, more
commonly, informal—when one action or state accompanies (or accompanied)
another: X to Y 'with the occurrence of X, Y' or 'when <u>or</u> if X, Y' or
'whenever <u>or</u> if ever X, Y.' Y may be non-past, past, imperative, etc.; it
has no restrictions as to form. Thus:

   Wa⌐ka⌐ru to, o⌐mosiro⌐i. 'Whenever I understand (lit. with being clear),
     it's interesting.'
   Go⌐-zi ni ⌐na⌐ru to, de⌐ma⌐sita. 'When it got to be 5 o'clock (lit. with
     becoming 5 o'clock), I left.'
   Sa⌐mu⌐i to, u⌐ti o demase⌐ñ. 'Whenever it's cold (lit. with being cold),
     I don't leave the house.'
   Ki⌐otuke⌐nai to, ko⌐warema⌐su yo⏌ 'If you're not careful (lit. with not
     being careful), it will break!'
   Hima da to, ho⌐ñ o yomimasu. 'When I'm free (lit. with being free), I
     read (a book).'

A non-past inflected form + <u>to</u> + <u>su⌐ḡu</u> means 'as soon as so-and-so happens <u>or</u> happened' (lit. 'immediately with the occurrence of so-and-so'):

   De⌐ñki o kesu to ⌐su⌐ḡu ne⌐te simaima⌐su. 'As soon as I turn off the
     lights (lit. immediately with turning off the lights), I fall asleep.'
   Byo⌐oki ni na⌐ru to ⌐su⌐ḡu o⌐isyasañ o yobima⌐sita. 'As soon as I got
     sick, I called the doctor.'

Compare and study the following groups of examples:

Past:

(a) Ma⌐do o a⌐keta⌐ra, sa⌐muku na⌐rima⌐sita. 'When I opened the win-
    dow, it got cold.'
(b) Ma⌐do o a⌐keta toki⌐ ni, ko⌐tori ḡa ha⌐itte ki⌐ma⌐sita. 'When I
    opened the window, a bird flew in.'
(c) Ma⌐do o akeru to, ku⌐sya⌐mi¹ o si⌐hazimema⌐sita. 'When I opened
    (lit. with the opening of) the window, I started sneezing.'

Habitual:

(a) Ma⌐do o a⌐keru toki⌐ ni wa, ki⌐otuke⌐te kudasai. '(At times) when
    you open the windows, be careful.'
(b) Ma⌐do o akeru to, so⌐to de asoñde iru ko⌐domo no ko⌐e ḡa ⌐yo⌐ku
    kikoemasu. 'When I open (lit. with the opening of) the windows,
    I can hear the voices of the children playing outside, very
    clearly.'

Future:

(a) Ma⌐do o a⌐kere⌐ba, sa⌐muku narimasu. 'It will get cold if (i.e.
    provided) you open the window.'
(b) Ma⌐do o a⌐keta⌐ra, sa⌐muku narimasu. 'If you [should] open the
    window, it will get cold.'
(c) Ma⌐do o akeru to, sa⌐muku na⌐rima⌐su yo⌐ 'If you open (lit. with
    the opening of) the window, it will get cold!'

To is also used in expressions indicating 'hope':

Iru to ⌐i⌐i desu ḡa ⌐ne⌐e.
    'I hope he's in, don't you.'
Wa⌐ka⌐ru to ⌐i⌐i desu ḡa ⌐ne⌐e.
    'I hope he understands, don't you.'

Additional examples:

Go-⌐zi-suḡi⌐ ni ⌐na⌐ru to, kono miti wa zi⌐do⌐osya de i⌐ppai ni nari-
    ma⌐su.
    'When it gets to be after five, this street becomes filled with cars.'
O⌐mosiro⌐i to, yo⌐ru o⌐soku na⌐ru made ⌐ho⌐ñ ya za⌐ssi o yo⌐ñde imasu.
    'When they're interesting, I read (lit. am reading) books and maga-
    zines in the evening until it gets late.'
Wa⌐kara⌐nai to, wa⌐ka⌐ru made ⌐nañ-do mo se⌐ñse⌐e ni ki⌐kima⌐su.
    'Whenever I don't understand, I ask the teacher over and over again,
    until I do (understand).'
Ha⌐yaku dekakenai to, o⌐soku narima⌐su yo⌐
    'If you don't start out in a hurry, you'll be late!'
A⌐mai mono⌐ da to, i⌐kura de⌐ mo tabemasu.
    'When it's something sweet, I eat any (large) amount.'
Te⌐ñki no ⌐i⌐i hi da to, ko⌐ko kara de⌐ mo ⌐Hu⌐zisañ ḡa ⌐yo⌐ku mie-
    masu.
    'When it's a nice day, you can see Fuji very well, even (being) from
    here.'
Syokuzi ḡa owaru to ⌐su⌐ḡu zi⌐mu⌐syo e ka⌐erima⌐sita.
    'As soon as dinner was over, I returned to the office.'

---

¹ Ku⌐sya⌐mi 'a sneeze'; ku⌐sya⌐mi o suru 'sneeze (verb).'

3. -zu⌐tu

-Zu⌐tu occurs immediately following numbers and indefinite quantity expressions, meaning 'each' or 'of each' or 'for each' or 'at a time.' Thus, hi⌐to-tu-zu⌐tu ya⌐rima⌐sita means 'I gave one of each' or 'I gave one for each [of them]' or 'I gave one at a time.'

Before -zu⌐tu, a word which is normally accented loses its accent.

Examples:

Na⌐ihu to ⌐ho⌐oku to su⌐pu⌐uñ o, i⌐p-poñ-zu⌐tu o⌐tori-kudasa⌐i.
'Take one each of the knives, forks, and spoons.'
Ma⌐initi nīhoñḡo to ēeḡo o ni-⌐zikañ-zu⌐tu beñkyoo-simasu.
'Every day I study Japanese and English two hours each.'
Wa⌐surenai yo⌐o ni ⌐ma⌐iasa kūsuri o hi⌐to-tu-zu⌐tu no⌐ma⌐sete kudasai.
'Don't forget to have him take one of each of the medicines every morning.'
Mi⌐na⌐sañ so⌐no kami⌐ o sa⌐ñ-mai-zu⌐tu ⌐to⌐tte kudasai.
'Everybody, please take three sheets each of that paper.'
Su⌐kosi-zu⌐tu i⌐rete kudasa⌐i.
'Put in a little at a time.'

4. uti Preceded by Negative

Uti occurs as a time word meaning 'interval' in combinations like wa⌐ka⌐i uti ni 'in the interval when [someone] is young,' asa no uti ni 'within the morning,' etc.

Uti is also frequently preceded by a sentence modifier consisting of, or ending with, a non-past negative. The combination means literally 'the interval during which so-and-so has not happened'—i.e. 'before so-and-so happens.'

Examples:

Byo⌐oki na⌐ra; hi⌐doku na⌐ra⌐nai uti ni, i⌐sya ni mi⌐te mo⌐rawana⌐kereba na⌐rimase⌐ñ.
'If you're sick, you must have the doctor see you before it gets serious (lit. during the interval when it hasn't become serious).'
O⌐kyakusañ ḡa ko⌐nai uti ni, kodomo ni ⌐go⌐hañ o ta⌐besa⌐sete si⌐ma-imasyo⌐o.
'I guess I'll finish feeding the children before the guests come (lit. during the interval when the guests haven't come).'
Deñsya ḡa tomarañai uti ni, o⌐rite wa i⌐kemase⌐ñ.
'You mustn't get off before the train stops (lit. during the interval when the train hasn't stopped).'

5. ——— ko⌐to⌐ wa ⌐na⌐i

Ko⌐to⌐ wa √⌐na⌐i preceded by a sentence modifier means 'there isn't any matter of ———,' 'it isn't that ———.' The sequence is frequently followed by ḡa or keredo meaning 'but.'

Examples:

I⌐kanai koto⌐ wa a⌐rimase⌐ñ ḡa, i⌐ku⌐ no wa o⌐soku na⌐ru to omoimasu.

'It isn't that I'm not going, but I think I'll go late (lit. the going will
be late).'

I⌐kitai koto⌐ wa ˧na˦i keredo, i⌐kana⌐kereba na⌐rimase˦n̄.

'It isn't that I want to go but I must go.'

O⌐naka ḡa ita˦i koto wa ˧na˦i n̄ desu ḡa, tyo⌐tto ⌐he˦n̄ na n̄ desu.

'It isn't that my stomach hurts, but it feels (lit. is) a little strange.'

De⌐ki⌐nai koto wa ˧na˦i to omoimasu.

'I don't think it's impossible.' (Lit. 'I think that there isn't im-
possibility.')

In this pattern, the negative following ko⌐to⌐ wa ordinarily has medium-
high [˦] pitch. Compare:

i⌐kanai koto⌐ wa ˧na˦i 'it isn't that I'm not going'

and:

i⌐kanai koto⌐ wa ⌐na˦i 'there's never a time when I don't go'

The first sequence—ending with ˧na˦i—is an example of the pattern described in this note, but the second sequence—ending with ⌐na˦i—is an example of a pattern described in Lesson 31, Grammatical Note 1. The contrast in accents is usual but not invariable.

DRILLS

A. Substitution Drill

1. I'm (a person) from Chiyoda Service . . .

   Ti⌐yoda-sa⌐abisu no mo˦no˦ de
   gozaimasu ḡa—

2. I'm (a person) from the
   American Embassy . . .

   A⌐merika-taisi⌐kan̄ no mo˦no˦ de
   gozaimasu ḡa—

3. I'm (a person) from the
   JTB . . .

   Ko⌐otuuko⌐osya no mo˦no˦ de go-
   zaimasu ḡa—

4. I'm (a person) from the
   insurance company . . .

   Ho⌐ken̄ḡa⌐isya no mo˦no˦ de gozaimasu ḡa—

5. I'm (a person) from the
   Ministry of Education . . .

   Mo⌐n̄bu⌐syoo no mo˦no˦ de gozai-
   masu ḡa—

6. I'm (a person) from the
   Bank of Japan . . .

   Ni⌐hon̄-gi⌐n̄koo no mo˦no˦ de go-
   zaimasu ḡa—

7. I'm (a person) from the
   Asahi Shimbun . . .

   A⌐sahi-si⌐n̄bun̄ no mo˦no˦ de go-
   zaimasu ḡa—

8. I'm (a person) from the
   electric company . . .

   De⌐n̄kiḡa⌐isya no mo˦no˦ de gozaimasu ḡa—

B. Substitution Drill

1. I'll send [him] here with
   his lunch.

   O⌐ben̄too (o) mota⌐sete yokosimasu.

2. I'll send [him] here with
   the estimate.

   Mi⌐tumori (o) mota⌐sete yokosimasu.

3. I'll send [him] here with
   a guide book.

   A⌐n̄naisyo⌐ (o) mo˦ta˦sete yokosimasu.

4. I'll send [him] here with
   the tickets.

   Ki⌐ppu (o) mota⌐sete yokosimasu.

5. I'll send [him] here with the receipt.

U⸠ketori (o) mota⸣sete yokosima-su.

6. I'll send [him] here with a letter.

Te⸠gami (o) mota⸣sete yokosima-su.

7. I'll send [him] here with the money.

O⸠kane (o) mota⸣sete yokosimasu.

8. I'll send [him] here with the key.

Ka⸠gi⸣ (o) mo⸠ta⸣sete yokosima-su.

C. Substitution Drill

1. Please pull that rope.

A⸠no nawa⸣ (o) hi⸠ite kudasa⸣i.

2. Please let go that rope. /ha⸠na⸣su/

A⸠no nawa⸣ (o) ha⸠na⸣site kudasai.

3. Please grab that rope. /nigiru/

A⸠no nawa⸣ (o) ni⸠gitte kudasa⸣i.

4. Please pick up that rope. /hirou/

A⸠no nawa⸣ (o) hi⸠rotte kudasa⸣i.

5. Please lower that rope. /sa⸠ge⸣ru/

A⸠no nawa⸣ (o) ⸠sa⸣gete kudasai.

6. Please tie that rope. /si⸠ba⸣ru/

A⸠no nawa⸣ (o) si⸠ba⸣tte kudasai.

7. Please take away that rope. /to⸣ru/

A⸠no nawa⸣ (o) ⸠to⸣tte kudasai.

8. Please hold that rope. /mo⸣tu/

A⸠no nawa⸣ (o) ⸠mo⸣tte kudasai.

9. Please raise that rope. /ageru/

A⸠no nawa⸣ (o) a⸠gete kudasa⸣i.

10. Please drop that rope. /o⸠to⸣su/

A⸠no nawa⸣ (o) o⸠to⸣site kudasai.

11. Please hand over that rope. /watasu/

A⸠no nawa⸣ (o) wa⸠tasite kudasa⸣i.

12. Please lend me that rope. /kasu/

A⸠no nawa⸣ (o) ka⸠site kudasa⸣i.

D. Substitution Drill

1. The <u>carpenter</u> collapsed.

Da⸣iku-sañ ga ta⸠orema⸣sita.

2. The <u>carpenter</u> knocked [it] over.

Da⸣iku-sañ ga ta⸠osima⸣sita.

3. [He] knocked over the ladder.

Ha⸠sigo⸣ o taosima⸣sita.

4. [He] stood the ladder up.

Ha⸠sigo⸣ o <u>tatema⸣sita</u>.

5. <u>I</u> stood [it] up <u>or</u> built [it].

Wa⸠takusi ga tatema⸣sita.

6. <u>I</u> stood up.

Wa⸠takusi ga <u>tatima⸣sita</u>.

7. <u>I</u> bent [it].

Wa⸠takusi ga <u>magema⸣sita</u>.

8. [I] bent a nail.

Ku⸠gi⸣ o magema⸣sita.

9. [I] dropped a nail.

Ku⸠gi⸣ o otosima⸣sita.

10. The <u>gardener</u> dropped [it].

U⸠ekiya⸣ ga otosima⸣sita.

E. Substitution Drill

1. I'd like to make this material into curtains . . .

    Ko⌐no ki⌉zi (o) ⌐ka⌉ateñ ni si⌐ta⌉i ñ desu g̃a—

2. I'd like to make this room into a study . . .

    Ko⌐no heya⌉ (o) <u>syo⌐sai</u> ni sita⌉i ñ desu g̃a—

3. I'd like to make this board into a shelf . . .

    Ko⌐no i⌉ta (o) <u>ta⌐na</u> ni sita⌉i ñ desu g̃a—

4. I'd like to make this Japanese room into a Western-style room . . .

    Ko⌐no zasiki⌉ (o) <u>yo⌐oma</u> ni sita⌉i ñ desu g̃a—

5. I'd like to make this house into a school . . .

    Kono <u>uti</u> (o) ga⌐kkoo</u> ni sita⌉i ñ desu g̃a—

6. I'd like to make this meat into sukiyaki . . .

    Ko⌐no <u>niku⌉</u> (o) <u>su⌐kiyaki</u> ni sita⌉i ñ desu g̃a—

7. I'd like to make this kimono into a dress . . .

    Kono <u>kimono</u> (o) <u>wa⌐ñpi⌉isu</u> ni si⌐ta⌉i ñ desu g̃a—

8. I'd like to make this fish into sashimi . . .

    Kono <u>sakana</u> (o) o⌐sasimi</u> ni si-ta⌉i ñ desu g̃a—

F. Substitution Drill

1. It doesn't warrant hiring an expert but . . .

    Se⌐ñmoñ no hito⌉ (o) ta⌐no⌉mu hodo zya ⌐na⌉i keredo—

2. It doesn't warrant building a new house but . . .

    A⌐tarasi⌉i uti (o) ta⌐te⌉ru hodo zya ⌐na⌉i keredo—

3. It doesn't warrant repainting the whole wall but . . .

    <u>Kabe (o)</u> ⌐ze⌉ñbu nu⌐rikae⌉ru hodo zya ⌐na⌉i keredo—

4. It doesn't warrant calling a doctor but . . .

    O⌐isyasañ (o) yobu</u> hodo zya na⌉i keredo—

5. It doesn't warrant quitting that company but . . .

    <u>Ano kaisya (o) ya⌐meru</u> hodo zya na⌉i keredo—

6. It doesn't warrant firing him but . . .

    A⌐no⌉ hito (o) ya⌐mesaseru</u> hodo zya na⌉i keredo—

7. It doesn't warrant going all the way back there but . . .

    A⌐suko ma⌉de mo⌐do⌉tte iku</u> hodo zya ⌐na⌉i keredo—

8. It doesn't warrant being in bed from morning till night but . . .

    A⌉sa kara ba⌐ñ ma⌉de ne⌐te (i)ru</u> hodo zya na⌉i keredo—

G. Substitution Drill

1. They're things like putting up shelves and moving heavy furniture.

    Ta⌐na (o) tutta⌉ri, o⌐moi ka⌉g̃u (o) u⌐g̃oka⌉sitari su⌐ru yo⌐o na ko-⌐to⌉ desu.

2. They're things like planting trees and weeding.
   /ki⌉ (o) ueru, ku⌐sa⌉ (o) ⌐to⌉ru/

    Ki⌉ (o) u⌐eta⌉ri, ku⌐sa⌉ (o) ⌐to⌉-ttari su⌐ru yo⌐o na ko⌐to⌉ desu.

3. They're things like repairing old houses and
   putting up new houses.
   /hu⌐ru˺i uti (o) na⌐o˺su,
   a⌐tarasi˺i uti (o) ta⌐te˺-
   ru/

   Hu⌐ru˺i uti (o) na⌐o˺sitari, a⌐tara-
   si˺i uti (o) ⌐ta˺tetari su⌐ru yo˺o
   na ko⌐to˺ desu.

4. They're things like taking care of the garden
   and cleaning the house.
   /ni⌐wa no teire˺ (o)
   suru, uti no soozi (o)
   suru/

   Ni⌐wa no teire˺ (o) si⌐ta˺ri, u⌐ti
   no soozi (o) sita˺ri su⌐ru yo˺o
   na ko⌐to˺ desu.

5. They're things like seeing the sights and buying souvenirs. /keñbutu-
   suru, omiyaḡe (o) kau/

   Ke⌐ñbutu-sita˺ri, o⌐miyaḡe (o) ka-
   tta˺ri su⌐ru yo˺o na ko⌐to˺ desu.

6. They're things like taking walks and going fishing. /sañpo-suru, turi
   ni iku/

   Sa⌐ñpo-sita˺ri, tu⌐ri ni itta˺ri su⌐ru
   yo˺o na ko⌐to˺ desu.

7. They're things like
   studying the language
   and reading history and
   geography books. /ko-
   toba˺ (o) beñkyoo-suru,
   re⌐kisi ya ti˺ri no ⌐ho˺ñ
   (o) ⌐yo˺mu/

   Ko⌐toba˺ (o) be⌐ñkyoo-sita˺ri, re-
   ⌐kisi ya ti˺ri no ⌐ho˺ñ (o) ⌐yo˺ñ-
   dari su⌐ru yo˺o na ko⌐to˺ desu.

8. They're things like reading advertisements and
   telephoning agents.
   /ko⌐okcku (o) yo˺mu, bu-
   ⌐ro˺okaa ni deñwa-suru/

   Ko⌐okoku (o) yo⌐ñdari, bu⌐ro˺okaa
   ni de⌐ñwa-sita˺ri su⌐ru yo˺o na
   ko⌐to˺ desu.

H. Substitution Drill

   (Add <u>no</u> following the substitution item, as required.)

   1. It's like its name.   Na⌐mae no to˺ori desu.
   2. It's as I said.   I⌐tta to˺ori desu.
   3. It's as you said.   O⌐ssya˺tta ⌐to˺ori desu.
   4. It's as I explained.   Se⌐tumee-sita to˺ori desu.
   5. It's as you know.   Go⌐zo˺ñzi no ⌐to˺ori desu.
   6. It's as I promised.   Ya⌐kusoku no to˺ori desu.
   7. It's as you ordered.   Go⌐tyuumoñ no to˺ori desu.
   8. It's as I thought.   O⌐mo˺tta ⌐to˺ori desu.
   9. It's like always.   I⌐tu mo no ⌐to˺ori desu.

I. Response Drill (based on Grammatical Note 5)

      Tutor: Si⌐mase˺ñ ka⌐ /mo⌐ñdai ḡa a˺ru/ 'Aren't you going to
              do it? /there are problems/'

Student: Si⌐nai koto¬ wa ˧na˦i ñ desu ḡa, mo⌐ñdai ḡa a˧ru ñ desu.
'It isn't that I'm not going to do it, but there are problems.'

1. Ta⌐rimase˧ñ ka⌐ /gu⌐ai
   ḡa waru˧i/
   Ta⌐rinai koto¬ wa ˧na˦i ñ desu
   ḡa, gu˧ai ḡa waru˧i ñ desu.

2. Wa⌐karimase˧ñ ka⌐
   /o⌐mosi¬roku ˧na˦i/
   Wa⌐kara˧nai koto wa ˧na˦i ñ desu
   ḡa, o⌐mosi¬roku ˧na˦i ñ desu.

3. Ki⌐koemase˧ñ ka⌐ /wa-
   ⌐kara˧nai/
   Ki⌐koenai koto¬ wa ˧na˦i ñ desu
   ḡa, wa⌐kara˧nai ñ desu.

4. Mi⌐emase˧ñ ka⌐ /yo⌐me-
   nai/
   Mi⌐e˧nai koto wa ˧na˦i ñ desu
   ḡa, yo⌐me˧nai ñ desu.

5. I⌐karemase˧ñ ka⌐ /i⌐ki-
   taku na˧i/
   I⌐karenai koto¬ wa ˧na˦i ñ desu
   ḡa, i⌐kitaku na˧i ñ desu.

6. Si⌐rimase˧ñ ka⌐ /su⌐ki¬
   zya ˧na˦i/
   Si⌐ranai koto¬ wa ˧na˦i ñ desu ḡa,
   su⌐ki¬ zya ˧na˦i ñ desu.

7. De⌐kimase˧ñ ka⌐ /si⌐ta-
   ku na˧i/
   De⌐ki˧nai koto wa ˧na˦i ñ desu
   ḡa, si⌐taku na˧i ñ desu.

J. Substitution Drill (based on Grammatical Note 4)

1. Before the chimney gets
   clogged (lit. in the non-
   clogged interval), let's
   fix it.
   E⌐ñtotu ḡa tumara˧nai uti ni, na-
   ⌐osimasyo¬o.

2. Before the nails come
   out, let's fix it.
   Ku⌐ḡi ḡa tore˧nai uti ni, na⌐osi-
   masyo¬o.

3. Before the handyman
   comes, let's fix it.
   Be⌐ñriya ḡa ko˧nai uti ni, na⌐osi-
   masyo¬o.

4. Before it goes bad, let's
   fix it.
   Da⌐me¬ ni na˧ra˦nai uti ni, na⌐osi-
   masyo¬o.

5. Before it breaks, let's
   fix it.
   Ko⌐ware¬nai uti ni, na⌐osimasyo¬o.

6. Before the children wake
   up, let's fix it.
   Ko⌐domo ḡa oki˧nai uti ni, na⌐osi-
   masyo¬o.

7. Before it collapses, let's
   fix it.
   Ta⌐ore˧nai uti ni, na⌐osimasyo¬o.

8. Before it falls, let's fix
   it.
   O⌐ti¬nai uti ni, na⌐osimasyo¬o.

9. Before it falls apart,
   let's fix it.
   Ha⌐nare¬nai uti ni, na⌐osimasyo¬o.

10. Before the secretary
    goes home, let's fix it.
    Hi⌐syo¬ ḡa ka˧era˦nai uti ni, na-
    ⌐osimasyo¬o.

K. Substitution Drill (based on Grammatical Note 2)

1. When it rains hard, it
   leaks.
   Hi˧doku ˧hu˦ru to, a˧me ḡa ⌐mo¬ru
   ñ desu.

2. When I move heavy fur-
   niture, my back hurts.
   /o⌐moi ka˧ḡu (o) u˧ḡoka˦su, se⌐naka
   ḡa i˧taku ˧na˦ru/
   O⌐moi ka˧ḡu (o) u˧ḡoka˦su to, se-
   ⌐naka ḡa i˧taku ˧na˦ru ñ desu.

3. When I break something,   Na⌐ni ka ko⌐wa⌐su to, na⌐o⌐site
   I have it fixed. /na⌐ni   mo⌐rau⌐ ñ desu.
   ka ko⌐wa⌐su, na⌐o⌐site
   morau/

4. When I have time, I   Hima da to, hi⌐rune (o) suru⌐ ñ
   take a nap. /hima da,   desu.
   hirune (o) suru/

5. When I don't understand,   Wa⌐kara⌐nai to, se⌐ñse⌐e ni ki-
   I ask the teacher. /wa-   ⌐ku⌐ ñ desu.
   ⌐kara⌐nai, se⌐ñse⌐e ni
   kiku/

6. When it's cold, I don't   Sa⌐mu⌐i to, de⌐kakena⌐i ñ desu.
   go out. /sa⌐mu⌐i, de-
   kakenai/

7. When I drink, I don't   O⌐sake (o) no⌐mu to, gu⌐ai ḡa
   feel well. /o⌐sake (o)   wa⌐ruku ⌐na⌐ru ñ desu.
   no⌐mu, gu⌐ai ḡa wa⌐ruku
   ⌐na⌐ru/

L. Grammar Drill (based on Grammatical Note 1)

        Tutor: Si⌐ma⌐sita. /da⌐re ka/ 'I did it. /someone/'
        Student: Da⌐re ka ni sa⌐sema⌐sita. 'I had someone do it.'

1. Ta⌐na (o) turima⌐sita.   Da⌐iku ni ta⌐na (o) turasema⌐-
   /da⌐iku/   sita.
2. Ki⌐ (o) u⌐ema⌐sita.   Uekiya ni ⌐ki⌐ (o) u⌐esasema⌐-
   /uekiya/   sita.
3. Na⌐ḡaku ma⌐tima⌐sita.   Ya⌐nusi ni ⌐na⌐ḡaku ma⌐tasema⌐-
   /ya⌐nusi/   sita.
4. Hu⌐de de kakima⌐sita.   Se⌐eto ni hu⌐de de kakasema⌐-
   /se⌐eto/   sita.
5. Ku⌐ruma (o) miḡakima⌐-   U⌐ñte⌐ñsyu ni ku⌐ruma (o) miḡa-
   sita. /u⌐ñte⌐ñsyu/   kasema⌐sita.
6. Syo⌐kuzi no sitaku (o)   Zyotyuu ni syo⌐kuzi no sitaku
   sima⌐sita. /zyotyuu/   (o) sasema⌐sita.
7. Mo⌐nooki⌐ no ka⌐ḡi⌐ (o)   Ka⌐nai ni mo⌐nooki⌐ no ka⌐ḡi⌐
   ka⌐kema⌐sita. /ka⌐nai/   (o) ka⌐kesasema⌐sita.
8. Ni⌐hoñḡo de hanasima⌐-   A⌐no⌐ hito ni ni⌐hoñḡo de hana-
   sita. /a⌐no⌐ hito/   sasema⌐sita.
9. A⌐sa ⌐ha⌐yaku ki⌐ma⌐sita.   Hi⌐syo ni ⌐a⌐sa ⌐ha⌐yaku ko⌐sa-
   /hi⌐syo⌐/   sema⌐sita.
10. Ki⌐mono (o) kima⌐sita.   Kodomo ni ki⌐mono o kisasema⌐-
    /kodomo/   sita.
11. U⌐suku kirima⌐sita.   Ni⌐ku⌐ya ni u⌐suku kirasema⌐-
    /ni⌐ku⌐ya/   sita.
12. Ze⌐ñbu ki⌐kima⌐sita.   Tomodati ni ⌐ze⌐ñbu ki⌐kasema⌐-
    /tomodati/   sita.

    a. For each of the causative sentences in the above exercise, give
        the corresponding sentence using a gerund + <u>morau</u>.

Example:

Tutor: A⌜no⌝ hito ni sa⌜sema⌝sita 'I had him do it.'
Student: A⌜no⌝ hito ni si⌜te moraima⌝sita. 'I had it done by him.' or 'He did it for me.'

M. Completion Drill (based on Grammatical Note 1)

Tutor: Si⌜ta⌝katta ñ desu ḡa, 'I wanted to do it but—'
Student: a⌜no⌝ hito wa sa⌜sete kuremase⌝ñ desita. 'he didn't let me (do).'

1.	Ka⌝ḡu (o) u⌜ḡokasita⌝katta ñ desu ḡa,	a⌜no⌝ hito wa u⌜ḡokasa⌝sete ku⊢remase⊣ñ desita.
2.	Ryo⌜koo-sita⌝katta ñ desu ḡa,	a⌜no⌝ hito wa ryo⌜koo-sasete kuremase⌝ñ desita.
3.	Siḡoto (o) tu⌜zuketa⌝katta ñ desu ḡa,	a⌜no⌝ hito wa tu⌜zukesasete kuremase⌝ñ desita.
4.	Eeḡo de i⌜ita⌝katta ñ desu ḡa,	a⌜no⌝ hito wa i⌜wasete kuremase⌝ñ desita.
5.	A⌜no dooḡu⌝ (o) tu⌜kaita⌝katta ñ desu ḡa,	a⌜no⌝ hito wa tu⌜kawasete kuremase⌝ñ desita.
6.	Yoohuku (o) ki⌜ta⌝katta ñ desu ḡa,	a⌜no⌝ hito wa ki⌜sasete kuremase⌝ñ desita.
7.	Geta (o) ha⌜kita⌝katta ñ desu ḡa,	a⌜no⌝ hito wa ha⌜kasete kuremase⌝ñ desita.
8.	Osasimi (o) ta⌜beta⌝katta ñ desu ḡa,	a⌜no⌝ hito wa ta⌜besa⌝sete ku⊢remase⊣ñ desita.
9.	Sono teḡami (o) yo⌜mita⌝katta ñ desu ḡa,	a⌜no⌝ hito wa yo⌜ma⌝sete ku⊢remase⊣ñ desita.
10.	Ra⌝zio (o) ki⌜kita⌝katta ñ desu ḡa,	a⌜no⌝ hito wa ki⌜kasete kuremase⌝ñ desita.
11.	Se⌜ñse⌝e ni a⌜ita⌝katta ñ desu ḡa,	a⌜no⌝ hito wa a⌜wa⌝sete ku⊢remase⊣ñ desita.

N. Grammar Drill (based on Grammatical Note 1)

Tutor: Si⌜te⌝ mo ⌜i⌝i desu ka⌣ 'May I do it?'
Student: Sa⌜sete itadakemase⌝ñ ka⌣ 'Would you let me do it?'

1.	Ko⌜ko de ma⌝tte mo ⌜i⌝i desu ka⌣	Ko⌜ko de mata⌝sete i⊢tadakemase⊣ñ ka⌣
2.	Ha⌝yaku ⌜ka⌝ette mo ⌜i⌝i desu ka⌣	Ha⌝yaku ka⌜era⌝sete i⊢tadakemase⊣ñ ka⌣
3.	E⌜ñpitu de ka⌝ite mo ⌜i⌝i desu ka⌣	E⌜ñpitu de kaka⌝sete i⊢tadakemase⌝ñ ka⌣
4.	Ni⌜ho⌝ñ ni tuite ki⌜ite⌝ mo ⌜i⌝i desu ka⌣	Ni⌜ho⌝ñ ni tuite ki⌜kasete itadakemase⌝ñ ka⌣
5.	De⌜ñwa (o) ka⌝kete mo ⌜i⌝i desu ka⌣	De⌜ñwa (o) kakesa⌝sete i⊢tadakemase⊣ñ ka⌣
6.	A⌜na⌝ta no ⊢se⊣etaa (o) ki⌜te⌝ mo ⌜i⌝i desu ka⌣	A⌜na⌝ta no ⊢se⊣etaa (o) ki⌜sasete itadakemase⌝ñ ka⌣

7. Asita ya⌐su⌐nde mo ⌐i⌐i   Asita ya⌐suma⌐sete i⌐tadakemase⌐ñ
   desu ka⌐   ka⌐
8. Hi⌐rune (o) site⌐ mo ⌐i⌐i   Hi⌐rune (o) sasete itadakemase⌐ñ
   desu ka⌐   ka⌐
9. A⌐na⌐ta no zi⌐biki⌐ (o)   A⌐na⌐ta no zi⌐biki⌐ (o) tu⌐kawasete
   tu⌐katte⌐ mo ⌐i⌐i desu   itadakemase⌐ñ ka⌐
   ka⌐
10. Raisyuu kara ⌐tyo⌐tto   Raisyuu kara ⌐tyo⌐tto ya⌐sumi⌐ (o)
    ya⌐sumi⌐ (o) ⌐to⌐tte mo   to⌐ra⌐sete i⌐tadakemase⌐ñ ka⌐
    ⌐i⌐i desu ka⌐

O. Expansion Drill

1. [He] had [him] do [it].   Sa⌐sema⌐sita.
    [He] had [him] do work.   Si⌐goto (o) sasema⌐sita.
    [He] had [him] do work   Daidokoro de si⌐goto (o) sase-
    in the kitchen.   ma⌐sita.
    [He] had the carpenter   Da⌐iku ni da̅idokoro de si⌐goto
    do work in the kitchen.   (o) sasema⌐sita.
    The handyman had the   Beñriya wa ⌐da⌐iku ni da̅idokoro
    carpenter do work in   de si⌐goto (o) sasema⌐sita.
    the kitchen.

2. I made [them] drink [it].   No⌐masema⌐sita.
    I made [them] drink   Ku⌐suri (o) nomasema⌐sita.
    medicine.
    I made [them] drink the   Kusuri (o) su⌐kosi-zu⌐tu no⌐ma-
    medicine a little at a   sema⌐sita.
    time.
    I made [them] drink the   Moratta kusuri (o) su⌐kosi-zu⌐tu
    medicine I had re-   no⌐masema⌐sita.
    ceived, a little at a
    time.
    I made [them] drink the   Oisyasañ ni moratta kusuri (o)
    medicine I had re-   su⌐kosi-zu⌐tu no⌐masema⌐sita.
    ceived from the doctor,
    a little at a time.
    I made the children drink   Kodomo ni o̅isyasañ ni moratta
    the medicine I had re-   kusuri (o) su⌐kosi-zu⌐tu no⌐ma-
    ceived from the doctor,   sema⌐sita.
    a little at a time.

3. I had [him] plant [them].   U⌐esasema⌐sita.
    I had [him] plant trees.   Ki⌐ (o) u⌐esasema⌐sita.
    I had [him] plant tall   Ta⌐ka⌐i ⌐ki⌐ (o) u⌐esasema⌐sita.
    trees.
    I had [him] plant trees   Ka⌐ki⌐ne yori ta⌐ka⌐i ⌐ki⌐ (o)
    taller than the fence.   u⌐esasema⌐sita.
    I had [him] plant trees   Mawari ni, ka⌐ki⌐ne yori ta⌐ka⌐i
    taller than the fence,   ⌐ki⌐ (o) u⌐esasema⌐sita.
    [all] around.

I had [him] plant trees taller than the fence, [all] around the fence.	Ka⌐ki⌐ne no mawari ni, ka⌐ki⌐ne yori ta⌐ka⌐i ⌐ki⌐ (o) u⌐esasema⌐sita.
I had the gardener plant trees taller than the fence, [all] around the fence.	Uekiya ni, ka⌐ki⌐ne no mawari ni, ka⌐ki⌐ne yori ta⌐ka⌐i ⌐ki⌐ (o) u⌐esasema⌐sita.

4.

I had [her] exchange [it].	To⌐rikaesasema⌐sita.
I had [her] exchange a necktie.	Ne⌐kutai (o) to⌐rikaesasema⌐sita.
I had [her] exchange a loud necktie.	Ha⌐de⌐ na ⌐ne⌐kutai (o) to⌐rikaesasema⌐sita.
I had [her] exchange a loud necktie I had received from a friend.	Tomodati ni moratta ha⌐de⌐ na ⌐ne⌐kutai (o) to⌐rikaesasema⌐sita.
I had [her] exchange a loud necktie I had received from a friend, for a more conservative one.	Tomodati ni moratta ha⌐de⌐ na ⌐ne⌐kutai (o) ⌐mo⌐tto zi⌐mi⌐ na no to to⌐rikaesasema⌐sita.
I had my wife exchange a loud necktie I had received from a friend, for a more conservative one.	Ka⌐nai ni tōmodati ni moratta ha⌐de⌐ na ⌐ne⌐kutai (o) ⌐mo⌐tto zi⌐mi⌐ na no to to⌐rikaesasema⌐sita.

SUPPLEMENTARY DIALOGUES

1. Smith: De⌐ki⌐tara, i⌐ma ⌐tyo⌐tto te⌐gami o ka⌐ite mo⌐raita⌐i ñ desu ḡa⌐
   Secretary: Ha⌐a, ka⌐sikomarima⌐sita.
   Smith: Hazime ni wa⌐tasi no iu to⌐ori ⌐ka⌐ite ⌐mi⌐te kudasai⌐ So⌐no ue⌐ de na⌐osima⌐su kara⌐ I⌐i desu ka⌐
   Secretary: Ha⌐i. Do⌐ozo o⌐ssya⌐tte kudasai.

2. Mrs. Smith: O⌐isii oka⌐si desu ⌐ne⌐e. Do⌐ko de o⌐kai ni narima⌐sita ka⌐
   Mrs. Yamamoto: Ta⌐naka-sañ no o⌐kusañ ḡa go⌐zibuñ de otukuri ni na⌐tte, zyo⌐tyuusañ ni mota⌐sete yo⌐ko⌐site ku⌐dasa⌐tta ñ desu yo⌐
   Mrs. Smith: *Zu⌐ibuñ o⌐zyoozu de⌐su ⌐ne⌐e.

3. Tanaka: Haisyaku-sita zassi ya⌐bu⌐ite si⌐maima⌐sita. Do⌐o mo su⌐mimase⌐ñ desita.
   Smith: Ka⌐maimase⌐ñ. Sore wa ⌐mo⌐o yo⌐ñde si⌐matta⌐ ñ desu kara⌐
   Tanaka: Na⌐ḡa⌐i aida o⌐kari-sita⌐ri ya⌐bu⌐itari, hoñtoo ni gōmeñ-nasai⌐[1]
   Smith: Ho⌐ñtoo ni kamawa⌐nai ñ desu yo. Tu⌐ḡi⌐ no ḡa ki⌐te⌐ masu kara, yo⌐mimase⌐ñ ka⌐
   Tanaka: Kore kara ki⌐otukema⌐su kara, ha⌐isyaku-sasete kudasa⌐i.

4. Smith: Ni⌐hoñ no rekisi o beñkyoo-sita⌐i ñ desu ḡa, da⌐re ka te⌐kitoo na señse⌐e o syo⌐okai-site kudasaimase⌐ñ ka⌐

---

[1] Go⌐meñ-nasa⌐i. 'Excuse me.'

Tanaka: Zya'a, Ya⌐mada-sañ to iu hito˥ o si⌐tte ima˩su ḡa— A⌐no˥ hito
   wa bḛtu ni re⌐kisi ḡa señmoñ to iu hodo zya na'i ñ desu ḡa; na-
   ⌐kanaka yo˥ku si⌐tte iru˩ si, sono ue, e⌐eḡo mo daibu hanase˥ru
   hi⌐to˩ desu kara—
Smith: Ze˥hi so⌐no kata˩ o syo⌐okai-site kudasaimase˩ñ ka⌐
Tanaka: E˥e, i˥i desu to mo. Su˥ḡu re⌐ñraku-simasyo˩o.

5. Tanaka: Ma˥initi do⌐no-ḡurai-zu˥tu be⌐ñkyoo-site ru˩ ñ desu ka⌐
Smith: Ga⌐kkoo de˥ wa go-⌐zikañ-zu˥tu desu.
Tanaka: Kañzi wa?
Smith: Kañzi wa ⌐ma˥initi i⌐ti-zikañ-zu˥tu de, taitee to⌐o-ḡurai-zu˥tu
   naraimasu.

6. Tanaka: Kono siḡoto kyo⌐o-zyuu ni site simaita˥i ñ desu ḡa, zi⌐kañ
   ḡa tarina˥i ka mo sirenai to o⌐mo˩tte, si⌐ñpai-site iru˩ ñ desu.
Smith: So⌐ñna ni isoḡa˥nakute mo ⌐i˥i ñ desu yo⌐ Ko⌐ñsyuu no uti ni
   sure˥ba ⌐i˩i ñ desu kara—
Tanaka: A⌐sita-zyuu ni sumase˥nai to, do⌐yoo ma˥de ni si⌐ña˥kereba na-
   ⌐rana˩i hŏka no siḡoto ḡa o⌐soku narima˥su kara—
Smith: Ma˥a, de⌐ki˩nai mono de⌐ki˩nai ñ desu kara. A⌐ñmari hata-
   rakisuḡi˥ru to, byo⌐oki ni narima˥su kara ⌐ne˩e.

7. Smith: Ko⌐no ki⌐zi wa ⌐do˥tira ḡa o⌐mote˩ de, do˥tira ḡa u⌐ra˩ ka wa-
   ⌐karimase˩ñ ⌐ne˩e.
Tanaka: A⌐kai ho˥o ḡa o⌐mote˩ zya ⌐na˩i desyoo ka.
Smith: Sa˥a. Wa⌐takusi ni˥ wa wa⌐karimase˩ñ ḡa—

8. Smith: Hutuu no ni⌐hoñḡo no ho˥ñ no o⌐mote˩ ni ⌐na⌐ru no wa, e⌐eḡo
   no ho˥ñ no u⌐ra˩ ni ⌐na⌐ru ñ desu ḡa, ro⌐omazi de ka⌐ita ⌐ho˩ñ wa
   ⌐do˩o desyoo.
Tanaka: Ro⌐omazi no ho˥ñ wa su⌐kuna˥i ñ desu ḡa, daitai e⌐eḡo no ho˥ñ
   to o⌐nazi da to omoima˥su ḡa—

9. Mrs. Tanaka: Tyo˥tto ko⌐no osakana ta˥bete ⌐mi˩te ne? He˥ñ na a˥zi ḡa
   suru˥ desyoo?
Maid: Ko⌐marima˥sita ⌐ne˩e. Mo˥o ⌐Ta⌐roo-tyañ ni ta⌐besa˥sete si⌐matta˩
   ñ desu keredo— Ho⌐ñtoo ni tyo˥tto ⌐he˩ñ desu ⌐ne˩e. Byo⌐oki ni na-
   ra˥nakereba ⌐i˩i desu ḡa—
Mrs. Tanaka: Ki⌐otuke˥te ite; gu⌐ai ḡa waru˥i yoo dattara, su˥ḡu o⌐isya-
   sañ ni turete ikimasyo˩o.

10. Smith: O⌐isyasañ de˥ mo ⌐da˩redare sa⌐ñ te iu˥ ñ desu ka⌐
Tanaka: Da⌐redare-señse˥e tte i⌐u˩ ñ desu yo⌐

11. Employee: Tyo˥tto gu⌐ai ḡa waru˥i ñ desu ḡa, ha˥yaku ka⌐era˥sete i⌐ta-
   dakemase˩ñ ka⌐
Employer: Gu⌐ai ḡa waru˥i? Zya˥a, hi˥doku na⌐ra⌐nai uti ni ⌐ka⌐etta
   hoo ḡa ⌐i˩i yo⌐
Employee: Sore kara; a⌐sita˥ mo, su⌐mimase˩ñ ḡa, ya⌐suma˥sete ku⌐da-
   saimase˩ñ ka⌐ O⌐isyasañ ni mi˥te mo⌐raita˩i ñ desu ḡa—
Employer: A⌐sita˥ wa be⌐tu ni isoḡa˥siku ⌐na˩i kara, ka⌐mawa˥nai yo⌐
Employee: Zya˥a; su⌐mimase˩ñ ḡa, ka⌐era˥sete itadakimasu. Si⌐tu˥ree-
   simasu.
Employer: Odaizi ni.

12. Tanaka: Eego wa wa⌐ka˥ru to o⌐mosiro˥i ñ desu ḡa, wa⌐kara˥nai to i⌐ya˥
    ni ⌐na˥tte simatte‿
    Smith: Na˥ñ de mo ⌐so˥o desyoo? Ma˥a ⌐to˥nikaku, ma˥initi su⌐kosi-zu˥tu
    be⌐ñkyoo-sita˥ra, su˥ḡu zyo⌐ozu˥ ni na⌐rima˥su yo‿

13. Smith: I⌐ñki˥[1] no bi⌐ñ˥ no hu⌐ta o site okana˥i to, ko⌐bosima˥su yo‿
    Tanaka: Sono huta wa ⌐ko⌐ruku˥[2] ḡa ⌐to˥rete si⌐matta˥ kara, da⌐me˥ na
    ñ desu.
    Smith: Zya˥a, ho⌐ka no bi˥ñ no hu⌐ta o tukatta˥ra ⌐do˥o desu ka‿
    Tanaka: A˥ru ka ⌐do˥o ka sa⌐ḡasite mimasyo˥o.

14. Mrs. Smith: Ta⌐iheñ ke⌐kkoo na o⌐ka˥si de gozaimasu ⌐ne˥e. Do˥tira no
    de gozaimasu ka‿
    Mrs. Tanaka: Do˥kodoko no ⌐na˥ninani to i⌐˥u yo˥o na yu⌐umee na mono˥
    de wa go⌐zaimase˥ñ. U⌐ti no so˥ba no o⌐ka˥siya no mo⌐no˥ de go-
    zaimasu ḡa, na⌐kanaka i˥i azi de gozaimasyoo?

English Equivalents

1. Smith: If you can, I'd like to have you write a letter now . . .
    Secretary: Yes, certainly.
    Smith: First, please try writing it as I say it. On the basis of that, I'll
    correct it (so . . .) All right?
    Secretary: Yes. Please go ahead (lit. say [it]).

2. Mrs. Smith: What delicious cake! Where did you buy it?
    Mrs. Yamamoto: Mrs. Tanaka made it herself and was kind enough to
    send the maid here with it.
    Mrs. Smith: She's very good [at baking], isn't she.

3. Tanaka: I've torn the magazine I borrowed from you. I'm very sorry.
    Smith: It doesn't matter. I've already finished reading that one (so . . .)
    Tanaka: What with borrowing it for a long time and tearing it, [I] really
    [must ask you to] excuse me.
    Smith: It really doesn't matter. The next [issue] has come. Wouldn't
    you [like to] read it?
    Tanaka: From now on I'll be careful so do let me borrow it.

4. Smith: I'd like to study Japanese history. Would you be kind enough to
    introduce [me to] some suitable teacher?
    Tanaka: Well, I know a man named Mr. Yamada . . . He isn't a real
    specialist in history (lit. he isn't especially so much that you say
    history [is] a specialty) but he knows it quite well and, what is more,
    he is a person who can speak a considerable amount of English too,
    so . . .
    Smith: By all means would you introduce [me to] him?
    Tanaka: Yes, of course, that will be fine. I'll get in touch with him
    right away.

---

[1] 'Ink.'

[2] 'Cork.'

5. Tanaka: About how long (each [day]) are you studying every day?
    Smith: At school, it's five hours (each [day]).
    Tanaka: What about kanji?
    Smith: Kanji is one hour (each time) every day, and we usually learn
       about ten each time.

6. Tanaka: I'd like to finish doing this work (within) today, but I've been
       worrying, thinking that there may not be enough time.
    Smith: You don't have to hurry so much. (Because) it will be all right
       provided you do it sometime this week.
    Tanaka: If I don't finish it (within) tomorrow, other work that I must do
       by Saturday will be late (so. . .)
    Smith: Well, things that are impossible are impossible (so. . .) When
       you overwork (too much), you get sick so—you know.

7. Smith: You can't tell which is the right side and which is the wrong side
       of this material, can you.
    Tanaka: Wouldn't the redder side be the right side?
    Smith: Hmm. . . It isn't clear to me but [maybe you can tell].

8. Smith: What is (lit. becomes) the front of the normal Japanese book is
       (lit. becomes) the back of an English book, but what about books
       written in romaji?
    Tanaka: There aren't many romaji books but I think that for the most
       part they are the same as English books . . .

9. Mrs. Tanaka: Say, taste (lit. try eating) this fish, would you? Doesn't
       it have a funny taste?
    Maid: Oh dear. I've already fed it to Taro . . . It really is a little
       strange, isn't it. I hope he doesn't get sick . . .
    Mrs. Tanaka: Let's be careful, and if he seems to have something the
       matter with him, let's take him to the doctor right away.

10. Smith: Even in the case of a doctor do you say 'So-and-so-<u>san</u>'?
    Tanaka: You say 'So-and-so-<u>sensei</u>.'

11. Employee: I don't feel well. May I go home early?
    Employer: You don't feel well? Then you'd better go home before you
       feel worse (lit. in the interval when it hasn't become bad).
    Employee: And I'm sorry but would you let me take tomorrow off too?
       I'd like to have the doctor look me over . . .
    Employer: Tomorrow we're not especially busy so it will be all right.
    Employee: Well then, I'm sorry but I'll leave now (lit. I'll accept your
       letting me go home). Goodbye.
    Employer: Take care of yourself.

12. Tanaka: English is fun when I understand it, but when I don't under-
       stand, I end up hating it . . .
    Smith: Isn't everything like that? In any case, if you study every day
       a little at a time, you'll get to be good at it very soon.

13. Smith: If you don't put the top on the ink bottle (now, for future refer-
       ence), you'll spill it.
    Tanaka: That top is no good because the cork has come out of it.
    Smith: Then why don't you use the top of another bottle?
    Tanaka: I'll look and see if there is [one] or not.

14. Mrs. Smith: This is very fine cake. Where is it from?
    Mrs. Tanaka: This isn't anything famous that you can describe as "so-
    and-so from such-and-such a place." (Lit. This isn't a famous thing
    of the kind "so-and-so from such-and-such a place.") It's something
    from a pastry shop near the house, but it has (lit. is) quite a nice
    flavor, hasn't it?

EXERCISES

1. You have just bought a house and are discussing repairs and changes to
   be made, with a handyman. Cover the following work which you want
   him to have done for you:

   a. putting up shelves in the kitchen
   b. replacing (i.e. exchanging) the mats in the zashiki and the fusuma
      that are torn
   c. cleaning the chimney
   d. repairing the wall in front of the house and the fence around the
      garden
   e. planting some big trees toward the back of the garden
   f. repairing the places in the roof that leak

   Ask the handyman to give you a rough estimate by Saturday, and tell him
   you will talk to him again next week, on the basis of that.

2. Tell Haruko:

   a. that your overcoat button (botañ) has come off.
   b. that your overcoat has a hole.
   c. that your overcoat is torn.
   d. that the screws in the door have come out.
   e. that this fish has a funny taste.
   f. that this milk has a funny smell.
   g. to put the lid on this box.
   h. to lock this box.
   i. to stuff some paper in this box.
   j. to put up the mosquito nets.

3. Make up ten short conversations, each one of which contains one of the
   following phrases:

   a. so⌐no ue⌐ de
   b. ka⌐era⌐nai uti ni
   c. su⌐kosi-zu⌐tu
   d. ya⌐kusoku no to⌐ori
   e. ya⌐meru hodo zya na⌐i
   f. mo⌐ta⌐sete yokosimasu
   g. uti no mawari ni
   h. i⌐kasete itadakemase⌐ñ ka
   i. a⌐me ḡa ⌐hu⌐ru to
   j. ta⌐to⌐eba

Lesson 34. Personal History

BASIC DIALOGUES: FOR MEMORIZATION

(a)

(An applicant for a position has come for an interview)

Applicant

a personal history record	ri⌐reki⌐syo

1. I've brought my personal history record. — Ri⌐reki⌐syo (o) mo⌐tte mairima⌐sita.

Employer

2. I'll take a look at it. — Tyo⌐tto haikeñ-simasu.

birth or place of birth (name of city and prefecture near Tokyo)	umare or oumare ⸼ Ti⌐ba

3. Oh, you were born in Chiba (lit. your place of birth is Chiba)—right? — A⌐a, oumare (wa) ⌐Ti⌐ba desu ne?

Applicant

be born	umareru /-ru/
grow up	so⌐da⌐tu /-u/

4. Yes. Chiba is the place (lit. one) where I was born, but the place where I grew up is not Chiba. — Ha⌐a. U⌐mareta⌐ no wa ⌐Ti⌐ba desu ḡa, so⌐da⌐tta no wa ⌐Ti⌐ba zya a⌐rimase⌐ñ.

Employer

5. What do you mean by that? — To iu to?

Applicant

in reality or the fact is	zi⌐tu⌐ wa
both parents	ryo⌐osiñ or go⌐ryo⌐osiñ ⸼
substitute	kawari
instead of parents	ryo⌐osiñ no kawari ni
grandfather	so⌐hu or o⌐zi⌐isañ ⸼
grandmother	so⌐bo or o⌐ba⌐asañ ⸼
bring up or raise	so⌐date⌐ru /-ru/
be brought up	so⌐daterare⌐ru /-ru/
be brought up by one's grandmother	so⌐bo ni so⌐daterare⌐ru

6. The fact is that until I entered school, I was brought up by my grandmother instead of my parents. — Zi⌐tu⌐ wa, ga⌐kkoo e ha⌐iru made wa, ryo⌐osiñ no kawari ni ⌐so⌐bo ni so⌐daterarema⌐sita.

296

place of one's permanent residence	ho⌐ńseki⌐ti
live <u>or</u> reside	su⌐mu /-u/
be living in the country	i⌐naka ni su⌐nde (i)ru

7. Therefore I lived in the country, where our permanent residence place is.

De⌐su kara, ho⌐ńseki⌐ti no i⌐naka ni su⌐nde (i)masita.

Employer

8. Oh, of course.

A⌐a, naruhodo.

one's permanent residence	hoñseki
Saitama Prefecture	Sa⌐itama⌐-keñ
Konosu City	Ko⌐onosu⌐-si
Ningyo Cho	Ni⌐ñḡyo⌐o-tyoo
Lot No. 8	ha⌐ti-ba⌐ñti

9. Your permanent residence is (Lot) No. 1638, Ningyo Cho, Konosu City, Saitama Prefecture—right?

Hoñseki (wa) Sa⌐itama⌐-keñ, Ko-⌐onosu⌐-si, Ni⌐ñḡyo⌐o-tyoo, se⌐ñ roppyaku ⌐sa⌐ñ-zyuu ha⌐ti-ba⌐ñti desu ne?

Applicant

10. Yes, that's right.

Ha⌐i, so⌐o desu.

Employer

oh! <u>or</u> my word! <u>or</u> hold on!	oya?
elementary school	syo⌐oḡa⌐kkoo
middle school	tyu⌐uḡaku
Kansai (the Kyoto-Osaka area, western Honshu)	Ka⌐ñsai
Kanto (the Kanto plain, central Honshu)	Ka⌐ñtoo

11. Oh! But [you went to] elementary school [in] Kansai, middle school [in] Shikoku, and university [in] Tokyo— right?

Oya? Si⌐ka⌐si; syo⌐oḡa⌐kkoo wa ⌐Ka⌐ñsai, tyu⌐uḡaku wa Si⌐ko⌐ku, daiḡaku wa To⌐okyoo na⌐ñ desu ne?

Applicant

Japan Broadcasting Company (NHK)	Ni⌐hoñhoosookyo⌐okai
often	tabitabi
change one's post	teñkiñ-suru
be made to change one's post <u>or</u> be transferred	teñkiñ-saserareru /-ru/

12. Yes. That's because my father worked for NHK and was transferred often.

Ha⌐i. Ti⌐ti⌐ ḡa Ni⌐hoñhoosoo-kyo⌐okai ni tu⌐to⌐mete (i)te, ta-⌐bitabi teñkiñ-saserareta⌐ kara desu.

Employer

| 13. | I see. | Naruhodo. |

(b)

Smith

(Smith is asking Tanaka about his military experiences.)

	let me see <u>or</u> well now	eeto
	armed forces	gu⌐ñtai
	join the armed forces	gu⌐ñtai ni ⌐ha⌐iru
14.	Well now . . . Did you join the armed forces immediately upon leaving the university?	Eeto_ Da⌐iḡaku (o) de⌐ru to ⌐su⌐-ḡu, gu⌐ñtai ni ⌐ha⌐itta ñ desu ka⌐

Tanaka

	army	ri⌐ku⌐ḡuñ
	be taken	to⌐rare⌐ru /-ru/
15.	Yes. I was taken into the army right away.	E⌐e. Su⌐ḡu ri⌐ku⌐ḡuñ ni to⌐rare-ma⌐sita.

Smith

| | during the war | señzityuu |
| 16. | During the war what kind of work were you doing? | Señzityuu wa ⌐do⌐ñna siḡoto (o) si⌐te (i)ma⌐sita ka⌐ |

Tanaka

	soon after <u>or</u> in no time	ma⌐mo⌐naku
	war	señsoo
	summon <u>or</u> draft	syoosyuu-suru
	be drafted	syoosyuu-sareru /-ru/
17.	I came back from military [service] and in no time the war began, so I was drafted again right away.	Gu⌐ñtai kara ⌐ka⌐ette ma⌐mo⌐-naku se⌐ñsoo ḡa hazimatta⌐ no de, su⌐ḡu ma⌐ta syoosyuu-sare-ma⌐sita.
	be defeated <u>or</u> be beaten	makeru /-ru/
	the end of war	syuuseñ
	the war ends (lit. become the end of war)	syu⌐useñ ni na⌐ru
	be made to work	hatarakaserareru /-ru/
18.	I was made to work in the armed forces without inter-ruption until Japan was de-feated and the war ended.	Ni⌐hoñ ḡa mǎkete, syu⌐useñ ni na⌐ru made; zu⌐tto gu⌐ñtai de ha⌐tarakaserarema⌐sita.

Smith

| 19. | Oh. | A⌐a, so⌐o. |

Tanaka

| | unfortunate <u>or</u> unfortunately | ainiku |

Manchuria	Maⁿ̄syuu
Siberia	Siberiya
be taken (of living beings)	turete ikareru /-ru/
give back or send back or return [something]	ka⌐esu /-u/
be returned	ka⌐esare⌐ru /-ru/

20. Unfortunately I was in Man-
    churia so I was taken to
    Siberia, and I was finally
    returned [to Japan] in Showa
    28 [1953].

    Ainiku ⌐Maⁿ̄syuu ni iᵗta⁴ no de,
    Siberiya e turete ikarete; syoowa
    ⌐ni⌐zyuu ha⌐ti⌐-neñ ni ya⌐tto kaesa-
    rema⌐sita.

Smith

hardship or troubles or an ordeal	ku⌐roo or go⌐ku⌐roo †
restricted or uncom- fortable or incon- venient	hu⌐ziyuu /na/

21. What an ordeal! It must have
    been awfully uncomfortable,
    wasn't it?

    So⌐re wa goku⌐roo desita ᵗne⁴e.
    Zu⌐ibuñ ⌐hu⌐ziyuu datta desyoo?

Tanaka

indeed or really or honestly	mattaku
too awful to talk about (lit. is severe to the extent that it doesn't become talk)	ha⌐nasi⌐ ni na⌐ra⌐nai hodo hiᵗdo⁴i
life or existence	seekatu
family	ka⌐zoku or go⌐ka⌐zoku †
one's family at home	ku⌐ni no ka⌐zoku
be patient or put up with	ga⌐mañ-suru

22. Yes. Honestly, it was too
    awful a life to talk about,
    but I thought about my family
    at home, and managed to put
    up with it.

    E⌐e. Mattaku, ohanasi ni na-
    ⌐ra⌐nai hodo hiᵗdo⁴i se⌐ekatu de⁴-
    sita ḡa; ku⌐ni no ka⌐zoku no koᵗto⁴
    (o) kaᵗ ñḡa⁴ete, ya⌐tto ga⌐mañ-site
    (i)masita.

Smith

23. Really! How terrible that was!
    How about after you came back?

    Sore wa sore wa. Ta⌐iheñ de⌐-
    sita ᵗne⌐e. Ka⌐ette kara wa?

Tanaka

uh—	anoo
is ashamed or is shy	ha⌐zukasi⌐i /-ku/ or o⌐hazukasi⌐i ⁺ /-ku/
burn [something]	yaku /-u/
be unfavorably affected by burning	yakareru /-ru/

have one's home burn	uti o yakareru
have a shop	mi˧se˧ o yaru
live <u>or</u> make a living	seekatu-suru

24. Uh—the fact is that I'm
    ashamed [to say it], but be-
    cause our home was wiped
    out by fire and there was no
    suitable work, I lived by
    having my wife run a small
    shop.

    Anoo— Zi˧tu˥ wa, o˧hazukasi˥i
    ñ desu ḡa; u˧ti (o) yakarete si-
    matta˥ si, te˧kitoo na siḡoto mo
    na˥katta no de; ka˥nai ni ti˧isa˥i
    mi˧se˥ (o) yarasete se˧ekatu-
    sima˥sita.

Smith

25. I see.   Naruhodo.

(c)

(Jones is interviewing Ikeda for a position as translator and has
    just finished discussing his experience and qualifications.)

Jones

by the way <u>or</u> well now	to˧koro˥ de
translation	hoñyaku

26. Well now, we want a person
    here now who will do trans-
    lating for us (lit. a person
    from whom we'll receive the
    doing of translation).

    To˧koro˥ de ˧i˥ma ko˧tira de˥
    wa, ho˧ñyaku (o) site morau
    hito˥ ḡa ho˧si˥i ñ desu.

Ikeda

27. I see.   Ha˥a.

Jones

circumstances <u>or</u> case	baai
in hurrying circumstances	i˧so˥ḡu baai ni
<u>or</u> in cases where	
[someone] is in a hurry	
middle of the night	yo˧naka˥

28. In cases where we're in a
    hurry, there may be times
    when we have [people] work
    until the middle of the night.
    Even so, would it be all
    right?

    I˧so˥ḡu baai ni wa, yo˧naka˥
    made ha˧taraite morau koto˥
    ḡa ˧a˥ru ka mo si˧remase˥ñ
    ḡa; so˧re de˥ mo ka˧maimase˥ñ
    ka⌐

Ikeda

be made to do	saserareru /-ru/
complaint	huhee
complain	huhee o iu

29. Certainly. No matter what
    kind of work I'm made to do
    [and] when [I'm made to do
    it], I'll never complain.

    Ha˥a. Do˥ñna siḡoto (o) ˧i˥tu
    sa˧serarete˥ mo, ke˧site huhee
    wa moosimase˥ñ.

a hundred times as many (or much) or hundred-fold	hyaku-bai
a thousand times as many (or much) or thou-sandfold	señ-bai
is hard to bear	turai /-ku/
even a hundred times even a thousand times as hard	hyaku-bai mo señ-bai mo turai

30. [That's] because I used to do work a hundred times and a thousand times as hard.

Hyaku-bai mo se⌐ñ⌐-bai mo turai siḡoto (o) sita mono⌐ desu kara‿

Jones

compare	kuraberu /-ru/

31. If you compare it to that [I guess it's not so bad], is it.

So⌐re ni kurabere⌐ba ⌐ne⌐e.

within one hour	i⌐ti-zikañ-i⌐nai ni
translate	hoñyaku-suru
translate into Japanese	nihoñḡo ni hoñyaku-suru

32. Well then, please try trans-lating this into Japanese within one hour.

Zya⌐a, kore (o) i⌐ti-zikañ-i⌐nai ni ni⌐hoñḡo ni hoñyaku-site mi⌐te kudasai.

question	situmoñ

33. If you have any questions, please ask me.

Na⌐ni ka si⌐tumoñ (ḡa) a⌐ttara ki⌐ite kudasa⌐i.

Ikeda

34. All right. I don't have any-thing to inquire about es-pecially.

Ha⌐i. Betu ni u⌐kaḡau koto⌐ (wa) a⌐rimase⌐ñ.

Jones

35. Well then, please begin right away.

Zya⌐a, su⌐ḡu ha⌐zimete kudasa⌐i.

ADDITIONAL VOCABULARY

Supplementary Questions:

live or exist	i⌐ki⌐ru /-ru/

1. Are your parents living?

Go⌐ryo⌐osiñ (ḡa) ⌐i⌐kite (i)masu ka‿

die	sinu /-u/
die or pass on	nakunaru [1] /-u/

---

[1] Less abrupt word than sinu.

2. When did your father die?

    O⌐to˺osañ (wa) ⌐i˺tu na┣kunarima⌐˺-sita ka↲

      education or schooling
      undergo

    kyooiku
    u⌐ke˺ru /-ru/

3. What kind of schooling have you had?

    Do⌐ñna kyo┣oiku (o) ukema⌐˺sita ka↲

      graduate (verb)

    sotuḡyoo-suru

4. When did you graduate from college?

    I⌐˺tu da┣iḡaku (o) sotuḡyoo-sima⌐˺-sita ka↲

      experience

    keekeñ or gokeekeñ┊

5. Do you have experience?

    Go⌐keekeñ (ḡa) arima⌐˺su ka↲

      interpreting

    tu⌐uyaku

6. Is(n't) there someone here who can interpret?

    Tu⌐uyaku no de┣ki⌐ru hito (wa) i⌐mase˺ñ ka↲

7. Did you join the <u>navy</u>?

    <u>Ka⌐iḡuñ</u> ni ha┣irima⌐˺sita ka↲

      air force
      marines
      Self-Defense Forces

    kuuḡuñ
    rikuseñtai
    zieetai

8. Were you a <u>soldier</u>?

    <u>He⌐etai</u> de⌐˺sita ka↲

      navy sailor
      military officer

    su⌐ihee
    syo⌐okoo

Definitions:

1. Schooling which you are required to have is called "compulsory education."

    U⌐ke˺nakereba na┣ra⌐nai kyooiku wa gi⌐mukyo˺oiku to iu.

2. (The act of) boys (or men) and girls (or women) getting their education together is called "coeducation."

    O⌐toko˺ mo o┣ñna⌐ mo i⌐ssyo ni kyooiku o uke⌐ru koto wa da⌐ñ-zyokyo˺oḡaku to iu.

3. The dress (i.e. clothing) that military personnel wear is called a "(military) uniform."

    Gu⌐ñziñ no kiru huku˺ wa ḡuñ-puku to iu.

NOTES ON THE BASIC DIALOGUES

1. One's ri⌐reki˺syo is regularly presented in Japan when applying for a job. It is written according to a standard form, and includes one's name, present address and permanent address, and a record of education, professional experience, awards, and punishments.

4. So͏ᒣda͏ᒣtu is the intransitive partner of transitive so͏ᒣdate͏ᒣru (Sentence 6).

5. **To iu to**: The first **to** is the quotative and the second **to** is the particle of accompaniment. The phrase means literally 'with saying quote'—that is, 'when one says what has just been said, what does one mean?' The quotative applies to what immediately precedes—in this case, Basic Sentence 4: 'When you say "Chiba is the place . . . is not Chiba," what do you mean?'

6. Remember that o͏ᒣzi͏ᒣisañ and o͏ᒣba͏ᒣasañ are also used as polite words for 'old man' and 'old woman' respectively.

7. The verbal ᒣsu͏ᒣmu occurs most commonly in its gerund form su͏ᒣnde + √iru.

9. **Hoñseki** denotes the permanent address of a Japanese—often the residence of his or her parents and/or grandparents or her husband's family. It designates the place where a Japanese is formally registered. Addresses in Japanese, like dates, begin with the largest division that is mentioned and end with the smallest; the parts follow each other directly without intervening particles (but note the contrast between Mi͏ᒣnato͏ᒣ-ku, Si͏ᒣba 'Shiba, Minato Ward' and Mi͏ᒣnato͏ᒣ-ku no ᒣSi͏ᒣba 'Shiba in Minato Ward'). Cities are si͏ᒣ, but Tokyo is a special kind of city called to͏ᒣ (hence To͏ᒣkyo͏ᒣo-to but Yo͏ᒣkohama͏ᒣ-si). Some other divisions which occur frequently in addresses are gu͏ᒣñ 'county,' mu͏ᒣra͏ᒣ 'village,' ku͏ᒣ 'ward,' ma͏ᒣti͏ᒣ 'town' or 'machi' (part of a city, same as 'cho'), and, of course, tyoome͏ᒣ 'chome.' Most—but not necessarily all—parts of an address consist of compounds made up of a proper name plus the type of division. Thus: X-guñ 'X County,' X-mura 'X Village,' etc. Note, however, the following typical Tokyo address, which includes a proper name without a division suffix: To͏ᒣokyo͏ᒣo-to Mi͏ᒣnato͏ᒣ-ku Ázabu Ta̋keya-tyoo na͏ᒣna-ba͏ᒣnti 'No. 7, Takeya-cho, Azabu, Minato Ward, (City of) Tokyo.'

11. The Japanese pre-war and post-war education systems differ considerably. Roughly speaking, they compare as follows:

	Pre-war	Post-war
Syo͏ᒣoḡa͏ᒣkkoo	6 years	6 years
Tyu͏ᒣuḡaku	5 years	3 years
Kookoo	3 years	3 years
Daiḡaku	3 years	4 years

There were six years of compulsory education before the war, nine years after.
Kookoo is an abbreviated form of ko͏ᒣotooḡa͏ᒣkkoo.

12. 'Change one's post' as applied to military personnel is teñniñ-suru.

16. With señzityuu, compare señzeñ 'before the war' and señḡo 'after the war.'

17. A verbal gerund + ma͏ᒣmo͏ᒣnaku means 'soon after doing so-and-so,' 'after doing so-and-so, in no time —— .'

18. Note: X ni makeru 'be defeated in X.' The past maketa (lit. 'I have been beaten') often occurs as the equivalent of 'I give up!' or 'You win!'

The transitive partner of intransitive <u>makeru</u> is <u>makasu</u> /-u/ 'beat [someone]' (<u>X de makasu</u> 'beat [someone] at X'). The opposite of <u>makeru</u> is <u>ka⌐tu</u> /-u/ 'win' (<u>X ni ⌐ka⌐tu</u> 'win in X' or 'win over X').

20. <u>Ka⌐esu</u> is the transitive partner of intransitive <u>ka⌐eru</u> /-u/ 'go back.'

21. <u>Hu⌐ziyuu</u> is the opposite of <u>zi⌐yu⌐u</u> /<u>na</u>/ 'free' or 'unrestricted.'

24. <u>Yaku</u> is also the equivalent of 'bake,' 'roast,' 'toast.' <u>Yaku</u> is the transitive partner of intransitive <u>yakeru</u> /-<u>ru</u>/ 'be burned,' 'be baked,' 'be roasted,' 'be toasted.'

26. <u>To⌐koro⌐ de</u> usually introduces a shift in subject.

31. Note also: <u>X to kuraberu</u> 'compare with X.'

33. Note also: <u>situmoñ-suru</u> 'question' (verb) or 'ask questions.'

GRAMMATICAL NOTES

1. The Passive

So⌐daterare⌐ru		so⌐date⌐ru 'bring up.'
Ka⌐esare⌐ru		ka⌐esu 'give back.'
Yakareru	is the PASSIVE of	yaku 'burn.'
Umareru		umu 'give birth to.'
To⌐rare⌐ru		to⌐ru 'take.'
Sareru		suru 'do.'

Most verbals have corresponding PASSIVE verbals meaning basically 'be affected by such-and-such an action or state.'

An informal non-past passive is accented if the verbal from which it is derived is accented; the accent of the citation form occurs on the next-to-last syllable.

To form the passive:

-<u>ru</u> Verbals: Substitute -<u>rare-ru</u> for the final -<u>ru</u> of the informal non-past.

                Example: <u>mi⌐ru</u> 'see': <u>mi⌐rare⌐ru</u> 'be affected by [someone's] seeing'

-<u>u</u> Verbals: Substitute -<u>are-ru</u> for the final -<u>u</u> of the informal non-past. When the informal non-past ends in two vowels, substitute -<u>ware-ru</u> for the final -<u>u</u>.

                Examples: <u>to⌐ru</u> 'take': <u>to⌐rare⌐ru</u> 'be affected by [someone's] taking'
                         <u>iu</u> 'say': <u>iwareru</u> 'be affected by [someone's] saying'

-<u>aru</u> Verbals: Passive does not ordinarily occur.

Irregular Verbals: <u>ku⌐ru</u> 'come': <u>ko⌐rare⌐ru</u> 'be affected by [someone's] coming'
                     <u>suru</u> 'do': <u>sareru</u> 'be affected by [someone's] doing'

The passives of verbals belonging to the -ru group and of iku and ku⌐ru
are identical in form with the commonly occurring alternants of the corresponding potentials.

All passives are themselves verbals belonging to the -ru group. Thus,
the passive of to⌐ru has such forms as:

Informal non-past:	to⌐rare⌐ru
Stem:	to⌐ra⌐re
Informal past:	to⌐ra⌐reta
Gerund:	to⌐ra⌐rete
Conditional:	to⌐rare⌐tara
Provisional:	to⌐rare⌐reba

What we call a passive in English is not the same as a Japanese passive.
The basic meaning of a Japanese passive is 'someone is directly or indirect-
ly, often unfavorably, affected by the action of someone else.' In conversational Japanese, the subject of a passive—i.e. the one who is affected—is
almost invariably a person;[1] if expressed, it is followed by particle wa or
ḡa. The agent by whom the action is performed, if expressed, is followed
by particle ni. The direct object of a non-passive verbal occurs as the direct object (followed by particle o) of the corresponding passive. Study the
following pairs:

1. (a) O⌐kosima⌐sita. 'I woke [someone] up.'
   (b) O⌐kosarema⌐sita. 'I was awakened.' (Lit. 'I was [directly] af-
       fected—perhaps unfavorably—by [someone's] waking [me] up.')

2. (a) Ko⌐domo o okosima⌐sita. 'I woke the children up.'
   (b) Ko⌐domo o okosarema⌐sita. 'The children were awakened and I
       was annoyed.' (Lit. 'I was unfavorably affected by the waking of
       the children [by someone].')

3. (a) Zyo⌐tyuu ḡa kodomo o okosima⌐sita. 'The maid woke the chil-
       dren up.'
   (b) Zyotyuu ni ko⌐domo o okosarema⌐sita. 'The children were awak-
       ened by the maid and I was annoyed.' (Lit. 'I was unfavorably af-
       fected by the waking of the children by the maid.')

4. (a) Zyo⌐tyuu ḡa yamema⌐sita. 'The maid quit.'
   (b) Zyo⌐tyuu ni yamerarema⌐sita. 'The maid quit and I was annoyed.'
       (Lit. 'I was unfavorably affected by quitting by the maid.')

The subject of every passive form in the preceding examples is the speaker
('I'), and if it were expressed, it would be followed by wa or ḡa, depending
on emphasis.

It is important to note the following contrast between English and Japanese
passives: if an English passive is transformed to the corresponding active,
the subject of the passive becomes the object of the active:

   'I (subject) was awakened by my mother' = 'My mother woke me (object).'
   'My son (subject) was awakened by the maid' = 'The maid woke my
   son (object).'

---

[1] A few passives occur with inanimate subjects in conversation. Thus: Kore
wa ⌐na⌐ni ni tu⌐kawarete ima⌐su ka◡ 'What is this being used for?'

In Japanese this is usually not true: see examples under 2, 3, and 4 above.

Even intransitive verbals have passive equivalents. Compare:

U⌐ñte⌐ñsyu wa o⌐soku kima⌐sita. 'The driver came late.'
and:
U⌐ñte⌐ñsyu ni o⌐soku korarema⌐sita. 'The driver came late and I was
    annoyed.' (Lit. 'I was unfavorably affected by coming late on the
    part of the driver.')

Passives based on intransitive verbals, and on transitive verbals denoting
an action which is never done to people, regularly have the unfavorable shade
of meaning. Thus:

ka⌐erare⌐ru 'be unfavorably affected by someone's returning'
ikareru 'be unfavorably affected by someone's going'
ta⌐berare⌐ru 'be unfavorably affected by someone's eating'
no⌐mare⌐ru 'be unfavorably affected by someone's drinking'

However, a passive based on a verbal which denotes an action which can be
directed toward a person, may or may not have the unfavorable shade of
meaning, depending on the individual verbal and/or on context. Thus:

umareru 'be born'
sirareru 'come to be known'
yobareru 'be called' or 'be unfavorably affected by someone's calling'
kikareru 'be asked' or 'be unfavorably affected by someone's asking'
o⌐kosare⌐ru 'be awakened' or 'be unfavorably affected by the waking of
    someone'

In English, an unfavorable shade of meaning is sometimes denoted by the
use of the pattern 'have so-and-so done.' Compare the following three examples:

Tanaka-sañ ni de⌐ñwa o ka⌐kete mo⌐raima⌐sita.
    'I had Mr. Tanaka telephone.' (he did it for me)
Tanaka-sañ ni de⌐ñwa o kakesasema⌐sita.
    'I had Mr. Tanaka telephone.' (I caused him to do it)
Tanaka-sañ ni de⌐ñwa o kakerarema⌐sita.
    'I had Mr. Tanaka telephone.' (I didn't want him to call)

In the few cases where the doer of the action of a Japanese passive is inanimate, it is regularly followed by particle de. Thus:

de⌐ñwa de okosare⌐ru 'be awakened by the telephone'

A commonly occurring exception is:

a⌐me ni hu⌐rare⌐ru 'be rained on'

Remember that in the Japanese equivalent of a sentence like 'My watch
was taken by a child,' the subject is the person affected, the direct object is
the thing taken, and the agent is the person who did the taking. Thus:

(Watakusi wa) ko⌐domo ni to⌐kee o torarema⌐sita.

In the Japanese equivalent of a sentence like 'The windows were opened by
the maid,' no passive occurs unless an unfavorable reaction is implied.
Thus:

Zyotyuu ḡa ˹ma˺do o a˥kema˧sita. 'The maid opened the windows.' or
'The windows were opened by the maid.'

but:

Zyotyuu ni ˹ma˺do o a˥kerarema˧sita. 'The maid opened the windows
and I was annoyed' or 'The windows were opened by the maid—but
I didn't want them opened.'

In the Japanese equivalent of sentences like 'The windows are opened,'
which contain an English passive that describes a state of being resulting
from an action, rather than the action itself, a transitive gerund + a˺ru occurs (cf. Lesson 16, Grammatical Note 1). Thus:

Ma˺do ḡa a˥kete arima˧su. 'The windows are opened.' or 'The windows have been opened.'

Additional examples:

Ta˹noma˺reta ˥yo˧o ḡa ˥a˺ru kara, Ta˹naka-sañ no uti ni yorana˺kereba
na˥rimase˧ñ.
'There's a matter I've been asked to attend to so I must stop in at
Mr. Tanaka's house.'
Gaiziñ ni mi˹ti o kikarema˺sita ḡa, e˹eḡo de setumee-dekimase˺ñ de-
sita.
'I was asked the way by an American (i. e. Westerner) but I couldn't
explain in English.'
A˺sa ˹ha˺yaku de˹ñwa de okosa˺reta kara, ne˹mu˺i ñ desu.
'I'm tired because I was awakened early in the morning by the tele-
phone.'
Watakusi wa na˹ni mo iwana˺katta no ni, he˹ñ na ko˥to˧ o i˹tta yo˺o ni
o˥mowa˧rete; ko˹marima˺sita.
'I'm upset because [people] think I said something strange when I
didn't say anything at all.' (Lit. 'I have become upset, being affected by [someone's] thinking as if I said a strange thing in spite
of the fact that I said nothing.')
Kyo˺neñ u˹ti o yakarete˺ kara, a˹pa˺ato ni imasu.
'I've been in an apartment from the time my house burned last year
(lit. after being unfavorably affected by the burning of my house
last year).'
Se˹kkaku ka˺ita teḡami o ko˹domo ni yabukarema˺sita.
'The children tore up the letters I took such trouble to write.' (Lit.
'I was unfavorably affected by the tearing of the specially written
letters, by the children.')
Sa˺too-sañ wa ˹da˺re ka ni ku˹ruma o tora˺reta soo desu.
'I hear that Mr. Sato had his car taken by someone.'
Ha˹nami˺ ni i˹ku tumori da˺tta no ni, a˹me ni hu˥ra˧rete i˹karemase˺ñ
desita.
'Although I planned to go to see the cherry blossoms, I couldn't go
because it rained (lit. I was unfavorably affected by the falling of
rain).'

2. The Passive Causative

Hatarakaserareru ⎱
Saserareru   ⎰ is the PASSIVE CAUSATIVE of ⎰ hataraku 'work.'
                                                     ⎱ suru 'do.'

Most verbals have a causative equivalent (cf. Lesson 32, Grammatical
Note 1) and most causatives, in turn, have a passive equivalent, made (as
are all passives derived from verbals of the -ru group) by replacing the final -ru of the informal non-past with -rare-ru. The resulting verbal,
which ends in -(s)ase-rare-ru, is called the PASSIVE CAUSATIVE and
means 'be affected by someone's making [me] do so-and-so,' 'be made to
do so-and-so.' A passive causative based on an accented causative is also
accented; the accent of the citation form is on the next-to-last syllable.
Thus:

	Causative	Passive Causative
ta⌐be⌐ru 'eat'	ta⌐besase⌐ru 'cause to eat'	ta⌐besaserare⌐ru 'be made to eat'
no⌐mu 'drink'	no⌐mase⌐ru 'cause to drink'	no⌐maserare⌐ru 'be made to drink'
iu 'say'	iwaseru 'cause to say'	iwaserareru 'be made to say'
iku 'go'	ikaseru 'cause to go'	ikaserareru 'be made to go'
ku⌐ru 'come'	ko⌐sase⌐ru 'cause to come'	ko⌐saserare⌐ru 'be made to come'
suru 'do'	saseru 'cause to do'	saserareru 'be made to do'

Some speakers of Japanese also use a slightly abbreviated form of the
passive causative in which the -(s)aserareru ending is replaced by -(s)asa-
reru. Thus: ta⌐besasare⌐ru 'be made to eat,' no⌐masare⌐ru 'be made to
drink,' etc.

When expressed, the subject of a passive causative—that is, the nominal
denoting the person who is made to do something—is followed by particle wa
or ḡa, and the agent—the person who causes the action—is followed by particle ni. Thus:

(Watakusi wa) se⌐ṅse⌐e ni i˥waserarema˥sita.
'I was made to say [it] by the teacher.'

The meaning of a passive causative resembles, but is not identical with,
that of a -nakereba na⌐ra⌐nai pattern. Compare:

(a) Ka⌐imono ni ikana˥kereba na˥rimase˥ṅ desita. 'I had to go shop-
        ping.'

and:

(b) Ka⌐imono ni ikaserarema˥sita. 'I was made to go shopping.'

Sentence (a) states simply that it was necessary for me to go shopping; anything from a shortage of supplies to a direct order may have been the cause
of my going. Sentence (b), however, implies that some person(s) made me
go, even though they are not necessarily identified in the sentence.

Some situations may be described in terms of either a causative or a passive causative, with the personal nominals occurring as subject and before particle <u>ni</u> reversed. Thus:

Ta⌐roo wa ⌐Zi⌐roo ni sa⌐sema⌐sita. 'Taro made Jiro do it.'
Zi⌐roo wa ⌐Ta⌐roo ni sa⌐serarema⌐sita. 'Jiro was made to do it by Taro.'

However, when the person made to do something is the speaker, the passive causative is regularly used:

Ta⌐roo ni sa⌐serarema⌐sita. 'I was made to do it by Taro' or 'Taro made me do it.'

Additional examples:

Ya⌐kusoku no zikañ ni itta⌐ no ni, i⌐ti-zi⌐kañ mo ma⌐tasera⌐rete si-⌐maima⌐sita.
'In spite of the fact that I went at the appointed time, I ended up being made to wait all of an hour.'
I⌐soḡasera⌐reta no de, hoñ o mo⌐tte ku⌐ru no o wa⌐surema⌐sita.
'Because I was made to hurry, I forgot to bring my book.'
Tanaka-sañ wa ka⌐isya o yamesasera⌐reta soo desu.
'I hear that Mr. Tanaka was fired (lit. was made to quit the company).'
Nihoñḡo de ha⌐nasi⌐ o sa⌐serarema⌐sita.
'I was made to give a talk in Japanese.'
Yuube tōmodati ni ⌐bi⌐iru o ta⌐kusañ nomasera⌐reta no de, ma⌐da o⌐naka no guai ḡa he⌐ñ desu.
'I was made to drink lots of beer by a friend last night so my stomach still feels strange.'

3. -i⌐nai ~ -i⌐ḡai

-I⌐nai 'within' or 'up to' or 'not more than' occurs directly following a number — most commonly one denoting a period of time or an amount of money.

The opposite of -i⌐nai is -i⌐ḡai 'outside of,' 'except for.' It occurs following nominals in general.

Before -i⌐nai and -i⌐ḡai, a word which is normally accented loses its accent.

Examples:

I⌐s-syuukañ-i⌐nai ni Ni⌐hoñ e ⌐ta⌐tu tumori desu.
'I expect to leave for Japan within a week.'
Se⌐ñ-eñ-i⌐nai dattara, ka⌐tte⌐ mo ⌐i⌐i desu.
'If it should be not more than ¥ 1000, you may buy it.'
Zyu⌐u-niñ-i⌐nai no ⌐ka⌐iḡi ni wa, ko⌐no heya⌐ o tukaimasu.
'For conferences of up to ten people, we use this room.'
Mo⌐kuyoobi-i⌐ḡai nara, i⌐tu de⌐ mo u⌐ti ni ima⌐su.
'I'll be at home anytime, if it's not Thursday (lit. provided it's outside of Thursday).'
To⌐okyoo-i⌐ḡai ni wa i⌐kitaku arimase⌐ñ.
'I don't want to go outside of Tokyo.'

Ni⌐hoñgo-i⌐gai wa wa⌐karimase⌐ñ.
'I don't understand [any language] except Japanese.'

4. Counters: -bai and -bañti

-Bai is the counter for multiples, meaning 'so-and-so many times (as much or as many).' It combines with numerals of Series I, from 'two' on:

ni-bai	'2 times (as much or as many)'
sañ-bai	'3 times (as much or as many)'
yoñ-bai	'4 times (as much or as many)'
go-bai	'5 times (as much or as many)'
roku-bai	'6 times (as much or as many)'
nana-bai or siti-bai	'7 times (as much or as many)'
hati-bai	'8 times (as much or as many)'
kyuu-bai	'9 times (as much or as many)'
zyuu-bai	'10 times (as much or as many)'
nañ-bai	'how many times (as much or as many)?'

A nominal X + particle no + a number ending in -bai means 'so-and-so many times as much or as many as X.' Thus:

Zyuu wa ⌐ni⌐ no go-⌐bai de⌐su. '10 is 5 times 2.'
A⌐tarasi⌐i zi⌐biki⌐ wa i⌐ma ma⌐de tu⌐katta zibiki⌐ no sa⌐ñ-bai a⌐ru
  soo desu. 'I hear that the new dictionary has 3 times [as much as]
  the dictionary I've used until now.'

Bai occurs as an independent word meaning 'double,' in combinations like ba⌐i ni na⌐ru 'become double,' '[something] doubles' and ba⌐i ni su⌐ru 'double [something].'

-Bañti combines with numerals of Series I to name lot numbers. The numbers from one to ten are:

i⌐ti-ba⌐ñti	'lot number one'
ni-⌐ba⌐ñti	'lot number two'
sa⌐ñ-ba⌐ñti	'lot number three'
yo⌐ñ-ba⌐ñti	'lot number four'
go-⌐ba⌐ñti	'lot number five'
ro⌐ku-ba⌐ñti	'lot number six'
na⌐na-ba⌐ñti	'lot number seven'
ha⌐ti-ba⌐ñti	'lot number eight'
kyu⌐u-ba⌐ñti	'lot number nine'
zyu⌐u-ba⌐ñti	'lot number ten'
na⌐ñ-ba⌐ñti	'lot number what?'

DRILLS

A. Substitution Drill

1. [We] beat Tokyo University.   To⌐odai o makasima⌐sita.
2. [We] beat [them] at tennis.   Te⌐nisu de ma⌐kasima⌐sita.

3. Tokyo University beat [us]. To⌐odai g̈a makasima¬sita.
4. Tokyo University won. To⌐odai g̈a katima¬sita.
5. Tokyo University lost. To⌐odai g̈a makema¬sita.
6. [We] lost in war. Se⌐ñsoo ni makema¬sita.
7. [We] won in war. Se⌐ñsoo ni katima¬sita.
8. [We] won over Tokyo University. To⌐odai ni katima¬sita.

B. Substitution Drill

1. We want someone (lit. a person) who will do translating for us (lit. [from whom] we will receive translating). Ho⌐ñyaku (o) site morau hito¬ g̈a ho⌐si⁴i ñ desu.

2. We want someone who will repair the roof for us. Ya⌐ne (o) na⌐o⁴site mo⌐rau hito¬ g̈a ho⌐si⁴i ñ desu.

3. We want someone who will repaint the walls for us. Ka⌐be (o) nurika¬ete mo⌐rau hito¬ g̈a ho⌐si⁴i ñ desu.

4. We want someone who will explain this for us. Ko⌐re (o) setumee-site morau hito¬ g̈a ho⌐si⁴i ñ desu.

5. We want someone who will move the piano for us. Pi¬ano (o) ug̈oka¬site mo⌐rau hito¬ g̈a ho⌐si⁴i ñ desu.

6. We want someone who will clean the chimney for us. E⌐ñtotu (o) soozi-site morau hito¬ g̈a ho⌐si⁴i ñ desu.

7. We want someone who will weed the garden for us. Ni⌐wa no kusa¬ (o) ⌐to⁴tte mo⌐rau hito¬ g̈a ho⌐si⁴i ñ desu.

8. We want someone who will put up some shelves for us. Ta⌐na (o) tutte morau hito¬ g̈a ho⌐si⁴i ñ desu.

9. We want someone who will do interpreting for us. Tu¬uyaku (o) si⌐te morau hito¬ g̈a ho⌐si⁴i ñ desu.

C. Substitution Drill

1. Instead of fish I used meat. Sakana no kawari ni ni⌐ku¬ (o) tu⌐kaima¬sita.

2. Instead of screws I used nails. Ne¬zi no kawari ni ku⌐g̈i (o) tukaima¬sita.

3. Instead of milk I used water. Mi⌐ruku no kawari ni mi¬zu (o) tukaima¬sita.

4. Instead of kanji I used kana. Kañzi no kawari ni ka⌐na (o) tukaima¬sita.

5. Instead of gas I used electricity. Ga¬su no kawari ni ⌐de¬ñki (o) tu⌐kaima¬sita.

6. Instead of a heater I used a hibachi. Su⌐to⁴obu no kawari ni ⌐hi¬bati (o) tu⌐kaima¬sita.

7. Instead of gasoline I used oil. Gasoriñ no kawari ni ⌐o¬iru (o) tu⌐kaima¬sita.

8. Instead of a (dusting) cloth I used a cleaning rag.

Hu⌐ki¬ñ no kawari ni zo⌐okiñ (o) tukaima¬sita.

9. Instead of hot water I used cold water.

Oyu no kawari ni mi¬zu (o) tukaima¬sita.

10. Instead of chopsticks I used a fork.

O⌐ha¬si no kawari ni ⌐ho¬oku (o) tu⌐kaima⁴sita.

D. Substitution Drill

1. It was too awful a life to talk about.

Ha⌐nasi¬ ni na⌐ra¬nai hodo hi⌐do⁴i se⌐ekatu de⁴sita.

2. It was too tough a life to talk about.

Ha⌐nasi¬ ni na⌐ra¬nai hodo tu⌐rai seekatu de⁴sita.

3. It was too upsetting a life to talk about.

Ha⌐nasi¬ ni na⌐ra¬nai hodo ko⌐ma⁴-tta se⌐ekatu de⁴sita.

4. It was too restricted a life to talk about.

Ha⌐nasi¬ ni na⌐ra¬nai hodo ⌐hu⁴zi-yuu na se⌐ekatu de⁴sita.

5. It was too dangerous a life to talk about.

Ha⌐nasi¬ ni na⌐ra¬nai hodo a⌐bunai seekatu de⁴sita.

6. It was too boring a life to talk about.

Ha⌐nasi¬ ni na⌐ra¬nai hodo tu⌐mara⁴-nai se⌐ekatu de⁴sita.

7. It was too troublesome a life to talk about.

Ha⌐nasi¬ ni na⌐ra¬nai hodo ⌐ku⁴roo no o⌐o⁴i se⌐ekatu de⁴sita.

E. Substitution Drill

1. The place where I was born is Chiba but the place where I grew up is not (Chiba).

U⌐mareta¬ no wa ⌐Ti⁴ba desu ḡa, so⌐da¬tta no wa ⌐Ti⁴ba zya a⌐ri-mase⁴ñ.

2. The place where I worked is the country but the place where I lived is not (country).

Ha⌐taraita¬ no wa i⌐naka de⁴su ḡa, su⌐ñda no wa i⌐naka zya arima-se⁴ñ.

3. The one I read is English but the one I wrote is not (English).

Yo⌐nda no wa e⌐eḡo de⁴su ḡa, ka⌐ita no wa e⌐eḡo zya arimase⁴ñ.

4. The one I checked is mine but the one I took is not (mine).

A⌐zu¬keta no wa wa⌐takusi no⁴ de-su ḡa, mo⌐tte i⁴tta no wa wa⌐ta-kusi no⁴ zya a⌐rimase⁴ñ.

5. The one who asked the question is a student but the one who answered is not (a student).

Si⌐tumoñ-sita¬ no wa ga⌐kusee de⁴-su ḡa, he⌐ñzi¬-sita no wa ga⌐ku-see zya arimase⁴ñ.

6. The one who broke it is a child but the one who fixed it is not (a child).

Ko⌐wa¬sita no wa ko⌐domo de⁴su ḡa, na⌐o¬sita no wa ko⌐domo zya arimase⁴ñ.

7. The place where they made it is a factory but the place where they sold it is not (a factory).

Tu⌐ku¬tta no wa ko⌐oba⁴ desu ḡa, u⌐tta¬ no wa ko⌐oba⁴ zya a⌐rima-se⁴ñ.

F. Substitution Drill

1. This one is simple if you compare it to that one . . .

   Kore wa aꞋre ni kurabereꞋba kaꞋñtañ naꞋ ñ desu ḡa—

2. Kana is easy if you compare it to kanji . . .

   Kana wa kaꞋñzi ni kurabereꞋba yaꞋsasiꞋi ñ desu ḡa—

3. The post-war [period] is free if you compare it to pre-war . . .

   Señgo wa seꞋñzeñ ni kurabereꞋba ziꞋyuꞋu na ñ desu ḡa—

4. This kind of cloth wears well if you compare it to that kind of cloth . . .

   KoꞋñna kiꞋzi wa aꞋñna kiꞋzi ni kuꞋrabereꞋba zyoꞋobu naꞋ ñ desu ḡa—

5. Life in the country is hard if you compare it to life in the city . . .

   Inaka no seekatu wa maꞋti no seekatu ni kurabereꞋba tuꞋraꞋi ñ desu ḡa—

6. This house is big if you compare it to that house . . .

   Kono uti wa aꞋno uti ni kurabereꞋba hiꞋroꞋi ñ desu ḡa—

7. The Japanese are small if you compare them to the Americans . . .

   NiꞋhoñziꞋñ wa AꞋmerikaꞋziñ ni kuꞋrabereꞋba tiꞋisaꞋi ñ desu ḡa—

8. This book is easy to read if you compare it to the newspapers . . .

   KoꞋno hoꞋñ wa siꞋñbuñ ni kurabereꞋba yoꞋmiyasuꞋi ñ desu ḡa—

G. Substitution Drill

1. In case you're in a hurry, what do you do?

   IꞋsoꞋḡu baꞋai niꞌ wa ꞋdoꞋo simasu Ꞌka—

2. In case you want to ask a question, what do you do?

   SiꞋtumoñ-sitai baai niꞋ wa ꞋdoꞋo simasu ka—

3. In case you've been beaten, what do you do?

   MaꞋketa baai niꞋ wa ꞋdoꞋo simasu ka—

4. In case you haven't understood, what do you do?

   WaꞋkaraꞋnakatta baꞋai niꞌ wa ꞋdoꞋo simasu ka—

5. In case you can't translate, what do you do?

   HoꞋñyaku-dekiꞋnai baꞋai niꞌ wa ꞋdoꞋo simasu ka—

6. In case of typhoon, what do you do?

   TaꞋihuꞋu no baꞋai niꞌ wa ꞋdoꞋo simasu ka—

7. In case you want to go home early, what do you do?

   HaꞋyaku kaꞋeritaꞌi baꞋai niꞌ wa ꞋdoꞋo simasu ka—

8. In case you can't hear, what do you do?

   KiꞋkoenai baai niꞋ wa ꞋdoꞋo simasu ka—

9. In that case, what do you do?

   SoꞋno baai niꞋ wa ꞋdoꞋo simasu ka—

10. In case of rain, what do you do?

    AꞋme no baꞋai niꞌ wa ꞋdoꞋo simasu ka—

H. Substitution Drill (based on Grammatical Note 4)

   (Insert the appropriate numeral with counter -bai.)

1. Four is twice two. Si⌐ wa hi⌐ no ni-⌐bai de⌐su.
2. Three is three times one. Sañ wa i⌐ti⌐ no sa⌐ñ-bai de⌐su.
3. Twelve is six times two. Zyu⌐uni⌐ wa hi⌐ no ro⌐ku-bai de⌐-su.
4. Twenty is four times five. Ni⌐zyuu wa go⌐ no yo⌐ñ-bai de⌐su.
5. Sixteen is eight times two. Zyu⌐uroku⌐ wa hi⌐ no ha⌐ti-bai de⌐su.
6. Fifty is five times ten. Go⌐zyu⌐u wa zyu⌐u no go-⌐bai de⌐-su.
7. Thirty-five is seven times five. Sa⌐ñzyuu ⌐go⌐ wa go⌐ no na⌐na-bai de⌐su.
8. One hundred is ten times ten. Hya⌐ku⌐ wa zyu⌐u no zyu⌐u-bai de⌐-su.

I. Substitution Drill

1. I plan to leave for Kyoto within a week. I⌐s-syuukañ-i⌐nai ni ⌐Kyo⌐oto e ⌐ta⌐tu tumori desu.
2. I plan to leave for Kyoto next week. Raisyuu ⌐Kyo⌐oto e ⌐ta⌐tu tumori desu.
3. I plan to leave for Kyoto by Thursday. Mo⌐kuyo⌐o made ni ⌐Kyo⌐oto e ⌐ta⌐tu tumori desu.
4. I plan to leave for Kyoto about Saturday. Do⌐yoobi-ḡo⌐ro ⌐Kyo⌐oto e ⌐ta⌐tu tumori desu.
5. I plan to leave for Kyoto on the tenth. Tooka ni ⌐Kyo⌐oto e ⌐ta⌐tu tumori desu.
6. I plan to leave for Kyoto before this month is over. Ko⌐ñgetu-zyuu ni ⌐Kyo⌐oto e ⌐ta⌐tu tumori desu.
7. I plan to leave for Kyoto during the morning. Asa no uti ni ⌐Kyo⌐oto e ⌐ta⌐tu tumori desu.
8. I plan to leave for Kyoto a little before four. Yo⌐-zi ⌐tyo⌐tto ⌐ma⌐e ni ⌐Kyo⌐oto e ⌐ta⌐tu tumori desu.
9. I plan to leave for Kyoto at 7:30. Si⌐ti-zi-ha⌐ñ ni ⌐Kyo⌐oto e ⌐ta⌐tu tumori desu.
10. I plan to leave for Kyoto at sharp nine. Tyo⌐odo ku⌐-zi ni ⌐Kyo⌐oto e ⌐ta⌐tu tumori desu.

J. Level Drill [1]

1. Ri⌐reki⌐syo (o) mo⌐tte mairima⌐sita. Ri⌐reki⌐syo (o) mo⌐tte kima⌐sita.
2. Ke⌐site huhee wa moosi-mase⌐ñ. Ke⌐site huhee wa iimase⌐ñ.

---

[1] In each case, the sentence on the right is a plain formal equivalent of the polite formal sentence on the left.

3. Ha⌐isyaku-site⌐ mo yo⌐ro-   Ka⌐rite⌐ mo ⌐i⌐i desu ka⌣
   si⌐i desu ka⌣
4. Ya⌐suma⌐sete i⌐tadakema-   Ya⌐suma⌐sete mo⌐raemase⌐ñ ka⌣
   se⌐ñ ka⌣
5. To o⌐ssya⌐ru to?   To iu to?
6. Do⌐tira de o⌐sodati ni   Do⌐ko de so⌐datima⌐sita ka⌣
   narima⌐sita ka⌣
7. Ni⌐hoñḡo ni hoñyaku-   Ni⌐hoñḡo ni hoñyaku-sima⌐sita
   nasaima⌐sita ka⌣   ka⌣

K. Expansion Drill

1. [She] was born.   U⌐marema⌐sita.
   [She] was born in Tokyo.   To⌐okyoo de umarema⌐sita.
   [She] was born in Tokyo   Syoowa ⌐zyu⌐ugo-neñ ni To⌐okyoo
   in Showa 15.   de umarema⌐sita.
   Mrs. Tanaka was born   Ta⌐naka-sañ no o⌐kusañ wa syŏ-
   in Tokyo in Showa 15.   owa ⌐zyu⌐ugo-neñ ni To⌐okyoo
                                     de umarema⌐sita.

2. Would you translate [it]   Ho⌐ñyaku-site kudasaimase⌐ñ ka⌣
   for me?
   Would you translate [it]   E⌐eḡo ni hoñyaku-site kudasai-
   into English for me?   mase⌐ñ ka⌣
   Would you translate this   Kono kookoku (o) e⌐eḡo ni hoñ-
   advertisement into   yaku-site kudasaimase⌐ñ ka⌣
   English for me?
   Would you translate this   Kono ni⌐hoñḡo no kookoku (o)
   Japanese advertisement   e⌐eḡo ni hoñyaku-site kudasai-
   into English for me?   mase⌐ñ ka⌣

3. [It] was defeated.   Ma⌐kema⌐sita.
   [It] was defeated in war.   Se⌐ñsoo ni makema⌐sita.
   [It] was defeated in war   Syoowa ni⌐zyu⌐u-neñ ni se⌐ñsoo
   in Showa 20.   ni makema⌐sita.
   Germany was defeated   Do⌐itu (wa) syŏowa ni⌐zyu⌐u-neñ
   in war in Showa 20.   ni se⌐ñsoo ni makema⌐sita.

4. Somebody broke some-   Ko⌐wasarema⌐sita.
   thing and I was annoyed.
   I had three plates broken.   Sara (o) ⌐sa⌐ñ-mai ko⌐wasarema⌐-
                                     sita.
   I had three plates broken   A⌐tarasi⌐i zyotyuu ni sǎra (o)
   by the new maid.   ⌐sa⌐ñ-mai ko⌐wasarema⌐sita.
   I had three plates broken   I⌐ti-zikañ-i⌐nai ni a⌐tarasi⌐i zyo-
   by the new maid within   tyuu ni sǎra (o) ⌐sa⌐ñ-mai ko-
   an hour.   ⌐wasarema⌐sita.

5. I used to be made to work.   Ha⌐tarakaserareta mon(o)⌐ desu.
   I used to be made to work   Hatake de ha⌐tarakaserareta
   in the fields.   mon(o)⌐ desu.

I used to be made to work   A⌐sa kara ba⌐n̄ ma⌐de hǎtake de
in the fields from morn-   ha⌐tarakaserareta mon(o)⌐ desu.
ing till night.

My father used to make   Ti⌐ti⌐ ni ⌐a⌐sa kara ba⌐n̄ ma⌐de
me work in the fields   hǎtake de ha⌐tarakaserareta
from morning till   mon(o)⌐ desu.
night.

L. Grammar Drill (based on Grammatical Note 1)

        Tutor: Da⌐re ka si⌐ma⌐sita. 'Somebody did it.'
        Student: Da⌐re ka ni sa⌐rema⌐sita. 'I was [unfavorably] affected
                 by someone's doing it.' or 'I had someone do it.'

    1. Tomodati ḡa o⌐soku kima⌐-   Tomodati ni o⌐soku korarema⌐-
       sita.   sita.
    2. Hi⌐syo⌐ ḡa ya⌐mema⌐sita.   Hi⌐syo⌐ ni ya⌐merarema⌐sita.
    3. Kodomo ḡa to⌐kee (o)   Kodomo ni to⌐kee (o) torarema⌐-
       torima⌐sita.   sita.
    4. Zyotyuu ḡa o⌐ka⌐si (o)   Zyotyuu ni o⌐ka⌐si (o) ta⌐berare-
       ta⌐bema⌐sita.   ma⌐sita.
    5. Da⌐re ka ⌐ma⌐do (o) a⌐ke-   Da⌐re ka ni ⌐ma⌐do (o) a⌐kerare-
       ma⌐sita.   ma⌐sita.
    6. Ta⌐roo-tyañ ḡa to ⌐(o) si-   Ta⌐roo-tyañ ni to ⌐(o) simerare-
       mema⌐sita.   ma⌐sita.
    7. Ga⌐kusee ḡa kikima⌐sita.   Ga⌐kusee ni kikarema⌐sita.
    8. O⌐ba ḡa sodatema⌐sita.   O⌐ba ni sodaterarema⌐sita.
    9. A⌐katyañ ḡa o⌐kosima⌐sita.   A⌐katyañ ni o⌐kosarema⌐sita.
   10. Se⌐n̄se⌐e ḡa ko⌐re (o) yo-   Se⌐n̄se⌐e ni ko⌐re (o) yomarema⌐-
       mima⌐sita.   sita.

M. Grammar Drill (based on Grammatical Note 2)

        Tutor: Si⌐ma⌐sita. /da⌐re ka/ 'I did it. /someone/'

        Student: Da⌐re ka ni | sa⌐serareta | mon(o)⌐ desu.[1] 'Someone used
                             | sa⌐sareta |
                 to make me do it.'

    1. Ya⌐sai (o) tabema⌐sita.   Ha⌐ha ni ya⌐sai (o) | tabesasera⌐reta |
       /ha⌐ha/ | tabesasa⌐reta |
                                     mo⌐n(o)⌐ desu.

    2. Hu⌐de de kakima⌐sita.   Se⌐n̄se⌐e ni hu⌐de de | kakasera⌐reta |
       /se⌐n̄se⌐e/ | kakasa⌐reta |
                                     mo⌐n(o)⌐ desu.

    3. Pa⌐ñku-sita taiya (o) to-   Ti⌐ti⌐ ni pa⌐ñku-sita taiya (o)
       rikaema⌐sita. /ti⌐ti⌐/ | torikaesasareta | mon(o)⌐ desu.
                                     | torikaesasareta |

    4. E⌐ḡo de hanasima⌐sita.   Oba ni e⌐ḡo de | hanasasera⌐reta |
       /oba/ | hanasasa⌐reta |
                                     mo⌐n(o)⌐ desu.

---

[1] Give the long and short forms for each.

5. Mi⌐ruku (o) no⌐mima⌐sita. Ryo⌐osiñ ni ⌐mi⌐ruku (o)
   /ryo⌐osiñ/   │ no⌐masera⌐reta │ mo⌐n(o)⌐ desu.
                             │ no⌐masa⌐reta   │

6. Pi⌐ano no reñsyuu (o)   Ha⌐ha ni pi⌐ano no reñsyuu (o)
   sima⌐sita. /ha⌐ha/   │ saserareta │ mon(o)⌐ desu.
                             │ sasareta   │

7. Yo⌐ku ha⌐tarakima⌐sita.   So⌐hu ni ⌐yo⌐ku │ ha⌐tarakaserareta │
   /so⌐hu/   │ ha⌐tarakasareta   │
                             mon(o)⌐ desu.

8. Ga⌐kkoo ni aru⌐ite i⌐ki-   Ti⌐ti⌐ ni ga⌐kkoo ni aru⌐ite
   ma⌐sita. /ti⌐ti⌐/   │ i⌐kaserareta │ mon(o)⌐ desu.
                             │ i⌐kasareta   │

9. Ma⌐initi ko⌐ko e kima⌐-   Se⌐ñse⌐e ni ⌐ma⌐initi ko⌐ko e
   sita. /se⌐ñse⌐e/   │ kosasera⌐reta │ mo⌐n(o)⌐ desu.
                             │ kosasa⌐reta   │

10. Ma⌐iasa ma⌐tima⌐sita.   Tomodati ni ⌐ma⌐iasa
    /tomodati/   │ ma⌐tasera⌐reta │ mo⌐n(o)⌐ desu.
                             │ ma⌐tasa⌐reta   │

For each sentence of the above exercise, give the corresponding sentence meaning 'I had to ———' with no reference to any person as the cause.

Example:
Tutor: Ha⌐ha ni ya⌐sai (o) tabesasera⌐reta mo⌐no(o)⌐ desu.
Student: Ya⌐sai (o) tabe⌐nakereba na⌐rimase⌐ñ desita.

N. Substitution Drill (based on Grammatical Note 2)

1. No matter what kind of   Do⌐ñna siḡoto (o) sa⌐serarete⌐ mo,
   work I'm made to do,   ke⌐site huhee wa iimase⌐ñ.
   I'll never complain.

2. No matter when I'm made   I⌐tu ha⌐tarakaserarete⌐ mo, ke-
   to work, I'll never com-   ⌐site huhee wa iimase⌐ñ.
   plain.

3. No matter where I'm   Do⌐ko e i⌐kaserarete⌐ mo, ke⌐site
   made to go, I'll never   huhee wa iimase⌐ñ.
   complain.

4. No matter what time I'm   Na⌐ñ-zi ni ko⌐sasera⌐rete mo,
   made to come, I'll never   ke⌐site huhee wa iimase⌐ñ.
   complain.

5. No matter what town I'm   Do⌐no ma⌐ti⌐ ni te⌐ñkiñ-sasera-
   transferred to, I'll never   rete⌐ mo, ke⌐site huhee wa iima-
   complain.   se⌐ñ.

6. No matter what kind of   Do⌐ñna tu⌐rai seekatu (o) sasera-
   tough life I'm made to   rete⌐ mo, ke⌐site huhee wa iima-
   live, I'll never com-   se⌐ñ.
   plain.

7. No matter what I'm made
to eat, I'll never com-
plain.

Na⌉ni (o) ta⌐besasera⌐rete mo,
ke⌐site huhee wa iimase⌉ñ.

8. No matter what kind of
medicine I'm made to
take, I'll never complain.

Do⌉ñna kusuri (o) no⌐masera⌐rete
mo, ke⌐site huhee wa iimase⌉ñ.

Do the above drill, with the tutor reading each of the sentences on
the right and the student repeating, substituting the short form of
the passive causative.
Example:
    Tutor: Do⌉ñna siḡoto (o) sa⌐serarete⌐ mo, ke⌐site huhee wa
              iimase⌉ñ.
    Student: Do⌉ñna siḡoto (o) sa⌐sarete⌐ mo, ke⌐site huhee wa
              iimase⌉ñ.

O. Substitution Drill

1. I came back and in no
time war began.

Ka⌉ette ma⌐mo⌉naku se⌐ñsoo ḡa
hazimarima⌉sita.

2. I came back and in no
time I began this.

Ka⌉ette ma⌐mo⌉naku ko⌉re (o)
hazimema⌉sita.

3. I came back and in no
time I joined the army.

Ka⌉ette ma⌐mo⌉naku ⌐gu⌉ñtai ni
ha⌐irima⌐sita.

4. I came back and in no
time I was taken into
the army.

Ka⌉ette ma⌐mo⌉naku ri⌐ku⌉ḡuñ
ni to⌐rarema⌐sita.

5. I came back and in no
time I was drafted.

Ka⌉ette ma⌐mo⌉naku syo⌉osyuu-
sarema⌉sita.

6. I came back and in no
time I quit.

Ka⌉ette ma⌐mo⌉naku ya⌐mema⌉-
sita.

7. I came back and in no
time he quit on me.

Ka⌉ette ma⌐mo⌉naku a⌐no⌉ hito ni
ya⌐merarema⌉sita.

8. I came back and in no
time I fired him.

Ka⌉ette ma⌐mo⌉naku a⌐no⌉ hito (o)
ya⌐mesasema⌉sita.

9. I came back and in no
time I was fired by him.

Ka⌉ette ma⌐mo⌉naku a⌐no⌉ hito ni
ya⌐mesaserarema⌉sita.

10. I came back and in no
time I was transferred.

Ka⌉ette ma⌐mo⌉naku te⌐ñkiñ-
saserarema⌉sita.

SUPPLEMENTARY DIALOGUES

1. Tanaka: Ta⌐bako ika⌉ḡa desu ka⌐
   Yamamoto: Se⌐kkaku⌉ desu ḡa, sake to tabako o to⌐merarete iru⌉ ñ de-
           su yo⌐
   Tanaka: Gobyooki de?
   Yamamoto: E⌉e. I⌐k-kaḡetu-ḡu⌉rai ⌐ma⌐e made ti⌐ti⌉ no mu⌐ra⌐ de ya-
           ⌐su⌐ñde i⌐ta⌐ ñ desu yo⌐
   Tanaka: So⌉o desu ka. I⌐kemase⌉ñ desita ⌐ne⌉e. Si⌐rimase⌉ñ desita ka-
     ra, si⌐tu⌉ree-simasita.

Yamamoto: Iie, do⌉o itasimasite. Kono-ḡoro wa ze⌈n̄zen̄ gu⌈a⌉i no waru⌉i to⊢koro⊣ wa ⌈na⌉i n̄ desu ḡa, ma⌉da su⌈ki⌉ na sake to tabako wa no⌈ma⌉sete mo⊢raena⊣i n̄ de ⌈ne⌉e.

Tanaka: Sore wa sore wa. Ma⌉a, byo⌉oki ni⌉ wa ka⌈temase⌉n̄ kara, mo⌉o suko⌉si ⊢ga⊣man̄-suru n̄ desu ⌈ne⌉e.

2. Tanaka: Do⌉o desu ka⌣—a⊢na⊣ta no ben̄kyoo wa.

Smith: Mo⌉o i⌈ya⌉ ni ⊢na⊣tte si⊢maima⊣sita yo.

Tanaka: Do⌉o site desu ka.

Smith: Ma⌉initi ⌈ma⌉initi ⌈a⌉sa kara ba⌈n̄ ma⌉de ni⌈hon̄ḡo o kakasera⌉retari, ha⌈nasasera⌉retari, ki⌈kasera⌉retari su⊢ru⊣ n̄ desu kara_

Tanaka: De⌉ mo, so⌉o sure⌉ba ⌈ha⌉yaku o⌈boerare⌉ru desyoo?

Smith: So⌈re wa so⌉o desu ḡa_

3. Tanaka: Ho⌈n̄yaku-sina⌉kereba na⊢ra⊣nai teḡami ḡa ⊢a⊣ru n̄ desu ḡa, o⌈siete kudasaimase⌉n̄ ka⌣

Smith: E⌈ḡo ni hon̄yaku-suru⌉ n̄ nara, o⌈te⌉tudai-sima⌉su yo⌣

Tanaka: Hi⌈to⌉ri de si⊢ta⊣ra; go-bai mo zyu⌉u-bai mo zikan̄ ḡa kaka⌉tte, yo⌈naka⌉ ni ⊢na⊣tte mo de⌈ki⌉nai ka mo si⊢remase⊣n̄ kara_

Smith: Zya, su⌉ḡu ha⊢zimemasyo⊣o.

Tanaka: Zya⌉a, su⌈mimase⌉n̄ ḡa, o⌈neḡai-sima⌉su.

4. Yamamoto: Tanaka-san̄. O⌈kosan̄ ḡa oumare ni na⌉tta soo de, o⌈medetoo gozaima⌉su.

Tanaka: A⌈ri⌉ḡatoo gozaimasu.

Yamamoto: Do⌉tira de irassyaimasu ka⌣

Tanaka: Mu⌈suko de gozaima⌉su.

Yamamoto: So⌈re wa i⌉i desu ⌈ne⌉e.

5. Mr. Smith: O⌈tokoro o itte kudasa⌉i. Bo⌉ku ḡa ka⊢kima⊣su kara. A. Ainiku ka⌈mi⌉ ḡa i⌈ti-mai mo na⌉kute_

Mr. Tanaka: Bo⌉ku arima⌉su. Do⌉ozo. To⌈okyo⌉o-to, Mi⌈nato⌉-ku, Azabu, Ho⌈n̄mura⌉-tyoo, sa⌈n̄-ba⌉n̄ti desu yo⌣

Mr. Smith: Mo⌉o suko⌉si yu⌈kku⌉ri i⊢tte kudasaimase⊣n̄ ka. Ka⌈kika⌉ta o⌈so⌉i kara_

6. Smith: Tanaka-san̄ wa ⌈ma⌉da go⌈byooki de⌉su ka⌣

Yamamoto: E⌉e. Mo⌉o ro⌈k-ka⌉getu ne⊢te ima⊣su yo⌣ Uti de ⌈na⌉ni ka hon̄yaku no siḡoto o site, so⌈re de seekatu-site iru so⌉o desu ḡa_

Smith: Go⌈ka⌉zoku wa?

Yamamoto: Ohanasi ni na⌈ra⌉nai hodo tu⌈rai so⌉o desu yo. Okane wa ta⌈rina⌉i si, byo⌉oki no koto⌉ o si⌈n̄pai-site iru⌉ si_

7. Smith: I⌉ma ⌈su⌉n̄de iru tokoro ho⌈n̄seki⌉ti desu ka⌣

Mr. Tanaka: Iie iie. Ho⌈n̄seki wa inaka no ho⌉o de, su⌉n̄da koto wa a⌈rimase⌉n̄.

Smith: To iu to?

Mr. Tanaka: Bo⌉ku ḡa u⊢mareru ma⊣e ni ti⌈ti⌉ ḡa To⌉okyoo e ten̄kin̄-saserarete, bo⌉ku wa zu⌈tto Tookyoo de sodatima⌉sita. So⌉hu ya ⊢so⊣bo wa ⌈ma⌉da inaka ni ite, so⌈tira ḡa ma⌉da ho⊢n̄seki na⊣ n̄ desu.

Smith: Naruhodo.

8. Conductor (announcing): Ma˺mo˺naku Yo˹kohama de gozaima˺su. O˹ori
ni na˺ru ka˥ta˥ wa o˺sitaku neḡaima˺su.
Male Passenger: Ni˺motu ḡa o˹o˺i ñ da ḡa, a˹kaboo wa iru daro˺o ne?
Conductor: Ha˺a. Ho˺omu[3] ni o˥rima˥su kara, go˹siñpai na˺ku.

9. Smith: A˺na˺ta wa ḡo˺zibuñ no o˹ka˺asañ ni tuite ha˥na˥su toki, na˺ñ te
yo˥bu˥ ñ desu ka⌐
Mr. Tanaka: Ba˹ai ni yotte tiḡau˺ ñ desu ḡa; tyu˹uḡaku no tomodati to
ha˥na˥su ba˥ai ni˥ wa o˹hukuro˺[1] tte itte, ka˺zoku to ha˥na˥su
ba˥ai ni˥ wa o˹ka˺asañ te itte, se˹ñse˺e nado ni ˹te˺enee[2] ni ha-
˥nasa˥nakereba na˥ra˥nai ba˥ai ni˥ wa ˹ha˥ha tte i˥u˥ ñ desu.
Smith: Naruhodo. O˹ka˺asañ ni wa a˹na˺ta tte i˥u˥ ñ desu ka⌐
Mr. Tanaka: Iie. Ti˹ti˺ ya ˥ha˥ha o a˹na˺ta tte yo˥bu koto˥ wa a˹rima-
se˹ñ. Taitee o˹to˺osañ o˹ka˺asañ te yo˥bu˥ ñ desu.

10. Smith: Se˹ñse˺e ni ri˹reki˺syo o mo˥tte ku˥ru yoo ni i˥wareta˥ ñ desu
ḡa, ri˹reki˺syo tte i˥u˥ no wa ˹do˺ñna mo˥no˥ desu ka⌐
Mr. Tanaka: Sore wa ˹ne˺e. So˺no hito no u˺mareta tokoro˺ ya u˺mareta
hi, sore kara ˹de˺ta gakkoo ya ˹do˺ñna siḡoto o si˥ta˥ ka to i˥u
yo˥o na koto o ˥ka˥ita mo˥no˥ na ñ desu.
Smith: Zya˺a, i˺ma ma˺de no ke˹ekeñ o ka˺keba ˥i˥i ñ desu ne?
Mr. Tanaka: Ma˺a ˥so˥o desu ḡa; da˹itai no kakika˺ta ḡa wa˥kara˥nai to
o˹komari desyo˺o kara, bo˺ku no o o˺mise-simasyo˺o ka.
Smith: Yo˹rosi˺kereba, ha˹ikeñ-sasete kudasa˺i.

English Equivalents

1. Tanaka: How about a cigarette?
Yamamoto: It's kind of you to ask but I'm not allowed to drink or smoke
(lit. I am affected by the stopping of sake and cigarettes).
Tanaka: Because you're ill?
Yamamoto: Yes. Until about a month ago I was away from work (lit.
resting), in my father's village.
Tanaka: Really. That was too bad. I didn't know so excuse my rudeness.
Yamamoto: That's all right. There's nothing wrong with me (lit. there
are no places at all where the condition is bad) these days but
they won't let me drink or smoke yet—things I love to do (lit. I
cannot yet receive their letting me take in sake and cigarettes
which I love). . .
Tanaka: Oh dear. I guess you should be patient a little longer since
you can't have the upper hand when it comes to sickness (lit.
over sickness you can't win). . .

2. Tanaka: How goes it—your studying?
Smith: I'm fed up with it already.
Tanaka: Why?

---

[1] Familiar way of referring to one's mother, comparable to English 'the old lady.' Used by young men.

[2] Te˺enee /na/ 'polite.'

[3] Ho˺omu 'platform.'

Smith: Because day after day, day after day, from morning until night, I'm made to write Japanese and speak it and listen to it.

Tanaka: But if you do that, you'll be able to learn it quickly, won't you?

Smith: That's true but . . .

3.   Tanaka: I have a letter that I must translate. Would you show me how?

Smith: If it's a matter of translating into English, I'll help you.

Tanaka: If I do it alone, it will take me five and ten times as much time, and even if I keep on until the middle of the night (lit. even if it becomes the middle of the night), I may not be able to finish it (so . . .)

Smith: Well, let's begin right away.

Tanaka: (Well) I'm sorry [to bother you] but would you [help me]?

4.   Yamamoto: Mr[s]. Tanaka! I hear that your baby has been born. Congratulations.

Tanaka: Thank you.

Yamamoto: Is it a boy or a girl? (Lit. Which is it?)

Tanaka: It's a boy.

Yamamoto: Isn't that nice!

5.   Mr. Smith: Please tell me your address. (Because) I'll write it down. Oh. Unfortunately I don't have a single sheet of paper . . .

Mr. Tanaka: I have. Here you are. It's No. 3, Hommura Cho, Azabu, Minato Ward, Tokyo (City).

Mr. Smith: Would you say it a little more slowly? (Because) I write slowly (lit. my way of writing is slow).

6.   Smith: Is Mr. Tanaka still sick?

Yamamoto: Yes. He's been in bed six months now. He is doing some translation work at home and is making his living with that, they say, but . . .

Smith: What about his family?

Yamamoto: I hear that they are having too difficult a time to talk about. They don't have enough money and they are worrying about his illness and . . .

7.   Smith: Is the place where you are living now your permanent residence (place)?

Mr. Tanaka: No no. My permanent residence is in the country and I've never lived there.

Smith: What do you mean by that?

Mr. Tanaka: My father was transferred to Tokyo before I was born and I grew up (all the time) in Tokyo. My grandfather and grandmother are still in the country and that is still our permanent residence.

Smith: I see.

8.   Conductor: Next stop Yokohama. (Lit. In no time it will be Yokohama.) All passengers getting off, please get ready. (Lit. I request preparation [from] persons who will get off.)

Male Passenger: I have a lot of luggage. I suppose there will be porters, won't there?

Conductor: Yes. They'll be on the platform so don't worry.

9. Smith: When you speak about your own mother, what is it you call her?
    Tanaka: It's different depending on circumstances. In cases where I'm
            speaking with friends from middle school, I say "ofukuro," and
            in cases where I'm speaking with the family, I say "okāsan,"
            and in cases where I must speak politely, to people like teach-
            ers, I say "haha."
    Smith: I see. [When speaking] to your mother do you say "anata"?
    Tanaka: No. There's never a time when I address my mother and fa-
            ther as "anata." I usually address them as "otōsan," "okāsan."

10. Smith: I was told by the teacher to bring my personal history; (but) what
            sort of thing is a personal history?
    Mr. Tanaka: Oh, that. It's a thing [that has] written [on it] things like
            the place where the person was born and the day when he was
            born, and then the schools he graduated (lit. went out) from and
            what kind of work he's done.
    Smith: Then as long as I write my experience up to now it will be all
            right, won't it?
    Mr. Tanaka: That's about it, but you'll probably have difficulty if you
            don't understand the general way of writing it, so shall I show
            you mine?
    Smith: If it's all right, please let me see it.

EXERCISES

1. Interview an applicant for a job. Check on his name, present address,
    permanent residence, educational background, military service, and
    experience. Tell him you will get in touch with him by next Monday.

2. Make up twelve short conversations, each one of which contains one of
    the following phrases:

     a. huhee o iu
     b. i⌐s-syuukañ-i¬nai ni
     c. wa⌐kara¬nai ba⌐ai ni⌐ wa
     d. o⌐hazukasi¬i ñ desu ḡa
     e. to⌐koro¬ de
     f. ma⌐mo¬naku
     g. ha⌐nasi¬ ni na⌐ra¬nai hodo turai
     h. —— no kawari ni
     i. ainiku
     j. uti o yakareru
     k. To⌐okyoo-i¬ḡai
     l. saserareru

Lesson 35. Among Friends

BASIC DIALOGUES: FOR MEMORIZATION

(a)

(Matsumoto and Tanaka are young men who are close friends.)

Tanaka

game or match	siai
do you go? or are you gonna go?	iku kai⌐

1. Matsumoto. Are you gonna go and see the game tomorrow? — Matumoto-kuñ. Asita no siai ⌐mi⌐ ni iku kai⌐

Matsumoto

2. Did you say (it's) a game? — Siai da tte?

baseball	yakyuu

3. You mean baseball, don't you? — Yakyuu daro?

Tanaka

4. Yeah. — N̄.

Matsumoto

it's tiresome, don't you agree?	tu⌐ma⌐ññai zya nai ka

5. Aren't you bored stiff by things like baseball? — Ya⌐kyuu na⌐ñka tu⌐ma⌐ññai zya nai ka.

generally speaking, on the whole, as a rule	oyoso
interest	kyo⌐omi⌐ [1]
have an interest	kyo⌐omi⌐ ḡa ⌐a⌐ru

6. As a rule, they don't appeal to me! — Oyoso | kyo⌐omi na⌐i ⌐ne⌐e.

Tanaka

oh, dear! or good heavens!	ma⌐a
don't say (imperative)	i⌐u⌐ na

7. Oh, don't say that! — Ma⌐a, so⌐o iu⌐ na yo.

seems to be good or is likely to be good	i⌐i rasi⌐i /-ku/

8. The one [i.e. game] tomorrow is likely to be good. — A⌐sita no⌐ (wa) i⌐i rasi⌐i yo⌐

---

[1] Alternate accent: kyo⌐omi.

323

once in a while <u>or</u>	tama ni
now and then	
associate with	tuᒥkiaᒣu /-u/
associate with (imperative)	tuᒥkiaᒣe

9. Keep me company once in a
    while.

Taᒥma niᒣ wa tuᒥkiaᒣe yo.

Matsumoto

10. What time does it begin?
    (Lit. From what time is it?)

Naᒣñ-zi kara dai.

Tanaka

11. Wasn't it (from) about one?

Iᒥti-zi-ḡoᒣro kara zya ᒥnaᒣkatta
ka na?

Matsumoto

12. I'm already booked up for
    tomorrow—to go swimming.

Aᒥsitaᒣ wa ᒥmoᒣo yaᒥkusoku-sityа-
ttaᒣ ñ da yo—oᒥyoᒣḡi ni iku tte.

swim (imperative)

oᒥyoᒣḡe

13. You come (lit. go) along and
    swim!

Kimi mo issyo ni itte, oᒥyoᒣḡe
yo.

sports	suᒥpoᒣotu
as for not being a sport	suᒥpoᒣotu de ᒥnaᒣkutyaa
it's no fun, don't you	oᒥmosiᒣroku ᒥnaᒣi zya nai ka
agree?	

14. When it's not a sport you take
    part in (lit. do) yourself,
    don't you agree it's no fun?

Ziᒥbuñ de yaru supoᒣotu de ᒥnaᒣ-
kutyaa, oᒥmosiᒣroku ᒥnaᒣi zya nai
ka.

Tanaka

15. I wonder what I should do!

Doᒣo siyoo ka ᒥnaᒣa_

after all

yaᒥhaᒣri <u>or</u> yaᒥppaᒣri

16. I'm going to make it baseball
    (lit. the baseball alternative)
    after all.

Boku (wa) yaᒥppaᒣri yaᒥkyuu no
hoᒣo ni suᒥruᒣ yo.

(b)

Wife

stoppage of electricity	teedeñ

17. Oh! The electricity is off!

Aᒥra, teedeñ yo⌐

Husband

18. Again?

Maᒥtaᒣ kai⌐

Wife

always <u>or</u> at all hours	syoᒣttyuu
<u>or</u> constant(ly)	
because it is constant	syoᒣttyuu desu mono

19. I hate it because it keeps happening.

Syo˙ttyuu desu mono, i⌐ya⌐a ⌐ne⌐e.

Husband

almost
it's every night, don't you agree?

ho⌐to⌐ndo
ma⌐ibañ zya⌐ nai ka

20. It's almost every night— isn't it.

Ho⌐to⌐ndo ma⌐ibañ zya⌐ nai ka.

Wife

I wonder if it will become attached

tu⌐ku⌐ ka sira

21. I wonder if it will go on soon.

Su͡gu tu⌐ku⌐ ka sira.

Husband

don't understand or can't tell

wa⌐ka⌐rya sinai

22. I can't tell.

Wa⌐ka⌐rya si⌐na⌐i sa.

is dark
candle

kurai /-ku/
ro⌐osoku⌐

23. In any case, it's dark so let's light a candle.

To⌐nikaku ku⌐ra⌐i kara, ro⌐osoku⌐ tu⌐keyo⌐o.

Wife

household altar (Shinto)
household altar (Buddhist)
kamidana or butsudan

kamidana
butudañ
kamidana ka butudañ

24. I think there's a big (lit. thick) candle (placed) in the kamidana or the butsudan.

Kamidana ka butudañ ni hu⌐to⌐i roosoku o⌐ite a⌐ru to o⌐mo⌐u no yo⌐

Husband

is it left?

no⌐ko⌐tte ru kai⌐

25. Is that still left?

Are ⌐ma⌐da no⌐ko⌐tte ru kai⌐

Wife

probably
one-third
about as much as one-third

ta⌐buñ
sa⌐ñ-buñ no iti⌐
sa⌐ñ-buñ no iti⌐ hodo

26. Yes. Probably there should be about a third [of it] left.

E⌐e. Ta⌐buñ sa⌐ñ-buñ no iti⌐ hodo no⌐ko⌐tte ru hazu yo⌐

Husband

go or come or be (imperative)
go and get (lit. come having taken) (imperative)

oide

tott(e) oide

27. (Then) would you go and get it?

Zya⌐a, tott(e) oide⌐

Wife (bringing candle)

accept or receive	tyoodai-suru ⁺
let me have (imperative)	tyoˈodaˈi
attach for me (imperative)	tuˈkeˈte tyoodai

28. Light it, would you?   Tuˈkeˈte tyoodai ne?

(c)

(Mrs. Yamamoto has just run into her good friend, Mrs. Ikeda.)

Mrs. Yamamoto

neglect to write or visit	gobusata-suru ⁺
excuse me	goˈmeñ-nasaˈi

29. Forgive me for not getting in   Gobusata-sityatte goˈmeñ-nasaˈi
touch with you.   ne?

Mrs. Ikeda

nothing but neglect	goˈbusata baˈkari
to write or visit	

30. I'm the one who keeps neglect-   Koˈtira koˈso goˈbusata baˈkari
ing to get in touch with you.   site—

Mrs. Yamamoto

while thinking or	oˈmoinaˈḡara
although thinking	
unintentionally or	tuˈi
carelessly	

31. While I kept thinking of tele-   Oˈdeˈñwa siˈyoˈo siˈyoˈo to oˈmoinaˈ-
phoning (lit. while thinking,   ḡara ˈtuˈi—
'I'll make a call, I'll make
[it]'), I unintentionally [let
it slip my mind].

make a business trip	syuttyoo-suru
exam or test	siˈkeˈñ
entrance exam	nyuˈuḡakusikeˈñ

32. My husband was away on   Syuˈziñ ḡa syuˈttyoo-sitaˈri, ko-
business, and there were   ˈdomo no nyuuḡakusikeˈñ ḡa ˈaˈtta-
my child's entrance exams,   ri site ˈneˈe.
and so on—you know . . .

Mrs. Ikeda

33. How did your son do?   Boˈttyañ ˈdoˈo nasutte?

Mrs. Yamamoto

thanks to you or	okaḡe de
thanks for asking	
parent	oˈyaˈ
grow thin	yaseru /-ru/

34. He was finally able to get   Okaḡe de, yaˈtto hairemaˈsita
into [school], thank you, but   kedo; siñpai-site, oˈyaˈ mo ko
parents and child wasted away   mo yaˈsetyaimaˈsita wa⌣
worrying!

Mrs. Ikeda

35. Wasn't it nice that he was
able to get in!

O⌐hairi ni na⌐rete, yo⌐katta wa
⌐ne⌐e.

have a good head <u>or</u>
be smart <u>or</u> be bright

a⌐tama⌐ ḡa ⌐i⌐⌐i

36. [It's] because your son is
bright.

Bo⌐ttyañ (wa) a⌐tama⌐ ḡa ⌐i⌐⌐i kara_

Mrs. Yamamoto

37. Oh, heavens no!

Ma⌐a, to⌐ñde mo na⌐i.

Mrs. Ikeda

a relief

hi⌐toa⌐ñsiñ [1]

38. You must be relieved [that the
got in]. (Lit. With this, a
relief, isn't it.)

Ko⌐re de hitoa⌐ñsiñ ⌐ne⌐e.

high school
with each passing year
<u>or</u> each year
competition <u>or</u> contest

kookoo
i⌐ti-neñ-ḡo⌐to ni

kyoosoo

39. Isn't it awful how the competition for both high school and
university gets [more] severe
each year.

Kookoo mo da⌐iḡaku mo i⌐ti-neñ-
ḡo⌐to ni kyo⌐osoo ḡa hi⌐doku
⌐na⌐tte, ko⌐ma⌐ru wa ⌐ne⌐e.

Mrs. Yamamoto

unless [someone] leaves
<u>or</u> graduates
find employment <u>or</u> get
a job
because it's a matter of
not being able to find
a job

de⌐nakeryaa

syuusyoku-suru

syu⌐usyoku-deki⌐nai ñ
desu mono

40. [It's] because you can't get a
job in a good place unless you
graduate from a good school,
isn't it . . .

I⌐i gakkoo (o) ⌐de⌐nakeryaa, i⌐i
toko e syu⌐usyoku-deki⌐nai ñ
desu mono ⌐ne⌐e.

Mrs. Ikeda

with this being the trend
(lit. as for being this
kind of manner)
pathetic <u>or</u> pitiful

ko⌐ñna hu⌐u de wa <u>or</u>
ko⌐ñna hu⌐u zya

ka⌐waiso⌐o /na/

41. But with this being the trend,
it's hard on the children (lit.
the children are pitiful),
isn't it.

De⌐ mo; ko⌐ñna hu⌐u zya, kodomo ḡa ka⌐waiso⌐o da wa ⌐ne⌐e.

---

[1] Alternate accent: hi⌐to⌐añsiñ.

Mrs. Yamamoto

be that as it may <u>or</u>   so⌐re wa so⌐o to
  to change the subject
42. To change the subject, your   So⌐re wa so⌐o to, o⌐taku no a⌐ka-
     baby must be (lit. have be-   tyañ ⌐mo⌐o ⌐zu⌐ibuñ ⌐o⌐okiku onari
     come) big by now, isn't he?   desyoo?

Mrs. Ikeda

something <u>or</u> anything   na⌐ñ ka
  act as if wanting to say   i⌐itaso⌐o ni suru
43. Yes. He has begun to eat   E⌐e. Mo⌐o ⌐gohañ (o) ta⌐behazi-
     (food) already, and he often   meta⌐ si, yo⌐ku ⌐na⌐ñ ka i⌐itaso⌐o
     acts as if he wants to say   ni su⌐ru⌐ no yo⌐
     something.

a word   hitokoto
44. But as far as language goes,   De⌐ mo, ko⌐toba⌐ wa ⌐ma⌐da hi-
     he doesn't say a single word   ⌐tokoto mo hanasa⌐nai kedo⌐
     yet. . .

Mrs. Yamamoto

birthday   ta⌐ñzyo⌐obi <u>or</u> o⌐tañzyo⌐-
                                          obi ⌐
45. Is his birthday soon now?   O⌐tañzyo⌐obi mo⌐o su⌐gu na no?

Mrs. Ikeda

46. No, not yet (not yet).   Iie, ma⌐da ⌐ma⌐da.

because he's nine months   ku-⌐ka⌐ḡetu desu mono
47. (Because) he's nine months   I⌐ma ku-⌐ka⌐ḡetu desu mono.
     old now.

Mrs. Yamamoto

in that case   so⌐re de⌐ wa <u>or</u> so⌐re
                                          zya⌐a
unreasonable <u>or</u> beyond   mu⌐ri /na/
  one's power
48. In that case, you can't expect   So⌐re zya⌐a, ohanasi wa ⌐ma⌐da
     him to talk yet (lit. talk is   ⌐mu⌐ri ⌐ne⌐e.
     still unreasonable), can
     you. . .

rapidly   do⌐ñdoñ
pleasure <u>or</u> enjoyment   ta⌐nosi⌐mi [1] or otanosimi ⌐
49. Babies grow up rapidly so   A⌐katyañ wa ⌐do⌐ñdoñ ⌐o⌐okiku
     they're fun [to watch], aren't   o⌐nari da⌐ kara, otanosimi ⌐ne⌐e.
     they.

go to someone else's home   aḡaru /-u/ ⌐
go to see   haikeñ ni aḡaru ⌐

─────────────
[1] Or ta⌐nosimi⌐.

50. I'll come (lit. go) to see him   Iti-do ha⌐ikeñ ni aḡaru⌐ wa ne?
    some (lit. one) time — all
    right?

Mrs. Ikeda

51. Yes. Come, by all means.   E⌐e. Ze⌐hi i⌐ra⌐site.

ADDITIONAL VOCABULARY

1. There was an <u>earthquake</u> this   Ke⌐sa zi⌐siñ ḡa arima⌐sita yo⌐
   morning.

   fire   ka⌐zi
   accident   zi⌐ko

2. Help!   Ta⌐suke⌐te.

3. It's set at about <u>5 per cent</u>.   Go⌐-bu hodo ni ⌐na⌐tte (i)masu.

   10 per cent   i⌐ti⌐-wari
   15 per cent   i⌐ti-wari go⌐-bu

4. That baby <u>cries</u> a lot, doesn't A⌐no a⌐katyañ (wa) ⌐yo⌐ku <u>na̱ku</u>
   he?   desyoo?

   laugh   warau /-u/

5. What a <u>frightening</u> expression! <u>Ko⌐wa⌐i</u> ka⌐o de⌐su ⌐ne⌐e.
   <u>or</u> What an angry look!

   is dreadful <u>or</u> terrible   su⌐go⌐i /-ku/
   <u>or</u> terrific <u>or</u> extraordinary
   is lonesome <u>or</u> cheer-   sa⌐bisi⌐i /-ku/
   less
   is happy   u⌐resi⌐i /-ku/

NOTES ON THE BASIC DIALOGUES

3. The loan-word <u>be⌐esubo⌐oru</u> is another word for 'baseball.'

9. Note: <u>hi⌐to to tukia⌐u</u> 'associate with a person.' The derivative nominal
   <u>tukiai</u> means 'association' or 'acquaintance.'

11. Note the use of the past. Compare English: 'Didn't I hear that it started
    at one?'

12. <u>Sityatta</u> is the contracted equivalent of <u>site simatta</u>. <u>Tte</u> is the quota-
    tive: lit. 'I've already made a promise for tomorrow — quote to go swim-
    ming.'

13. <u>Kimi</u> is an informal man's word used in reference to one's equals or in-
    feriors. It is also used as an informal term of address.

Note all the following less formal equivalents of watakusi and a⌐na⌐ta:

'I':   watasi (men and women)
       bo⌐ku   (men only)
       atasi   (women only)
       wasi   (older men only)
       ore   (rough word; men only)

'you': a⌐nta   (men and women)
       omae   (used more commonly by men, in addressing inferi-
               ors, particularly children)

14. Na⌐kutya/a/ is the contracted equivalent of na⌐kute wa. The combina-
    tion e + consonant + a (in the same word or consecutive words) is
    regularly contracted to ya/a/ in contracted speech. When such a con-
    traction yields the combination d + ya, it is regularly spelled zya in
    this text. Thus:

        sore wa   > sorya/a/
        —eba [1]   > —a/a/
        —kereba [1] > —kerya/a/ (cf. Sentence 40, below)
        de⌐ wa   > zya⌐/a/

    The zya which occurs in the negative equivalent of a nominal + da com-
    bination (for example, ho⌐n zya ⌐na⌐i 'it isn't a book') is also a contrac-
    tion of de + wa. The wa is sometimes omitted, leaving de alone: so⌐o
    de ⌐na⌐kereba 'unless it's so'; su⌐po⌐otu de ⌐na⌐kute wa 'as for not being
    a sport.'

15. In men's speech, na⌐a occurs as an alternant of ne⌐e, and na as an al-
    ternant of ne, particularly in deliberative questions addressed to one-
    self.

16. Ya⌐ppa⌐ri is an informal, more emphatic alternant of ya⌐ha⌐ri.

19. I⌐ya⌐a is an alternant of i⌐ya⌐.

23. The opposite of kurai is akarui /-ku/ 'is light.'

26. Following a number, hodo regularly means 'about (as much as).'

29. Gobusata-sityau is the contracted equivalent of gobusata-site simau.

32. Note: si⌐ke⌐n-suru 'test' 'put [something] to a test' and si⌐ke⌐n o u⌐ke⌐-
    ru /-ru/ 'undergo a test,' 'take a test.'

33. The use of a sentence-final gerund with question intonation as a substi-
    tute for a past-tense form is typical of women's informal speech. Na-
    ⌐su⌐tte is an alternant of na⌐sa⌐tte, gerund of na⌐sa⌐ru [1].

34. Okage de is a less polite equivalent of okagesama de.
    The opposite of yaseru is hu⌐to⌐ru /-u/ 'grow fat.' Note: ya⌐seta hi-
    to⌐ 'thin person'; hu⌐to⌐tta hito 'fat person.'
    Ya⌐setyaima⌐sita is the contracted equivalent of ya⌐sete simaima⌐sita.

37. As an expression of pleasure, ma⌐a is typical of women's speech. In its
    various other uses (for example, Sentence 7 above), it occurs in the
    speech of both men and women.

---
[1] Ending of the provisional.

39. Note: kyoosoo-suru 'compete.'

40. See note on Sentence 14 above. The -kerya/a/ ending may be further contracted to -kya/a/. Thus, na῾kereba has as its contracted equivalents na῾kerya/a/ and na῾kya/a/.

43. Nañ ka is a contraction of na῾ni ka and is used by men and women. I῾itaso῾o is made up of the stem of iitai 'want to speak,' and -soo 'looking as if —— .'

48. Note: mu῾ri ni saseru 'force [someone] to do.'

49. Note also the verbal ta῾nosi῾mu /-u/ 'take pleasure in,' 'enjoy' and the adjectival ta῾nosi῾i 'is merry or pleasant or enjoyable.'

50. Do not confuse plain aḡaru 'go up' with humble polite aḡaru↑ 'go to someone else's home.'

Additional Vocabulary

2. Ta῾suke῾ru /-ru/ is a transitive verbal meaning 'save' or 'rescue' or 'help.' Its intransitive partner is ta῾suka῾ru /-u/ 'be saved' or 'be helped' or 'survive.'

3. The counter for units of per cent is -bu and for tens of per cent is -wari. Both counters take numerals of Series I. Examples:

i῾ti῾-bu	'1%'	i῾ti῾-wari	'10%'
ni῾-bu	'2%'	ni῾-wari	'20%'
sañ-bu	'3%'	sañ-wari	'30%'
yoñ-bu	'4%'	yoñ-wari	'40%'
go῾-bu	'5%'	go῾-wari	'50%'
ro῾ku῾-bu	'6%'	ro῾ku῾-wari	'60%'
nana῾-bu or		nana῾-wari or	
si῾ti῾-bu	'7%'	si῾ti῾-wari	'70%'
ha῾ti῾-bu	'8%'	ha῾ti῾-wari	'80%'
ku῾-bu	'9%'	ku῾-wari	'90%'
		zyu῾u-wari [1]	'100%'

nañ-bu 'how many per cent?'   nañ-wari 'how many tens of per cent?'

Percentages equaling ten or more, which are not multiples of ten, are regularly expressed in terms of -wari and -bu. Thus, '38 per cent' is sa῾ñ-wari hati῾-bu.

4. Naku is a verbal of the -u group.

5. Ko῾wa῾i is an adjectival.

GRAMMATICAL NOTES

1. ra῾si῾i

X ra῾si῾i means 'is apparently or evidently X,' 'is typical of X.' X may be:

---

[1] Rare.

(1) a sentence consisting of (or ending with) a non-past or past informal verbal or adjectival
(2) a sentence ending with da⌉tta
(3) a nominal, with or without preceding modifiers
(4) a sequence ending with a particle

Ra⌐si⌉i is itself an adjectival, but unlike other adjectivals, it never occurs
at the beginning of a phrase. The word or phrase that immediately precedes
ra⌐si⌉i regularly loses its accent.

Ra⌐si⌉i resembles -soo and yo⌉o, but there are specific differences:

(1) Grammar

    (a) -Soo is a suffix which enters into compounds with verbal and ad-
jectival stems and a few nominals. -Soo compounds are themselves na nominals.

    (b) Ra⌐si⌉i is an adjectival (ra⌉siku, ra⌉sikute, ra⌉sikatta, etc.). For
what precedes it, see above.

    (c) Yo⌉o is a na nominal. It is preceded by a demonstrative (kono,
sono, etc.), a phrase ending in particle no, or a sentence modifier (cf. Lesson 24, Grammatical Note 1).

(2) Meaning

    (a) -Soo words usually refer to physical appearance, whereas ra⌐si⌉i
and yo⌉o patterns rely on any kind of evidence.

    (b) For a comparison of -soo and yo⌉o, see Lesson 26, Grammatical
Note 5.
Yo⌉o refers to similarity or likeness, whereas ra⌐si⌉i indicates
apparent equivalence. Ko⌐domo no yo⌉o, for example, can refer
only to someone who is childlike BUT NOT A CHILD, whereas
ko⌐domo rasi⌉i refers ONLY TO A CHILD who is 'just like a
child.' Similarly, a male can be o⌐ñna no yo⌉o 'like a woman,'
but only a female can be o⌐ñna rasi⌉i 'ladylike'; summer, fall,
and winter can be ha⌉ru no ⌐yo⌉o, but only spring can be ha⌉ru
rasi⌉i.

Examples:

De⌐pa⌉ato ni wa, na⌐ñ de mo aru rasi⌉i desu ⌐ne⌉e.
    'Apparently there is everything in department stores, isn't there.'
Kinoo no siai wa ma⌐ketyatta rasi⌉i ⌐ne⌉e.
    'Apparently they lost yesterday's game, didn't they.'
A⌐no zibiki⌉ wa nākanaka i⌐i rasi⌉i.
    'That dictionary is apparently quite good.'
Ta⌐kakatta rasi⌉i kedo, ka⌐tta so⌉o desu ⌐ne⌉e.
    'They say he bought it, although apparently it was expensive.'
Amerika no he⌐etai rasi⌉i hi⌐to⌉ ḡa ki⌐ma⌉sita yo‿
    'Someone who is evidently an American soldier is here (lit. has
    come).'
A⌐merika⌉ziñ desu ḡa, A⌐merikaziñ ra⌉siku a⌐rimase⌉ñ ⌐ne⌉e.
    'He's an American but he doesn't seem like one (lit. like an Amer-
    ican).'
Kono teḡami wa A⌐merika kara rasi⌉i desu ⌐ne⌉e.
    'This letter is apparently from America.'

2. ──── zya nai ka

X + zya nai[1] ka means 'X is true, isn't it'; 'surely you agree that X is true, don't you'; 'you see, don't you, that X is true!'; 'I <u>knew</u> that X was true!' X, in this construction, is usually a non-past or past verbal or adjectival, the past copula da⌐tta, a nominal, or a sequence ending with a particle.

Be sure to distinguish among the following kinds of sentences:

(a) O⌐mosi⌐roku ⌐na⌐i? 'Isn't it interesting?' or 'It's not interesting?'
(b) O⌐mosiro⌐i zya nai ka. 'It <u>is</u> interesting, isn't it.' or 'Surely you agree it's interesting, don't you.'
(c) O⌐mosi⌐roku ⌐na⌐i zya nai ka. 'It <u>isn't</u> interesting, is it.' or 'Surely you agree it isn't interesting, don't you.'

In general, ──── zya nai ka in sentence-final position occurs in men's speech. Women use ──── zya nai no as an equivalent. Both men and women also use more polite and more formal equivalents (──── zya arimaseñ ka and ──── de⌐ wa gozaimaseñ ka).

Examples:

Gu⌐ai ḡa waru⌐i soo da ḡa, yo⌐ku ta⌐berare⌐ru zya nai ka.
'I hear you don't feel well, but you can eat well, can't you!'
Bo⌐ku ḡa itta to⌐ori, Kyo⌐ziñ[2] ḡa katta zya⌐ nai ka.
'Just as I told you, the Giants <u>did win</u>, didn't they.'
So⌐ñna ni isoḡa⌐nakute mo ⌐i⌐i zya nai ka.
'Surely you don't have to hurry so much, do you.'
Ha⌐ya⌐i ⌐ne⌐e. Sa⌐ñzyu⌐p-puñ sika ka⌐kara⌐nai zya nai ka.
'It's early, isn't it. It <u>does</u> take only 30 minutes, doesn't it.'
Tanaka-sañ wa tu⌐mara⌐nai tte i⌐tta⌐ keredo, na⌐kanaka omosiro⌐i ⌐ho⌐ñ zya nai ka.
'Mr. Tanaka said it was dull, but surely you agree that it <u>is</u> an interesting book, don't you.'
Sa⌐ñ-zi kara da tte i⌐tta⌐ keredo, ni⌐-zi kara zya nai ka.
'He said it started at (lit. was from) three but it <u>does</u> start at two, doesn't it.'

3. Honorific and Humble Nominals

A nominal consisting of polite prefix <u>o-</u> + a verbal stem is an HONORIFIC NOMINAL. (Examples: <u>omati</u> from <u>ma⌐tu</u> 'wait,' <u>oake</u> from <u>akeru</u> 'open,' etc.) An honorific nominal is unaccented.

Honorific nominals occur:

(1) + ni √⌐na⌐ru (Lesson 9, Grammatical Note 2)
(2) + √da (Lesson 23, Grammatical Note 2)
(3) + √-suru (Lesson 13, Grammatical Note 4)
(4) + -kudasa⌐i(ma⌐se) (Lesson 18, Grammatical Note 3)
(5) In sentence-final position as a request (Lesson 18, Grammatical Note 3).

---

[1] Regularly unaccented in this construction. The accent pattern of X + zya nai ka is parallel to that of X + ka mo sirenai.

[2] Kyoziñ 'giant.'

Some honorific nominals are irregular. For example, goran̄ (occurring in patterns 1, 4, 5 above) is the honorific nominal for the verbal mi⌐ru, and oide (occurring in patterns 1, 2, 4, and 5) is the honorific nominal for verbals ku⌐ru 'come,' iku 'go,' and iru 'be.'

Note also the nominal gomen̄ 'your pardon,' which occurs in patterns 2, 4, and 5, although it is not directly linked with any particular verbal.

Contrasting with the above honorific nominals is a small group of HUMBLE NOMINALS which occur in patterns 3 and 5 above, and refer politely (i. e. humbly) to the actions of the speaker:

> tyo⌐oda⌐i: tyoodai-suru (humble equivalent of morau 'receive,' 'accept,' 'eat,' 'drink'; usage resembles that of itadaku)
> Tyo⌐oda⌐i. 'Let me have [it].'
> haiken̄: haiken̄-suru (humble equivalent of mi⌐ru 'see')
> Haiken̄. 'Let me see [it].'
> haisyaku: haisyaku-suru (humble equivalent of kariru 'borrow'; usage resembles that of okari-suru)
> Haisyaku. 'Let me borrow [it].'

4. Informal Imperatives

A. Affirmative

The affirmative informal imperative of a verbal consists of:

(1) -ru Group: the citation form with final -u changed to -o [2]
                    (but note ku⌐re⌐ 'give me!' from kureru).

                    Example: ta⌐be⌐ru 'eat': ta⌐be⌐ro 'eat!'

(2) -u Group: the citation form with final -u changed to -e [2]

                    Example: ma⌐tu 'wait': ma⌐te 'wait!'

(3) -aru Group: the stem alone

                    Example: na⌐sa⌐ru 'do': na⌐sa⌐i 'do!'

(4) Irregular Group: suru 'do': si⌐ro⌐ 'do!'
                      ku⌐ru 'come': ko⌐i 'come!'

All may be followed by particle yo.

Except for those of Group (3), all the imperatives listed above are used only by men, in abrupt speech, when they are addressing close friends, intimates, and inferiors. As a slightly less abrupt imperative, men use a verbal gerund + ku⌐re⌐ (the informal imperative of kureru 'give me'): [3]

> Ta⌐bete kure. 'Eat (for me).' (Lit. 'Give me eating.')
> No⌐n̄de kure. 'Drink (for me).'
> Itte kure. 'Go (for me).'

---

[1] For further comments on tyo⌐oda⌐i see Grammatical Note 4, following.

[2] An imperative of an unaccented verbal is accented on the final syllable.

[3] This is less polite than gerund + honorific nominal okure.

These differ from gerund + ku⌐dasa⌐i only in that ku⌐re⌐ 'give me' is plain informal, whereas ku⌐dasa⌐i 'give me' is polite informal.

Informal imperatives based on honorific verbals of Group (3) above (i⌐rassya⌐i, na⌐sa⌐i, o⌐ssya⌐i, and ku⌐dasa⌐i) are used by men and women. They are informal but polite.

Another informal affirmative imperative pattern, used by women and, less commonly, men, consists of a verbal stem or an honorific nominal (Note 3 above) + -nasa⌐i. Examples:

Ta⌐benasa⌐i.	or	O⌐tabe-nasa⌐i.	'Eat!'
No⌐minasa⌐i.	or	O⌐nomi-nasa⌐i.	'Drink!'
I⌐kinasa⌐i.	or	O⌐ide-nasa⌐i.[1]	'Go!'

Such imperatives occur most commonly in addressing children, close relatives, maids, etc. They are never used in addressing a superior. Other examples of the pattern are:

O⌐yasumi-nasa⌐i. 'Goodnight.' (Lit. 'Rest!')

and

O⌐kaeri-nasa⌐i. 'Welcome home.' (Lit. 'Return!')

Remember that verbal gerunds and honorific and humble nominals in sentence-final position[2] also occur as informal affirmative requests (cf. Lesson 18, Grammatical Note 3, and Note 3 above). Tyo⌐oda⌐i, like ku⌐dasa⌐i, may be preceded by a nominal object or a verbal gerund:

O⌐ka⌐si (o) tyoodai. 'Give me (lit. let me have) some candy.'

Ma⌐tte tyoodai. 'Wait (for me).' (Lit. 'Let me have waiting.')

Tyo⌐oda⌐i requests are informal and familiar. They are frequently used by men and women in addressing children, but in general occur much more commonly in the speech of women.

B. Negative

A verbal in its citation form (the informal non-past) + particle na is an abrupt, informal negative imperative used by men in addressing close friends, intimates, and inferiors. An accented verbal retains its original accent before na, but a normally unaccented verbal acquires an accent on its final syllable. Na may be followed by yo.

Examples:

Ta⌐be⌐ru na. 'Don't eat!'

No⌐mu na. 'Don't drink!'

Su⌐ru⌐ na. 'Don't do [it]!'

Corresponding negative imperatives of honorific verbals are rare.

The following kinds of negative requests, consisting of — or including — a -nai negative + de, are less abrupt but still informal:

---

[1] Also means 'Come!' or 'Stay!'

[2] Or pre-final before yo and ne.

—nai de.	(Men and women)
—nai de kure.	(Men only)
—nai de okure.	(Men and older women)
—nai de kudasai.	(Men and women)
—nai de tyoodai.	(See tyoᶜodaˀi under affirmative above)

5. -naḡara 'although'

Reread Lesson 31, Grammatical Note 2.

-Naḡara, like English 'while,' has two different meanings: (1) 'while' = 'during' and (2) 'while' = 'although.' It is introduced with the first meaning in Lesson 31, and with the second meaning in this lesson.

-Naḡara meaning 'although' is compounded not only with verbal stems but also with some nominals (particularly na words). It is sometimes followed by particle mo 'even.'

The accent of -naḡara words is the same, regardless of which meaning -naḡara has.

Examples:

Oᶜtaku no maˀe o ᶜmaˀiniti toᶜorinaˀḡara, hiᶜma ḡa naˀkute oᶜyori-dekiˀ-
    nai ñ desu.
    'While I pass (the front of) your house every day, I can't stop in be-
    cause I have no (free) time.'
Oᶜisiku naˀi to iinaḡara, miᶜñna taˀbete siᵗmaimaˀsita.
    'While he said it wasn't good, he ended up eating everything.'
Uᶜti no maˀe made ikinaḡara, haᶜirimaseˀñ desita.
    'While he walked all the way to (the front of) the house, he didn't
    come in.'
Siᶜtureenaˀḡara, oᶜtosi o ukaḡaimasyoˀo.
    'While it's rude, let's ask his age.'

6. Fractions

The Japanese equivalent of an English fraction X/Y is Y-buñ no X: lit. 'X-many of Y-many parts,' in which X and Y are numerals of Series I, and -buñ is the counter for 'parts.'

A numeral + counter -buñ is unaccented.

1/3	saᶜñ-buñ no itiˀ
1/4	yoᶜñ-buñ no itiˀ or si-ᶜbuñ no itiˀ
2/5	go-ᶜbuñ no niˀ
5/6	roᶜku-buñ no goˀ
3/7	siti-buñ no sañ or nana-buñ no sañ
5/8	haᶜti-buñ no goˀ
2/9	kyuᶜu-buñ no niˀ
9/10	zyuᶜu-buñ no kyuᶜu

Ni-ᶜbuñ no itiˀ is the equivalent of mathematical '1/2'; for conversational 'half,' there is the special word haᶜñbuˀñ.

A nominal + particle <u>no</u> + a fraction means 'a fraction of so-and-so.' Thus: <u>roosoku no sa⌐n-buñ no iti⌐</u> 'one-third of the candle(s).'

<u>Kono</u> + a fraction means 'a fraction of this' and <u>sono</u> + a fraction means 'a fraction of that': for example, <u>kono sa⌐n-buñ no ni⌐</u> 'two-thirds of this.'

Additional examples:

Ni⌐ wa ro⌐ku⌐ no sa⌐n-buñ no iti⌐ desu.
'Two is one-third of 6.'
Ro⌐ku⌐ no sa⌐n-buñ no ni⌐ wa ⌐si⌐ desu.
'Two-thirds of 6 is 4.'
So⌐no ho⌐ñ no yo⌐n-buñ no sañ hodo yomima⌐sita.
'I read about three-quarters of that book.'
Ko⌐no hañbu⌐ñ wa so⌐no sa⌐n-buñ no iti⌐ yori su⌐kuna⌐i desu.
'Half of this is less than one-third of that.'

7. Particles: <u>ka</u> 'or,' <u>ba⌐kari</u> 'only,' <u>mono</u> 'because'

a. <u>ka</u> 'or'

<u>Ka</u> connects nominals and means 'or':

kore ka so⌐re 'this or that'
nihoñ̄go ka e⌐ego 'Japanese or English'
pe⌐ñ ka e⌐ñpitu 'a pen or pencil'

Be sure to distinguish between the following two kinds of sentences:

Pe⌐ñ ka e⌐ñpitu o tukaima⌐sita ka˩ 'Did you use (either) a pen or a pencil?' (anticipating answer 'yes' or 'no')
Pe⌐ñ o tu⌐kaima⌐sita ka, e⌐ñpitu o tukaima⌐sita ka˩ 'Did you use a pen—or (did you use) a pencil?' (i.e. which one did you use?)

Examples:

Ho⌐ñ ka za⌐ssi o kasite kudasa⌐i.
'Please let me borrow a book or a magazine.'
Kyo⌐o wa Ta⌐naka-sañ ka Ya⌐mamoto-sañ ḡa ku⌐ru hazu desu.
'Today Mr. Tanaka or Mr. Yamamoto is supposed to come.'
A⌐sita⌐ ka a⌐sa⌐tte i⌐kimasyo⌐o.
'Let's go tomorrow or the next day.'
Raisyuu ⌐Ni⌐kkoo ka ⌐Kyo⌐oto e i⌐ku tumori de⌐su.
'I plan to go to Nikko or Kyoto next week.'

b. <u>Ba⌐kari</u> 'only'

<u>Ba⌐kari</u> (or, more emphatic, <u>ba⌐kkari</u>) means 'little else but,' 'just.' Some of its more common occurrences are:

1. Preceded by a non-past or past verbal and followed by √da.

Examples: Be⌐ñkyoo-suru ba⌐kari desu. 'He just studies.' or 'All he does is study.' or 'He does little else but study.'
Tu⌐ita ⌐ba⌐kari desu. 'He (only) just arrived.'

2. Preceded by a verbal gerund and followed by √iru.

Examples: Aˡsa kara baˡñ maˡde haˡtaraite baˡkari imasu. 'All
            I'm doing is working, from morning till night.'
          Teˡrebi o ˡmiˡte ˡbaˡkari iˡmaˡsita. 'All he was do-
            ing was watching television.'

3. Preceded by a nominal.

A verbal compound consisting of a nominal + <u>suru</u>—for example,
<u>beñkyoo-suru</u> 'study'—occurs as two independent words with <u>baˡka-
ri</u> between them: for example, beˡñkyoo baˡkari suru 'do nothing
but study.'

Examples:

    Kuˡ-zi kara beˡñkyoo-suruˡ no wa, Taˡnaka-sañ baˡkari desu.
    'Mr. Tanaka is about the only one who studies at (lit. from)
    nine o'clock.'
    Kodomo wa oˡkaˡsi ˡbaˡkari taˡbemaˡsita. 'The children ate
    little else but sweets.'
    Ueda-sañ wa ryoˡkoo baˡkari simasu. 'Mr. Ueda does little
    else but travel.'

Following a nominal, the meaning of <u>baˡkari</u> resembles that of <u>dake</u>
and <u>sika</u>. Compare the following examples:

    Taˡnaka-sañ dake tabemaˡsita. 'Just Mr. Tanaka (no one
    else) ate.'
    Oˡkaˡsi ˡbaˡkari taˡbemaˡsita. 'I ate little else but candy.'
    (i.e. lots of candy, a little of other things)
    Oˡkaˡsi sika taˡbemaseˡñ desita. 'I didn't eat anything except
    candy.' (a negative approach, emphasizing that nothing else
    was eaten)

Following a nominal which is a number or indefinite quantity word, [1]
<u>baˡkari</u> means 'about,' 'only about': <u>mi-ˡttu baˡkari</u> 'about 3 (units),'
<u>ni-ˡneñ baˡkari</u> 'about 2 years.' Compare:

    Zyuˡu-niñ baˡkari kiˡmaˡsita. '(Only) about ten people came.'
    Zyuˡu-niñ-ǧuˡrai kiˡmaˡsita. 'About ten people came.'
    Zyuˡu-niñ hodo kiˡmaˡsita. 'About (as many as) ten people
    came.'

c. <u>mono</u> 'because'

The particle <u>mono</u> occurs as a more familiar, informal equivalent of
<u>kara</u> 'because,' in sentences where the emphasis is on the reason or justifi-
cation for an action which is contrary to expectation. It occurs more commonly, though not exclusively, in the speech of women.

Examples:
    Are kaˡitaˡkatta kedo, yaˡmetaˡ no yo⌣—taˡkaˡi ñ desu mono— (W)
    'I wanted to buy it but I gave up the idea—because it's expensive.'

----

[1] An accented number or quantity expression loses its accent before <u>baˡkari</u>.

Ko⌐ñna e⌐ega tu⌐ma⌐ñnai mono, mo⌐o de⌐yo⌐o yo. (M)
'This kind of movie is boring so let's leave now.'
I⌐ti-zi⌐kañ mo a⌐ru⌐ku ñ nara, i⌐kana⌐i wa◡—tu⌐kare⌐ru mono◡ (W)
'If it's a matter of walking for all of an hour I'm not going—because I'll get tired.'

8. Sentence Particles: kai, sa

a. kai

Kai is an interrogative sentence particle used by men in informal speech, as a more conversational, less abrupt equivalent of ka. It follows non-past, past, and tentative informal inflected words (but da is lost before kai just as it is lost before ka).

Examples:

Formal (MW)	Informal (M; abrupt)	Informal (M)	Informal (Predomi- nantly W)	Informal (MW)
Wa⌐karima⌐su ka◡	Wa⌐ka⌐ru ka.	Wa⌐ka⌐ru kai◡	Wa⌐ka⌐ru no?	Wa⌐ka⌐ru?
Sa⌐mu⌐i desu ka◡	Sa⌐mu⌐i ka.	Sa⌐mu⌐i kai◡	Sa⌐mu⌐i no?	Sa⌐mu⌐i?
So⌐o desu ka◡	So⌐o ka.	So⌐o kai◡	So⌐o na no?	So⌐o?
So⌐o desita ka◡	So⌐o datta ka.	So⌐o datta kai◡	So⌐o datta no?	So⌐o da- tta?

In informal questions containing a question word (na⌐ni, da⌐re, i⌐tu, etc.), dai occurs in men's speech in sentence-final position as a more conversational, less abrupt equivalent of sentence-final da.

Examples:

Formal (MW)	Informal (M; abrupt)	Informal (M)	Informal (Predomi- nantly W)	Informal (MW)
Do⌐o desu ka◡	Do⌐o da.	Do⌐o dai◡	Do⌐o na no?	Do⌐o?
Do⌐ko desu ka◡	Do⌐ko da.	Do⌐ko dai◡	Do⌐ko na no?	Do⌐ko?
Da⌐re no desu ka◡	Da⌐re no da.	Da⌐re no dai◡	Da⌐re no na no?	Da⌐re no?
Na⌐ñ-zi kara desu ka◡	Na⌐ñ-zi kara da.	Na⌐ñ-zi kara dai◡	Na⌐ñ-zi kara na no?	Na⌐ñ-zi kara?

b. sa

Sa is a sentence particle of emphasis which occurs, in the standard language, in men's informal speech. Its meaning is similar to that of yo but it is softer and less assertive. It does not follow imperative form.

Before sa, da is lost:

So⌐o da yo.
So⌐o da ne?

but:

So⌐o sa.

9. -ḡo⌐to⌐ ni

-Ḡo⌐to ni, directly following a nominal—particularly a number denoting a
period of time—means 'each so-and-so,' 'each and every so-and-so,' 'with
the occurrence of each so-and-so.' Before -ḡoto ni, a word which is regularly accented loses its accent. Thus:

    hu⌐tu-ka-ḡo⌐to ni 'every two days'
    sa⌐ñ-syuukañ-ḡo⌐to ni 'every three weeks'
    hi-⌐ḡo⌐to ni 'with each passing day'

Examples:

    Sa⌐ñ-neñ-ḡo⌐to ni ku⌐ni e kaerima⌐su.
    'Every three years, I return to my country.'
    Yo-⌐zikañ-ḡo⌐to ni ko⌐no kusuri o no⌐ñde kudasai.
    'Please take this medicine every four hours.'
    Ba⌐su wa sa⌐ñzyup-puñ-ḡo⌐to ni ⌐de⌐ru soo desu.
    'They say the bus leaves every 30 minutes.'
    Tanaka-sañ no eeḡo wa hi-⌐ḡo⌐to ni zyo⌐ozu⌐ ni na⌐rima⌐su yo↲
    'Mr. Tanaka's English improves with each passing day.'
    Tu⌐kia⌐u hi⌐to-ḡo⌐to ni so⌐o iima⌐su yo↲
    'He says that to every person he associates with.'

10. —— ka sira

Ka sira occurs at the end of sentences following inflected words—non-
past, past, and tentative—and means 'I wonder if ——.' It occurs more
commonly, but not exclusively, in the speech of women. The more common
men's equivalent is ka na (cf. Sentence 11 of the Basic Dialogues).

For accentuation, see ka mo siremaseñ (Lesson 30, Grammatical Note 2).

Remember that before ka, da is lost.

Examples: [1]

    Wa⌐ka⌐ru ka sira. 'I wonder if he understands.'
    Wa⌐ka⌐tta ka sira. 'I wonder if he understood.'
    I⌐ko⌐o ka sira. 'I wonder if I should go.'
    Sa⌐mu⌐i ka sira. 'I wonder if it's cold.'
    Sa⌐mukatta ka sira. 'I wonder if it was cold.'
    So⌐o ka sira. [2] 'I wonder if that's so.'
    So⌐o datta ka sira. 'I wonder if it was like that.'

11. wa⌐ka⌐rya sinai

A verbal stem + wa + √sinai occurs as a more emphatic equivalent of
the corresponding negative of the verbal. The stem of an unaccented verbal
acquires an accent on its final syllable.

---

[1] The examples are all in the informal style. Formal inflected forms also
occur before ka sira.

[2] So⌐o da + ka sira = So⌐o ka sira.

Examples:

    ta⌐be¬nai: ta⌐be¬ wa sinai 'doesn't eat'
    no⌐ma¬nakatta: no¬mi wa si⌐na⌐katta 'didn't drink'
    ko¬nai: ki¬ wa sinai 'doesn't come'
    si⌐mase¬n̄:   si¬ wa si⌐mase¬n̄ 'doesn't do'

In more familiar speech, <u>wa</u> becomes <u>ya</u>, resulting in combinations like:

    ta⌐be¬ ya sinai
    no¬mi ya si⌐na⌐katta
    ki¬ ya sinai

In contracted speech, a verbal stem of two or more syllables ending in <u>i</u>
loses its final <u>-i</u>; the <u>-a</u> of particle <u>ya</u> is often lengthened.

Examples:

    no¬mya *[a]* sinai 'doesn't drink'
    ha⌐na¬sy *[a]* sinai 'doesn't talk'

DRILLS

A. Substitution Drill

1.	I'm so glad (lit. wasn't it nice) that you were able to get into that school!	A⌐no gakkoo ni ha¬irete ⌐yo¬katta desu ⌐ne¬e.
2.	I'm so glad that you were able to buy tickets for tomorrow's game!	<u>Asita no siai no kippu ḡa kaete</u> ⌐yo¬katta desu ⌐ne¬e.
3.	I'm so glad that you passed the entrance examination!	<u>Nyu⌐uḡakusike¬n̄ ni ⌐pa¬su-site</u> [1] ⌐yo¬katta desu ⌐ne¬e.
4.	I'm so glad that you got a job at a good place!	<u>I¬i to⌐koro⌐ e syůusyoku-site</u> ⌐yo¬katta desu ⌐ne¬e.
5.	I'm so glad that there wasn't a fire!	<u>Ka¬zi ḡa ⌐na¬kute</u> ⌐yo¬katta desu ⌐ne¬e.
6.	I'm so glad that you didn't get sick!	<u>Byo⌐oki ni nara¬nakute</u> ⌐yo¬katta desu ⌐ne¬e.
7.	I'm so glad that Tokyo University won!	<u>To⌐odai ḡa ka¬tte</u> ⌐yo¬katta desu ⌐ne¬e.
8.	I'm so glad that you transferred to a place where it's pleasant to live!	<u>Su⌐mii¬i to⌐koro⌐ e těnkin̄-site</u> ⌐yo¬katta desu ⌐ne¬e.

B. Substitution Drill

1.	Once in a while we go together.	Ta⌐ma ni¬ wa i⌐ssyo ni ikima⌐su.

----

[1] <u>Pasu-suru</u> 'pass (an examination).'

2. We sometimes go together. To⌐kidoki issyo ni ikima⌐su.

3. We go together almost every day. Ho⌐to¬ndo ⌐ma¬initi i⌐ssyo ni ikima¬su.

4. We often go together. Ta⌐bitabi issyo ni ikima⌐su.

5. We always go together. I⌐tu mo i⌐ssyo ni ikima¬su.

6. We usually go together. Ta⌐itee issyo ni ikima⌐su.

7. We ordinarily go together. Hu⌐tuu issyo ni ikima⌐su.

8. We go together a good deal. Yo⌐ku i⌐ssyo ni ikima¬su.

C. Substitution Drill

1. I'm already booked up for tomorrow — to go swimming. A⌐sita⌐ wa ⌐mo⌐o ya⌐kusoku-sityaima⌐sita yo — o⌐yo¬ḡi ni i⌐ku¬ tte.

2. I'm already booked up for tomorrow — to come here again. A⌐sita⌐ wa ⌐mo⌐o ya⌐kusoku-sityaima⌐sita yo — ma⌐ta koko e ku¬ru tte.

3. I'm already booked up for tomorrow — to go to the teacher's house. A⌐sita⌐ wa ⌐mo⌐o ya⌐kusoku-sityaima⌐sita yo — se⌐ñse¬e no otaku ni a⌐ḡaru¬ tte.

4. I'm already booked up for tomorrow — to go to see the cherry blossoms. A⌐sita⌐wa ⌐mo⌐o ya⌐kusoku-sityaima⌐sita yo — ha⌐nami¬ ni i⌐ku¬ tte.

5. I'm already booked up for tomorrow — to work all day. A⌐sita⌐ wa ⌐mo⌐o ya⌐kusoku-sityaima⌐sita yo — i⌐tiniti-zyuu hataraku¬ tte.

6. I'm already booked up for tomorrow — to play tennis. A⌐sita⌐ wa ⌐mo⌐o ya⌐kusoku-sityaima⌐sita yo — te⌐nisu (o) su⌐ru¬ tte.

7. I'm already booked up for tomorrow — to take the children to the doctor's (place). A⌐sita⌐ wa ⌐mo⌐o ya⌐kusoku-sityaima⌐sita yo — ko⌐domo (o) oisyasañ no toko¬ e tu⌐rete iku¬ tte.

8. I'm already booked up for tomorrow — to go to the Ginza to shop. A⌐sita⌐ wa ⌐mo⌐o ya⌐kusoku-sityaima⌐sita yo — Gi⌐ñza e kaimono ni iku¬ tte.

D. Level Drill [1]

1. So⌐o sitya⌐a i⌐kemase¬ñ yo⌐ So⌐o site⌐ wa i⌐kemase¬ñ yo⌐

2. A⌐me ḡa hu⌐ra¬nakeryaa ⌐i¬i desu ḡa ⌐ne⌐e. A⌐me ḡa hu⌐ra¬nakereba ⌐i¬i desu ḡa ⌐ne⌐e.

---

[1] Each sentence on the right is the uncontracted equivalent of the sentence on the left.

3. Kodomo (wa) ⌐moᒣo ne-
   ⌐tyaimaᒣsita yo⌐⌐
4. A⌐ñna hikoᒣoki nya noᒣryaᒣa
   siᒣhaᒣi yo.
5. Ze⌐ñzeñ wakaᒣñnai.
6. Ko⌐ñna huᒣu zya tuᒣmaᒣ-
   ñnai zya nai ka.
7. Si⌐tiᒣ-zi made ni ⌐koᒣ-
   nakyaa aᒣwaᒣnai.
8. Saᒣke (o) noᒣñzyatta.

Kodomo (wa) ⌐moᒣo neᒣte simai-
maᒣsita yo⌐⌐
A⌐ñna hikoᒣoki ni wa noᒣriᒣ wa
siᒣhaᒣi yo.
Ze⌐ñzeñ wakaraᒣnai.
Ko⌐ñna huᒣu de wa tuᒣmaraᒣnai
zya [1] nai ka.
Si⌐tiᒣ-zi made ni ⌐koᒣnakereba
aᒣwaᒣnai.
Saᒣke (o) noᒣñde simatta.

E. Grammar Drill (based on Grammatical Note 1)

> Tutor: Waᒣkarimaᒣsu ᒥneᒣe. 'He understands, doesn't he.'
> Student: Waᒣkaru rasiᒣi desu ᒥneᒣe. 'He apparently understands,
>   doesn't he.'

1. Kinoo no siai (wa) ⌐yoᒣ-
   katta desu ᒥneᒣe.
2. Kyoᒣo (wa) siᒣkeᒣñ de-
   sita ᒥneᒣe.
3. A⌐noᒣ ko (wa) ⌐iᒣtu mo
   waᒣratte (i)maᒣsu ᒥneᒣe.
4. Koᒣno zibikiᒣ (wa) hoᒣñyaku-sita hitoᒣ no desu
   ᒥneᒣe.
5. Ziᒣko (ḡa) aᒣrimaᒣsita
   ᒥneᒣe.
6. Ze⌐ñzeñ gaᒣmañ deᒣki-
   maseᒣñ ᒥneᒣe.
7. Añna seekatu (wa) sa-
   ⌐bisiᒣi desu ᒥneᒣe.
8. Oᒣtoᒣosañ no siᒣriai deᒣsu
   ᒥneᒣe.
9. Kono mati no otera (wa)
   yuᒣumee deᒣsu ᒥneᒣe.
10. Aᒣsuko no osoᒣba (wa)
    oᒣisiᒣi desu ᒥneᒣe.
11. Suᒣpoᒣotu ni wa kyoᒣomiᒣ
    ḡa aᒣrimaseᒣñ ᒥneᒣe.

Kinoo no siai (wa) yoᒣkatta rasiᒣi
desu ᒥneᒣe.
Kyoᒣo (wa) siᒣkeñ datta rasiᒣi desu ᒥneᒣe.
A⌐noᒣ ko (wa) ⌐iᒣtu mo waᒣratte
(i)ru rasiᒣi desu ᒥneᒣe.
Koᒣno zibikiᒣ (wa) hoᒣñyaku-sita
hito no rasiᒣi desu ᒥneᒣe.
Ziᒣko (ḡa) aᒣtta rasiᒣi desu
ᒥneᒣe.
Ze⌐ñzeñ gaᒣmañ deᒣkinai rasiᒣi
desu ᒥneᒣe.
Añna seekatu (wa) saᒣbisii rasiᒣi
desu ᒥneᒣe.
Oᒣtoᒣosañ no siᒣriai rasiᒣi desu
ᒥneᒣe.
Kono mati no otera (wa) yuᒣumee rasiᒣi desu ᒥneᒣe.
Aᒣsuko no osoᒣba (wa) oᒣisii rasiᒣi desu ᒥneᒣe.
Suᒣpoᒣotu ni wa kyoᒣomiᒣ ḡa naᒣi
rasiᒣi desu ᒥneᒣe.

F. Substitution Drill

1. Apparently golf has become popular in Japan.
2. They say that golf has
   become popular in Japan.

Niᒣhoᒣñ de wa ⌐goᒣruhu ḡa saᒣkañ
ni natta rasiᒣi desu.
Niᒣhoᒣñ de wa ⌐goᒣruhu ḡa saᒣkañ
ni <u>naᒣtta soo desu.</u>

---

[1] This <u>zya</u> rarely occurs in its uncontracted equivalent in informal conversation.

3. Golf is supposed to have
   become popular in Japan.

Ni⌐hoꜝñ de wa ⌐goꜝruhu ḡa sa⌐kañ
ni naꜝtta hazu desu.

4. I think that golf has become popular in Japan.

Ni⌐hoꜝñ de wa ⌐goꜝruhu ḡa sa⌐kañ
ni naꜝtta to omoimasu.

5. Don't you agree that
   golf has become popular
   in Japan?

Ni⌐hoꜝñ de wa ⌐goꜝruhu ḡa sa⌐kañ
ni naꜝtta ñ zya arimaseñ ka.

6. Golf seems to have be-
   come popular in Japan.

Ni⌐hoꜝñ de wa ⌐goꜝruhu ḡa sa⌐kañ
ni naꜝtta yoo desu.

G. Substitution Drill

1. I'm to go on a business
   trip every month from
   now on.

Kore kara ma⌐ituki syuttyoo-suruꜝ
ñ desu.

2. I plan to go on a business
   trip every month from
   now on.

Kore kara ma⌐ituki syuttyoo-suru
tumori deꜝsu.

3. I've decided to go on a
   business trip every
   month from now on.

Kore kara ma⌐ituki syuttyoo-suru
kotoꜝ ni si⌐maꜝsita.

4. I think he'll go on a
   business trip every
   month from now on.

Kore kara ma⌐ituki syuttyoo-suruꜝ
to omoimasu.

5. They say he's going to
   go on a business trip
   every month from now
   on.

Kore kara ma⌐ituki syuttyoo-suru
soꜝo desu.

6. He's supposed to go on
   a business trip every
   month from now on.

Kore kara ma⌐ituki syuttyoo-suru
hazu deꜝsu.

7. Apparently he's going
   to go on a business
   trip every month from
   now on.

Kore kara ma⌐ituki syuttyoo-suru
rasiꜝi desu.

H. Grammar Drill (based on Grammatical Note 2)

Tutor: I⌐ꜝi desu ⌐neꜝe. 'Isn't it nice!'
Student: I⌐ꜝi zya arimaseñ ka. 'Don't you agree that it's nice?' or
         'Isn't it true that it's nice?'

1. Añna ⌐maꜝdo no su⌐kunaꜝi
   uti (wa) ku⌐raꜝi desu ⌐neꜝe.

Añna ⌐maꜝdo no su⌐kunaꜝi uti (wa)
ku⌐raꜝi zya arimaseñ ka.

2. Tu⌐rai seekatu deꜝsu
   ⌐neꜝe.

Tu⌐rai seekatu zyaꜝ arimaseñ ka.

3. Ma⌐ꜝe yori zu⌐tto yase-
   maꜝsita ⌐neꜝe.

Ma⌐ꜝe yori zu⌐tto yasetaꜝ zya arimaseñ ka.

4. Añna hi⌐doꜝi zisiñ (wa)
   ko⌐waꜝi desu ⌐neꜝe.

Añna hi⌐doꜝi zisiñ (wa) ko⌐waꜝi zya
arimaseñ ka.

5. A⌐na⌐ta no tokee (wa)   A⌐na⌐ta no tokee (wa) ⌐da⌐re ka
   ⌐da⌐re ka ni to⌐rarema⌐-   ni to⌐ra⌐reta zya arimaseñ ka.
   sita ⌐ne⌐e.

6. A⌐merika⌐ziñ to ze⌐ñzeñ   A⌐merika⌐ziñ to ze⌐ñzeñ tukiawa⌐-
   tukiaimase⌐ñ ⌐ne⌐e.   nai zya arimaseñ ka.

7. A⌐no⌐ hito (wa) ⌐yo⌐ku   A⌐no⌐ hito (wa) ⌐yo⌐ku te⌐ñkiñ-
   te⌐ñkiñ-saserarema⌐su   saserareru⌐ zya arimaseñ ka.
   ⌐ne⌐e.

8. Soñna siḡoto (wa) to⌐si-   Soñna siḡoto (wa) to⌐siyori⌐ ni wa
   yori⌐ ni wa ⌐mu⌐ri desu   ⌐mu⌐ri zya arimaseñ ka.
   ⌐ne⌐e.

I. Substitution Drill (based on Grammatical Note 5)

1. While he said he under-   Wa⌐ka⌐ru tte iinaḡara, hoñtoo wa
   stood, he really didn't   wa⌐kara⌐nakatta ñ desu.
   (understand).

2. While he said he'd do it,   Su⌐ru⌐ tte iinaḡara, hoñtoo wa
   he really didn't (do).   si⌐na⌐katta ñ desu.

3. While he said he didn't   Si⌐rana⌐i tte iinaḡara, hoñtoo wa
   know, he really did   si⌐tte (i)ta⌐ ñ desu.
   (know).

4. While he said he'd give   Ku⌐reru⌐ tte iinaḡara, hoñtoo wa
   it to me, he really didn't   ku⌐rena⌐katta ñ desu.
   (give).

5. While he said he could   Ga⌐mañ de⌐ki⌐ru tte iinaḡara, hoñ-
   stand it, he really   too wa ⌐ga⌐mañ de⌐ki⌐nakatta ñ
   couldn't (stand it).   desu.

6. While he said he could   U⌐ḡokase⌐ru tte iinaḡara, hoñtoo
   move it, he really   wa u⌐ḡokase⌐nakatta ñ desu.
   couldn't (move it).

7. While he said he hadn't   Wa⌐surena⌐katta tte iinaḡara, hoñ-
   forgotten, he really had   too wa wa⌐sureta⌐ ñ desu.
   (forgotten).

8. While he said it would   Ya⌐ku⌐ ni ⌐ta⌐tu tte iinaḡara, hoñ-
   be useful, it really   too wa ya⌐ku⌐ ni ta⌐ta⌐nakatta ñ
   wasn't (of use).   desu.

J. Level Drill (based on Grammatical Note 4)

Tutor: No⌐ñde kudasai. 'Please drink.'

Male Student: No⌐me yo. 'Drink!'
Female Student: No⌐minasa⌐i yo. 'Drink!'

1. Ta⌐ma ni⌐ wa tu⌐kia⌐tte   Ta⌐ma ni⌐ wa tu⌐kia⌐e yo.
   kudasai.   Ta⌐ma ni⌐ wa tu⌐kiainasa⌐i yo.

2. Tyo⌐tto ⌐ma⌐tte kudasai.   Tyo⌐tto ⌐ma⌐te yo.
                                   Tyo⌐tto ma⌐tinasa⌐i yo.

3. Ko⌐no sakana (o) yaite   Ko⌐no sakana (o) yake⌐ yo.
   kudasa⌐i.   Ko⌐no osakana (o) yakinasa⌐i yo.

4. Ta⌐bako (o) katte¬ kite   Ta⌐bako (o) katte ko¬i yo.
   kudasai.   Ta⌐bako (o) katte kinasa¬i yo.

5. A⌐sita ha¬yaku yo⌐ko¬site   A⌐sita ha¬yaku yo⌐ko¬se yo.
   kudasai.   A⌐sita ha¬yaku yo⌐kosinasa¬i yo.

6. Ro⌐osoku¬ (o) tu�ke⁺te   Ro⌐osoku¬ (o) tu�ke⌐ro¬ yo.
   kudasai.   Ro⌐osoku¬ (o) tu�kenasa⁺i yo.

7. U⌐ta¬ (o) u�tatte kudasa⁺i. U⌐ta¬ (o) u�tae⁺ yo.
                                    U⌐ta¬ (o) u�tainasa⁺i yo.

8. Ko⌐re kara sitaku (o)   Ko⌐re kara sitaku (o) siro¬ yo.
   site kudasa¬i.   Ko⌐re kara sitaku (o) sinasa¬i yo.

9. A⌐ma¬do (o) a�kete ku-   A⌐ma¬do (o) a�kero⁺ yo.
   dasa⁺i.   A⌐ma¬do (o) a�kenasa⁺i yo.

10. Kore (o) ka⌐midana ni   Kore (o) ka⌐midana ni oke¬ yo.
    oite kudasa¬i.   Kore (o) ka⌐midana ni okinasa¬i
                                    yo.

K. Level Drill (based on Grammatical Note 4)

Tutor: So⌐o iwana¬i de kudasai. 'Please don't say that.'

Male Student: So⌐o iu¬ na yo. 'Don't say that!'
Female Student: So⌐o iwana¬i de yo. 'Don't say that!'

1. Wa⌐surena¬i de kudasai.   Wa⌐sureru¬ na yo.
                                  Wa⌐surena¬i de yo.

2. Sore wa ⌐mi¬nai de ku-   Sore wa ⌐mi¬ru na yo.
    dasai.   Sore wa ⌐mi¬nai de yo.

3. Dare ni mo mi⌐se¬nai   Dare ni mo mi⌐se¬ru na yo.
    de kudasai.   Dare ni mo mi⌐se¬nai de yo.

4. Sa⌐waḡa¬nai de kudasai.   Sa⌐waḡu¬ na yo.
                                  Sa⌐waḡa¬nai de yo.

5. Si⌐ṅpai-sina¬i de kudasai.   Si⌐ṅpai-suru¬ na yo.
                                  Si⌐ṅpai-sina¬i de yo.

6. Ma⌐kena¬i de kudasai.   Ma⌐keru¬ na yo.
                                  Ma⌐kena¬i de yo.

7. Kore wa tu⌐kawana¬i de   Kore wa tu⌐kau¬ na yo.
    kudasai.   Kore wa tu⌐kawana¬i de yo.

8. A⌐no sakana (o) tabe¬nai   A⌐no sakana (o) tabe⌐ru na yo.
    de kudasai.   A⌐no osakana (o) tabe¬nai de yo.

9. O⌐kane (o) karina¬i de   O⌐kane (o) kariru¬ na yo.
    kudasai.   O⌐kane (o) karina¬i de yo.

10. O⌐kane (o) kasana¬i de   O⌐kane (o) kasu¬ na yo.
    kudasai.   O⌐kane (o) kasana¬i de yo.

L. Response Drill (based on Grammatical Note 4)

Tutor: So⌐re (o) site aḡemasyo⌐o ka. 'Shall I do that one
                 for you?'

Male Student: N̄, si⌐te kure¬ yo. 'Yes, please do.'
Female Student: E⌐e, si⌐te tyooda¬i.[1] 'Yes, please do.'

─────────────────────────
[1] Remember that <u>tyoodai</u> imperatives are familiar and informal.

1. De⌐ñwaba¬ñḡoo (o) ki⌐ite   N̄, ki⌐ite kure¬ yo.
   aḡemasyo⌐o ka.   E¬e, ki⌐ite tyooda⌐i.

2. Na⌐mae (o) ka⌐ite a⌐ḡe-   N̄, ka⌐ite ku⌐re¬ yo.
   masyo⌐o ka.   E¬e, ka⌐ite tyoodai.

3. Syo⌐ozi (o) si⌐mete a⌐ḡe-   N̄, si⌐mete ku⌐re¬ yo.
   masyo⌐o ka.   E¬e, si⌐mete tyoodai.

4. A⌐ñna⌐i-site a⌐ḡemasyo⌐o   N̄, a⌐ñna⌐i-site ku⌐re¬ yo.
   ka.   E¬e, a⌐ñna⌐i-site tyoodai.

5. Ku⌐suri (o) aḡemasyo⌐o   N̄, ku⌐re¬ yo.
   ka.   E¬e, tyo⌐oda⌐i.

6. Hu⌐rosiki ni tutu⌐ñde   N̄, tu⌐tu⌐ñde ku⌐re¬ yo.
   a⌐ḡemasyo⌐o ka.   E¬e, tu⌐tu⌐ñde tyoodai.

7. So⌐no ni⌐motu (o) ⌐mo⌐tte   N̄, mo⌐tte ku⌐re¬ yo.
   a⌐ḡemasyo⌐o ka.   E¬e, mo⌐tte tyoodai.

8. Ka⌐ya (o) tutte aḡema-   N̄, tu⌐tte kure¬ yo.
   syo⌐o ka.   E¬e, tu⌐tte tyooda⌐i.

M. Level Drill [1]

Tutor: Ka⌐erima⌐sita ka⌐ 'Has he gone home?'
Student: O⌐kaeri ni narima⌐sita ka⌐ 'Has he gone home?'

1. Mo⌐o mi⌐ma⌐sita ka⌐   Mo⌐o go⌐rañ ni narima⌐sita ka⌐

2. Do⌐ko e i⌐kima⌐sita ka⌐   Do⌐tira e o⌐ide ni narima⌐sita
                                    ka⌐

3. Ho⌐ñ (o) ka⌐esima⌐sita   Ho⌐ñ (o) o⌐kaesi ni narima⌐sita
   ka⌐   ka⌐

4. Ta⌐naka-sañ ima⌐su ka⌐   Ta⌐naka-sañ oide ni narima⌐su
                                    ka⌐

5. Na⌐ñ-zi-ḡo⌐ro de⌐ma⌐su   Na⌐ñ-zi-ḡo⌐ro o⌐de ni narima⌐su
   ka⌐   ka⌐

6. A⌐sita mata kima⌐su ka⌐   A⌐sita mata oide ni narima⌐su
                                    ka⌐

7. Na⌐ñ-zi ni o⌐kima⌐su   Na⌐ñ-zi ni o⌐oki ni narima⌐su
   ka⌐   ka⌐

8. Do⌐ko de so⌐datima⌐sita   Do⌐tira de o⌐sodati ni narima⌐-
   ka⌐   sita ka⌐

N. Substitution Drill (based on Grammatical Note 6)

1. One-third of three is one.   Sañ no sa⌐ñ-buñ no iti¬ wa i⌐ti¬
                                    desu.

2. Two-fifths of five is two.   Go¬ no go-⌐buñ no ni¬ wa ⌐ni¬
                                    desu.

3. One-fifth of ten is two.   Zyu⌐u no go-⌐buñ no iti¬ wa ⌐ni¬
                                    desu.

4. One-fourth of eight is two.   Ha⌐ti¬ no yo⌐ñ-buñ no iti¬ wa ⌐ni¬
                                    desu.

---

[1] In each case, the sentence on the right contains √na⌐ru and is the polite equivalent of the sentence on the left.

5. Two-thirds of six is   Ro⌐ku⌐ no sa⌐ñ-buñ no ni⌐ wa ⌐si⌐
   four.   desu.

6. Three-fourths of four   Si⌐ no yŏñ-buñ no sañ wa sa⌐ñ
   is three.   de⌐su.

7. One-third of twelve is   Zyu⌐uni⌐ no sa⌐ñ-buñ no iti⌐ wa
   four.   ⌐si⌐ desu.

8. One-tenth of twenty is   Ni⌐zyuu no zyu⌐u-buñ no iti⌐ wa
   two.   ⌐ni⌐ desu.

O. Expansion Drill (based on Grammatical Note 7)

Tutor: So⌐re (o) kudasa⌐i. /are/ 'Give me that. /that one over there/'

Student: So⌐re ka are (o) kudasa⌐i. 'Give me that one or that one over there.'

1. Ka⌐midana ni oite ari-   Ka⌐midana ka butudañ ni oite
   ma⌐su. /butudañ/   arima⌐su.

2. Ko⌐ohi⌐i (o) tyo⌐oda⌐i.   Ko⌐ohi⌐i ka o⌐tya (o) tyooda⌐i.
   /otya/

3. E⌐ñpitu de ka⌐ite kuda-   E⌐ñpitu ka pe⌐ñ de ⌐ka⌐ite kudasai. /pe⌐ñ/   sai.

4. Re⌐kisi (ḡa) beñkyoo-   Re⌐kisi ka ti⌐ri (ḡa) be⌐ñkyoo-
   sita⌐i ñ desu. /ti⌐ri/   sita⌐i ñ desu.

5. Ne⌐zi (ḡa) irimasu.   Ne⌐zi ka ku⌐ḡi (ḡa) irima⌐su.
   /kuḡi/

6. Maineñ ya⌐ma⌐ e ikima-   Maineñ ya⌐ma⌐ ka ⌐u⌐mi e iki-
   su. /u⌐mi/   masu.

7. Ge⌐tuyo⌐o ni i⌐ku tumori   Ge⌐tuyo⌐o ka ka⌐yo⌐o ni i⌐ku tu-
   de⌐su. /ka⌐yo⌐o/   mori de⌐su.

8. Ka⌐iḡuñ ni ha⌐irita⌐i ñ   Ka⌐iḡuñ ka ku⌐uḡuñ ni hairita⌐i
   desu. /kuuḡuñ/   ñ desu.

P. Level Drill (based on Grammatical Note 8)

Tutor: I⌐kima⌐su ka⌐ 'Are you going?'

Male Student: Iku kai⌐ 'Are you going?'
Female Student: I⌐ku⌐ no?[1] 'Are you going?'

1. Wa⌐karima⌐sita ka⌐   Wa⌐ka⌐tta kai⌐
                              Wa⌐ka⌐tta no?

2. Ta⌐sukarima⌐sita ka⌐   Ta⌐suka⌐tta kai⌐
                              Ta⌐suka⌐tta no?

3. I⌐tu desu ka⌐   I⌐tu dai⌐
                              I⌐tu na no?

4. Ko⌐wa⌐i desu ka⌐   Ko⌐wa⌐i kai⌐
                              Ko⌐wa⌐i no?

---

[1] Remember that this pattern is used more frequently, but not exclusively by women.

5. Syo˹ttyuu desu ka⌟   Syo˹ttyuu kai⌟
                               Syo˹ttyuu na no?

6. Tu˹ra˺katta desu ka⌟   Tu˹ra˺katta kai⌟
                               Tu˹ra˺katta no?

7. Ma˹kema˺sita ka⌟   Maketa kai⌟
                               Ma˹keta˺ no?

8. Mu˹ri desita ka⌟   Mu˹ri datta kai⌟
                               Mu˹ri datta no?

Q. Grammar Drill (based on Grammatical Note 7)

> Tutor: Ha˹irima˺sita. 'He came in.'
> Student: Ha˹itta ˹ba˺kari desu. 'He (only) just came in.'

1. Ku˹suri (o) nomima˺sita.   Ku˹suri (o) no˹nda ˹ba˺kari desu.
2. Da˹iɡaku (o) dema˺sita.   Da˹iɡaku (o) de˹ta ˹ba˺kari desu.
3. Nyu˹uɡakusike˺ñ (o) u˹ke-   Nyu˹uɡakusike˺ñ (o) ˹u˺keta ˹ba˺-
   ma˺sita.   kari desu.
4. I˹i to˹koro˺ ni syu˹usyoku-   I˹i to˹koro˺ ni syu˹usyoku-sita
   sima˺sita.   ba˹kari desu.
5. Ri˹ku˺ɡuñ ni syo˹osyuu-   Ri˹ku˺ɡuñ ni syo˹osyuu-sareta
   sarema˺sita.   ba˹kari desu.
6. Ku˹ni ni kaerima˺sita.   Ku˹ni ni ka˹etta ˹ba˺kari desu.
7. So˹no kookoku (o) mima˺-   So˹no kookoku (o) mi˹ta ˹ba˺kari
   sita.   desu.
8. Ni˹ho˺ñ ni tu˹kima˺sita.   Ni˹ho˺ñ ni ˹tu˹ita ˹ba˺kari desu.

R. Grammar Drill (based on Grammatical Note 7)

> Tutor: Mi-˹ttu hodo kaima˺sita. 'I bought about (as many as)
>   three.'
> Student: Mi-˹ttu ba˹kari ka˹ima˺sita. 'I bought (only) about
>   three.'

1. Zyu˹u-niñ hodo mi˹ema˺-   Zyu˹u-niñ ba˹kari mi˹ema˺sita.
   sita.
2. Ro˹osoku˺ (ɡa) ˹sa˺ñ-boñ   Ro˹osoku˺ (ɡa) sa˹ñ-boñ ba˹kari
   hodo no˹ko˺tte (i)masu.   no˹ko˺tte (i)masu.
3. Sore wa sa˹ñzeñ-eñ hodo   Sore wa sa˹ñzeñ-eñ ba˹kari ka-
   kaka˺ru to omoimasu.   ˹ka˺ru to omoimasu.
4. Kippu (o) ha˹ti˺-mai hodo   Kippu (o) ha˹ti-mai ba˹kari ka-
   ka˹ima˺sita.   ˹ima˺sita.
5. Ta˹kusii ɡa go-˹dai hodo   Ta˹kusii ɡa go-˹dai ba˹kari na-
   narañde (i)ma˺su.   ˹rañde (i)ma˺su.
6. Ki˹ (ɡa) go-˹hoñ hodo   Ki˹ (ɡa) go-˹hoñ ba˹kari u˹ete
   uete arima˺su.   arima˺su.

S. Substitution Drill (based on Grammatical Note 9)

1. Each year the competi-   I˹ti-neñ-ɡo˺to ni kyo˹osoo ɡa hi˹-
   tion gets more severe.   doku narimasu.

2. Each month the competi-   I⌐k-kaḡetu-ḡo⌐to ni kyo⌐osoo ḡa hi⌐-
   tion gets more severe.   doku narimasu.
3. Each month the teacher   I⌐k-kaḡetu-ḡo⌐to ni se⌐ñse⌐e ḡa ka-
   changes.   warimasu.
4. Every two hours the   Ni-⌐zikañ-ḡo⌐to ni se⌐ñse⌐e ḡa ka-
   teacher changes.   warimasu.
5. Every two hours I take   Ni-⌐zikañ-ḡo⌐to ni ku⌐suri (o) nomi-
   medicine.   ma⌐su.
6. Every thirty minutes I   Sa⌐ñzip-puñ-ḡo⌐to ni ku⌐suri (o) no-
   take medicine.   mima⌐su.
7. They say there's an ac-   Sa⌐ñzip-puñ-ḡo⌐to ni ⌐zi⌐ko ḡa ⌐a⌐ru
   cident every thirty min-   soo desu.
   utes.

T. Grammar Drill

   Tutor: Wa⌐karimase⌐ñ. 'I don't understand.'
   Student: Wa⌐ka⌐rya sinai. [1] 'I don't understand.'

   1. I⌐kimase⌐ñ.   I⌐kya⌐a sinai.
   2. Ki⌐mase⌐ñ.   Ki⌐ ya sinai.
   3. Si⌐mase⌐ñ.   Si⌐ ya sinai.
   4. Ta⌐bemase⌐ñ.   Ta⌐be⌐ ya sinai.
   5. No⌐mimase⌐ñ.   No⌐mya sinai.
   6. Si⌐rimase⌐ñ.   Si⌐rya⌐a sinai.
   7. Mi⌐mase⌐ñ.   Mi⌐ ya sinai.
   8. Yo⌐mimase⌐ñ.   Yo⌐mya sinai.
   9. Ka⌐kimase⌐ñ.   Ka⌐kya sinai.
  10. Ha⌐nasimase⌐ñ.   Ha⌐na⌐sya sinai.

U. Variation Drill [2] (based on Grammatical Note 10)

   Left Column: I⌐i ka sira. 'I wonder if it's all right.'
   Right Column: I⌐i ka na? 'I wonder if it's all right.'

   1. Da⌐izyo⌐obu ka sira.   Da⌐izyo⌐obu ka na?
   2. I⌐ko⌐o ka sira.   I⌐ko⌐o ka na?
   3. Sa⌐bisi⌐i ka sira.   Sa⌐bisi⌐i ka na?
   4. Do⌐ko ni ⌐su⌐ñde (i)ru   Do⌐ko ni ⌐su⌐ñde (i)ru ka na?
      ka sira.
   5. Mu⌐ri datta ka sira.   Mu⌐ri datta ka na?
   6. Ya⌐mesaserareta⌐ ka sira.   Ya⌐mesaserareta⌐ ka na?

---

[1]
 Emphatic, informal, contracted form. Based on Grammatical Note 11.

[2]
 The sentences on the left occur more commonly (though not exclusively) in
women's speech, and the sentences on the right are typical of men's speech.
For men students, the tutor reads the sentences on the left and the student
gives the sentences on the right. For women students, the reverse procedure is used.

7. De⌐ki⌐ru ka sira.   De⌐ki⌐ru ka na?
8. Te⌐edeñ ka⌐ sira.   Teedeñ ka na?

SUPPLEMENTARY DIALOGUES

1. Mr. Tanaka (meeting Mr. Yamada late at night): Yamada-kuñ, i⌐ma oka-
   eri kai⌐
   Mr. Yamada: Ma⌐iban, ka⌐isya no okyaku no tukia⌐i de, o⌐soku na⌐ru ñ
   da yo.
   Mr. Tanaka: Ya⌐ppa⌐ri ki⌐mi mo so⌐o kai. Bo⌐ku mo ⌐syo⌐ttyuu na ñ de,
   i⌐ya⌐ ni ⌐na⌐ttyau yo. Ka⌐isya no okyaku to tukia⌐u yori, uti
   de ⌐ka⌐nai ya kŏdomo to yu⌐kku⌐ri ta⌐beta⌐i yo.
   Mr. Yamada: So⌐o da yo. Hito o ryo⌐ori⌐ya e a⌐ñna⌐i-saseraretari,
   syu⌐ttyoo-saserareta⌐ri, i⌐ya⌐ da ⌐ne⌐e —kaisyaiñ wa.
   Mr. Tanaka: De⌐ mo; ho⌐ka no toko⌐ e syu⌐usyoku-site⌐ mo, onazi sa⌐

2. Mr. Tanaka: Do⌐ñdoñ mo⌐no⌐ no nedañ ḡa aḡaru ⌐ne⌐e.
   Mr. Yamamoto: Sa⌐to⌐o nañka i⌐s-syuukañ-ḡo⌐to ni ⌐ḡo⌐-eñ mo aḡatte
   iru yo⌐
   Mr. Tanaka: Na⌐ñ de⌐ mo so⌐o ta⌐kaku ⌐na⌐ttyaa ko⌐ma⌐ru ⌐ne⌐e.
   Mr. Yamamoto: Gekkyuu wa o⌐nazi na⌐ ñ da kedo—

3. Mr. Tanaka: Bu⌐ra⌐uñ-sañ [1] a⌐merika⌐ziñ na no ni hi⌐tokoto mo eeḡo
   tukawana⌐katta yo⌐
   Mr. Yamamoto: Ze⌐ñbu ni⌐hoñḡo de hana⌐sita no kai⌐
   Mr. Tanaka: So⌐o da yo. Sono ue, na⌐kanaka uma⌐i kotoba tu⌐kau⌐
   ñ da yo. Bi⌐kku⌐ri-sityatta.
   Mr. Yamamoto: Taitee ḡaiziñ no hanasi ⌐he⌐ñ na mo⌐no⌐ da ḡa ⌐ne⌐e.

4. Mrs. Tanaka: Tyo⌐tto zi⌐biki tyooda⌐i.
   Maid: Ko⌐re de gozaima⌐su ka⌐
   Mrs. Tanaka: A⌐a, so⌐re zya na⌐i no yo. Mo⌐tto ătui ku⌐ro⌐i no da ke-
   do, so⌐ko ni na⌐i?
   Maid: Ku⌐ro⌐i no wa ko⌐re sika gozaimase⌐ñ ḡa, ko⌐re de go-
   zaima⌐su ka⌐
   Mrs. Tanaka: So⌐o ⌐so⌐o, sore. Do⌐o mo.

5. Father: O⌐mosiroso⌐o na ⌐e⌐eḡa ḡa ⌐a⌐ru yo⌐ O⌐mae mo itte mi⌐nai
   kai⌐
   Son: Do⌐ñna ⌐e⌐eḡa? O⌐to⌐osañ tu⌐rete⌐ tte ku⌐reru⌐ no?
   Father: A⌐a. Kyo⌐o wa hi⌐ma da⌐ kara ne?
   Son: I⌐i ⌐na⌐a. O⌐to⌐osañ ḡa ⌐i⌐i to o⌐mo⌐u mo⌐no⌐ nara, na⌐ñ de mo
   i⌐i yo⌐ Bo⌐ku ⌐su⌐ḡu ki⌐kae⌐ru kara, ma⌐tte te ne?
   Father: I⌐i to mo. Yu⌐kku⌐ri ki⌐ka⌐ete oide⌐

6. Mrs. Tanaka: Bo⌐ttyañ o⌐ge⌐ñki?
   Mrs. Yamamoto: Okaḡesama de. De⌐ mo, ze⌐ñzeñ beñkyoo-sina⌐i ñ de,
   ko⌐ma⌐ttyau no yo⌐
   Mrs. Tanaka: Ma⌐da ti⌐isa⌐i kara desyoo?

---

[1] 'Brown.'

Mrs. Yamamoto: Mo῭o zyu῭uni⌐ na ñ desu mono, su⌐ko῭si wa be⌐ñkyoo-
            sasena῭kutyaa—

Mrs. Tanaka: Si⌐taku na῭i no ni ⌐mu῭ri ni sa⌐sete⌐ mo, da⌐me῭ zya
            nai ka sira.

Mrs. Yamamoto: So῭o ῭ne῭e. Syu῭ziñ mo, beñkyoo si⌐ro῭ si⌐ro῭ tte ⌐mu῭ri
            ni sa⌐sete⌐ mo o⌐boe῭nai kara, na῭ni mo iwanai ho῭o ḡa ⌐i⌐i
            tte i⌐u⌐ ñ da kedo; mo῭o su⌐ḡu ⌐tyu῭uḡaku desyoo? Si⌐ñpai
            na῭ no yo.

Mrs. Tanaka: Soñna ni si⌐ñpai-sina῭kute mo da⌐izyo῭obu yo⌐

7. Mr. Tanaka: Mu῭ri ka mo si⌐rena῭i kedo, a῭sita ma῭de ni ko῭no te-
            ḡami ho⌐ñyaku-site kurena῭i kai.

Mr. Yamamoto: Do⌐ñna ñ dai. Ya⌐sasi῭i ñ nara de⌐ki⌐ru yo⌐

Mr. Tanaka: Ki῭mi ni⌐ nara mu⌐zukasiku na῭i sa. Bo῭ku ni wa ze⌐ñ-
            zeñ waka῭ñnai kedo sa⌐

Mr. Yamamoto: Ma῭a, si⌐te mi῭ru yo.

Mr. Tanaka: I῭tu mo ki῭mi ni yarasetyatte, su⌐ma῭nai [1] kedo; ta῭no-
            mu yo.

Mr. Yamamoto: Ya⌐raserareru῭ no wa ⌐i῭i beñkyoo sa. De῭ mo; si⌐te
            mi῭nakutya, de⌐ki῭ru ka ⌐do῭o ka wa⌐kara῭nai yo⌐—hoñtoo
            ni. De⌐kitara a῭sita no a῭sa mo⌐tte ku῭ru yo.

Mr. Tanaka: Su⌐ma῭nai [1] kedo, ze῭hi ta῭no῭mu yo.

8. Taro: Ano hu⌐to῭tta hito ⌐da῭re ka na?

Jiro: Si⌐rana῭i kai⌐ Masao-kuñ da yo⌐

Taro: Masao-kuñ? Hu⌐to῭ttyatta ῭na῭a.

Jiro: Kinoo ga⌐kkoo de a῭tta ñ da kedo, boku mo bi⌐kku῭ri-sityatta yo.
            I῭k-ka῭ḡetu hodo ⌐Ni῭kkoo de ya⌐su⌐ñde, ta῭be῭ru no ḡa i⌐ti-
            bañ tanosimi῭ datta tte.

Taro: Ha῭yaku ya῭seta ho῭o ḡa ⌐i῭i ῭na῭a.

9. Mr. Smith: Kono-ḡoro i῭s-syuukañ-ḡo῭to ni kãñzi go-⌐zyu῭u hodo oboe-
            saserare῭ru ñ da ḡa, mu῭ri da to o⌐mo⌐u yo.

Mr. Tanaka: So῭o daroo ⌐ne⌐e.

Mr. Smith: Be⌐ñkyoo ba῭kari site, tyo῭tto a⌐tama῭ ḡa ⌐he῭ñ ni ⌐na⌐tta
            yo.

10. Man: Ueda-kuñ o⌐mosiro῭i hito da ⌐na῭a.

Woman: E῭e. Tu⌐kia῭eba tu⌐kia῭u hodo ⌐i⌐i hito da wa⌐

Man: Ano῭ hito to ha⌐na⌐su no ḡa tanosimi῭ da ⌐ne⌐e. O⌐mosiro῭i
            ko⌐to ba⌐kari itte—

11. Tanaka: O⌐zyo῭osañ o⌐ḡe῭ñki?

Smith: Okaḡesama de. Ma῭initi ⌐so῭to de ya⌐kyuu ba῭kari site—

Tanaka: Yakyuu o?

Smith: E῭e. Ano῭ ko wa o῭ñna rasi῭i koto wa ze⌐ñzeñ sina῭i de, i῭tu
            mo o⌐toko⌐ no ko to a῭sobu⌐ ñ desu yo⌐

12. Tanaka: *I῭i o⌐te῭ñki desu ⌐ne῭e.

Smith: Hoñtoo ni ha⌐ru ra῭siku na⌐rima⌐sita ⌐ne῭e.

Tanaka: Mo῭o sa⌐kura ḡa sakihazime῭ta soo desu yo⌐

Smith: So῭o desu ka. Kotosi wa ⌐tyo῭tto ha⌐ya῭i yoo zya arimaseñ ka⌐

---

[1] Informal equivalent of su⌐mimase῭ñ.

13. American Student (male): Mo'o ni⌐hoñgo na'ñka be⌐ñkyoo-sitaku na'i yo.
     Japanese Friend (male): Na'ze dai.
     American: Su⌐re'ba su'ru hodo muzukasiku na'tte, i'ya' ni ⌐na'ttyatta ñ
         da yo.
     Japanese: Ma'a, so'o iu' na yo. Kimi wa i⌐tibañ ñma'i ñ zya nai ka.
         Ki⌐mi ḡa yametyatta'ra, mi⌐ñna yametyau' zya nai ka.
     American: Do'o site ko⌐ñna meñdookusa'i ka⌐ñzi na'ñka tu⌐kau' ñ da-
         roo ⌐na'a.
     Japanese: Boku mo ⌐do'o site ka si⌐rya'a si⌐na'i kedo—

14. (Mr. Tanaka and his wife have dropped in to see Mr. and Mrs. Yamamo-
     to. Mr. Yamamoto is Mr. Tanaka's former boss.[1])

     Mrs. Yamamoto: A'ra i⌐rassya'i. A⌐ha'ta,[2] me⌐zurasi'i kata o⌐mie ni
         na'tta wa—

     Mr. Yamamoto: A'a, Ta⌐naka-kuñ ka. O'kusañ mo ḡo'issyo? Yo'ku
         ⌐ki'ta ⌐ne'e. E⌐ñryo na'ku a⌐ḡatte kure' yo.

     Mr. Tanaka: Do'o mo go⌐busata-itasima'sita. Mi⌐na'sama o⌐ge'ñki
         de irassyaimasu ka—

     Mr. Yamamoto: A'a, okaḡe de. Ki⌐mi ñ[3] toko' mo mi⌐ñna ge⌐ñki kai—

     Mr. Tanaka: Ha'a, okaḡesama de.

     Mrs. Tanaka: O⌐bo'ttyama mo o⌐ge'ñki de irassyaimasyoo?

     Mrs. Yamamoto: E'e. Ma⌐sao mo ge⌐ñki yo— De' mo ⌐ne'e. Mo'o su⌐ḡu
         ko'okoo no nyuuḡakusike'ñ desyoo? Ma⌐ibañ yo⌐naka ma'de
         be⌐ñkyoo-sina'kereba na⌐ra'nai no de, ka⌐waiso'o na no yo.

     Mrs. Tanaka: Gakkoo wa ⌐i'i to⌐koro' ni ⌐na'reba ⌐na'ru hodo kyo-
         osoo ḡa ⌐hi'doo gozaimasu kara ⌐ne'e.

     Mr. Yamamoto: Mu'ri ni ⌐i'i gakkoo e i⌐rete' mo, a'to de ko⌐ma'ru ñ
         da kara; mu'ri na be⌐ñkyoo wa su⌐ru' na tte i⌐u' ñ da ḡa—

     Mrs. Yamamoto: Kono-ḡoro ⌐syo'ttyuu teedeñ-suru desyoo? Se⌐kkaku
         be⌐ñkyoo-site ru' no ni, ko⌐ma'ttyau no yo—

     Mr. Yamamoto: Ro'osoku' zya be⌐ñkyoo-deki'nai kara ⌐ha'a.

     Mrs. Tanaka: O⌐bo'ttyama wa ⌐yo'ku o⌐deki ni na'ru kara, go⌐siñ-
         pai-nasara'nakute mo—

     Mrs. Yamamoto: To⌐ñde mo na'i wa— Si⌐ke'ñ ḡa ⌐su'meba hi⌐toa'ñsiñ
         de⌐ki'ru kedo; so're ma'de wa, o'ya no ho'o mo ⌐i'tu mo
         si⌐ke'ñ no ko⌐to ba⌐kari ka⌐ñḡa'ete i⌐na'kerya na⌐ra'nai ñ
         de, ra⌐ku' zya ⌐na'i no yo—

     Mr. Yamamoto: So're wa so'o to, ki'mi no oto'osañ ko'no-ḡoro ⌐do'o?

     Mr. Tanaka: Okaḡesama de, da⌐ibu yo'ku na⌐rima'sita. I'ma wa
         I⌐zu no oñseñ de yasu'ñde orimasu.

     Mr. Yamamoto: So're wa yo'katta ⌐ne'e.

     Mr. Tanaka: Su⌐ko'si ya⌐seta yo'o desu ḡa; isya wa ⌐mo'o si⌐ñpai
         na'i to i⌐tte orima'su no de, hi⌐toa'ñsiñ-itasimasita.

     Mrs. Yamamoto: A'katyañ wa? Tu⌐rete ku⌐reba ⌐yo'katta no ni—

     Mrs. Tanaka: No⌐rimono ḡa komima'su no de, kyo'o wa tu⌐rete mai-
         rimase'ñ desita. Ma⌐ta aḡarasete itadakima'su kara—

---

[1] Note the differences of politeness and formality level in the Japanese text,
reflecting the difference of position.

[2] A wife regularly addresses her husband as a⌐na'ta.

[3] Contraction of no.

Mrs. Yamamoto: Ze⌐hi tu⌐rete⌐ kite tyoodai⌐ Mo⌐o o⌐tañzyo⌐obi wa
⌐su⌐nda no ne?
Mrs. Tanaka:　　Ha⌐a, se⌐ñgetu de gozaimasita.
Mrs. Yamamoto: A⌐katyañ wa ta⌐hosi⌐mi ⌐ne⌐e. . . . I⌐ma ⌐gohañ tu⌐ku-
ra⌐sete ru kara, ta⌐bete itte tyoodai ne?
Mr. Tanaka:　　A⌐ri⌐gatoo gozaimasu ḡa, ko⌐domo ḡa ma⌐tte orimasu
kara‿
Mr. Yamamoto: Ma⌐a, soñna koto iwazu ni, ta⌐bete itte ku⌐re⌐ yo.
Su⌐ḡu daroo?
Mrs. Yamamoto: E⌐e, su⌐ḡu yo‿ Da⌐ kara, ta⌐bete ra⌐ssya⌐i yo.
Mr. Tanaka:　　O⌐so⌐reirimasu. Se⌐kkaku⌐ de gozaimasu kara, tyo-
⌐odai-site mairima⌐su.
Mrs. Yamamoto: So⌐o site⌐ ne? Na⌐rubeku iso⌐ide sa⌐seru⌐ kara‿

English Equivalents

1. Mr. Tanaka:　Yamada, are you going home now?
   Mr. Yamada: I'm (lit. I get) late every night entertaining (lit. because
   of association of) company clients.
   Mr. Tanaka:　Then it's the same with you? I get sick of it too because
   it's happening all the time. Instead of mixing with company
   clients, I'd prefer to eat leisurely at home, with my wife
   and children.
   Mr. Yamada: That's right. Having to take (lit. lead) people to restaurants and go away on business trips is awful, isn't it—for
   company employees.
   Mr. Tanaka:　But even if you take a job in another place it will be just
   the same.

2. Mr. Tanaka:　　Prices (of things) go up fast, don't they.
   Mr. Yamamoto: Sugar, for example, is going up as much as ¥5 every
   week.
   Mr. Tanaka:　　With everything getting expensive like that, it's awful,
   isn't it.
   Mr. Yamamoto: Salaries are the same but [nothing else is].

3. Mr. Tanaka:　　Even though Mr. Brown is an American, he didn't use
   a single word of English.
   Mr. Yamamoto: Did he say everything in Japanese?
   Mr. Tanaka:　　That's right. What's more, he uses quite good (lit.
   skillful) language. I was amazed.
   Mr. Yamamoto: Usually Westerners' speech is (something) strange
   (but)—you know.

4. Mrs. Tanaka: Say, let me have the dictionary.
   Maid:　　　　Do you mean this one?
   Mrs. Tanaka: Oh, not that. It's a thicker, black one. Isn't it right
   over there?
   Maid:　　　　If it's (lit. as for) a black one, there's only this one. Is
   this the one?
   Mrs. Tanaka: That's right, that's right, that one. Thanks.

5. Father: There's an interesting(-looking) movie. Wouldn't you like to go
             and see it (too)?
    Son: What kind of movie? Will you (lit. father) take me?
    Father: Yes, I'm free today so . . .
    Son: That's wonderful. Everything is good that you think is good
             (lit. provided it's a thing that father thinks is good). I'll
             change clothes right away so wait (lit. be waiting) for me,
             will you?
    Father: Sure. Take your time changing. (Lit. Come having changed
             slowly.)

6. Mrs. Tanaka: Is your son well?
    Mrs. Yamamoto: Yes, thank you. But I get upset because he doesn't
                    study at all.
    Mrs. Tanaka: Isn't that because he's still young (lit. small)?
    Mrs. Yamamoto: He's twelve already, so unless I make him study a
                    little [there will be trouble—i.e. I must make him study a
                    little].
    Mrs. Tanaka: I wonder if it isn't bad, forcing him to do it (lit. even
                    forcibly making him do it) when (lit. in spite of the fact that)
                    he doesn't want to (do).
    Mrs. Yamamoto: Hmmm. My husband too says that even if you force
                    him to do it by saying 'Study! Study!' he won't learn, so
                    it's better not to say anything, but soon now it will be [time
                    for] middle school—right? It's a worry.
    Mrs. Tanaka: You don't have to worry like that.

7. Mr. Tanaka: This may be unreasonable but would you translate this
                   letter for me by tomorrow?
    Mr. Yamamoto: What kind (of one) is it? If it's an easy one I can do it.
    Mr. Tanaka: For you it won't be hard. It's completely beyond me . . .
                   (Lit. For me, it's completely incomprehensible but . . .)
    Mr. Yamamoto: Well, I'll try and do it.
    Mr. Tanaka: I'm sorry, always ending up having you do it, but would
                   you?
    Mr. Yamamoto: Having to do it is good practice (lit. study). But unless
                   I try doing it, I can't tell whether I can or not—really. If I
                   can, I'll bring it tomorrow morning.
    Mr. Tanaka: I'm sorry to bother you, but I really need it (lit. I re-
                   quest it by all means).

8. Taro: I wonder who that fat fellow is.
    Jiro: Don't you know? It's Masao.
    Taro: Masao? Hasn't he put on weight!
    Jiro: I saw him at school yesterday. I was surprised too. He took a
           vacation at Nikko for about (as much as) a month and eating
           was his greatest pleasure, he says.
    Taro: He'd better get thin in a hurry!

9. Mr. Smith: We have to learn about (as many as) fifty kanji each week
                 nowadays. I think it's unreasonable.
    Mr. Tanaka: It probably is.
    Mr. Smith: My head is reeling (lit. has become strange) because all I
                 do is study.

10. Man: Isn't Ueda an interesting man!
    Woman: Yes. The more you see of him the nicer (person) he is.
    Man: Talking with him is a pleasure, isn't it! (Because) everything
            he says is interesting. (Lit. Saying nothing but interesting
            things.)

11. Tanaka: How is your daughter?
    Smith: Fine, thank you. She does nothing every day but [play] base-
            ball outside . . .
    Tanaka: Baseball?
    Smith: Yes. Instead of doing anything at all that's ladylike, she al-
            ways plays with the boys.

12. Tanaka: Isn't it nice weather!
    Smith: It's really (become) like spring, isn't it.
    Tanaka: I hear that the cherry trees have begun to bloom already.
    Smith: Really? Don't they seem a little early this year?

13. American Student (male): I don't want to study anything like Japanese
                any more.
    Japanese Friend (male):   Why?
    American: The more I do it the harder it gets, and I'm good and sick of
            it.
    Japanese: Come now, don't say that! Aren't you the best [in the group]?
            If you quit, you know that everybody will quit.
    American: I wonder why you use things like these kanji that are such a
            nuisance.
    Japanese: I don't know why either . . .

14. Mrs. Yamamoto: Oh, come in! /To Mr. Yamamoto/ (You,) someone
                unexpected has come.
    Mr. Yamamoto: Oh, Tanaka? Is your wife with you? I'm glad you
                came. Come right in (lit. up).
    Mr. Tanaka: Excuse us for not having been in touch with you. Are
                you all well?
    Mr. Yamamoto: Yes, thanks. Is everyone well at your place, too?
    Mr. Tanaka: Yes, thank you.
    Mrs. Tanaka: Your son is well too, isn't he?
    Mrs. Yamamoto: Yes, Masao is fine, too. But you know—[he'll be tak-
                ing] entrance exams for high school soon now. He has to
                study every night until the middle of the night; (so) I feel
                sorry for him.
    Mrs. Tanaka: [That's] because the better the school is, the keener
                the competition.
    Mr. Yamamoto: (Even) if you do get him into a good school with a
                struggle, you have trouble later on, so I say 'Don't do
                studying that's too much for you,' but [it does no good].
    Mrs. Yamamoto: The electricity goes off constantly these days, doesn't
                it? It gets to be annoying just when he is taking the trouble
                to study.
    Mr. Yamamoto: (Because) you can't study with candles!
    Mrs. Tanaka: Your son does very well so you don't have to worry.
    Mrs. Yamamoto: Heavens no! We'll be able to relax once the test is
                over, but until then, even (the side of) the parents must al-
                ways be thinking of nothing but the exams so it's not easy.

Mr. Yamamoto: To change the subject, how is your father these days?
Mr. Tanaka: He's much better, thank you. Right now, he's taking
                it easy at an Izu hot spring.
Mr. Yamamoto: Wasn't it fine [that it turned out that way].
Mr. Tanaka: He seems a little thin but the doctor keeps saying
                there's nothing more to worry about so we are relieved.
Mrs. Yamamoto: How is the baby? I wish you had brought him.
Mrs. Tanaka: The trains (and busses, etc.) are crowded so we didn't
                bring him today.. We'll (accept your letting us) come again
                so [we'll bring him then].
Mrs. Yamamoto: Please do bring him.   His birthday has passed (lit.
                finished) already, hasn't it?
Mrs. Tanaka: Yes, it was last month.
Mrs. Yamamoto: What a joy babies are! . . . I'm having dinner made
                now so do eat before you go (lit. go having eaten), won't
                you?
Mr. Tanaka: Thank you but the children are waiting, so . . .
Mr. Yamamoto: Oh, don't say that. Do eat before you go. (Lit. With-
                out saying that kind of thing, go having eaten.) (To Mrs. Ya-
                mamoto) It will be [ready] soon, won't it?
Mrs. Yamamoto: Yes, right away. That's why [you should] eat before
                you go.
Mr. Tanaka: Thank you very much. Since you've been so kind as to
                ask us, we will (eat and then go).
Mrs. Yamamoto: Fine. (Lit. Do that, will you?) I'll have it made as
                quickly as possible (so . . .)

EXERCISES

1. Read the following in Japanese:

a.	2/3	k.	10%
b.	3/4	l.	3%
c.	1/2	m.	14%
d.	9/10	n.	68%
e.	3/5	o.	50%
f.	4/7	p.	72%
g.	3/10	q.	99%
h.	1/9	r.	85%
i.	5/6	s.	90%
j.	3/8	t.	11%

2. Go through the Supplementary Dialogues of this lesson, changing all the
    typically feminine utterances to corresponding men s utterances if you
    are a man, and vice versa if you are a woman.

3. Make up twelve short conversations, each of which contains one of the
    following:

a. ta⌐ma ni¬ wa   g. to⌐ñde mo na¬i
b. ya⌐ppa¬ri   h. i⌐k-kaḡetu-ḡo¬to ni
c. ho⌐to¬ndo   i. so⌐re wa so¬o to
d. otya ka ko⌐ohi¬i   j. mu⌐ri ni saseru
e. tu¬i   k. do¬ñdoñ
f. be⌐ñkyoo ba¬kari   l. wa⌐ka¬ru to iinaḡara

4. Make up informal conversations according to the following outlines:

a. You have just met a close friend whom you haven't seen for a long
    time. Discuss what you've been doing, why you haven't been in
    touch, how the family is, when you can get together again, etc.
    Use your imagination and keep the conversation lively!

b. You are planning a weekend trip with a close friend. He wants to
    go to Kyoto, stay at a Western-style hotel, visit temples and
    shrines, and shop for souvenirs. You want to go to Izu, stay at a
    Japanese inn, and swim and fish and rest. Have a friendly discus-
    sion and reach some final agreement.

c. There is to be a baseball game next Saturday. You want a close
    friend of yours to go to the game with you, but he wants to watch
    it on television. Argue about the matter until one of you gives in.

Appendix I

A. Summary of Verbals

Every Japanese verbal is assigned to one of four sub-classes: -ru, -u, -aru, or irregular. Most verbals belong to one of the first two classes, since there are only five -aru verbals (go⌐za⌐ru⁺, i⌐rassya⌐ru⁺, ku⌐dasa⌐ru⁺, na⌐sa⌐ru⁺, and o⌐ssya⌐ru⁺) and two irregular verbals (ku⌐ru and suru). Verbals belonging to the -u class are further divided according to the sound that precedes final -u: k, ḡ, b, m, n, s, r, t, or a vowel.

The following is a summary of informal forms introduced in this text, with samples of each subclass. Where possible, an accented and unaccented sample are given for each. In every row across, Forms 2–9 are derived forms of the verbal whose citation form (the informal non-past) is Form 1; Form 10 is a verbal derivative but is itself an adjectival whose inflection is summarized in Appendix IB below; Forms 11–14 are verbal derivatives and are themselves the citation forms of verbals belonging to the -ru group, having their own inflected forms 2–9. When a particular form of a sample verbal occurs only rarely (or never)—for example, yo⌐roko⌐bu 'take pleasure in' does not ordinarily occur in the imperative—the rare (or hypothetical) form is enclosed in parentheses in the chart on pages 360–61.

359

SAMPLE

	1.	2.	3.	4.	5.	6.	7.
Subclass	Non-past	Stem	Gerund	Past	Conditional	Representative	Provisional

-ru

(accented)	ta⌐be¬ru 'eat'	ta⌐be	ta⌐bete	ta⌐beta	ta⌐betara	ta⌐betari	ta⌐be¬reba
(unaccented)	ireru 'insert'	ire	irete	ireta	i⌐reta¬ra	i⌐reta¬ri	i⌐rere¬ba

-u

-ku

(accented)	a⌐ru¬ku 'walk'	a⌐ru¬ki	a⌐ru¬ite	a⌐ru¬ita	a⌐ru¬itara	a⌐ru¬itari	a⌐ru¬keba
(unaccented)	kiku 'ask'	kiki	kiite	kiita	ki⌐ita¬ra	ki⌐ita¬ri	ki⌐ke¬ba

-g̃u

(accented)	o⌐yo¬g̃u 'swim'	o⌐yo¬g̃i	o⌐yo¬ide	o⌐yo¬ida	o⌐yo¬idara	o⌐yo¬idari	o⌐yo¬g̃eba

-bu

(accented)	yo⌐roko¬bu 'take pleasure in'	yo⌐roko¬bi	yo⌐roko¬nde	yo⌐roko¬nda	yo⌐roko¬ndara	yo⌐roko¬ndari	yo⌐roko¬beba
(unaccented)	yobu 'call'	yobi	yoñde	yoñda	yo⌐ñda¬ra	yo⌐ñda¬ri	yo⌐be¬ba

-mu

(accented)	no⌐mu 'drink'	no⌐mi	no⌐ñde	no⌐ñda	no⌐ñdara	no⌐ñdari	no⌐meba
(unaccented)	yamu 'cease'	yami	yañde	yañda	ya⌐ñda¬ra	ya⌐ñda¬ri	ya⌐me¬ba

-nu

(unaccented)	sinu 'die'	sini	siñde	siñda	si⌐ñda¬ra	si⌐ñda¬ri	si⌐ne¬ba

-su

(accented)	ha⌐na¬su 'talk'	ha⌐na¬si	ha⌐na¬site	ha⌐na¬sita	ha⌐na¬sitara	ha⌐na¬sitari	ha⌐na¬seba
(unaccented)	kasu 'lend'	kasi	kasite	kasita	ka⌐sita¬ra	ka⌐sita¬ri	ka⌐se¬ba

-ru

(accented)	tu⌐ku¬ru 'make'	tu⌐ku¬ri	tu⌐ku¬tte	tu⌐ku¬tta	tu⌐ku¬ttara	tu⌐ku¬ttari	tu⌐ku¬reba
(unaccented)	noru 'ride'	nori	notte	notta	no⌐tta¬ra	no⌐tta¬ri	no⌐re¬ba

-tu

(accented)	ma⌐tu 'wait'	ma⌐ti	ma⌐tte	ma⌐tta	ma⌐ttara	ma⌐ttari	ma⌐teba

Vowel + -u

(accented)	ha⌐ra¬u 'pay'	ha⌐ra¬i	ha⌐ra¬tte	ha⌐ra¬tta	ha⌐ra¬ttara	ha⌐ra¬ttari	ha⌐ra¬eba
(unaccented)	arau 'wash'	arai	aratte	aratta	a⌐ratta¬ra	a⌐ratta¬ri	a⌐rae¬ba

-aru [1]

(accented)	o⌐ssya¬ru ' 'say'	o⌐ssya¬i	o⌐ssya¬tte	o⌐ssya¬tta	o⌐ssya¬ttara	o⌐ssya¬ttari	o⌐ssya¬reba

Irregular

(accented)	ku⌐ru 'come'	ki¬	ki⌐te¬	ki⌐ta¬	ki⌐ta¬ra	ki⌐ta¬ri	ku⌐reba
(unaccented)	suru 'do'	si	site	sita	si⌐ta¬ra	si⌐ta¬ri	su⌐re¬ba

[1] Go⌐za¬ru belongs to this subclass but occurs only in the formal style—i.e. the stem go⌐zai compounds with √-ma⌐su. I⌐rassya¬ru has alternate gerunds i⌐rassya¬tte ~ i⌐ra¬site, na⌐sa¬ru has alternate gerunds na⌐sa¬tte ~ na⌐su¬tte, and ku⌐dasa¬ru has alternate gerunds ku⌐dasa¬tte ~ ku⌐dasu¬tte. Parallel alternation occurs in Forms 4–6 of these three verbals.

VERBALS

8. Tentative	9. Imperative	10. Negative Non-past	11. Potential Non-past	12. Causative Non-past	13. Passive Non-past	14. Passive Causative Non-past
taˈbeyoˈo ireyoo	taˈbeˈro iˈreroˈ	taˈbeˈnai irenai	taˈberareˈru irerareru	taˈbesaseˈru iresaseru	taˈberareˈru irerareru	taˈbesaserareˈru iresaserareru
aˈrukoˈo kikoo	aˈruˈke kiˈkeˈ	aˈrukaˈnai kikanai	aˈrukeˈru kikeru	aˈrukaseˈru kikaseru	aˈrukareˈru kikareru	aˈrukaserareˈru kikase.reru
oˈyogoˈo	oˈyoˈge	oˈyogaˈnai	oˈyogeˈru	oˈyogaseˈru	oˈyogareˈru	oˈyogaserareˈru
(yoˈrokoboˈo) yoboo	(yoˈrokoˈbe) yoˈbeˈ	yoˈrokobaˈnai yobanai	(yoˈrokobeˈru) yoberu	(yoˈrokobaseˈru) yobaseru	(yoˈrokobareˈru) yobareru	(yoˈrokobaserareˈru) yobaseraseru
noˈmoˈo (yamoo)	noˈme (yaˈmeˈ)	noˈmaˈnai yamanai	noˈmeˈru (yameru)	noˈmaseˈru (yamaseru)	noˈmareˈru yamareru	noˈmaserareˈru (yamaserareru)
(sinoo)	(siˈneˈ)	sinanai	(sineru)	(sinaseru)	sinareru	(sinaserareru)
haˈnasoˈo kasoo	haˈnaˈse kaˈseˈ	haˈnasaˈnai kasanai	haˈnaseˈru kaseru	haˈnasaseˈru kasaseru	haˈnasareˈru kasareru	haˈnasaserareˈru kasaserareru
tuˈkuroˈo noroo	tuˈkuˈre noˈreˈ	tuˈkuraˈnai noranai	tuˈkureˈru noreru	tuˈkuraseˈru noraseru	tuˈkurareˈru norareru	tuˈkuraserareˈru noraseraseru
maˈtoˈo mate	maˈte	maˈtaˈnai matanai	maˈteˈru materu	maˈtaseˈru matase.ru	maˈtareˈru matareru	maˈtaserareˈru mataseraseru
haˈraoˈo araoo	haˈraˈe aˈraeˈ	haˈrawaˈnai arawanai	haˈraeˈru araeru	haˈrawaseˈru arawaseru	haˈrawareˈru arawareru	haˈrawaserareˈru arawaseraseru
oˈssyaroˈo	oˈssyaˈi	oˈssyaraˈnai	oˈssyareˈru	(oˈssyaraseˈru)	(oˈssyarareˈru)	(oˈssyaraserareˈru)
koˈyoˈo siyoo	koˈi siˈroˈ	koˈnai sinai	koˈrareˈru deˈkiˈru	koˈsaseˈru saseru	koˈrareˈru sareru	koˈsaserareˈru saseraseru

362   Appendix I

Remarks on accent:

FORM 1 (Non-past): Before particles g̱a, ka, kara, keredo, si, and yori, [1]
  sentence particles ka, kai, sa, and wa, nominal no, and various forms
  of the copula, [2] an unaccented non-past acquires a final-syllable accent.
  Examples: no⌐ru⌐ kara, a⌐rau⌐ keredo, ki⌐ku⌐ kai, su⌐ru⌐ no, etc.

FORM 3 (Gerund): Before particles mo and wa, and sentence particle yo,
  an unaccented gerund acquires a final-syllable accent. Examples: no⌐tte⌐
  mo, a⌐ratte⌐ wa, ki⌐ite⌐ yo, etc.

FORM 4 (Past): See remarks under Form 1 above. Examples: no⌐tta⌐ kara,
  a⌐ratta⌐ keredo, ki⌐ita⌐ kai, si⌐ta⌐ no, etc.

FORM 8 (Tentative): The informal tentative of an unaccented verbal has an
  accented alternant. Thus: no⌐ro⌐o, a⌐rao⌐o, etc.

GENERAL: When, according to the regular pattern, an accent would occur on
  the voiceless syllable of a verbal, it may shift to a neighboring voiced
  syllable.

  Examples:

  ku⌐ru 'come':   gerund ki⌐te⌐
  hu⌐ru 'fall, rain': gerund hu⌐tte⌐ (or hu⌐tte)
  ki⌐ru 'cut':   gerund ki⌐tte⌐ (or ki⌐tte)

  Formal verbals are made by combining the stem (Form 2 above) with
  √-ma⌐su. The inflection of √-ma⌐su is as follows:

  1   2   3   4   5   6   7
-ma⌐su ———   -ma⌐site -ma⌐sita -ma⌐sitara -ma⌐sitari (-masu⌐reba)

                        8   9   10
                    -masyo⌐o   -ma⌐se   -mase⌐n̄

---

[1] Alternate accent: unaccented verbal + accented yo⌐ri.

[2] Alternate accent: unaccented verbal and accented √da. Example: i⌐ku⌐ desyoo or i⌐ku desyo⌐o.

B. Summary of Adjectivals

An adjectival is an inflected word which ends in -ai, -ii, -ui, or -oi in its citation form (informal non-past) and has a derivative form (the adverbial) ending in -ku.

Negative adjectivals end in -nai and are derived from verbals; they have, in addition to a -ku adverbial, an alternate adverbial ending in -zu, but they have no polite adverbial form.

-Tai 'want to' adjectivals are also derived from verbals; except for accent differences, they are identical with -ai adjectivals in general.

The following is a summary of adjectival forms introduced in this text, with samples of each type. Note that Form 11, the negative form of non-negative adjectivals, is the adverbial + na'i; na'i is itself inflected like any negative adjectival except that it has no -zu adverbial.

SAMPLI

	1.	2.	3. Alternate Negative Adverbial	4. Polite Adverbial	5.
	Non-past	Adverbial			Gerund
-ai					
(accented)	ta⌐ka¬i 'is high'	ta⌐kaku	——	ta⌐koo	ta⌐kakute
(unaccented)	tumetai 'is cold'	tumetaku	——	tumetoo	tu⌐meta⌐ku◆
-ii					
(accented)	su⌐zusi¬i 'is cool'	su⌐zu¬siku	——	suzusyuu	su⌐zu¬sikut◆
(unaccented)	oisii 'is delicious'	oisiku	——	oisyuu	o⌐isi¬kute
-ui					
(accented)	a⌐tu¬i 'is hot'	a¬tuku	——	a¬tuu	a¬tukute
(unaccented)	atui 'is thick'	atuku	——	atuu	a⌐tu¬kute
-oi					
(accented)	hi⌐ro¬i 'is wide'	hi¬roku	——	hi¬roo	hi⌐rokute
(unaccented)	tooi 'is far'	tooku	——	tooo	to⌐o¬kute
-tai					
(accented)	ta⌐beta¬i 'want to eat'	ta⌐beta¬ku	——	ta⌐beto¬o	ta⌐beta⌐ku◆
(unaccented)	ikitai 'want to go'	ikitaku	——	ikitoo	i⌐kita⌐kute
-nai					
(accented)	ta⌐be¬nai 'doesn't eat'	ta⌐be¬naku	ta⌐be¬zu	——	ta⌐be¬naku◆
(unaccented)	ikanai 'doesn't go'	ikanaku	ikazu	——	i⌐kana¬kut◆

.DJECTIVALS

6. Past	7. Conditional	8. Representative	9. Provisional	10. Tentative [1]	11. Negative
aˀkakatta	taˀkakattara	taˀkakattari	taˀkakereba	taᶜkakaroˀo	taˀkaku ˀnaˀi
ᴉˀmetaˀkatta	tuˀmetaˀkattara	tuˀmetaˀkattari	tuˀmetaˀkereba	tuˀmetakaroˀo	tuˀmetaku naˀi
uˀzuˀsikatta	suˀzuˀsikattara	suˀzuˀsikattari	suˀzuˀsikereba	suˀzusikaroˀo	suˀzuˀsiku ˀnaˀi
ˀisiˀkatta	oˀisiˀkattara	oˀisiˀkattari	oˀisiˀkereba	oˀisikaroˀo	oˀisiku naˀi
ˀtukatta	aˀtukattara	aˀtukattari	aˀtukereba	aˀtukaroˀo	aˀtuku ˀnaˀi
ᶜtuˀkatta	aᶜtuˀkattara	aᶜtuˀkattari	aᶜtuˀkereba	aᶜtukaroˀo	aᶜtuku naˀi
iˀrokatta	hiˀrokattara	hiˀrokattari	hiˀrokereba	hiˀrokaroˀo	hiˀroku ˀnaˀi
ɔᶜoˀkatta	toᶜoˀkattara	toᶜoˀkattari	toᶜoˀkereba	toᶜokaroˀo	toᶜoku naˀi
aᶜbetaˀkatta	taᶜbetaˀkattara	taᶜbetaˀkattari	taᶜbetaˀkereba	taᶜbetakaroˀo	taᶜbetaˀku ˀnaˀi
ᶜkitaˀkatta	iᶜkitaˀkattara	iᶜkitaˀkattari	iᶜkitaˀkereba	iᶜkitakaroˀo	iᶜkitaku naˀi
aᶜbeˀnakatta	taᶜbeˀnakattara	taᶜbeˀnakattari	taᶜbeˀnakereba	taᶜbenakaroˀo	——
ᶜkanaˀkatta	iᶜkanaˀkattara	iᶜkanaˀkattari	iᶜkanaˀkereba -	iᶜkanakaroˀo	——

The alternate informal tentative adjectival pattern — consisting of a non-past adjectival + aroo — is the pattern regularly drilled in the text.

Remarks on accent:

FORM 1 (Non-past): Before particles g̱a, ka, kara, keredo, si, and yori, [1]
sentences particles ka, kai, sa, and wa, nominal no, and forms of the
copula, an unaccented non-past acquires an accent on its next-to-last syllable. [2] Examples: tu⌐meta¬i kara, i⌐kita¬i keredo, i⌐kana¬i no, etc.

In sentence-final position, a normally unaccented non-past adjectival occurs with both accented and unaccented alternants. Example: Abunai. or
A⌐buna¬i.

GENERAL: Many of the accented adjectival forms in the chart above have
alternate accents in current use in the Tokyo area. Some of these have
occurred in the text.

Examples:

ta¬kakute   or   ta⌐ka¬kute
hi¬rokute   or   hi⌐ro¬kute
mi⌐zi¬kaku   or   mi⌐zika¬ku
u⌐re¬syuu   or   u⌐resyu¬u

In each case, the second form is a newer form.

---

[1] Alternate accent: unaccented adjectival + accented yo¬ri.

[2] But tooi acquires an accent on its final syllable.

C. Summary of the Copula da

The following forms of √da have been introduced:

	1. Non-past	2. Pre-nominal	3. Gerund	4. Past	5. Condi-tional	6. Repre-sentative	7. Provi-sional	8. Ten-tative
Inform-al	da	na~no	de	da˺tta	da˺ttara	da˺ttari	nara/ba/	da⌐ro˺o
Form-al	de˺su	——	de˺site	de˺sita	de˺si-tara	de˺si-tari	de˺sita-raba	de⌐syo˺o

Remarks on accent:

accented form of √da regularly loses its accent following an accented word or phrase.

FORM 2 (Pre-nominal) is regularly unaccented except that na following an unaccented word or phrase and preceding nominal no acquires an accent. Example: byo⌐oki na˺ no.

FORM 3 (Gerund) following an unaccented nominal (or nominal + particle) acquire an accent before particles mo and wa.   Examples: so⌐re de˺ mo, so⌐re de˺ wa, ko⌐ko kara de˺ mo, etc.

FORM 8 (Tentative) following an unaccented verbal has alternate accents: either the verbal remains unaccented (with da⌐ro˺o/de⌐syo˺o accented) or the verbal acquires a final-syllable accent (with daroo/desyoo unaccented).

Examples:

i⌐ku daro˺o	or	i⌐ku˺ daroo
i⌐ku desyo˺o	or	i⌐ku˺ desyoo
i⌐tta daro˺o	or	i⌐tta˺ daroo
i⌐tta desyo˺o	or	i⌐tta˺ desyoo

Appendix II

A. na Nominals [1]

be⌐ñri	'convenient'	me⌐ewaku	'troublesome'
betu [2]	'separate'	mu⌐ri	'unreasonable'
da⌐isuki	'very pleasing'	o⌐oki [3]	'big'
da⌐izi⌐	'valuable,' 'important'	rippa	'splendid'
da⌐izyo⌐obu	'safe'	sakañ	'flourishing'
da⌐me⌐	'no good'	si⌐tu⌐ree	'rude'
ge⌐ñki	'good health,' 'high	si⌐zuka	'quiet'
	spirits'	-soo [4]	'looking as if'
ha⌐de⌐	'bright,' 'loud,' 'flashy'	su⌐ki⌐	'pleasing'
heeki	'unconcerned'	syo⌐oziki⌐	'honest'
he⌐ñ	'strange'	taiheñ	'dreadful,' 'awful'
hima	'free time'	taisetu	'important'
hu⌐beñ	'inconvenient'	te⌐enee	'polite'
hukuzatu	'complicated'	tekitoo	'suitable'
hu⌐u	'manner'	ti⌐isa [3]	'small'
hu⌐ziyuu	'inconvenient,'	yo⌐o	'manner'
	'restricted'	yuumee	'famous'
iroiro [2]	'various'	zi⌐mi⌐	'subdued,'
i⌐ya⌐	'unpleasant'		'conservative'
kañtañ	'simple'	zi⌐yu⌐u	'free'
ka⌐waiso⌐o	'pitiful'	zyoobu	'sturdy'
ke⌐kkoo	'fine'	zyo⌐ozu⌐	'proficient'
kirai	'dislike'	zyu⌐ubu⌐ñ	'enough'
ki⌐ree	'pretty,' 'clean'		

Examples of usage:

    Ki⌐ree desu. '[It]'s pretty.'
    Ki⌐ree zya a⌐rimase⌐ñ. '[It] isn't pretty.'
    Ki⌐ree na o⌐zyo⌐osañ desu. '[She]'s a pretty girl.'
    Ki⌐ree ni na⌐rima⌐sita. '[She]'s grown to be pretty.'
    Ki⌐ree ni ka⌐kima⌐sita. '[He] wrote beautifully.'

---

[1] The list below includes all na nominals introduced in this text.

[2] Occurs with na or no as the modifier of a following nominal.

[3] With following na, alternates with -i form of related adjectival as modifier of a following nominal. Thus: $\left| \frac{ti⌐isa\ na}{ti⌐isa⌐i} \right|$ ⌐ko⌐e 'low voice'; $\left| \frac{o⌐oki\ na}{o⌐oki⌐i} \right|$ ⌐ko⌐e 'loud voice.'

[4] For example, de⌐kiso⌐o 'looking as if it would be possible,' a⌐tuso⌐o 'looking as if it would be hot,' zyo⌐obuso⌐o 'sturdy-looking,' etc.

B. Counters [1]

	Counter for:	Numerals of Series I [2]	Numerals of Series II [3]	Irregular	Counts	Names	Counts and Names
-bai (34)	multiples	X			X		
-bañ (12)	serial numbers	X				X	
-bañ (21)	nights		X		X		
-bañ-señ (19)	track numbers	X				X	
-ba'ñti (34)	lot numbers	X				X	
-bu (35)	units of per cent	X			X		
-buñ (35)	fraction denominators	X				X	
-dai (20)	vehicles	X			X		
-do (1)	number of times	X			X		
-eñ (3)	yen	X			X		
-ḡatu (8)	months of the year	X				X	
-ḡo'o-sya (19)	train car numbers	X				X	
-gu'ramu (22)	grams	X			X		
-hai (14)	glassfuls	X			X		
-heñ (32)	number of times	X			X		
-hoñ (5)	long, cylindrical objects	X			X		
-huñ (8)	minutes	X					X
-ka/-niti (8)	days			X			X
-ka'ḡetu (8)	months	X			X		
-kai (16)	floors	X					X
-kai (32)	number of times	X			X		
-ma (21)	rooms		X		X		
-mai (5)	thin, flat objects	X			X		
-neñ (8)	years	X					X
-niñ-mae (15)	portions	X			X		
-ri/-niñ (10)	people			X	X		
-ri'ttoru (20)	liters	X			X		
-satu (5)	volumes	X			X		
-syu'ukañ (8)	weeks	X			X		
-too (19)	classes	X				X	
-tu (5, 10)	units of inanimate objects; years of age (people)		X		X		

---

[1] The list below includes all the counters introduced in this text. The parenthesized numbers tell in what lesson each appeared first. An accent mark indicates a consistently accented counter.

[2] I'ti', ni', sañ, etc.

[3] Hi'to', huta, mi', etc.

[4] A number which counts tells <u>how many</u>; a number which names tells <u>which one</u>. Thus: ni-'ka'ḡetu '2 months' counts, ni'-ḡatu 'February' names, and ni'-neñ '2 years' or 'the year 2' counts and names.

Counters (cont.)

| | | Occurs with: | | | Usage: | | |
	Counter for:	Numerals of Series I	Numerals of Series II	Irreg-ular	Counts	Names	Counts and Names
-tubo (30)	tsubo (app. 6' x 6')		X[1]		X		
-tyoome (7)	chome	X				X	
-wari (35)	tens of per cent	X			X		
-zi (8)	hours of the day	X				X	
-zikañ (8)	hours	X			X		
-zyoo (30)	jo (app. 3' x 6')	X			X[2]		

---

[1] Also occurs with some numerals of Series I.

[2] Also occurs as a name for a room having the given number of mats.

C. Table of Time Expressions [1]

		Present	Next	Next-after-next	Last	Last-before-last	Every
'day'	hi	kyo'o 'today'	a'sita 'tomorrow'	a'sa'tte 'day after tomorrow'	ki'no'o 'yesterday'	o'toto'i 'day before yesterday'	ma'initi 'every day'
'morning'	a'sa	ke'sa 'this morning'	a'sita no a'sa 'tomorrow morning'	a'sa'tte no a'sa 'morning after next'	ki'ñoo no a'sa 'yesterday morning'	o'totoi no a'sa 'morning before last'	ma'iasa 'every morning'
'night'	bañ	ko'ñbañ 'tonight'	asita no bañ 'tomorrow night'	a'sa'tte no bañ 'night after next'	yu'ube 'last night'	ototoi no bañ 'night before last'	ma'ibañ [2] 'every night'
'week'	syu'u	koñsyuu 'this week'	raisyuu 'next week'	saraisyuu 'week after next'	señsyuu 'last week'	se'ñse'ñsyuu 'week before last'	maisyuu 'every week'
'month'	tu'ki'	koñgetu 'this month'	raigetu 'next month'	saraigetu 'month after next'	señgetu 'last month'	se'ñse'ñgetu 'month before last'	maituki or maigetu 'every month'
'year'	to'si'	kotosi 'this year'	raineñ 'next year'	saraineñ 'year after next'	kyo'neñ 'last year'	o'to'tosi 'year before last'	maitosi or maineñ 'every year'

[1] There are many formal alternants which are not listed here; only the more common conversational expressions are included.

[2] Has unaccented alternant.

Japanese-English Glossary

Except for proper names, the following list contains all the vocabulary introduced in this text, Parts I and II—words occurring in the Notes and as additional vocabulary as well as those occurring in the Basic Dialogues. Numbers following the entries refer to lessons: a number alone means that the entry first occurs in the Basic Dialogues of that lesson; a number followed by '-A' refers to the Additional Vocabulary of that lesson; a number followed by '-N' indicates that the item first occurs in the Notes or any later section of that lesson. CI, Int, and App. refer to Classroom Instructions, [1] Introductory Lesson, and Appendix respectively. An asterisk means that the item is included in the Index to the Grammatical Notes, with a reference to the location of the appropriate note(s).

Except in special cases, verbals and adjectivals are listed in their citation form only. Every verbal—except a compound ending in -suru—is identified as transitive /tr/ or intransitive /intr/ [2] and is assigned to the appropriate subclass; [3] its gerund is also given. For example, akeru /tr:-ru: akete/ identifies akeru as a transitive verbal belonging to the -ru subclass (i.e. the subclass to which ta⌐be┐ru 'eat' and mi┐ru 'see' belong), with gerund akete. All compound verbals ending in -suru have the same inflection as that of suru alone; accordingly, they are identified only as /tr/ or /intr/.

Every adjectival is identified by '/-ku/' [4] after the citation form. Thus, the adjectival meaning 'is big' appears as o⌐oki┐i /-ku/.

All forms of the copula which occur in the text are listed and identified.

Nominals occur with no special designation, except that the members of the subclass of na-nominals [5] are identified by a following '/na/.'

Particles and quotatives are so identified. All are marked with asterisks, since all are included in the index.

Pre-nominals are identified by the designation '/+ nom/.'

Counters are so identified and are listed with a preceding hyphen.

---

[1] Words designated as CI are those which occur only in the Classroom Instructions.

[2] For a description of transitive and intransitive verbals, see Part I, Lesson 16, Grammatical Note 1.

[3] For a description of verbal subclasses, see Part I, Lesson 11, Grammatical Note 1.

[4] See Part I, Lesson 2, Grammatical Note 1.

[5] See Part I, Lesson 12, Grammatical Note 4.

373

'/M/' and '/W/' follow entries typical of men's or women's speech respectively.

Except in a few special cases, words having a polite alternant that differs from the plain alternant only in the addition of the polite prefix o- or go- are listed only in the plain alternant.

For purposes of alphabetizing, hyphens and the macron of ḡ are ignored. Syllabic ñ is assigned to the position immediately following nonsyllabic n.

In most cases, combinations occurring as indented sublistings match the first occurrence in the lessons; but a simpler, more generally occurring example of the pattern is cited in cases where the combination which occurs first in the lessons seems less desirable as the model for a pattern of wide general use.

A

a oh! 4
a⌐a oh! Int.
a⌐a that way 29-N
a⌐a yes 16
abunai /-ku/ is dangerous 7
aḡaru /intr:-u:aḡatte/ go up, come up, enter 18
aḡaru⁺ /intr:-u:aḡatte/ go to someone else's home 35
aḡeru* /tr:-ru:aḡete/ give (to someone other than the speaker) 17; raise 29-N
site aḡeru do for someone 17
aida* space between 7; interval of time, while 31
kono aida the other day, recently 31
Tookyoo to Yokohama no aida between Tokyo and Yokohama 7
tu⌐tu¬nde moratte (i)ru aida while [someone] is having [something] wrapped 31
ainiku unfortunate(ly) 34
airoñ pressing iron, pressing 21
a⌐iroñ o kake¬ru iron, press 21
akaboo porter, redcap 20
akai /-ku/ is red 4
akañboo baby 26-N
akarui /-ku/ is light (i.e. not dark) 35-N
a⌐katyañ baby 26
akeru /tr:-ru:akete/ open [something] 16
a⌐ki autumn, fall 18
a⌐kiya¬sumi autumn vacation 25-N
aku /intr:-u:aite/ [something] opens 16; become vacant 29
aite (i)ru be open 16; be free for use or unoccupied 21
a⌐ma¬do sliding storm-door 18
a⌐maḡa¬sa rain umbrella 29-N
amai /-ku/ is sweet or sugary or insufficiently salted 14-A
a⌐me rain 18
a⌐me ḡa ⌐hu⌐ru it rains 18
a⌐merika¬ziñ an American 10
a⌐mi¬do screens 30
a⌐na¬ hole 33
a⌐na¬ o akeru make a hole 33-N
a⌐na¬ ḡa aku get a hole in something 33-N
a⌐na¬ta you Int

ane older sister 11-A
a⌐ni older brother 11-A
ano* /+ nom/ that — over there 3
Ano ne! Say! Hey there! 13
anoo uh... 34
añmari /+ negative/ not very much, not so much, not too much 3; /+ affirmative/ so much, too much 14
añna* that kind, that kind of 5
añna ni to that extent 28-N
a⌐ñna¬i-suru /tr/ guide, show the way 31
a⌐ñnaisyo¬ guidebook 32
añnaizyo, a⌐ñnaizyo¬ information booth 19
a⌐ñta you 35-N
a⌐o blue, green 16
a⌐o¬i /-ku/ is blue or green 4; is pale 14
a⌐pa¬ato apartment house 16
a⌐ra /W/ oh! you don't say! not really! 33
arare hail 26-A
a⌐rasi storm 26-A
arau /tr:-u:aratte/ wash 17
are* that thing over there 2
A⌐ri¬ḡatoo (gozaimasita).⁺ Thank you (for what you did). Int.
A⌐ri¬ḡatoo (gozaimasu).⁺ Thank you. Int.
a⌐ru* /intr:-u:a⌐tte;neg-na¬i/ be located (of inanimate objects), have 2
si⌐mete ⌐a⌐ru have been closed 16
a⌐ru¬ku /intr:-u:a⌐ru¬ite/ walk 20
a⌐sa morning 9
a⌐sa¬ flax, linen 23-A
a⌐sago¬hañ breakfast 15-N
asamesi /M/ breakfast 24-N
a⌐sa¬tte day after tomorrow 30
a⌐si¬ leg, foot 17-A
a⌐sita¬, asita tomorrow 1
asobu /intr:-u:asoñde/ play, amuse oneself, be at leisure, have a good time; visit (for pleasure); loaf, be unemployed 27
asoko that place over there, over there 6
asuko /see asoko/ 6
a⌐tama¬ head 17

a⌐tama¬ (cont.)
  a⌐tama¬ g̃a ⌐i⌐i have a good head,
    be smart or bright 35
  a⌐tama¬ g̃a i⌐ta⌐i have a headache 17
a⌐tarasi⌐i /-ku/ is new or fresh 2
atarimae natural, proper, reasonable
    32-N
atasi /W/ I, me 35-N
a⌐t(a)taka⌐i /-ku/ is warm 16
atira that one (of two); that way,
    thereabouts, over there 6
a⌐to* later, afterward 4
  a⌐to de later, at a later time 4
  su⌐ma¬seta ato de after having
    finished 31
  a⌐to no i⌐k-ka⌐g̃etu the remaining
    month 29
  A⌐to ⌐na¬ni o simasyoo ka. What

a⌐to* (cont.)
  shall I do next? 17
a⌐tti¬ /see atira/ 6
atui /-ku/ is thick (of flat objects) 22-N
a⌐tu¬i /-ku/ is hot 14
a⌐tusug̃i¬ru /intr:-ru:a⌐tusu⌐g̃ite/ be
    too hot 21
a⌐u /intr:-u:a⌐tte/ meet, see (and talk
    to) a person 11
  Ya⌐mada-sañ ni a⌐u meet or see
    Mr. Yamada 11
azi flavor, taste 32
  azi g̃a suru have a flavor 33-N
a⌐zuka¬ru /tr:-u:a⌐zuka¬tte/ receive in
    custody, take charge of, keep 20-N
a⌐zuke¬ru /tr:-ru:a⌐zu¬kete/ put into some-
    one else's keeping temporarily,
    check, deposit 20

B

baai circumstances, case 34
  i⌐so¬g̃u baai ni in case [someone]
    is in a hurry 34
bai double 34-N
  ba⌐i ni na⌐ru [something] doubles
    34-N
  bai ni suru double [something] 34-N
-bai /counter for multiples/ 34
ba⌐kari* /particle/ nothing but,
    little else but, only, just 35
  go⌐busata ba⌐kari nothing but
    neglect to write or visit 35
ba⌐kkari /see ba⌐kari/ 35-N
bañ night 19
-bañ /counter for nights/ 21
-bañ /counter for naming numbers
    in a series/ 12
bañdo (man's) belt 23-A
  bañdo o suru wear a belt 23-A
ba⌐ñg̃o¬hañ evening meal, dinner 15-N
ba⌐ñg̃o¬o number 12
bañmesi /M/ dinner 24-N
-bañ-señ /counter for naming track
    numbers/ 19
-bañti /counter for naming lot
    numbers/ 34
ba⌐ree ballet 28-A
ba⌐su bus 8
ba⌐ta butter 14-A
ba⌐tterii battery 20-N
be⌐ekoku⌐ziñ an American 10-A
be⌐esubo¬oru baseball 35-N
be⌐ñg̃o¬si lawyer 24-A

beñkyoo-suru /tr/ study 11
be⌐ñri /na/ convenient 29-N
beñriya handyman 33
be⌐ñto⌐o box lunch 27
be⌐ñzyo¬ /M/ toilet 6-A
beruto (woman's) belt 23-A
  beruto o suru wear a belt 23-A
be⌐tto bed 17-A
betu /na ~ no/ separate 21
betu ni /+ negative/ not especially 13
bi⌐iru beer 14
bi⌐kku¬ri-suru /intr/ be surprised, be
    amazed, be startled 29
bi⌐ru building (Western style) 6
bo⌐ku, boku /M/ I, me 5
bo⌐kutati /M/ we, us 27
boo stick 33-A
bo⌐eki¬syoo foreign trader 24-A
bo⌐ohu¬u gale 26-A
booi waiter, steward, barboy, office
    boy 24-A
boosi hat 23
botañ button 33-N
bo⌐ttyañ ‡ son 11-A
bu part 28
  hiru no bu daytime performance
    28-N
  yo⌐ru no bu evening performance 28
-bu /counter for units of per cent/ 35
bukka commodity prices 29
bu⌐kkyoo Buddhism 32
-buñ /counter for fraction denominator/
    35

-buñ (cont.)

sa⌐ñ-buñ no iti¬ one third 35

bu⌐ñbo¬oḡu writing materials 31-A

bu⌐ñpo¬oḡu writing materials 31-A

bu⌐ñraku (traditional Japanese puppet theater) 28-A

bu⌐ra¬usu blouse 23-A

bu⌐re¬eki brakes 20

bu⌐ro¬okaa agent 30

buta pig 17-A

butaniku pork 22-N

butudañ household altar (Buddhist) 35

byoobu screen 31-A

byooiñ hospital 7

byooki sickness, sick 11

D

da* /copula: informal non-past/

da¬ kara therefore, so, for that reason, that is why 27

dai charge, cost 22

dai* /M/ /interrogative alternant of da/ 35

-dai /counter for vehicles/ 20

daibu a good deal, a good many 33

daidokoro kitchen 17

da⌐idokorodo¬oḡu kitchen utensils 31-A

daiḡaku university 13

da⌐iku carpenter 24-A

da⌐isuki /na/ very pleasing 15

daitai for the most part, by and large, generally 33

da⌐izi /na/ important, valuable 11-N

Odaizi ni.† Take care /of yourself/! 11

da⌐izyo¬obu /na/ safe, all right 7

da⌐ke¬* just, only 4

so⌐re dake¬ just that, that's all 4

mi-⌐ttu¬ dake just three (units) 5

da⌐kuroñ dacron 23

da⌐me¬ /na/ no good, bad, broken 2

dañboo heating 30

da⌐ñboose¬tubi heating equipment, central heating 30

dañdañ gradually 27

da⌐ñnasa¬ma† master 12

da⌐ñsu dance, dancing (Western style) 28-A

da⌐ñzyokyo¬oḡaku coeducation 34-A

da⌐re who? 10

da⌐re ka someone, somebody 25

dare mo /+ negative/ nobody 13

da⌐redare so-and-so (a person) 33-N

da⌐ro¬o* /copula: informal tentative/ 24

da⌐su /tr:-u:da¬site/ put out, send out, take out 17

te⌐gami o da¬su mail a letter 25-N

da⌐tta* /copula: informal past/

de* /copula: gerund/

de¬ mo however, but, even so 29

zyo⌐tyuu no hanasi¬ de wa according to what the maid says 22

si⌐na¬i de without doing, instead of doing 24

wa⌐surena¬i de /kudasai/ don't forget 22

de* /particle/ by means of 7; at, in 7

de⌐guti exit 20

dekakeru /intr:-ru:dekakete/ set out, go out 13

de⌐ki¬ru /intr:-ru:de¬kite/ be possible, can do 9; come into being, be(come) completed 15

ko⌐maka¬ku de⌐ki⌐ru can change [money]; can make into small units 22

ni⌐hoñḡo ḡa deki¬ru can [speak] Japanese 9

de⌐ñki electricity, electric light 16

de⌐ñkiḡa¬isya electric company 24

de⌐ñkisuto¬obu electric heater 30

de⌐ñsya, deñsya electric train, street car 8

deñwa telephone 6

de⌐ñwa o kake¬ru telephone (verb) 12

de⌐ñwaba¬ñḡoo telephone number 12

deñwa-suru /intr/ make a telephone call 12

deñwatyoo telephone book 12

de⌐pa¬ato department store 6

de⌐ru /intr:-ru:de¬te/ go out, leave 9; go out (for a special occasion) 27

de⌐te kuru emerge 26

de⌐sita* /copula: formal past/

de⌐su* /copula: formal non-past/

de¬su kara /formal equivalent of da¬ kara/ 27

de⌐syo¬o* /copula: formal tentative/

de⌐te kuru emerge 26

-do /counter for number of times/ 1
do˺a door (Western-style) 16
doituᷓo German language 11-A
do˹ituˎziñ a German 10-A
do˺ko what place? where? 6
  do˺ko ka somewhere, some place
  25
  do˺ko e mo ikanai not go anywhere
  27
do˺kodoko such-and-such a place 33-N
do˺nata˺ who? 10
do˺no* /+ nom/ which ── ? 3
dono-ᷓurai about how long? about how
  much? 8
do˺ñdoñ rapidly 35
do˺nna* what kind? what kind of? 5
  do˺ñna ni to what extent? 28-N
do˺o how? what way? 2
  Do˺o itasimasite. ˺ Don't mention it.
    You're welcome. Int.
  do˺o mo in every way Int.
  Do˺o mo. [Thanks] very much. Int.
  do˺o sita what happened? 14
  do˺o site why? how? 11
  do˹o site˺ mo whatever happens,
    by all means 26
  do˺o suru do what? act how? 13
  a˺ru ka ˺do˺o ka wa˹kara˺nai isn't

do˺o (cont.)
    clear whether there are or not
    29
doobutu animal 17-A
do˹oᷓu˺ implement, tool, utensil 31-N
-doori /see to˹ori˺/ avenue, street
    7-N
-doori in accordance with 19
    zi˹kañ-do˺ori on time 19
do˺ozo please Int.
dorai dry cleaning 23-N
do˹raikuri˺iniñᷓu dry cleaning 23
do˺re* which thing (of three or more)?
    2
  do˹re de˺ mo whichever (of three or
    more) it is, any one at all 15
  do˺re ka any one (of three or more)
    25-N
do˺tira which one (of two)?; which way?
    whereabouts? where? 6
  do˹tira de˺ mo whichever one (of
    two) it is, either one 15
  do˺tira ka either one 25-N
  do˺tira mo both 10
  do˺tira no ˺ho˺o which alternative? 15
do˺tirasama˺ who? 12
do˺tti /see do˺tira/ 6
doy̆o˺o(bi), doyoo Saturday 8

E

e˺ picture 31-A
e* /particle/ to, into, onto 7
e? what? 33
ebi shrimp, prawn 14
e˺e yes; that's right Int.
e˺eᷓa movie 25
e˹eᷓa˺kañ movie theater 7
eeᷓo English language 11-A
e˹ekoku˺ziñ Englishman 10-A

eeto let me see, well now 34
e˺ki station 6
-eñ /counter for yen/ 3
eñpitu pencil 2
eñryo reserve, restraint 18
  Go˹eñryo na˺ku. ˺ Don't hold back.
    Don't stand on ceremony. 18
eñtotu chimney 30-A
e˺ñziñ engine 20-N

G

ᷓa* /particle/
  Ha˹iza˺ra ᷓa arimasu. There's an
    ashtray. 4
  Ki˺ree desu ᷓa_ It's pretty but . . . '
    4
gaikoku foreign country 11-N
gaikokuᷓo foreign language 11
ga˹ikoku˺ziñ foreigner 11-N
ga˹iko˺okañ diplomat 24-A
ga˹imu˺syoo Foreign Office 11
-ᷓaisya /see kaisya/ company 12-N

gaiziñ foreigner, Westerner, Ameri-
    can 11-N
gakkoo school 6-A
gakusee student 24-A
ga˺mañ-suru /intr/ be patient, put up
    with 34
ga˺ñneñ the year 1, first year of an
    emperor's reign 8-N
gara pattern 23
ga˹re˺ezi garage (commercial) 20
gasoriñ gasoline 20

gaˈsoriñsutaˈñdo   gas station   20
gaˈsugaˈisya   gas company   12-N
-ḡata⁺ /pluralizing suffix/   27-N
  aˈnatagaˈta   you (plural)   27-N
-ḡatu /counter for naming the months
    of the year/   8
geesya   geisha   28-N
gekizyoo   theater   6-A
geˈñkañ   entry hall   16
geˈñki /na/   health, pep, good spirits
    Int.
  (O)ˈgeˈñki desu ka↵   Are you well?
    How are you?   Int
geta   wooden clogs   23-A
geˈtuyoˈo(bi), getuyoo   Monday   8
giˈmukyoˈoiku   compulsory education   34-A
giñkoo   bank   6
giˈñkoˈoiñ   bank employee   24-A
goˈ   five   3
goˈ   (Japanese game)   31
gobusata-suru⁺ /intr/   neglect to
    write or visit   35
Goˈeñryo naˈku.⁺   Don't hold back.
    Don't stand on ceremony.   18
goˈḡo   afternoon, p.m.   9
goˈhañ   cooked rice; food   14-A; meal
    15
gohukumono   yard goods, dry goods
    31-A
Goˈkuˈroosama (desita).⁺   Thanks for
    your trouble.   1
Goˈmeñ-kudasaˈi(maˈse).   Excuse me
    (for breaking away or interrupting).
    12; Is anybody here?   22
Goˈmeñ-nasaˈi.   Excuse me.   33-N
goˈmiˈ   trash   30
gomibako   box for trash   33
goˈmiˈya   trash collector   30
-ḡoo-sya /counter for naming train
    car numbers/   19

goˈrañ ni naˈru⁺   see (a thing); look at
    28
-goˈro*   approximate point of time,
    about   8
  haˈti-ḡatu-ḡoˈro   about August   8
goˈruhu   golf   32-A
Goˈsiñpai naˈku.⁺   Don't worry.   30
gotisoo   a feast, delicious food and/or
    drink   14-N
  Goˈtisoosama (deˈsita).⁺   It was a
    feast.   Thank you for the delicious
    refreshments.   14
-ḡoˈto ni*   every ——   35
  iˈti-neñ-ḡoˈto ni   with every passing
    year   35
Goˈyukkuˈri.⁺   Take it easy.   Don't rush.
    Have a pleasant, unhurried time.
    31
goˈzaˈru⁺ * /intr:-aru/   be located (of
    inanimate objects); have   Int.
goˈzeñ   a.m.   9-N
goˈzoˈñzi da⁺   know   13
guai   condition   20
  guˈai ḡa iˈi   be in good condition, be
    fine, be in good health   20-N
  guˈai ḡa waruˈi   be in bad condition, be
    out of order, feel unwell, feel sick
    20
guñ   county   34-N
guñpuku   military uniform   34-A
guˈñtai   armed forces   34
guñziñ   serviceman (i.e. man in the
    armed forces)   24-A
-ḡuˈrai*   approximate extent, about   8
  dono-ḡurai   about how much?   8
  ni-ˈsyuukañ-ḡuˈrai   about two weeks   8
  koˈtatu-ḡuˈrai   about as much as a ko-
    tatsu   30
-guramu /counter for grams/   22
gyuuniku   beef   22
gyuunyuu   cow's milk   14-A

H

haˈ   tooth   17-A
haˈaˈ⁺   yes; that's right   4
haˈdeˈ /na/   gaudy, bright, loud   23
haˈeˈru /intr:-ru:haˈete/   come out,
    spring up, grow   26
haˈha   mother   11-A
haˈi   yes; that's right   Int; here you
    are   3
-hai /counter for glassfuls and cup-
    fuls/   14

haiiro   gray   16
haikeñ-suru⁺ /tr/   see (a thing); look at
    28
haˈikiñḡu   hiking   32-A
haˈiru /intr:-u:haˈitte/   enter, go in
    17
  haˈitte (i)ru   be inside   17; be in-
    cluded   21
haˈisya   dentist   24-A
haisyaku-suru⁺ /tr/   borrow   32

haiyuu   actor, actress   28-A
ha꜔iza꜔ra   ashtray   3
ha꜔ka꜔ru /tr:-u:ha꜔ka꜔tte/   measure   23
   su꜔ṅpoo o haka꜔ru   take measure-
      ments   23
ha꜔kki꜔ri   clearly, distinctly, precisely
   18
hako   box   17
haku /tr:-u:haite/   put on, wear (on
   feet or legs)   23
ha꜔ma꜔   beach   32-A
hameru /tr:-ru:hamete/   put on, wear
   (on hands)   23-A
hana   nose   17-A
ha꜔na꜔   flower   6-A; flower arrangement   18
ha꜔nami꜔   cherry-blossom viewing   27
ha꜔nare꜔ru /intr:-ru:ha꜔na꜔rete/   become separated, part from, fall
   apart   33-A
ha꜔nasi꜔   talking, a talk, a story   13
   a꜔no꜔ hito no ha꜔nasi꜔ de wa   ac-
      cording to what he says   22
hanasi-tyuu   in the middle of talking;
   the line is busy   13
ha꜔na꜔su /tr:-u:ha꜔na꜔site/   speak, talk
   13
ha꜔na꜔su /tr:-u:ha꜔na꜔site/   let go, set
   free   33-A
ha꜔na꜔ya   flower shop, florist   6-A
hanazi   nosebleed   24-N
-haṅ   half   8
   sa꜔ṅ-zikaṅ-ha꜔ṅ   three hours and a
      half   8
   go-꜔zi-ha꜔ṅ   5:30   9
ha꜔ṅbu꜔ṅ   half, half part   14
ha꜔ṅdoba꜔kku   handbag   23-A
haṅkati   handkerchief   23-A
ha꜔ṅniti꜔   half-day   25
haṅtai   opposite   19
haṅtai-suru /intr/   oppose   19-N
haṅtoo   peninsula   32
haori   coat (Japanese style)   23-A
ha꜔ra꜔u /tr:-u:ha꜔ra꜔tte/   pay   22
ha꜔re꜔ru /intr:-ru:ha꜔rete/   clear up   26
ha꜔reso꜔o /na/   looking as if it would
   clear up   26
ha꜔ru   spring (season)   18-N
ha꜔ruya꜔sumi   spring vacation   25-N
ha꜔si   chopsticks   14-A
ha꜔si꜔   bridge   20
hasiḡo   ladder   33-A
hatake   non-rice field, dry field   29

ha꜔tarakisuḡi꜔ru /intr:-ru:ha꜔tarakisu꜔-
   ḡite/   overwork   25
hataraku /intr:-u:hataraite/   work   24
ha꜔tati   twenty years of age   10-N
ha꜔ti꜔   eight   3
ha꜔ti-zyo꜔o   eight-mat area or room   30
hatu   leaving   19
   zyu꜔uiti꜔-zi hatu   leaving at eleven
      o'clock   19
   Ko꜔obe hatu   leaving Kobe, coming
      from Kobe   19
hatu-ka   twenty days; twentieth day of
   the month   8
ha꜔ya꜔i /-ku/   is fast or early   9
ha꜔ya꜔ru /intr:-u:ha꜔ya꜔tte/   become
   prevalent   26
hayasi   forest   32-A
hazimaru /intr:-u:hazimatte/   [some-
   thing] begins   26-N
hazime   beginning   24
Ha꜔zimema꜔site.   How do you do?   11
hazimeru* /tr:-ru:hazimete/   begin
   [something]   26
   hu꜔rihazime꜔ru   begin raining or
      snowing   26
   Naḡasaki o hazime   beginning with
      Nagasaki, from Nagasaki on down,
      to say nothing of Nagasaki   32
ha꜔zi꜔mete   the first time   11
   Ha꜔zi꜔mete ome ni kakarimasu. ⁺
      How do you do?   11
hazu*   expectation   22
   kasu hazu da   is supposed to rent,
      is expected to rent   22
   na꜔i hazu wa na꜔i   there's no reason
      to suppose that there isn't any,
      there should be some   22-N
ha꜔zukasi꜔i /-ku/   is shamed, is shy
   34
he꜔bi   snake   17-A
hee   wall   30
hee?   really? you don't say! no kidding!   33
heeki /na/   unconcerned, indifferent,
   unmoved   27
   heeki de suru   do with unconcern,
      make nothing of [it]   27-N
   heeki na kao o suru   look uncon-
      cerned   27-N
heetai   soldier   34-A
heeti   a plain   32-A
heṅ   area, section, part   6
   kono heṅ   this area, around here   6

heñ (cont.)
　　do˺no heñ　what part? what section?
　　　19
he˺ñ /na/　strange　13
-heñ　/counter for number of times/
　　32
he˹ñzi˺　a reply, an answer　24
　　he˹ñzi˺ o suru　answer, reply (verb)
　　24
he˹ta˺ /na/　unskilled, poor at　18
he˹ya˺　room　13
hi, hi˺　day　15; sun　26
hiatari　exposure to the sun　30
　　hi˹atari ga i˺i　is sunny　30
hi˺bati　brazier　21
hidari　left　6
　　hi˹dari no ho˺o　left side; toward the
　　　left　6
hi˹do˺i /-ku/　is severe　21
hi˹gasi˺　east　30-A
higasimuki　facing east　30-N
hige　beard, hair on the face　22
hikidasi　drawer　17
hi˹ko˺oki　airplane　8
hikoozyoo　airport　20
hiku /tr:-u:hiite/　pull　33-A
　　kaze o hiku　catch a cold　26-N
hi˹ku˺i /-ku/　is low　31
hima /na/　free time, leisure　12
　　hi˹ma na toki˺　time when [someone]
　　　is free　12
hi˹ro˺i /-ku/　is broad or wide or
　　spacious or big in area　21
hi˺rosa　area; width　23-N
hirou /tr:-u:hirotte/　pick up　33-A
hi˹ru˺　noon, daytime　15-N
　　hiru no bu　daytime performance
　　　28-N
hi˹rugo˺hañ　noon meal, lunch　15
hirumesi /M/　lunch　24
hirune　nap　27
　　hirune o suru　take a nap　27
hi˹ru-sugi˺　past noon, afternoon　31
hi˹syo˺　secretary　24
hito, hi˹to˺　person　10
　　o˹ñna˺ no hito　woman　10
　　o˹toko˺ no hito　man　10
hi˹to˺añsiñ, hi˹toa˺ñsiñ　a relief　35
hi˹to˺koto　a word　35
hi˹to˺-ri　one person, single (person)
　　10
　　hi˹to˺-ri de　alone, by oneself　17
hi˹to˺-tu　one unit　5

hodo*　approximate extent　15
　　sa˹ñ-buñ no iti˺ hodo　about as much
　　　as one-third　35
　　teñpura hodo su˹ki˺ zya ˹na˺i　[I] don't
　　　like [it] as much as tempura　15
　　ta˹no˺mu hodo zya ˹na˺i　isn't worth
　　　hiring, doesn't warrant hiring　33
　　ha˹nasi˺ ni na˹ra˺nai hodo hi˺do˺i　is
　　　too awful to talk about　34
　　si˹tte (i)re˺ba iru hodo　the more
　　　someone knows　32
hoka　other, another, other than　4
　　hoka ni　in addition　4
　　Tanaka-sañ no hoka ni　in addition
　　　to Mr. Tanaka, other than Mr. Ta-
　　　naka　15-N
　　hoka no hi　another day　15
ho˹keñga˺isya　insurance company　24
ho˺ñ　book　2
-hoñ　/counter for long, cylindrical
　　units/　5
ho˹ñbako　bookcase　24-N
ho˹ñdana　bookshelf　17
hoñseki　one's permanent residence　34
ho˹ñseki˺ti　place of one's permanent
　　residence　34
hoñtoo　truth, true　3
ho˹ñya　book store, book dealer　6-A
hoñyaku　translation　34
hoñyaku-suru /tr/　translate　34
ho˹o*　side; direction; alternative　6
　　hi˹dari no ho˺o　left side, toward
　　　the left　6
　　ko˹tira no ho˺o　this side, this di-
　　　rection　6
　　mi˹gi no ho˺o　right side, toward
　　　the right　6
　　i˺i hoo no ryokañ　rather good inn,
　　　inn on the good side　21
　　si˹ta ho˺o ga ˹i˺i　it will be better to
　　　have done [it], [you]'d better do [it]
　　　20
hoo?　oh? really?　32
ho˹oboo　all directions, everywhere　32
ho˹oku　fork　14-A
ho˹omu　platform　34-N
ho˹oñ　horn　20-N
hooseki　jewel　31-A
hosi　star　26-A
ho˹si˺i /-ku/　want　31
　　bo˹ku ga hosi˺i　I want [it]　31
　　te˹eburu ga hosi˺i　[I] want a table　31
ho˹so˺i /-ku/　is thin or small in circum-
　　ference　31-N

ho⌐sonağa⌐i /-ku/   is long and slender
    or long and narrow   31
ho⌐su /tr:-u:ho⌐site/   dry [something]
    out, air [something]   23
ho⌐teru   hotel   6
ho⌐toñdo   almost   35
hu⌐beñ /na/   inconvenient   29
hu⌐buki   snow storm   26-A
hude   writing brush   31
huhee   complaint   34
    huhee o iu   complain   34
hu⌐ki⌐ñ   dishrag, dish cloth, cloth   17
huku /tr:-u:huite/   wipe   17
hu⌐ku /intr:-u:hu⌐ite/   blow   26
hu⌐ku⌐   clothing   34-A
hukuzatu /na/   complicated   28
hu⌐ne   ship, boat   8
-huñ /counter for naming and counting
    minutes/   8
hurañsuğo   French language   11-A
hu⌐rañsu⌐ziñ   Frenchman   10-A
hu⌐rihazime⌐ru /intr:-ru:hu⌐rihazi⌐mete/
    begin falling (of rain or snow)   26
hu⌐ro⌐   bath   21-N
hu⌐roba⌐   bathroom (not toilet)   17-A
huroba-tuki   with bath   21
hurosiki   furoshiki (cloth square for
    wrapping)   4

hu⌐ru /intr:-u:hu⌐tte, hu⌐tte⌐/   fall (of
    rain or snow)   18
    a⌐me ğa ⌐hu⌐ru   it rains   18
hu⌐ru⌐i /-ku/   is old (i. e. not new) or
    stale   2-A
hu⌐suma⌐, husuma   sliding door (opaque)
    18
huta   lid, cover   33
    huta o suru   put a lid on   33
hu⌐ta-tu⌐   two units   5
hu⌐to⌐i /-ku/   is thick or big in circum-
    ference   31-N
hutoñ   Japanese quilt   21
    hutoñ o siku   spread the quilts (for
    sleeping)   21
hu⌐to⌐ru /intr:-u:hu⌐to⌐tte/   grow fat   35-N
    hu⌐to⌐tta hito   fat person   35-N
hutuu   usual, regular, ordinary   21
hu⌐u /na/   manner, style   22
    do⌐ñna huu   what (kind of) style?   22
hu⌐yu⌐   winter   18-N
hu⌐yuya⌐sumi   winter vacation   25-N
hu⌐ziyuu /na/   restricted, uncomfortable,
    inconvenient   34
hya⌐ku⌐   one hundred   3
-hyaku /counter for hundreds/   3
hya⌐kusyo⌐o   farmer   24-A
hyo⌐o   hail   26-A

I

-i⌐ğai*   outside of, except for   34-N
    mo⌐kuyoobi-i⌐ğai   except for Thurs-
    day   34-N
i⌐ğirisu⌐ziñ   Englishman   10-A
-i⌐ğo   later than, after   28
    so⌐re-i⌐ğo   after that, later than
    that   28
i⌐i /yo⌐ku/   is good or fine or all
    right; never mind   2
    i⌐tte⌐ mo ⌐i⌐i   is all right to go,
    [someone] may go   22
    i⌐kana⌐kute mo ⌐i⌐i   is all right not
    to go, [someone] doesn't have to
    go   22-N
    su⌐zu⌐sikute ⌐i⌐i   is nice and cool   29
    ku⌐reba ⌐i⌐i desu ğa ⌐ne⌐e   [I] hope
    [someone] comes   32-N
-i⌐i* /-yo⌐ku/   is easy to —   28-N
    tu⌐kaii⌐i   is easy to use   28-N
iie   no; that's not right   Int.
i⌐ka⌐ğa+   how?   4
    I⌐ka⌐ğa desu ka⌐   How are you? How
    are things? How about it (offering
    something)?   4

i⌐ke⌐   pond   32-A
I⌐kemase⌐ñ ⌐ne⌐e.   That's too bad.   11
ikenai   it won't do, that's too bad
    11
    si⌐te⌐ wa ĩkenai   must not do   25
    si⌐ha⌐kereba ĩkenai   must do   32-N
    si⌐ha⌐kute wa (or si⌐ha⌐kutya/a/)
    ĩkenai   must do   32-N
-iki   -bound   19
    Kyooto-iki   bound for Kyoto   19
i⌐ki⌐ru /intr:-ru:i⌐kite/   live, exist,
    be alive   34-A
iku* /intr:-u:itte/   go   1
i⌐kura   how much?   3
i⌐kutu   how many units?   5; how old
    (of people)?   10
i⌐ma   now   7
i⌐ma⌐   living room   17-A
i⌐mi   meaning   21
    do⌐o iu ⌐i⌐mi   what meaning?   21
i⌐mo⌐oto   younger sister   11-A
i⌐habi⌐kari   lightning   26-A
    i⌐habi⌐kari ğa suru   there is light-
    ning   26-A

-i⌐nai* within 34
  i⌐ti-zikañ-i⌐nai within one hour 34
inaka the country 27
i⌐hu⌐ dog 17
i⌐ñdo⌐ziñ an Indian (from India) 10-A
i⌐ñki ink 33-N
ippai full 20
  i⌐ppai ni na⌐ru become full 20-N
  ippai ni suru fill [something] 20
  hi⌐to⌐ de ippai filled with people 27
i⌐rassya⌐ru ꜚ* /intr:-aru:i⌐rassya⌐tte ~
    i⌐ra⌐site/ be 6; go 7; come 8
  I⌐rassya⌐i(ma⌐se). Welcome! 4
  Do⌐nata de (i)rassyaimasu ka꜔ ꜚ
    Who is it? Who are you? 10
ireru /tr:-ru:irete/ put in, insert 17
iri⌐guti entrance 20-N
i⌐ro⌐ color 5
  do⌐ñna iro what (kind of) color? 5
iroiro /na~no/ various[ly] 25
iroñ na various 28
iru* /intr:-ru:ite/ be located (of
    animate beings) 6
  beñkyoo-site (i)ru be studying 11
  hu⌐tte (i)ru be raining 18
  kekkoñ-site (i)ru be married 10
iru /intr:-u:itte/ be necessary, need,
    want 4
iru /intr:-u:itte/ enter 29
  ki ni iru be pleasing, appeal 29
i⌐sogasi⌐i /-ku/ is busy 13
i⌐so⌐gu /intr:-u:i⌐so⌐ide/ be in a hurry 7
issyo together 15
  Sa⌐itoo-sañ to issyo together with
    Mr. Saito 15
isu chair 17-A
isya doctor (medical) 24-A
i⌐ta board 33-A
itadaku ꜚ* /tr:-u:itadaite/ eat, drink
    14; receive, accept 17

itadaku ꜚ* (cont.)
  si⌐te itadakemase⌐ñ ka ꜚ would you be
    kind enough to do [it]? 25
  sa⌐sete itadakemase⌐ñ ka ꜚ would you
    be kind enough to let me do [it]
    33
i⌐ta⌐i /-ku/ is painful 17
i⌐ta⌐mu /intr:-u:i⌐ta⌐ñde/ be(come) hurt
    or spoiled or damaged or worn
    out or painful 14
  i⌐ta⌐ñda ebi spoiled shrimp 14
itasu ꜚ /tr:-u:itasite/ make, do 13
  Do⌐o itasimasite. Don't mention it.
    You're welcome. Int.
i⌐ti⌐ one (numeral) 3
itibañ, i⌐ti⌐bañ* to the highest degree 15
  i⌐tibañ taka⌐i is most expensive 15
iti-niti-zyuu all day long 25
i⌐to⌐ko cousin 11-A
I⌐tte irassya⌐i. Goodbye. (Lit. Go and
    come.) 20
I⌐tte kima⌐su. Goodbye. (Lit. I'll go
    and come.) 20-N
I⌐tte mairima⌐su. ꜚ Goodbye. (Lit. I'll
    go and come.) 20
i⌐tto⌐osya first-class car 19-A
i⌐tu when? 8
  i⌐tu ka some time 25-N
  i⌐tu mo always 9
i⌐tu⌐-tu five units 5
iu /tr:-u:itte/ say, be named, be
    called 1
  To iu to? What do you mean by that?
    34
  su⌐ru yo⌐o ni iu tell [someone] to do
    24
i⌐ya /M/ no; that's not right 16
iya⌐ /na/ unpleasant 26
-i⌐zeñ before 28-N
  so⌐re-i⌐zeñ before that 28-N

K

ka* /particle/ (question) Int.
  O⌐geñki desu ka꜔ ꜚ Are you well?
    Int.
  do⌐o iu ka si⌐ranai not know how one
    says it 18
  a⌐ru ka ꜛdo⌐o ka wa⌐kara⌐nai isn't
    clear whether there are or not 29
ka* /particle/ or 35
  pe⌐ñ ka e⌐ñpitu pen or pencil 35
ka mo sirenai* maybe — 30
  i⌐i ka mo sirenai maybe it's good,
    it may be good 30

ka sira* I wonder — 35
  su⌐ru⌐ ka sira I wonder if [someone]
    will do [it] 35
-ka ~ -niti /counter for naming and
    counting days/ 8
ka⌐ateñ curtain 33
kabe wall of a room 30
kabi mildew 26
kabuki (form of traditional Japanese
    theater) 28
ka⌐bu⌐ru /tr:-u:ka⌐bu⌐tte/ put on or
    wear (on head) 23

ka┐do   street corner   7
ka┌eri┐   return (noun)   27
ka┌eru   /intr:-u:ka┐ette/   return (home)
   9
kaeru   /tr:-ru:kaete/   change [some-
   thing]   21-N
ka┐esu   /tr:-u:ka┐esite/   give back, send
   back, return [something]   34
ka┐ette kuru   come back   22
ka┌g̃eki   opera   28-A
-kag̃etu   /counter for number of months/
   8
ka┌g̃i┐   key   16
   ka┌g̃i┐ g̃a ka┌ka┐ru   [something]
   locks   16
   ka┌g̃i┐ o ka┌ke┐ru   lock [something]
   16
ka┌g̃u   furniture   17-A
kai*   /M/   /sentence particle/   (question)   35
   I┌ku┐ kai⌐   Are you gonna go?   35
-kai   /counter for naming and counting
   floors/   16
-kai   /counter for number of times/   31
kaidañ   stairway   17-A
ka┌ig̃i, ka┌ig̃i┐   conference   25
   kaig̃i-tyuu   in the middle of a conference, in conference   25
ka┌ig̃uñ   navy   34-A
kaikee   bill, accounting, check   15
kaimono   shopping   26
ka┌iniku┐i   /-ku/   is difficult to buy   28
kaisya   business company, company
   office   12
ka┌isya┐iñ   company employee   24
ka┌ka┐ru   /intr:-u:ka┌ka┐tte/   be required, take   8; be suspended   11
   ka┌g̃i┐ g̃a ka┌ka┐ru   [something]
   locks   16
   o┐me ni kaka┐ru⌐   see (a person),
   meet   11
   Ha┌zi┐mete ome ni kakarimasu.⌐
   How do you do.   11
   zi┌kañ g̃a kaka┐ru   take time   8
ka┌ke┐mono   hanging scroll   31-A
ka┌ke┐ru   /tr:-ru:ka┐kete/   hang, suspend, apply [something]   12; sit
   down   25
   a┌iroñ o kake┐ru   press with an iron
   21
   de┌ñwa o kake┐ru   telephone (verb)
   12
   ka┌g̃i┐ o ka┌ke┐ru   lock [something]
   16

ka┌ke┐ru (cont.)
   me┌g̃ane o ka┌ke┐ru   wear eyeglasses
   23-A
ka┌kika┐ta   way or style of writing   31
ka┌ki┐ne   fence   30
ka┐ku   /tr:-u:ka┐ite/   write, draw   7
ka┌ma┐u   /intr:-u:ka┌ma┐tte/   mind, care
   about   18-N
   ka┌mawa┐nai   doesn't matter, makes
   no difference, is all right   9
ka┌mi┐   paper   5
ka┌mi┐   hair (on head)   22
kamidana   household altar (Shinto)   35
ka┌minari┐   thunder   26-A
   ka┌minari┐ g̃a naru   it thunders   26-A
kana   Japanese written syllabary   31
ka┐nai   (one's own) wife   11
ka┐nari   fairly, rather   32
ka┌nazu┐ti   hammer   33-A
kane   money   22
ka┌ñg̃ae┐ru   /tr:-ru:ka┌ñg̃a┐ete/   consider,
   think over   29
ka┌ñg̃o┐hu   nurse   24-A
ka┌ñkoku┐ziñ   a South Korean   10-A
kañkoo   sightseeing   32-N
   kañkoo ni iku   go sightseeing   32-N
ka┌ñkooba┐su   sightseeing bus   32-A
ka┌ñko┐okyaku   sightseer   32-A
ka┌ñkoore┐ssya   sightseeing train   32-A
kañtañ   /na/   simple   28
kañzi   Chinese written character   31
kao   face; expression   14
   a┌o┐i kao o suru   be pale   14
kara*   /particle/   from   8; because   11;
   after   16
   sore kara   from that point, after that,
   and then, and   4
ka┌ra┐   empty   20-N
karada   body   17-A
ka┌ra┐i   /-ku/   is spicy or salty   14
kariru   /tr:-ru:karite/   borrow, rent
   [from someone]   13
karu   /tr:-u:katte/   clip, mow   22
karui   /-ku/   is light (i.e. not heavy)   20-N
ka┐sa   umbrella   23
kaseñ   synthetic fibers   23
Ka┌sikomarima┐sita.   Certainly.   I'll do
   as you have asked.   4
kasiya   house for rent   29
kasu   /tr:-u:kasite/   lend, rent [to some-
   one]   22
ka┌ta┐⌐   person   10
   o┌ñna no kata┐⌐   woman   10
   o┌toko no kata┐⌐   man   10
ka┌ta┐   shape, style   23

katai /-ku/ is hard or tough or stiff
   or firm 22-N
katamiti one-way 19
katati shape, style 23
ka ͨtazuke ͺru /tr:-ru:ka ͨtazu ͺkete/
   straighten up, put in order 16
katte kitchen 31-N
ka ͨttedo ͺo ͞gu kitchen utensils 31-A
ka ͺtu /intr:-u:ka ͺtte/ win 34-N
kau /tr:-u:katte/ buy 4
ka ͟wa ͺ river 32-A
ka ͟wai ͺi /-ku/ is cute 31
ka ͟waiso ͺo /na/ pathetic, pitiful 35
ka ͟waka ͺsu /tr:-u:ka ͟waka ͺsite/ dry
   [something] 31-N
ka ͟wa ͺku /intr:-u:ka ͟wa ͺite/ become
   dry 15
   no ͺdo ͞ga ka ͭwa ͣita I'm thirsty 15
kawari a change; a substitute 34; a
   second helping 18
   ryo ͺosiñ no kawari ni instead of
   parents 34
kawaru /intr:-u:kawatte/ undergo
   change 24
kaya mosquito net 21
ka ͟yo ͺo(bi), kayoo Tuesday 8
kayou /intr:-u:kayotte/ commute 29
ka ͺzañ volcano 32-A
kaze wind 21
   ka ͟ze ͞ga hu ͺku the wind blows 26
kaze a cold 26
   kaze o hiku catch a cold 26
ka ͺzi a fire 35-A
ka ͺzoku family 11-A
kedo /see keredo/ 20
ke ͺdo /see ke ͺredo/ 22
keekeñ experience 34-A
ke ͺezai economics 32-A
kekkoñ-suru /intr/ marry 10
   kekkoñ-site (i)ru be married 10
ke ͺkkoo /na/ fine, all right 9
   Mo ͺo ͺke ͺkkoo desu. I'm fine as I am.
   I've had enough already. 14
-keñ prefecture 34
   Sa ͨitama ͺ-keñ Saitama Prefecture 34
keñbutu-suru /tr/ see the sights, go
   sightseeing 27
ke(re)do* /particle/ although 20
ke ͺ(re)do however 22
ke ͺsa this morning 9
ke ͺsiki scenery 29
kessite never 29

kesu /tr:-u:kesite/ turn off, extinguish,
   erase 16
ki ͺ tree 27; wood 33-A
ki spirit, mind, attention 25
   ki ͞ga tu ͺku notice 25
   ki ni iru be pleasing, appeal 29
kieru /intr:-ru:kiete/ become extin-
   guished, go out 16-N
kiiroi /-ku/ is yellow 4
ki ͨkae ͺru, ki ͨka ͺeru /tr:-ru:ki ͨka ͺete/
   change clothes 23
kikoeru /intr:-ru:kikoete/ be audible,
   can hear 13
kikoo climate 26
kiku /tr:-u:kiite/ ask a question, listen,
   hear 12
kimaru /intr:-u:kimatte/ be(come) decided 23-N
kimeru /tr:-ru:kimete/ decide [some-
   thing] 23
kimi you 27
kimono kimono, Japanese clothing 23-A
kimoti feeling, mood 18
   ki ͺmoti ͞ga i ͺi is pleasant or agreeable 18
ki ͺho ͺo, kinoo yesterday 1
ki ͺnu silk 23-A
ki ͨñyo ͺo(bi), kiñyoo Friday 8
ki ͺotuke ͺru /intr:-ru:ki ͺotuke ͺte/ be
   careful 17
kippu ticket 19
kirai /na/ displeasing 15
ki ͺree /na/ pretty, clean 3
kirisutokyoo Christianity 32
kiru /tr:-ru:kite/ put on, wear (on
   body) 23
ki ͺru /tr:-u:ki ͺtte, ki ͨtte ͺ/ cut, cut off,
   hang up (the telephone) 13
ki ͺssa ͺteñ, kissateñ tearoom 14-A
ki ͺsya ͺ (steam) train 8
ki ͺsya ͺ newspaperman 24-A
ki ͨta ͺ north 30-A
kitamuki facing north 30-N
ki ͨtana ͺi /-ku/ is dirty 16
kitto surely, positively, certainly 24
kitui /-ku/ is tight 23
ki ͺzi material, cloth 23
ko child 10
   o ͨñna ͺ no ko little girl 10
   o ͺtoko ͺ no ko little boy 10
ko ͨbore ͺru /intr:-ru:ko ͺbo ͺrete/ [some-
   thing] spills 17
ko ͨbo ͺrete (i)ru be spilled 17

koꞈboꞈsu /tr:-u:koꞈboꞈsite/   spill [some-
     thing] 17-N
kodomo child 10
koꞈe voice 13
   oꞈokiꞈi ꞈkoꞈe de or ꞈoki na ꞈkoꞈe
     de with a loud voice 13
koꞈi /-ku/ is strong or thick (of liq-
     uids); is dark (of colors) 14-A
koko this place, here 6
koꞈkoꞈno-tu nine units 5
koꞈmakaꞈi /-ku/ is small or fine or
     detailed 17
koꞈmaꞈru /intr:-u:koꞈmaꞈtte/ be(come)
     distressing or troublesome or
     annoying or inconvenient or
     perplexing 9
   aꞈtukute koꞈmaꞈru be annoying be-
     cause it's hot 29
koꞈmeꞈ uncooked rice 14-A
koꞈmu /intr:-u:koꞈnde/ be(come)
     crowded 20
   koꞈnde (i)ru be crowded 20
konaida the other day, recently 31
kono* /+ nom/ this — 3
kono aida the other day, recently 31
kono-ḡoro these days, nowadays 18
koꞈñ navy blue 23
koꞈñbañ this evening, tonight 13
   Koñbañ wa. Good evening. Int.
koñdo this time (i.e. this next time or
     this last time) 28
koñḡetu this month 10
koñna* this kind, this kind of 5
   koñna ni to this extent 28-N
Koñniti wa. Good afternoon. Int.
koñsyuu this week App.
koꞈo thus, this way 29
   koꞈo iu tokoroꞈ place like this 29
koꞈobaꞈ factory 24
koobañ police box 7
kooeñ park 6-A
kooiñ factory worker 24-A
koꞈohiꞈi coffee 14
koꞈohiizyaꞈwañ cup (with handles) 14-A
kookoku advertisement 30
koꞈokaꞈñsyu telephone operator 12
kookoo high school 34-N
koꞈomuꞈiñ government employee 24
koori ice 14-A
kooru freeze 26
   kootte (i)ru be frozen 26
koꞈotooḡaꞈkkoo high school 34-N
koꞈotuukoꞈosya Japan Travel Bureau 12

kootya black tea 14-A
koozyoo, koꞈozyoꞈo factory 24
koppu glass for drinking 14-A
kore* this thing 2
koꞈruku cork 33-N
koꞈsa strength or thickness (liquids);
     darkness (colors) 23-N
koꞈsiꞈ lower part of the back 17-A
koꞈsyoꞈo pepper 14-A
kosyoo out of order 13
kosyoo-suru /intr/ break down 13-N
koꞈtaeꞈru, koꞈtaꞈeru /intr:-ru:koꞈtaꞈete/
     answer CI
kotatu quilt-covered warming place 30
kotira this one (of two); this way, here-
     abouts, here 6; this person 11;
     the person speaking 12
   koꞈtira no hoꞈo this side, this di-
     rection 6
koꞈtoꞈ* thing (intangible), act, fact 24
   aꞈruꞈku koto ḡa deꞈkiꞈru can walk 25-N
   saꞈñpo-suru kotoꞈ ḡa suꞈkiꞈ da like to
     take walks 24-N
   iꞈku kotoꞈ ḡa ꞈaꞈru do sometimes go
     31-N
   iꞈtta kotoꞈ ḡa ꞈaꞈru have at some
     time gone 31
   iꞈku kotoꞈ ni suru decide to go 32
   aꞈru koto wa ꞈaꞈru do exist, do have 32
   taꞈrinai kotoꞈ wa ꞈnaꞈi isn't that it's
     not enough 33
koꞈtobaꞈ word, language 32-A
kotori bird 17-A
kotosi this year 8
kotozuke message; the giving of a mes-
     sage 13
koꞈttiꞈ /see kotira/ 6
kottoohiñ curios, antiques 31-A
koꞈwaꞈi /-ku/ is frightening 35-A
koꞈwareꞈru /intr:-ru:koꞈwaꞈrete/ be-
     come broken 31
   koꞈwaꞈrete (i)ru be broken 31
koꞈwaꞈsu /tr:-u:koꞈwaꞈsite/ break [some-
     thing] 31-N
kuꞈ nine 3
kuꞈ ward 34-N
   Miꞈnatoꞈ-ku Minato Ward 34-N
kubi neck 17-A
kuꞈdaꞈmono fruit 14-A
kudari down-train (i.e. going away from
     Tokyo) 19
kuꞈdasaꞈi* /imperative of kuꞈdasaꞈru/
     give me 1

ku⌐dasa⌐i* (cont.)
 Ko⌐re o kudasa⌐i. Please give me
  this one. 4
 Ma⌐tte kudasai. Please wait. 1
 I⌐so⌐ga⌐nai de kudasai. Please don't
  hurry. 7
ku⌐dasa⌐ru ⌐ * /tr:-aru:ku⌐dasa⌐tte ~ ku-
  ⌐dasu⌐tte/ give me 4
 ka⌐ite ku⌐dasaimase⌐ñ ka ⌐ would
  (lit. won't) you be kind enough to
  write (or draw) for me? 7
ku⌐gi nail 33
ku⌐mo cloud 26-A
ku⌐mo⌐ru /intr:-u:ku⌐mo⌐tte/ cloud up
  26
kuni a country; one's native land or
  area 32
-kuñ /M/ /suffix attached to men's
  and boys' names; familiar/ 13
ku⌐ra⌐ storehouse, godown 33-A
kuraberu /tr:-ru:kurabete/ compare
  34
kurai /-ku/ is dark 35
kureru* /tr:-ru:kurete/ give me 17
 ta⌐no⌐ñde kureru request (or order)
  for me 17, ~ for you 33
 o⌐ko⌐site kurenai ka would(n't) you
  wake me? 21
ku⌐ro⌐i /-ku/ is black 4
ku⌐roo hardship, troubles, ordeal 34
 Go⌐ku⌐roosama (desita). Thanks for
  your trouble. 1
ku⌐ru* /intr:irreg:ki⌐te⌐/ come 8
 hu⌐tte kuru begin to fall 26
 ta⌐no⌐ñde kuru come having en-
  gaged, go and engage 20

kuruma car, cart 7
ku⌐sa⌐ a grass, weed 33
 ni⌐wa no kusa⌐ o ⌐to⌐ru weed the
  garden 33
ku⌐si⌐ a comb 23-A
kusuri medicine 6-N
kusuriya drugstore, druggist 6-A
ku⌐sya⌐mi a sneeze 33-N
 ku⌐sya⌐mi o suru sneeze (verb)
  33-N
kuti mouth 17-A
ku⌐tu⌐ shoes 21
ku⌐tu⌐sita socks, stockings 23
kuuguñ air force 34-A
ku⌐uki air 20
kya⌐burettaa carburetor 20-N
kyaku guest, customer 18
kyo⌐o today 1
kyo⌐odai brothers and/or sisters 11-A
kyooiku education, schooling 34
kyookai church 32
kyo⌐omi⌐, kyo⌐omi an interest 35
 kyo⌐omi⌐ ga ⌐a⌐ru have an interest
  35
kyoosoo competition, contest 35
kyoosoo-suru /intr/ compete 35-N
kyoozyu professor 24-A
kyoziñ giant 35-N
kyu⌐u nine 3
kyu⌐uke⌐esitu rest room, lounge 31-A
kyuukoo express 19
kyu⌐uko⌐okeñ express ticket 19-A
kyu⌐uryoo salary 24
kyu⌐uzi waiter/waitress, steward[ess],
  barboy, office boy 24-A

M

-ma /counter for number of rooms/
  21
ma⌐a oh well, I guess, you might say
  4; oh dear, good heavens 35
ma⌐da* /+ affirmative/ still, yet 18;
  /+ negative/ not yet 14
 ma⌐da da it is yet to happen; not
  yet 14
made* /particle/ as far as 7;
  until 9
 To⌐okyo⌐o-eki made as far as Tokyo
  Station 7
 na⌐ñ-zi made until what time? 9
 zyu⌐u-ḡatu⌐ made ni by October 9
 tu⌐ku made until arriving 27

ma⌐do window 16
ma⌐do⌐ḡuti ticket window 19
ma⌐e* front 6; before 8
 e⌐ki no ⌐ma⌐e front of the station 6
 ma⌐e no kaisya previous company
  24
 zi⌐p-pu⌐ñ mae ten minutes before
  the hour 8
 zi⌐p-puñ ma⌐e, zi⌐p-puñ ⌐ma⌐e ten
  minutes ago 8
 ta⌐be⌐ru ⌐ma⌐e (time) before eating
  31
maeuri advance sale 28
maḡaru /intr:-u:maḡatte/ make a turn
  7

mag̅aru (cont.)
  ka⌉do o mag̅aru turn at the corner, turn the corner 7
mag̅eru /tr:-ru:mag̅ete/ bend [something] 33-A
ma⌈g̅o⌉ grandchild 11-A
-mai /counter for thin, flat units/ 5
ma⌉iasa every morning 9-N
ma⌉iban̄ every night 19-N
maido every time 4
  Ma⌉ido ari⌉g̅atoo gozaimasu. Thank you again and again. 4
maig̅etu every month 9-N
mainen̄ every year 9-N
ma⌉initi every day 9
  ma⌉initi no ⌐yo⌉o ni almost every day 24
ma⌉iru↓* /intr:-u:ma⌉itte/ go 7; come 8
maisyuu every week 9-N
maitosi every year 9-N
maituki every month 9-N
makasu /tr:-u:makasite/ beat [someone in something] 34-N
makeru /intr:-ru:makete/ be defeated, be beaten 34
  maketa I give up! you win! 34-N
ma⌈kita⌉bako cigarette 3-N
ma⌈ku⌉ curtain, act 28
  maku no aida between acts 28
makuai between acts 28
ma⌈ma⌉ condition 16
  so⌈no mama⌉ de being that condition as it is 16
ma⌈mo⌉naku soon after, in no time 34
-man̄ /counter for ten thousands/ 3
man̄naka middle 23
maru circle 31-N
marui /-ku/ is round 31
ma⌈ssu⌉g̅u straight 7
mata again 4
  Ma⌈ta do⌉ozo. Please [come] again. 4
ma⌈ti⌉ town 29; machi (part of a city) 34-N
ma⌈tia⌉isitu waiting room 20
ma⌈tig̅ae⌉ru /tr:-ru:ma⌈tig̅a⌉ete/ make a mistake 24
ma⌈tig̅a⌉u /intr:-u:ma⌈tig̅a⌉tte/ be wrong 24-N
ma⌉tinee daytime performance 28-N
mattaku indeed, really, honestly 34
ma⌉tti match 3

ma⌉tu /tr:-u:ma⌉tte/ wait, await, wait for 1
maturi festival 32
mawari circumference 33
  ka⌈ki⌉ne no mawari ni around the fence 33
mawaru /intr:-u:mawatte/ go around 20
mawasu /tr:-u:mawasite/ send around, turn [something] around 20
ma⌈ze⌉ru /tr:-ru:ma⌉zete/ mix [something] 33-A
ma⌈zi⌉ru /intr:-u:ma⌈zi⌉tte/ [something] mixes 33-A
ma⌈zu⌉i /-ku/ is bad-tasting 14
me⌉ eye 17-A
-me* /ordinal number suffix/ 31
me⌉e niece 11-A
me⌉g̅osan̄↑ niece 11-A
meesi name card, calling card 13
me⌉ewaku /na/ troublesome, annoying 32
  go⌈me⌉ewaku zya ⌐na⌉kereba↑ if it isn't [too much] trouble for you 32
me⌉ezi Meiji Era (1868–1912) 8
me⌉g̅ane eyeglasses 23-A
  me⌉g̅ane o ka⌐ke⌉ru wear eyeglasses 23-A
me⌉isya eye doctor, oculist 24-A
me⌈n̄dookusa⌉i /-ku/ is troublesome, tiresome 27
me⌈si⌉ cooked rice, meal 24-N
mesiag̅aru↑ /tr:-u:mesiag̅atte/ eat; drink; smoke 14
me⌈zurasi⌉i /-ku/ is amazing, unusual, unexpected 27
  me⌈zura⌉siku ⌈i⌉i is unusually good 27
mi⌉dori green 16-N
mi⌈e⌉ru* /intr:-ru:mi⌉ete/ be visible, can see; put in an appearance, show up, come 18; appear, seem, look 26
mig̅aku /tr:-u:mig̅aite/ shine <u>or</u> polish [something] 21
mig̅i right (i.e. not left) 6
  mi⌈g̅i no ho⌉o right side, toward the right 6
mi⌉kosi portable shrine carried about during festivals 32
mi⌈mi⌉ ear 17-A
  mi⌈mi⌉ g̅a to̅oi is hard of hearing 27

minami south 30
minamimuki facing south 30
mi⌐na˩sañ ⌐ everyone 11
minato harbor, port 32
mi⌐ñna˩ everyone; everything 11
mi⌐ru* /tr:-ru:mi˩te/ look at, see 12
    si⌐te mi˩ru try doing, do and see
    19
mi⌐ruku milk 14
misaki cape, promontory 32-A
mi⌐se˩ store, shop 6-A
    mi⌐se no hito˩ shop employee 24-A
    mi⌐se˩ o yaru have a shop 34
mi⌐se˩ru /tr:-ru:mi˩sete/ show, let
    [someone] see 4
miti street, road, way 7
mi-⌐ttu˩ three units 5
mitukaru /intr:-u:mitukatte/ be(come)
    found 24
mitukeru /tr:-ru:mitukete/ find [some-
    thing] 24-N
mitumori estimate 33
    daitai no mitumori rough estimate
    33
mituriñ jungle 32-A
miyage souvenir 31-A
mi⌐zika˩i /-ku/ is short 22
mizu cold water 14
mi⌐zuu˩mi lake 32-A
mo* /particle/ also, too 4; even
    22
    a⌐o˩i no mo blue one(s) too 4
    de⌐pa˩ato ni mo in the department
    store too 6
    o⌐oki˩i no mo ti⌐sa˩i no mo both
    big ones and small ones 5
    iti-neñ mo /+ affirmative/ all of
    a year, a whole year 24;
    /+ negative/ not even a year 24
    i⌐tte˩ mo even if [someone] goes
    22
    i⌐tte˩ mo ⌐i˩i is all right to go,
    [someone] may go 22
    i⌐tte˩ mo i⌐kana˩kute mo whether
    [someone] goes or not 22
    do⌐ko e i⌐tte˩ mo wherever [some-
    one] goes 27
    do⌐o mo in every way Int.
    i⌐tu mo always 9
    dotira mo both 10
    dare mo /+ negative/ nobody 13
mo⌐do˩ru /intr:-u:mo⌐do˩tte/ go back,
    back up 7

mo⌐kuyo˩o(bi), mokuyoo Thursday 8
momeñ cotton 23
momoiro pink 16-N
mo⌐no˩* thing (tangible) 14; used to
    32
    ka⌐tta mono˩ da used to buy 32
mo⌐no˩ ⌐ person 33
mono* /particle/ because 35
    syo⌐ttyuu desu mono because it's
    all the time 35
mo⌐nooki˩ storeroom 33-A
mo⌐ñ gate 30-A
mo⌐ñ /see mo⌐no˩/ 32
mo⌐ñbu˩syoo Ministry of Education 25
moñdai problem 28
moo* /+ quantity expression/ more,
    additional 1
    moo iti-do one time more 1
    mo⌐o suko˩si a little more, a few
    more 4
mo⌐o* /+ affirmative/ already, yet,
    now already, soon now 14;
    /+ negative/ no more 18
    mo⌐o su˩gu soon now, any minute
    now 15
moosiageru ⌐ /tr:-ru:moosiagete/ say
    (to you) 32-N
mo⌐osu ⌐ /tr:-u:mo⌐osite/ say, be
    named, be called 18
morau* /tr:-u:moratte/ receive, get
    17
    site morau have [someone] do [it],
    have [something] done 17
    ki⌐te˩ moraenai? can('t) I have you
    come? would you come? 25
mo⌐ru /intr:-u:mo⌐tte/ leak 33
mo⌐si supposing 28
mo⌐simosi hello (on the telephone); say
    there! 12
mo⌐tase˩ru /tr:-ru:mo⌐ta˩sete/ cause
    [someone] to have 33
    be⌐ñto˩o o mo⌐ta˩sete yo⌐ko˩su
    send [someone] here with a lunch
    33
mo⌐tiage˩ru /tr:-ru:mo⌐tia˩gete/ lift
    33-A
mo⌐ti˩roñ of course 15
mo⌐to former time 24
motte iku take [something somewhere]
    14-N
mo⌐tte ku˩ru bring [something]
    14
mo⌐tto* more 5

moˀtu /tr:-u:moˀtte/ hold, take hold
     of, have 32
mukoo   beyond, over there; the far
     side 6
   biˀru no mukoo   beyond the build-
     ing 6
   muˁkoo no biˀru   the building over
     there 6
muˀne˺   chest (part of the body) 17-A
muˀra˺   village 34-N
muˀra˺saki   purple 16-N

N

na* /pre-nominal alternant of da/ 12
   hiˁma na toki˺   time when [someone]
     is free 12
na* /negative imperative particle/ 35
   iˁu˺ na   don't say 35
na? /sentence particle/ /M/ isn't
     it true? do you agree? 35
naˀa /sentence particle/ /M/ isn't
     it true! don't you agree! 35
naˀdo*   and so forth, etc. 31
   ni˺ŋgyoo naˀdo   dolls and so forth,
     a doll for example, something
     like a doll 31
naɡaɡutu   boots 24-N
naˁɡaˀi /-ku/   is long 22
naɡaisu   couch, sofa 17-A
naˁɡame˺   view 32
-naɡara*   while, during 31; while,
     although 35
   noˁminaˀɡara   while drinking 31
   oˀmoinaˀɡara   while or although
     thinking 35
naˀɡasa   length 23
naˁɡasi˺   a sink 17-A
naˀi /-ku/   there isn't 15
naˀihu   knife 14-A
naiseñ   telephone extension 12
naˀka   inside 17
   hiˁkidasi no naˀka   inside the
     drawer 17
naˁkaba˺   middle 26
nakanaka /+ affirmative/   consider-
     ably, more than expected 11;
     /+ negative/   not easily, not
     readily 28
naku /intr:-u:naite/   cry 35-A
nakunaru /intr:-u:nakunatte/   die,
     pass away 34-A
namae   name 10
naˀna   seven 3

muˀri /na/   unreasonable, beyond one's
     power 35
muˀri ni saseru   force [someone] to
     do 35
musi   bug, insect 21
muˁsiatuˀi /-ku/   is muggy, sultry 26
musuko   son 11-A
muˁsume˺   daughter 11-A
mu-ˁttu˺   six units 5
muˀzi   solid color 23
muzukasii /-ku/   is difficult 11

naˀna˺-tu   seven units 5
naˀni   what? 2
   naˀni ka   something, anything 4
   naˀni ka ˁyoˀo   some business, some
     matter to be attended to 25
   nani mo /+ negative/   nothing 18
naniiro   what color? 5-N
naˀninani   so-and-so 33
naniziñ   what nationality? 10-A
naˀñ /alternant of naˀni/   what? 2
   naˁñ de˺ mo   no matter what it is,
     anything at all 15
   naˁñ de mo aˀru   there's every-
     thing 29
   naˁñ de mo naˀi   it's nothing 29
   naˀñ ka   something, anything 35
   naˀñ te iˀtte˺ mo   whatever [some-
     one] says 27
naˀñ-do mo   any number of times 27
naˀñka* /alternant of naˀdo/ 31
nañni mo /see nani mo/ 18
naˁoˀru /intr:-u:naˀoˀtte/   get well, re-
     cover 14
naˁoˀsu /tr:-u:naˀoˀsite/   fix, repair 13
naˀpukiñ   napkin 14-A
nara(ba) /provisional of da/ 32
naraberu /tr:-ru:narabete/   line [some-
     thing or someone] up 20-N
narabu /intr:-u:narañde/   [something
     or someone] lines up 20
naˁraˀnai*   it won't do 32
   siˁnaˀkereba naˀraˀnai   must do 32
naˁraˀu /tr:-u:naˁraˀtte/   learn, take
     lessons 18
naˀru* /intr:-u:naˀtte/   become, get
     to be 10
   naˀtte (i)ru   it has become or been
     set at or been made into 29
   oˀokiku naˀruˀ   get big 10
   ya-ˁttu˺ ni ˀnaˀru   get to be eight

naꟸru* (cont.)
    years old 10
    oꜝkaeri ni naꟸru ꞈ /honorific equiva-
      lent of kaꟸeru/ 9
naru /intr:-uːnatte/ sound, ring, roar,
    rumble 26-A
    kaꜝminariꟸ ḡa naru it thunders
    26-A
narubeku as much as possible 22
    naꜝrubeku usuku kiꟸru cut as thin
      as possible 22
naruhodo I see, to be sure, of course
    32
naꜝsaꟸru ꞈ /tr:-aruːnaꜝsaꟸtte ~ naꜝsuꟸtte/
    do, make 13
naꜝtuꟸ summer 18-N
naꜝtuyaꟸsumi summer vacation 25
naꟷwaꟸ rope 33-A
ne?* /sentence particle/ isn't it
    true? do you agree? 13
nedañ price 31
neꟸe* /sentence particle/ isn't it
    true! don't you agree! 1
    Doꟸko desyoo ka ꞈneꟷe. Where would
      it be! I wonder where it is! 11
neꟸesañ ꞈ older sister 11-A
neꜝḡaꟸu ꞈ /tr:-uːneꜝḡaꟸtte/ request Int.
    Oꞈnegai-simaꟸsu. ꞈ I'd like it. Please
    let me have it. Please do so. I have
    a request to make of you. Int.
neꟸko cat 17-A
neꟸkutai necktie 23-A
    neꟸkutai o suru wear a necktie
    23-A
nemui /-ku/ is sleepy 21
-neñ /counter for naming and counting
    years/ 8
neru /intr:-ruːnete/ go to bed, go to
    sleep 21
    nete (i)ru be in bed, be asleep 21
neꟸzi screw 33
neꟷzimaꟸwasi screwdriver 33-A
niꟸ two 3
ni* /particle/ in, on, at 6; into,
    onto, to 7; by 17
    hoka ni in addition 4
    sezu ni without doing, instead of
      doing 24
    Toꟸokyoo ni aꟸru be in Tokyo 6
    saꟸñ-zi ni iku go at three o'clock 8
    ya-ꜝttuꟸ ni ꞈnaꟷru become eight
      years old 10

ni* (cont.)
    teñpura ni suru make it tempura,
      decide on tempura 14
    koko ni oku put here 17
    tomodati ni iu say to a friend 18
    aꟸi ni ꞈkuꟷru come to see 25
    daꟸre ka ni naꞈosaseꟷru make some-
      one fix 33
    toꜝmodati ni tukuꟸtte morau have a
      friend make [it] 17
    soꟸbo ni soꞈdatererareꟷru be brought
      up by one's grandmother 34
    daꟸre ka ni saserareru be made to
      do [something] by someone 34-N
niꜝaꟸu /intr:-uːniꜝaꟸtte/ suit, be be-
    coming 23
niꜝḡaꟸi /-ku/ is bitter 14-A
niḡiru /tr:-uːniḡitte/ grasp 33-A
nihoñḡo Japanese language 11
Niꜝhoñ-hoosookyoꟸokai Japan Broad-
    casting Company 34
nihoñma Japanese-style room 21
niꜝhoñziꟸñ a Japanese 10
niꜝisañ ꞈ older brother 11-A
niꜝkuꟸ meat 6-N
-nikuꟸi* /-ku/ cause difficulty in do-
    ing 28
    kaꜝinikuꟸi is difficult to buy 28
niꜝkuꟸya meat market, butcher 6-A
niꟸmotu baggage, things to carry 20
-niñ /counter for people/ 10
niñḡyoo doll 31
-niñmae /counter for portions/ 15
niꜝoꟸi smell, odor 33
    niꜝoꟸi ḡa suru have an odor 33
nippoñḡo Japanese language 11
niꞈppoñziꟸñ a Japanese 10-A
nisi west 30-A
nisimuki facing west 30-N
nisyoku-tuki with two meals, including
    two meals 21
-niti /counter for naming and counting
    days/ 10
niꜝtiyoꟸo(bi), nitiyoo Sunday 8
niꜝtoꟸosya second-class car 19
niwa garden 17-A
niꟷwakaaꟸme sudden shower 26-A
niꟷziꟸ, nizi rainbow 26-A
no* one, ones 4; act, fact 28; mat-
    ter, case 7-N
    aꜝkaꟸi no red one(s) 4
    kyoꟸo no wa as for today's (one) 5

no* (cont.)
ka⌜u⌉ no the act of buying, the buying, buying 28
ka⌜u⌉ no ni in the process of buying, for buying 28; in spite of the fact that [someone] buys 29
i⌜kita⌉i no desu it is a case of wanting to go, I want to go 7-N
ka⌜rita⌉i no de being a case of wanting to rent, because [someone] wants to rent 29
no* /particle/
To⌜okyoo no ti⌉zu map of Tokyo 5
kyo⌉o no siñbuñ today's newspaper 5
watakusi no siñbuñ my newspaper 5
ni⌜to⌉osya no tomaru tokoro the place where the second-class cars stop 19
no* /pre-nominal alternant of da/ 19-N
byooki no kodomo sick child 19-N
nobori up-train (i.e. going toward Tokyo) 19
noboru /intr:-u:nobotte/ climb 32-N
ya⌜ma⌉ ni noboru climb a mountain 32-N
no⌉do throat 15
no⌉do ḡa ka⊢wa⊣ku become thirsty 15
no⌜koḡiri⌉ saw (tool) 33-A
no⌜ko⌉ru /intr:-u:no⌜ko⌉tte/ be(come) left over or left behind 20
no⌜ko⌉su /tr:-u:no⌜ko⌉site/ leave behind, leave over (for another time) 20-N
no⌜mi⌉mizu drinking water 21
no⌜mi⌉mono a drink, beverage 15
no⌉mu /tr:-u:no⌉ñde/ drink; smoke; take (medicine) 14
no⌉o (form of classical Japanese drama) 28-A
noriba place for boarding vehicles 20
norikae a transfer (from one vehicle to another) 19
no⌜rikae⌉ru, no⌜rika⌉eru /intr:-ru:no⌜rika⌉ete/ change vehicles, transfer 19-N
norimono vehicle 29
noru /intr:-u:notte/ get on (a vehicle), take (a vehicle), ride 19
noseru /tr:-ru:nosete/ give [someone] a ride, carry, take on board 19-N
notihodo later 12
nozoku /tr:-u:nozoite/ look in at, peek at 31
nu⌜rikae⌉ru, nu⌜rika⌉eru /tr:-ru:nu⌜rika⌉ete/ repaint 30
nuru /tr:-u:nutte/ paint 30
nu⌜ru⌉i /-ku/ is lukewarm 21
nya[a] /contraction of ni wa/ 27
nyu⌜uḡakusike⌉ñ entrance exam 35
ñ /M/ yeah 14
ñ* /contraction of no/ 7
i⌜kita⌉i ñ desu it is a matter of wanting to go, I want to go 7
de⌜kakeru⌉ ñ da it is a matter of going out, [someone] goes out 23
ñ⌜ma⌉ /see u⌜ma⌉/ 17-A
ñ⌜ma⌉i /see u⌜ma⌉i/ 22

O

o* /particle/
Hu⌜rosiki o mi⌉sete kudasai. Please show me a furoshiki. 4
Kono miti o ma⌜ssu⌉ḡu i⊢tte kudasa⊣i. Please go straight along this street. 7
oba aunt 11-A
o⌜ba⌉asañ† grandmother; old lady 11-A
obasañ† aunt; woman 11-A
o⌉bi Japanese sash 23-A
o⌉bi o si⊢me⊣ru tie an obi 23-A
o⌜boe⌉ru /tr:-ru:o⌜bo⌉ete/ commit to memory 24
o⌜bo⌉ete (i)ru remember 24
oboñ+ tray 14-A
Odaizi ni.† Take care [of yourself]! 11
odori dance, dancing (Japanese style) 28-A
O⌜hayoo (gozaima⌉su).+ Good morning. Int.
ohukuro /M—familiar/ my mother, the old lady 34-N
o⌜hu⌉ro+ bath 21
o⌜hu⌉ro ni ⊢ha⊣iru go into the bath, take a bath 21
oi nephew 11-A
oide† /honorific nominal/ 9-N
Oide. Come! Go! Stay! 35
o⌜ide ni na⌉ru† be, come, go 9-N

oiḡosañ ⁺ nephew 11-A

oimotosañ ⁺ younger sister 11-A

o˼iru oil (for automobiles) 20

oisii /-ku/ is delicious 14

oisyasañ ⁺ doctor (medical) 24-A

oite iku leave behind 26-N

o˼ka˼asañ ⁺ mother 11-A

O˼kaeri-nasa˺i. Welcome home. Hello.
   20

okaḡe de ⁺ /informal equivalent of
   okaḡesama de/ 35

okaḡesama de ⁺ thanks to you; thanks
   for asking Int.

O˼kamai na˺ku. ⁺ Don't bother. Don't
   go to any trouble. 18

okane ⁺ money 22

o˼ka˺si ⁺ cake, sweets 14-A

o˼kasi˺i /-ku/ is funny (either strange
   or amusing) 20

o˼ki˺ru /intr:-ru:o˼kite/ get up, wake
   up 21
   o˺kite (i)ru be up, be awake 21

okosañ ⁺ child 10

o˼ko˺su /tr:-u:o˼ko˺site/ wake [some-
   one] up 21

oku* /tr:-u:oite/ put, place 17
   site oku do in advance, do now for
   later reference 17

okureru /intr:-ru:okurete/ fall behind,
   become late 19
   okurete (i)ru be late 19

okurimono gift 31

okuru /tr:-u:okutte/ send 23

o˼kusañ ⁺ wife; madam; mistress 11

okuzyoo roof garden 31-A

omae /M/ you 35-N

O˼matase-(ita)sima˺sita. ⁺ I'm sorry to
   have kept you waiting. 4

O˼matidoosama de˺sita. ⁺ I'm sorry you
   were kept waiting. 20

o˼me ni kaka˺ru ⁺ see (a person), meet
   11
   Ha˼zi˺mete ome ni kakarimasu. ⁺
   How do you do? 11

omoi /-ku/ is heavy 20

o˼moida˺su /tr:-u:o˼moida˺site/ call to
   mind, recall 24

o˼mosiro˺i /-ku/ is interesting, is unusual, is fun 2

o˼mote˺ front surface, outside, right
   side 33-N

o˼mo˺tya toy 31

o˼motyau˺riba toy counter, toy department 31

o˼mo˺u* /tr:-u:o˼mo˺tte/ think 26
   i˼i to o⁺mo⁴u think it's good 26
   i˼koo to omo˺u think I'll go 26
   i˼ko˺o ka to o⁺mo⁴u wonder if I
   should go 26-N
   Do˺o omoimasu ka。 What do you
   think? 26

onaka stomach 15
   onaka ḡa suku become hungry 15

onazi same 2
   onazi kusuri same medicine 17
   kore to onazi same as this 17

O˼neḡai-sima˺su. ⁺ Please (speaker requesting something; lit. I make a
   request). Int.

o˺no hatchet, ax 33-A

o˼ñḡaku music 28-A

oñḡakuka musician 28-A

o˼ñḡaku˺kai concert 28-A

o˼ñna˺ female 10
   o˼ñna˺ no hito woman 10
   o˼ñna˺ no kata˺ ⁺ woman 10
   o˼ñna˺ no ko little girl 10

oñseñ hot spring, hot-spring resort
   32

o˼oa˺me heavy rain 26-A

o˺obaa (full-length) coat 23

oohuku round trip 19

o˼o˺i /-ku/ is frequent, is much, are
   many 21

o˼oi˺soḡi de in a big hurry 32

o˼oka˺ze strong wind 26-A

o˼oke˺sutora orchestra 28-A

o˺oki* /na/ big 13
   o˺oki na ⁺ko⁴e loud voice 13

o˼oki˺i /-ku/ is big 2

ookisa size 23-N

ooyuki heavy snow 26-A

o˺pera opera 28-A

ore /M/ I, me 35-N

o˼ri˺ru /intr:-ru:o˺rite/ go down, de-
   scend, get off (a vehicle) 20

o˼ro˺su /tr:-u:o˼ro˺site/ lower, let
   down, discharge (from a vehicle)
   20-N

o˺ru ⁺* /intr:-u:o˺tte/ be located (of
   animate beings) 6
   ke˼kkoñ-site o˺ru ⁺ be married 10
   be˼ñkyoo-site o˺ru ⁺ be studying 11
   hu˼tte ⁺o⁴ru ⁺ be raining 18

Osaki ni. ⁺ [Excuse me for going] ahead.
   18

Do˺ozo, osaki ni. ⁺ Please [go] ahead.
   18-N

osieru /tr:-ru:osiete/ teach, inform
    7
osiire closet (for clothing, quilts, etc.)
    17-A
osoi /-ku/ is late or slow 11
osoku late 31-N
Osoreirimasu. Thank you. I'm sorry.
    18
ossyaru† /tr:-aru:ossyatte/ say, be
    named, be called 13
osu /tr:-u:osite/ push 33-A
otaku† home, household 9
    otaku no† pertaining or belonging
        to your household 10
otiru /intr:-ru:otite/ fall, drop
    33-A
otoko male 10
    otoko no hito man 10
    otoko no kata† man 10
    otoko no ko little boy 10
otoosañ† father 11
otooto younger brother 11-A
otosu /tr:-u:otosite/ drop [some-
    thing] 33-A

ototoi, ototoi day before yesterday
    8
otootosi year before last 24
otya† tea 14
owari the end 28
owaru /intr:-u:owatte/ come to an
    end 28
oya parent 11-A
oya? oh! my word! hold on! 34
oyagosañ† parent 11-A
Oyasumi-nasai. Good night. Int.
oyogi swimming 32-A
oyogu /intr:-u:oyoide/ swim 27
oyoso generally speaking, on the
    whole, as a rule 35
oyu† hot water 14-A
ozeñ† eating tray 21
    ozeñ o dasu bring out the trays,
        serve dinner 21
ozi uncle 11-A
oziisañ† grandfather; old man 11-A
ozisañ† uncle; man 11-A
ozyoosañ† daughter; young girl; little
    girl 11-A

P

pañ bread 14-A
pañku-suru /intr/ become punctured
    20
    taiya ga pañku-suru have a flat
        tire 20

pasu-suru /intr/ pass (an exam)
    35-N
peñ pen 2
peñti pliers 33-A
puroguramu program 28-N

R

raigetu next month 16-N
raineñ next year 16-N
raisyuu next week 16
raitaa lighter 4
rasii* /-ku/ seems to be 35
    ii rasii seems to be good 35
razio radio 16
ree zero 12
reezooko refrigerator 17-A
rekisi history 32
reñga brick 33-A
reñraku-suru /tr/ get in touch, con-
    tact, communicate 24
reñsyuu practice 31
reñsyuu-suru /tr/ practice (verb) 31
reñzi stove (for cooking) 17-A
reñzu lens 24
resutorañ restaurant 14-A
-ri ~niñ /counter for people/ 10
riku land 32-N

rikuguñ army 34
rikuseñtai marines 34-A
rippa /na/ fine, handsome, magnificent,
    imposing 18
rireki'syo personal history record 34
-rittoru /counter for liters/ 20
roku six 3
roku-zyoo six-mat area or room 30
roodoosya laborer 24-A
rooka hall, corridor 17-A
roomazi romanization 31-N
roosoku candle 35
rosiago Russian language 11-A
rosia'ziñ a Russian 10-A
rusu away from home 12
    rusu-tyuu ni during [someone's] ab-
        sence from home 18
rusubañ care-taking 27
    rusubañ o suru take care of house
        during absence of others 27

ryokañ inn (Japanese style) 6-A
ryokoo a trip 32
ryokoo-suru /intr/ take a trip, travel
    32

S

sa* /sentence particle/ /M/ 35
sa'a hmm... 6
sa'abisu service 33
sabaku desert 32-A
sa'bisi'i /-ku/ is lonesome or cheer-
    less 35-A
sa⌐ga'ru /intr:-u:sa⌐ga'tte/ go down
    29-N
saḡasu /tr:-u:saḡasite/ look for 22
sa⌐ḡe'ru /tr:-ru:sa⌐ḡete/ lower [some-
    thing] 29-N
sakaba saké bar 29-N
sakana fish 6-N
sakanaya fish market, fish man 6-A
sakañ /na/ flourishing, prosperous,
    thriving, popular 32
sakaya saké shop 29
sake rice wine 14
sakezuki saké lover, drinker 24-N
saki ahead 6
    kono saki up ahead from here 7
saku /intr:-u:saite/ bloom 27
    saite (i)ru be in bloom 27
sakura cherry tree, cherry blossom
    27
-sama† (more polite alternant of -sañ)
    12
sa'mu'i /-ku/ is cold (of weather or
    atmosphere) 14
sañ three 3
-sañ† Mr., Mrs., Miss Int.
sa⌐ndoi'tti sandwich 28-N
sañpo a walk 18
sañpo-suru /intr/ take a walk 18-N
sa⌐ñto'osya third-class car 19-A
sa⌐ñ-zyo'o three-mat area or room
    30
sara plate, dish 14-A
saraiḡetu month after next App.
saraineñ year after next App.
saraisyuu week after next App.
sa⌐rari'imañ salaried man, white-
    collar worker 24-A
sa⌐simi' sashimi (raw fish) 14-A
sa⌐to'o sugar 14-A
-satu /counter for books, magazines,
    etc./ 5

ryo⌐ori'ya restaurant (Japanese style) 14-A
ryo⌐osi fisherman 24-A
ryo⌐osiñ both parents 11-A
ryo⌐ozi'kañ consulate 6

sa⌐wa'ḡu /intr:-u:sa⌐wa'ide/ make noise,
    be boisterous 27
Sayonara. Goodbye. Int.
sayoo that way, thus, so 12
Sayoonara. Goodbye. Int.
sebiro man's suit 21
-see -made 23
    Amerika-see American-made 23
seekatu life, existence 34
seekatu-suru /intr/ live, make a living
    34
seereki Western calendar, Christian
    Era 8-N
se'etaa sweater 23
se'eto pupil 24-A
seezi politics 32-A
se⌐ka'i world 32-A
se'ki, seki seat, assigned place 12
se⌐kita'ñ coal 30
se⌐kkaku' with much trouble, on pur-
    pose; with special kindness 26
se⌐kkaku' desu ḡa it's kind of you
    to ask [me] but 26
se⌐kkaku ku'ru come on purpose,
    take the trouble to come, come
    specially 26
sekkeñ soap 17
se⌐ma'i /-ku/ is narrow or cramped
    or small in area 21-N
senaka back (part of the body) 17-A
se'ñ thousand 3
-señ /counter for thousands/ 3
se'ñḡetu last month 14
señḡo post-war 34-N
se⌐ñkyo'osi missionary 24-A
se⌐ñme'ñki wash basin 17-A
señmeñzyo washroom, lavatory 17-A
señmoñ specialty 33
    señmoñ no hito specialist, expert
        33
se⌐ñse'e teacher, doctor 16
se⌐ñse'ñḡetu month before last App.
se⌐ñse'ñsyuu week before last App.
señsoo war 34
señsu (folding) fan 31-A
señsyuu last week 26
señtaku laundering 23-N

señtakumono laundry (i. e. things to be
    laundered) 23-N
señtaku-suru /tr/ launder 23
señtakuya laundry (store), laundryman
    23-N
señzeñ pre-war 34-N
señzitu the other day 18
señzi-tyuu during war 34
setomono china, pottery 31-A
se⌐tubi equipment, facilities, accom-
    modations 30
setumee explanation 28-N
setumee-suru /tr/ explain 28
se⌐wa⌐ helpful service 25
    Iroiro o⌐se⌐wa ni na⌐rima⌐sita. ⌐
    I'm much obliged to you. 25
si⌐ four 3
si⌐ city 34
    Ko⌐onosu⌐-si Konosu City 34
si* /particle/ and 23
    zyo⌐obu da⌐ si it is strong and what
    is more 23
siai game, match 35
siba lawn 33
sibai a play, show 28
si⌐ba⌐raku a while (short or long) 11
    Si⌐ba⌐raku desita. It's been a long
    time [since I last saw you]. 11
si⌐ba⌐ru /tr:-u:si⌐ba⌐tte/ tie, bind
    33-A
sigoto work 10
    sigoto-tyuu in the middle of work
    12
si⌐ha⌐iniñ manager 24-A
sika* /particle/ /+ negative/ nothing
    but, only 21
    ko⌐re sika na⌐i there's nothing but
    this, there's only this 21
si⌐kaku⌐ square 31-N
si⌐kaku⌐i /-ku/ is square 31
si⌐ka⌐si however, but 15
sikata method, way of doing 23
    si⌐kata ga na⌐i it can't be helped,
    nothing can be done 23
si⌐ke⌐ñ exam, test 35
    si⌐ke⌐ñ o u⌐ke⌐ru take an exam 35
sikeñ-suru /tr/ put to a test, examine
    35-N
sikiti building lot 30
siku /tr:-u:siite/ spread out (on floor,
    ground, etc.) 21
    hutoñ o siku spread out the futon
    (for sleeping) 21

si⌐ma⌐ island 32
si⌐ma⌐ru /intr:-u:si⌐ma⌐tte/ [something]
    closes or shuts 16
simau* /tr:-u:simatte/ put away, store
    17
    irete simau finish putting in, put in
    for good, end up by putting in 17
si⌐me⌐ru /tr:-ru:si⌐mete/ close or shut
    [something] 16
    o⌐bi o si⌐me⌐ru wear an obi 23
sinu /intr:-u:siñde/ die 34-A
siñbuñ newspaper 2
si⌐ñbuñki⌐sya newspaperman 24-A
siñdai bed 17-A
si⌐ñda⌐ikeñ berth ticket 19-A
si⌐ñda⌐isya sleeping car 19-A
siñgeki modern drama 28-A
siñpai worry 23
    Go⌐siñpai na⌐ku. ⌐ Don't worry. 23
siñpai-suru /tr/ worry 23-N
siñsitu bedroom 17-A
si⌐ñtoo Shintoism 32
siñzyu pearl 31-A
si⌐o⌐ salt 14-A
si⌐rabe⌐ru /tr:-ru:si⌐ra⌐bete/ look into,
    check, investigate 20
siraseru /tr:-ru:sirasete/ cause to
    know, let [someone] know 33
sirenai* it can't be known 30
    i⌐i ka mo sirenai maybe it's good,
    it may be good 30
siriai acquaintance 29
si⌐ro⌐i /-ku/ is white 4
siru /tr:-u:sitte/ come to know 10
    sitte (i)ru know 10
sita under, below, bottom, youngest
    10
    si⌐ta no ho⌐ñ bottom book 10-N
    ho⌐ñ no sita under the book 10-N
sitagi underwear 23-A
sitaku preparation 16
    sitaku o suru prepare 16
si⌐ti⌐ seven 3
situmoñ question 32-N
situmoñ-suru /intr/ question, ask
    questions 34-N
si⌐tu⌐ree /na/ rudeness, rude 10
    Si⌐tu⌐ree desu ga_ Excuse me
    but . . . 10
    Si⌐tu⌐ree(-simasu). Excuse me (on
    leaving). Int.
    Si⌐tu⌐ree(-simasita). Excuse me
    (for what I did). Int.

siyoo /see syoo/ 23-N
si'zuka /na/ quiet 21
so'ba vicinity 6
  e'ki no 'so'ba near the station 6
  so'ba no 'e'ki a nearby station 6
  su'gu 'so'ba immediate vicinity 6
so'ba noodles 14-A
so'ba'ya noodle shop 14-A
so'bo grandmother 11-A
so'date'ru /tr:-ru:so'da'tete/ bring up, raise 34
so'da'tu /intr:-u:so'da'tte/ grow up 34
so'hu grandfather 11-A
soko that place, there 6
sono* /+ nom/ that— 3
  sono ue on top of that, what is more 23
  so'no ue' de on the basis of that 33
sonna* that kind, that kind of 5
  sonna ni to that extent 28
so'o that way, thus, so 2
  So'o desu. That's right. 2
  So'o desu ka. Is that right? Oh? 2
  So'o desu 'ne'e. That's right, isn't it. 2; Let me see... Hmmm... 4
so'o da* it is said 22
  i'ku so'o da it is said that [he] is going to go; they say that [he] is going to go; I hear that [he] is going to go 22
-soo* /na/ looking as if 26
  ha'reso'o /na/ looking as if it would clear up 26
soodañ discussion 28-N
soodañ-suru /tr/ discuss, talk over 28
soozi-suru /tr/ clean (verb) 16
so'ra sky 26-A
sore* that thing 2
  sore de that being the case, accordingly 32
  so're de' wa in that case 35
  sore kara after that, and then, and 4
  so're wa so'o to be that as it may, to change the subject 35
Sore wa sore wa. Oh, my goodness! You don't say! Really! 27
sorezore respectively, severally 32
so'ru /tr:-u:so'tte/ shave 22
sosite and, then, and then 27
sotira that one (of two); that way, thereabouts, there 6; that person 11; the person addressed 12

so'to outside 17
so'tti /see sotira/ 6
sotug̃yoo-suru /tr/ graduate 34-A
su'barasi'i /-ku/ is wonderful 32
su'gi' past, after 8
  ni-'hu'ñ sugi two minutes after the hour 8
su'gi'ru* /intr:-ru:su'gite/ exceed 21-N
  a'tusugi'ru be too hot 21
su'go'i /-ku/ is dreadful, terrible, terrific, extraordinary 35-A
su'gu soon, any minute, right away 5; readily, easily 28
  su'gu 'so'ba immediate vicinity 6
suidoo running water, water pipes 30
su'ihee navy sailor 34-A
suiseñ flushing 30
su'iyo'o(bi), suiyoo Wednesday 8
su'ka'ato skirt 23-A
su'ki' /na/ pleasing; like [something] 15
sukiyaki sukiyaki (stew of vegetables with meat or chicken or fish) 14-A
su'kka'ri completely 27
su'ko'si a little, a few 4
  mo'o suko'si a little more, a few more 4
suku /intr:-u:suite/ become empty 15
  onaka g̃a suku become hungry 15
su'kuna'i /-ku/ is rare, scarce; are few 21-N
su'mai residence 16
su'mase'ru /tr:-ru:su'ma'sete/ finish [something] 26
su'mi corner (of a room) 17
su'mi' ink stick 31
Su'(m)imase'ñ. I'm sorry. Thank you for your trouble. Int.
Su'(m)imase'ñ desita. I'm sorry (for what I did). Thank you (for the trouble you took). Int.
sumu /intr:-u:suñde/ come to an end 26-N
su'mu /intr:-u:su'ñde/ live, reside 34
suna sand 33-A
suñpoo measurements 23
supeiñg̃o Spanish language 11-A
su'po'otu sports 35
su'ppa'i /-ku/ is acid or sour 14-A
su'pu'uñ spoon 14-A
suru* /tr:irreg:site/ do, perform, make 1; make into, decide on 14; practice a profession 24; play (a game or instrument) 31-N

suru* (cont.)
  ikoo to suru   be about to go; try to
    go   26
  i⌐itaso˥o ni suru   act as if wanting to
    say   35
  teñpura ni suru   make it tempura,
    decide on tempura   14
  i⌐ku koto˥ ni suru   decide to go   32
  uti to site   as a house   29
  u⌐ti to site˥ mo   even as a house   29
su⌐si˥   sushi (rice with fish, seaweed,
    egg, etc.)   14-A
su⌐si˥ya   sushi shop   14-A
su⌐ta˥a   star (i. e. leading player)   28-A
sutañdo   lamp   17-A
suteru /tr:-ru:sutete/   throw away   17
su⌐to˥obu   heater   16
suu /tr:-u:sutte/   smoke (cigarettes,
    cigars, etc.)   14
su˥utu   woman's suit   23-A
suwaru /intr:-u:suwatte/   sit (Japanese
    style, on floor or ground)   25-N
su˥zi   plot   28
su⌐zuri˥   ink stone   31
su⌐zusi˥i /-ku/   is cool   18
syasyoo   train conductor   19
syatyoo   company president   24-A
syokudoo   dining room   14-A
syo⌐kudo˥osya   dining car   19-A
syokuryoohiñ   foodstuffs, groceries
    31-A
syoku-tuki   with meals   21
syokuzi   dining, a meal   15
  syokuzi o suru   dine, eat a meal   15
syoo   method, way of doing   23
  syo⌐o˥ ḡa na˥i   it can't be helped,

ta˥   rice field   29-N
tabako   cigarette, tobacco   3
tabakoya   cigar store   6-A
ta⌐bemo˥no, ta⌐bemono˥   food, edibles
    15-N
ta⌐be˥ru /tr:-ru:ta˥bete/   eat   14
ta⌐besase˥ru /tr:-ru:ta⌐besa˥sete/   feed   33
ta˥bi   socks (Japanese style)   23-A
ta⌐bi˥   time, occasion   32
  ryo⌐koo-suru tabi˥ ni   everytime
    [someone] travels   32
tabitabi   often   34
ta˥buñ   probably   35
Tadaima. Hello, I'm back.   20
taiheñ /na/   awful, dreadful, terrible,
    a nuisance; very   20

syoo (cont.)
  nothing can be done   23
syoobai   business, occupation   33
syo⌐oḡa˥kkoo   elementary school   34
syooḡi   shogi (Japanese chess)   31
syookai   introduction   25
syookai-suru /tr/   introduce   25-N
syookoo   military officer   34-A
syo˥oniñ   merchant, shopkeeper   29
syo⌐osyoo   a little   4
syoosyuu-suru /tr/   summon; draft   34
syooti-suru /tr/   consent to, agree to
    21
  Syo⌐oti-(ita)sima˥sita. Certainly. I
    agree to your request.   21
syoowa   Showa Era (1926-   )   8
syooyu   soy sauce   14-A
syoozi   sliding door (translucent)   18
syo⌐oziki˥ /na/   honest   29
syosai   study (i. e. a room)   17
syo˥ttyuu   always, at all hours, con-
    stantly   35
syuttyoo-suru /intr/   make a business
    trip   35
syuu   week   App.
-syuukañ   /counter for number of weeks/
    8
syuumatu   weekend   29
syuuseñ   end of war   34
  syu⌐useñ ni na˥ru   war ends   34
syuusyoku-suru /intr/   find employment,
    get a job   35
syuuzeñ   repairs   30
syuuzeñ-suru /tr/   repair, fix   30-N
syuuzi   calligraphy   31
syu˥ziñ   husband   11-A

T

ta⌐ihu˥u   typhoon   26-A
ta˥iriku   continent   32-A
ta˥iru   tile   33-A
taisetu /na/   important   20
ta⌐isi˥kañ   embassy   6
taisyoo   Taisho Era (1912-1926)   8
taitee   usual, usually   9
  ta⌐itee no amerika˥ziñ   most Ameri-
    cans   15
taiya, ta˥iya   a tire   20
ta⌐ka˥i /-ku/   is expensive   3; is high
    31-N
ta⌐kusa˥ñ, takusañ   much, many   5
ta˥kusii   taxi   7
tama ni   once in a while, now and then
    35

ta⌐ma¬go egg 14-A
tana shelf 17-A
ta⌐ni¬ valley 32-A
ta⌐no¬mu /tr:-u:ta⌐no¬nde/ make a re-
    quest, place an order 14; engage,
    hire 20
ta⌐nosi¬i /-ku/ is merry or pleasant
    or enjoyable 35-N
ta⌐nosi¬mi, ta⌐nosimi¬ pleasure, enjoy-
    ment 35
ta⌐nosi¬mu /tr:-u:ta⌐nosi¬nde/ take
    pleasure in, enjoy 35-N
ta⌐nbi¬ /see ta⌐bi¬/ 32-N
tañsu chest of drawers 17-A
ta⌐ñze¬ñ quilted kimono 23-A
ta⌐ñzyo¬obi birthday 35
ta⌐ore¬ru /intr:-ru:ta⌐o¬rete/ fall over,
    collapse 33-A
ta⌐o¬su /tr:-u:ta⌐o¬site/ throw over,
    knock down 33-A
tariru /intr:-ru:tarite/ be sufficient
    20
ta⌐suka¬ru /intr:-u:ta⌐suka¬tte/ be saved,
    be helped, survive 35-N
ta⌐suke¬ru /tr:-ru:ta⌐suke¬te/ rescue,
    save 35-N
    Tasukete_ Help! 35-A
tatami rice-straw floor mat 18
    ta⌐tami no heya¬ room with tatami
    18
ta⌐temo¬no, ta⌐te¬mono building 6
ta⌐te¬ru /tr:-ru:ta⌐tete/ build, erect
    32
-tati /pluralizing suffix/ 27
    bo⌐kutati we, us 27
ta⌐to¬eba for example 33
ta⌐toe¬ru /tr:-ru:ta⌐to¬ete/ give an ex-
    ample 33-N
ta⌐tu /intr:-u:ta¬tte/ depart, leave for
    a trip 19
ta⌐tu /intr:-u:ta¬tte/ stand up 27
    ta¬tte (i)ru be standing 27
    ya⌐ku¬ ni ⌐ta¬tu be useful, serve a
    purpose 32
te¬ hand 17-A
te⌐a¬rai toilet 6-A
te⌐bu¬kuro gloves 23
    te⌐bu¬kuro o hameru put on or wear
    gloves 23-A
teeburu table 17
teedeñ stoppage of electricity 35
te⌐enee /na/ polite 34-N
tegami letter 25
    te⌐gami o da¬su mail a letter 25-N

te⌐ire¬ care, repair 33
    te⌐ire¬ o suru care for, repair 33
tekitoo /na/ suitable, appropriate 33
temae this side 6
    byooiñ no temae this side of the
    hospital 6
te⌐nisu tennis 32-A
teñiñ shop employee 24-A
te⌐ñki weather; good weather 18
teñkiñ-suru /intr/ change one's post
    34
teñniñ-suru /intr/ change one's post
    (military) 34-N
teñpura tempura (batter-fried fish or
    vegetables) 14
teñpuraya tempura shop 14-A
teñzyoo ceiling 30-A
tera Buddhist temple 32
te⌐rebi television 16
te⌐tuda¬u /tr:-u:te⌐tuda¬tte/ help, lend
    a hand 17
ti blood 24-N
tiḡau /intr:-u:tiḡatte/ be wrong; be
    different 2
    tiḡatta azi different taste 32
    sore to tiḡau be different from
    that 17
    Ti⌐ḡaima¬su. Wrong number (on the
    telephone). 13
ti¬isa /na/ small 13-N
    ti¬isa na ⌐ko¬e a low voice 13-N
ti⌐isa¬i /-ku/ is small 2
ti⌐ka¬i /-ku/ is near 20
ti⌐ka¬ku vicinity 31
ti⌐ka¬situ basement 31-A
tikatetu subway 20
ti¬ri geography 32
ti⌐ti¬ father 11
ti⌐tto¬ mo /+ negative/ not a bit 24
ti¬zu map 5
to* /particle/ and 4; with 15; as
    29
    ho¬ñ to zassi book and magazine 4
    Sa⌐itoo-sañ to issyo together with
    Mr. Saito 15
    sa⌐muku ⌐na⌐ru to when it gets cold
    (lit. with getting cold) 33
    uti to site as a house 29
    u⌐ti to site¬ mo even as a house
    29
to* /quotative/ 18
    na¬ñ to iu say what? be named or
    called what? 18
to door 16

to⌐ city, metropolis (Tokyo only) 34-N
   To⌐kyoo-to the city of Tokyo 34-N
to mo* /particle sequence/ certainly,
   positively, of course 32
   A⌐rima⌐su to mo. Certainly there
   are. 32
todana cupboard (with shelves) 17
to⌐doke⌐ru /tr:-ru:to⌐do⌐kete/ deliver
   22
to⌐do⌐ku /intr:-u:to⌐do⌐ite/ reach, be
   delivered 22-N
to⌐ire(tto) toilet 6-A
tokee clock, watch 8
to⌐ki⌐* time, occasion 12
   no⌐ru toki⌐ /ni/ when [someone]
   rides 19
to⌐kidoki⌐ sometimes 9
tokkyuu special express 19
to⌐kkyu⌐ukeñ special-express ticket
   19-A
tokonoma Japanese-style alcove 18
to⌐ko(ro)⌐* place 18; place where one
   lives 22; time, occasion 25
   yo⌐nda to⌐koro⌐ da just read 30
   to⌐koro⌐ de by the way, well now 34
   O⌐isogasii tokoro⌐ (o) ⌐do⌐o mo a⌐ri⌐-
   gatoo gozaimasu. Thank you for
   your time when you are [so] busy.
   25
tokoya barber, barbershop 22
to⌐ku ni in particular 29
tokubetu special 19-N
to⌐kubetukyu⌐ukoo special express 19
to⌐kubetuni⌐too special second class
   19-N
tokuni special second class 19-N
tomaru /intr:-u:tomatte/ come to a
   halt; stop at, lodge 19
tomeru /tr:-ru:tomete/ bring to a
   halt 7
tomodati friend 10
tonari next door, adjoining 6
   e⌐ki no tonari next door to the
   station 6
to⌐nikaku anyway, at any rate 28
To⌐nde mo na⌐i. Heavens no! 8
to⌐o ten units 5
to⌐o tower, pagoda 32
-too /counter for naming classes/ 19
Toodai Tokyo University 13
tooi /-ku/ is far 13
   deñwa ga tooi have trouble hearing
   (on the telephone) 13

tooi (cont.)
   mi⌐mi⌐ ga tooi is hard of hearing
   27
to⌐oku⌐ far distance, the far away 31-N
to⌐ori⌐ avenue, wide street 7
to⌐ori way, manner 33
   na⌐mae no to⌐ori like its name, in
   accordance with its name 33
tooroo lantern 32-A
to⌐oru /intr:-u:to⌐otte/ pass through, go
   through, pass in front of 19
to⌐osuto toast 14-A
to⌐otoo finally, in the end 24
to⌐re⌐ru /intr:-ru:to⌐rete/ come off,
   come out, be taken 33
tori bird 17-A; chicken, fowl 14-A
torii gateway to Shinto shrine 32-A
torikaeru /tr:-ru:torikaete/ exchange
   20
to⌐ru /tr:-u:to⌐tte/ take up, take away,
   remove, take off, pass [to some-
   one] 17
   na⌐tuya⌐sumi o ⌐to⌐ru take a summer vacation 25
to⌐si⌐ year 26
to⌐siyori⌐, to⌐siyo⌐ri old person 27
totemo exceedingly, very 8
to⌐tte oku put aside for future use 28
tottemo exceedingly, very 8
to⌐zi⌐ru /tr:-ru:to⌐zite/ close [some-
   thing] CI
/t/te* /quotative/ 18
   na⌐ñ te iu say what? be named or
   called what? 18
-/t/tu /counter for number of units/ 5;
   /counter for years of people's
   age/ 10
-tubo /counter for tsubo [approximately
   6' x 6']/ 30
tu⌐gi⌐ next 7
   tu⌐gi⌐ no ⌐ka⌐do next corner 7
tugoo circumstances, conditions 25
   tu⌐goo ga i⌐i is convenient [for
   someone] 25-N
   tu⌐goo ga waru⌐i is inconvenient [for
   someone] 25-N
tu⌐i unintentionally, carelessly 35
tu⌐itati⌐ first day of the month 8
tu⌐ite* concerning 32
   re⌐kisi ni tu⌐ite concerning history
   32
tu⌐kare⌐ru /intr:-ru:tu⌐ka⌐rete/ become
   tired 17

tukau /tr:-u:tukatte/ use 22
  sukiyaki ni takau use for sukiyaki
    22
tu⌐ke˥ru /tr:-ru:tu⌐ke˥te/ attach, turn
    [something] on 16
tu⌐ki˥ moon; month 26-A
tukiai association, acquaintance 35-N
tukiatari end of a street <u>or</u> corridor
    7
tu⌐kia˥u /intr:-u:tu⌐kia˥tte/ associate
    with 35
tu˥ku /intr:-u:tu˥ite/ arrive 9; [some-
    thing] becomes attached <u>or</u> turned
    on 16
  ki ⌐ga tu˥ku notice 25
tukue desk 17
tu⌐ku˥ru /tr:-u:tu⌐ku˥tte/ make 23
tu⌐ma˥ñnai /<u>see</u> tu⌐mara˥nai/ 24
tu⌐mara˥nai /-ku/ is dull <u>or</u> boring; is
    trifling 2
tu⌐ma˥ru /intr:-u:tu⌐ma˥tte/ become
    blocked <u>or</u> clogged 33
tu⌐me˥ru /tr:-ru:tu˥mete/ cram, stuff,
    stop up 33-N
tumetai /-ku/ is cold 14
tumori* intention, plan 20
  iku tumori da [I] intend to go, [I]
    plan to go 20
turai /-ku/ is hard to bear 34
tureru /tr:-ru:turete/ lead 28
  turete (i)ku take (people <u>or</u> ani-
    mals) 28
turi fishing 32
turu /tr:-u:tutte/ suspend, hang by a
    string 33
  tana o turu hang a shelf 33
tutaeru /tr:-ru:tutaete/ report, com-
    municate, convey a message 13
tu⌐ti˥ dirt 33-A
tu⌐tome˥ru /intr:-ru:tu⌐to˥mete/ be-
    come employed 10
  tu⌐to˥mete (i)ru be employed 10
tu⌐tu˥mu /tr:-u:tu⌐tu˥nde/ wrap 31

tu˥uyaku interpreting 34-A
tu⌐yo˥i /-ku/ is strong 17
tuyu rainy season 26
tuzukeru /tr:-ru:tuzukete/ continue
    [something] 24
tuzuku /intr:-u:tuzuite/ [something]
    continues 24-N; adjoin 28
  tu⌐zuita se˥ki adjoining seats 28
tyairo brown 16
tyaku arriving 19
  i⌐ti˥-zi tyaku arriving at one o'clock
    19
tyanoma family room (Japanese style)
    17-A
-tyañ ꜛ /suffix added to children's given
    names/ 10
tyawañ cup <u>or</u> small bowl (Japanese
    style) 14-A
-tyoo cho (section of a city) 34
  Ni⌐ñgyo˥o-tyoo Ningyo Cho 34
tyoodai-suru ꜛ* accept, receive 35
  Tyo⌐oda˥i. Let me have [it]. 35
  Tu⌐ke˥te tyoodai. Attach for me.
    35
tyoodo exactly 8
-tyoome /counter for naming chomes/
    7
tyooseñgo Korean language 11-A
tyo⌐oseñzi˥ñ a Korean 10-A
tyo⌐oti˥ñ paper lantern 32-A
tyo˥tto a bit, a little 1; just 5
  Tyo⌐tto. Say there! 4
  tyo˥tto— I'm afraid it won't do . . .
    4
-tyuu in the middle of ——, now busy
    with —— 12
  si⌐goto-tyuu in the middle of work
    12
tyu˥ugaku middle school 34
tyuugokugo Chinese language 11-A
tyu⌐ugoku˥ziñ a Chinese 10-A
tyuumoñ-suru /tr/ place an order
    14

U

u⌐de˥ arm 17-A
u⌐e˥, ue over, above, top, topmost,
    oldest 10
  u⌐e no ho˥ñ top book 10-N
  ho˥ñ no ue top of the book 10-N
  sono ue on top of that, what is
    more 23
  so⌐no ue˥ de on the basis of that 33

uekiya gardener 24-A
ueru /tr:-ru:uete/ plant 33
u⌐goka˥su /tr:-u:u⌐goka˥site/ move
    [something] 33
u⌐go˥ku /intr:-u:u⌐go˥ite/ [someone
    <u>or</u> something] moves 33-N
ukagau ꜛ /tr:-u:ukagatte/ inquire
    6

ukaḡau ⁱ (cont.)
  tyoꜜtto uˡkaḡaimaˡsu ḡa excuse me
    but; I'm just going to ask [you
    something] but 6
ukaḡau ⁱ /intr:-u:ukaḡatte/ visit 16
uˡkeˡru /tr:-ru:uˡkete/ undergo 34-A
uketori receipt 22
uketuke reception desk 25
uˡmaˡ horse 17-A
uˡmaˡi /-ku/ is delicious; is skilled 22
umare birth, place of birth 34
umareru /intr:-ru:umarete/ be born
  34
uˡmi sea, ocean 18
uˡn̄ḡa canal 32-A
uˡn̄teˡn̄syu driver, chauffeur 24-A
uˡraˡ back, lining, wrong side 33
uˡresiˡi /-ku/ is happy 35-A
uriba counter, selling place 31
urikire sellout 28
uriko salesgirl 24-A
uru /tr:-u:utte/ sell 22
usaḡi rabbit 17-A
usi bull, cow 17-A
usiro back, rear 7
  taˡisiˡkan̄ no usiro back of the

usiro (cont.)
  embassy 7
usui /-ku/ is weak or thin (of liquids);
  is light (of colors) 14; is thin (of
  flat objects) 22
uˡtaˡ song 27
utau /tr:-u:utatte/ sing 27
uˡtiˡ, uti home, house, household
  9
  uti no our household's, our
    10
uti* among 15; interval, within,
  during 27; /preceded by nega
  tive/ before 33
  A to B to C no uti /de/ /being/
    among A and B and C 15
  asa no uti /ni/ within the morning,
    during the morning 33
  tuˡmaraˡnai uti ni before it gets
    clogged 33
  waˡkaˡi uti while [someone] is
    young 27
uˡtiˡwa (non-folding) fan 31-A
uˡtu /tr:-u:uˡtte/ hit, strike 33-A
uˡuru wool 23-A
uwaḡi jacket 23

W

wa* /sentence particle/ /W/ 16
wa* /particle/ as for, comparatively
  speaking Int.
  Aˡnaˡta wa? How about you? Int.
  Sore wa ˡhaˡn̄ desu ka‿ What is
    that? (Lit. As for that, what is
    it?) 2
  Siˡn̄bun̄ wa kaimaseˡn̄ desita. A
    newspaper I didn't buy. 4
  Koˡko niˡ wa aˡrimaseˡn̄. Here
    there isn't one. 6
  siˡteˡ wa iˡkenai must not do 25
  siˡnaˡkute wa iˡkenai must do 32-N
wahuku Japanese-style clothing 23-A
waisyatu shirt 23
waˡkaˡi /-ku/ is young 27
waˡkaˡru /intr:-u:waˡkaˡtte/ be com-
  prehensible, understand, can
  tell 1
waˡke cause, reason, circumstance
  32
  siˡranai waˡke zya ˡnaˡi isn't the

waˡke (cont.)
  case that I don't know 32
  Doˡo iu ˡwaˡke desu ka‿ What is
    the reason? 32-N
wan̄ bowl 14-A
waˡn̄ bay 32-A
waˡn̄piˡisu (one-piece) dress 23-A
warau /tr:-u:waratte/ laugh 35-A
-wari /counter for units of ten per
  cent/ 35-A
  iˡti-wari goˡ-bu 15 per cent 35-A
wari ni comparatively 31
waˡruˡi /-ku/ is bad 2-A
wasi /M/ I, me 35-N
wasureru /tr:-ru:wasurete/ forget 4
wasyoku Japanese-style food 21
wata(ku)si I, me 5
  wata(ku)si no my, mine 5
wataru /intr:-u:watatte/ go over, go
  across 20
watasu /tr:-u:watasite/ hand over
  20-N

Y

ya* /particle/ and 17
  hoñ ya zassi books and magazines
  and the like 17
ya⌐buˈku /tr:-u:ya⌐buˈite/ tear [some-
  thing] 33
ya⌐bureˈru /intr:-ru:ya⌐buˈrete/ [some-
  thing] tears 33-N
ya⌐buˈru /tr:-u:ya⌐buˈtte/ tear [some-
  thing] 33-N
yaˈgi goat 17-A
ya⌐haˈri after all 35
ya⌐kamasiˈi /-ku/ is noisy 21
yakeru /intr:-ru:yakete/ be burned
  or baked or roasted or toasted
  34-N
yaku /tr:-u:yaite/ burn, bake, roast,
  toast [something] 34
ya⌐kuˈ ni ⌐taˈtu be useful, serve a
  purpose 32
yakusoku promise, appointment, engagement, reservation 21
yakusoku-suru /tr/ promise 21-N
yakusya actor, actress 28-A
yakyuu baseball 35
ya⌐maˈ mountain 18
ya⌐manoˈbori mountain-climbing 32-A
yameru /tr:-ru:yamete/ quit, give up
  14
yamu /intr:-u:yañde/ cease 26
yaˈne roof 30
yaˈnusi, yanusi home owner, landlord 29
yaoya vegetable store 6-A
ya⌐ppaˈri after all 35
yaru* /tr:-u:yatte/ give (to someone
  other than the speaker) 17
  site yaru do for someone 17-N
yaru /tr:-u:yatte/ do 33
  mi⌐seˈ o yaru have a shop 34
yasai vegetable 14-A
yasasii /-ku/ is easy 11
yaseru /intr:-ru:yasete/ grow thin
  35
  ya⌐seta hitoˈ thin person 35-N
ya⌐suˈi /-ku/ is cheap 3
-yasuˈi* /-ku/ is easy to do 28-N
  ka⌐iyasuˈi is easy to buy 28-N
ya⌐sumiˈ vacation, holiday, time off
  8
  ya⌐sumi no hiˈ day off 27
ya⌐suˈmu /tr:-u:ya⌐suˈñde/ rest, re-
  lax, take time off 17

yaˈtiñ the rent 29
ya⌐toˈu /tr:-u:ya⌐toˈtte/ employ 24
yatto finally, barely, with difficulty
  24
yattoko pliers 33-A
ya-⌐ttuˈ eight units 5
ya⌐warakaˈi /-ku/ is soft or tender or
  pliable 22
yo* /sentence particle/ 2
  Peñ desu yo. It's a pen (I tell you).
  2
yobu /tr:-u:yoñde/ call, summon 13
yoˈi /-ku/ is good 2-N
yoko side 6
  de⌐paˈato no yoko the side of the department store 6
yokosu /tr:-u:yokosite/ send here,
  hand over to speaker 33
yoˈku /adverbial of iˈi ~ yoˈi/ well, a
  good deal, often 1
yoˈmu /tr:-u:yoñde/ read 13
yo⌐nakaˈ middle of the night 34
yoˈñ four 3
yoˈo business affairs, matter to attend
  to 22
yoˈo* /na/ manner, way; seem, look
  24
  a⌐naˈta no ⌐yoˈo na hito a person
  like you 24
  mu⌐zukasii yoˈo da seem to be difficult 24
  de⌐kiˈru yoo ni ⌐naˈru reach the
  point where it is possible 24
  ki⌐ite miˈru yoo ni iu tell [some-
  one] to try asking 24
  ma⌐initi no yoˈo ni almost every
  day 24
yoohuku Western-style clothing 23
yookañ Western-style building 30
yooma Western-style room 21
yoosyoku Western-style food 21-N
yoozi business affairs, matter to
  attend to 22
yori* /particle/ more than 15
  ko⌐re yoˈri ⌐iˈi is better than
  this 15
yo⌐rokoˈbu /intr:-u:yo⌐rokoˈñde/ take
  pleasure in 16
yo⌐rokoˈñde /gerund of yo⌐rokoˈbu/
  gladly, with pleasure
  16

yorosii /-ku/ is good or fine or all
   right; never mind 5
   Do꜖ozo yorosiku. (Lit.) Please
   (treat me) favorably. 11
   Mi꜖ha꜒sañ ni yorosiku. Give my
   regards to everyone. 11
   yo꜖rosi꜒kereba provided it's all
   right or agreeable or convenient
   32
yo꜖ru night, night-time 16
   yo꜖ru no bu evening performance
   28
yoru /intr:-u:yotte/ stop in 22
yoru* /intr:-u:yotte/ depend, rely 26
   to꜖si꜒ ni yotte depending on the
   year, according to the year 26
   zyo꜖tyuu no hanasi꜒ ni yoru to
   according to what the maid says
   30
yo-꜖ttu꜒ four units 5
yotukado intersection 20
yo꜖wa꜒i /-ku/ is weak or frail or
   delicate or in poor health 26

yoyaku-suru /tr/ reserve 28
yo꜖zyo꜒o-hañ four-and-a-half-mat
   area or room 30
yu꜖bi꜒ finger 17-A
yuka floor 30-A
yukata summer kimono 23-A
yu꜖ki꜒ snow 23
-yuki -bound 19
   Yokosuka-yuki Yokosuka-bound
   19
yu꜖kku꜒ri slowly 13
yuku /alternant of iku/ 19-N
yu꜖ube꜒ last night 11
yuubiñ mail 24
yu꜖ubi꜒ñkyoku post office 6
yuudati sudden (evening) shower
   26-A
yuūgata early evening 23
yuumee /na/ famous 32
yu꜖za꜒masi water which has been
   boiled 21-N

Z

za꜖siki꜒ Japanese-style room or
   parlor 21
zassi magazine 2
ze꜖hi by all means 28
zeñ Japanese eating tray 21-N
ze꜖ñbu all, the whole thing 1
zeñzeñ /+ negative/ not at all 22
ze꜖ro zero 12
-zi /counter for naming o'clocks/ 8
zi꜖biki꜒ dictionary 2
zibuñ oneself 20
   zibuñ de by oneself 20
   zibuñ no one's own 20
zi꜖do꜒osya automobile 7
zieetai Self-Defense Forces 34-A
zikañ time 18
   zi꜖kañ ga a꜒ru have time 18
   zi꜖kañ-do꜒ori on time 19
-zikañ /counter for number of hours/
   8
zi꜖ko an accident 35-A
zi꜖mi /na/ plain, subdued, quiet 23
zi꜖mu꜒iñ office worker 24-A
zi꜖mu꜒syo office 9
zi꜖ñzya Shinto shrine 32
zisiñ earthquake 35-A
zi꜖syo dictionary 2
zi꜖te꜒ñsya, ziteñsya bicycle 22

ziteñsyaya bicycle shop, bicycle
   dealer 22
zi꜖tu꜒ wa in reality, the fact is 34
ziŷu꜒u /na/ free, unrestricted 34-N
zo꜖ñzi꜒nai ↓ /-ku/ don't know 13
zo꜖ñzite ꜖o꜒ru ↓ know 13
zookiñ cleaning rag 17
zoori sandals 23-A
zu꜖bo꜒ñ trousers 23
zu꜖ibuñ extremely, to a considerable
   degree 3
zutto by far 15; without interruption
   24
   zu꜖tto ma꜒e kara since a long time
   ago 15
-zu꜖tu* each, of each, for each, at a
   time 33
   hi꜖to-tu-zu꜒tu one of each, one for
   each, one at a time 33
zya /contraction of de꜒ wa/ 2
   e꜖ñpitu zya na꜒i it isn't a pencil 2
   tu꜖ma꜒ñnai zya nai ka it's tiresome—don't you agree? surely
   you agree that it's tiresome 35
zya꜖[a] then, well then, in that case 2
zyama /na/ hindrance, bother 17
   zya꜖ma ni na꜒ru become a bother,
   get in the way 17

zyari gravel 33-A

-zyoo /counter for number of units of
   one-tatami area [= 1/2 tsubo or
   app. 18 sq. ft.] and for naming
   rooms/ 30

zyoobu /na/ strong, firm, durable,
   healthy 23

zyoʾobusoʾo /na/ sturdy-looking,
   healthy-looking 26

zyoʾosyaʾkeñ passenger ticket 19-A

zyoʾozuʾ /na/ skilled, skillful 18

zyotyuu maid 22

zyotyuubeya maid's room 33

zyoyuu actress 28-A

zyuʾñsa, zyuñsa policeman 7

zyuʾu ten 3

-zyuu* throughout 25
   iti-niti-zyuu all day long 25
   kyoo-zyuu ni within today, before
      today is over 25

zyuʿubuʾñ /na/ enough 20

zyuʿu-zyoʾo ten-mat area or room
   30

Index to the Grammatical Notes